-7. [

BROMLEY COLLEGE LIBRARY

B23612

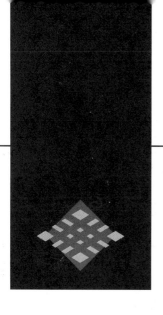

*O*rganization
Theory and Design

FIFTH EDITION

Richard L. Daft
Vanderbilt University

West Publishing Company
Minneapolis/St. Paul   New York   Los Angeles   San Francisco

Interior design   Paula Goldstein

Copyediting   Marilynn Taylor

Composition   Parkwood Composition Services, Inc.

Art   Parkwood Composition Services, Inc.

Index   JoAnne Naples

Cover image   H. Armstrong Roberts/Eurostock

Cover design   Roslyn Stendahl, Dapper Design

Photo credits follow index

BROMLEY COLLEGE OF FURTHE & HIGHER EDUCATION		
ACCN.		B23612
CLASSN.		658·4
CAT.		LOCN. TH

West's Commitment to the Environment

In 1906, West Publishing Company began recycling materials left over from the production of books. This began a tradition of efficient and responsible use of resources. Today, up to 95 percent of our legal books and 70 percent of our college and school texts are printed on recycled, acid-free stock. West also recycles nearly 22 million pounds of scrap paper annually—the equivalent of 181,717 trees. Since the 1960s, West has devised ways to capture and recycle waste inks, solvents, oils, and vapors created in the printing process. We also recycle plastics of all kinds, wood, glass, corrugated cardboard, and batteries, and have eliminated the use of Styrofoam book packaging. We at West are proud of the longevity and the scope of our commitment to the environment.

Production, Prepress, Printing and Binding by West Publishing Company.

TEXT IS PRINTED ON 10% POST CONSUMER RECYCLED PAPER

Printed with **Printwise**
Environmentally Advanced Water Washable Ink

British Library Cataloguing-in-Publication Data. A catalogue record for this book is available from the British Library.

COPYRIGHT © 1983,
1986, 1989, 1992   By WEST PUBLISHING COMPANY
COPYRIGHT © 1995   By WEST PUBLISHING COMPANY
                          610 Opperman Drive
                          P.O. Box 64526
                          St. Paul, MN 55164-0526

All rights reserved

Printed in the United States of America

02 01 00 99 98 97 96   8 7 6 5 4 3 2

Library of Congress Cataloging-in-Publication Data

Daft, Richard L.
    Organization theory and design / Richard L. Daft. –– 5th ed.
        p. cm.
    Includes index.
    ISBN 0-314-04452-3
    1. Organization. I. Title.
HD31.D135   1995   94-34070
658.4—dc20   CIP

To B. J. *AND KAITLYN*
For bringing so much joy into my life

Contents

PART 4   *Organization Design Processes*   259

CHAPTER 8   **Innovation and Change**   261

Preface

My vision for the fifth edition of *Organization Theory and Design* is to present the most recent thinking about organizations in a way that is interesting and enjoyable for students. Things are changing fast in the world of organizations. My mission is to integrate new concepts and models from organization theory with changing events in the real world of organizations to provide the most up-to-date view of organizations available. The field of organization studies is intriguing, rich, and helpful. Organization theory frameworks presented in this book have been developed from research on real organizations. The concepts help students and managers explain their organizational world and solve real-life problems.

FEATURES NEW TO THE FIFTH EDITION

Many students in a typical organization theory course do not have extensive organizational experience, especially at the middle and upper levels where organization theory is most applicable. To engage students in today's world of organizations, the fifth edition incorporates or expands significant features: a new chapter on learning organizations, a new feature called "Paradigm Busters," new concepts, new book reviews, new case examples, and new video and integrative cases for student analysis. The total set of features substantially improves and expands the book's content and accessibility. A glossary has been added to the fifth edition.

Paradigm Buster The Paradigm Buster boxes describe companies that have undergone a major shift in strategic direction, values, or culture to cope with today's turbulent, competitive international environment. The Paradigm Buster items illustrate company transformations toward empowerment, new structures, new cultures, new technologies, new ways of making decisions, breaking down barriers between departments and divisions, and joining all employees together in a common mission. Examples of Paradigm Busters include *John Deere, Imperial Oil, United Parcel Service, Ciba-Geigy Canada, Amoco Corporation, Texas Instruments, The Body Shop, Reflexite Corporation,* and *General Electric.*

New Chapter Chapter 14 has been changed to "Toward the Learning Organization." This chapter describes this new organizational phenomenon called the learning organization. The chapter integrates materials from previous chapters into an over-all model, and then extends that thinking toward the learning organization, includ-ing the nature of leadership, employee involvement, information sharing, and cor-porate culture. The learning organization represents the newest thinking about organizational design.

New Concepts Many concepts have been added or expanded in this edition. These concepts include *chaos theory, paradigm shift,* and both the Miles and Snow and the Porter frameworks for *business level strategy.* Material on *strategies for survival* has been added to the population ecology section. Other new material includes an expanded discussion of *organizational downsizing and decline, the horizontal corporation, reengi-neering, total quality management,* and *organizational development.* Other new concepts include the use of *information technology for networking, adaptive and non-adaptive cor-porate cultures, strategic control, elements of empowering employees, strategic uses of advanced information technology,* and *small versus large organization size.*

New Book Marks Another unique feature of this book is the book reviews includ-ed in 13 chapters. These book reviews reflect issues of current concern to scholars and managers. The books signal issues that managers are dealing with and that scholars are researching. New Book Marks in this edition include *Leadership and the New Science, Vital Signs, Reinventing the Factory, Busting Bureaucracy, Reengineering the Corporation, The Virtual Corporation, The New Leaders,* and *Managing with Power.*

New Case Examples This edition contains many new examples of organizations to illustrate theoretical concepts. Many examples are international, and all are about real organizations. Perhaps the major change has been to replace the opening case about *Joseph Schlitz Brewing Company* with a new case about *IBM.* The Schlitz case was a favorite among readers, but it has gradually become dated, and the IBM case reflects organization theory concepts relevant to companies today. Other new chap-ter opening cases include *Compaq Computer, WQED Pittsburgh, General Motors, Xerox Corporation, Chrysler Corporation, General Electric, Black & Decker, Connor Formed Metal Products,* and *Pepsi Cola.* In addition, many new In Practice cases are used with-in chapters to illustrate specific concepts. These new cases include *Ameritech, Que-becor Printing, Granite Rock Company, Safeway, Kodak, J.C. Penney, Browning Ferris Industries, Toshiba, Zoom Telephonics, Four Seasons Hotels, RailTex Service Company, Time Warner, San Diego Zoo, Hewlett-Packard, Autodesk, Inc., Southwest Airlines, Urgences Santé,* and "*Casablanca.*"

New Video and Integrative Cases This edition introduces the use of video cases. Video footage relevant to organization theory concepts has been shot at four com-panies: *Price Costco, IBAX Healthcare Systems, Lanier Worldwide, Inc.,* and the *Min-nesota Twins.* Written descriptions of these four organizations are included at the end of the text. The students can read about the company before class, and then see the video during class. Teaching notes about these cases are available. We welcome feed-back about these cases and hope to expand the role of video cases in future editions. In addition, several new integrative cases have been added to enable student dis-cussion and involvement. The new integrative cases include both national and inter-national situations, such as *The Pierre Dux Case, Turnaround at Petrus Consumer Goods*

Division, The Audubon Zoo, Common Utility System Team, and *The Charge of the Nueces Task Force.*

OTHER FEATURES

Many of the features from previous editions have been so well received that the general approach has been retained.

1. Multiple pedagogical devices are used to enhance student involvement in text material. "A Look Inside. . ." introduces each chapter with a relevant and interesting organizational example. "In Practice" cases illustrates theoretical concepts in organizational settings. Frequent exhibits are used to help students visualize material and relationships, and the artwork has been redone to communicate concepts ever more clearly. The "Summary and Interpretation" section tells students which points are important in the broader context of organization theory. "Guides to Action" tells students how to use material to analyze cases and manage organizations. "Cases for Analysis" are tailored to chapter concepts and provide a vehicle for student analysis and discussion.
2. Each chapter is highly focused and is organized into a logical framework. Many organization theory books treat material in sequential fashion, such as, "Here's View A. Here's View B. Here's View C," and so on. This book integrates diverse views and shows how they apply to organizations. Moreover, each chapter sticks to the essential point. Students are not introduced to extraneous material or confusing methodological squabbles that occur among organizational researchers. The body of research in most areas points to a major trend, which is reported here. Several chapters develop a framework that organizes major ideas into an overall scheme.
3. This book has been extensively tested on students. Feedback from students and faculty members has been used in the revision. The combination of organization theory concepts, book reviews, examples of paradigm busting organizations, case illustrations, and other teaching devices is designed to meet student learning needs, and students have responded very favorably.

ACKNOWLEDGMENTS

Textbook writing is a team enterprise. The fifth edition has integrated ideas and hard work from many people to whom I am very grateful. The reviewers of the fourth edition made an especially important contribution. They praised many features, were critical about things that didn't work well, and offered several suggestions. I thank the following individuals for their significant contribution to this text.

Janet Barnard
Rochester Institute of Technology

Marian Clark
New Mexico State University

Sara L. Keck
Texas A & M University

Robert T. Keller
University of Houston-University Park

Ronald A. Klocke
Mankato State University

Steven K. Paulson
University of North Florida

Carleton J. Whitehead
Texas Tech University

Jack Wimer
Baylor University

I also remain grateful to the focus group participants and the reviewers of the previous edition. Many of the changes suggested for the previous edition were carried through to this new edition and continue to enhance the quality of the text. I again thank these people for their contributions to this book.

Peggy Anderson
University of Wisconsin-Whitewater

Douglas G. Arnold
City University of Bellevue

Allen Bluedorn
University of Missouri

Marta Calas
University of Massachusetts

Bruce H. Drake
Lewis and Clark College

Lorraine Dyke
Carleton University

James E. Estes
University of South Carolina

Lawrence Gales
University of Cincinnati

Robert P. Gephart
University of Alberta

Royston Greenwood
University of Alberta

Geoffrey Hoare
University of Washington

Mohammad Jamal
Concordia University

Ronald A. Klocke
Mankato State University

Arie Y. Lewin
Duke University

Stephen J. Markell
University of Houston-Clear Lake

John G. Maurer
Wayne State University

Edward F. McDonough, III
Northeastern University

Diana D. Mrotek
Sacred Heart University

Theodore H. Rosen
University of Maryland

Borje O. Saxberg
University of Washington

Sheldon C. Snow
Pepperdine University

Mike Stebbins
California State Polytechnic-San Luis Obispo

Mary S. Thibodeaux
University of North Texas

David L. Torres
University of Arizona

Harold Welsch
DePaul University

I especially thank and acknowledge Karen Dill Bowerman, California State University-Fresno, for her terrific contribution to the *Instructor's Manual* that accompanies *Organization Theory and Design*. Karen did a superb job developing new questions for the test bank, creating new teaching ideas and auxiliary lectures, and writing teaching notes for the cases. Karen's work provides many additional resources for instructors to use in class.

Among my professional colleagues, I owe a special debt to Arie Lewin, who over the last few years has been both friend and collaborator. His suggestions for new material about international structures, advanced information technology, and top management direction had major impact on this book. I also appreciate the intellectual stimulation and emotional support from friends and colleagues here at the Owen School—Bruce Barry, Vickie Buenger, Tom Mahoney, Rich Oliver, and Greg Stewart. Marty Giesel, the Dean here at Owen, maintained a positive scholarly atmosphere and supported me with the time and resources needed to complete this book.

I want to extend special thanks to my editorial assistant, Pat Lane. Working with an assistant was a new step for me, and Pat provided outstanding help throughout the revision of this text. Pat skillfully drafted materials on a variety of cases and topics, found sources, and did an outstanding job with the copyedited manuscript, galley proofs, and ancillary materials. Pat's personal enthusiasm and caring for the text added to the high level of excellence in the fifth edition.

I also thank Rita Carswell, Art Del Buono, and Kelly Allen. Rita plowed through the typing of chapters on time every time, and worked on a variety of other tasks to give me time to write. Art Del Buono, an MBA student at Vanderbilt, did a wonderful job of researching and drafting materials for the Book Marks and other cases in the text. I also want to acknowledge the hard work and superb organization skills of Kelly Allen, my personal assistant, who somehow provided me with free time and a high quality of life during the revision.

The editors at West also deserve special mention. Rick Leyh is the new Senior Editor for *Organization Theory and Design,* and he facilitated the dream for the project. The transition from Richard Fenton to Rick Leyh was seamless. Esther Craig, Developmental Editor, did her usual great job of keeping all parts of the project moving, and provided significant ideas for improvements. The helpfulness and support of Esther and Rick were critical to the revision. In addition, Peggy Brewington, Production Editor for this edition, combined creativity and a smooth organizational style to facilitate the book's on-time completion.

Finally, I want to acknowledge the love and support of my daughters and their families. We have grown close over the period of this revision, and I am very appreciative of the good times I've spent with Amy, Gary, Danielle, and Brian. I also appreciate the infusion of joy and surprise into my life from the visits of B. J. and Kaitlyn, which is why I dedicate this book to them.

Organization Theory and Design

FIFTH EDITION

Introduction to Organizations

CHAPTER 1
Organizations and Organization Theory

CHAPTER

1

Organizations and Organization Theory

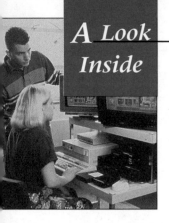

International Business Machines Corporation

Owning stock in IBM was like owning a gold mine. The overwhelming success of the IBM PC sent the company's already high profits soaring, and IBM was ranked as the world's largest company in terms of stock market value. Big Blue, as the company was known, was creating jobs around the world, its work force ultimately swelling to 407,000.

A decade later, those who had invested their lives—or their money—in a company they thought could never fail watched long-cherished dreams go down the drain. The company went from earning a $6 billion profit to reporting a whopping $5 billion loss two years later. IBM stock lost more than $75 billion in value, an amount equal to the gross domestic product of Sweden. Everyone associated with the once-great company suffered.

- More than 140,000 IBM workers lost their jobs. Entire towns that sprang up because of IBM watched their economies disappear. New York's middle Hudson Valley was devastated, and when IBM announced layoffs in 1993, local officials requested that gun shops close for the day.
- As IBM stock fell from $176 to the low $40s, so did the retirement hopes of hundreds of thousands of investors, from IBM executives to the small-town grandmother who thought she'd made the safest investment in the world.
- By the time IBM gave up its no-layoffs policy, damaged employee morale was reinforced by former employees who sold T-shirts with the IBM logo spelling out "I've Been Mislead."
- After a long career of rising to the top of one of the world's greatest companies, the chairman of IBM, John Akers, resigned under heavy pressure, taking other top executives with him. But more than careers were tarnished that day. On the same day, the company shook up the financial world by announcing that for the first time in history, it was slashing its quarterly dividend from $1.21 to $.54 a share.

The fall of IBM, the giant of the computer industry for eighty years, is a classic story of organizational failure. The company went from literally being at the top of the world to fighting for its life. How did it happen?

Background

IBM grew out of a conglomerate formed in 1911 that primarily made scales, coffee grinders, cheese slicers, and time clocks. The so-called "Computer-Tabulating-Recording" component of the conglomerate grew quickly, and the name change to International Business Machines Corporation in 1924 signaled a significant shift in focus.

For fifty-seven years, until 1971, IBM was led by the Thomas Watsons (senior and junior). The leaders who followed them were not as forceful or visionary as the Watsons, but they inherited a strong company that clearly dominated the computer market. In the mid-1960s, IBM introduced the System/360 family of mainframe computers—six models launched simultaneously, requiring five new factories and creating thousands of new jobs. An outstanding success, the 360 sealed IBM's leadership in the computer industry. Some think it may have marked another turning point as well.

"Bureaucracy Run Amok"

Retired IBM executive Malcolm Robinson, who rose to a senior post in IBM Europe, said, "The scale of the [System/360 project] created a complexity in the business that almost couldn't be handled. It was chaos for awhile. So an organization had to be created to bring things under control and make sure that kind of breakdown never happened again. And that really may have been what made the bureaucracy take off."[1] Statistics indicate that Robinson was right. IBM's personnel count went up almost 130 percent between 1963 and 1966, while sales rose about 97 percent.

Many mistakes made by IBM executives were caused by too many people and too many meetings. Decisions that should have been made quickly in response to changes in the computer market were delayed or ignored because of the cumbersome management system that demanded everything be done "the IBM way." For one thing, the IBM way demanded consensus through meetings, so anytime a participating staff member "non-concurred," in the jargon of the company, decisions were referred to another meeting. IBM choked on the bureaucratic culture. When IBM's new chairman took over after the resignation of John Akers, he said of the troubled company he would try to revive, "It was bureaucracy run amok."

The IBM culture led to such things as the ridiculous—but relatively harmless—file of IBM-approved jokes for executives to tell at luncheons or other speaking engagements. But it also led to disaster.

"The Times They Are A-Changin'"

Around the time IBM introduced its 360 line of computers in the mid-1960s, folk singer Bob Dylan's song "The Times They Are A-Changin'" was released. Unfortunately, IBM didn't change with the times. The company staked its claim in the world of multimillion-dollar mainframes. It was late getting into the personal computer market, choosing to steer what company leaders in the 1970s thought was a safe course—preserving the company's mainframe profits.

By the time IBM decided to enter the personal computer game in earnest, the death knell was already starting to toll on the profits from mainframes. The values that guided IBM and its mainframe leadership—the caution, the obsessive training of employees, a focus on following rather than anticipating customer needs, and a guarantee of lifetime employment to its workers—didn't work when IBM moved into the fast-paced, ever-changing, competitive world of personal computers.

It's Not What They Did; It's What They Didn't Do

The IBM PC was an instant success for IBM. But it's what the company *didn't* do, both before and after the introduction of the PC, that ultimately caused its downfall.

The first big mistake IBM made was in not taking advantage of a new technology the company itself invented in the mid-1970s. The reduced instruction-set computing (RISC) microprocessor offered simplified, faster computing, well-suited to the minicomputers that were gaining popularity. But the new technology threatened the huge profits from the company's mainframe business. The decision to develop smaller, less expensive machines with new technology kept getting delayed until the competition stepped way ahead of IBM at its own game.

At least as damaging to IBM's future was its subsequent failure to grab a larger share of PC profits when it finally had the opportunity. The company signed on with Microsoft for the PC's software and Intel for the microprocessor. IBM might, at the time, have purchased all or part of both of these companies, allowing Big Blue to cash in on the huge profits that are now accruing to the two smaller firms.

Bill Gates, chairman of Microsoft, had actually encouraged IBM to buy outright the MS-DOS operating system he found for it in 1980. When IBM declined—an executive said the company didn't want to get bogged down in the software—Microsoft bought the system for a mere $75,000. That move helped the small company grow to the point of making $700 million in profits in 1992. In the same year, Intel reported earnings of $1.1 billion, and the combined market value of Microsoft and Intel outpaced IBM by over $15 million.

IBM's bureaucratic culture again got in the way. When IBM and Microsoft worked to co-develop a new operating system for a new line of PCs, IBM assigned such a large number of people to the project that they had to spend as much time communicating with one another as they did working toward a new system.

In addition, IBM's way of measuring productivity—by the number of lines of code someone wrote—encouraged its programmers to write inefficient operating code. As IBM's horde of programmers labored away, one member of Microsoft's small team rewrote a piece of IBM operating code requiring 33,000 characters by using just 200 characters. The team then began rewriting other parts of IBM's cumbersome code, making it smaller and thus faster. Rather than recognizing the benefits of the changes, IBM managers complained that Microsoft was performing "negative" work by condensing the lines of code and, therefore, that Microsoft should be paying IBM rather than the other way around.

Soon afterward, IBM passed up another opportunity. Believing it would be beneficial to his own company as well as to IBM, Microsoft's chairman suggested that the larger company purchase around 10 percent of Microsoft. Again, IBM declined—a very expensive mistake. If IBM had bought 10 percent of Microsoft then, the company would today have turned a $100 million investment into $3 billion.

Another thing IBM didn't do quickly was accept that its no-layoffs policy was simply no longer working in the fast-paced world in which the company was operating. As one former manager put it, the policy was defended "like virginity." Rather than admitting the organization needed to be streamlined and the work force cut, IBM began several years of "reorganizing"—eliminating positions here, firing employees there for the slightest infractions of the rules. The company gradually increased the pressure for workers to accept severance offers. All the time, IBM's then-Chairman John Akers kept insisting that no one was being laid off. Though some championed Akers's efforts to maintain this distinctive piece of IBM's culture, employee morale and company image were severely damaged by these word games by the time IBM finally gave up its sacred no-layoffs policy.

IBM Today

In January 1993, John Akers finally announced that he was stepping down as chairman of IBM, a move that many thought was long overdue. Though Akers wasn't responsible for the problems at IBM, he failed to solve them. The media attention surrounding the announcement of his resignation tarnished IBM's image even further.

One of the tasks ahead for IBM's new CEO, Louis V. Gerstner, Jr., is to shine up that image and somehow emphasize the IBM brand name as the primary computer resource for consumers. Though IBM still has a good name, Gerstner doesn't have an easy job ahead of remaking IBM culturally as well as technologically. He plans to create a culture in which IBM people will waste fewer opportunities, minimize bureaucracy, and put the good of the company ahead of their divisions.

Technologically, IBM will focus its energies on the Power system, a set of superfast microprocessors that can be used in anything from hand-held computers to large supercomputers. The system represents the first time since the System/360 mainframe line in the 1960s that IBM has focused its energy and risked its future on a single technology. The PowerPC chip helped IBM come out with its most successful laptop, the ThinkPad.

Can IBM rebound from its many mistakes and once again be a leader in the computer industry? Or was it too far gone to ever come back? Watching the answer unfold will be one of the top organizational stories of the next decade.[2]

W elcome to the real world of organization theory. The rise and fall of IBM illustrates organization theory in action. IBM managers were deeply involved in organization theory each day of their working lives—but they never realized it. Company managers didn't fully understand how the organization related to the environment or how it should function internally. Familiarity with organization theory would have enabled IBM's managers to understand their situation and to analyze and diagnose what was happening to them. Organization theory gives us the tools to explain what happened to IBM. Organization theory also helps us understand what may happen in the future, so we can manage our organizations more effectively.

Organization Theory in Action

TOPICS
Each of the topics to be covered in this book is illustrated in the IBM case. Consider, for example, IBM's failure to respond to or control such elements as customers, suppliers, and competitors in the fast-paced external environment; its inability to coordinate departments and design control systems that promoted efficiency; slow decision making, such as delaying action on exploiting the potential of new technology; handling the problem of large size; the absence of a forceful top management team that allowed IBM to drift further and further into chaos; and an outmoded corporate culture that strangled efforts to renew or revitalize the company. These are the subjects with which organization theory is concerned.

Of course, organization theory is not limited to IBM. Every organization, every manager in every organization, is involved in organization theory. Two other organizations that were giants along with IBM in the 1960s—General Motors and Sears Roebuck—also fell from greatness primarily because their leaders didn't analyze and respond to what was happening both outside and inside their companies.[3]

There are success stories, too. Hewlett-Packard Company—which was beginning to suffer from some of the same "big company" problems as IBM in the 1980s—went through a major, highly successful reorganization in 1990, using concepts based in organization theory. By mid-1993, HP was one of the fastest growing PC companies around.[4] Interestingly, Hewlett-Packard was one of the two companies to first pick up on the RISC technology IBM ignored for so long. Ford Motor Company, John Deere, Timex, and AT&T have undergone similar successful structural transformations.

Organization theory draws lessons from these organizations and makes those lessons available to students and managers of organizations. The story of IBM is important because it demonstrates that large organizations are vulnerable, that lessons are not learned automatically, and that organizations are only as strong as their decision makers.

CURRENT ISSUES

Research into hundreds of organizations provides the organizational knowledge base to make IBM and other organizations more effective. For example, issues facing organizations in the 1990s are different from those of the 1960s and 1970s. Some of the issues IBM and other organizations must confront today are:

1. Global Competition   Every company, large and small, faces international competition on their home turf at the same time they confront the need to be competitive in international markets. IBM was always fairly successful in selling computers internationally, but the company's concern about Japanese computer companies may have contributed to its failure to respond to domestic competitors. After Westinghouse sold its lamp operations to a Holland-based company, rival General Electric quickly saw the need to get into the international market; by 1993, approximately 40 percent of GE Lighting's sales came from abroad.[5] But while U.S. investment abroad rose 35 percent from 1987 to 1992, foreign investment in the United States more than doubled.[6] People who work for Burger King, Standard Oil, Pillsbury, Shell Oil, or CBS Records are already working for foreign bosses.

2. Organization Design   As IBM learned, bigger doesn't always mean better. In the 1990s, smaller means better in many industries, and downsizing and decline are considered as natural and important as growth.[7] One of the hottest trends is often called "reengineering," a radical redesign of business processes that leads to big results—and usually big layoffs.[8] Managers need lean, adaptive organizations, often subdividing a large firm into a series of small, freestanding divisions.

   Structures are flatter, with middle management being eliminated. Organization designs today are structured around teams of employees that become primary work units and are empowered to make decisions. General Electric's factory in Bayamón, Puerto Rico, has one manager, fifteen salaried "advisers" and 172 hourly workers. Hourly workers are organized into teams of ten or so; they change jobs every six months so that each worker knows his or her own job as well as how it affects the next person. There are no supervisors; "advisers" speak up only when teams ask for help.[9]

3. Empowering Employees   As organization design changes, so do the ways of motivating employees. Organization members in many enlightened organizations are considered partners or associates, not employees. Organization leaders are rejecting the by-the-numbers approach to management, recognizing that an increasingly important part of their job is showing others they really care.[10] When Union Carbide went through a total restructuring, top management set the guidelines for new processes, but they wisely allowed the details of how to work within those processes to come from workers on the floor of the pilot plant in Taft, Louisiana. Those employees found savings for the company of more than $20 million.[11]

   Some 10 percent of U.S. employees are now covered by employee stock ownership plans (ESOPs) that empower employees to share in the company's success. Other human resource innovations include Merck's encouragement of employees to change careers within the company, Pepsico's letting employees move laterally across divisions, and Taco Bell's rotation of store employees through all the jobs, from making tacos to greeting customers.[12] Symmetrix, a consulting firm in Lexington, Massachusetts, offers stress-reduction classes to its employees.[13]

4. Speed   The 1980s saw dramatic increases in product and service quality by U.S. and Canadian companies. Although quality will still be important, the distinguishing competitive issue in the 1990s will be how fast products and services can be delivered to customers. The Limited can have ten thousand dresses reflecting a new fashion into stores within forty-one days, long before the original runway fashion is sold. 3M's giant electronics operation in Austin, Texas, reduced its product development time from two years to about two months. Ford middle managers reduced the time required for commercial credit approval from one month to one week, then tackled the problem again and reduced it to one day. Customers want things fast, and organizations must be designed to encourage quick collaboration and instant response, all the time keeping quality high.[14] In his efforts to turn IBM around, one of Lou Gerstner's top priorities is getting products to market faster than competitors.[15]

5. Communication Technology   Today, employees can be linked up with everyone else through the use of personal computers and networks. Indeed, vendors and customers can be brought into the loop for instant communication. Technology facilitates communication and group formation in whatever way is needed to accomplish tasks or projects. Technology dramatically flattens organization structures, so that there may be hundreds of far-flung sites, such as stores or offices, all transmitting information to a single headquarters.[16] Publisher McGraw Hill maintains worldwide circulation files for sixteen of its magazines from an office in Ireland, where employees work at computer terminals linked to the company's mainframes in Highstown, New Jersey.[17] New communications technology also empowers employees, giving them access to complete information, which enables them to get the job done in less time than if they had to solicit information from superiors or colleagues.

PURPOSE OF THIS CHAPTER

The purpose of this chapter is to explore the nature of organizations and organization theory today. Organization theory has developed from the systematic study of organizations by scholars. Concepts are obtained from living, ongoing organizations. Organization theory can be very practical, as illustrated in the IBM case. It helps people understand, diagnose, and respond to emerging organizational needs and problems.

The next section begins with a formal definition of organization and then explores introductory concepts for describing and analyzing organizations. Next, the scope and nature of organization theory are discussed more fully. Succeeding sections consider what organization theory can and cannot do, its usefulness, and how organization theory models can help people manage complex organizations. The chapter closes with a brief overview of the important themes to be covered in this book.

What Is an Organization?

Organizations are hard to see. We see outcroppings, such as a tall building or a computer workstation or a friendly employee; but the whole organization is vague and abstract, and may be scattered among several locations. We know organizations are there because they touch us every day. Indeed, they are so common we take them for granted. We hardly notice that we are born in a hospital, have our birth records registered in a government agency, are educated in schools and universities, are raised on food produced on corporate farms, are treated by doctors engaged in a joint practice, buy a house built by a construction company and sold by a real estate agency, borrow money from a bank, turn to police and fire departments when trouble erupts, use moving companies to change residences, receive an array of benefits from government agencies, spend forty hours a week working in an organization, and are even laid to rest by an undertaker.[18]

DEFINITION

Organizations as diverse as a church, a local hospital, and the International Business Machines Corporation have characteristics in common. The definition used in this book to describe organizations is as follows: **organizations** are social entities that are goal-directed, deliberately structured activity systems with a permeable boundary.[19] There are four key elements in this definition.

1. *Social Entities*   Organizations are composed of people and groups of people. The building blocks of an organization are people and their roles. People interact with each other to perform essential functions in organizations. Recent trends in management indicate the importance of human resources, with most new management approaches designed to empower employees with greater opportunities to contribute. The importance of human resources will be discussed throughout this book.

2. *Goal-Directed*   Organizations exist for a purpose. An organization and its members are trying to achieve an end or mission. Participants may have goals different from those of the organization, and the organization may have several goals; but organizations exist for one or more purposes without which they would cease to exist. The notion of organizational strategy and goals will be discussed in Chapter 2.

3. *Deliberately Structured Activity Systems*   An activity system simply means that organizations perform work activities. Organizational tasks are deliberately subdivided into separate departments and sets of activities. Subdivision achieves efficiencies in the work process. The deliberate structure is used to coordinate and direct separate groups and departments. The structuring of organizations will be discussed in Chapters 4 through 7.

4. *Permeable Boundary*   All organizations have boundaries that separate them from other organizations. Membership is distinct. The boundary determines who and what is inside or outside the organization. But in today's rapidly changing world, the boundaries of competitive organizations are becoming permeable rather than rigid as organizations share information and technology to their mutual advantage. IBM joined with both Motorola and Apple in bringing the new PowerPC chip to the market in the fall of 1993.[20] One reason boundaries are becoming more permeable is the emphasis on speed. Consider, for example, the linkage between Wal-Mart and Procter and Gamble's order-fulfillment processes. A box of washing detergent rung up on a Wal-Mart cash register is at the same time registered in Procter and Gamble's warehouse, enabling P&G to know how many boxes need to be replenished on Wal-Mart's shelves.[21] Jack Welch, CEO of General Electric, wants to eliminate boundaries among GE's many divisions.[22]

IMPORTANCE

Organizations are not just all around us; they are the prominent social institution of our time. Charles Perrow proposed that organizations are the key phenomenon in existence today.[23] Most people assume that social forces such as politics, economics, and religion shape organizations. Perrow argues the opposite, suggesting that large organizations have changed politics, because politicians come from organizations and are beholden to them. Social class is determined by rank and position within organizations, not vice versa. Sophisticated new technologies for producing goods and services have no life without large organizations. The family has been shaped to cope with the organizational phenomenon, with most families being dependent on organizations for wages and livelihood. Religion has even become a large organization phenomenon. The most rapidly growing denominations take advantage of television and of modern marketing and management techniques to increase membership and raise millions of dollars.

However, it is not just the presence of organizations that is important, but knowledge of *organizing*. Consider the awesome accomplishments of organizing during the Persian Gulf war. All air assets reported to a single general, unlike in the Vietnam War, where each service controlled its own aircraft. This enabled the extraordinary coordination of up to three thousand flights a day by a ground team using personal computers combined with four AWACS planes in the air, together keeping the armada of planes from running into each other while carrying out the daily list of target runs, ordnance deliveries, and refueling stops that often ran to three hundred pages. A rapid reaction team was created to acquire custom-built bombs for hard-to-penetrate targets. Within thirty-six hours after ordering a special bomb from the United States, it was being loaded on a warplane in the Gulf. U.S. commando teams sneaked behind enemy lines on dune buggies and motorcycles, sending targeting information to satellites overhead. A new problem arose somewhere in the Gulf every minute, and someone invented a way of organizing to solve it.[24]

Thus, organizations shape our lives, and well-informed managers can shape organizations. We are truly a society of organizations, and a systematic study and understanding of organizations can enable us to use and control this important resource.

Organizations as Systems

OPEN SYSTEMS

One significant development in the study of organizations was the distinction between closed and open systems.[25] A **closed system** would not depend on its environment; it would be autonomous, enclosed, and sealed off from the outside world. Although a true closed system cannot exist, early organization studies focused on internal systems. Early management concepts, including scientific management, leadership style, and industrial engineering, were closed-system approaches because they took the environment for granted and assumed the organization could be made more effective through internal design. The management of a closed system would be quite easy. The environment would be stable and predictable and would not intervene to cause problems. The primary management issue would be to run things efficiently.

An **open system** must interact with the environment to survive; it both consumes resources and exports resources to the environment. It cannot seal itself off. It must continuously change and adapt to the environment. Open systems can be enormously complex. Internal efficiency is just one issue—and sometimes a minor one. The organization has to find and obtain needed resources, interpret and act on environmental changes, dispose of outputs, and control and coordinate internal activities in the face of environmental disturbances and uncertainty. Every system that must interact with the environment to survive is an open system. The human being is an open system. So is the planet Earth, the city of New York, and IBM. Indeed, one problem at IBM was that top managers seemed to forget they were part of an open system. They isolated themselves within the IBM culture and failed to pay close attention to what was going on with their customers, suppliers, and competitors.

To understand the whole organization, it should be viewed as a system. A **system** is a set of interacting elements that acquires inputs from the environment, transforms them, and discharges outputs to the external environment. The need for inputs and outputs reflects dependency on the environment. Interacting elements mean that people and departments depend upon one another and must work together.

Exhibit 1.1 illustrates an open system. Inputs to an organization system include employees, raw materials and other physical resources, information, and financial resources. The transformation process changes these inputs into something of value that can be exported back to the environment. Outputs include specific products and services for customers and clients. Outputs may also include employee satisfaction, pollution, and other by-products of the transformation process.

ORGANIZATIONAL SUBSYSTEMS

An organization is composed of several **subsystems,** also illustrated in Exhibit 1.1. The specific functions required for organization survival are performed by departments that act as subsystems. Organizational subsystems perform five essential functions: boundary spanning, production, maintenance, adaptation, and management.[26]

Exhibit 1.1   An Open System and Its Subsystems.

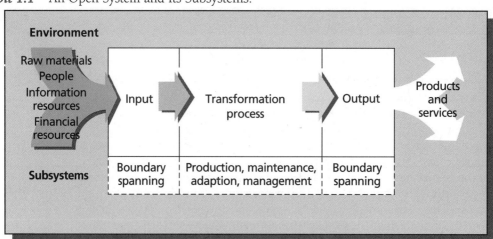

Boundary Spanning　Boundary subsystems handle input and output transactions; in other words, they are responsible for exchanges with the environment. On the input side, boundary departments acquire needed supplies and materials. On the output side, they create demand and market outputs. Boundary departments work directly with the external environment. At IBM, boundary departments include marketing on the output side and purchasing on the input side.

Production　The production subsystem produces the product and service outputs of the organization. This is where the primary transformation takes place. This subsystem is the production department in a manufacturing firm, the teachers and classes in a university, and the medical activities in a hospital. At IBM, the production subsystem actually manufactures computers, software, and workstations.

Maintenance　The maintenance subsystem is responsible for the smooth operation and upkeep of the organization. Maintenance includes the cleaning and painting of buildings and the repair and servicing of machines. Maintenance activities also try to meet human needs, such as morale, compensation, and physical comfort. Maintenance functions in a corporation like IBM are performed by such subsystems as the personnel department, the employee cafeteria, and the janitorial staff.

Adaptation　The adaptive subsystem is responsible for organizational change. The adaptive subsystem scans the environment for problems, opportunities, and technological developments. It is responsible for creating innovations and for helping the organization change and adapt. At IBM, the technology, research, and marketing research departments are responsible for the adaptive function.

Management　Management is a distinct subsystem, responsible for directing and coordinating the other subsystems of the organization. Management provides direction, strategy, goals, and policies for the entire organization. In addition, the managerial subsystem is responsible for developing organization structure and directing tasks within each subsystem. At IBM, the management subsystem consists of the chairman, the vice-president, and the managers of it several divisions.

In ongoing organizations, the five subsystems are interconnected and often overlap. Departments often have multiple roles. Marketing is primarily a boundary spanner but may also sense problems or opportunities for innovation. Managers coordinate and direct the entire system, but they are also involved in maintenance, boundary spanning, and adaptation. People and resources in one subsystem may perform other functions in organizations.

CHAOS THEORY

The new science of **chaos theory** tells us that we live in a complex world full of randomness and uncertainty. Our world is characterized by surprise, rapid change, and confusion, and often seems totally out of our control. Managers can't measure, predict, or control in traditional ways the unfolding drama inside or outside the organization. However, chaos theory recognizes that this randomness and disorder occurs within certain constraints or larger patterns of order.[27]

One characteristic of chaotic systems, called the butterfly effect, is relevant for today's managers. The butterfly effect means small events can have giant effects. A butterfly flapping its wings over Peking can cause air disturbances that will eventually affect the weather in the United States. Today's companies are like the weather—small events may have consequences far beyond their initial strength. For example, an insignificant lawsuit against AT&T had far-reaching effects, resulting in the emergence of MCI and other long-distance carriers and ultimately creating a whole new world of telecommunications. More about chaos theory and its importance for managers is described in Book Mark 1.0.

Today's businesses must be able to respond to the completely unpredictable, within certain bounds of the organization's mission and guiding principles. The rapid change in our world requires organizations to be fluid, perhaps replacing jobs, roles, structures, and even products or services weekly or monthly. In a chaotic world, the big picture is more important than the parts. Managers must imprint the organization's larger mission and values in the minds of employees, thus enabling empowered employees to respond on their own to a random, unpredictable environment. Managers can also flood the organization with information, keeping everyone fully informed. Trends associated with managing chaotic organizations are a shift to worker teams, staying connected to the customer, the empowerment of employees, and a structure based on horizontal work processes rather than vertical functions. Consider the following example of how Ameritech is handling the chaos in today's organizations.

IN PRACTICE ◆ 1.1

Ameritech

Ameritech, one of the top-performing "Baby Bells" born in the revolutionary breakup of AT&T, is now facing competition not only from other Baby Bells but from long-distance carriers and cable television operators. Leaders at Ameritech know that in the current volatile environment, with regulatory authorities opening up the telecommunications business to more competitors, the company simply can't predict how many customers it can attract or keep. In response, Ameritech is reinventing itself, with its major emphasis on serving the customer. It is doing so through "Team Ameritech," in which teams of workers are assigned to stay in touch with and meet the needs of each large customer. The team approach has sharply cut response time to customer concerns.

As has been true at other companies facing chaotic changes, the reorganization at Ameritech has also meant job losses, and for employees used to the old, paternalistic Bell culture, the layoffs are a big shock. To help keep employees aware of what's happening and ease resistance to the widespread changes, Ameritech holds regular seminars for employees and management to talk to one another face-to-face. This hasn't allayed all the fears, but Ameritech continues to emphasize employee empowerment even as management stays committed to the necessity for constant change.[28]

As the pace of change in our society accelerates, the changes faced by organizations accelerate as well. Change and problem solving by everyone have replaced stability and efficiency as the key traits of successful organizations, and the skill needed most by leaders in the 1990s is the ability to manage chaos. To do so requires seeing the organization as a fluid, ever-changing social system that often cannot be managed with traditional, top-down techniques.

BOOKMARK
1.0

HAVE YOU READ ABOUT THIS?
Leadership and the New Science
by Margaret J. Wheatley

In the world of Newtonian physics, every atom moves in a unique, predictable trajectory determined by the forces exerted on it. Prediction and control are gained by reducing wholes into small parts and carefully regulating the forces that act on those parts. In the world of organizations, vertical hierarchy, division of labor, task descriptions, and operating procedures represent the application of Newtonian logic to obtain predictable, controlled results.

Just as Newton's laws broke down as physics explored ever smaller elements of matter and ever wider expanses of the universe, rigid, control-oriented organizations do not work well in a world of instant information, constant change, and global competition. The physical sciences responded to the failure of Newtonian mechanics with a new paradigm called quantum mechanics. And according to Margaret Wheatley in *Leadership and the New Science,* organizations are finding new ways of designing themselves to survive in a quantum world.

Chaos, Relationships, and Fields

Chaos theory underlies quantum mechanics. Disorder underlies apparent order. Individual actions, whether by atoms or people, cannot be easily predicted and controlled. Here's why:

- Nothing exists except in relationship to everything else. Relationships among things are the key determinants of a well-ordered system we perceive. Order emerges through a web of relationships that make up the whole, not as the result of controls on individual parts.
- The empty space between things is filled with fields, invisible material that connects elements together. In organizations, the fields that bind people include a vision, shared values, culture, caring, and information. These fields give an organization its "feel" and are the source of leader influence.

- A system, especially an organization, is defined by the relationships and fields that bind the parts together into a whole. The system cannot be understood by analyzing just tangible parts because relationships and fields are what produce the whole.

Implications for Leadership

Chaos theory provides a new way to see, understand, and lead organizations. Wheatley believes that the new science can influence leaders to:

- Nurture relationships and fields with a clear vision, statements of value, expressions of caring, and the sharing of information.
- Free employees from strict rules and controls so they can develop bonds and relationships that will create a strong, successful organization.
- Concentrate on the whole and not worry about parts in isolation.
- Not waste time unraveling single cause-effect relationships, because they don't exist, or spend time creating elaborate plans and time lines that assume perfect top-down control.
- Design organization structures with an eye to how they facilitate strong relationships among people.
- Remember that the universe will not accede to a desire for tight control and perfectly determined outcomes.

Wheatley believes that large organizations can use this new approach to manage even in a world of constant flux. The new science emphasizes the importance of leadership that enables individuals to create a desirable order and company success.

Leadership and the New Science by Margaret J. Wheatley is published by Berrett-Koehler Publishers.

Dimensions of Organizations

The systems view pertains to dynamic, ongoing activities within organizations. The next step for understanding organizations is to look at dimensions that describe specific organizational traits. These dimensions describe organizations much the same way that personality and physical traits describe people.

Organizational dimensions fall into two types: structural and contextual. **Structural dimensions** provide labels to describe the internal characteristics of an organization. They create a basis for measuring and comparing organizations. **Contextual dimensions** characterize the whole organization, including its size, technology, environment, and goals. They describe the organizational setting that influences the structural dimensions. Contextual dimensions can be confusing because they represent both the organization and the environment as the context within which the structural dimensions occur. Both structural and contextual dimensions are necessary to evaluate and understand organizations.[29] Key structural and contextual dimensions are listed in Exhibit 1.2.

STRUCTURAL DIMENSIONS

1. *Formalization* pertains to the amount of written documentation in the organization. Documentation includes procedures, job descriptions, regulations, and policy manuals. These written documents describe behavior and activities. Formalization is often measured by simply counting the number of pages of documentation within the organization. Large state universities, for example, tend to be high on formalization because they have several volumes of written rules for such things as registration, dropping and adding classes, student associations, dormitory governance, and financial assistance. A small, family-owned business, in contrast, may have almost no written rules and would be considered informal.

2. *Specialization* is the degree to which organizational tasks are subdivided into separate jobs. If specialization is extensive, each employee performs only a narrow range of tasks. If specialization is low, employees perform a wide range of tasks in their jobs. Specialization is sometimes referred to as the *division of labor.*

3. *Standardization* is the extent to which similar work activities are performed in a uniform manner. In a highly standardized organization like McDonald's, work content is described in detail, and similar work is performed the same way at all locations.

4. *Hierarchy of authority* describes who reports to whom and the span of control for each manager. The hierarchy is depicted by the vertical lines on an organization chart, as illustrated in Exhibit 1.3. The hierarchy is related to *span of control* (the number of employees reporting to a supervisor). When spans of control are narrow, the hierarchy tends to be tall. When spans of control are wide, the hierarchy of authority will be shorter.

5. *Complexity* refers to the number of activities or subsystems within the organization. Complexity can be measured along three dimensions: vertical, horizontal, and spatial. Vertical complexity is the number of levels in the hierarchy. Horizontal complexity is the number of job titles or departments existing horizontally across the organization. Spatial complexity is the number of geographical locations. The organization in Exhibit 1.3 has a vertical complexity of five levels. The horizontal complexity can be calculated as either thirty-four job titles or seven major departments. Spatial complexity is low because the organization is located in one place.

6. *Centralization* refers to the hierarchical level that has authority to make a decision. When decision making is kept at the top level, the organization is centralized.

Structural
1. Formalization
2. Specialization
3. Standardization
4. Hierarchy of authority
5. Complexity
6. Centralization
7. Professionalism
8. Personnel ratios

Contextual
1. Size
2. Organizational technology
3. Environment
4. Goals and strategy
5. Culture

Exhibit 1.2
Structural and Contextual Dimensions of Organizations.

When decisions are delegated to lower organizational levels, it is decentralized. Organizational decisions that might be centralized or decentralized include purchasing equipment, establishing goals, choosing suppliers, setting prices, hiring employees, and deciding marketing territories.

7. *Professionalism* is the level of formal education and training of employees. Professionalism is considered high when employees require long periods of training to hold jobs in the organization. Professionalism is generally measured as the average number of years of education of employees, which could be as high as twenty in a medical practice and less than ten in a construction company.

8. *Personnel ratios* refer to the deployment of people to various functions and departments. Personnel ratios include the administrative ratio, the clerical ratio, the professional staff ratio, and the ratio of indirect to direct labor employees. A personnel ratio is measured by dividing the number of employees in a classification by the total number of organizational employees.

CONTEXTUAL DIMENSIONS

1. *Size* is the organization's magnitude as reflected in the number of people in the organization. It can be measured for the organization as a whole or for specific components, such as a plant or division. Since organizations are social systems, size is typically measured by the count of employees. Other measures such as total sales or total assets also reflect magnitude, but they do not indicate the size of the human part of the social system.

2. *Organizational technology* is the nature of the production subsystem, and it includes the actions and techniques used to change organizational inputs into outputs. An assembly line, a college classroom, and an oil refinery are technologies, although they differ from one another.

3. The *environment* includes all elements outside the boundary of the organization. Key elements include the industry, government, customers, suppliers, and the financial community. Environmental elements that affect an organization the most are often other organizations.

4. The organization's *goals and strategy* define the purpose and competitive techniques that set it apart from other organizations. Goals are often written down as an enduring statement of company intent. A strategy is the plan of action that describes resource allocation and activities for dealing with the environment and for reaching the organization's goals. Goals and strategies define the scope of operations and the relationship with employees, clients, and competitors.

Exhibit 1.3   Organization Chart Illustrating the Hierarchy of Authority and the Structural Complexity for a Community Job Training Program.

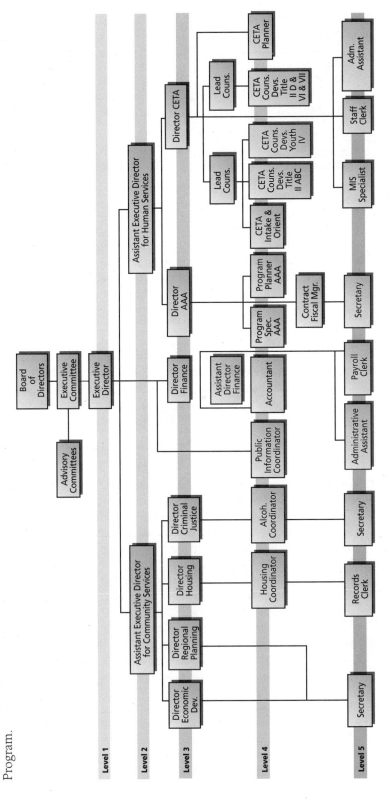

5. An organization's *culture* is the underlying set of key values, beliefs, understandings, and norms shared by employees. These underlying values may pertain to ethical behavior, commitment to employees, efficiency, or customer service, and they provide the glue to hold organization members together. An organization's culture is unwritten but can be observed in its stories, slogans, ceremonies, dress, and office layout.

The thirteen contextual and structural dimensions discussed here are interdependent. For example, large organization size, a routine technology, and a stable environment all tend to create an organization that has greater formalization, specialization, and centralization. More detailed relationships among the thirteen dimensions are explored in later chapters of this book.

These dimensions provide a basis for the measurement and analysis of characteristics that cannot be seen by the casual observer, and they reveal significant information about an organization. Consider, for example, the dimensions of W. L. Gore & Associates compared with those of Wal-Mart and a welfare agency.

IN PRACTICE ◆ 1.2
W. L. Gore & Associates

When Jack Dougherty began work at W. L. Gore & Associates, Inc., he reported to Bill Gore, the company's founder, to receive his first assignment. Gore told him, "Why don't you find something you'd like to do." Dougherty was shocked at the informality, but quickly recovered and began interrogating various managers about their activities. He was attracted to a new product called Gore-Tex, a membrane that was waterproof but breathable when bonded to fabric. The next morning, he came to work dressed in jeans and began helping feed fabric into the maw of a large laminator. Five years later, Dougherty was responsible for marketing and advertising in the fabrics group.

Bill Gore died in 1986, but the organization he designed still runs without official titles, orders, or bosses. People are expected to find a place where they can contribute and manage themselves. The company has some 4,200 associates (not employees) in twenty-nine plants. The plants are kept small—up to 200 people—to maintain a family atmosphere. "It's much better to use friendship and love than slavery and whips," Bill Gore said. Several professional employees are assigned to develop new products, but the administrative structure is lean. Good human relations is a more important value than is internal efficiency, and it works. New plants are being built almost as fast as the company can obtain financing.

Contrast that approach to Wal-Mart's, where efficiency is the goal. Wal-Mart achieves its competitive edge through employee commitment and internal cost efficiency. A standard formula is used to build each store, with uniform displays and merchandise. Wal-Mart has more than 1,300 stores, and its administrative expenses are the lowest of any chain. The distribution system is a marvel of efficiency. Goods can be delivered to any store in less than two days after an order is placed. Stores are controlled from the top, but store managers are also given some freedom to adapt to local conditions. Performance is high, and employees are satisfied because the pay is good and more than half of them share in corporate profits.

An even greater contrast is seen in the welfare office at Newark, New Jersey. The office is small, but workers are overwhelmed with rules. One employee pointed to a four-inch stack of memos about recent rule changes resulting from Congress rewriting the laws concerning food stamp distribution. Employees don't have time to read the memos, much less learn the new rules. Applicants have to fill out four-page forms without a single mistake or food stamps will be delayed for weeks. Along with the rules, the number of applicants has also been increasing. Most office employees have been thrown into the role of serving clients, and there is little staff to do typing and filing. Employees are frustrated, and so are welfare applicants. Fights break out occasionally. One employee commented, "We're lucky we don't have a riot."[30]

Several structural and contextual dimensions of Gore & Associates, Wal-Mart, and the welfare agency are illustrated in Exhibit 1.4. Gore & Associates is a medium-sized manufacturing organization that ranks very low with respect to formalization, standardization, and centralization. A number of professional staff are assigned to nonworkflow activities to do the research and development needed to stay abreast of changes in the fiber industry. Wal-Mart is much more formalized, standardized, and centralized. Efficiency is more important than new products, so most activities are guided by standard regulations. The percentage of nonworkflow personnel is kept to a minimum. The welfare agency, in contrast to the other organizations, reflects its status as a small part of a large government bureaucracy. The agency is overwhelmed with rules and standard ways of doing things. Rules are dictated from the top. Most employees are assigned to workflow activities, although in normal times a substantial number of people are devoted to administration and clerical support.

Structural and contextual dimensions can thus tell a lot about an organization and about differences among organizations. Organization dimensions are examined in more detail in later chapters to determine the appropriate level of each dimension needed to perform effectively in each organizational setting.

What Is Organization Theory?

Organization theory is not a collection of facts; it is a way of thinking about organizations. Organization theory is a way to see and analyze organizations more accurately and deeply than one otherwise could. The way to see and think about organizations is based upon patterns and regularities in organizational design and behavior. Organization scholars search for these regularities, define them, measure them, and make them available to the rest of us. The facts from the research are not as important as the general patterns and insights into organizational functioning.

HISTORY

You may recall from an earlier management course that the modern era of management theory began early in this century with the classical management perspective, which included both scientific management and administrative principles approaches. **Scientific management,** pioneered by Frederick Taylor, claimed decisions about organization and job design should be based on precise, scientific procedures after careful study of individual situations. **Administrative principles** focused more on the total organization and grew from the insights of practitioners. For example, Henry Fayol proposed fourteen principles of management, such as "each subordinate receives orders from only one superior" (unity of command) and "similar activ-

Exhibit 1.4   Characteristics of Three Organizations.

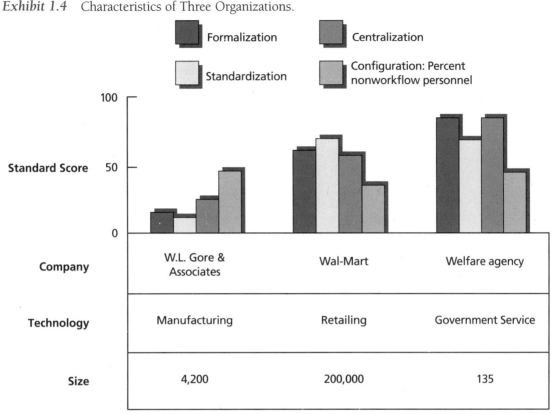

ities in an organization should be grouped together under one manager" (unity of direction).[31] Scientific management and administrative principles were closed systems approaches that did not anticipate the chaos facing companies in the 1990s.

Following classical management theory, other academic approaches emerged. The Hawthorne studies showed that positive treatment of employees increased motivation and productivity and laid the groundwork for subsequent work on leadership, motivation, and human resource management. The work of sociologists on bureaucracy, beginning with Weber, appeared in the 1950s and 1960s and helped establish the notions of bureaucracy that will be discussed in Chapter 5. Later organizations came to be characterized as rational, problem-solving, decision-making systems.[32]

Scientific management, administrative principles, and bureaucratic approaches to organizing seemed to work well into the 1950s and 1960s. Now we see that success during this period occurred because the economies of Europe and Japan had been shattered by World War II, so North American companies had the playing field to themselves. Organizations became horrendously overmanaged, with bloated administrative ratios and professional staff ratios that would sink many organizations in the 1970s and 1980s. International competition from Europe and Japan provided the rude awakening. For example, Xerox discovered it was using 1.3 overhead workers for every direct worker, while its Japanese affiliate needed only 0.6 overhead workers. By the 1980s, North American companies had to find a better way. AT&T

cut 30,000 managers during the 1980s. The merger of Chevron and Gulf led to the dismissal of 18,000 employees, many of whom were managers. GE laid off 50,000 salaried employees.[33]

The 1980s produced new corporate cultures that valued lean staff, flexibility, rapid response to the customer, motivated employees, caring for customers, and quality products. The world was changing fast because corporate boundaries were altered by waves of merger activity, much of it international, and increased international competition.

The net effect of the evolving business environment and evolving study of organization theory has produced two outcomes: a more organic approach to management and the use of contingency theory and models to describe and convey organizational concepts.

PARADIGM SHIFT

A **paradigm** is a shared mind-set that represents a fundamental way of thinking, perceiving, and understanding the world. Our beliefs and understandings direct our behavior. In today's fast-paced society, a number of shifts in ways of thinking and understanding are occurring, and these in turn are associated with shifts in understanding and behavior taking place in organizations.

Shifts in Society   Some of the shifts occurring in society are reflected in Exhibit 1.5 as old versus new paradigms. In today's uncertain world, which seems to grow smaller and more interconnected even as it becomes more fragmented and divided, the scope of reference is by necessity international rather than domestic. In addition, the general population, and thus the work force, is increasingly culturally diverse, and workers are becoming more interested in opportunities for personal and professional growth than in guarantees of economic security. Perhaps one of the greatest shifts has been from an exploitative approach to our world's natural resources to an ecologically sensitive approach. Moreover, there has been a subtle increase in feminine values of feeling, relationship building, openness, understanding, and flexibility, compared to masculine values of competitiveness, rationality, individuality, aggressiveness, and control.[34]

Shifts in Organizations   Significant changes are occurring in organizations in response to changes in the society at large. These are reflected in Exhibit 1.6 as a shift from a mechanistic paradigm to an organic paradigm. A tightly controlled approach is associated with a **mechanistic management.** A loose, flexible approach is typically associated with **organic management.**

Exhibit 1.5
Old vs. New
Paradigms in
Society.

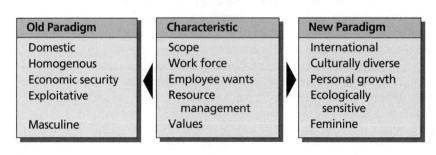

Old Paradigm	Characteristic	New Paradigm
Domestic	Scope	International
Homogenous	Work force	Culturally diverse
Economic security	Employee wants	Personal growth
Exploitative	Resource management	Ecologically sensitive
Masculine	Values	Feminine

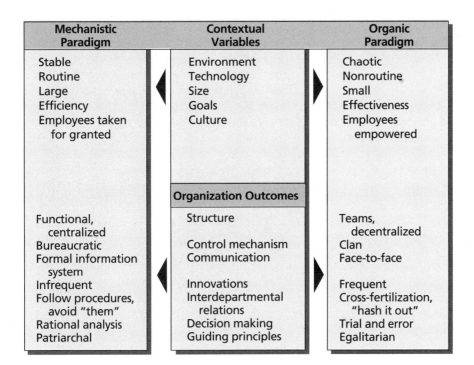

Exhibit 1.6
Mechanistic vs.
Organic Organi-
zational Para-
digms.

In the old paradigm, environments were more certain than they are today, technologies tended to be routine manufacturing processes, and organizations were suited to large size and efficient production in which employees were treated as just another exploitable resource. Internal structures tended to be vertical, functional, and bureaucratic. The organization could use rational analysis and be guided by patriarchal values reflected in the vertical hierarchy and superior-subordinate power distinctions.[35]

The new paradigm recognizes the unstable, even chaotic nature of the external environment. Technologies are typically nonroutine, and small size is as important as large size, with more emphasis on effectiveness and work cultures that empower employees and nurture a multicultural work force. In the new paradigm, organizations are based more on teamwork, clan control, face-to-face interactions, frequent innovations, and a learning approach. Qualities traditionally considered egalitarian—equality, empowerment, horizontal relationships, and consensus building—are particularly important in the new, organic paradigm. One example of the new paradigm is John Deere, as described in the Paradigm Buster.

CONTINGENCY

Despite the changes in the environment, organizations are not all alike. A great many problems occur when all organizations are treated as similar, which was the case with both the administrative principles and bureaucratic approaches that tried to design all organizations alike. The organization charts and financial systems that work in the retail division of a conglomerate will not be appropriate in the manufacturing division.

Paradigm Buster

John Deere

When is a blue-collar worker not a blue-collar worker? When he's traveling around the country acting like a salesman on a corporate expense account, that's when. Or perhaps when she's training customers or dealers in the proper maintenance of a machine she recently helped assemble on the shop floor. Or when he's working with the plant's engineers to figure out ways to eliminate production problems.

Assembly-line workers at John Deere & Company are performing all these functions and more as Deere redefines the role of blue-collar workers. These efforts are in response to a tough environment and years of downsizing that reduced the company's employee base, particularly white-collar supervisors. As the company continues to face decreasing demand for farm equipment and increasing competition from other companies, Deere Chief Executive Hans W. Becherer believes "reaching out to the workers" is the quickest way to fight back. And, so far, it is working as Deere's costs have gone down and its profits up. Much of the cost-cutting has resulted from the assembly-line workers themselves.

But the biggest changes have been in worker relations. Reflecting a new trend in management, Becherer believed his company had a lot to learn about quality and costs from the people who worked daily on the shop floor. So he instituted aggressive, paradigm-shifting programs, such as the following:

- In partnership with the United Auto Workers (UAW), the company assigns factory workers to temporary jobs in customer service, marketing, and dealer and customer training to diversify their skills.
- An experimental program ties the pay raises of hourly workers to their successful completion of college courses and subsequent demonstration of new skills on the job.
- Hourly workers make unsupervised visits to local farms to see how customers are using the equipment and, more important, to see what needs aren't being met by farm equipment companies.
- Assembly-line workers meet regularly with suppliers to help suppliers cut costs and improve delivery times.

It's a new world of cooperation between labor and management at John Deere and one that requires a new level of harmony and trust. UAW leaders and Deere managers spent three days with a human relations consultant at a rural retreat to forge a better relationship. At the retreat, the two sides were forced to trust each other and work together to traverse a difficult obstacle course. Indeed, both sides may feel they're facing an obstacle course each day as they continue to work for peaceful and cooperative relationships in a fast-changing world.

Source: Based on Kevin Kelly, "The New Soul of John Deere," *Business Week,* 31 January 1994, 64–66.

Contingency means that one thing depends upon other things, and for organizations to be effective, there must be a "goodness of fit" between their structure and the conditions in their external environment.[36] What works in one setting may not work in another setting. There is not one best way. Contingency theory means "it depends." For example, the terms in Exhibit 1.6 illustrate contingency theory. Some organizations may experience a certain environment, use a routine technology, and desire efficiency. In this situation, a mechanistic approach to management that uses bureaucratic control procedures, a functional structure, and formal communication would be appropriate. Likewise, organic, free-flowing management processes work best in an uncertain environment with a nonroutine technology. The correct management approach is contingent upon the organization's situation.

MODELS

Theories and models are tools for understanding organizations. A **theory** is a description that explains how organizational characteristics or variables are causally related. For scientists, this description may be a written set of formal statements. For managers, a theory reflects the manager's understanding of how the organization works, and it is not written down. A **model** is a simple representation that describes a few important dimensions of an organization. Many types of models exist. For example, a small-scale physical model was constructed for every set in the movie *Raiders of the Lost Ark*. The models were used to diagnose potential filming problems before the real sets were constructed.

Referring once again back to Exhibit 1.6, the mechanistic and organic paradigms represent two models. Each model contains several variables. **Variables** are organizational characteristics that can be measured or that vary in magnitude across organizations. **Independent variables** have causal impact on other organizational characteristics. **Dependent variables** are caused by other phenomena. For example, the environment and technology can be considered independent variables that influence the dependent variables of structure, control mechanisms, and communications in organizations. A stable environment and routine technology will tend to cause different structures, control mechanisms, and communications than will uncertain environments and nonroutine technologies.

Organization Theory Has Multiple Perspectives

Organization theorists—and some managers—tend to align themselves with distinct perspectives or frames of reference toward organizations. The perspective adopted throughout most of this book is sometimes called the rational-contingency perspective. Two alternative perspectives are radical-Marxism and transaction-cost economics.

RATIONAL-CONTINGENCY PERSPECTIVE

The **rational-contingency perspective** carries an implicit manager orientation toward efficiency and maintenance of the organizational status quo.[37] Researchers adopting this perspective accept the organization status quo as given and simply search for regularities to test to predict and control the organization toward greater efficiency and performance. This perspective assumes that managers are intendedly rational. Managers may not always have the correct answer, but they try to do what is logically best for the organization. Rationality means that goals are selected, effectiveness criteria are established, and managers adopt strategies to achieve designated outcomes in the manner best for the organization. Moreover, managers try to logically design structure and processes to fit the contingencies of environment, technology, and other factors in the organization's situation. The rational-contingency view is widely held, and adherents believe that organizations are instruments for accomplishing tasks that benefit everyone in the organization.[38] Again, most of the concepts in this book are based on the rational-contingency perspective.

RADICAL-MARXISM PERSPECTIVE

Organization theorists who adopt a **radical-Marxism** perspective agree that managers are intendedly rational, but with a twist. Managers are believed to make decisions to maintain themselves in the capitalist class, keeping power and resources for themselves. Managers make decisions not for organizational efficiency and productivity but to maintain or increase their positions. Thus, workers are given small jobs not to increase output but because it "de-skills" workers and prevents them from having a larger claim on the organization. The radical-Marxism perspective is driven by egalitarian values, and CEO salaries that can be two hundred times larger than employee salaries add legitimacy to this argument.

A second aspect of this perspective is the belief in changing the status quo. The goal of organizational theory should be to free organization employees from alienation, exploitation, and repression. Radical-Marxists believe organization theory should have a political agenda that examines the legitimacy of what organizations do and uncovers power and resource distortions. Indeed, the most extreme proponents of this view would like to see a societal transformation that would stop members high in the social hierarchy from dominating lower members.[39]

TRANSACTION-COST ECONOMICS PERSPECTIVE

This approach developed out of the field of economics and has received attention from a number of organizational theorists and organization sociologists.[40] The **transaction-cost economics** perspective assumes that individuals act in their self-interest and that exchanges of goods and services could theoretically occur in the free marketplace. However, as environments become complex and uncertain, the transaction costs become prohibitive. Contracts become lengthy, number in the hundreds, and cannot all be supervised; hence, transactions are brought within the hierarchy of an organization. Behavior can be monitored through supervision, control systems, and audits less expensively than through contracts. A particular organization structure occurs because it is most cost efficient. The goal of individuals in organizations is to reduce transaction costs.

Thus, the focus of this perspective is on the exchange of goods and services rather than on production, and it takes a rather narrow, economic view of organization events. Proponents of the transaction-cost perspective agree it cannot explain all behavior in organizations. Most people and organizations want to behave in ways that minimize costs. However, many activities within organizations are based on trust and social relationships rather than on supervision, contracts, and economic relationships.

What Organization Theory Can Do

Why study organizations? Most people who study organization theory belong to one of two groups: those who are organization managers or potential managers, and those who will not be managers. For the second group, the reason is to appreciate and understand more about the world around them. Organization theory can provide an appreciation and understanding of what is happening in organizations. As described earlier, North America is a society of organizations, and organizations are the key social entities of our time. By studying organizations, you can learn more about a significant aspect of your environment, just as you would by studying geography, astronomy, or music.

For people who are or will be managers, organization theory provides significant insight and understanding to help them become better managers. As in the case of IBM, many managers learn organization theory by trial and error. At IBM, the managers did not understand the situation they were in or the contingencies to which they should respond. The same thing happened at People Express Airlines. In 1984, it was considered one of the best managed companies; twenty-four months later, it flopped. People Express's informal organization structure and control systems were not suited to a large airline. Organization theory identifies variables and provides models so managers know how to diagnose and explain what is happening around them and thus can organize for greater effectiveness.

In a very real sense, organization theory can make a manager more competent and more influential. Understanding how and why organizations act lets managers know how to react. The study of organizations enables people to see and understand things other people cannot see and understand. The topic of organizational culture has been increasingly important in recent years as organizations shift to structures emphasizing teamwork and consensus building. Companies such as Xerox are finding that by using social scientists to help them understand their culture, they can improve productivity and cut costs.

IN PRACTICE ◆ 1.3

Xerox

When Xerox set out in the 1980s to devise less expensive and more productive training programs for its service technicians, it asked for the help of anthropologist Julian Orr. By going on service calls himself, Orr found that repairing copy machines wasn't the technicians' most difficult job—it was handling the people who were trying to use the machines. He found that a large number of service calls were from customers who simply didn't know how to use the complex copiers, not from users whose machines broke down. The technicians often found themselves acting as teachers. While Xerox was focusing on adding more in-depth and complex technological training, the problems service technicians encountered most often were problems of relationships. With this new knowledge, Xerox could develop methods for helping technicians deal with both the machine and the human aspects of their jobs.[41]

The experience at Xerox shows the positive side of what organization theory can do in the area of corporate culture. Organization theory also covers many additional topics that are discussed in this book. The next section provides an overview of these topic areas.

Framework for the Book

What topic areas are relevant to organization theory and design? How does a course in management or organizational behavior differ from a course in organization theory? The answer is related to the concept called level of analysis.

LEVELS OF ANALYSIS

In systems theory, each system is composed of subsystems. Systems are nested within systems, and one **level of analysis** has to be chosen as the primary focus. Four levels of analysis normally characterize organizations, as illustrated in Exhibit 1.7. The individual human being is the basic building block of organizations. The human being is to the organization what a cell is to a biological system. The next higher system level is the group or department. These are collections of individuals who work together to perform group tasks. The next level of analysis is the organization itself. An organization is a collection of groups or departments that combine into the total organization. Organizations themselves can be grouped together into the next higher level of analysis, which is the interorganizational set and community. The interorganizational set is the group of organizations a single organization interacts with. Other organizations in the community also make up an important part of an organization's environment.

Organization theory focuses on the organizational level of analysis but with concern for groups and the environment. To explain the organization, one should look not only at its characteristics but also at the characteristics of the environment and of the departments and groups that make up the organization. The focus of this book is to help you understand organizations by examining their specific characteristics, the nature and relationships among groups and departments that make up the organization, and the collection of organizations that make up the environment.

Are individuals included in organization theory? Organization theory does consider the behavior of individuals, but in the aggregate. People are important, but they are not the primary focus of analysis. Organization theory is distinct from organizational behavior. **Organizational behavior** is the micro approach to organizations because it focuses on the individuals within organizations as the relevant units of analysis. Organizational behavior examines concepts such as motivation, leadership style, and personality and is concerned with cognitive and emotional differences among people within organizations. **Organization theory** is a macro exami-

Exhibit 1.7
Levels of Analysis in Organizations.

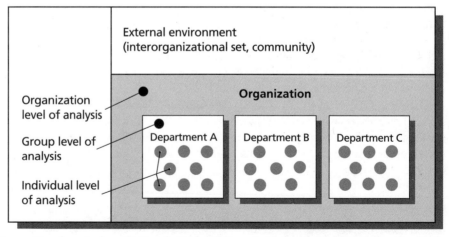

Source: Based on Andrew H. Van de Ven and Diane L. Ferry, *Measuring and Assessing Performance* (New York: Wiley, 1980), p. 8; and Richard L. Daft and Richard M. Steers, *Organizations: A Micro/Macro Approach* (Glenview, Ill.: Scott, Foresman, 1986), p. 8.

nation of organizations because it analyzes the whole organization as a unit. Organization theory is concerned with people aggregated into departments and organizations and with the differences in structure and behavior of the organization level of analysis. Organization theory is the sociology of organizations, while organizational behavior is the psychology of organizations.

Organization theory is directly relevant to top- and middle-management concerns and partly relevant to lower management. Top managers are responsible for the entire organization and must set goals, develop strategy, interpret the external environment, and decide organization structure and design. Middle management is concerned with major departments, such as marketing or research, and must decide how the department relates to the rest of the organization. Middle managers must design their departments to fit work-unit technology and deal with issues of power and politics, intergroup conflict, and information and control systems, each of which is part of organization theory. Organization theory is only partly concerned with lower management because this level of supervision is concerned with employees who operate machines, type letters, teach classes, and sell goods. Organization theory is concerned with the big picture of the organization and its major departments.

PLAN OF THE BOOK

The topics within the field of organization theory are interrelated. Chapters are presented so that major ideas unfold in logical sequence. The framework that guides the organization of the book is shown in Exhibit 1.8. Part I introduces the basic idea of organizations as social systems and the nature of organization theory. This discussion provides the groundwork for Part II, which is about top management, goals and effectiveness, and the external environment. Organizations are open systems that exist for a purpose. The nature of the environment and the achievement of that purpose are the topics of Part II. Part III describes how to design the organization's structure. Organization design is related to such factors as organizational technology and size. This section includes a chapter that explains how to design organization charts and reporting relationships for product, functional, and matrix structures. It concludes with a chapter on new team-based and international designs.

Parts IV and V look at processes inside the organization. Part IV describes how structure can be designed to influence internal systems for innovation and change and for information and control. Part V shifts to dynamic behavioral processes that exist within and between major organizational departments. The management of intergroup conflict, decision making, power and politics, and organizational leadership and culture are covered there. Part VI considers leadership and designs for the future.

PLAN OF EACH CHAPTER

Each chapter begins with an organizational case to illustrate the topic to be covered. Theoretical concepts are introduced and explained in the body of the chapter. Several "In Practice" segments are included in each chapter to illustrate the concepts and show how they apply to real organizations. "Book Marks" are included in most chapters to present organizational issues managers face right now. These book reviews discuss current concepts and applications to deepen and enrich your understanding of organizations. The "Paradigm Busters" illustrate the dramatic changes taking place in management thinking and practice. Each chapter closes with a "Summary and Interpretation"

Exhibit 1.8   Framework for the Book.

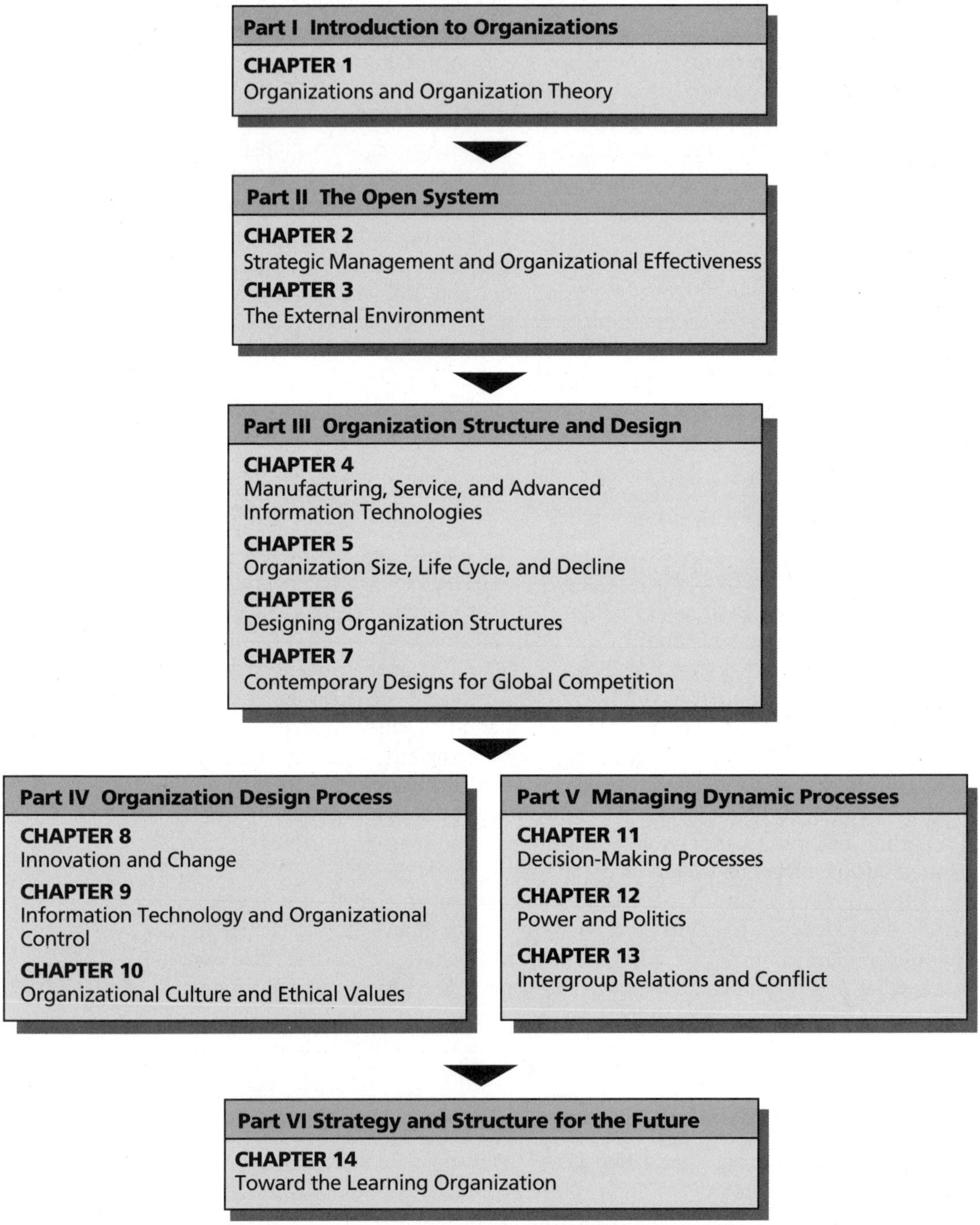

Part I Introduction to Organizations

CHAPTER 1
Organizations and Organization Theory

Part II The Open System

CHAPTER 2
Strategic Management and Organizational Effectiveness
CHAPTER 3
The External Environment

Part III Organization Structure and Design

CHAPTER 4
Manufacturing, Service, and Advanced
Information Technologies
CHAPTER 5
Organization Size, Life Cycle, and Decline
CHAPTER 6
Designing Organization Structures
CHAPTER 7
Contemporary Designs for Global Competition

Part IV Organization Design Process

CHAPTER 8
Innovation and Change
CHAPTER 9
Information Technology and Organizational
Control
CHAPTER 10
Organizational Culture and Ethical Values

Part V Managing Dynamic Processes

CHAPTER 11
Decision-Making Processes
CHAPTER 12
Power and Politics
CHAPTER 13
Intergroup Relations and Conflict

Part VI Strategy and Structure for the Future

CHAPTER 14
Toward the Learning Organization

section and a "Guides to Action" section. "Summary and Interpretation" reviews and interprets important theoretical concepts. "Guides to Action" highlight key points for use in designing and managing organizations.

Summary and Interpretation

One important idea in this chapter is that organizations are systems. In particular, they are open systems that must adapt to the environment to survive. Change has replaced stability as a key trait in today's organizations. The new science of chaos theory reminds managers that organizations must remain constantly vigilant of the environment and be continuously primed to adapt to random, unpredicted events. A number of paradigm shifts are occurring in our society and in organizations. The trend in organizations today is away from mechanistic, highly structured approaches to management toward looser, more flexible organic approaches. Important issues relevant to organizations today are international competition; flatter, team-based structures; permeable boundaries; face-to-face communication between management and workers; and doing things fast.

The focus of analysis for organization theory is not individual people but the organization itself. Relevant concepts include the dimensions of organization structure and context. The dimensions of formalization, specialization, standardization, hierarchy of authority, complexity, centralization, professionalism, personnel ratios, size, organizational technology, environment, goals and strategy, and culture provide labels for measuring and analyzing organizations. These dimensions vary widely from organization to organization. Subsequent chapters provide frameworks for analyzing organizations with these concepts.

Another important idea is that organization theory consists of multiple perspectives. This book tends to adopt the managerial, rational-contingency approach to organization theory. Other equally valid approaches include the radical-Marxist and the transaction-cost economics perspectives.

Finally, most concepts pertain to the top- and middle-management levels of the organization. This book is concerned more with the topics of those levels than with the operational level topics of supervision and motivation of employees, which are discussed in courses on organizational behavior.

KEY CONCEPTS

administrative principles	organizational behavior
chaos theory	organizations
closed system	organization theory
contextual dimensions	paradigm
contingency	radical-Marxism
dependent variables	rational-contingency perspective
independent variables	scientific management
level of analysis	structural dimensions
mechanistic management	subsystems
model	system
open system	theory
organic management	transaction-cost economics

DISCUSSION QUESTIONS

1. What is the definition of *organization*? Briefly explain each part of the definition.
2. What is the difference between an open system and a closed system? Can you give an example of a closed system?

3. What are the five subsystems in organizations? If an organization had to give up one system, which one could it survive the longest without? Explain.

4. Why might human organizations be considered more complex than machine-type systems? What is the implication of this complexity for managers?

5. What is the difference between formalization, specialization, and standardization? Do you think an organization high on one of these three dimensions would also be high on the others? Discuss.

6. Have you ever gone through a paradigm shift? Describe it. What advantages or disadvantages do you see in working for a leading-edge company like John Deere?

7. What does *contingency* mean? What are the implications of contingency theories for managers?

8. What levels of analysis are typically studied in organization theory? How would these contrast with the level of analysis studied in a course in psychology? Sociology? Political science?

9. What is the value of organization theory for nonmanagers? For managers?

10. Early management theorists believed that organizations should strive to be logical and rational, with a place for everything and everything in its place. Discuss the pros and cons of this approach for today's organizations.

 GUIDES TO ACTION

As an organization manager, keep the following guides in mind:

1. Do not ignore the external environment or protect the organization from it. Because the environment is unpredictable, do not expect to achieve complete order and rationality within the organization. Strive for a balance between order and flexibility.

2. Assign people and departments to perform the subsystem functions of production, boundary spanning, maintenance, adaptation, and management. Do not endanger the organization's survival and effectiveness by overlooking these functions.

3. Think of the organization as an entity distinct from the individuals who work in it. Describe the organization according to its size, formalization, decentralization, complexity, specialization, professionalism, personnel ratios, and the like. Use these characteristics to analyze the organization and to compare it with other organizations.

4. Be cautious when applying something that works in one situation to another situation. All organizational systems are not the same. Use organization theory to identify the correct structure, goals, strategy, and organic versus mechanistic control for each organization.

5. Make yourself a competent, influential manager by using the frameworks and models that organization theory provides to interpret and understand the organization around you. Be aware of which perspective you adopt and believe in. Use organization theory to handle such things as intergroup

conflict, power and politics, organization structure, environmental change, and organizational goals.

Consider these guides when analyzing the following case.

Pierce County*

CASE FOR ANALYSIS

Pierce County, the second largest county in Washington, is located in the west central part of the state. It contains 1,676 square miles of land and 279 square miles of water. The county includes extremely varied topography, ranging from sea level to the 14,410-foot summit of Mount Rainier. The current population is approximately 420,000, of which about 205,000, or 49 percent, reside in the eighteen incorporated towns and cities within the county. These towns and cities range in size from South Prairie with a population of 210 to Tacoma, the third largest city in the state, with a population of about 157,000. Approximately 215,000 persons, or 51 percent of the county's population, live in the unincorporated areas of the county.

Pierce County has a strong economic base; the three dominant forces are wood products, aerospace, and military support. The lumber and wood products industry has become much more sophisticated, with plywood and paper production assuming greater importance. Aerospace activity, mainly related to Boeing, is currently strong as a result of a substantial backlog of commercial aircraft orders. Military support activity has fluctuated, although it is currently quite strong with indications of continued strength. The county is served by three major transcontinental railroads, excellent highways, modern airport facilities, one of the finest deep-water ports in the world, and it is well situated for continued residential, commercial, and industrial growth. Several urban centers have developed throughout the county, and a continued and steady population growth is anticipated in all areas of the county, which will exert a considerable impact on the need for governmental services to ensure orderly development in the future.

Pierce County is governed by a board of three commissioners elected, one each, from three commissioner districts. The present county organization consists of approximately 1,200 employees, of which about 450 work under the county engineer in the department of public works. The overall organization is structured such that approximately forty department or other budget heads report directly to the board of county commissioners. A partial list of these departments and their responsibilities appears in Exhibit 1.9.

*This is an abbreviated version of the Pierce County case prepared by Professor Davis W. Carvey at Pacific Lutheran University, Tacoma, Wash. Preparation of this case was made possible by a grant from the Univar Corporation. Copyright © 1980. Reprinted with permission.

Exhibit 1.9   Partial List of Departments Reporting to the Board of County Commissioners.

The primary responsibility of each department is described below. The approximate number of full-time employees is shown in parentheses.

Assigned Counsel (9)
Provides defense services for those without legal counsel.
Annex Manager (17)
Provides maintenance, security, and fire protection for the County Annex (a large suburban county office building).
Board of Equalization (7)
Conducts property assessment and appeals hearings.
Leases (1)
Negotiates and prepares county lease agreements.
Building Maintenance (45)
Maintains County-City Building (downtown Tacoma office building) operations and grounds (excluding gardens).
Community Action Agency (34)
Administers services for low-income residents.
Community Development (3)
Plans, administers, and evaluates programs using federal community development monies.
Cooperative Extension Service (11)
Offers continuing adult education, primarily related to farming.
County Fair (1)
Responsible for yearly county fair, primarily with parks and recreation workers.
Building Inspection (21)
Issues permits and performs building inspections.
Equipment Rental and Revolving (28)
Purchases equipment and provides maintenance, primarily related to county road department.
Inter-County River Improvement (6)
Cares for and maintains rivers crossing county boundaries.
River Improvement (13)
Cares for and maintains rivers flowing only within the county.
Roads (236)
Supervises road construction and maintenance.
Sewers (7)
Designs and supervises sewer system construction.
Solid Waste Management (31)
Disposes of refuse.
Weed Control (2)
Controls weeds, primarily toxic weeds along county roads.
County Operations (7)
Maintains buildings other than the County-City Building.
County Properties (6)
Maintains county buildings' grounds.

Social Services (9)
Contracts with outside agencies for social services.
Communications (5)
Operates and maintains all county communications systems (except telephone) and coordinates communications of surrounding fire districts, small-town police, etc.
District Court Probation
Provides presentence reports, probation, and parole services for Pierce County district courts.
Fire Prevention Bureau (15)
Conducts fire inspections and provides related enforcement.
Information and Research (2)
Completes research, analysis, and report preparation.
Involuntary Commitment (6)
Takes actions related to arranging care and hospitalization for the mentally ill.
Law Enforcement Support Agency (43)
Answers Pierce County emergency telephone number and dispatches the Pierce County Sheriff and the Tacoma Police Department.
Law and Justice Planning (6)
Controls crime-reduction planning and improvement of the criminal justice system.
License (6)
Issues business and occupational licenses.
Manpower Planning (34)
Conducts employment and training programs.
Parks and Recreation (65)
Oversees parks and recreation.
Planning (23)
Conducts comprehensive planning for the county, and administers zoning and related codes.
Purchasing (6)
Purchases supplies and equipment for county operations.
Central Stores, Print Shop, and Mail Room (18)
Controls office supplies, printing, and mail collection and distribution, respectively.
Remann Hall (104)
Administers juvenile court and related services.
Veteran's Aid (4)
Provides veteran's emergency services.
Area Agency on Aging (7)
Provides services for older citizens.
Equal Employment Opportunity (3)
Implements and monitors effectiveness of the Pierce County affirmative action plan.

At least some of the hodgepodge nature of the present organizational structure can be attributed to the rapid growth of both federal and state programs impinging upon county government and services. Frequently, to obtain monies channeled through these programs, the county has had to establish a separate administrative unit to apply for funds and then administer that particular program. Many of these programs have overlapping responsibilities and relationships with a variety of other programs, governmental (federal, state, and local) units, and numerous planning and advisory groups. The result has been a growing bureaucracy consisting of many semiautonomous "fiefdoms" reporting to the commissioners. This system has been subject to increasing citizen criticism in recent years as more and more county residents become disenchanted with what they apparently consider to be an inadequate governmental response to their problems.

Citizen criticism of Pierce County government in general, and of individual commissioners from time to time, continued to mount through the 1970s. During this period, a substantial and growing pressure for change developed, eventually culminating in a 1976 freeholder election to determine whether a *board of freeholders* (that is, a group of fifteen county residents) should be elected for the purpose of studying various forms of government and framing a charter for Pierce County (which would then be put to a vote, for approval or rejection). The most vocal support for the charter plan came from a group called Citizens for a Freeholder Election, chaired by attorney Robert Deutscher. This group conducted a year-long campaign to have the freeholder plan approved. The major opposition came from civic affairs leader Virginia Shackelford and the Factual Information on Freeholder Elections Committee, which she headed. The Pierce County Central Labor Council also came out strongly against the plan.

The 1976 election showed that the citizens of Pierce County did want a change, although, judging from the election results, not as drastic a change as some had hoped. On the one hand, the freeholder proposition was defeated, capturing approximately 48 percent of the vote. On the other hand, the single commissioner up for reelection, two-term incumbent George Sheridan, was soundly beaten by state senator Joe Stortini. Stortini suggested the voters were convinced that meaningful changes were possible within the framework of the present county governmental system and that his own anti-incumbent campaign may have contributed to the freeholder drive's defeat.

One of Commissioner Stortini's first acts after being sworn in was to begin following through on his major reform campaign promises by announcing the appointment of two citizen task forces. One group was to be charged with designing a centralized personnel system, while the other would focus on developing a plan for restructuring the organization (both plans to be implemented within the present commissioner system framework). This action immediately drew the wrath of the local League of Women Voters. Stortini, in spite of this early hostility to his methods, went ahead with his task force program.

The Task Force on Reorganization soon found that the actual workings of the existing organization were so complex and yet so uncoordinated that it was difficult to get complete information concerning each county program in a reasonable length of time. Thus, after several meetings, the task force decided to proceed using the information shown in Exhibit 1.9 as a starting point from which to begin developing a meaningful organizational structure.

QUESTIONS

1. In addition to drafting a proposed chart, analyze and discuss the contextual and structural dimensions of the Pierce County government organization.
2. What are the forces acting on the county commissioners? Will these forces result in a loose or tight management approach? Explain.
3. How might you restructure the departments that report to the county board of commissioners to achieve greater efficiencies and improve responsiveness to county residents?

NOTES

1. Carol J. Loomis, "Dinosaurs?" *Fortune,* 3 May 1993, 36–42.
2. The analysis of IBM was based on Paul Carroll, *Big Blues: The Unmaking of IBM* (New York: Crown Publishers, 1993); Judith H. Dobrzynski, "Rethinking IBM," *Business Week,* 4 October 1993, 86–97; David Kirkpatrick, "Breaking Up IBM," *Fortune,* 27 July 1992, 44–55, "Gerstner's New Vision for IBM," *Fortune,* 15 November 1993, 119–26, and "Big Blue and Dumb," Review of Paul Carroll's *Big Blues, Fortune,* 20 September 1993, 159; Carol J. Loomis, "Dinosaurs?" *Fortune,* 3 May 1993, 36–42; Michael W. Miller and Laurence Hooper, "Akers Quits at IBM under Heavy Pressure; Dividend Is Slashed," *Wall Street Journal,* 27 January 1993, A1, A6; John W. Verity, "IBM: A Bull's-Eye and a Long Shot," *Business Week,* 13 December 1993, 88–89; and G. Pascal Zachary and Stephen Kreider Yoder, "Computer Industry Divides into Camps of Winners and Losers," *Wall Street Journal,* 27 January 1993, A1, A4.
3. Loomis, "Dinosaurs?"
4. Catherine Arnst, "Now HP Stands for Hot Products," *Business Week,* 14 June 1993, 36.
5. Thomas A. Stewart, "Welcome to the Revolution," *Fortune,* 13 December 1993, 66–77.
6. Stewart, "Welcome to the Revolution."
7. Kim S. Cameron, "Organizational Downsizing," paper presented to the Army Research Center, February 1991.
8. Thomas A. Stewart, "Reengineering: The Hot New Managing Tool," *Fortune,* 23 August 1993, 41–48.
9. Thomas A. Stewart, "The Search for the Organization of Tomorrow," *Fortune,* 18 May 1992, 92–98.
10. Walter Kiechel III, "How We Will Work in the Year 2000," *Fortune,* 17 May 1993, 38–52.
11. Thomas A. Stewart, "Reengineering."
12. Joseph Weber, "Farewell, Fast Track," *Business Week,* 10 December 1990, 192–200.
13. Kiechell III, "How We Will Work," 38–52.
14. Tom Peters, "Time-Obsessed Competition," *Management Review,* September 1990, 16–20.
15. Dobrzynski, "Rethinking IBM," 86–97.
16. Kiechel III, "How We Will Work," 38–52.
17. Bernard Wysocki, Jr., "American Firms Send Office Work Abroad to Use Cheaper Labor," *Wall Street Journal,* 14 August 1991, A1, A4.
18. Howard Aldrich, *Organizations and Environments* (Englewood Cliffs, N.J.: Prentice-Hall, 1979), 3.
19. Arthur G. Bedeian and Raymond F. Zamnuto, *Organizations: Theory and Design* (Chicago: Dryden, 1991), 9; Aldrich, *Organizations and Environments,* 4–6.
20. Kirkpatrick, "Gerstner's New Vision for IBM," 119–26.
21. Stewart, "The Search for the Organization of Tomorrow," 92–98.
22. Noel M. Tichy and Stratford Sherman, *Control Your Destiny or Someone Else Will* (New York: Currency Doubleday, 1993).
23. Charles Perrow, "A Society of Organization," paper presented at the Macro Organizational Behavior Society, Northwestern University, October 1987.
24. Tom Mathews, "The Secret History of the War," *Newsweek,* 18 March 1991, 28–39.
25. James D. Thompson, *Organizations in Action* (New York: McGraw-Hill, 1967), 4–13.
26. Daniel Katz and Robert L. Kahn, *The Social Psychology of Organizations* (New York: Wiley, 1978).
27. Richard L. Daft and Robert H. Lengel, "The Challenge of Chaos," *Owen Manager* 14 (Spring 1993): 2–7.
28. John Huey, "Managing in the Midst of Chaos," *Fortune,* 5 April 1993, 38–48.
29. The following discussion was heavily influenced by Richard H. Hall, *Organizations: Structures, Processes, and Outcomes* (Englewood Cliffs, N.J.: Prentice-Hall, 1991); D. S. Pugh, "The Measure-

ment of Organization Structures: Does Context Determine Form?" *Organizational Dynamics* 1 (Spring 1973): 19–34; and D. S. Pugh, D. J. Hickson, C. R. Hinings, and C. Turner, "Dimensions of Organization Structure," *Administrative Science Quarterly* 13 (1968): 65–91.

30. Adapted from John Huey, "The New Post-Heroic Leadership," *Fortune,* 21 February 1994, 42–50; John Huey, "Wal-Mart: Will It Take over the World?" *Fortune,* 30 January 1989, 52–61. Howard Rudnitsky, "How Sam Walton Does It," *Forbes,* 16 August 1982, 42–44; and Janet Guyan, "Food-Stamp Red Tape Raises Tension Levels in Understaffed Offices," *Wall Street Journal,* 27 June 1984, 1, 16.

31. Richard L. Daft, *Management,* 3d ed. (Chicago: Dryden, 1994).

32. Richard L. Daft and Arie Y. Lewin, "Can Organization Studies Begin to Break out of the Normal Science Strait-jacket? An Editorial Essay," *Organization Science* 1 (1990): 1–9.

33. Amanda Bennett, *The Death of the Organization Man* (New York: William Morrow, 1990).

34. John A. Byrne, "Paradigms for Postmodern Managers," *Business Week*, special edition *Reinventing America,* 1992, 62–63; Audrey Edwards, "Cultural Diversity in Today's Corporation: The Enlightened Manager," *Working Woman,* January 1991, 45–51; Brian Dumaine, "The New Non-Managers," *Fortune,* 22 February 1993, 80–84.

35. Kathleen B. Iannello, *Decisions Without Hierarchy* (New York: Routledge, 1992).

36. Johannes M. Pennings, "Structural Contingency Theory: A Reappraisal," *Research in Organizational Behavior* 14 (1992): 267–309.

37. Dennis A. Gioia and Evelyn Pitre, "Multiparadigm Perspectives on Theory Building," *Academy of Management Review* 15 (1990): 584–602.

38. Richard H. Hall, *Organizations: Structures, Processes, and Outcomes* (Englewood Cliffs, N.J.: Prentice-Hall, 1991).

39. Gioia and Pitre, "Multiparadigm Perspectives on Theory Building."

40. William S. Hesterly, Julia Liebeskind, and Todd R. Zenger, "Organizational Economics: An Impending Revolution in Organization Theory?" *Academy of Management Review* 15 (1990): 402–20; Oliver E. Williamson, *Markets and Hierarchy: Analysis and Antitrust Implications* (New York: Free Press, 1975) and *The Economic Institutions of Capitalism* (New York: Free Press, 1985); Oliver E. Williamson and William G. Ouchi, "The Markets and Hierarchy Program of Research: Origins, Implications, Prospects," in Andrew H. Van de Ven and William E. Joyce, eds., *Perspectives on Organizational Design and Behavior* (New York: Wiley-Interscience, 1981).

41. Christina Elnora Garza, "Studying the Natives on the Shopfloor," *Business Week,* 30 September 1991, 74–78.

PART

2

*T*he Open System

CHAPTER 2

Strategic Management and Organizational Effectiveness

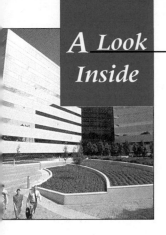

Compaq Computer

When Eckhard Pfeiffer took over as CEO of Compaq Computer, his first priority was to develop new goals and strategies for the company. Compaq traditionally sold computers to corporations through middlemen. Manufacturing costs continued to climb, but sales weren't keeping up. Then Compaq posted its first-ever quarterly loss and laid off 1,700 workers. Employee morale hit rock bottom.

Compaq's ambitious new mission is to be number one in PC and workstation market share by 1996. This will mean changing from a supplier of PCs to corporations into a maker of computers for every market, from small, hand-held communicators to home computers, all at low prices. To achieve this new mission, Compaq's new goals include the following:

1. Design and make competitively priced computers for specific market segments and advertise them aggressively. Television ads are already running for Compaq's new Pressario line of home computers. The machines have such user-friendly features as factory-installed software and a built-in telephone answering machine.
2. Improve distribution: Compaq computers must be accessible to every consumer. Compaq has already added thousands of retailers, including Wal-Mart.
3. Cut manufacturing and inventory costs. Subassembly work will be performed by contractors to cut costs. And rather than stockpile computers in inventory, Compaq is shifting to a "build to order" manufacturing system.
4. Establish strong alliances with other computer-related companies. As Compaq moves into new markets, it will need alliances with software companies, such as Microsoft, which is fine-tuning a version of its Windows software for Compaq's "mobile companion," a tiny notebook computer.

So far, Compaq's new mission and goals seem to fit the marketplace. Competitors were stunned when Compaq cut prices on some computers by one-third and rushed new models to market. Compaq has more than doubled its share of the $35 billion-a-year PC and workstation market, from 3.8 percent to 10 percent, and it made more money in 1993 than Apple and IBM combined. Employee morale is way up also, which helps productivity. With volume doubling, total manufacturing costs fell by almost $10 million. Compaq Computer is moving boldly into the future.[1]

A n **organizational goal** is a desired state of affairs that the organization attempts to reach.[2] A goal represents a result or end point toward which organizational efforts are directed. The goals for Compaq Computer include new, competitively priced computers for all markets, better distribution of products, money-saving manufacturing systems, and alliances with other computer-related companies.

PURPOSE OF THIS CHAPTER

Top managers give direction to organizations. They set goals and develop the strategies for their organization to attain those goals. The purpose of this chapter is to help you understand the types of goals organizations pursue and some of the competitive strategies managers develop to reach those goals. The chapter also describes the most popular approaches to measuring the effectiveness of organizational efforts. To manage organizations well, managers need a clear sense of how to measure effectiveness. The last part of the chapter discusses some characteristics common to effective organizations.

Top Management Strategic Direction

An organization is created and designed to achieve some end, which is decided by the chief executive officer and/or the top management team. Organization structure and design is an outcome of this purpose. Indeed, *the primary responsibility of top management is to determine an organization's goals, strategy, and design, therein adapting the organization to a changing environment.*[3] Middle managers do much the same thing for major departments within the guidelines provided by top management. The relationships through which top managers provide direction and then design are illustrated in Exhibit 2.1.

The direction setting process typically begins with an assessment of the opportunities and threats in the external environment, including the amount of change, uncertainty, and resource availability, which will be discussed in more detail in Chapter 3. Top management also assesses internal strengths and weaknesses to define the company's distinctive competence compared with other firms in the industry.[4] The assessment of internal environment often includes an evaluation of each department and is shaped by past performance and the leadership style of the

Exhibit 2.1 Top Management Role in Organization Direction, Design, and Effectiveness.

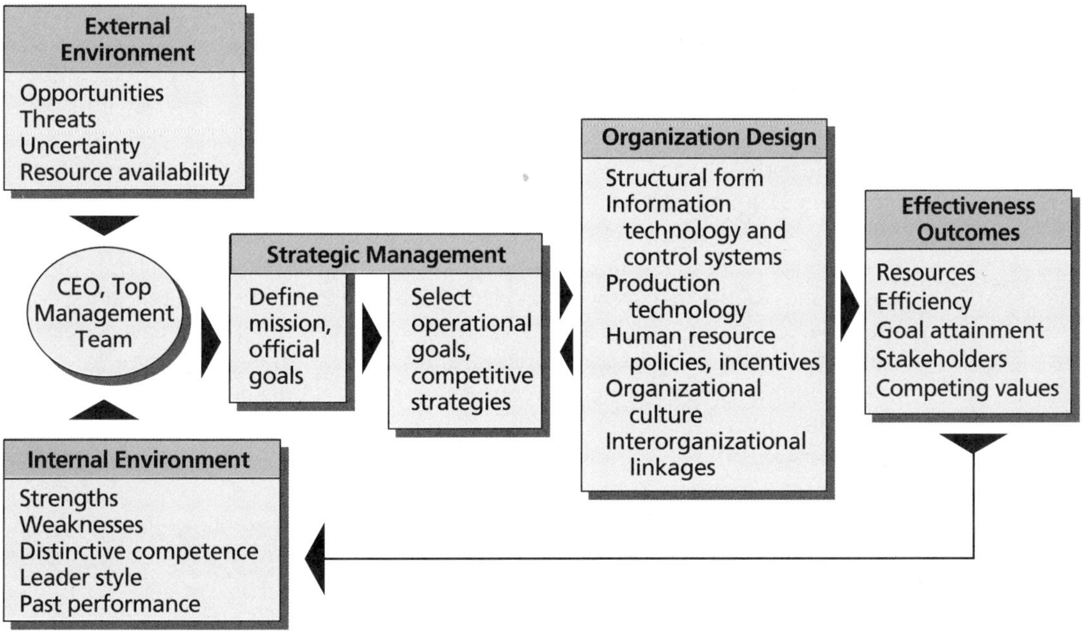

Source: Adapted from Arie Y. Lewin and Carroll U. Stephens, "Individual Properties of the CEO as Determinants of Organization Design," unpublished manuscript, Duke University, 1990.

CEO and top management team. The next step is to define overall mission and official goals based upon the correct fit between external opportunities and internal strengths. Specific operational goals or strategies can then be formulated to define how the organization is to accomplish its overall mission.

In Exhibit 2.1, organization design reflects the way goals and strategies are implemented. Organization design is the administration and execution of the strategic plan. *This is the role of organization theory.* Organization direction is achieved through decisions about structural form, information technology and control systems, the type of production technology, human resource policies, culture, and linkages to other organizations. Changes in structure, technology, human resource policies, culture, and interorganization linkages will be discussed in subsequent chapters. Also note the arrow in Exhibit 2.1 running from organization design back to strategic management. This means that strategies often are made within the current structure of the organization, so that current design constrains or puts limits on goals and strategy. More often than not, however, as we saw at Compaq Computer, the new goals and strategy are selected based on environmental needs, and then the top management attempts to redesign the organization to achieve those ends.

Finally, Exhibit 2.1 illustrates how managers evaluate the effectiveness of organizational efforts—that is, the extent to which the organization realizes its goals. This chart reflects the most popular ways of measuring performance, each of which is discussed later in this chapter. It is important to note here that performance measurements feed back into the internal environment, so that past performance of the organization is assessed by top management in setting new goals and strategies for the future.

The role of top management is important because managers can interpret the environment differently and develop different goals. For example, immediately after World War II, Sears Roebuck and Montgomery Ward were similar in size and reputation. Sears expected economic prosperity and a population migration to the suburbs and adopted goals of growth and expansion. Montgomery Ward expected a depression and retrenched to save money. Sears' managers were correct, and Sears grew to be several times larger than Ward's. Today, Wal-Mart interpreted the retail environment to need cost efficiency and service to smaller cities. This interpretation has allowed Wal-Mart to surpass Sears in size because Sears was designed for high prices and a slow response to environmental changes. Top management choices about goals, strategies, and organization design made the difference.

Remember that goals and strategy are not fixed or taken for granted. Top managers and middle managers must select goals for their respective units, and the ability to make these choices largely determines firm success. Organization design is used to implement goals and strategy and also determines organizational success. We will now discuss further the concept of organizational goals and strategy, and in the latter part of this chapter, we will discuss various ways to evaluate organizational effectiveness.

Organizational Goals

Many types of goals exist in an organization, and each type performs a different function. One major distinction is between the officially stated goals of the organization and the operative goals the organization actually pursues.

OFFICIAL GOALS

The overall goal for an organization is often called the **mission**—the organization's reason for existence. The mission describes the organization's vision, its shared values and beliefs, and its reason for being. It can have a powerful impact on an organization.[5] The mission is sometimes called the **official goals,** which are the formally stated definition of business scope and outcomes the organization is trying to achieve. Official goal statements typically define business operations and may focus on values, markets, and customers that distinguish the organization. Whether called a mission statement or official goals, the organization's general statement of its purpose and philosophy often is written down in a policy manual or the annual report. The mission statement for the Toro Company is shown in Exhibit 2.2. Note how the overall mission, values, and goals are all defined.

OPERATIVE GOALS

Operative goals designate the ends sought through the actual operating procedures of the organization and explain what the organization is actually trying to do.[6] Operative goals describe specific measurable outcomes and are often concerned with the

---

THE TORO DIFFERENCE

THE TORO MISSION

We will produce the most distinctive and the best outdoor maintenance and beautification products in the world.

THE TORO DIFFERENCE

We believe that to be the best, we must be different. The Toro difference is an attitude that says we care—a commitment to every action and business decision we make—and a sense of pride in who we are, what we do and what we mean to each other. We are individuals with unique talents and strengths, working as a team to serve Toro's customers, employees and stockholders.

Our Beliefs Will Guide Us

Our beliefs will help us shape the present and pave a path into the future. We believe:
- Our employees will always be our most valuable asset
- Excellent service and superior quality are Toro's priorities
- Achieving maximum productivity is critical to our success
- Prudent risk-taking is vital to our long term success and growth
- Innovation and creativity are vital attributes we must encourage and reinforce

These beliefs must be our foundation for building relationships, directing actions and working as a team.

Our People Count

The Toro Company's greatest asset is its employees. Therefore we:
- Care about and support each other as individuals
- Communicate openly, honestly and supportively
- Build trust and display integrity in our actions as well as our words
- Demonstrate compassion and respect for each other
- Provide every opportunity for professional growth and enrichment

We will accept nothing less from ourselves or from our co-workers.

EXCELLENCE IN ACTION

By serving Toro employees and customers with excellence, an attractive return on investment will be a natural product of our efforts.

Exhibit 2.2
Mission Statement of the Toro Company.

Source: Used with permission of the Toro Company.

short run. Operative versus official goals represent actual versus stated goals. Operative goals typically pertain to the primary tasks an organization must perform, similar to the subsystem activities identified in Chapter 1.[7] These goals concern overall performance, boundary spanning, maintenance, adaptation, and production activities. Specific goals for each primary task provide direction for the day-to-day decisions and activities within departments.

Overall Performance   Profitability reflects the overall performance of for-profit organizations. Profitability may be expressed in terms of net income, earnings per share, or return on investment. Other overall goals are growth and output volume. Growth pertains to increases in sales or profits over time. Volume pertains to total sales or the amount of products or services delivered. For the fibers unit of Dupont Company, CEO Edgar Woolard has set a goal of increasing sales to $9 million by 1996. But the company has fallen short of his overall performance goal of raising return on equity to an average of 16 percent.[8]

Not-for-profit organizations such as labor unions do not have goals of profitability, but they do have goals that attempt to specify the delivery of services to members within specified budget expense levels. Growth and volume goals also may be indicators of overall performance in not-for-profit organizations.

Resources   Resource goals pertain to the acquisition of needed material and financial resources from the environment. They may involve obtaining financing for the construction of new plants, finding less expensive sources for raw materials, or hiring top-quality college graduates.

Market   Market goals relate to the market share or market standing desired by the organization. Market goals are the responsibility of marketing, sales, and advertising departments. An example of a market goal is Bausch & Lomb's desire to capture at least 50 percent of every segment of the contact lens market. Hitachi has 60 percent of the world market for special laser devices that send voice signals down fiber-optic phone lines, and Frito-Lay controls about half the market share for salty snacks.[9] All three companies have operative goals of having the largest market share in a specific industry.

Employee Development   Employee development pertains to the training, promotion, safety, and growth of employees. It includes both managers and workers. MMI, which manages fourteen hotels and resorts, has a goal of increasing its human resource department budget by 20 percent to $450,000 to increase employee training, picnics, and get-togethers.[10] These activities improve morale and help employees develop the skills for higher-level jobs.

Innovation   Innovation goals pertain to internal flexibility and readiness to adapt to unexpected changes in the environment. Innovation goals are often defined with respect to the development of specific new services, products, or production processes. For example, Rubbermaid has a goal of generating enough new products so that 30 percent of sales come from products no more than five years old. A related goal is to launch one hundred products annually, one-third of which are new from the ground up.[11]

Productivity Productivity goals concern the amount of output achieved from available resources. They typically describe the amount of resource inputs required to reach desired outputs and are thus stated in terms of "cost for a unit of production," "units produced per employee," or "resource cost per employee." For example, Rubbermaid has a productivity goal of increasing the number of units produced per worker per day. Total output increased from three hundred units per worker per day in 1952 to five hundred units in 1980 and 750 in 1988. Another productivity goal was to reduce the number of sales representatives and to increase the work force by only 50 percent while doubling sales. The resulting increases in productivity have produced fresh profits for Rubbermaid.

MANAGING MULTIPLE GOALS

How do managers accomplish the goal-setting process when each department manager, for example, may champion a different goal? The focus of managers on different goals can create heated conflicts and the desire to serve different environmental demands. To resolve these differences, managers typically engage in bargaining and "satisficing."

Bargaining engages managers with different goals in a give-and-take discussion to find a workable basis for achieving their joint interests. This process leads to a **coalition,** which is an alliance among several managers who agree about organizational goals.[12] Coalitions arise through the bargaining process to give managers a way to bridge their differences. A coalition will support certain goals. The term *coalition* describes the political nature of the goal-agreement process. Through discussion and negotiation, most interest groups are able to attain some part of their goals.

Satisficing means organizations accept a "satisfactory" rather than a maximum level of performance.[13] By accepting satisfactory performance across several criteria, the organization can achieve several goals simultaneously. Ralston Purina tries to attain satisfactory levels of profit, market share, and new products. It doesn't maximize any of these goals. University students have multiple goals, including a livable income, good grades, and social activities. Instead of maximizing income, getting straight As, and spending large amounts of time with family and friends, which would be goal maximization, most students "satisfice." They earn enough money to get through the next semester, achieve a few As but accept some Bs and Cs, and try to see the family on weekends. Organizations use a similar process to satisfice across multiple goals.

PURPOSES OF GOALS

Both official goals and operative goals are important for the organization, but they serve very different purposes. Official goals provide legitimacy, while operative goals provide employee direction, decision guidelines, and criteria of performance. These purposes are summarized in Exhibit 2.3.

Legitimacy A mission statement (or official goals) symbolizes legitimacy to external and internal stakeholders. The official goals describe the purpose of the organization so people know what it stands for and accept its existence. Moreover, employees join and become committed to an organization when they identify with the organization's stated goals.

Exhibit 2.3
Goal Type and
Purpose.

Type of Goals	Purpose of Goals
Official goals, mission:	Legitimacy
Operative goals:	Employee direction and motivation Decision guidelines Standard of performance

Most top managers want their company to look good to other companies in their environment. Managers want customers, competitors, suppliers, and the local community to look upon them in a favorable light. The officially stated goals help create this positive impression. For example, each year *Fortune* magazine reflects the corporate concern for legitimacy with ratings of the reputations of corporations in each of thirty-two industries. Not all of a company's reputation can be traced to tangible financial facts. While financial status alone would predict that UST (U.S. Tobacco Company) would rank as a highly admired company, the declining legitimacy of cigarettes pushed it to number ninety-four on *Fortune's* reputation scale.[14] Not-for-profit and heavily regulated government agencies also work to win the goodwill of external groups. For example, telephone companies recently were criticized for offering sexually explicit dial-up message services. Public sentiment caused many phone companies to shut them down. Telephone companies as well as cigarette manufacturers develop mission and goal statements that are legitimate and socially responsible.

Employee Direction and Motivation   Goals give a sense of direction to organization participants. The stated end toward which an organization is striving and strategies for how to get there tell employees what they are working for. Goals help motivate participants, especially if participants help select the goals. At 3M, for example, the overall goal that "25 percent of sales should come from products developed in the past five years" is widely accepted and pursued by employees. All employees work toward innovation.

Decision Guidelines   The goals of an organization also act as guidelines for employee decision making. Organizational goals are a set of constraints on individual behavior and decisions.[15] They help define the correct decisions concerning organization structure, innovation, employee welfare, or growth. When Owens-Illinois, a glass container manufacturer, established the goal of reducing volume to improve profits, internal decisions were redirected. Owens-Illinois had been running marginal plants just to maintain volume. The new goal of increased profits provided decision guidelines that led to the closing of these marginal plants.

Criteria of Performance   Goals provide a standard for assessment. The level of organization performance, whether in terms of profits, units produced, or number of complaints, needs a basis for evaluation. Is a profit of 10 percent on sales good enough? The answer lies in goals. Goals reflect past experience and describe the desired state for the future. If the profit goal is 8 percent, then a 10 percent return is excellent. When Owens-Illinois shifted from volume to profit goals, profits increased by 30 percent. This occurred during the period when two competitors reported profit declines of 61 percent and 76 percent. Profit thus replaced production volume as the criterion of performance.[16]

SUMMARY

Official goals and mission statements describe a value system for the organization, while operative goals represent the primary tasks of the organization. Official goals legitimize the organization, while operative goals are more explicit and well defined. For example, when Datapoint Corporation was trying to achieve greater efficiency in customer service, managers adopted the operative goals of schedule, cost, and quality. Manufacturing was expected to "deliver a product to the customer on time, deliver it at minimal cost, and deliver a good quality product."[17] These operative goals provided direction to employees and helped attain the overall company goal of continuing to have consecutive quarterly increases in net revenues, net earnings, and shipments.

Organizational Strategies

A **strategy** is a plan for interacting with the competitive environment to achieve organizational goals. Some managers think of goals and strategies as interchangeable, but for our purposes, goals define where the organization wants to go and strategies define how it will get there. For example, a goal may be to achieve 15 percent annual sales growth; strategies to reach that goal might include aggressive advertising to attract new customers, motivating salespeople to increase the average size of customer purchases, and acquiring other businesses that produce similar products. Strategies can include any number of techniques to achieve the goal. Two models for formulating strategies are the Porter model of competitive strategies and Miles and Snow's strategy typology. Each provides a framework for competitive action.

PORTER'S COMPETITIVE STRATEGIES

Michael E. Porter studied a number of businesses and introduced a framework describing three competitive strategies.[18] These strategies and the organizational characteristics associated with each are summarized in Exhibit 2.4.

1. Low-Cost Leadership   The **low-cost leadership** strategy tries to increase market share by emphasizing low cost compared to competitors. With a low-cost leadership strategy, the organization aggressively seeks efficient facilities, pursues cost reductions, and uses tight controls to produce products more efficiently than its competitors. For example, Scottish Inn and Motel 6 are low-priced alternatives to Holiday Inn and Ramada. Gallo has achieved a low-cost leadership position in the wine industry and remained a profitable company by consistently holding at least a 15 percent cost advantage over its largest domestic competitors.[19] Low cost is an effective strategy, but getting there can be a difficult shift for a high-cost company, as described in the Paradigm Buster.

2. Differentiation   In a **differentiation** strategy, organizations attempt to distinguish their products or services from others in the industry. An organization may use

Exhibit 2.4
Organizational
Characteristics
for Porter's
Competitive
Strategies.

Strategy	Commonly Required Skills and Resources
Low-cost leadership	Tight cost control Process engineering skills Intense supervision of labor Products designed for ease in manufacture Frequent, detailed control reports
Differentiation	Strong marketing abilities Strong coordination among functional departments Creative flair Strong capability in basic research Corporate reputation for quality or technological leadership
Focus	Combination of the above policies directed at a specific strategic target

Source: Reprinted with permission of The Free Press, a division of Macmillan, Inc., from *Competitive Strategy: Techniques for Analyzing Industries and Competitors* by Michael E. Porter. Copyright © 1980 by The Free Press.

advertising, distinctive product features, exceptional service, or new technology to achieve a product perceived as unique. This strategy usually targets customers who are not particularly concerned with price, so it can be quite profitable. Mercedes-Benz automobiles, Maytag appliances, and Tylenol are the products of companies that have benefited from a differentiation strategy. However, companies must remember that successful differentiation strategies require a number of costly activities, such as product research and design and extensive advertising.

3. Focus   With Porter's third strategy, the **focus** strategy, the organization concentrates on a specific regional market or buyer group. The company will try to achieve either a low-cost advantage or a differentiation advantage within a narrowly defined market. One example of focus strategy is the brokerage firm of Edward D. Jones & Company. It focused on the investment needs of rural America, moving into small towns where Merrill Lynch representatives wouldn't even stop for gas. In this ignored market niche, Jones has opened more than 1,300 offices and serves over 1 million customers with its conservative investment philosophy.[20]

MILES AND SNOW'S STRATEGY TYPOLOGY

Another business strategy typology was developed from the study of business strategies by Raymond Miles and Charles Snow.[21] The Miles and Snow typology is based on the idea that managers seek to formulate strategies that will be congruent with the external environment. Organizations strive for a fit among internal characteristics, strategy, and the external environment. The four strategies that can be developed are the prospector, the defender, the analyzer, and the reactor. These strategies, their environments, and the internal organizational characteristics associated with each are shown in Exhibit 2.5.

1. Prospector   The **prospector** strategy is to innovate, take risks, seek out new opportunities, and grow. This strategy is suited to a dynamic, growing environment,

Paradigm Buster

Imperial Oil

Nothing shifts goals and strategy so fast as learning your refinery has eleven months to live. Ken Ball, director of Imperial Oil Limited's refinery in Dartmouth, Nova Scotia, received a performance report placing his refinery near the bottom of North American refineries. Costs were too high, inefficiency was rampant, and he was given eleven months to go from among the worst to among the best, or Imperial would shut his refinery down.

Ball and his management team saw that the refinery had to become a low-cost leader, because retail prices were fixed. Seeking the cooperation of supervisors and employees, he pinpointed the problem as the wrong organization structure. People were organized by what they did, with pipefitters reporting to pipefitters and electricians reporting to electricians. People were so narrowly focused that a pipefitter would never help an electrician.

To achieve low-cost leadership, Ball threw out the rule book and redesigned the plant into four main work teams. Each team was composed of forty to fifty workers and was responsible for an entire horizontal chunk of the refinery operation—such as the conversion of crude oil into useful forms or finished oil movement and storage. Each team contained a spectrum of trades and skills.

As the team concept took hold, the efficiencies became obvious. Fewer supervisors were needed. The refinery shed an amazing 46 percent of the work hours required to run the plant. Seniority was replaced with emphasis on individual performance.

The change in strategy followed by refinery redesign produced striking results. Overall costs fell by 30 percent, and the Dartmouth refinery is now performing in the top quarter of all refineries in North America. Ken Ball and his associates in the Imperial Oil refinery now know the meaning of global competition. It means they have to be among the best in the world, and it is something that is achieved at home within the gates of their own plant.

Source: Based on Merle Macisaac, "Born-Again Basket Case," *Canadian Business,* May 1993, 38–44.

---

where creativity is more important than efficiency. The internal organization is fluid and decentralized, reflecting an organic approach. Federal Express Corporation, which innovates in both services and production techniques in the rapidly changing overnight mail industry, exemplifies the prospector strategy.

2. Defender   The **defender** strategy is almost the opposite of the prospector. Rather than taking risks and seeking out new opportunities, the defender strategy is concerned with stability or even retrenchment. This strategy seeks to hold onto current customers, but it neither innovates nor seeks to grow. The defender is concerned primarily with internal efficiency and control to produce reliable, high-quality products for steady customers. The defender strategy can be successful when the organization exists in a declining industry or a stable environment. Chrysler Corporation, led by Lee Iacocca, shifted to a defender strategy when sales slumped drastically in the 1980s. The company began dramatic cost-cutting efforts, including eliminating nearly a quarter of its white-collar labor force, cutting out white-collar training such as Dale Carnegie courses, and slashing the product-development budget. During the 1990s, Chrysler has shifted to a prospector strategy with new car lines to fight off Japanese imports.[22]

Exhibit 2.5   Miles and Snow's Strategy Typology.

	Strategy	Environment	Organizational Characteristics
Prospector	Innovate. Find new market opportunities. Grow. Take risks.	Dynamic, growing	Creative, innovative, flexible, decentralized
Defender	Protect turf. Retrench, hold current market.	Stable	Tight control, centralized, production efficiency, low overhead
Analyzer	Maintain current market plus moderate innovation	Moderate change	Tight control and flexibility, efficient production, creativity
Reactor	No clear strategy. React to specific conditions. Drift.	Any condition	No clear organizational approach; depends on current needs

Source: Based on Raymond E. Miles, Charles C. Snow, Alan D. Meyer, and Henry L. Coleman, Jr., "Organizational Strategy, Structure, and Process," *Academy of Management Review* 3 (1978), 546–562.

3. Analyzer   The **analyzer** tries to maintain a stable business while innovating on the periphery. It seems to lie midway between the prospector and the defender. Some products will be targeted toward stable environments in which an efficiency strategy designed to keep current customers is used. Others will be targeted toward new, more dynamic environments, where growth is possible. The analyzer attempts to balance efficient production for current lines of products with the creative development of new product lines. Anheuser-Busch is a good example of this, with its stable beer line and innovation of snack foods as a complementary line. Apple Computer, which lost a differentiation advantage based on its user-friendly software when Microsoft developed Windows, has shifted to an analyzer strategy, recognizing its core business will be the Macintosh but moving aggressively into development of innovative products and services to keep the company growing.[23]

4. Reactor   The **reactor** strategy is really not a strategy at all. Rather, reactors respond to environmental threats and opportunities in an ad hoc fashion. In a reactor strategy, top management has not defined a long-range plan or given the organization an explicit mission, so the organization takes whatever actions seem to meet the immediate needs. Though the reactor strategy can sometimes be successful, failed companies are often the result of its use. The Joseph A. Schlitz Brewing Company went through a period in which it dropped from first to seventh in the brewing industry because of poor strategic decisions. The large retailer Macy's, now attempting to make a comeback, went bankrupt largely because managers failed to adopt a strategy consistent with the consumer trend toward moderately priced merchandise and strong customer service.[24]

An example of a successful prospector strategy in the Miles and Snow typology is Quebecor Printing, an aggressive company based in Montreal.

IN PRACTICE ♦ 2.1
Quebecor Printing

The commercial printing industry is struggling to survive, and companies are dropping like flies. But in this volatile and competitive environment, Canadian-based Quebecor, Inc. is not only surviving, it's expanding, acquiring ailing printing companies and moving into markets in Mexico, India, and Europe. Quebecor is the largest printer in Canada, the second-largest in North America, and a growing competitor in Europe. The company prints everything from the *National Enquirer* and *Time* magazine to DC Comics.

The company, started in 1950 and still run by Pierre Peladeau, has a goal to be number one in niche markets. Quebecor has made more than one hundred mergers and buyouts since 1972. But Quebecor's main focus in on customers.

Peladeau's motto might be: "Don't look at your competitors. Look at your customers." By focusing on highly customized service, Quebecor hasn't had to worry about the competition. For example, by using "selective binding" techniques, one Quebecor plant can print almost two dozen versions of *Reader's Digest* for regional and urban markets. That kind of service keeps customers coming back.

Innovative customer service requires new technology and services. In 1992, the company spent more than $62 million on new presses and equipment, much of it designed for personalized printing and selective binding. Quebecor Destination Services offers customers the benefits of Quebecor's economies of scale on such services as central mailing list management, bulk postal rates, and foreign mailings.

Quebecor is a creative, innovative, flexible company, and its top managers are employing a prospector strategy to fuel the company's growth into the future.[25]

Organizational Effectiveness

Understanding organizational goals and strategies is the first step toward understanding organizational effectiveness. Organizational goals represent the reason for an organization's existence and the outcomes it seeks to achieve. The next few sections of the chapter explore the topic of effectiveness and how effectiveness is measured in organizations.

Goals were defined earlier as the desired future state of the organization. Organizational **effectiveness** is the degree to which an organization realizes its goals.[26] Effectiveness is a broad concept. It implicitly takes into consideration a range of variables at both the organizational and departmental levels. Effectiveness evaluates the extent to which multiple goals—whether official or operative—are attained.

Efficiency is a more limited concept that pertains to the internal workings of the organization. Organizational efficiency is the amount of resources used to produce a unit of output.[27] It can be measured as the ratio of inputs to outputs. If one organization can achieve a given production level with fewer resources than another organization, it would be described as more efficient.[28] For example, the Honda plant in Marysville, Ohio, used just 2,423 workers to produce 870 cars per day— 2.8 employees per car. This plant is considered much more efficient than the Jeep plant in Toledo, Ohio, which required 5,400 workers to produce 750 cars per day— an average of 7.2 employees per car.

Sometimes efficiency leads to effectiveness. In other organizations, efficiency and effectiveness are not related. An organization may be highly efficient but fail to achieve its goals because it makes a product for which there is no demand. Likewise, an organization may achieve its profit goals but be inefficient.

Overall effectiveness is difficult to measure in organizations. Organizations are large, diverse, and fragmented. They perform many activities simultaneously. They pursue multiple goals. And they generate many outcomes, some intended and some unintended.[29] However, when managers tie performance measurement to strategy execution, it can be a valuable tool for helping organizations reach their goals.[30] For example, Federal Express developed a list of "service quality indicators"—service problems ranked according to their seriousness based on customer satisfaction surveys. By giving workers specific goals to shoot for, Federal Express ties performance measurement to the everyday operation and success of the company.[31] Federal Express is an example of the importance of performance measurement as described in a new book, *Vital Signs,* discussed in Book Mark 2.0. A variety of frameworks have evolved to measure performance, and each examines a different criterion for effectiveness.

Traditional Effectiveness Approaches

The measurement of effectiveness has focused on different parts of the organization. Organizations bring resources in from the environment, and those resources are transformed into outputs delivered back into the environment, as shown in Exhibit 2.6. The **goal approach** to organizational effectiveness is concerned with the output side and whether the organization achieves its goals in terms of desired levels of output.[32] The **system resource approach** assesses effectiveness by observing the beginning of the process and evaluating whether the organization effectively obtains resources necessary for high performance. The **internal process approach** looks at internal activities and assesses effectiveness by indicators of internal health and efficiency.

This section first examines effectiveness as evaluated by the goal approach. Then it turns to the system resource and internal process approaches to effectiveness. The following section of this chapter examines contemporary approaches that integrate these perspectives.

GOAL APPROACH

The goal approach to effectiveness consists of identifying an organization's output goals and assessing how well the organization has attained those goals.[33] This is a logical approach because organizations do try to attain certain levels of output, profit, or client satisfaction. The goal approach measures progress toward attainment of those goals.

Indicators   The important goals to consider are operative goals. Efforts to measure effectiveness have been more productive using operative goals than using official goals.[34] Official goals tend to be abstract and difficult to measure. Operative goals reflect activities the organization is actually performing.

BOOKMARK 2.0

HAVE YOU READ ABOUT THIS?

Vital Signs
by Steven M. Hronec

When author Steven Hronec saw a good mission statement—"This organization provides products and services which consistently meet or exceed standards set by our customers, on time and at the lowest cost"—he immediately asked the CEO how it was measured. The CEO admitted that he had no way of knowing whether people in the organization were working toward that mission. Compare that with Federal Express, where the goals are 100 percent customer satisfaction and 100 percent service performance on every package handled. Fed Ex uses a twelve-item statistical survey of customer satisfaction and service quality. The twelve items are tracked every day and communicated to employees.

Performance measures are the vital signs of an organization. Without correct measures, people may work on things not vital to company success.

The Best Vital Signs

The best measures focus on process and outputs. Process performance measures monitor a sequence of activities designed to produce some part of a product or service. These measures should motivate people within the process to collaborate by measuring such things as setup time, response time to meet a customer request, time to develop a new product, or order fulfillment cycle time.

Output performance measures report the results or outcome of a process. Output measures include net income, customer satisfaction, percentage returns, and percentage of sales from new products.

In the new world of organizations, both process and output performance measures should reflect a horizontal rather than a vertical view. It is not what happens in the accounting or marketing departments alone that is important, but how fast orders are received and processed across departments, how products are made and delivered, and how customer complaints are handled. Departments must work together to satisfy customer needs.

Getting Started

Goals should be established with an eye toward stakeholders, including customers, shareholders, and employees.

Review the goals of the organization and make certain they are the driving force for determining performance measurement.

Select the types of performance measures that support the goals. When developing a new measurement system, primary processes are those that touch the customer. These should be identified and measured first.

An Example

Consider a company that has product innovation as its mission. This translates into goals of developing two new products each year and reducing development time by 50 percent. The critical horizontal process here is clearly new product development, and key activities for measurement include the conceptual design, product design, and prototype development. Output measures might include number of parts used in new products, actual costs, number of vendors used, and date of completion.

Vital signs can help a company achieve competitive advantage. The measurement system can also be used to measure total quality management and the organization's emphasis on reducing time for customers. And remember, performance measurements can be used to cause desirable changes rather than be the outcome of changes.

Vital Signs by Steven M. Hronec is published by American Management Association.

One example of multiple goals is from a survey of U.S. business corporations.[35] Their reported goals are shown in Exhibit 2.7. Twelve goals were listed as being important to these companies. These twelve goals represent outcomes that cannot be achieved simultaneously. They illustrate the array of outcomes organizations attempt to achieve.

Exhibit 2.6
Traditional
Approaches
to the
Measurement of
Organizational
Effectiveness.

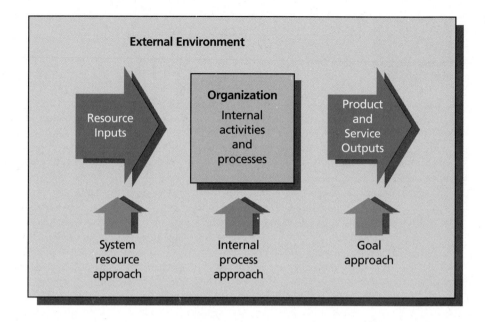

Application   The goal approach is used in business organizations because output goals can be readily measured. Business firms typically evaluate performance in terms of profitability, growth, market share, and return on investment. However, identifying operative goals and measuring performance of an organization are not always easy. Two problems that must be resolved are the issues of multiple goals and subjective indicators of goal attainment.

Since organizations have multiple and conflicting goals, effectiveness often cannot be assessed by a single indicator. High achievement on one goal may mean low achievement on another. Moreover, there are department goals as well as over- all performance goals. The full assessment of effectiveness should take into consid- eration several goals simultaneously.

The other issue to resolve with the goal approach is how to identify operative goals for an organization and how to measure goal attainment. For business organi- zations, there are often objective indicators for certain goals. The stated objectives of top management and such measures as profit or growth are available in published reports. Subjective assessment is needed in business organizations for such out- comes as employee welfare or social responsibility. The following example shows how Granite Rock Company measures goal performance related to customer satis- faction and ties this information back into its daily operations.

IN PRACTICE ◆ 2.2
Granite Rock Company

Granite Rock believes if something is worth doing, it's worth measuring. The century-old, family-owned company tracks its various operations in about forty different ways. Graphs and charts are plotted and posted on bulletin boards at company headquarters and at each plant.

One of these charts shows employees how they measure up in the eyes of their customers. Granite Rock charges premium rates for high-quality construction materials and has to work hard to convince customers that its products and services are worth the extra cost.

The company regularly surveys customers to find out not only how they rate Granite Rock but how they rate the company's major competitors as well. Granite Rock's operations then aim to out-perform the group average by at least 33 percent.

- On-time delivery is at the top of the list of factors customers are concerned about, and therefore, it's at the top of the list of Granite Rock's customer-satisfaction goals. Recent performance measurement charts told workers they ranked 59 percent above the average for on-time delivery.
- Maintaining high product quality is a goal Granite Rock reached easily: 69 percent above the norm.
- But the company ranked highest of all on scheduling, or the ability to deliver needed products on short notice. Customers rated the company 76 percent better than the average.

Granite Rock has to be rated effective based on achieving its customer satisfaction goals. Ratings are not always so high in a company that tracks its performance forty different ways. When they're not, a top manager says, it "sounds an alarm. We believe you don't stress a negative—you chart it. Our people. . .will look at that negative and want to do something about it."[36]

For not-for-profit and some business organizations, many goals cannot be measured objectively. Someone has to go into the organization and learn what are the actual goals. Since goals reflect the values of top management, the best informants are members of the top management coalition.[37] These managers can report on the actual goals of the organization. Once goals are identified, subjective perceptions of goal achievement can be obtained if quantitative indicators are not available.

The goal approach seems to be the most logical way to assess organizational effectiveness. Effectiveness is defined as the ability of an organization to attain its goals. However, the actual measurement of effectiveness is a complex problem. Organizations have many goals, so there is no single indicator of effectiveness. Some goals are subjective and must be identified by managers within the organization. The assessment of organizational effectiveness using the goal approach requires that the evaluator be aware of these issues and allow for them in the evaluation of effectiveness.

SYSTEM RESOURCE APPROACH

The system resource approach looks at the input side of the transformation process shown in Exhibit 2.6. It assumes organizations must be successful in obtaining resource inputs and in maintaining the organizational system to be effective. Organizations must obtain scarce and valued resources from other organizations. From a systems view, organizational effectiveness is defined as the ability of the organization, in either absolute or relative terms, to exploit its environment in the acquisition of scarce and valued resources.

Indicators Obtaining resources to maintain the organization system is the criterion by which organizational effectiveness is assessed. In a broad sense, indicators of system resource effectiveness encompass the following dimensions:

Exhibit 2.7
Reported
Goals of U.S.
Corporations.

Goal	% Corporations
Profitability	89
Growth	82
Market share	66
Social responsibility	65
Employee welfare	62
Product quality and service	60
Research and development	54
Diversification	51
Efficiency	50
Financial stability	49
Resource conservation	39
Management development	35

Source: Adapted from Y. K. Shetty, "New Look at Corporate Goals," *California Management Review* 22, no. 2 (1979), pp. 71–79.

1. Bargaining position—the ability of the organization to exploit its environment in the acquisition of scarce and valued resources
2. Ability of the system's decision maker to perceive and correctly interpret the real properties of the external environment
3. Maintenance of internal day-to-day organizational activities
4. Ability of the organization to respond to changes in the environment.[38]

Usefulness   The system resource approach is valuable when other indicators of performance are difficult to obtain. In many not-for-profit and social welfare organizations, for example, it is hard to measure output goals or internal efficiency. George Mason University recently received a lot of attention for increasing its academic reputation. The indicators used to evaluate George Mason's effectiveness were its ability to obtain scarce and valued resources. At one time, its faculty was considered second-rate, but George Mason has since been able to hire top professors to fill endowed chairs in several departments. Another indicator is the ability to obtain gifts of money. In four years, George Mason went from an endowment of less than $1 million and no professorships to an endowment of $20 million and twenty-nine professorships. Another scarce and valued resource is students. George Mason was able to increase the diversity of its student body and attract students with higher scholastic aptitude test scores. The ability to attract better students and faculty, plus winning large gifts from businesses and foundations, are used by George Mason administrators to indicate effective performance.[39]

Although the system resource approach is valuable when other measures of effectiveness are not available, it does have shortcomings. Often the ability to acquire resources seems less important than the utilization of those resources. For example, a college football program that recruits many star players would not be considered effective if the program did not develop the players to produce a winning team. This approach is most valuable when measures of goal attainment cannot be obtained.

INTERNAL PROCESS APPROACH

In the internal process approach, effectiveness is measured as internal organizational health and efficiency. An effective organization has a smooth, well-oiled internal process. Employees are happy and satisfied. Departmental activities mesh with one another to ensure high productivity. This approach does not consider the external environment. The important element in effectiveness is what the organization does with the resources it has, as reflected in internal health and efficiency.

Indicators The best-known proponents of a process model are from the human relations approach to organizations. Such writers as Chris Argyris, Warren G. Bennis, Rensis Likert, and Richard Beckhard have all worked extensively with human resources in organizations and emphasize the connection between human resources and effectiveness.[40] Writers on corporate culture and organizational excellence have stressed the importance of internal processes. Results from a recent study of nearly two hundred secondary schools showed that both human resources and employee-oriented processes were important in explaining and promoting effectiveness in those organizations.[41]

Indicators of an effective organization as seen from an internal process approach are:

1. Strong corporate culture and positive work climate
2. Team spirit, group loyalty, and teamwork
3. Confidence, trust, and communication between workers and management
4. Decision making near sources of information, regardless of where those sources are on the organizational chart
5. Undistorted horizontal and vertical communication; sharing of relevant facts and feelings
6. Rewards to managers for performance, growth, and development of subordinates and for creating an effective working group
7. Interaction between the organization and its parts, with conflict that occurs over projects resolved in the interest of the organization.[42]

A second indicator of internal process effectiveness is the measurement of economic efficiency. William Evan developed a method that uses quantitative measures of efficiency.[43] The first step is to identify the financial cost of inputs (I), transformation (T), and outputs (O). Next, the three variables can be combined in ratios to evaluate various aspects of organizational performance. The most popular assessment of efficiency is O/I. For an automaker, this would be the number of cars produced per employee. For a hospital, the O/I ratio is the number of patients per annual budget. For a university, it is the number of students graduated divided by the resource inputs. The O/I ratio indicates overall financial efficiency for an organization.

Usefulness The internal process approach is important because the efficient use of resources and harmonious internal functioning are ways to measure effectiveness. As discussed in Chapter 1, a significant recent trend in management is the empowerment of human resources as a source of competitive advantage. Most managers believe participative management approaches and positive corporate culture are important components of effectiveness.

The financial approach to efficiency is useful for measuring the performance of departments concerned with efficiency, such as manufacturing. For example, the manufacturing efficiency of Chrysler enabled it to become the low-cost producer in the automobile industry. The assembly line was reorganized, and the number of robots was increased from 300 to 1,242. The payoff in productivity was an increase from 4,500 to 8,000 cars and trucks a day, while the number of worker-hours to build a vehicle shrank from 175 to 102.[44]

The internal process approach does have shortcomings. Total output and the organization's relationship with the external environment are not evaluated. Also, evaluations of internal health and functioning are often subjective, because many aspects of inputs and internal processes are not quantifiable. Like the other approaches to organizational effectiveness, the internal process approach has something to offer, but managers should be aware that efficiency alone represents a limited view of organizational effectiveness.

Contemporary Effectiveness Approaches

The three approaches—goal, system resource, internal process—to organizational effectiveness described earlier all have something to offer, but each one tells only part of the story. Recently, integrative approaches to organizational effectiveness have been introduced. These new approaches acknowledge that organizations do many things and have many outcomes. These approaches combine several indicators of effectiveness into a single framework. They include the stakeholder and competing values approaches.

STAKEHOLDER APPROACH

One proposed approach integrates diverse organizational activities by focusing on organizational stakeholders. A **stakeholder** is any group within or outside an organization that has a stake in the organization's performance. Creditors, suppliers, employees, and owners are all stakeholders. In the **stakeholder approach** (also called the constituency approach), the satisfaction of such groups can be assessed as an indicator of the organization's performance.[45] Each stakeholder will have a different criterion of effectiveness because it has a different interest in the organization. Each stakeholder group has to be surveyed to learn whether the organization performs well from its viewpoint.

Indicators   The initial work on evaluating effectiveness on the basis of stakeholders included ninety-seven small businesses in Texas. Seven stakeholder groups relevant to those businesses were surveyed to determine the perception of effectiveness from each viewpoint.[46] Each stakeholder and its criterion of effectiveness are:

Stakeholder	Effectiveness Criteria
1. Owners	Financial return
2. Employees	Worker satisfaction, pay, supervision
3. Customers	Quality of goods and services
4. Creditors	Creditworthiness
5. Community	Contribution to community affairs
6. Suppliers	Satisfactory transactions
7. Government	Obedience to laws, regulations

The survey of stakeholders showed that a small business found it difficult to simultaneously fulfill the demands of all groups. One business may have high employee satisfaction, but the satisfaction of other groups may be lower. Nevertheless, measuring all seven stakeholders provides a more accurate view of effectiveness than any single measure. Evaluating how organizations perform across each group offers an overall assessment of effectiveness.

Usefulness   The strength of the stakeholder approach is that it takes a broad view of effectiveness and examines factors in the environment as well as within the organization. The stakeholder approach includes the community's notion of social responsibility, which was not formally measured in traditional approaches. The stakeholder approach also handles several criteria simultaneously—inputs, internal processing, outputs—and acknowledges that there is no single measure of effectiveness. The well-being of employees is just as important as attaining the owner's goals.

The stakeholder approach is gaining in popularity, based on the view that effectiveness is a complex, multidimensional concept that has no single measure.[47] Recent research has shown that the assessment of multiple stakeholder groups is an accurate reflection of effectiveness, especially with respect to organizational adaptability.[48] Moreover, research shows that firms really do care about their reputational status and do attempt to shape stakeholders' assessments of their performance.[49] If an organization performs poorly according to several interest groups, it is probably not meeting its effectiveness goals. However, satisfying some stakeholders may alienate others, as illustrated by the following example of the Safeway grocery chain.

IN PRACTICE ◆ 2.3

Safeway, Inc.

Safeway, Incorporated's new chief executive is just the kind of man shareholders like to see leading the Oakland-based supermarket chain. By slashing costs, reducing prices, and steadily improving service, Steve Burd has turned Safeway into a tough competitor in the struggling supermarket business. The company reported a 110 percent increase in profits and a 3 percent rise in sales in the third quarter of 1993, and analysts predicted a tripling of income for the entire year. As a result, the price of Safeway's stock increased more than 70 percent.

The drastic cost-cutting has benefited customers as well, and employees have been cautiously satisfied with their role in the restructuring. But suppliers are complaining, as cutting costs for Safeway sometimes means transferring more expenses to vendors. Competition for shelf space is fierce, and although Safeway denies charging vendors for space, it admits it might ask them to help pay for advertising. And suppliers gasped at a recent convention when Safeway's director of marketing suggested the chain take goods from vendors on consignment, to be returned if they don't sell promptly.

Safeway's new CEO has obviously improved the company's operating success. But there may be a limit to how far suppliers will go in the effort to cut costs within the organization.[50]

COMPETING VALUES APPROACH

Recall that organizational goals and performance criteria are defined by top and middle managers. The **competing values approach** to organizational effectiveness was developed by Robert Quinn and John Rohrbaugh to combine the diverse indicators of performance used by managers and researchers.[51] Using a comprehensive list of performance indicators, a panel of experts in organizational effectiveness rated the indicators for similarity. The analysis produced underlying dimensions of effectiveness criteria that represented competing management values in organizations.

Indicators   The first value dimension pertains to organizational **focus,** which is whether dominant values concern issues that are *internal* or *external* to the firm. Internal focus reflects a management concern for the well-being and efficiency of employees, and external focus represents an emphasis on the well-being of the organization itself with respect to the environment. The second value dimension pertains to organization **structure,** and whether *stability* versus *flexibility* is the dominant structural consideration. Stability reflects a management value for top-down control, similar to the mechanistic approach described in Chapter 1. Flexibility represents a value for adaptation and change and is similar to the organic approach to structure.

The value dimensions of structure and focus are illustrated in Exhibit 2.8. The combination of dimensions provides four models of organizational effectiveness, which, though seemingly different, are closely related. In real organizations, these competing values can and often do exist together. Each model reflects a different management emphasis with respect to structure and focus.[52]

The **open systems model** reflects a combination of external focus and flexible structure. Management's primary goals are growth and resource acquisition. The organization accomplishes these goals through the subgoals of flexibility, readiness, and a positive external evaluation. The dominant value in this model is establishing a good relationship with the environment to acquire resources and grow. This model is similar in some ways to the system resource model described earlier.

The **rational goal model** represents management values of structural control and external focus. The primary goals are productivity, efficiency, and profit. The organization wants to achieve output goals in a controlled way. Subgoals that facilitate these outcomes are internal planning and goal setting, which are rational management tools. The rational goal model is similar to the goal approach described earlier.

The **internal process model** is in the lower left section of Exhibit 2.8; it reflects the values of internal focus and structural control. The primary outcome is a stable organizational setting that maintains itself in an orderly way. Organizations that are well established in the environment and simply want to maintain their current position would fit this model. Subgoals for this model include mechanisms for efficient communication, information management, and decision making.

The **human relations model** incorporates the values of an internal focus and a flexible structure. Here, management concern is on the development of human resources. Employees are given opportunities for autonomy and development. Management works toward the subgoals of cohesion, morale, and training opportunities. Organizations adopting this model are more concerned with employees than with the environment.

The four models in Exhibit 2.8 represent opposing organizational values. Managers must decide which goal values will take priority in their organizations. The way two organizations are mapped onto the four models is shown in Exhibit 2.9.[53] Organization A is a young organization concerned with finding a niche and becoming established in the external environment. Primary emphasis is given to flexibility,

Exhibit 2.8 Four Models of Effectiveness Values.

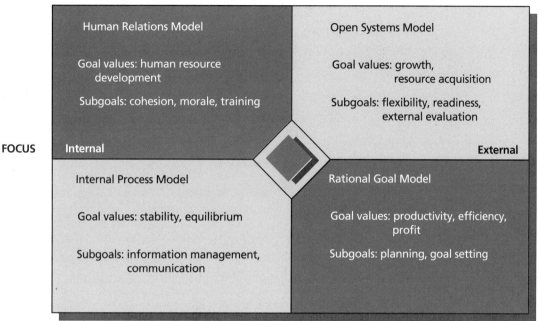

STRUCTURE

Flexibility

Human Relations Model	**Open Systems Model**
Goal values: human resource development	Goal values: growth, resource acquisition
Subgoals: cohesion, morale, training	Subgoals: flexibility, readiness, external evaluation

FOCUS   Internal   External

Internal Process Model	**Rational Goal Model**
Goal values: stability, equilibrium	Goal values: productivity, efficiency, profit
Subgoals: information management, communication	Subgoals: planning, goal setting

Control

Source; Adapted from Robert E. Quinn and John Rohrbaugh, "A Spatial Model of Effectiveness Criteria: Toward a Competing Values Approach to Organizational Analysis," *Management Science* 29 (1983), pp. 363–77; and Robert E. Quinn and Kim Cameron, "Organizational Life Cycles and Shifting Criteria of Effectiveness: Some Preliminary Evidence," *Management Science* 29 (1983), pp. 33–51.

innovation, the acquisition of resources from the environment, and the satisfaction of external constituencies. This organization gives moderate emphasis to human relations and even less emphasis to current productivity and profits. Satisfying and adapting to the environment are more important. The emphasis given to open systems values means that the internal process model is practically nonexistent. Stability and equilibrium receive little emphasis.

Organization B, in contrast, is an established business in which the dominant value is productivity and profits. This organization is characterized by planning and goal setting. Organization B is a large company that is well established in the environment and is primarily concerned with successful production and profits. Flexibility and human resources are not major concerns. This organization prefers stability and equilibrium to readiness and innovation because it wants to take advantage of its established customers.

Usefulness   The competing values approach makes two contributions. First, it integrates diverse concepts of effectiveness into a single perspective. It incorporates the ideas of output goals, resource acquisition, and human resource development as goals the organization tries to accomplish. Second, the model calls attention to effectiveness

Exhibit 2.9
Effectiveness
Values for Two
Organizations.

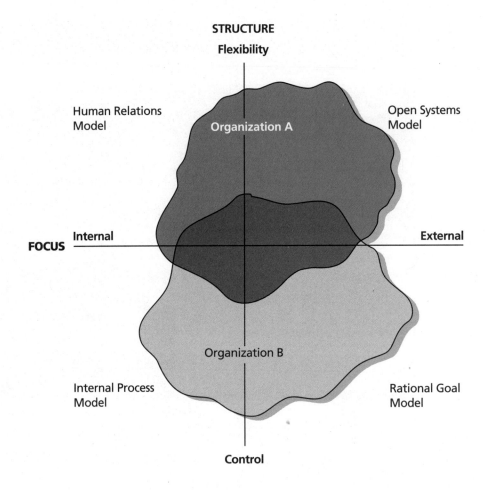

Exhibit 2.9
Effectiveness
Values for Two
Organizations.

criteria as management values and shows how opposing values exist at the same time. Managers must decide which values they wish to pursue and which values will receive less emphasis. The four competing values exist simultaneously, but not all will receive equal priority. For example, a new, small organization that concentrates on establishing itself within a competitive environment will give less emphasis to developing employees than to the external environment.

The dominant values in an organization often change over time as organizations experience new environmental demands or new top leadership. Eastman Kodak Company is in the midst of shifting its values to a growth-oriented strategy, following the hiring of a new chairman.

IN PRACTICE ◆ 2.4
Kodak

Eastman Kodak Company is an old, established business, a one-time giant in the world of chemical photography. But Kodak failed to make the shift to a fast-paced multimedia world, and 1992 profits barely matched those of a decade earlier. Though Kodak developed a visionary growth-oriented strategy based on technology for merging photography and compact disks several years ago, that strategy was downplayed in favor of short-term efforts to maintain the company's status in chemical photography. Kodak's managers preferred stability and equilibrium as reflected in the internal process and rational goal models in Exhibit 2.8.

Kodak's new chairman, George M. C. Fisher, is reviving the long-term growth-oriented vision and trying to lead Kodak fully into the multimedia revolution. Kodak's most ambitious new product is the Photo CD, which allows photographs to be read by a computer. Kodak's researchers have plenty of other ideas; for example, a home thermal printer that connects to the Photo CD and a digital television so that images can be printed out for a multitude of uses, from student term papers to customized Christmas cards.

Kodak's innovations in world-class technology represent a shift in values to the open systems model. Fisher is also changing the company's stodgy culture. This means more concern with employees, including training and empowerment, who will take more responsibility for future changes. The increased flexibility and morale reflect the values in the human relations model of Exhibit 2.8.[54]

Achieving Organizational Effectiveness

Many things contribute to an organization's success. As we saw in Chapter 1, today's effective organizations reflect a number of paradigm shifts in response to changes in society. Successful organizations recognize the chaotic nature of the international environment and remain flexible to adapt quickly. Another shift is a concern for empowering employees and a stronger interest in corporate culture.

Recent books, such as *Reengineering the Corporation* about corporate redesign, and *Control Your Destiny or Someone Else Will* about Jack Welch's revolution at General Electric, have added new understanding about these shifts and their importance.[55] These books suggest a number of management ideas based on the experiences of large American corporations, small businesses, and high-tech companies. Some of the major ideas from these publications are summarized in Exhibit 2.10. They are organized into four categories: strategic orientation, top management, organization design, and corporate culture.

STRATEGIC ORIENTATION

Three characteristics identified in corporate research pertain to an organization's strategic orientation: being *close to the customer, fast response,* and having a *clear business focus.*

Effective organizations are customer-driven. Organizations are increasingly looking at customers as their most important stakeholders, and a dominant value in successful organizations is satisfying customer needs.[56] Today's top managers often call customers directly to learn their needs. For example, the president of Pepsi Cola North America makes a point of calling at least four customers directly per day.[57]

A fast response means successful companies respond quickly to problems and opportunities. They lead rather than follow. They take chances. They don't study things to death. Successful companies seek opportunities and encourage change. They learn through trial and error.

Moreover, successful organizations are clearly focused. They know whether they want to be a prospector or a defender. They know that to be successful, they

Exhibit 2.10   Factors Associated with Organization Effectiveness.

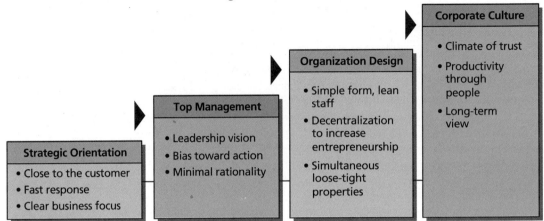

should do what they do best, sticking close to the business they know and understand. At Gerber, the motto is "Babies are our business . . . our only business."

TOP MANAGEMENT

Management techniques and processes are another dimension of effective organizations. Three factors unique to managers are part of a highly successful company: *leadership vision, a bias toward action,* and *minimal rationality.*

To be effective, an organization needs a special kind of leadership vision that provides leadership of the organization, not just leadership within the organization. Leaders must provide a vision of what can be accomplished and give employees a sense of direction, shared purpose, and meaning. Visionary leaders are willing to roll up their sleeves and become involved in problems at all levels.

Managers and employees in effective organizations are also oriented toward action—they don't talk problems to death before making decisions or creating solutions. Successful companies "do it, try it, fix it." The decision philosophy at Pepsi-Co, for example, is "Ready, Fire, Aim."[58]

Research into effective, adaptive organizations indicates that they minimize rationality rather than rely too much on objective, quantitative decision rules. Managers in effective organizations recognize that rational methods alone may not be fast enough, accurate enough, or able to handle ambiguity.

ORGANIZATION DESIGN

Effective organizations are characterized by three design attributes: *simple form and lean staff, decentralization to increase entrepreneurship,* and *simultaneous loose-tight properties.*

Simple form and lean staff means that the underlying form and systems of effective organizations are elegantly simple and few personnel are in staff positions. There is little bureaucracy. Large companies are divided into small divisions for simplicity and adaptability.

Organization structure is decentralized to encourage innovation and change. Creativity and innovation by employees at all levels are encouraged and rewarded. Technical people are located near marketing people so they can lunch together. Organizational units are kept small to create a sense of belonging and shared problem solving.

Simultaneous loose-tight properties may seem like a paradox, but effective organizations use tight controls in some places and loose controls in others. Tight, centralized control is used for the firm's core values. At McDonald's, for example, no exceptions are made to the core values of quality, service, cleanliness, and value. Yet in other areas, employees are free to experiment, to be flexible, and to take risks in ways that can help the company reach its goals.

CORPORATE CULTURE

One lesson from research on Japanese companies is that employee commitment is a vital component of organization success. Effective companies manage to harness employee energy and enthusiasm. They do so by creating a *climate of trust,* encouraging *productivity through people,* and taking a *long-term view.*

A climate of trust is necessary so that employees can deal openly and honestly with one another. Collaboration across departments requires trust. Managers and workers must trust one another to work together in joint problem solving. At Ford Motor Company, where workers were historically suspicious of management, a new climate of trust has led to increased productivity and reduced costs.[59]

Productivity through people simply means that everyone must participate. Rank-and-file workers are considered the root of quality and productivity. People are empowered to participate in production, marketing, and new product improvements. Conflicting ideas are encouraged rather than suppressed. The ability to move ahead through consensus preserves the sense of trust, increases motivation, and facilitates both innovation and efficiency.

Another lesson learned from the Japanese is the importance of a long-term view. Organizational success is not built in a day. Effective companies realize they must invest in training employees and commit to employees for the long term. Career paths are designed to give employees broad backgrounds rather than rapid upward mobility.

The ideas summarized in Exhibit 2.10 are important, but recent research suggests that they are not always successful. Organizations that have these characteristics often go through periods of lower performance.[60] But a preponderance of these characteristics is generally a part of the management culture of successful organizations. The important point is that the concepts and models from organization theory can be used to manage organizations to high performance.

Summary and Interpretation

This chapter discussed organizational goals and the strategies top managers use to help organizations achieve those goals. Goals specify the mission or purpose of an organization and its desired future state; strategies define how the organization will reach its goals. The chapter also discussed the most popular approaches to measuring effectiveness, that is, how well the organization realizes its purpose and attains its desired future state. Finally, we talked about the characteristics most commonly found in effective organizations today.

Organizations exist for a purpose; top managers define a specific mission or task to be accomplished. Official goals make explicit the purpose and direction of an organization. Goals are not given or fixed. They are defined through bargaining and coalition building. Official and operative goals are a key element in organizations because they meet these needs—establishing legitimacy with external groups and setting standards of performance for participants.

Managers must develop strategies that describe the actions required to achieve goals. Two models for formulating strategies are the Porter model of competitive strategies and Miles and Snow's strategy typology.

No easy, simple, guaranteed measure will provide an unequivocal assessment of performance. The complexity of measuring effectiveness reflects the complexity of organizations as a topic of study. Organizations must perform diverse activities well—from obtaining resource inputs to delivering outputs—to be successful. Traditional approaches used output goals, resource acquisition, or internal health and efficiency as the criteria of effectiveness. Contemporary approaches consider multiple criteria simultaneously. Organizations can be assessed by surveying constituencies that have a stake in organizational performance, or by evaluating competing values for effectiveness. No approach is suitable for every organization, but each offers some advantage that the others may lack.

From the point of view of managers, the goal approach to effectiveness and measures of internal efficiency are useful when measures are available. The attainment of output and profit goals reflects the purpose of the organization, and efficiency reflects the cost of attaining those goals. Other factors such as top management preferences, the extent to which goals are measurable, and the scarcity of environmental resources may influence the use of effectiveness criteria. In not-for-profit organizations, where internal processes and output criteria often are not quantifiable, stakeholder satisfaction or resource acquisition may be the only available indicators of effectiveness.

From the point of view of people outside the organization, such as academic investigators or government researchers, the stakeholder and competing values approaches to organizational effectiveness may be preferable. The stakeholder approach evaluates the organization's contribution to society. The competing values approach acknowledges different areas of focus (internal, external) and structure (flexibility, stability) and allows for managers to choose one value to emphasize.

Many things contribute to the effectiveness of organizations. Today's high-performing organizations recognize the unstable, even chaotic nature of the environment and remain flexible. The final section of the chapter described the qualities of strategic orientation, top management, organization design, and corporate culture that enable companies to be successful.

KEY CONCEPTS

analyzer	differentiation
bargaining	effectiveness
coalition	efficiency
competing values approach	focus
defender	focus strategy

goal approach	prospector
human relations model	rational goal model
internal process approach	reactor
internal process model	satisficing
low-cost leadership	stakeholder
mission	stakeholder approach
official goals	strategy
open systems model	structure
operative goals	system resource approach
organizational goal	

DISCUSSION QUESTIONS

1. Discuss the role of top management in setting organizational direction.

2. How do operative market goals differ from resource and productivity goals?

3. Compare the twelve qualities associated with organizational effectiveness with the internal process, goal, and competing values approaches to *measuring* effectiveness. Which approach would seem to best measure those twelve qualities in a company?

4. "A Look Inside" at the beginning of this chapter described several goals pursued by Compaq Computer. How is it possible for an organization to pursue multiple goals simultaneously?

5. What is the difference between a goal and a strategy?

6. Discuss the similarities and differences in the specific strategies described in Porter's competitive strategies and Miles and Snow's strategy typology. Which framework do you prefer? Why?

7. Do you believe mission statements and official goal statements provide an organization with genuine legitimacy in the external environment? Discuss.

8. Suppose you have been asked to evaluate the effectiveness of the police department in a medium-sized community. Where would you begin, and how would you proceed? What effectiveness approach would you prefer?

9. What are the advantages and disadvantages of the system resource approach versus the goal approach for measuring organizational effectiveness?

10. What are the similarities and differences between assessing effectiveness on the basis of competing values versus stakeholders? Explain.

11. A noted organization theorist once said, "Organizational effectiveness can be whatever top management defines it to be." Discuss.

GUIDES TO ACTION

As an organization manager, keep these guides in mind:

1. Establish and communicate organizational mission and goals. Communicate official goals to provide a statement of the organization's mission to external constituents. Communicate operational goals to provide internal direction, guidelines, and standards of performance for employees.

2. Discuss multiple goals with other managers, and develop a coalition that agrees on which goals to emphasize. Set priorities. Expect to engage in bargaining and satisficing.
3. After goals have been defined, select strategies for achieving those goals. Define a specific strategy based on Porter's competitive strategies or Miles and Snow's strategy typology.
4. Assess the effectiveness of the organization. Use the goal approach, internal process approach, and system resource approach to obtain specific pictures of effectiveness. Assess stakeholder satisfaction or competing values to obtain a broader picture of effectiveness.
5. Implement those factors associated with organization effectiveness appropriate for your company. Strategic orientation, top management, organization design, and corporate culture are factors that strongly influence successful companies.

Consider these guides when analyzing the following case.

CASE FOR ANALYSIS

The Paradoxical Twins: Acme and Omega Electronics*

Part I

In 1965, Technological Products of Erie, Pennsylvania, was bought out by a Cleveland manufacturer. The Cleveland firm had no interest in the electronics division of Technological Products and subsequently sold to different investors two plants that manufactured printed circuit boards. One of the plants, located in nearby Waterford, was renamed Acme Electronics; the other plant, within the city limits of Erie, was renamed Omega Electronics, Inc.

Acme retained its original management and upgraded its general manager to president. Omega hired a new president who had been a director of a large electronic research laboratory and upgraded several of the existing personnel within the plant. Acme and Omega often competed for the same contracts. As subcontractors, both firms benefited from the electronics boom of the early 1970s, and both looked forward to future growth and expansion. Acme had annual sales of $10 million and employed 550 people. Omega had annual sales of $8 million and employed 480 people. Acme regularly achieved greater net profits, much to the chagrin of Omega's management.

Inside Acme

The president of Acme, John Tyler, was confident that, had the demand not been so great, Acme's competitor would not have survived. "In fact," he said, "we have been able to beat Omega regularly for the most profitable contracts, thereby increasing our profit." Tyler credited his firm's greater effectiveness to his managers'

*Adapted from John F. Veiga, "The Paradoxical Twins: Acme and Omega Electronics," in John F. Veiga and John N. Yanouzas, *The Dynamics of Organization Theory* (St. Paul: West, 1984), 132–38.

abilities to run a "tight ship." He explained that he had retained the basic structure developed by Technological Products because it was most efficient for the high-volume manufacture of printed circuits and their subsequent assembly. Acme had detailed organization charts and job descriptions. Tyler believed everyone should have clear responsibilities and narrowly defined jobs, which would lead to efficient performance and high company profits. People were generally satisfied with their work at Acme; however, some of the managers voiced the desire to have a little more latitude in their jobs.

Inside Omega

Omega's president, Jim Rawls, did not believe in organization charts. He felt his organization had departments similar to Acme's, but he thought Omega's plant was small enough that things such as organization charts just put artificial barriers between specialists who should be working together. Written memos were not allowed since, as Rawls expressed it, "the plant is small enough that if people want to communicate, they can just drop by and talk things over."

The head of the mechanical engineering department said, "Jim spends too much of his time and mine making sure everyone understands what we're doing and listening to suggestions." Rawls was concerned with employee satisfaction and wanted everyone to feel part of the organization. The top management team reflected Rawls's attitudes. They also believed that employees should be familiar with activities throughout the organization so that cooperation between departments would be increased. A newer member of the industrial engineering department said, "When I first got here, I wasn't sure what I was supposed to do. One day I worked with some mechanical engineers and the next day I helped the shipping department design some packing cartons. The first months on the job were hectic, but at least I got a real feel for what makes Omega tick."

QUESTIONS

1. What are the goals at Acme? At Omega?
2. What impact do top managers have on these goals? Discuss.
3. Are these goals to be achieved with different strategies? Describe.

Part II

In 1976, integrated circuits began to cut deeply into the demand for printed circuit boards. The integrated circuits (ICs) or "chips" were the first step into microminiaturization in the electronics industry. Because the manufacturing process for ICs was a closely guarded secret, both Acme and Omega realized the potential threat to their futures, and both began to seek new customers aggressively.

In July 1976, a major photocopier manufacturer was looking for a subcontractor to assemble the memory unit for its new experimental copier. The projected contract for the job was estimated to be $5 to $7 million in annual sales.

Both Acme and Omega were geographically close to this manufacturer, and both submitted highly competitive bids for the production of one hundred prototypes. Acme's bid was slightly lower than Omega's; however, both firms were asked to produce one hundred units. The photocopier manufacturer told both firms speed was critical because its president had boasted to other manufacturers that the firm would have a finished copier available by Christmas. This boast, much to the designer's dismay, required pressure on all subcontractors to begin prototype production before final design of the copier was complete. This meant Acme and Omega would have at most two weeks to produce the prototypes or delay the final copier production.

QUESTIONS

1. Which firm do you think will produce the best results? Why?

Part III

Inside Acme

As soon as John Tyler was given the blueprints (Monday, July 11, 1976), he sent a memo to the purchasing department asking it to move forward on the purchase of all necessary materials. At the same time, he sent the blueprints to the drafting department and asked that it prepare manufacturing prints. The industrial engineering department was told to begin methods design work for use by the production department supervisors. Tyler also sent a memo to all department heads and executives indicating the critical time constraints of this job and how he expected that all employees would perform as efficiently as they had in the past.

The departments had little contact with one another for several days, and each seemed to work at its own speed. Each department also encountered problems. Purchasing could not acquire all the parts on time. Industrial engineering had difficulty arranging an efficient assembly sequence. Mechanical engineering did not take the deadline seriously and parceled its work to vendors so the engineers could work on other jobs scheduled previously. Tyler made it a point to stay in touch with the photocopier manufacturer to let it know things were progressing and to learn of any new developments. He traditionally worked to keep important clients happy. Tyler telephoned someone at the photocopier company at least twice a week and got to know the head designer quite well.

On July 15, Tyler learned that mechanical engineering was way behind in its development work, and he "hit the roof." To make matters worse, purchasing did not obtain all the parts, so the industrial engineers decided to assemble the product without one part, which would be inserted at the last minute. On Thursday, July 21, the final units were being assembled, although the process was delayed several times. On Friday, July 22, the last units were finished while Tyler paced around the plant. Late that afternoon, Tyler received a phone call from the head designer of the photocopier manufacturer, who told Tyler that he had received a call on Wednesday from Jim Rawls of Omega. He explained that Rawls's workers had found an error in the design of the connector cable and taken corrective action on their prototypes. He told Tyler that he had checked out the design error and that Omega was right. Tyler, a bit overwhelmed by this information, told the designer that he had all the memory units ready for shipment and that, as soon as they received the missing component on Monday or Tuesday, they would be able to deliver the final units. The designer explained that the design error would be rectified in a new blueprint he was sending over by messenger and that he would hold Acme to the Tuesday delivery date.

When the blueprint arrived, Tyler called in the production supervisor to assess the damage. The alterations in the design would call for total disassembly and the unsoldering of several connections. Tyler told the supervisor to put extra people on the alterations first thing Monday morning and to try to finish the job by Tuesday. Late Tuesday afternoon, the alterations were finished and the missing components were delivered. Wednesday morning, the production supervisor discovered that the units would have to be torn apart again to install the missing component. When John Tyler was told this, he again "hit the roof." He called industrial engineering and asked if it could help out. The production supervisor and the methods engineer couldn't agree on how to install the component. John Tyler settled the argument by ordering that all units be taken apart again and the missing component installed. He told shipping to prepare cartons for delivery on Friday afternoon.

On Friday, July 29, fifty prototypes were shipped from Acme without final inspection. John Tyler was concerned about his firm's reputation, so he waived the final inspection after he personally tested one unit and found it operational. On Tuesday, August 2, Acme shipped the last fifty units.

Inside Omega

On Friday, July 8, Jim Rawls called a meeting that included department heads to tell them about the potential contract they were to receive. He told them that as soon as he received the blueprints, work could begin. On Monday, July 11, the prints arrived and again the department heads met to discuss the project. At the end of the meeting, drafting had agreed to prepare manufacturing prints, while industrial engineering and production would begin methods design.

Two problems arose within Omega that were similar to those at Acme. Certain ordered parts could not be delivered on time, and the assembly sequence was difficult to engineer. The departments proposed ideas to help one another, however, and department heads and key employees had daily meetings to discuss progress. The head of electrical engineering knew of a Japanese source for the components that could not be purchased from normal suppliers. Most problems were solved by Saturday, July 16.

On Monday, July 18, a methods engineer and the production supervisor formulated the assembly plans, and production was set to begin on Tuesday morning. On Monday afternoon, people from mechanical engineering, electrical engineering, production, and industrial engineering got together to produce a prototype just to ensure that there would be no snags in production. While they were building the unit, they discovered an error in the connector cable design. All the engineers agreed, after checking and rechecking the blueprints, that the cable was erroneously designed. People from mechanical engineering and electrical engineering spent Monday night redesigning the cable, and on Tuesday morning, the drafting department finalized the changes in the manufacturing prints. On Tuesday morning, Rawls was a bit apprehensive about the design changes and decided to get formal approval. Rawls received word on Wednesday from the head designer at the photocopier firm that they could proceed with the design changes as discussed on the phone. On Friday, July 22, the final units were inspected by quality control and were then shipped.

QUESTIONS

1. Which organization was more effective at developing the prototype and meeting the deadlines? Was its level of effectiveness due to the goals chosen by top management?

2. Predict which organization will get the final contract. Why?

Part IV

Ten of Acme's final memory units were defective, while all of Omega's units passed the photocopier firm's tests. The photocopier firm was disappointed with Acme's delivery delay and incurred further delays in repairing the defective Acme units. However, rather than give the entire contract to one firm, the final contract was split between Acme and Omega with two directives added: (1) maintain zero defects and (2) reduce final cost. In 1977, through extensive cost-cutting efforts, Acme reduced its unit cost by 20 percent and was ultimately awarded the total contract.

QUESTIONS

1. How can Acme's success be explained? Did Acme's goals seem more appropriate? Did stakeholder satisfaction play a role?
2. Overall, who was more effective, Acme or Omega? Explain.

NOTES

1. Stephanie Losee, "How Compaq Keeps the Magic Going," *Fortune,* 21 February 1994, 88–92.
2. Amitai Etzioni, *Modern Organizations* (Englewood Cliffs, N.J.: Prentice-Hall, 1964), 6.
3. John P. Kotter, "What Effective General Managers Really Do," *Harvard Business Review* (November-December 1982): 156–67; Henry Mintzberg, *The Nature of Managerial Work* (New York: Harper & Row, 1973).
4. Charles C. Snow and Lawrence G. Hrebiniak, "Strategy, Distinctive Competence, and Organizational Performance," *Administrative Science Quarterly* 25 (1980): 317–35.
5. David L. Calfee, "Get Your Mission Statement Working!" *Management Review,* January 1993, 54–57; John A. Pearce II and Fred David, "Corporate Mission Statements: The Bottom Line," *Academy of Management Executive* 1 (1987): 109–16; Fred R. David, "How Companies Define Their Mission," *Long-Range Planning* 22 (1989): 90–97.
6. Charles Perrow, "The Analysis of Goals in Complex Organizations," *American Sociological Review* 26 (1961): 854–66.
7. Johannes U. Stoelwinder and Martin P. Charns, "The Task Field Model of Organization Analysis and Design," *Human Relations* 34 (1981): 743–62; Anthony Raia, *Managing by Objectives* (Glenview, Ill.: Scott, Foresman, 1974).
8. Joseph Weber, "DuPont's Trailblazer Wants to Get out of the Woods," *Business Week*, 31 August 1992, 70–71.
9. Neil Gross, "Inside Hitachi," *Business Week,* 28 September 1992, 92-100; Patricia Sellers, "Pepsi Keeps on Going after No. 1," *Fortune,* 11 March 1991, 64; and "Bausch & Lomb: Hardball Pricing Helps It to Regain Its Grip in Contact Lenses," *Business Week,* 16 July 1984, 78–80.
10. Tom Richman, "Mississippi Motivators," *Inc.,* October 1986, 83–88.
11. Alex Taylor III, "Why the Bounce at Rubbermaid," *Fortune,* 13 April 1987, 77–78.
12. William B. Stevenson, Joan L. Pearce, and Lyman W. Porter, "The Concept of 'Coalition' in Organization Theory and Research," *Academy of Management Review* 10 (1985): 256–68.
13. James G. March and Herbert A. Simon, *Organizations* (New York: Wiley, 1958); Richard M. Cyert and James G. March, *A Behavioral Theory of the Firm* (Englewood Cliffs, N.J.: Prentice-Hall, 1963); James D. Thompson, *Organizations in Action* (New York: McGraw-Hill, 1967), 83–98.
14. Jennifer Reese, "America's Most Admired Corporations," *Fortune,* 8 February 1993, 44–54.
15. Thompson, *Organizations in Action.*
16. "Owens-Illinois: Giving up Market Share to Improve Profits," *Business Week,* 11 May 1981, 81–82.
17. Richard Crone, Bruce Snow, and Ricky Waclawcayk, "Datapoint Corporation," unpublished manuscript, Texas A&M University, 1981.
18. Michael E. Porter, *Competitive Strategy: Techniques*

for Analyzing Industries and Competitors (New York: Free Press, 1980).

19. A. Miller and G. G. Dess, "Assessing Porter's (1980) Model in Terms of Its Generalizability, Accuracy, and Simplicity," *Journal of Management Studies* 30 (1993): 553–85.

20. Nathaniel Gilbert, "John W. Bachmann: Securities Well in Hand," *Management Review,* January 1988, 17–19.

21. Raymond E. Miles and Charles C. Snow, *Organizational Strategy, Structure, and Process* (New York: McGraw-Hill, 1978).

22. Alex Taylor III, "Can Iacocca Fix Chrysler—Again?" *Fortune,* 8 April 1991, 50–54.

23. Andrew Kupfer, "Apple's Plan to Survive and Grow," *Fortune,* 4 May 1992, 68–72.

24. Susan Caminiti, "A High-Priced Game of Catch Up," *Fortune,* 6 September 1993, 73–74.

25. Michael Crawford, "Prey for the Paper Tiger," *Canadian Business,* November 1993, 22–33.

26. Etzioni, *Modern Organizations,* 8.

27. Etzioni, *Modern Organizations,* 8; Gary D. Sandefur, "Efficiency in Social Service Organizations," *Administration and Society* 14 (1983): 449–68.

28. Richard M. Steers, *Organizational Effectiveness: A Behavioral View* (Santa Monica, Calif.: Goodyear, 1977), 51.

29. Karl E. Weick and Richard L. Daft, "The Effectiveness of Interpretation Systems," in Kim S. Cameron and David A. Whetten, eds., *Organizational Effectiveness: A Comparison of Multiple Models* (New York: Academic Press, 1982).

30. Craig Eric Schneider, Douglas G. Shaw, and Richard W. Beatty, "Performance Measurement and Management: A Tool for Strategy Execution," *Human Resource Management* 30 (Fall 1991): 279–301.

31. Frank Rose, "New Quality Means Service Too," *Fortune,* 22 April 1991, 99–108.

32. Steven Strasser, J. D. Eveland, Gaylord Cummins, O. Lynn Deniston, and John H. Romani, "Conceptualizing the Goal and Systems Models of Organizational Effectiveness—Implications for Comparative Evaluation Research," *Journal of Management Studies* 18 (1981): 321–40.

33. James L. Price, "The Study of Organizational Effectiveness," *Sociological Quarterly* 13 (1972): 3–15.

34. Richard H. Hall and John P. Clark, "An Ineffective Effectiveness Study and Some Suggestions for Future Research," *Sociological Quarterly* 21 (1980): 119–34; Price, "Study of Organizational Effectiveness;" Perrow, "Analysis of Goals."

35. George W. England, "Organizational Goals and Expected Behaviors in American Managers," *Academy of Management Journal* 10 (1967): 107–17.

36. Edward O. Welles, "How're We Doing?" *Inc.*, May 1991, 80–83.

37. Johannes M. Pennings and Paul S. Goodman, "Toward a Workable Framework," in Paul S. Goodman, Johannes M. Pennings, et al., *New Perspectives on Organizational Effectiveness* (San Francisco: Jossey-Bass, 1979), 152.

38. J. Barton Cunningham, "A Systems-Resource Approach for Evaluating Organizational Effectiveness," *Human Relations* 31 (1978): 631–56; Ephraim Yuchtman and Stanley E. Seashore, "A System Resource Approach to Organizational Effectiveness," *Administrative Science Quarterly* 12 (1967): 377–95.

39. David Shribeman, "University in Virginia Creates a Niche, Aims to Reach Top Ranks," *Wall Street Journal,* 30 September 1985, 1, 9.

40. Chris Argyris, *Integrating the Individual and the Organization* (New York: Wiley, 1964); Warren G. Bennis, *Changing Organizations* (New York: McGraw-Hill, 1966); Rensis Likert, *The Human Organization* (New York: McGraw-Hill, 1967); Richard Beckhard, *Organization Development Strategies and Models* (Reading, Mass.: Addison-Wesley, 1969).

41. Cheri Ostroff and Neal Schmitt, "Configurations of Organizational Effectiveness and Efficiency," *Academy of Management Journal* 36 (1993): 1345–61; Peter J. Frost, Larry F. Moore, Meryl Reise Louis, Craig C. Lundburg, and Joanne Martin, *Organizational Culture* (Beverly Hills, Calif.: Sage, 1985).

42. J. Barton Cunningham, "Approaches to the Evaluation of Organizational Effectiveness," *Academy of Management Review* 2 (1977): 463–74; Beckhard, *Organization Development.*

43. William M. Evan, "Organization Theory and Organizational Effectiveness: An Exploratory Analysis," *Organization and Administrative Sciences* 7 (1976): 15–28.

44. Alex Taylor III, "Lee Iacocca's Production Whiz," *Fortune,* 22 June 1987, 36–44.

45. Anne S. Tusi, "A Multiple-Constituency Model of Effectiveness: An Empirical Examination at the Human Resource Subunit Level," *Administrative Science Quarterly* 35 (1990): 458, 483; Charles Fombrun and Mark Shanley, "What's in a Name? Reputation Building and Corporate Strategy," *Academy of Management Journal* 33 (1990):

233–58; Terry Connolly, Edward J. Conlon, and Stuart Jay Deutsch, "Organizational Effectiveness: A Multiple-Constituency Approach," *Academy of Management Review* 5 (1980): 211–17.

46. Frank Friedlander and Hal Pickle, "Components of Effectiveness in Small Organizations," *Administrative Science Quarterly* 13 (1968): 289–304.

47. Kim S. Cameron, "The Effectiveness of Ineffectiveness," in Barry M. Staw and L. L. Cummings, eds., *Research in Organizational Behavior* (Greenwich, Conn.: JAI Press, 1984), 235–86; Rosabeth Moss Kanter and Derick Brinkerhoff, "Organizational Performance: Recent Developments in Measurement," *Annual Review of Sociology* 7 (1981): 321–49.

48. Tusi, "A Multiple-Constituency Model of Effectiveness."

49. Fombrun and Shanley, "What's in a Name?"

50. Russell Mitchell, "Safeway's Low-Fat Diet," *Business Week,* 18 October 1993, 60–61.

51. Robert E. Quinn and John Rohrbaugh, "A Spatial Model of Effectiveness Criteria: Toward a Competing Values Approach to Organizational Analysis," *Management Science* 29 (1983): 363–77.

52. Regina M. O'Neill and Robert E. Quinn, "Editor's Note: Applications of the Competing Values Framework," *Human Resource Management* 32 (Spring 1993): 1–7.

53. Robert E. Quinn and Kim Cameron, "Organizational Life Cycles and Shifting Criteria of Effectiveness: Some Preliminary Evidence," *Management Science* 29 (1983): 33–51.

54. Mark Maremont with Gary McWilliams, "Kodak: Shoot the Works," *Business Week,* 15 November 1993, 30–32; Joan E. Rigdon, G. Christian Hill and Gautam Naik, "Hiring Fisher, Kodak Gambles on a Future in a Multimedia World," *Wall Street Journal,* 29 October 1993, A1, A7.

55. Michael Hammer and James Champy, *Reengineering the Corporation* (New York, HarperCollins, 1993); Noel M. Tichy and Stratford Sherman, *Control Your Destiny or Someone Else Will* (New York: Currency Doubleday, 1993).

56. Oren Harari, "You're Not in Business to Make a Profit," *Management Review,* July 1992, 53–55.

57. Sellers, "Pepsi Keeps on Going after No. 1."

58. Amy Dunkin, "Pepsi's Marketing Magic: Why Nobody Does It Better," *Business Week,* 10 February 1986, 52–57.

59. Neil Templin, "A Decisive Response to Crisis Brought Ford Enhanced Productivity," *Wall Street Journal,* 15 December 1992, A1, A8.

60. Michael A. Hitt and R. Duane Ireland, "Peters and Waterman Revisited: The Unended Quest for Excellence," *Academy of Management Executive* 1 (1987): 91–98.

CHAPTER

3

The External Environment

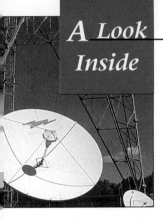

WQED Public Television

The station that gave Mister Rogers his start is in trouble. Pittsburgh's WQED initiated the now-famous children's series "Mister Rogers' Neighborhood" and worked with National Geographic to produce fifteen years' worth of documentaries that were some of the most-watched programs on the Public Broadcasting System (PBS). The station was a $36 million operation and earned twenty eight Emmy awards.

But the once relatively stable world of public television has turned topsy-turvy. Today's cable networks, such as the Discovery Channel, offer viewers the same kinds of programs once seen only on PBS. Public stations are facing increasing competition for viewers and decreasing corporate and government funding. Most public television stations have cut back staff and slashed executives' salaries as they come to grips with this harsh new environment.

In WQED's case, however, station executives either failed to see the environmental danger signals or ignored them. Though most stations recognized that massive corporate support was drying up, WQED blithely carried on as usual when the station lost both its major corporate sponsor, Gulf Oil, and its principal co-producer, National Geographic. Station executives continued to receive handsome salaries and benefits, amounting to as much as sixty thousand dollars more each than what was disclosed in public filings, along with generous car allowances and other expensive perks. As the station continued to appeal on air to viewers for support, word of these excesses began to surface, creating more trouble from the environment. Loyal long-time subscribers are furious, and WQED faces a $4.8 million deficit and no prospects for major new sponsorship.

WQED is now taking drastic steps under the leadership of acting CEO Donald Korb, a retired Westinghouse treasurer and former head of WQED's finance committee. But even Korb admits that a turnaround won't be easy. For WQED to survive, he recently said, "We need a lot of skill and a little bit of luck."[1]

W QED learned the hard way that its station is not a permanent fixture in a stable environment. Its board and acting CEO are struggling to save the once-mighty station by drastically reducing staff and cutting top salaries and benefits. In an effort to redeem the station's reputation in the community, they have turned over financial records for investigation. By failing to heed the warning signs about cable network competition and declining funding, WQED now faces a struggle just to survive.

The problem of a changing environment is not unique to public television stations. Companies in all industries confront difficulties because of changes in the environment. Automobile manufacturers such as Chrysler and General Motors continue to face tough foreign competition, including an increasing number of foreign-owned manufacturing plants built on U.S. soil. Small retailers have long suffered threats from huge discount stores, such as Wal-Mart. But even the mighty Wal-Mart is vulnerable to changes in the environment. Small retailers are challenging some of the giant chain's competitive tactics in court, claiming it is violating antitrust laws, and stubborn New Englanders have slowed the expansion of Wal-Mart into that region largely with zoning requirements and legal arguments that it will have a detrimental impact on the local environment.[2]

Firms that attempt to grow through mergers and acquisitions have run into brick walls in the form of tough regulations in many states. For other firms, new technology such as digital communications, microrobots from Japan, or Nucor's highly efficient thin-slab steel casting poses major threats. Also, firms in all industries agree that international competition worries everyone. The list could go on and on. The external environment is the source of important threats facing major corporations today.[3]

PURPOSE OF THIS CHAPTER

The purpose of this chapter is to develop a framework for assessing environments and how organizations can respond to them. First, we will identify the organizational domain and the sectors that influence the organization. Then, we will explore two major environmental forces on the organization—the need for information and the need for resources. Organizations respond to these forces through structural design, planning systems, imitation, and attempts to change and control elements in the environment. Finally, the chapter examines a recent perspective on organization-environment relationships, which is described in the population ecology model.

The Environmental Domain

In a broad sense, the environment is infinite and includes everything outside the organization. However, the analysis presented here considers only the aspects of the environment to which the organization is sensitive and must respond to survive. Thus, **organizational environment** is defined as all elements that exist outside the boundary of the organization and have the potential to affect all or part of the organization.

The environment of an organization can be understood by analyzing its domain within external sectors. An organization's **domain** is the chosen environmental field of action. It is the territory an organization stakes out for itself with respect to products, services, and markets served. Domain defines the organization's niche and defines those external sectors with which the organization will interact to accomplish its goals. For example, the domain of WQED brought it into contact with customers (viewers), competitors, corporate funders, and government rules and regulations.

The environment comprises several **sectors** or subdivisions of the external environment that contain similar elements. Ten sectors can be analyzed for each organization: industry, raw materials, human resources, financial resources, market, technology, economic conditions, government, sociocultural, and international. The sectors and a hypothetical organizational domain are illustrated in Exhibit 3.1. For most companies, the sectors in Exhibit 3.1 can be further subdivided into the task environment and general environment.

TASK ENVIRONMENT

The **task environment** includes sectors with which the organization interacts directly and that have a direct impact on the organization's ability to achieve its goals. The task environment typically includes the industry, raw materials, and market sectors, and perhaps the human resources and international sectors. For example, in the industry sector, Intel Corporation, still the king of computer chips, now faces major

Exhibit 3.1
An
Organization's
Environment.

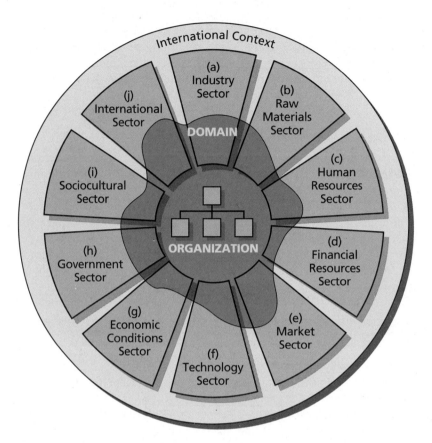

(a) Competitors, industry size and competitiveness, related industries

(b) Suppliers, manufacturers, real estate, services

(c) Labor market, employment agencies, universities, training schools, employees in other companies, unionization

(d) Stock markets, banks, savings and loans, private investors

(e) Customers, clients, potential users of products and services

(f) Techniques of production, science, research centers, automation, new materials

(g) Recession, unemployment rate, inflation rate, rate of investment, economics, growth

(h) City, state, federal laws and regulations, taxes, services, court system, political processes

(i) Age, values, beliefs, education, religion, work ethic, consumer and green movements

(j) Competition from and acquisition by foreign firms, entry into overseas markets, foreign customs, regulations, exchange rate

new competition from such large companies as Texas Instruments, Sun Microsystems, and Digital Equipment Corporation, as well as continuing competition from such clone-makers as Advanced Micro Devices and Cyrix. In addition, looming on the chip horizon is the triumvirate of Apple, IBM, and Motorola, which recently began shipping its PowerPC chips.[4] Businesses also have to keep a close watch on the market sector. Toy companies such as Mattel and Tyco have introduced African-American dolls in response to the growing population and buying power of African-Americans, while cosmetic companies such as Maybelline are developing products geared to darker skins.[5]

GENERAL ENVIRONMENT

The **general environment** includes those sectors that may not have a direct impact on the daily operations of a firm but will indirectly influence it. The general environment often includes the government, sociocultural, economic conditions, technology, and financial resources sectors. These sectors affect all organizations eventually. For example, general economic conditions eventually change ways of doing business. An era of low inflation means that furniture maker Ethan Allen, for example, hasn't raised prices in three years. To remain competitive, the company has to keep prices low, so it strives to increase its profit margins by turning to simpler furniture designs and increasing technological efficiency.[6] In the sociocultural sector, decreasing leisure time and the swelling ranks of women in the work force have contributed to a boom in the televised "home shopping" industry. Even prestigious retailers such as Saks Fifth Avenue are now offering clothes and other goods on screen.[7]

INTERNATIONAL CONTEXT

The international sector can directly affect many organizations, and it has become extremely important in the last few years. In addition, all domestic sectors can be affected by international events. Despite the significance of international events for today's organizations, many students fail to appreciate the importance of international events and still think domestically. Think again. Even if you stay in your hometown, your company may be purchased tomorrow by the English, Canadians, Japanese, or Germans. The Japanese alone own more than one thousand U.S. companies, including steel mills, rubber and tire factories, automobile assembly plants, and auto parts suppliers. Nationwide, more than 350,000 Americans work for Japanese companies. People employed by Pillsbury, Shell Oil, Firestone, and CBS Records are working for foreign bosses.[8]

Another possibility is that the company you work for will be targeted for competition by a foreign company that may produce better quality goods for sale in your backyard. This occurred when giant NEC from Japan made a better product than small Florod Corporation for a market with only forty business customers. Further, consider the following predictions:[9]

- Japan, United Germany, and the European Economic Community of 1992 may spawn large, powerful companies that compete easily with U.S. firms. These companies could reshape the industry and market sectors as we now know them.
- Newly industrialized countries such as Korea, Taiwan, Singapore, and Spain produce huge volumes of low-cost, high quality commodities that will have an impact on the competitiveness of many industries, markets, and raw materials in North America.
- Eastern Europe, Russia, and China are all shifting toward market economies that also will affect markets, raw materials, industry competition, and worldwide economic conditions.

- Nine of ten of the world's largest banks are Japanese, sharply affecting the world's financial resources sector.
- Hundreds of partnerships are taking place between North American firms and firms in all parts of the world, facilitating the exchange of technology and production capability, thereby redefining the technology, raw materials, and industry sectors.
- Many companies in the United States build twin plants—one in Texas and one in Mexico. The Mexican plants provide component assembly, and that helps combat Mexico's high unemployment. Called maquiladoras, these plants reshape the human resources and raw materials sectors.
- All of these international connections are spawning new state and federal regulations, thereby affecting the government sector, and beliefs and values are becoming shared worldwide, shaping the sociocultural sector.[10]

What kind of chaos does global competition create for organizations? Consider this. By making and designing more of their autos in the United States, Japanese auto firms are intensifying their challenge to Detroit. Honda, Nissan, Toyota, Mazda, Mitsubishi, Subaru, and Isuzu have all shifted manufacturing to the United States, and they already own a 30 percent share of the U.S. car market. In addition, the United States is sinking like a rock in the consumer electronics industry. In the 1990s, production in Japan grew three times and production in Europe grew nearly two times faster than in the United States. Zenith is the only remaining U.S. maker of television sets, and it will soon be producing all of its televisions in Mexico, while foreign-owned companies such as Sony and Thomson (once General Electric) produce TVs in the United States. And while AT&T is still the world's largest telecommunications company, Alcatel of France has already surpassed it in sales of equipment.[11]

Today's environment pays no respect to national borders. Organizations must learn new rules to cope with the T-shirts, Nikes, notepad computers, business strategies, and takeover plans that are traveling around the planet right now by telephone, fax, and overnight mail. Of course, there is a positive side, too; when companies tailor their products to the unique needs of foreign countries and when they withstand tough foreign competition in domestic markets, they find that they can succeed and that the whole world is their marketplace.

The North American Free Trade Agreement is spurring many U.S. retailers to move into Canada and Mexico. Wal-Mart recently bought 120 stores from Woolworth to gain a foothold in Canada. The following example of J.C. Penney shows how an American company is positioning itself to be competitive in the international marketplace. Note also how the company is paying attention to other sectors in its environment.

IN PRACTICE ◆ 3.1

J.C. Penney Company

Ambitious expansion and aggressive marketing are turning a stodgy old-timer into a snazzy international competitor. Something happened the day Liz Claiborne, Estee Lauder, and other upscale brand-name companies turned up their noses at J.C. Penney Company. Caught between discount stores and specialty stores, Penney decided to get a new attitude. It started turning its own private labels into brand names by designing exclusive lines, rejecting substandard goods, and aggressively marketing the labels. It's a strategy that has paid off not only at home but increasingly overseas as well. Penney's house brands now form the core of a growing business on foreign soil.

Penney offers catalogs in Iceland, Brazil, and Russia and is translating a catalog into Spanish to tap into a growing Latin American catalog market. Licensed J.C. Penney shops are showing major sales in the United Arab Emirates and Singapore. Company executives are talking with potential partners in Portugal and Greece and checking into opportunities in Taiwan, Thailand, and Indonesia.

Rather than buying existing retail chains or purchasing property in foreign countries, Penney generally links up with local partners—a point that has helped it avoid costly cultural blunders. Its Chilean retail partners, for instance, know that men there consider short pants suitable only for children.

The biggest gamble so far, though, is in Mexico, where Penney plans to open seven stores and where it has decided it doesn't need a local partner. For this gamble to pay off, J.C. Penney will have to be vigilant and adaptable as retail competition in Mexico intensifies and as the global environment for retailers keeps changing.[12]

J.C. Penney has coped with several changes in the industry, raw materials, market, and international sectors. When it found itself betwixt and between in the 1980s—unable to compete with either discounters or specialty stores—J.C. Penney aggressively developed and marketed its own lines, such as Hunt Club, Worthington, St. John's Bay, and Arizona jeans. Success with these lines at home led the company to expand into overseas markets. In the next section, we will discuss in greater detail how organizations respond to the environmental uncertainty facing them.

Environmental Uncertainty

How does the environment influence an organization? The patterns and events occurring across environmental sectors can be described along several dimensions, such as whether the environment is stable or unstable, homogeneous or heterogeneous, concentrated or dispersed, simple or complex; the extent of turbulence; and the amount of resources available to support the organization.[13] These dimensions boil down to two essential ways the environment influences organizations: (1) the need for information about the environment and (2) the need for resources from the environment. The environmental conditions of complexity and change create a greater need to gather information and to respond based on that information. The organization also is concerned with scarce material and financial resources and with the need to ensure availability of resources. Each sector can be analyzed relative to these three analytical categories. The remainder of this section will discuss the information perspective, which is concerned with the uncertainty that environmental complexity and change creates for the organization. Later in the chapter, we will discuss how organizations control the environment to acquire needed resources.

Organizations must cope with and manage uncertainty to be effective. **Uncertainty** means that decision makers do not have sufficient information about environmental factors, and they have a difficult time predicting external changes. Uncertainty increases the risk of failure for organizational responses and makes it difficult to compute costs and probabilities associated with decision alternatives.[14] Characteristics of the environmental domain that influence uncertainty are the extent to which the external domain is simple or complex and the extent to which events are stable or unstable.[15]

SIMPLE-COMPLEX DIMENSION

The **simple-complex dimension** concerns environmental complexity, which refers to heterogeneity, or the number and dissimilarity of external elements relevant to an organization's operations. In a complex environment, many diverse external elements interact with and influence the organization. In a simple environment, as few as three or four similar external elements influence the organization.

Public television stations like WQED have a complex environment, as do universities. Universities span a large number of technologies and are a focal point for cultural and value changes. Government regulatory and granting agencies interact with a university, and so do a variety of professional and scientific associations, alumni, parents, foundations, legislators, community residents, international agencies, donors, corporations, and athletic teams. A large number of external elements thus make up the organization's domain, creating a complex environment. On the other hand, a hardware store in a suburban community is in a simple environment. The only external elements of any real importance are a few competitors, the parent company (for supplies), and customers. Government regulation is minimal, and cultural change has little impact. Human resources are not a problem because the store is run by family members or part-time help.

STABLE-UNSTABLE DIMENSION

The **stable-unstable dimension** refers to whether elements in the environment are dynamic. An environmental domain is stable if it remains the same over a period of months or years. Under unstable conditions, environmental elements shift abruptly. Instability may occur when competitors react with aggressive moves and countermoves regarding advertising and new products. Sometimes specific, unpredictable events—such as reports of syringes in cans of Pepsi or glass shards in Gerber's baby foods, the poisoning of Tylenol, or Union Carbide's gas leak in Bhopal, India—create unstable conditions. The Church of Scientology's attack on the antidepression drug Prozac, which it claimed drove people to murder and suicide, caused sales of the drug to weaken considerably before rebounding.[16]

An example of a stable environment is a public utility.[17] In the rural Midwest, demand and supply factors for a public utility are stable. A gradual increase in demand may occur, which is easily predicted over time. Toy companies, by contrast, have an unstable environment. Hot new toys are difficult to predict, a problem compounded by the fact that toys are subject to fad buying. Coleco Industries, makers of the once-famous Cabbage Patch Kids, and Worlds of Wonder, creators of Teddy Ruxpin, went bankrupt because of the unstable nature of the toy environment, their once-winning creations replaced today by Bandai's Mighty Morphin Power Rangers or Playmate Toys' Teenage Mutant Ninja Turtles.[18]

FRAMEWORK

The simple-complex and stable-unstable dimensions are combined into a framework for assessing environmental uncertainty in Exhibit 3.2. In the *simple, stable* environment, uncertainty is low. There are only a few external elements to contend with, and they tend to remain stable. The *complex, stable* environment represents somewhat greater uncertainty. A large number of elements have to be scanned, analyzed, and acted upon for the organization to perform well. External elements do not change rapidly or unexpectedly in this environment.

Exhibit 3.2   Framework for Assessing Environmental Uncertainty.

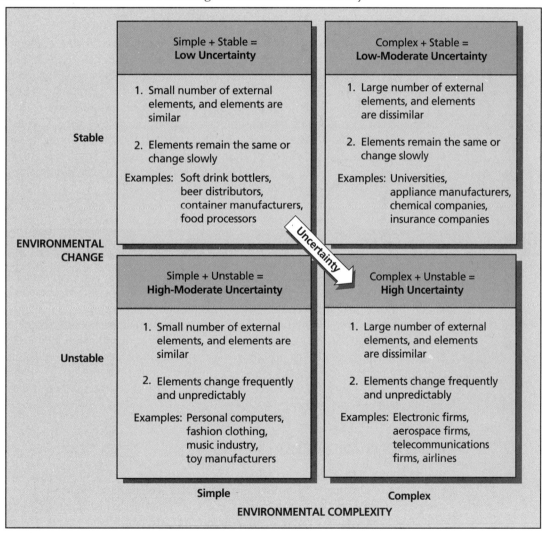

Source: Adapted and reprinted from "Characteristics of Perceived Environments and Perceived Environmental Uncertainty" by Robert B. Duncan, published in *Administrative Science Quarterly* 17 (1972): 313–27, by permission of *The Administrative Science Quarterly.* Copyright © 1972 by Cornell University.

Even greater uncertainty is felt in the *simple, unstable* environment.[19] Rapid change creates uncertainty for managers. Even though the organization has few external elements, those elements are hard to predict, and they react unexpectedly to organizational initiatives. The greatest uncertainty for an organization occurs in the *complex, unstable* environment. A large number of elements impinge upon the organization, and they shift frequently or react strongly to organizational initiatives. When several sectors change simultaneously, the environment becomes turbulent.[20]

A beer distributor functions in a simple, stable environment. Demand for beer changes only gradually. The distributor has an established delivery route, and supplies of beer arrive on schedule. State universities, appliance manufacturers, and insurance companies are in somewhat stable, complex environments. A large number of external elements are present, but although they change, changes are gradual and predictable.

Toy manufacturers are in simple, unstable environments. Organizations that design, make, and sell toys, as well as those that are involved in the clothing or music industry, face shifting supply and demand. Mattel is currently trying to regain ground in the toy business with an ambitious push into designing and marketing toys for boys.[21]

The oil industry and the airline industry face complex, unstable environments. Many external sectors are changing simultaneously. In the case of airlines, in just a few years they have been confronted with deregulation, the growth of regional airlines, surges in fuel costs, price cuts from competitors such as Southwest Airlines, shifting customer demand, an air-traffic controller shortage, overcrowded airports, and a reduction of scheduled flights.[22]

Adapting to Environmental Uncertainty

Once you see how environments differ with respect to change and complexity, the next question is, "How do organizations adapt to each level of environmental uncertainty? Environmental uncertainty represents an important contingency for organization structure and internal behaviors. An organization in a certain environment will be managed and controlled differently from an organization in an uncertain environment with respect to positions and departments, organizational differentiation and integration, control processes, institutional imitation, and future planning and forecasting. Organizations need to have the right fit between internal structure and the external environment.

POSITIONS AND DEPARTMENTS

As the complexity in the external environment increases, so does the number of positions and departments within the organization, which in turn increases internal complexity. This relationship is part of being an open system. Each sector in the external environment requires an employee or department to deal with it. The personnel department deals with unemployed people who want to work for the company. The marketing department finds customers. Procurement employees obtain raw materials from hundreds of suppliers. The finance group deals with bankers. The legal department works with the courts and government agencies.

BUFFERING AND BOUNDARY SPANNING

The traditional approach to coping with environmental uncertainty was to establish buffer departments. The **buffering role** is to absorb uncertainty from the environment.[23] The technical core performs the primary production activity of an organization. Buffer departments surround the technical core and exchange materials, resources, and money between the environment and the organization. They help the technical core function efficiently. The purchasing department buffers the technical core by stockpiling supplies and raw materials. The personnel department buffers the technical core by handling the uncertainty associated with finding, hiring, and training production employees.

A newer approach some organizations are trying is to drop the buffers and expose the technical core to the uncertain environment. These organizations no longer create buffers because they believe being well connected to customers and suppliers is more important than internal efficiency. Thus, as we saw in the first chapter, John Deere has assembly-line workers visiting local farms to determine and respond to customer concerns. Whirlpool pays hundreds of customers to test computer-simulated products and features.[24] Opening up the organization to the environment makes it more fluid and adaptable.

Boundary-spanning roles link and coordinate an organization with key elements in the external environment. Boundary spanning is primarily concerned with the exchange of information to (1) detect and bring into the organization information about changes in the environment and (2) send information into the environment that presents the organization in a favorable light.[25]

To detect important information, boundary personnel scan the environment.[26] For example, a market research department scans and monitors trends in consumer tastes. Boundary spanners in engineering and research and development (R&D) departments scan new technological developments, innovations, and raw materials. Boundary spanners prevent the organization from stagnating by keeping top managers informed about environmental changes. Often, the greater the uncertainty in the environment, the greater the importance of boundary spanners.[27]

The boundary task of sending information into the environment to represent the organization is used to influence other people's perception of the organization. In the marketing department, advertising and sales people represent the organization to customers. Purchasers may call on suppliers and describe purchasing needs. The legal department informs lobbyists and elected officials about the organization's needs or views on political matters.

All organizations have to stay in touch with the environment. Here's how the nation's number two garbage hauler is staying close to the customer.

IN PRACTICE ◆ 3.2
Browning Ferris Industries, Inc.

Rapid customer turnover was once accepted as part of the job in the garbage hauling business. But in today's lean times, with the industry facing stiffer competition from regional haulers and municipalities handling their own trash, Browning-Ferris Industries (BFI) realized it needed to stop losing 14 percent of its customer base per year. To keep growing, the company knew it had to become dedicated to satisfying customers. Using outside consultants, the company surveyed thirty thousand customers to rate the performance of each of its two hundred hauling districts. BFI now asks customers each month to respond in writing to questions about its service.

Common customer complaints included reckless, noisy drivers; rusted, bent, or otherwise damaged dumpsters; dumpsters left blocking driveways; and inconsiderate people using their neighbors' dumpsters to discard smelly trash. Not all customers complained, of course. One, after praising BFI's service, even gave the number two company a friendly tip: "Want you to know that Waste Management [the number one company] is coming to town and marketing like crazy." BFI executives used that timely information to their advantage.[28]

DIFFERENTIATION AND INTEGRATION

Another response to environmental uncertainty is the amount of differentiation and integration among departments. Organization **differentiation** is "the differences in cognitive and emotional orientations among managers in different functional departments, and the difference in formal structure among these departments."[29] When the external environment is complex and rapidly changing, organizational departments become highly specialized to handle the uncertainty in their external sector. Success in each sector requires special expertise and behavior. Employees in a research and development department thus have unique attitudes, values, goals, and education that distinguish them from employees in manufacturing or sales departments.

A study by Paul Lawrence and Jay Lorsch examined three organizational departments—manufacturing, research, and sales—in ten corporations.[30] This study found that each department evolved toward a different orientation and structure to deal with specialized parts of the external environment. The market, scientific, and manufacturing subenvironments identified by Lawrence and Lorsch are illustrated in Exhibit 3.3. Each department interacted with different external groups. The differences that evolved among departments within the organizations are shown in Exhibit 3.4. To work effectively with the scientific subenvironment, R&D had a goal of quality work, a long-time horizon (up to five years), an informal structure, and task-oriented employees. Sales was at the opposite extreme. It had a goal of customer satisfaction, was oriented toward the short term (two weeks or so), had a very formal structure, and was socially oriented.

One outcome of high differentiation is that coordination between departments becomes difficult. More time and resources must be devoted to achieving coordination when attitudes, goals, and work orientation differ so widely. **Integration** is the quality of collaboration between departments.[31] Formal integrators are often required to coordinate departments. When the environment is highly uncertain, frequent changes require more information processing to achieve coordination, so integrators become a necessary addition to the organization structure. Sometimes integrators are called liaison personnel, brand managers, or coordinators. As illustrated in Exhibit 3.5, organizations with highly uncertain environments and a highly differentiated structure assign about 22 percent of management personnel to integration activities, such as serving on committees, on task forces, or in liaison roles.[32] In organizations characterized by very simple, stable environments, almost no managers are assigned to integration roles. Exhibit 3.5 shows that, as environmental

Exhibit 3.3   Organizational Departments Differentiate to Meet Needs of Subenvironments.

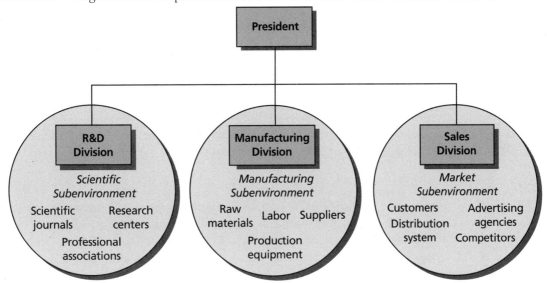

uncertainty increases, so does differentiation between departments; hence, the organization must assign a larger percentage of managers to coordinating roles.

Lawrence and Lorsch's research concluded that organizations perform better when the levels of differentiation and integration match the level of uncertainty in the environment. Organizations that performed well in uncertain environments had high levels of both differentiation and integration, while those performing well in less uncertain environments had lower levels of differentiation and integration.

ORGANIC VERSUS MECHANISTIC MANAGEMENT PROCESSES

Another response to environmental uncertainty is the amount of formal structure and control imposed on employees. Tom Burns and G. M. Stalker observed twenty industrial firms in England and discovered that external environment was related to internal management structure.[33] When the external environment was stable, the internal organization was characterized by rules, procedures, and a clear hierarchy of authority. Organizations were formalized. They were also centralized, with most decisions made at the top. Burns and Stalker called this a **mechanistic** organization system.

In rapidly changing environments, the internal organization was much looser, free-flowing, and adaptive. Rules and regulations often were not written down or, if written down, were ignored. People had to find their own way through the system to figure out what to do. The hierarchy of authority was not clear. Decision-making authority was decentralized. Burns and Stalker used the term **organic** to characterize this type of management structure.

Exhibit 3.6 summarizes the differences in organic and mechanistic systems. As environmental uncertainty increases, organizations tend to become more organic, which means decentralizing authority and responsibility to lower levels, encouraging employees to take care of problems by working directly with one another,

Exhibit 3.4   Differences in Goals and Orientations among Organizational Departments.

Characteristic	R & D Department	Manufacturing Department	Sales Department
Goals	New developments, quality	Efficient production	Customer satisfaction
Time horizon	Long	Short	Short
Interpersonal orientation	Mostly task	Task	Social
Formality of structure	Low	High	High

Source: Based on Paul R. Lawrence and Jay W. Lorsch, *Organization and Environment* (Homewood, Ill.: Irwin, 1969), pp. 23–29.

encouraging teamwork, and taking an informal approach to assigning tasks and responsibility. Thus, the organization is more fluid and is able to adapt continually to changes in the external environment.[34]

INSTITUTIONAL IMITATION

An emerging view, called the **institutional perspective,** argues that under high uncertainty, organizations mimic or imitate other organizations in the same institutional environment. The institutional environment includes other similar organizations in the industry that deal with similar customers, suppliers, and regulatory agencies.[35]

Managers in an organization experiencing great uncertainty assume that other organizations face similar uncertainty. These managers will copy the structure, management techniques, and strategies of other firms that appear successful. Such mimicking serves to reduce uncertainty for managers, but it also means that organizations within an industry will tend to look alike over time. For example, all retail department stores will tend to operate in a similar way, as will airlines, banks, and drug companies.

In general, corporations do not want to be criticized by shareholders for being too different. As a result, if a successful company in an industry establishes a formal intelligence department, other firms are likely to do likewise. Organizations thus experience fads and fashions just as people do. Recent organization fads include acquiring other companies to show rapid growth, downsizing to eliminate excess personnel, MBWA (managing by walking around), and "intrapreneuring" (promoting change from within).[36]

Exhibit 3.5   Environmental Uncertainty and Organizational Integrators.

	Plastics	Industry Foods	Container
Environmental uncertainty	High	Moderate	Low
Departmental differentiation	High	Moderate	Low
Percent management in integrating roles	22%	17%	0%

Source: Based on Jay W. Lorsch and Paul R. Lawrence, "Environmental Factors and Organizational Integration," *Organization Planning: Cases and Concepts* (Homewood, Ill.: Irwin and Dorsey, 1972), 45.

Exhibit 3.6   Mechanistic and Organic Organization Forms.

Mechanistic	Organic
1. Tasks are broken down into specialized, separate parts.	1. Employees contribute to the common task of the department.
2. Tasks are rigidly defined.	2. Tasks are adjusted and redefined through employee teamwork.
3. There is a strict hierarchy of authority and control, and there are many rules.	3. There is less hierarchy of authority and control, and there are few rules.
4. Knowledge and control of tasks are centralized at the top of organization.	4. Knowledge and control of tasks are located anywhere in the organization.
5. Communication is vertical.	5. Communication is horizontal.

Source: Adapted from Gerald Zaltman, Robert Duncan, and Jonny Holbek, *Innovations and Organizations* (New York: Wiley, 1973), 131.

PLANNING AND FORECASTING

The final organizational response to uncertainty is to increase planning and environmental forecasting. When the environment is stable, the organization can concentrate on current operational problems and day-to-day efficiency. Long-range planning and forecasting are not needed because environmental demands in the future will be the same as they are today.

With increasing environmental uncertainty, planning and forecasting become necessary.[37] Planning can soften the adverse impact of external shifting. Organizations that have unstable environments often establish a separate planning department. In an unpredictable environment, planners scan environmental elements and analyze potential moves and countermoves by other organizations. Planning can be extensive and may forecast various scenarios for environmental contingencies. As time passes, plans are updated through replanning. However, planning does not substitute for other actions, such as boundary spanning. Indeed, under conditions of extraordinarily high uncertainty, planning may not be helpful because the future is so difficult to predict.

Framework for Organizational Responses to Uncertainty

The ways environmental uncertainty influences organizational characteristics are summarized in Exhibit 3.7 The change and complexity dimensions are combined and illustrate four levels of uncertainty. The low uncertainty environment is simple and stable. Organizations in this environment have few departments and a mechanistic structure. In a low-moderate uncertainty environment, more departments are needed along with more integrating roles to coordinate the departments. Some planning and imitation may occur. Environments that are high-moderate uncertainty are unstable but simple. Organization structure is organic and decentralized. Planning is emphasized and managers are quick to imitate successful attributes of competitors. The high uncertainty environment is both complex and unstable and is the most difficult environment from a management perspective. Organizations are large and have many departments, but they are also organic. A large number of management

Exhibit 3.7   Contingency Framework for Environmental Uncertainty and Organizational Responses.

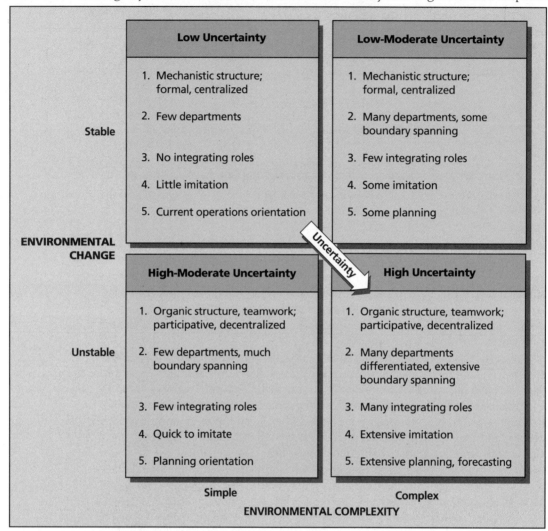

personnel are assigned to coordination and integration, and the organization uses boundary spanning, imitation, planning, and forecasting. Book Mark 3.0 reports additional ideas for responding to an uncertain environment.

Resource Dependence

Thus far, this chapter has described several ways in which organizations adapt to the lack of information and to the uncertainty caused by environmental change and complexity. Now, we turn to the third characteristic of the organization-environment relationship that affects organizations, which is the need for material and financial resources. The environment is the source of scarce and valued resources essential to

BOOKMARK 3.0

The Age of Unreason
by Charles Handy

Will we as a society simply react to an uncertain environment, or will we welcome change and use it to our advantage? Charles Handy believes

> . . . we are entering an Age of Unreason, when the future, in so many areas, is there to be shaped, by us and for us—a time when the only prediction that will hold true is that no predictions will hold true; a time, therefore, for bold imaginings in private life as well as public, for thinking the unlikely and doing the unreasonable.

Handy argues we are entering "the age of unreason," a time in which we will have to deal with discontinuous change—change with no pattern. Even the smallest changes will make big differences both the way we work and the way we live. To deal with this uncertainty, we must learn "discontinuous, upside-down thinking." This thinking will make all things possible by considering the unlikely as well as the absurd.

Application to Organizations

Handy identifies three new types of organizations that will be successful in the Age of Unreason—the shamrock, federal, and triple I. All three can exist simultaneously or to various degrees in one company or corporation.

- *Shamrock* The shamrock is made up of three parts, similar to the leaves on the shamrock plant. The first leaf is the organization's core, composed of essential, qualified, professional employees. The second leaf is composed of independent contractors—employees who contract for specific, often temporary, jobs. The third leaf is composed of a flexible labor force, including part-timers, single parents, and others who provide a range of skills. Handy feels the structure of the shamrock organization is changing due to global competition. The core leaf is shrinking, and the second and third leaves are expanding.
- *Federal* Federalism combines autonomy with cooperation through delegation of tasks and duties to the outlying parts of the organization.

The center—typically, headquarters—does not direct or control so much as it coordinates, advises, influences, and suggests. In a reversal from traditional, centralized organizations, the initiative, energy, and drive come from the outlying parts rather than the center.

- *Triple I* The three I's are intelligence, information, and ideas. In today's competitive information society, intelligence must be combined with quality information and ideas to give knowledge value. For organizations to deal successfully with uncertainty and rapid change, employees must possess all three I's.

Management Implications

In a highly uncertain environment, management has the somewhat overwhelming task of transforming existing organizations into learning organizations that learn and change with the environment. Handy discusses several methods through which learning and change can be accomplished.

- *Decentralization* Delegate decision-making power and responsibility to employees located in diverse locations.
- *Creative Thinking* Involve more employees in the decision-making process, thereby increasing the flow of creative ideas.
- *Trusting and Caring Climate Open to Change* Trust employees, encourage risk-taking, and be open to the changes that result from the risks taken.
- *Higher Levels of Responsibility* Avoid groupthink and provide challenging opportunities for employees by pushing them into new areas of responsibility. Horizontal transfers allow employees to gain a wider view of the organization.

Handy recognizes that the environment surrounding organizations is more uncertain than ever. The unstructured, upside-down thinking he describes will enable organizations to adapt and survive.

The Age of Unreason by Charles Handy is published by Harvard Business School Press.

organizational survival. Research in this area is called the resource dependence perspective. **Resource dependence** means that organizations depend on the environment but strive to acquire control over resources to minimize their dependence.[38] Organizations are vulnerable if vital resources are controlled by other organizations, so they try to be as independent as possible. However, when costs and risks are high, companies also team up to reduce resource dependence and the possibility of bankruptcy.

INTERORGANIZATIONAL COLLABORATION

North American organizations, both profit and not-for-profit, traditionally have worked alone, competing with each other, believing in the individualism and self-reliance that has been our tradition. But today, collaboration is the name of the game, as companies join together to be more competitive and to share scarce resources. As a new wave of technology based on digital communications builds, for example, computer manufacturers, local phone companies, cable television operators, cellular phone companies, and even water and gas utilities are teaming up. Companies all over the world are racing into alliances to share the risks in this uncharted territory and ultimately cash in on the rewards.[39] In today's volatile environment, companies are more willing to undertake ventures they don't completely own or control. Consider the following examples:

- AT&T, the world's largest telecommunications company, is reaching out everywhere these days, dropping its traditional do-it-from-scratch approach to team up with such major, established companies as Viacom, Inc., as well as small pioneering companies, ensconcing itself in almost every corner of the rapidly changing communications industry.[40]
- Many big companies, such as Motorola, Sony, Time Warner, IBM, and Kodak, are joining forces with smaller firms to explore new technologies and markets. Small, pioneering companies thus get the benefit of the larger firms' financing and marketing capabilities.[41]
- Canada's garment manufacturers and retailers have formed high levels of strategic partnerships. These linkages help retailers have the right products at the right times, and they give Canadian manufacturers a competitive speed and flexibility advantage over low-cost factories in other parts of the world.[42]
- Strategic partnerships were pioneered in North America by automakers in the 1980s. Ford Motor Company, for example, engaged in more than forty coalitions with other corporate organizations in 1987, the most famous of which was the partnership with Mazda to develop the Escort, the world's first global car.[43]

Partnerships are a major avenue for entering global markets, with both large and small firms developing partnerships overseas and in North America.

Why all this interest in **interorganizational coordination?** The major reasons are to share risks in entering new markets or in mounting new programs and to reduce the cost and enhance organizational profile in selected industries or technologies.[44]

Another reason is that North Americans have learned from competitors in Japan and Korea how effective interorganizational relationships can be. For example, Japan has corporate clans or industrial groups called *keiretsu*. A *keiretsu* is a collection of companies that share holdings in one another, have interlocking boards of directors, and undertake joint ventures in long-term business relationships. A *keiretsu* has long-term historical linkages through educational backgrounds of executives that literally create a family of companies.[45] North Americans typically have considered interdependence a bad thing, believing it would reduce competition. In a *keiretsu*, no single company dominates, and competition is fierce. It's as if the brothers and sisters of a single family went into separate businesses and want to outdo one another, but they still love one another and will help each other when needed. Companies in a *keiretsu* enjoy a safety net that encourages long-term investment and risk-taking for entering new markets and trying new technologies. The interorganizational linkage is so powerful that it is believed to be one of the major reasons for Japan's success in world markets. Perhaps the most famous *keiretsu* is Mitsubishi.

IN PRACTICE ◆ 3.3
Mitsubishi

The Mitsubishi group is well-known in North America. This *keiretsu* extends all the way back to prewar industrial Japan. The group comprises literally hundreds of companies, but at its heart are twenty-eight core members whose company presidents regularly meet. The three major companies are Mitsubishi Corporation, Mitsubishi Bank, and Mitsubishi Heavy Industry. Other companies—heavily connected by cross-ownership, other financial ties, interlocking directors, and long-term business relationships—are Mitsubishi Plastic Industries, Mitsubishi Petro Chemical, Kirin Brewery, Mitsubishi Oil, Mitsubishi Construction, Asahi Glass, Tokio Marine and Fire Insurance, Mitsubishi Motors, and Mitsubishi Rayon. From 17 percent to 50 percent of each of the twenty-eight core companies is owned by other companies in the family.

The coalition of companies, partially illustrated in Exhibit 3.8, gives Mitsubishi enormous clout. Mitsubishi Estate Company recently paid almost $1 billion for 58 percent of Rockefeller Center. Mitsubishi Corporation bought control of Aristech Chemical Corporation for about $875 million, and other Mitsubishi companies bought most of Verbatim from Kodak for $200 million, closed a $400 million power plant deal in Virginia, bought a San Francisco oil company for $75 million, and invested hundreds of million dollars in other ventures. Mitsubishi Trust and Banking was the main lender in the almost $1 billion deal to purchase the famed Pebble Beach Golf Course in California. This kind of clout is unattainable by a single company operating alone in North America. To reach the ultimate in interorganizational coordination, Mitsubishi has linked up with Germany's Daimler-Benz, one of the largest and most powerful industry groups in Europe.[46]

Although North American companies may never collaborate to the extent of Mitsubishi, interorganizational linkages can help firms make better use of scarce resources to achieve higher levels of innovation and performance.[47]

POWER AND DEPENDENCE

Formal relationships with other organizations present a dilemma to managers. North American organizations seek to reduce vulnerability with respect to resources by developing links with other organizations, but they also like to maximize their own autonomy and independence. Organizational linkages require coordination,[48] and they reduce the freedom of each organization to make decisions without concern for

Exhibit 3.8
A Portion of the
Mitsubishi
Keiretsu.

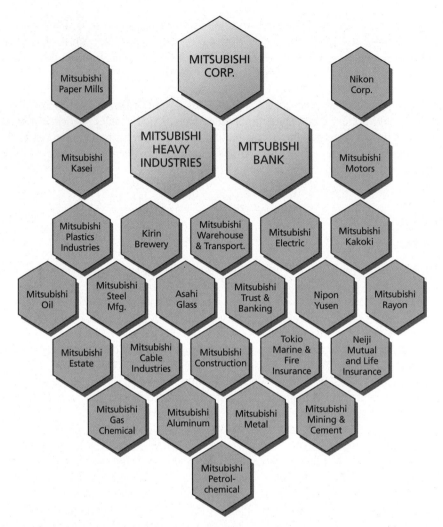

Source: Based on Robert Neff, "Mighty Mitsubishi Is on the Move," *Business Week,* 24 September 1990, 98–101.

the needs and goals of other organizations. Interorganizational relationships thus represent a trade-off between resources and autonomy. To maintain autonomy, organizations that already have abundant resources will tend not to establish new linkages. Organizations that need resources will give up independence to acquire those resources.

Dependence on shared resources gives power to other organizations. Once an organization relies on others for valued resources, those other organizations can influence managerial decision-making. When a large company like DuPont, Motorola, or Xerox forges a partnership with a supplier for parts, both sides benefit, but each loses a small amount of autonomy. For example, some of these large companies are now putting strong pressure on vendors to lower costs, and the vendors have few alternatives but to go along.[49] In much the same way, dependence on shared resources gives advertisers power over print and electronic media companies. For example, as newspapers face increasingly tough financial times, they are less likely to run stories that are critical of advertisers. Though newspapers insist advertisers don't get special treatment, some editors admit there is growing talk around the country of the need for "advertiser-friendly" newspapers.[50]

In another industry, Microsoft is so large and powerful that it has a virtual monopoly in personal computer operating systems, so its every technical change adversely affects producers of application software. Microsoft has been accused of abusing this power and of squashing small competitors that would like to link up with it. Gradually, Microsoft is learning to use these dependencies in a positive way.[51]

Controlling Environmental Resources

In response to the need for resources, organizations try to maintain a balance between linkages with other organizations and their own independence. Organizations maintain this balance through attempts to modify, manipulate, or control other organizations.[52] To survive, the focal organization often tries to reach out and change or control elements in the environment. Two strategies can be adopted to manage resources in the external environment: (1) establish favorable linkages with key elements in the environment and (2) shape the environmental domain.[53] Techniques to accomplish each of these strategies are summarized in Exhibit 3.9. As a general rule, when organizations sense that valued resources are scarce, they will use the strategies in Exhibit 3.9 rather than go it alone. Notice how dissimilar these strategies are from the responses to environmental change and complexity described in Exhibit 3.7. The dissimilarity reflects the difference between responding to the need for information rather than to the need for resources.

ESTABLISHING INTERORGANIZATIONAL LINKAGES

Ownership   Companies use ownership to establish linkages when they buy a part of or a controlling interest in another company. This gives the company access to technology, products, or other resources it doesn't currently have. The communications industry has become particularly complex, and many companies have been teaming up worldwide. AT&T has been attempting to purchase one-third of McCaw Cellular, which projects a $16 billion cellular phone market by 1996.[54] The telephone company US West is talking with Time Warner about investing up to $2 billion for an equity stake in return for access to Time Warner's entertainment properties.[55]

A greater degree of ownership and control is obtained through acquisition or merger. An *acquisition* involves the purchase of one organization by another so that

Establishing Interorganizational Linkages	Controlling the Environmental Domain
1. Ownership	1. Change of domain
2. Contracts, joint ventures	2. Political activity, regulation
3. Cooptation, interlocking directorates	3. Trade associations
4. Executive recruitment	4. Illegitimate activities
5. Advertising, public relations	

Exhibit 3.9
Organization Strategies for Controlling the External Environment.

the buyer assumes control. A *merger* is the unification of two or more organizations into a single unit.[56] In the world of computer software, Novell and Digital Research merged in an $80 million deal. The creation of Bristol Myers Squibb from the Bristol Myers and Squibb companies was a merger. Acquisition occurred when Philip Morris Company purchased Kraft Foods and when Maytag bought Magic Chef.[57] These forms of ownership reduce uncertainty in an area important to the acquiring company.

Formal Strategic Alliances   When there is a high level of complementarity between the business lines, geographical positions, or skills of two companies, the firms often go the route of a strategic alliance rather than ownership through merger or acquisition.[58] Such alliances are formed through contracts and joint ventures.

Contracts and joint ventures reduce uncertainty through a legal and binding relationship with another firm. Contracts come in the form of *license agreements* that involve the purchase of the right to use an asset (such as a new technology) for a specific time and *supplier arrangements* that contract for the sale of one firm's output to another. Contracts can provide long-term security by tying customers and suppliers to specific amounts and prices. For example, McDonald's contracts for an entire crop of russet potatoes to be certain of its supply of french fries. McDonald's also gains influence over suppliers through these contracts and has changed the way farmers grow potatoes and the profit margins they earn, which is consistent with the resource dependence perspective.[59] Large retailers such as Wal-Mart, K Mart, Toys 'R' Us, and Home Depot are gaining so much clout that they can almost dictate contracts telling manufacturers what to make, how to make it, and how much to charge for it. As one manufacturing representative put it, "Most suppliers would do absolutely anything to sell Wal-Mart." Totes, Inc., a maker of umbrellas, slipper socks, and other products, is producing a special, less costly brand for sale only in mass outlets.[60] *Joint ventures* result in the creation of a new organization that is formally independent of the parents, although the parents will have some control.[61] In a joint venture, organizations share the risk and cost associated with large projects or innovations, such as when Pratt & Whitney joined a consortium to develop a new engine or Tenneco created a joint venture with other oil companies to drill for oil in Africa.

Cooptation, Interlocking Directorates   **Cooptation** occurs when leaders from important sectors in the environment are made part of an organization. It takes place, for example, when influential customers or suppliers are appointed to the board of directors, such as when the senior executive of a bank sits on the board of a manufacturing company. As a board member, the banker may become psychologically coopted into the interests of the manufacturing firm. Community leaders also can be appointed to a company's board of directors or to other organizational committees or task forces. These influential people are thus introduced to the needs of the company and are more likely to include the company's interests in their decision-making.

An **interlocking directorate** is a formal linkage that occurs when a member of the board of directors of one company sits on the board of directors of another company. The individual is a communications link between companies and can influence policies and decisions. When one individual is the link between two companies, this is typically referred to as a **direct interlock.** An **indirect interlock** occurs when a director of company A and a director of company B are both directors of company C. They have access to one another but do not have direct influence over their respective companies.[62] Recent research shows that, as a firm's financial fortunes decline, direct interlocks with financial institutions increase. Financial uncertainty facing an industry also has been associated with greater indirect interlocks between competing companies.[63]

Executive Recruitment   Transferring or exchanging executives also offers a method of establishing favorable linkages with external organizations. For example, each year the aerospace industry hires retired generals and executives from the Department of Defense. These generals have personal friends in the department, so the aerospace companies obtain better information about technical specifications, prices, and dates for new weapon systems. They can learn the needs of the defense department and are able to present their case for defense contracts in a more effective way. Companies without personal contacts find it nearly impossible to get a defense contract. Having channels of influence and communication between organizations serves to reduce financial uncertainty and dependence for an organization.

Advertising and Public Relations   A traditional way of establishing favorable relationships is through advertising. Organizations spend large amounts of money to influence the taste of consumers. Advertising is especially important in highly competitive consumer industries and in industries that experience variable demand. Because of the declining demand for health care, hospitals have begun to advertise through billboards, newspapers, and broadcast commercials to promote special services and bonuses, such as steak dinners and champagne. Dow Chemical used skillful advertising to create a new image on college campuses. It invested $50 million over five years in its "Dow lets you do great things" advertising campaign, the success of which has enabled Dow to hire excellent college graduates, an important resource.[64]

Public relations is similar to advertising, except that stories often are free and aimed at public opinion. Public relations people cast an organization in a favorable light in speeches, in press reports, and on television. Public relations shapes the company's image in the minds of customers, suppliers, and government officials.

Summary   Organizations can use a variety of techniques to establish favorable linkages that ensure the availability of scarce resources. Linkages provide control over vulnerable environmental elements. Strategic alliances, interlocking directorates, and outright ownership provide mechanisms to reduce resource dependency on the environment. American companies like IBM, Apple, AT&T, and Motorola have been quick in recent years to turn rivalry into partnership. Perhaps surprisingly, Japan's electronic companies have been slower to become involved in joint ventures and other strategic alliances. Toshiba, however, has been living in the age of high-tech alliances for years and has the competitive edge to show for it.

IN PRACTICE ◆ 3.4
Toshiba

Strategic alliances have been a key element in Toshiba's corporate strategy since the early 1900s, when then, company contracted to make light bulb filaments for General Electric. Since then, Toshiba has taken advantage of partnerships, licensing agreements, and joint ventures to become one of the world's leading manufacturers of electronic products. A joint venture with Motorola has made Toshiba the top maker of large-scale memory chips. Other partnerships aid the company in producing computers, fax machines, copiers, medical equipment, advanced semiconductors, home appliances, and nuclear and steam power-generating equipment, just for starters. Exhibit 3.10 shows some of the many linkages Toshiba shares with other companies.

Toshiba is involved in more than two dozen major partnerships or joint ventures for two reasons. One is money: the company estimates that the next-generation dynamic random-access memory chip will cost more than $1 billion to develop (it is working with IBM and Siemens on the project). The other is speed: Toshiba's management thinks that carefully chosen partners offer the best means of harnessing the resources needed to move quickly in today's volatile high-tech marketplace.[65]

Toshiba illustrates how linkages can be used to control resources and reduce dependency. The other major strategy companies can use to manage resource dependency is to control or redefine the external environmental domain.

CONTROLLING THE ENVIRONMENTAL DOMAIN

In addition to establishing favorable linkages to obtain resources, organizations often try to change the environment. There are four techniques for influencing or changing a firm's environmental domain.

Change of Domain   The ten sectors described earlier in this chapter are not fixed. The organization decides which business it is in, the market to enter, and the suppliers, banks, employees, and location to use, and this domain can be changed.[66] An organization can seek new environmental relationships and drop old ones. An organization may try to find a domain where there is little competition, no government regulation, abundant suppliers, affluent customers, and barriers to keep competitors out.

Acquisition and divestment are two techniques for altering the domain. Rockwell International felt vulnerable with 63 percent of its revenues coming from the federal government; thus, it acquired Allen Bradley to move into factory automation—a new domain that was not dependent on the government. Robert Mercer, CEO of Goodyear Tire & Rubber Company, changed Goodyear's domain to get the company away from the cutthroat competition in tires. He did this by reallocating resources into nontire lines of businesses, such as auto parts, aerospace products, and plastics. Goodyear also acquired an oil and gas company. Entering these new domains has taken the pressure off the tire business and enabled Goodyear to prosper.[67] When British conglomerate Grand Metropolitan acquired Pillsbury, it also sold Bennigans, Steak & Ale, and Bumble Bee fish-canning operations, thereby redefining its domain in the food processing industry.

Political Activity, Regulation   Political activity includes techniques to influence government legislation and regulation. In one technique, organizations pay lobbyists to express their views to members of federal and state legislatures. Many CEOs

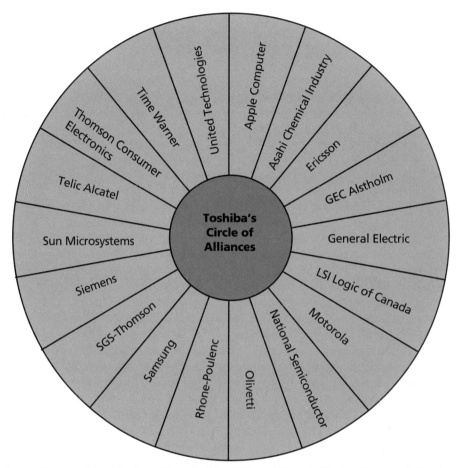

Exhibit 3.10
Interorganiza-
tional Linkages
of Toshiba Cor-
poration.

Source: Brenton R. Schlender, "How Toshiba Makes Alliances Work," *Fortune,* 4 October 1993, 116–120.

believe they should do their own lobbying. CEOs do have easier access than lobby-ists and can be especially effective when they do the politicking. For example, in 1990, a dozen CEOs from American electronic firms flew to Washington to persuade Congress to cut the capital gains tax. The CEOs gained access to their representa-tives and senators, persuading them that a lower capital gains tax would encourage long-term investment. Political activity is so important that "informal lobbyist" is an unwritten part of almost any CEO's job description.[68]

Political strategy can be used to erect regulatory barriers against new competi-tors or to squash unfavorable legislation. Corporations also try to influence the appointment to agencies of people who are sympathetic to their needs. The value of political activity is illustrated by Bethlehem Steel's effort to roll back foreign steel imports by 15 percent. Assuming domestic consumption remained the same, the average price for steel would have increased about $50 a ton, and the increase in tons for Bethlehem would have meant a quarter of a billion dollars of new business.

Trade Associations   Much of the work to influence the external environment is accomplished jointly with other organizations that have similar interests. Most manufacturing companies are part of the National Association of Manufacturers and also belong to associations in their specific industry. By pooling resources, these organizations can pay people to carry out activities such as lobbying legislators, influencing new regulations, developing public relations campaigns, and making campaign contributions. For example, the U.S. League of Savings Institutions had great influence over the Federal Home Loan Bank Board. The league provided good meals and chauffeurs for the bank board's officials when they traveled. In return, the league received agency briefings and internal drafts of regulations before they became law. The league also helped rewrite regulations it did not like.[69] This influence over the regulatory agency is one reason so many savings and loan associations failed, creating the savings and loan crisis.

Illegitimate Activities   Illegitimate activities represent the final technique companies sometimes use to control their environmental domain. Certain conditions, such as low profits, pressure from senior managers, or scarce environmental resources, may lead managers to adopt behaviors not considered legitimate. Many well-known companies have been found guilty of behavior considered unlawful. Example behaviors include payoffs to foreign governments, illegal political contributions, promotional gifts, and wire tapping. Intense competition among cement producers and in the oil business during a period of decline led to thefts and illegal kickbacks.[70] In the defense industry, the intense competition for declining contracts for major weapon systems led some companies to do almost anything to get an edge, including schemes to peddle inside information and to pay off officials.[71] One study found that companies in industries with low demand, shortages and strikes were more likely to be convicted for illegal activities, implying that illegal acts are an attempt to cope with resource scarcity.[72] In another study, social movement organizations such as Earth First! and the AIDS Coalition to Unleash Power (ActUp) were found to have acted in ways considered illegitimate or even illegal to bolster their visibility and reputation.[73]

SUMMARY FRAMEWORK

The relationships illustrated in Exhibit 3.11 summarize the two major themes about organization-environment relationships discussed in this chapter. One theme is that the amount of complexity and change in an organization's domain influences the need for information and hence the uncertainty felt within an organization. Greater information uncertainty is resolved through greater structural flexibility, the assignment of additional departments and boundary roles, and imitation. When uncertainty is low, management structures can be more mechanistic, and the number of departments and boundary roles can be fewer. The second theme pertains to the scarcity of material and financial resources. The more dependent an organization is on other organizations for those resources, the more important it is to either establish favorable linkages with those organizations or control entry into the domain. If dependence on external resources is low, the organization can maintain autonomy and does not need to establish linkages or control the external domain.

The Population Perspective

This final section introduces a different perspective on organization-environment relationships, called the **population ecology model** (also known as the natural

Exhibit 3.11   Relationship between Environmental Characteristics and Organizational Actions.

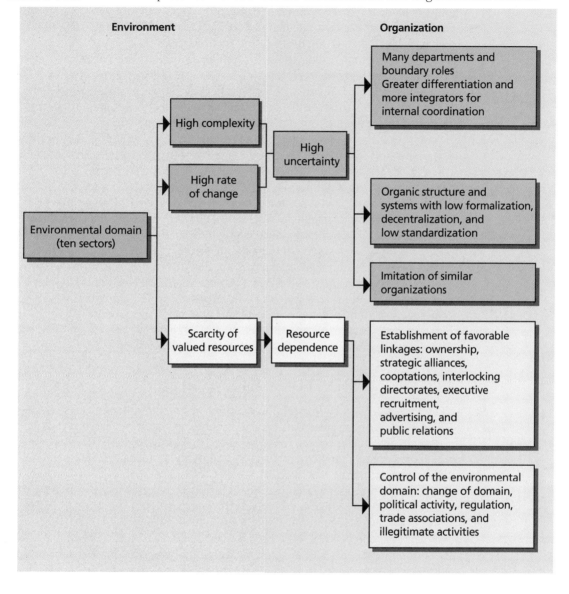

selection model).[74] This model differs from other models in this chapter because its focus is not on how individual organizations adapt to the environment but on organizational diversity and adaptation within a community or population of organizations.[75]

A population of organizations becomes diverse because new forms of organization are created. Thus, organization theorists who study population ecology focus on a community of organizations and investigate how social conditions influence the creation of new organizational forms and the demise of old organizational forms.

According to the model, when looking at an organizational population as a whole, the environment determines which organizations survive or fail. The assumption is that individual organizations suffer from structural inertia and find it difficult to adapt to environmental changes. Thus, when environmental change occurs, some organizations are likely to decline or fail, and new organizations emerge that are better suited to the needs of the environment.

The population ecology model is developed from theories of natural selection in biology, and the terms *evolution* and *selection* are used to refer to the underlying behavioral processes. Theories of biological evolution try to explain why certain life forms appear and survive while others perish. Such theories suggest the forms that survive are typically best fitted to the immediate environment.

Forbes magazine recently reported a study of American businesses over seventy years, from 1917 to 1987. Do you recall Baldwin Locomotive, Studebaker, and Lehigh Coal & Navigation? These companies were among 78 percent of the top one hundred in 1917 that did not see 1987. Of the twenty-two that remained in the top one hundred, only 11 did so under their original names. The environment of the 1940s and 1950s was suitable to Woolworth, but new organizational forms like Wal-Mart and K Mart became dominant in the 1980s. In 1917, most of the top one hundred companies were huge steel and mining industrial organizations, which were replaced by high-technology companies such as IBM and Merck.[76] Two companies that seemed to prosper over the entire period were Ford and General Motors, but they are now being threatened by world changes in the automobile industry. No company is immune to the processes of social change. From just 1979 to 1989, 187 of the companies on the Fortune 500 list ceased to exist as independent companies. Some were acquired, some merged, and some were liquidated.[77]

ORGANIZATIONAL FORM AND NICHE

The population ecology model is concerned with organizational forms. **Organizational form** is an organization's specific technology, structure, products, goals, and personnel, which can be selected or rejected by the environment. Each new organization tries to find a **niche** (a domain of unique environmental resources and needs) sufficient to support it. The niche is usually small in the early stages of an organization, but may increase in size over time if the organization is successful. If a niche is not available, the organization will decline and may perish.

From the viewpoint of a single firm, luck, chance, and randomness play important parts in survival. New products and ideas are continually being proposed by both entrepreneurs and large organizations. Whether these ideas and organizational forms survive or fail is often a matter of chance—whether external circumstances happen to support them. A woman who started a small electrical contracting business in a rapidly growing Florida community would have an excellent chance of success. If the same woman were to start the same business in a declining community elsewhere in the United States, the chance of success would be far less. Success or failure of a single firm thus is predicted by the characteristics of the environment as much as by the skills or strategies used by the organization.

PROCESS OF CHANGE

The population ecology model assumes that new organizations are always appearing in the population. Thus, organization populations are continually undergoing change. The process of change in the population is defined by three principles that occur in stages: **variation, selection,** and **retention.** These stages are summarized in Exhibit 3.12.

- *Variation.*   New organizational forms continually appear in a population of organizations. They are initiated by entreprenuers, established with venture capital by large corporations, or set up by a government seeking to provide new services. Some forms may be conceived to cope with a perceived need in the external environment. In your own neighborhood, for example, a new restaurant may be started to meet a perceived need. In recent years, a large number of new firms have been initiated to develop computer software, to provide consulting and other services to large corporations, and to develop new kinds of toys. Other new organizations produce a traditional product such as steel, but do it using minimal technology and new management techniques that make the new steel companies far more able to survive. Organizational variations are analogous to mutations in biology, and they add to the scope and complexity of organizational forms in the environment.
- *Selection.*   Some variations will suit the external environment better than others. Some prove beneficial and thus are able to find a niche and acquire the resources from the environment necessary to survive. Other variations fail to meet the needs of the environment and perish. When there is insufficient demand for a firm's product and when insufficient resources are available to the organization, that organization will be "selected out." Only a few variations are "selected in" by the environment and survive over the long term.
- *Retention.*   Retention is the preservation and institutionalization of selected organizational forms. Certain technologies, products, and services are highly valued by the environment. The retained organizational form may become a dominant part of the environment. Many forms of organizations have been institutionalized, such as government, schools, churches, and automobile manufacturers. McDonald's, which owns a huge share of the fast-food market and provides the first job for many teenagers, has become institutionalized in American life.

Institutionalized organizations like McDonald's seem to be relatively permanent features in the population of organizations, but they are not permanent in the long run. The environment is always changing, and, if the dominant organizational forms do not adapt to external change, they will gradually diminish and be replaced by other organizations. Already, Taco Bell, owned by PepsiCo, has been drawing in McDonald's customers because the Mexican fast-food chain kept lowering prices while McDonald's consistently raised them. Unless it adapts, McDonald's might no longer be price-competitive in the fast-food market.[78]

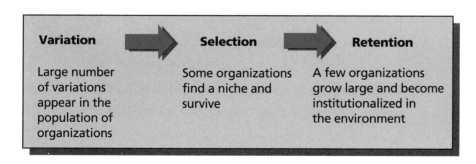

Exhibit 3.12 Elements in the Population Ecology Model of Organizations.

From the population ecology perspective, the environment is the important determinant of organizational success or failure. The organization must meet an environmental need, or it will be selected out. The process of variation, selection, and retention leads to the establishment of new organizational forms in a population of organizations.

STRATEGIES FOR SURVIVAL

Another principle that underlies the population ecology model is the **struggle for existence.** Organizations and populations of organizations are engaged in a competitive struggle over resources, and each organizational form is fighting to survive. The struggle is most intense among new organizations, and both the birth and survival frequencies of new organizations are related to factors in the larger environment. Factors such as size of urban area, percentage of immigrants, political turbulence, industry growth rate, and environmental variability have influenced the launching and survival of newspapers, telecommunication firms, railroads, government agencies, labor unions, and even voluntary organizations.[79]

In the population ecology perspective, **generalist** and **specialist** strategies distinguish organizational forms in the struggle for survival. Organizations with a wide niche or domain, that is, those that offer a broad range of products or services or that serve a broad market, are generalists. Organizations that provide a narrower range of goods or services or that serve a narrower market are specialists. An example of a specialist is Olmec Corporation, a New York-based toy manufacturer that markets more than sixty African-American and Hispanic dolls. Mattel, on the other hand, is a generalist, marketing a broad range of toys, including a Disney line, Barbie, and a new African-American doll that is more than a Barbie with darker skin.[80]

Specialists are generally more competitive than generalists in the narrow area in which their domains overlap. However, the breadth of the generalist's domain serves to protect it somewhat from environmental changes. Though demand may decrease for some of the generalist's products or services, it usually increases for others at the same time. In addition, because of the diversity of products, services, and customers, generalists are able to reallocate resources internally to adapt to a changing environment, whereas specialists are not. However, because specialists are often smaller companies, they can sometimes move faster and be more flexible in adapting to a changing environment.[81]

Managerial impact on company success may come from selecting a strategy that fits the larger environment. The following "In Practice" illustrates how a specialist organization emerged in a new form in response to environmental changes.

IN PRACTICE ♦ 3.5

Zoom Telephonics

Zoom Telephonics saw a perfect niche. People all over the country who hoped to save money by subscribing to MCI, Sprint, or other alternatives to AT&T were having to dial a long sequence of numbers to access their new carrier. Then came the Demon Dialer—Zoom's sales of this little automatic phone dialer truly zoomed. But along came equal access for all long-distance carriers, and sales just as quickly plummeted. Who needed a Demon Dialer to dial a 1?

Zoom saw its larger competitors go out of business, but Zoom is still going strong. How'd it do it? It adapted to a new environment by manufacturing and selling modems—devices that allow personal computers to send and retrieve data over phone lines. Today, Zoom is among the key players in the name-brand modem market. By finding a new niche, Zoom survived after suffering a devastating disintegration of its market.[82]

Zoom's original product was selected by the environment but that environment changed drastically. Changes are constantly threatening the niches of even well-established organizations. Zoom, like other companies, has to adapt quickly when conditions change.

Summary and Interpretation

The external environment has an overwhelming impact on management uncertainty and organization functioning. Organizations are open social systems. Most are involved with hundreds of external elements. The change and complexity in environmental domains have major implications for organizational design and action. Most organizational decisions, activities, and outcomes can be traced to stimuli in the external environment.

Organizational environments differ in terms of uncertainty and resource dependence. Organizational uncertainty is the result of the stable-unstable and simple-complex dimensions of the environment. Resource dependence is the result of scarcity of the material and financial resources needed by the organization.

Organization design takes on a logical perspective when the environment is considered. Organizations try to survive and achieve efficiencies in a world characterized by uncertainty and scarcity. Specific departments and functions are created to deal with uncertainties. The organization can be conceptualized as a technical core and departments that buffer environmental uncertainty. Boundary-spanning roles provide information about the environment.

The concepts in this chapter provide specific frameworks for understanding how the environment influences the structure and functioning of an organization. Environmental complexity and change, for example, have specific impact on internal complexity and adaptability. Under great uncertainty, more resources are allocated to departments that will plan, deal with specific environmental elements, and integrate diverse internal activities. Moreover, when risk is great or resources are scarce, the organization can establish linkages through the acquisition of ownership and through strategic alliances, interlocking directorates, executive recruitment, or advertising and public relations that will minimize risk and maintain a supply of scarce resources. Other techniques for controlling the environment include a change of the domain in which the organization operates, political activity, participation in trade associations, and perhaps illegitimate activities.

Two important themes in this chapter are that organizations can learn and adapt to the environment and that organizations can change and control the environment. These strategies are especially true for large organizations that command many resources. Such organizations can adapt when necessary but can also neutralize or change problematic areas in the environment.

Another important idea in this chapter is the concept of population ecology. The focus here is on an entire population of organizations, and the concepts are especially relevant to new, emerging organizations. The concepts of variation, selection, and retention suggest that the needs of the overall environment are important for organization success and survival. In this view, the appropriate role of management is to find a niche where products and services are desired by the environment. Generalist organizations operate within a wide niche—that is, they provide a broad range of products and services, or they serve a broad market. Specialist organizations operate within a narrow niche, offering a very limited range of products and services or serving a limited market. Both specialists, like Zoom Telephonics, and generalists must be ready to adapt and find new niches when the environment changes.

KEY CONCEPTS

boundary-spanning roles	organic
buffering roles	organizational environment
cooptation	organizational form
differentiation	population ecology model
direct interlock	resource dependence
domain	retention
indirect interlock	sectors
general environment	selection
generalist	simple-complex dimension
institutional perspective	specialist
integration	stable-unstable dimension
interlocking directorate	struggle for existence
interorganizational coordination	task environment
mechanistic	uncertainty
niche	variation

DISCUSSION QUESTIONS

1. Define *organizational environment*. Is it appropriate to include only the elements that actually interact with the organization?

2. What is environmental uncertainty? Which has the greatest impact on uncertainty—environmental complexity or environmental change? Why?

3. Why does environmental complexity lead to organizational complexity? Explain.

4. Is changing the organization's domain a feasible strategy for coping with a threatening environment? Explain.

5. Describe differentiation and integration. In what type of environmental uncertainty will differentiation and integration be greatest? Least?

6. Under what environmental condition is organizational planning emphasized? Is planning an appropriate response to a turbulent environment?

7. What is an organic organization? A mechanistic organization? How does the environment influence organic and mechanistic structures?

8. Why do organizations become involved in interorganizational relationships? Do these relationships affect an organization's dependency? Performance?

9. Assume you have been asked to calculate the ratio of staff employees to production employees in two organizations—one in a simple, stable environment and one in a complex, shifting environment. How would you expect these ratios to differ? Why?

10. How do the processes of variation, selection, and retention explain the evolution of a population of organizations?

GUIDES TO ACTION

As an organization designer, keep these guides in mind:

1. Scan the external environment for threats, changes, and opportunities. Organize elements in the external environment into ten sectors for analysis: industry, raw materials, human resources, financial resources, market, technology, economic, government, sociocultural, and international. Focus on sectors that may experience significant change at any time.

2. Match internal organization structure to the external environment. If the external environment is complex, make the organization structure complex. Reflect the rate of environmental change in the internal structure. Associate a stable environment with a mechanistic structure and an unstable environment with an organic structure. If the external environment is both complex and changing, make the organization highly differentiated and organic, use mechanisms to achieve coordination across departments, and be prepared to imitate other organizations.

3. Reach out and control external sectors that threaten needed resources. Influence the domain by engaging in political activity, joining trade associations, and establishing favorable linkages. Establish linkages through ownership, strategic alliances, cooptation, interlocking directorates, executive recruitment, advertising, and public relations. Reduce the amount of change or threat from the external environment so the organization will not have to change internally.

4. Adapt the organization to new variations being selected and retained in the external environment. If you are starting a new organization, find a niche that contains a strong environmental need for the products and services you provide and be prepared for a competitive struggle over scarce resources.

Consider these guides when analyzing the following case.

Jarrett and Maynard International*

CASE FOR ANALYSIS

Jarrett and Maynard International dominated the wheelchair industry for nearly fifty years. J&M developed the lightweight folding wheelchair in the 1940s and cornered 75 percent of the world market. After the founders retired in 1965, a second generation from the Jarrett and Maynard families kept the company profitable with an average return on equity of 20 percent. Things went so well it was hard to understand how they came apart starting in 1982. J&M's market share dwindled to 35 percent of the U.S. market and 30 percent of the overseas market, and in 1986, the company lost $5 million. At this point, the family owners decided to

---

*This case is based on material reported in Ellen Paris, "The Perils of Being Too Successful," *Forbes,* 9 February 1987, 88–90; and "Uses Nylon to Inject Mold One-Piece Spokeless Wheels for Wheelchairs," *Modern Plastics,* September 1986, 41.

bring in an outsider, Carter Estes, to be the new CEO. Carter spent the first three weeks talking to people in the company, visiting dealers, and listening.

He has just called together four executives to discuss his findings and diagnose problems. Joining him in the meeting are controller Dianne Schultz, manufacturing vice president Samuel Goodman, marketing vice president Kristen Johnson, and personnel vice president Robert Calabrese.

Estes started the discussion. "We all know the pain of declining sales and market share, and it's time to figure out what has gone wrong and how to correct it. When talking to dealers, one theme that kept coming up was the Scooter."

"Scooter?" responded Goodman.

"Yes, it's a three-wheel device used by older people, many of whom don't yet need a wheelchair. You know, Sam, I'm surprised you are not familiar with it. I was talking to your engineering people about the cost to design one, and only one engineer had seen a newspaper article about it."

Goodman replied somewhat red-faced, "Our job here is to manufacture wheelchairs as efficiently and as rapidly as possible. It's marketing's job to know what goes on in the marketplace and to keep us informed."

Before Kristin Johnson could respond, Carter said, "Let's stick with identifying consumer trends applicable to our business."

Bob Calabrese jumped in. "Well, I don't know if this is a trend exactly, but I am interested in government actions because of equal employment issues. My wife mentioned that her aunt, who purchased a new wheelchair from us, had her wheelchair reimbursement reduced. She had to pay an extra one hundred dollars out of her pocket. She said . . . ."

"Oh, my gosh," interrupted Johnson, "That may explain why those cheap Taiwanese chairs are selling so well to Medicare patients. They only cost two hundred dollars compared to our least expensive four hundred dollar model. At a trade show, I saw that a Japanese manufacturer is producing a model comparable to ours for $349. I wasn't too concerned because government reimbursements typically let people buy our chairs."

"Well, I hate to admit it, but I wasn't aware of these government changes or of the foreign imports," admitted Schultz.

"Me, too," said Goodman.

"An area I've noticed both on TV and at trade shows is the desire for the handicapped to lead active lives by participating in sports," said Goodman. "I see people playing basketball in wheelchairs and running races, including marathons. Their small, brightly colored chairs provide great mobility but are expensive to produce, and I'm not sure we can do it competitively. Our chairs are first quality, but they are heavy and hard to maneuver. The light, mobile chairs take new technology, but they could sell for as much as twelve hundred dollars retail, which might allow a sizable profit."

"Have you started research and development on these chairs?" asked Estes.

"No, it simply hasn't been on our list because we've been working to produce our current line of chairs more efficiently."

"What I hear you saying," responded Estes, looking at each person briefly, "is that we have lost the low end of the business to foreign competition, partly because they have cheaper chairs and partly because the government is reducing reimbursements. And it sounds like we have given away the profitable upper end of the wheelchair market to our domestic competitors who jumped on the trend toward wheelchair athletics. I can't believe you people haven't acted to do something about this. The great name of Jarrett and Maynard could have helped us be market leader in both areas."

Kristen Johnson, feeling defensive, argued, "We don't miss every trend. The problem is that when my salespeople talk to manufacturing and engineering people, they get the cold shoulder. Those people seem so deaf to new ideas that we've given up trying. All we hear is efficiency, efficiency, efficiency! We're going to be efficient all the way into Chapter 11 bankruptcy."

Sam Goodman exploded, "That's b.s. We listen, but your people's ideas are so off the wall. No one in the field has any appreciation of engineering difficulties or manufacturing expenses. A sport wheelchair would cost two thousand dollars to please you people."

"That would be better than the designs those engineers are working on that are unrelated to what customers want or to what is hot in the marketplace," Johnson retorted.

"Let's thrash this out later," interceded Estes. "Dianne, what do you feel about all this?"

"Well, it's been terrible watching our market share slide to 30 percent in the last few years. You are all aware that the stock price is only eight dollars compared to twenty-six dollars a few years ago. What you may not know is that trading has picked up at the eight-dollar price, which suggests potential raiders are buying the stock. We've announced no positive financial news, so someone may try to take us over assuming they can do a better job. We'll all probably be looking for jobs then. At any rate, our financial and accounting systems are in pretty good shape, and I've done some analysis on industry data that makes me believe our internal manufacturing costs are too high. I know people don't buy J&M wheelchairs for low prices, but we at least need to be in the ballpark and still show some markup on a sale. Also, Southwest Center Bank is acting edgy about our working-capital loan. Joe Bensen talked the other day about putting a cap on our loan and the possibility of increasing our interest rate. We are also getting pressure from suppliers to pay within thirty days. We've let some accounts drag out to sixty days or ninety days, and the suppliers don't think we look like a good accounts receivable risk. I don't mean to be too gloomy, because we can hold things together for at least another year and maybe two, but it sure would be nice to see things turn around."

"The high cost of manufacturing has to be addressed and solved," responded Estes. "You know, Sam, I think the problem is too many product variations. In the pacemaker business in Atlanta, we saved thousands of dollars by offering a limited product line, and many manufacturers are following this trend. Maybe we have to simplify, then use fewer suppliers, sticking to those that are reliable with high quality. This means we would have to carefully define the few products we want to produce and the markets we want to chase. The idea that we can produce more than four thousand different wheelchairs was a wonderful thing in the past, but I don't think it makes sense today. We're acting like a custom wheelchair shop rather than a manufacturing plant.

"The other place we're getting killed is in filling dealer orders so slowly. We are running up to three months late. One dealer told me he was so frustrated, he switched to another manufacturer, believing we simply can't deliver. Somehow we've got to deal realistically with dealers about what to expect. We've got to simplify, move faster, and innovate. It seems simple, but it's going to take some doing to get ourselves in touch with and responding to all aspects of the environment."

Estes decided to bring the meeting to a close. "Would you each think about the issues discussed here? We'll meet again in a couple of days and see what we can come up with to get everyone operating on the same wavelength, especially on the wavelength of customers and competitors. Remember, we've got to simplify, speed things up, innovate, and keep quality high without working in a vacuum."

"One thing I've been thinking about," said Goodman, "is to have employees ride around in wheelchairs on the shop floor when they go to lunch or take a break. That way they will get a feel for what the chairs are like and how to simplify them. We would even encourage them to take wheelchairs home."

"Yeah," said Schultz, "like the movie, 'Guess Who's Coming to Dinner.'"

As the laughter subsided, Estes agreed, "That's a great idea. The engineers and marketing people could do the same thing. Think about how we could get everyone involved so they understand the product, what's needed in the environment, and work together to meet those needs. I'm sure there are a lot of ideas we haven't thought of yet. For next time, don't constrain your thinking to your own areas."

Assume you are Dianne Schultz, controller. Answer the following questions.

QUESTIONS

1. Analyze the environment of Jarrett and Maynard International with respect to the environmental sectors, uncertainty, and resource dependence. What concepts from the chapter can explain what happened to J&M?
2. What ideas would you propose to help solve the problems at J&M? Come up with several suggestions and try to link each suggestion to a concept from this chapter.

NOTES

1. Valerie Reitman, "Pittsburgh's WQED Failed to See Change in Public-TV Industry," *Wall Street Journal,* 17 January 1994, A1, A5.
2. Wendy Zellner, "Not Everyone Loves Wal-Mart's Low Price," *Business Week,* 12 October 1992, 36–38; Suzanne Alexander, "Feisty Yankees Resist Wal-Mart's Drive to Set Up Shops in New England Towns," *Wall Street Journal,* 16 September 1993, B1, B6.
3. Alan Deutschman, "What 25-Year-Olds Want," *Fortune,* 27 August 1990, 42–50; Dean Foust and Tim Smart, "The Merger Parade Runs into a Brick Wall," *Business Week* 14 May 1990; Michael Schroeder and Walecia Konrad, "Nucor: Rolling Right into Steel's Big Time," *Business Week,* 19 November 1990, 76–81.
4. Catherine Arnst with Peter Burrows, "Showdown in Silicon Alley," *Business Week,* 1 November 1993, 146.
5. Maria Mallory with Stephanie Anderson Forest, "Waking Up to a Major Market," *Business Week,* 23 March 1992, 70–73.
6. Lucinda Harper and Fred R. Bleakley, "An Era of Low Inflation Changes the Calculus for Buyers and Sellers," *Wall Street Journal,* 14 January 1994, A1, A3.
7. Laura Zinn with Gail De George, Rochelle Shortz, Dorie Jones Yang, and Stephanie Anderson Forest, "Retailing Will Never Be the Same," *Business Week,* 26 July 1993, 54–60.
8. Andrew Kupfer, "How American Industry Stacks Up," *Fortune,* 9 March 1992, 36–46.
9. Tom Peters, "Prometheus Barely Unbound," *Academy of Management Executive* 4 (1990): 70–84.
10. Richard L. Daft, *Management* 3d ed. (Chicago: Dryden, 1994).
11. Kupfer, "How American Industry Stacks Up."
12. Bob Ortega, "Penney Pushes Abroad in an Unusu-

ally Big Way as It Pursues Growth," *Wall Street Journal,* 1 February 1994, A1, A6.

13. Allen C. Bluedorn, "Pilgrim's Progress: Trends and Convergence in Research on Organizational Size and Environment," *Journal of Management* 19 (1993): 163–91; Howard E. Aldrich, *Organizations and Environments* (Englewood, Cliffs, N.J.: Prentice-Hall, 1979); Fred E. Emery and Eric L. Trist, "The Casual Texture of Organizational Environments," *Human Relations* 18 (1965): 21–32.

14. Christine S. Koberg and Gerardo R. Ungson, "The Effects of Environmental Uncertainty and Dependence on Organizational Structure and Performance: A Comparative Study," *Journal of Management* 13 (1987): 725–37; Frances J. Milliken, "Three Types of Perceived Uncertainty about the Environment: State, Effect, and Response Uncertainty," *Academy of Management Review* 12 (1987): 133–43.

15. Robert B. Duncan, "Characteristics of Organizational Environment and Perceived Environmental Uncertainty," *Administrative Science Quarterly* 17 (1972): 313–27; Gregory G. Dess and Donald W. Beard, "Dimensions of Organizational Task Environments," *Administrative Science Quarterly* 29 (1984): 52–73; Ray Jurkovich, "A Core Typology of Organizational Environments," *Administrative Science Quarterly* 19 (1974): 380–94.

16. Thomas M. Burton, "Anti-Depression Drug of Eli Lilly Loses Sales after Attack by Sect," *Wall Street Journal,* 19 April 1991, A1, A2.

17. J. A. Litterer, *The Analysis of Organizations,* 2d ed. (New York: Wiley, 1973), 335.

18. Joseph Pereira, "Toy Industry Finds It Harder and Harder to Pick the Winners," *Wall Street Journal,* 21 December 1993, A1, A5.

19. Rosalie L. Tung, "Dimensions of Organizational Environments: An Exploratory Study of Their Impact on Organizational Structure," *Academy of Management Journal* 22 (1979): 672–93.

20. Joseph E. McCann and John Selsky, "Hyperturbulence and the Emergence of Type 5 Environments," *Academy of Management Review* 9 (1984): 460–70.

21. Eric Schine with Gary McWilliams, "Mattel: Looking for a Few Good Boy Toys," *Business Week,* 17 February 1992, 116–18.

22. Judith Valente and Asra Q. Nomani, "Surge in Oil Price has Airlines Struggling, Some Just to Hang on," *Wall Street Journal,* 10 August 1990, A1, A4.

23. James D. Thompson, *Organizations in Action* (New York: McGraw-Hill, 1967), 20–21.

24. Sally Solo, "Whirlpool: How to Listen to Consumers," *Fortune,* 11 January 1993, 77–79.

25. David B. Jemison, "The Importance of Boundary Spanning Roles in Strategic Decision-Making," *Journal of Management Studies* 21 (1984): 131–52; Mohamed Ibrahim Ahmad At-Twaijri and John R. Montanari, "The Impact of Context and Choice on the Boundary-Spanning Process: An Empirical Extension," *Human Relations* 40 (1987): 783–98.

26. James E. Svatko "Analyzing the Competition," *Small Business Reports,* January 1989: 21–28; R. T. Lenz and Jack L. Engledow, "Environmental Analysis Units and Strategic Decision Making: A Field Study of Selected 'Leading-Edge' Corporations," *Strategic Management Journal* 7 (1986): 69–89.

27. Robert C. Schwab, Gerardo R. Ungson, and Warren B. Brown, "Redefining the Boundary-Spanning Environment Relationship," *Journal of Management* 11 (1985): 75–86.

28. Jeff Bailey, "Why Customers Trash the Garbage Men," *Wall Street Journal,* 17 March 1993, B1, B11.

29. Jay W. Lorsch, "Introduction to the Structural Design of Organizations," in Gene W. Dalton, Paul R. Lawrence, and Jay W. Lorsch, eds., *Organizational Structure and Design* (Homewood, Ill.: Irwin and Dorsey, 1970), 5.

30. Paul R. Lawrence and Jay W. Lorsch, *Organization and Environment* (Homewood, Ill.: Irwin, 1969).

31. Lorsch, "Introduction to the Structural Design of Organizations," 7.

32. Jay W. Lorsch and Paul R. Lawrence, "Environmental Factors and Organizational Integration," in J. W. Lorsch and Paul R. Lawrence, eds., *Organizational Planning: Cases and Concepts* (Homewood, Ill.: Irwin and Dorsey, 1972), 45.

33. Tom Burns and G. M. Stalker, *The Management of Innovation* (London: Tavistock, 1961).

34. John A. Courtright, Gail T. Fairhurst, and L. Edna Rogers, "Interaction Patterns in Organic and Mechanistic Systems," *Academy of Management Journal* 32 (1989): 773–802.

35. Paul J. DiMaggio and Walter W. Powell, "The Iron Cage Revisited: Institutional Isomorphism and Collective Rationality in Organizational Fields," *American Sociological Review* 48 (1983): 147–60; Richard H. Hall, *Organizations: Structures, Processes, and Outcomes* (Englewood, Cliffs, N.J.: Prentice-Hall, 1987); Christine Oliver, "Strategic Responses to Institutional Processes," *Academy of Management Review* 16 (1991): 145–79.

36. "Business Fads: What's In—and Out," *Business*

Week, 20 January 1986, 52–61.

37. Thomas C. Powell, "Organizational Alignment as Competitive Advantage," *Strategic Management Journal* 13 (1992): 119-34. Mansour Javidan, "The Impact of Environmental Uncertainty on Long-Range Planning Practices of the U.S. Savings and Loan Industry," *Strategic Management Journal* 5 (1984): 381–92; Tung, "Dimensions of Organizational Environments," 672–93; Thompson, *Organizations in Action.*

38. David Ulrich and Jay B. Barney, "Perspectives in Organizations: Resource Dependence, Efficiency, and Population," *Academy of Management Review* 9 (1984): 471–81; Jeffrey Pfeffer and Gerald Salancik, *The External Control of Organizations: A Resource Dependent Perspective* (New York: Harper & Row, 1978).

39. Kathy Rebello with Richard Brandt, Peter Coy, and Mark Lewyn, "Your Digital Future," *Business Week,* 7 September 1992, 56–64.

40. Edmund L. Andrews, "AT&T Reaches Out (and Grabs Everyone)," *New York Times,* 8 August 1993, Sec. 3, 1, 6.

41. Rebello, et al. "Your Digital Future"; Mark Landler with Bart Ziegler and Ronald Grover, "Time Warner's Techie at the Top," *Business Week,* 10 May 1993, 60–63.

42. Mark Stevenson, "Virtual Mergers," *Canadian Business,* September 1993, 20–26.

43. James B. Treece, "How Ford and Mazda Shared the Driver's Seat," *Business Week,* 26 March 1990, 94–95.

44. Christine Oliver, "Determinants of Interorganizational Relationships: Integration and Future Directions," *Academy of Management Review* 15 (1990): 241–65.

45. Michael L. Gerlach, "The Japanese Corporate Network: A Blockmodel Analysis," *Administrative Science Quarterly* 37 (1992): 105–39.

46. Robert Neff, "Mighty Mitsubishi Is on the Move," *Business Week,* 24 September 1990, 98–101.

47. Timothy M. Stearns, Alan N. Hoffman, and Jan B. Heide, "Performance of Commercial Television Stations as an Outcome of Interorganizational Linkages and Environmental Conditions," *Academy of Management Journal* 30 (1987): 71–90; Keith G. Provan, "Technology and Interorganizational Activity as Predictors of Client Referrals," *Academy of Management Journal* 27 (1984): 811–29; David A. Whetten and Thomas K. Kueng, "The Instrumental Value of Interorganizational Relations: Antecedents and Consequences of Linkage Formation," *Academy of Management*

Journal 22 (1979): 325–44.

48. Andrew H. Van de Ven and Gordon Walker, "The Dnyamics of Interorganizational Coordination," *Administrative Science Quarterly* (1984): 598–621; Huseyin Leblebici and Gerald R. Salancik, "Stability in Interoganizational Exchanges: Rulemaking Processes of the Chicago Board of Trade," *Administrative Science Quarterly* 27 (1982): 227–42.

49. Kevin Kelly and Zachary Schiller with James B. Treece, "Cut Costs or Else: Companies Lay Down the Law to Suppliers," *Business Week,* 22 March 1993, 28–29.

50. G. Pascal Zachary, "Many Journalists See a Growing Reluctance to Criticize Advertisers," *Wall Street Journal,* 6 February 1992, A1, A9.

51. Richard Brandt, "Microsoft Is Like an Elephant Rolling around, Squashing Ants," *Business Week,* 30 October 1989, 148–52.

52. Judith A. Babcock, *Organizational Responses to Resource Scarcity and Munificence: Adaptation and Modification in Colleges within a University* (Ph.D. diss., Pennsylvania State University, 1981).

53. Peter Smith Ring and Andrew H. Van de Ven, "Developmental Processes of Corporative Interorganizational Relationships," *Academy of Management Review* 19 (1994): 90–118; Jeffrey Pfeffer, "Beyond Management and the Worker: The Institutional Function of Management," *Academy of Management Review* 1 (April 1976): 36–46; John P. Kotter, "Managing External Dependence," *Academy of Management Review* 4 (1979): 87–92.

54. Andrews, "AT&T Reaches Out."

55. Landler, et al., "Time Warner's Techie at the Top."

56. Bryan Borys and David B. Jemison, "Hybrid Arrangements as Strategic Alliances: Theoretical Issues in Organizational Combinations," *Academy of Management Review* 14 (1989): 234–49.

57. Brian Bremmer with Kathy Rebello, Zachary Schiller, and Joseph Weber, "The Age of Consolidation," *Business Week,* 14 October 1991, 86–94.

58. Julie Cohen Mason, "Strategic Alliances: Partnering for Success," *Management Review* (May 1993): 10–15.

59. John F. Love, *McDonald's: Behind the Arches* (New York: Bantam Books, 1986).

60. Zachary Schiller and Wendy Zellner with Ron Stodghill II and Mark Maremont, "Clout! More and More, Retail Giants Rule the Marketplace," *Business Week,* 21 December 1992, 66–73.

61. Borys and Jemison, "Hybrid Arrangements as Strategic Alliances."

62. Donald Palmer, "Broken Ties: Interlocking Direc-

torates and Intercorporate Coordination," *Administrative Science Quarterly* 28 (1983): 40–55; F. David Shoorman, Max H. Bazerman, and Robert S. Atkin, "Interlocking Directorates: A Strategy for Reducing Environmental Uncertainty," *Academy of Management Review* 6 (1981): 243–51; Ronald S. Burt, *Toward a Structural Theory of Action* (New York: Academic Press, 1982).

63. James R. Lang and Daniel E. Lockhart, "Increased Environmental Uncertainty and Changes in Board Linkage Patterns," *Academy of Management Journal* 33 (1990): 106–28; Mark S. Mizruchi and Linda Brewster Stearns, "A Longitudinal Study of the Formation of Interlocking Directorates," *Administrative Science Quarterly* 33 (1988): 194–210.

64. "Dow Chemical: From Napalm to Nice Guy," *Fortune,* 12 May 1986, 75.

65. Brenton R. Schlender, "How Toshiba Makes Alliances Work," *Fortune,* 4 October 1993, 116–20.

66. Kotter, "Managing External Dependence."

67. "Goodyear Feels the Heat," *Business Week,* 7 March 1988, 26–28.

68. David B. Yoffie, "How an Industry Builds Political Advantage," *Harvard Business Review* (May-June 1988): 82–89; Jeffrey H. Birnbaum, "Chief Executives Head to Washington to Ply the Lobbyist's Trade," *Wall Street Journal,* 19 March 1990, Al, A16.

69. Monica Langley, "Thrift's Trade Group and Their Regulators Get Along Just Fine," *Wall Street Journal,* 16 July 1986, 1,14.

70. Bryan Burrough, "Oil-Field Investigators Say Fraud Flourishes from Wells to Offices," *Wall Street Journal,* 15 January 1985, 1, 20; Irwin Ross, "How Lawless Are Big Companies?" *Fortune,* 1 December 1980, 57–64.

71. Stewart Toy, "The Defense Scandal," *Business Week,* 4 July 1988, 28–30.

72. Barry M. Staw and Eugene Szwajkowski, "The Scarcity-Munificence Component of Organizational Environments and the Commission of Illegal Acts," *Administrative Science Quarterly* 20 (1975): 345–54.

73. Kimberly D. Elsbach and Robert I. Sutton, "Acquiring Organizational Legitimacy through Illegitimate Actions: A Marriage of Institutional and Impression Management Theories," *Academy of Management Journal* 35 (1992): 699–738.

74. Jitendra V. Singh, *Organizational Evolution: New Directions* (Newbury Park, Calif.: Sage, 1990); Howard Aldrich, Bill McKelvey, and Dave Ulrich, "Design Strategy from the Population Perspective," *Journal of Management* 10 (1984): 67–86; Aldrich, *Organizations and Environments;* Michael Hannan and John Freeman, "The Population Ecology of Organizations," *American Journal of Sociology* 82 (1977): 929–64; Dave Ulrich, "The Population Perspective: Review, Critique, and Relevance," *Human Relations* 40 (1987): 137–52.

75. Jitenda V. Singh and Charles J. Lumsden, "Theory and Research in Organizational Ecology," *Annual Review of Sociology* 16 (1990): 161–95; Howard E. Aldrich, "Understanding, Not Integration: Vital Signs from Three Perspectives on Organizations," in Michael Reed and Michael D. Hughes, eds., *Rethinking Organizations: New Directories in Organizational Theory and Analysis* (London: Sage: forthcoming); Jitendra V. Singh, David J. Tucker, and Robert J. House, "Organizational Legitimacy and the Liability of Newness," *Administrative Science Quarterly* 31 (1986): 171–93; Douglas R. Wholey and Jack W. Brittain, "Organizational Ecology: Findings and Implications," *Academy of Management Review* 11 (1986): 513–33.

76. Peter Newcomb, "No One Is Safe," *Forbes,* 13 July 1987, 121; "It's Tough Up There," *Forbes,* 13 July 1987, 145–60.

77. Stuart Feldman, "Here One Decade, Gone the Next," *Management Review* (November 1990): 5–6.

78. Patricia Sellers, "Pepsi Keeps on Going after No. 1," *Fortune,* 11 March 1991, 61–70.

79. David J. Tucker, Jitendra V. Singh, and Agnes G. Meinhard, "Organizational Form, Population Dynamics, and Institutional Change: The Founding Patterns of Voluntary Organizations," *Academy of Management Journal* 33 (1990): 151–78; Glenn R. Carroll and Michael T. Hannan, "Density Delay in the Evolution of Organizational Populations: A Model and Five Empirical Tests," *Administrative Science Quarterly* 34 (1989): 411–30; Jacques Delacroix and Glenn R. Carroll, "Organizational Foundings: An Ecological Study of the Newspaper Industries of Argentina and Ireland," *Administrative Science Quarterly* 28 (1983): 274–91; Johannes M. Pennings, "Organizational Birth Frequencies: An Empirical Investigation," *Administrative Science Quarterly* 27 (1982): 120–44; David Marple, "Technological Innovation and Organizational Survival: A Population Ecology Study of Nineteenth-Century American Railroads," *Sociological Quarterly* 23 (1982): 107–16; Thomas G. Rundall and John O. McClain, "Environmental Selection and Physician Supply," *American Journal of Sociology* 87 (1982):

1090–1112.

80. Maria Mallory with Stephanie Anderson Forest, "Waking Up to a Major Market," *Business Week,* 23 March 1992, 70–73.

81. Arthur G. Bedeian and Raymond F. Zammuto, *Organizations: Theory and Design* (Orlando, Fla.: Dryden Press, 1991); Richard L. Hall, *Organizations: Structure, Process and Outcomes* (Englewood Cliffs, N.J.: Prentice-Hall, 1991).

82. Jenny C. McCune, "Shake, Rattle, and Roll," *Small Business Reports,* September 1992, 29–39.

PART

3

Organization Structure and Design

CHAPTER 4

Manufacturing, Service, and Advanced Information Technologies

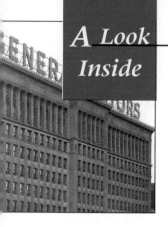

General Motors

The world's largest manufacturer is shifting to round-the-clock production and flexible factories to try to close the manufacturing-cost gap with Japan. General Motors plans to shift work to flexible, higher-volume operations that can produce more cars in fewer factories. The company's Lordstown, Ohio, assembly plant became the first facility in North America to go to high-capacity production, aiming to boost output by 18 percent, up to 450,000 cars a year.

Instead of the workerless, robot-run factories envisioned by GM in the 1980s, the new plan calls for a more efficient combination of workers and technology. The Lordstown plant is rehiring fifteen hundred laid-off workers for a third shift. Rather than buying new and expensive equipment, GM is reprogramming robots and other machinery for greater flexibility. Workers are being retrained to handle a variety of jobs rather than a few, monotonous tasks. Changes in car design and engineering mean cars will be easier to make. For example, GM is redesigning its small cars to use a one-size-fits-all chassis rather than the three sizes now in use. In the future, the plan calls for all factories to be laid out alike for additional flexibility.

GM feels confident that its new plan for round-the-clock, high-capacity operations can greatly boost output yet maintain quality. By changing its technology, the company expects to build 14 percent more cars in four plants than it built in seven when GM sales last peaked in 1986.[1]

Technology is the tools, techniques, and actions used to transform organizational inputs into outputs.[2] Technology is an organization's production process and includes machinery and work procedures. The technology at General Motors produces cars and trucks.

Organization technology begins with raw materials of some type (for example, unfinished steel castings in a valve manufacturing plant). Employees take action on the raw material to make a change in it (they machine steel castings), which transforms the raw material into the output of the organization (control valves ready for shipment to oil refineries). For Federal Express, the production technology includes the equipment and procedures for delivering overnight mail.

Exhibit 4.1 features an example of production technology for a manufacturing plant. Note how the technology consists of raw material inputs, a transformation process that changes and adds value to these items, and the ultimate product or service output that is sold to consumers in the environment. In today's large, complex organizations, it can be hard to pinpoint technology. Technology can be partly assessed by examining the raw materials flowing into the organization,[3] the variability of work activities,[4] the degree to which the production process is mechanized,[5] the extent to which one task depends upon another in the work flow,[6] or the number of new product outputs.[7]

Recall from the last chapter that organizations have a technical core that reflects the organization's primary purpose. The technical core contains the transformation process that represents the organization's technology. As today's organizations try to become more flexible in a changing environment, new technology may influence organizational structure, but decisions about organizational structure may also shape or limit technology. Thus, the interaction between core technology and structure leads to a patterned relationship in many organizations.[8]

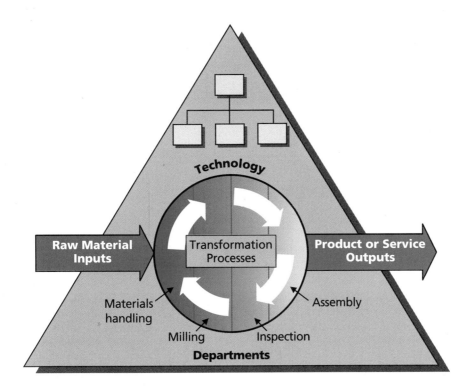

Exhibit 4.1
Transformation
Process for a
Manufacturing
Company.

In today's large, complex organizations, many departments exist and each may employ a different technology for its own function. Thus, research and development transforms ideas into new product proposals, and marketing transforms inventory into sales, each using a different technology. Moreover, the administrative technology used by managers to run the organization represents yet another technology. Computers and advanced information technology have impact on the administrative arena.

PURPOSE OF THIS CHAPTER

In this chapter, we will explore the nature of organizational technologies and the relationship between technology and organization structure. Chapter 3 described how the environment influences organization design. The question addressed in this chapter is, "How should the organization structure be designed to accommodate and facilitate the production process?" Form usually follows function, so the form of the organization's structure should be tailored to fit the needs of the production technology.

The remainder of the chapter will unfold as follows. First, we will examine how the technology for the organization as a whole influences organization structure and design. This discussion will include both manufacturing and service technologies and will introduce new concepts about advanced manufacturing technology. Next, we will examine differences in departmental technologies and how the technologies influence the design and management of organizational subunits. Third, we will explore how interdependence—flow of materials and information—among departments affects structure. Finally, we will examine how new computer-based information technologies are influencing organization design by their impact on administration and management of the organization.

Organization-Level Technology

Organization-level technologies are of two types—manufacturing and service. Manufacturing technologies include traditional manufacturing processes and new computer-based manufacturing systems.

MANUFACTURING FIRMS

Woodward's Study   The first and most influential study of manufacturing technology was conducted by Joan Woodward, a British industrial sociologist. Her research began as a field study of management principles in south Essex. The prevailing management wisdom at the time (1950s) was contained in what was known as universal principles of management. These principles were "one best way" prescriptions that effective organizations were expected to adopt. Woodward surveyed one hundred manufacturing firms firsthand to learn how they were organized.[9] She and her research team visited each firm, interviewed managers, examined company records, and observed the manufacturing operations. Her data included a wide range of structural characteristics (span of control, levels of management) and dimensions of management style (written versus verbal communications, use of rewards) and the type of manufacturing process. Data were also obtained that reflected commercial success of the firms.

Woodward developed a scale and organized the firms according to technical complexity of the manufacturing process. **Technical complexity** represents the extent of mechanization of the manufacturing process. High technical complexity means most of the work is performed by machines. Low technical complexity means workers play a larger role in the production process. Woodward's scale of technical complexity originally had ten categories, as summarized in Exhibit 4.2. These categories were further consolidated into three basic technology groups:

- *Group I: Small-Batch and Unit Production.*   These firms tend to be job shop operations that manufacture and assemble small orders to meet specific needs of customers. Custom work is the norm. **Small-batch production** relies heavily on the human operator; it is thus not highly mechanized. Examples include many types of made-to-order manufactured products, such as specialized construction equipment, custom electronic equipment, and custom clothing.
- *Group II: Large-Batch and Mass Production.*   **Large-batch production** is a manufacturing process characterized by long production runs of standardized parts. Output often goes into inventory from which orders are filled, because customers do not have special needs. Examples include most assembly lines, such as for automobiles or trailer homes.
- *Group III: Continuous Process Production.*   In **continuous process production** the entire process is mechanized. There is no starting and stopping. This represents mechanization and standardization one step beyond those in an assembly line. Automated machines control the continuous process, and outcomes are highly predictable. Examples would include chemical plants, oil refineries, liquor producers, and nuclear power plants.

Exhibit 4.2   Woodward's Classification of 100 British Firms According to Their Systems of Production.

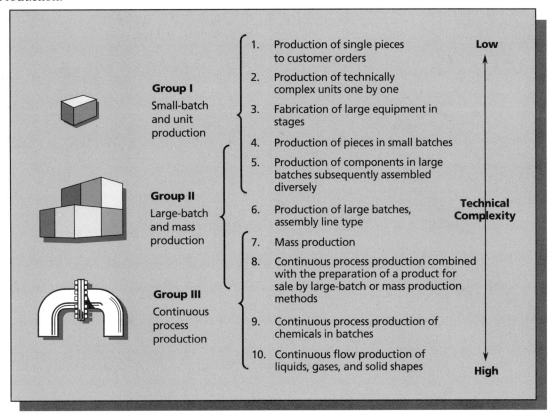

Group I
Small-batch and unit production

1. Production of single pieces to customer orders
2. Production of technically complex units one by one
3. Fabrication of large equipment in stages
4. Production of pieces in small batches

Group II
Large-batch and mass production

5. Production of components in large batches subsequently assembled diversely
6. Production of large batches, assembly line type
7. Mass production

Group III
Continuous process production

8. Continuous process production combined with the preparation of a product for sale by large-batch or mass production methods
9. Continuous process production of chemicals in batches
10. Continuous flow production of liquids, gases, and solid shapes

Low ↑ Technical Complexity ↓ High

Source: Adapted from Woodward, *Management and Technology* (London: Her Majesty's Stationery Office, 1958). Used with permission of Her Britannic Majesty's Stationery Office.

Using this classification of technology, Woodward's data made sense. A few of her key findings are given in Exhibit 4.3. The number of management levels and the manager/total personnel ratio, for example, show definite increases as technical complexity increases from unit production to continuous process. This indicates that greater management intensity is needed to manage complex technology. Direct/indirect labor ratio decreases with technical complexity because more indirect workers are required to support and maintain complex machinery. Other characteristics, such as span of control, formalized procedures, and centralization, are high for mass production technology but low for other technologies because the work is standardized. Unit production and continuous process technologies require highly skilled workers to run the machines and verbal communication to adapt to changing conditions. Mass production is standardized and routinized, so few exceptions occur, little verbal communication is needed, and employees are less skilled.

Overall, the management systems in both unit production and continuous process technology are characterized as organic. They are more free-flowing and adaptive, with fewer procedures and less standardization. Mass production, however, is mechanistic, with standardized jobs and formalized procedures. Woodward's

Exhibit 4.3
Relationship
between Techni-
cal Complexity
and Structural
Characteristics.

Structural Characteristic	Technology		
	Unit Production	Mass Production	Continuous Process
Number of management levels	3	4	6
Supervisor span of control	23	48	15
Direct/indirect labor ratio	9:1	4:1	1:1
Manager/total personnel ratio	Low	Medium	High
Workers' skill level	High	Low	High
Formalized procedures	Low	High	Low
Centralization	Low	High	Low
Amount of verbal communication	High	Low	High
Amount of written communication	Low	High	Low
Overall structure	Organic	Mechanistic	Organic

Source: Joan Woodward, *Industrial Organization: Theory and Practice* (London: Oxford University Press, 1965). Used with permission.

discovery about technology thus provided substantial new insight into the causes of organization structure. In Joan Woodward's own words, "Different technologies impose different kinds of demands on individuals and organizations, and those demands had to be met through an appropriate structure."[10]

Technology and Performance   Another portion of Woodward's study examined the success of the firms along dimensions such as profitability, market share, stock price, and reputation. As indicated in Chapter 2, the measurement of effectiveness is not simple or precise, but Woodward was able to rank firms on a scale of commercial success according to whether they displayed above-average, average, or below-average performance.

Woodward compared the structure-technology relationship against commercial success and discovered that successful firms tended to be those that had complementary structures and technologies. Many of the organizational characteristics of the successful firms were near the average of their technology category, as shown in Exhibit 4.3. Below-average firms tended to depart from the structural characteristics for their technology type. Another conclusion was that structural characteristics could be interpreted as clustering into organic and mechanistic management systems. Successful small-batch and continuous process organizations had organic structures, and successful mass production organizations had mechanistic structures. Subsequent research has replicated her findings.[11]

Today, finding the correct structure and management approach to fit production technology is still a major issue. Consider the management of nuclear power plants.

IN PRACTICE ◆ 4.1

Northeast Utilities and Boston Edison Company

Northeast Utilities' Millstone 1 nuclear plant, located in Waterford, Connecticut, is considered by the Nuclear Regulatory Commission (NRC) to be one of the best-managed plants in the industry. Northeast Utilities' management long ago realized that managing a nuclear power plant is different from managing a fossil fuel plant. Nuclear plants are bigger and more complex, and their complex technical systems and safety features require extensive maintenance. For these reasons, a large number of skilled workers are on the payroll, and each worker spends one week of every six in training classes. Northeast Utilities also assigns its best people to manage Millstone. The superintendent stays personally involved with employees by visiting the control room each day and chatting face-to-face with the staff.

Boston Edison Company's Pilgrim nuclear power plant, located just eight miles to the north of Millstone, is comparable in size, design, and vintage, but is considered by the NRC to be one of the worst-managed nuclear plants in the United States. Pilgrim hasn't had a major accident, but it was criticized by the NRC and has been shut down. Boston Edison didn't seem to realize that the complexity of nuclear technology required special management, that a nuclear plant is not just another boiler. At Pilgrim, operators rarely saw the superintendent face-to-face in the control room. A backlog of twelve thousand maintenance items indicated the need for more maintenance people. Moreover, Boston Edison traditionally did not assign its best managers to the nuclear plant. Edison is now trying to overcome its shortcomings by hiring a new plant manager, recruiting highly skilled operators, and doubling the maintenance staff.

The problem of managing nuclear plants was illustrated by the chairman of Georgia Power Company, who emphasized that "the world of a utility executive that has a nuclear power plant is different from one who doesn't, and if he doesn't understand that, he's in trouble."[12]

The nuclear power plant is a continuous process technology. Its automated equipment is highly complex and requires skilled employees along with a high number of maintenance personnel. Greater management skills and intensity are required to ensure close supervision and to provide backup expertise in a crisis. The failure of Boston Edison's management to diagnose the special management needs of nuclear technology cost the company and its ratepayers dearly. When the Pilgrim plant was closed for upgrading, Boston Edison spent $200,000 a day to buy electricity to replace what Pilgrim would have generated.[13]

ADVANCED MANUFACTURING TECHNOLOGY

In the years since Woodward's research, new developments have occurred in manufacturing technology. New manufacturing technologies include robots, numerically controlled machine tools, and computerized software for product design, engineering analysis, and remote control of machinery. The ultimate technology is called **advanced manufacturing technology** (AMT).[14] Also called *computer-integrated manufacturing,* the *factory of the future, smart factories,* or *flexible manufacturing systems,* AMT links together manufacturing components that previously stood alone. Thus, robots, machines, product design, and engineering analysis are coordinated by a single computer.

The result has already revolutionized the shop floor, enabling large factories to deliver a wide range of custom-made products at low mass production costs.[15]

Advanced manufacturing technology is typically the result of three subcomponents.

- Computer-aided design (CAD). Computers are used to assist in the drafting, design, and engineering of new parts. Designers guide their computer to draw specified configurations on the screen, including dimensions and component details. Hundreds of design alternatives can be explored, as can scaled-up or scaled-down versions of the original.[16]
- Computer-aided manufacturing (CAM). Computer-controlled machines in materials handling, fabrication, production, and assembly greatly increase the speed at which items can be manufactured. CAM also permits a production line to shift rapidly from producing one product to any variety of other products by changing the instruction tapes or software in the computer. CAM enables the production line to quickly honor customer requests for changes in product design and product mix.[17]
- Administrative automation. The computerized accounting, inventory control, billing, and shop-floor tracking systems allow managers to use computers to monitor and control the manufacturing process.

The combination of CAD, CAM, and administrative automation components is illustrated in Exhibit 4.4. This combination represents the highest level of advanced manufacturing technology. A new product can be designed on the computer, and a prototype can be produced untouched by human hands. The ideal factory can switch quickly from one product to another, working fast and with precision, without paperwork or recordkeeping to bog down the system.[18]

A company can adopt CAD in its engineering design department and/or CAM in its production area and make substantial improvements in efficiency and quality. However, when all three components are brought together in a truly advanced plant, the results are breathtaking. Companies such as Xerox, Westinghouse, Texas Instruments, Hewlett-Packard, and Northrop are leading the way. The most dramatic evidence of what can happen was Northrop's building of the B-2 Stealth bomber, one of the most complex products ever made. It was conceived, designed, and produced without a shred of paper, relying totally upon computer design. When the first B-2 was assembled, 97 percent of the thirty thousand parts fit perfectly the first time. The best Northrop had ever done before was 50 percent.[19]

This ultra-advanced system is not achieved piecemeal. AMT does not reach its ultimate level to improve quality and reduce cost until all parts are in place and used interdependently.

Some U.S. business leaders envision a time when even cars can be custom-made in as little as three days. An example from Ford illustrates the technology that could eventually enable this. Ford Motor Company's computer recently sent the design for a car's connecting rod to a computer at AlliedSignal Incorporated's plant in Kansas City. The computer there transformed the design into instructions that it then fed into a machine tool on the shop floor without human intervention.[20]

Performance   The awesome advantage of AMT is that products of different sizes, types, and customer requirements freely intermingle on the assembly line. Bar codes imprinted on a part enable machines to make instantaneous changes—such as

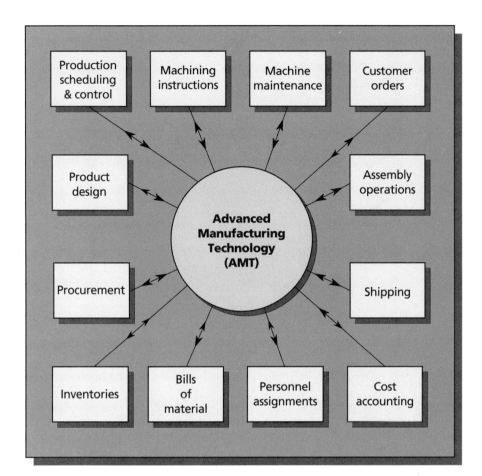

Exhibit 4.4
Coordination of
AMT-Related
Activities.

putting a larger screw in a different location—without slowing the production line. This means a single manufacturing plant can be both small batch and mass production at the same time, as illustrated in Exhibit 4.5. In traditional manufacturing systems studied by Woodward, management's choices were limited to the diagonal. Small batch allowed for high product variety and custom orders, but batch size was necessarily small. Mass production could have large batch size but less product variety. Continuous process could produce a single standard product in unlimited quantities. Advanced manufacturing technology allows plants to break free of this diagonal and to increase both batch size and product variety at the same time. The computer will tailor each product to a customer order.

Findings from early studies suggest that with AMT, machine utilization is more efficient, labor productivity increases, scrap rates decrease, and product variety and customer satisfaction increase.[21] Many United States manufacturing companies are reinventing the factory using AMT and associated management systems to increase productivity, as discussed in Book Mark 4.0.

Structural Implications   Research into the relationship between AMT and organizational characteristics is beginning to emerge, and the patterns are summarized in Exhibit 4.6. Compared with traditional mass production technologies, AMT has a

Exhibit 4.5   Relationship of Advanced Manufacturing Technology to Traditional Technologies.

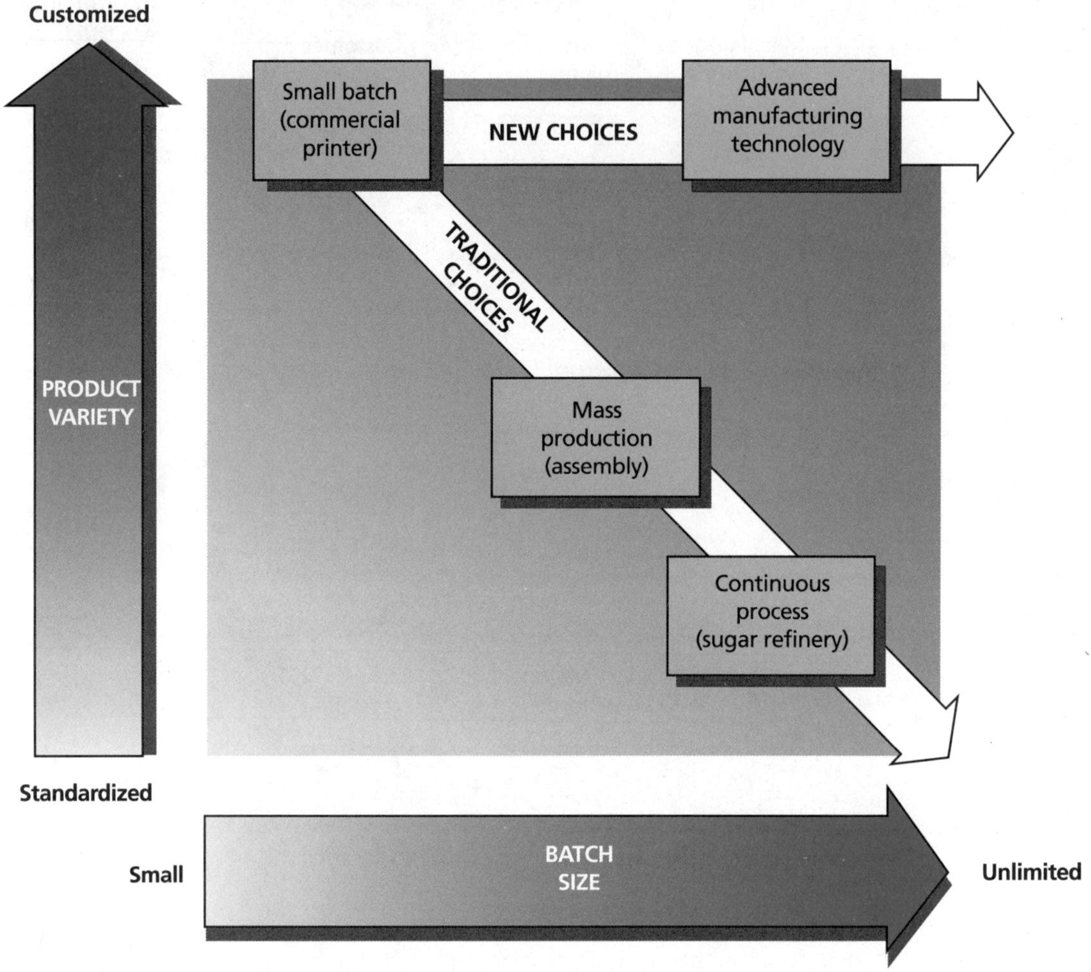

Source: Based on Jack Meredith, "The Strategic Advantages of New Manufacturing Technologies for Small Firms," *Strategic Management Journal* 8 (1987): 249–58; Paul Adler, "Managing Flexible Automation," *California Management Review* (Spring 1988): 34–56.

narrow span of control, few hierarchical levels, adaptive tasks, low specialization, decentralization, and the overall environment is characterized as organic and self-regulative. Employees need the skills to participate in teams, training is broad (so workers are not overly specialized) and frequent (so workers are up-to-date). Expertise tends to be cognitive so workers can process abstract ideas and solve problems. Interorganizational relationships in AMT firms are characterized by changing demand from customers—which is easily handled with the new technology—and close relationships with a few suppliers that provide top-quality raw materials.[22]

Recent research suggests that organizational structures should be carefully examined and altered if necessary before major changes are made in manufacturing technology. In organizations that have underlying problems with organizational

BOOKMARK 4.0

HAVE YOU READ ABOUT THIS?

Reinventing the Factory: Productivity Breakthroughs in Manufacturing Today

by Roy Harmon and Leroy Peterson

During the 1980s, the business press reported the demise of American manufacturing. Products were poor and cost too much. American firms were being driven out of many industries, including consumer electronics, steel, autos, and microelectronics.

Then many U.S. companies got to work rebuilding themselves to achieve world class status. By the early 1990s, the U.S. became the world's leading exporter, led by manufacturers of such items as airplanes, machine tools, and computer systems. American firms today produce steel for less per ton than their Japanese rivals, and U.S. auto and microchip producers have regained the largest share of their respective world markets.

Focused Factories

Harmon and Peterson offer the "focused factory" as the model managers can use to make their plants world class. A focused factory is a small factory within a larger plant. "For superior results, the reorganization of existing plants into multiple, smaller 'factories within a factory' is the single most important feature of productivity improvements." Characteristics of a focused factory include:

- Superb communications, including reliance on cross-functional design teams: people talk to one another.
- Managers lead from the shop floor, not from the front office.
- Managers and workers wear many hats.
- Administrative staff is lean, knowledgeable, and on-site.
- All employees are involved and dedicated to the firm's goals.

Components of Productivity Improvement

Modernizing plant operations begins with management commitment to ambitious improvement goals for the long term. Then a plan is created to reorganize the plant into focused factories. The plan is implemented by a dedicated team of top performers who are willing to get their hands dirty achieving higher productivity.

The authors identify three key components of productivity improvement.

Simplicity. "The single most important secret of leading-edge, productive manufacturing is simplification." Simplification takes three forms:

- Reduction in the number of components designed into the product.
- Reduction in the number of steps in a process flow.
- Reduction in the number of components in the fixtures and tooling.

Simplicity orients a firm's focus toward incremental improvement. The resulting designs in products and processes often have elegant simplicity.

Automation. Automating manufacturing processes and support functions reduces lead time and labor costs, improves quality, eliminates tedious and hazardous tasks, and provides timely and accurate information. However, massive expenditures in elaborate new facilities typically are not necessary. The authors argue that big productivity gains result most often from inexpensive equipment upgrades.

Integration. Integration links together all processes and focused factories by computers, networks, and material handling systems. The objective is to break down barriers between departments. The various tools of modern manufacturing, such as just-in-time and computer-aided manufacturing, can also be integrated into the system to solve various problems.

Conclusion

Reinventing the Factory is a straightforward guide to modern manufacturing. It concludes with a list of over 100 firms from around the world that have initiated major plant reorganizations. These firms report dramatic productivity and quality increases, and labor cost, floor space, and lead time reductions. Companies that follow the book's prescriptions can join the list.

Reinventing the Factory by Roy Harmon and Leroy Peterson is published by The Free Press.

Characteristic	Mass Production	AMT
Structure		
Span of control	Wide	Narrow
Hierarchical levels	Many	Few
Tasks	Routine, repetitive	Adaptive, craftlike
Specialization	High	Low
Decision making	Centralized	Decentralized
Overall	Bureaucratic, mechanistic	Self-regulation, organic
Human Resources		
Interactions	Stand alone	Teamwork
Training	Narrow, one time	Broad, frequent
Expertise	Manual, technical	Cognitive, social
		Solve problems
Interorganizational		
Customer demand	Stable	Changing
Suppliers	Many, arm's length	Few, close relations

Source: Based on Patricia L. Nemetz and Louis W. Fry, "Flexible Manufacturing Organizations: Implications for Strategy Formulation and Organization Design," *Academy of Management Review* 13 (1988): 627–38; Paul S. Adler, "Managing Flexible Automation," *California Management Review* (Spring 1988): 34–56; Jeremy Main, "Manufacturing the Right Way," *Fortune,* 21 May 1990, 54–64.

structure, advanced manufacturing technology may serve to institutionalize ineffective procedures. Organizations with highly mechanistic structures will likely not reap the benefits of advanced manufacturing technology.[23]

The other major change occurring in the technology of organizations is a growing service sector. Service technologies are different from manufacturing technologies and, in turn, require a specific organization structure.

SERVICE FIRMS

Some experts have argued that Canada and the United States are becoming service-oriented economies. New services such as overnight delivery, housecleaning, data base management, financial, and amusement mean service organizations are increasing at a more rapid rate than manufacturing firms.

Definition   Recent studies of service organizations focused on the unique dimensions of service technologies. **Service technologies** are defined based on the five elements in Exhibit 4.7. The first major difference is *simultaneous production and consumption,* which means a customer and an employee interact to provide the service. A client meets with a doctor or attorney, for example, and students and teachers come together in the classroom. This also means that customers tend to receive *customized output* and that *customers participate* in the production process. In manufacturing, by contrast, goods are produced at one time and inventoried for sale and con-

Exhibit 4.7 Examples of Service Technology versus Manufacturing Technology.

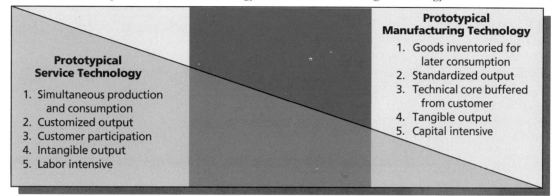

Service	Product and Service	Product
Airlines	Fast-food outlets	Soft drink companies
Hotels	Banks	Steel companies
Consultants	Cosmetics	Automobile manufacturers
Teachers	Real estate	Mining corporations
Health clinics	Stockbrokers	Food processing plants
Law firms	Retail stores	

Source: Based on David E. Bowen, Caren Siehl, and Benjamin Schneider, "A Framework for Analyzing Customer Service Orientations in Manufacturing," *Academy of Management Review* 14 (1989): 75–95.

sumption at another time; outputs tend to be standardized, and the production process tends to be removed and buffered from customers.

Another major difference is *intangible output* in a service firm. A service is abstract and often consists of information or knowledge in contrast with the tangible physical products made by manufacturing firms. This typically means service firms are *labor intensive,* with many employees needed to meet the needs of customers, while manufacturing firms tend to be capital intensive, relying on mass production, continuous process, and AMT technologies.[24]

The characteristics in Exhibit 4.7 are prototypical, or the standard case, but exceptions arise. Some service firms try to take on characteristics of manufacturers, and vice versa. Some firms end up in the middle—such as fast-food outlets, banks, and stockbrokers, which provide both a product and service. These firms do not actually make a product, they provide it as a service, but a tangible product is part of the transaction. The important point is that organizations can be classified along a continuum that includes both manufacturing and service characteristics, as illustrated in Exhibit 4.7.

Structure   The feature of service technologies with a distinct influence on organizational structure and control systems is the need for technical core employees to be close to the customer.[25] The differences between service and product organizations necessitated by customer contact are summarized in Exhibit 4.8.

The impact of customer contact on organization structure is reflected in the use of boundary roles and structural disaggregation.[26] Boundary roles are used extensively in manufacturing firms to handle customers and to reduce disruptions for the technical core. They are used less in service firms because a service is intangible and

Exhibit 4.8
Configuration
and Structural
Characteristics
of Service
Organizations
versus Product
Organizations.

Structure	Service	Product
1. Separate boundary roles	Few	Many
2. Geographical dispersion	Much	Little
3. Decision making	Decentralized	Centralized
4. Formalization	Lower	Higher
Human Resources		
1. Employee skill level	Higher	Lower
2. Skill emphasis	Interpersonal	Technical

cannot be passed along by boundary spanners, so service customers must interact directly with technical employees, such as doctors or brokers.

A service firm deals in information and intangible outputs and does not need to be large. Its greatest economies are achieved through disaggregation into small units that can be located close to customers. Stockbrokers, doctors' clinics, fast-food franchises, consulting firms, and banks disperse their facilities into regional and local offices. Manufacturing firms, on the other hand, tend to aggregate operations in a single area that has raw materials and an available work force. A large manufacturing firm can take advantage of economies derived from expensive machinery and long production runs.

Service technology also influences internal organization characteristics used to direct and control the organization. For one thing, the skills of technical core employees need to be higher. These employees need enough knowledge and awareness to handle customer problems rather than just enough to perform a single, mechanical task. Some service organizations give their employees the knowledge and freedom to make decisions and do whatever is needed to satisfy customers, while others, such as McDonald's, have set rules and procedures for customer service. Yet in all cases, service employees need social and interpersonal skills as well as technical skills.[27] Because of higher skills and structural dispersion, decision making often tends to be decentralized in service firms, and formalization tends to be low.

Understanding the nature of service technology enables managers to adopt an appropriate structure that is often quite different from the structure for a product-based or traditional manufacturing technology. Unlike manufacturing, service industries have traditionally not had to face the need to compete internationally. This is changing, however, and service industries are increasingly having to think globally. The following example illustrates how Four Seasons Hotels is attempting to maintain its record of quality service cross-culturally.

IN PRACTICE ◆ 4.2

Four Seasons Hotels

From the opening of its first hotel in 1961, the Toronto-based Four Seasons chain has put customer service first. Today, Four Seasons symbolizes all a luxury hotel stands for and, following recent acquisitions, will be operating forty-three hotels in seventeen countries.

The chain's emphasis on first-rate customer service has given it a decided edge with travel agents and meeting planners, who book most luxury hotel business.

Many of the newly acquired properties are in the Far East, and the Four Seasons Hotel Chinzan-so in Tokyo will be a model for other hotels in the region. Developing a level of service to appeal to both Eastern and Western travelers has perhaps been the company's greatest challenge. Managers found that Japanese workers were highly service-oriented, moving throughout the hotel quickly to do their jobs. However, Western travelers often misinterpreted their quick movements, suspecting problems at the hotel because employees were "rushing around." On the other hand, Japanese travelers perceived the slower pace of Western workers to mean they didn't care about their jobs or about serving their guests. The hotel management is attempting to slowly build into its employees the ability to distinguish between different guests' needs and respond to them appropriately.

The company hopes that its program of having approximately fifty Chinzan-so staff members observe and work in North American hotels for periods of up to a year will foster that ability. By seeing how the chain adapts its services to fit different guests' needs, the Chinzan-so workers then have a base for making similar adjustments in the hotel back in Tokyo.

Founder and chairman of the Four Seasons chain, Isadore Sharp, has always believed in the importance of customer service. In the increasingly competitive 1990s, he says, it "will become sacred."[28]

The Four Seasons hotel chain is determined to carry its sterling reputation for first-rate customer service into the Eastern as well as the Western world. It is emphasizing extensive training for employees, including observing and working in North American hotels.

Now let's turn to another perspective on technology, that of production activities within specific organizational departments. Departments often have characteristics similar to those of service technology, providing services to other departments within the organization.

Departmental Technology

This section shifts to the department level of analysis for departments not necessarily within the technical core. Each department in an organization has a production process that consists of a distinct technology. General Motors has departments for engineering, R&D, personnel, advertising, quality control, finance, and dozens of other functions. This section analyzes the nature of departmental technology and its relationship with departmental structure.

The framework that has had the greatest impact on the understanding of departmental technologies was developed by Charles Perrow.[29] Perrow's model has been useful for a broad range of technologies, which made it ideal for research into departmental activities.

VARIETY

Perrow specified two dimensions of departmental activities that were relevant to organization structure and process. The first is the number of exceptions in the work. This refers to task **variety,** which is the frequency of unexpected and novel events that occur in the conversion process. When individuals encounter a large number of unexpected situations, with frequent problems, variety is considered high. When there are few problems, and when day-to-day job requirements are repetitious, technology contains little variety. Variety in departments can range from repeating a single act, such as on an assembly line, to working on a series of unrelated problems or projects.

ANALYZABILITY

The second dimension of technology concerns the **analyzability** of work activities. When the conversion process is analyzable, the work can be reduced to mechanical steps and participants can follow an objective, computational procedure to solve problems. Problem solution may involve the use of standard procedures, such as instructions and manuals, or technical knowledge, such as that in a textbook or handbook. On the other hand, some work is not analyzable. When problems arise, it is difficult to identify the correct solution. There is no store of techniques or procedures to tell a person exactly what to do. The cause of or solution to a problem is not clear, so employees rely on accumulated experience, intuition, and judgment. The final solution to a problem is often the result of wisdom and experience and not the result of standard procedures. The brewmaster department at Heineken Brewery has an unanalyzable technology. Brewmasters taste each batch of product to identify the mix of ingredients and to see whether it fits within acceptable flavor limits. These quality control tasks require years of experience and practice. Standard procedures will not tell a person how to do such tasks.

FRAMEWORK

The two dimensions of technology and examples of departmental activities on Perrow's framework are shown in Exhibit 4.9. The dimensions of variety and analyzability form the basis for four major categories of technology: routine, craft, engineering, and nonroutine.

Routine technologies are characterized by little task variety and the use of objective, computational procedures. The tasks are formalized and standardized. Examples include an automobile assembly line and a bank teller department.

Craft technologies are characterized by a fairly stable stream of activities, but the conversion process is not analyzable or well understood. Tasks require extensive training and experience because employees respond to intangible factors on the basis of wisdom, intuition, and experience. Although advances in machine technologies seem to have reduced the number of craft technologies in organizations, a few craft technologies remain. For example, steel furnace engineers continue to mix steel based on intuition and experience, pattern makers at apparel firms still convert rough designers' sketches into salable garments, and gas and oil explorationists use their internal divining rod to determine where millions will be spent on drilling operations.

Engineering technologies tend to be complex because there is substantial variety in the tasks performed. However, the various activities are usually handled on the basis of established formulas, procedures, and techniques. Employees normally refer to a well-developed body of knowledge to handle problems. Engineering and accounting tasks usually fall in this category.

Exhibit 4.9   Framework for Department Technologies.

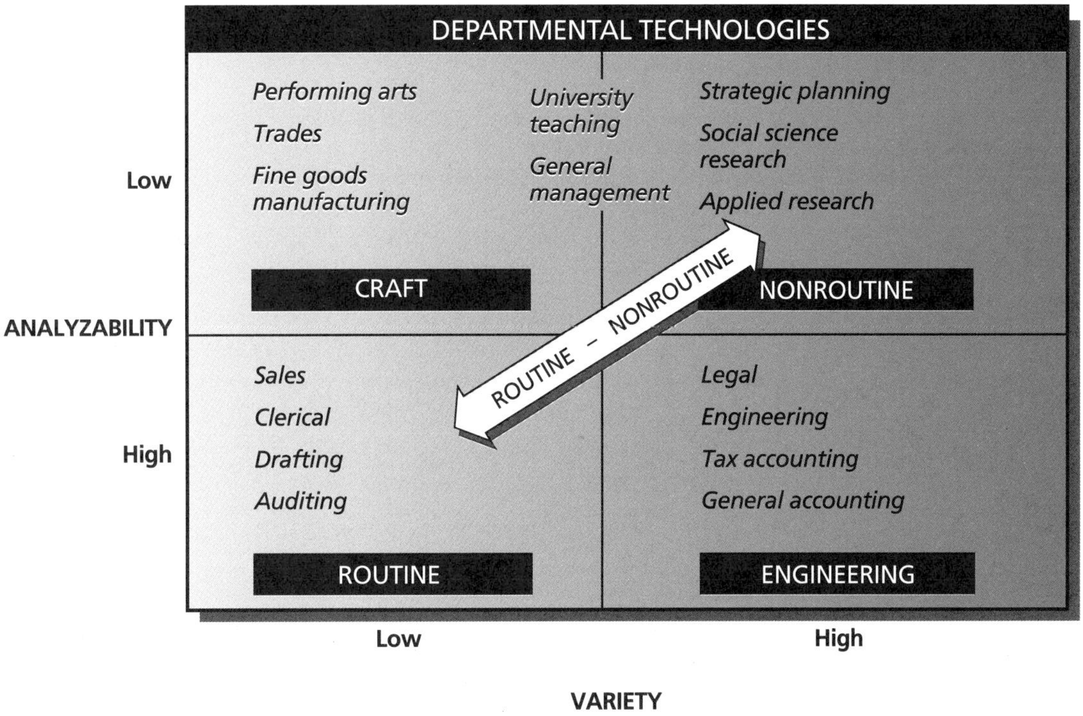

Source: Adapted with permission from Richard Daft and Norman Macintosh, "A New Approach to Design and Use of Management Information," *California Management Review* 21 (1978): 82–92. Copyright © 1978 by the Regents of the University of California. Reprinted by permission of the Regents.

Nonroutine technologies have high task variety, and the conversion process is not analyzable or well understood. In nonroutine technology, a great deal of effort is devoted to analyzing problems and activities. Several equally acceptable options typically can be found. Experience and technical knowledge are used to solve problems and perform the work. Basic research, strategic planning, and other work that involves new projects and unexpected problems are nonroutine.

Routine versus Nonroutine   Exhibit 4.9 also illustrates that variety and analyzability can be combined into a single dimension of technology. This dimension is called routine versus nonroutine technology, and it is the diagonal line in Exhibit 4.9. The analyzability and variety dimensions are often correlated in departments, meaning that technologies high in variety tend to be low in analyzability, and technologies low in variety tend to be analyzable. Departments can be evaluated, along a single dimension of routine versus nonroutine that combines both analyzability and variety, which is a useful shorthand measure for analyzing departmental technology.

The following questions show how departmental technology can be analyzed for determining its placement on Perrow's technology framework in Exhibit 4.9.[30] Employees normally circle a number from one to seven in response to each question.

Variety
1. To what extent would you say your work is routine?

2. Does most everyone in this unit do about the same job in the same way most of the time?
3. Are unit members performing repetitive activities in doing their jobs?

Analyzability
1. To what extent is there a clearly known way to do the major types of work you normally encounter?
2. To what extent is there an understandable sequence of steps that can be followed in doing your work?
3. To do your work, to what extent can you actually rely on established procedures and practices?

If answers to the above questions indicate high scores for analyzability and low scores for variety, the department would have a routine technology. If the opposite occurs, the technology would be nonroutine. Low variety and low analyzability indicate a craft technology, and high variety and high analyzability indicate an engineering technology. As a practical matter, most departments fit somewhere along the diagonal and can be most easily characterized as routine or nonroutine.

Department Design

Once the nature of a department's technology has been identified, then the appropriate structure can be determined. Department technology tends to be associated with a cluster of departmental characteristics, such as the skill level of employees, formalization, and pattern of communication. Definite patterns do exist in the relationship between work unit technology and structural characteristics, which are associated with departmental performance.[31] Key relationships between technology and other dimensions of departments are described in this section and are summarized in Exhibit 4.10.

1. *Organic versus Mechanistic.*   The single most persistent pattern is that routine technologies are associated with a mechanistic structure and processes and nonroutine technologies with an organic structure and processes. Formal rules and centralized management apply to routine units. When work is nonroutine, department administration is more organic and free-flowing. In the R&D lab at Datapoint Corporation, employees wear T-shirts and sandals, may wear beards, and ride to work on motorcycles. In the production department, employees wear more traditional dress, including shoes, shirts, and short haircuts, which reflects the more structured nature of the work.[32]
2. *Formalization.*   Routine technology is characterized by standardization and division of labor into small tasks that are governed by formal rules and procedures. For nonroutine tasks, the structure is less formal and less standardized. When variety is high, as in a research department, fewer activities are covered by formal procedures.[33]
3. *Decentralization.*   In routine technologies, most decision making about task activities is centralized to management.[34] In engineering technologies, employees with technical training tend to acquire moderate decision authority because technical knowledge is important to task accomplishment. Production employees who have long experience obtain decision authority in craft technologies

Exhibit 4.10   Relationship of Department Technology to Structural and Management Characteristics.

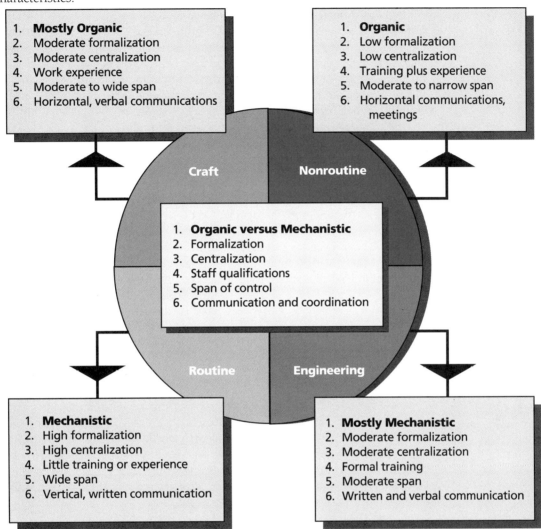

1. **Mostly Organic**
2. Moderate formalization
3. Moderate centralization
4. Work experience
5. Moderate to wide span
6. Horizontal, verbal communications

1. **Organic**
2. Low formalization
3. Low centralization
4. Training plus experience
5. Moderate to narrow span
6. Horizontal communications, meetings

Craft   **Nonroutine**

1. **Organic versus Mechanistic**
2. Formalization
3. Centralization
4. Staff qualifications
5. Span of control
6. Communication and coordination

Routine   **Engineering**

1. **Mechanistic**
2. High formalization
3. High centralization
4. Little training or experience
5. Wide span
6. Vertical, written communication

1. **Mostly Mechanistic**
2. Moderate formalization
3. Moderate centralization
4. Formal training
5. Moderate span
6. Written and verbal communication

because they know how to respond to problems. Decentralization to employees is greatest in nonroutine settings, where many decisions are made by employees.

4. *Worker Skill Level.*   Work staff in routine technologies typically require little education or experience, which is congruent with repetitive work activities. In work units with greater variety, staff are more skilled and often have formal training in technical schools or universities. Training for craft activities, which are less analyzable, is more likely to be through job experience. Nonroutine activities require both formal education and job experience.[35]

5. *Span of Control.*   Span of control is the number of employees who report to a single manager or supervisor. This characteristic is normally influenced by departmental technology. The more complex and nonroutine the task, the more problems arise in which the supervisor becomes involved. Although the span of

control may be influenced by other factors, such as skill level of employees, it typically should be smaller for complex tasks because on such tasks the supervisor and subordinate must interact frequently.[36]

6. *Communication and Coordination.* Communication activity and frequency increase as task variety increases.[37] Frequent problems require more information sharing to solve problems and ensure proper completion of activities. The direction of communication is typically horizontal in nonroutine work units and vertical in routine work units.[38] The form of communication varies by task analyzability.[39] When tasks are highly analyzable, statistical and written forms of communication (memos, reports, rules, and procedures) are frequent. When tasks are less analyzable, information typically is conveyed face-to-face, over the telephone, or in group meetings.

Two important points are reflected in Exhibit 4.10. First, departments do differ from one another and can be categorized according to their workflow technology.[40] Second, structural and management processes differ based on departmental technology. Managers should design their departments so that requirements based on technology can be met. Design problems are most visible when the design is clearly inconsistent with technology. Studies have found that when structure and communication characteristics did not reflect technology, departments tended to be less effective.[41] Employees could not communicate with the frequency needed to solve problems. Sometimes employees have to deviate from misplaced rules to behave as needed to fit the technology, as in the following case.

IN PRACTICE ♦ 4.3
"M*A*S*H"

The "M*A*S*H" television series illustrated how well-intentioned army managers who imposed a tight, mechanistic structure on nonroutine hospital units worked against the requirements of the unit's technology. The humor in the "M*A*S*H" programs resulted from the efforts of Hawkeye, Potter, and O'Reilly to get their work done despite the army's bureaucracy, which was designed for routine infantry activities. Colonel Potter's ability to let the MASH unit run in free-flowing, organic fashion enabled the unit to be far more effective than would be the case if all rules and procedures were followed.[42]

The same kind of relationship can be observed in hospital emergency rooms. Employees are highly skilled and have the authority to respond on their own initiative and discretion based on problems that arise. Following strict procedures would inhibit them from responding correctly to unexpected problems. On the other hand, strict rules are appropriate for routine hospital activities.

logical Interdependence among Departments

So far, this chapter has explored how organization and department technologies influence structural design. The final characteristic of technology that influences structure is called interdependence. **Interdependence** means the extent to which departments depend upon each other for resources or materials to accomplish their tasks. Low interdependence means that departments can do their work independently of each other and have little need for interaction, consultation, or exchange of materials. High interdependence means departments must constantly exchange resources.

TYPES

James Thompson defined three types of interdependence that influence organization structure.[43] These interdependencies are illustrated in Exhibit 4.11 and are discussed in the following sections.

Pooled **Pooled interdependence** is the lowest form of interdependence among departments. In this form, work does not flow between units. Each department is part of the organization and contributes to the common good of the organization, but works independently. McDonald's restaurants or branch banks are examples of pooled interdependence. An outlet in Chicago need not interact with an outlet in Urbana. The connection between branches is that they share financial resources from a common pool, and the success of each branch contributes to the success of the organization.

Thompson proposed that pooled interdependence would exist in firms with what he called a mediating technology. A **mediating technology** provides products or services that mediate or link clients from the external environment and, in so

Exhibit 4.11   Thompson's Classification of Interdependence and Management Implications.

Form of Interdependence	Demands on Horizontal Communication, Decision Making	Type of Coordination Required	Priority for Locating Units Close Together
Pooled (bank) / Clients	Low communication	Standardization, rules, procedures	Low
Sequential (assembly line) / Client	Medium communication	Plans, schedules, feedback	Medium
Reciprocal (hospital) / Client	High communication	Mutual adjustment, cross-departmental meetings, teamwork	High

doing, allows each department to work independently. Banks, brokerage firms, and real estate offices all mediate between buyers and sellers, but the offices work independently within the organization.

The management implications associated with pooled interdependence are quite simple. Thompson argued that managers should use rules and procedures to standardize activities across departments. Each department should use the same procedures and financial statements so the outcomes of all departments can be measured and pooled. Very little day-to-day coordination is required among units.

Sequential   When interdependence is of serial form, with parts produced in one department becoming inputs to another department, then it is called **sequential interdependence.** The first department must perform correctly for the second department to perform correctly. This is a higher level of interdependence than pooled, because departments exchange resources and depend upon others to perform well.

Sequential interdependence occurs in what Thompson called **long-linked technology,** which "refers to the combination in one organization of successive stages of production; each stage of production uses as its inputs the production of the preceding stage and produces inputs for the following stage."[44] Large organizations that use assembly line production, such as in the automobile industry, use long-linked technologies and are characterized by sequential interdependence.

The management requirements of sequential interdependence are more demanding than for pooled interdependence. Coordination among the linked plants or departments is required. Since the interdependence implies a one-way flow of materials, extensive planning and scheduling are generally needed. Plant B needs to know what to expect from Plant A so both can perform effectively. Some day-to-day communication among plants is also needed to handle unexpected problems and exceptions that arise.

Reciprocal   The highest level of interdependence is **reciprocal interdependence.** This exists when the output of operation A is the input to operation B, and the output of operation B is the input back again to operation A. The outputs of departments influence those departments in reciprocal fashion.

Reciprocal interdependence tends to occur in organizations with what Thompson called **intensive technologies,** which provide a variety of products or services in combination to a client. Hospitals are an excellent example because they provide coordinated services to patients. A patient may move back and forth between X-ray, surgery, and physical therapy as needed to be cured. A firm developing new products is another example. Intense coordination is needed between design, engineering, manufacturing, and marketing to combine all their resources to suit the customer's product need.

Management requirements are greatest in the case of reciprocal interdependence. The structure must allow for frequent horizontal communication and adjustment. Extensive planning is required in hospitals, for example, but plans will not anticipate or solve all problems. Daily interaction and mutual adjustment among departments are required. Managers from several departments are jointly involved in face-to-face coordination, teamwork, and decision making. Reciprocal interdependence is the most complex interdependence for organizations to handle.

STRUCTURAL PRIORITY

As indicated in Exhibit 4.11, since decision making, communication, and coordination problems are greatest for reciprocal interdependence, reciprocal interdependence should receive first priority in organization structure. Activities that are reciprocally interdependent should be grouped close together in the organization so managers have easy access to one another for mutual adjustment. These units should report to the same person on the organization chart and should be physically close so the time and effort for coordination can be minimized. Poor coordination will result in poor performance for the organization. If the reciprocally interdependent units cannot be located close together, the organization should design mechanisms for coordination, such as daily meetings between departments or an electronic mail network to facilitate communication. The next priority is given to sequential interdependencies, and finally to pooled interdependencies.

This strategy of organizing keeps the communication channels short where coordination is most critical to organizational success. For example, Boise Cascade Corporation experienced poor service to customers because customer service reps located in New York City were not coordinating with production planners in Oregon plants. Customers couldn't get delivery as needed. Boise was reorganized, and the two groups were consolidated under one roof, reporting to the same supervisor at division headquarters. Now customer needs are met because customer service reps work with production planning to schedule customer orders.

STRUCTURAL IMPLICATIONS

Most organizations experience various levels of interdependence, and structure can be designed to fit these needs, as illustrated in Exhibit 4.12.[45] In a manufacturing firm, new product development entails reciprocal interdependence among the design, engineering, purchasing, manufacturing, and sales departments. Perhaps a cross-departmental team could be formed to handle the back-and-forth flow of information and resources. Once a product is designed, its actual manufacture would be sequential interdependence, with a flow of goods from one department to another, such as between purchasing, inventory, production control, manufacturing, and assembly. The actual ordering and delivery of products is pooled interdependence, with warehouses working independently. Customers could place an order with the nearest facility, which would not require coordination among warehouses, except in unusual cases such as a stock outage.

When consultants analyzed NCR to learn why new products were so slow being developed, they followed the path from initial idea to implementation. The problem was that the development, production, and marketing of products took place in separate divisions, and communication across the three interdependent groups was difficult. NCR broke up its traditional organization structure and created several stand-alone units of about 500 people, each with its own development, production, and marketing people. This enabled new products to be introduced in record time.

A recent study of athletic teams reported that differences in team structure are closely related to interdependency among players. The following "In Practice" section illustrates how interdependence influences other aspects of baseball, football, and basketball teams.

IN PRACTICE ◆ 4.4

Athletic Teams

A major difference among baseball, football, and basketball is the interdependence among players. Baseball is low in interdependence, football is medium, and basketball represents the highest player interdependence. The relationships among interdependence and other characteristics of team play are illustrated in Exhibit 4.13.

Pete Rose said, "Baseball is a team game, but nine men who reach their individual goals make a nice team." In baseball, interdependence among team players is low and can be defined as pooled. Each member acts independently, taking a turn at bat and playing his or her own position. When interaction does occur, it is between only two or three players, as in a double play. Players are physically dispersed, and the rules of the game are the primary means of coordinating players. Players practice and develop their skills individually, such as by taking batting practice and undergoing physical conditioning. Management's job is to select good players. If each player is successful as an individual, the team should win.

In football, interdependence among players is higher and tends to be sequential. The line first blocks the opponents to enable the backs to run or pass. Plays are performed sequentially from first down to fourth down. Physical dispersement is medium, which allows players to operate as a coordinated unit. The primary mechanism for coordinating players is developing a game plan along with rules that govern the behavior of team members. Each player has an assignment that fits with other assignments, and management designs the game plan to achieve victory.

In basketball, interdependence tends to be reciprocal. The game is free-flowing, and the division of labor is less precise than in other sports. Each player is involved in both offense and defense, handles the ball, and attempts to score. The ball flows back and forth among players. Team members interact in a dynamic flow to achieve victory. Management skills involve the ability to influence this dynamic process, either by substituting players or by working the ball into certain areas. Players must learn to adapt to the flow of the game and to one another as events unfold.

Interdependence among players is a primary factor explaining the difference among the three sports. Baseball is organized around an autonomous individual, football around groups that are sequentially interdependent, and basketball around the free flow of reciprocal players.[46]

	Baseball	**Football**	**Basketball**
Interdependence	Pooled	Sequential	Reciprocal
Physical dispersion of players	High	Medium	Low
Coordination	Rules that govern the sport	Game plan and position roles	Mutual adjustment and shared responsibility
Key management job	Select players and develop their skills	Prepare and execute game	Influence flow of game

Source: Based on William Passmore, Carol E. Francis, and Jeffrey Haldeman, "Sociotechnical Systems: A North American Reflection on the Empirical Studies of the 70s," *Human Relations* 35 (1982): 1179–1204.

Exhibit 4.12   Primary Means to Achieve Coordination for Different Levels of Task Interdependence in a Manufacturing Firm.

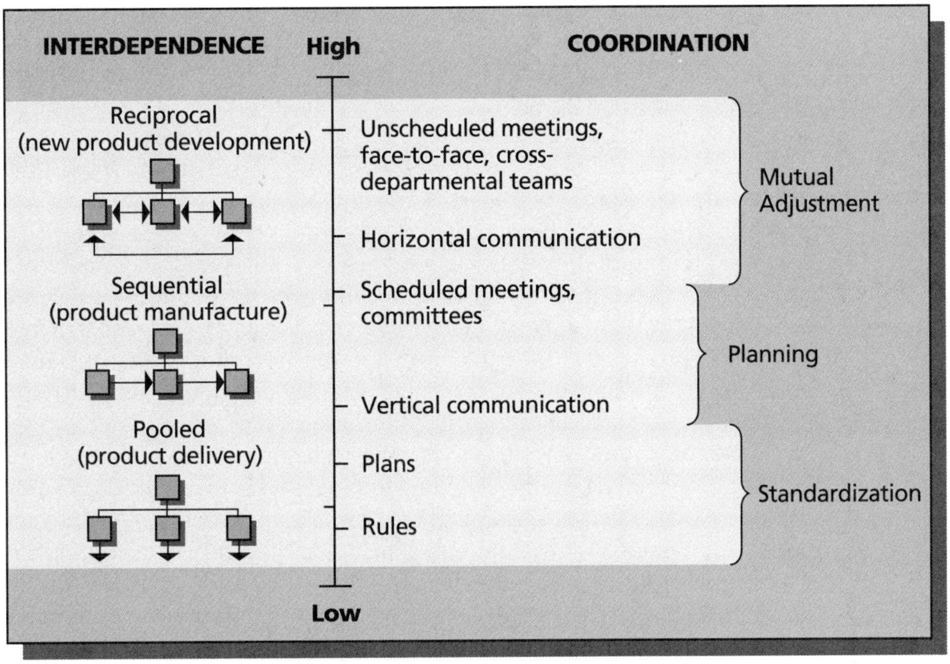

Source: Adapted from Andrew H. Van de Ven, Andre Delbecq, and Richard Koenig, "Determinants of Communication Modes within Organizations," *American Sociological Review* 41 (1976): 330.

Advanced Information Technology

Organizations are rapidly moving from the computer age of the 1970s to the information age of the 1990s, brought about by the microprocessor revolution. A typical microprocessor contains semiconductor chips that can execute tens of thousands of calculations in the blink of an eye, all in a space no larger than a fingernail. This revolution enabled the emergence of advanced manufacturing technology (AMT) systems described earlier in this chapter.

Microprocessors also enabled the disaggregation of large centralized computers into personal computers and workstations scattered around the organization, each having enormous computing power. Moreover, the solitary machines have become networks of interacting computers that greatly magnify their power and impact. Indeed, the impact of advanced information technologies on the administrative side of organizations is just as significant as that of advanced manufacturing technologies on manufacturing. New corporate structures have combined with advanced information technology to increase productivity in many corporations.[47] Companies that once ignored new information technologies have been able to revolutionize their operations by adopting them. One example is UPS, described in the Paradigm Buster.

Those aspects of **advanced information technology**(AIT) most significant for administration are executive information systems, groupware, and workflow automation. An **executive information system** is the use of computer technology to support the information needs of senior managers. For example, the CEO of

Duracell was able to use his personal computer to compare the performance of work forces in the United States and overseas. His computer produced a crisp table in color showing differences in productivity. Digging for more data, he discovered that overseas sales people were spending too much time calling on small stores, prompting a decision to service small stores in less expensive ways.[48] Executive information systems have the capacity for supporting nonroutine decisions, such as company strategy and competitive responses.

Groupware enables employees on a network to interact with one another through their personal computers. The simplest form of groupware is *electronic mail,* which allows one-on-one communication from one PC to another. Other, more complex groupware programs allow numerous employees to communicate simultaneously. For example, a team of employees might sit around a conference table or even remain in their separate offices while each uses a computer terminal through which the comments of other members are registered. All participants may view the same display on their screens, thereby removing communication barriers in group meetings and facilitating the sharing of information.[49]

Workflow automation is a growing niche in advanced information technology. Workflow software enables computer networks to automatically send documents, such as invoices, check requests, or customer inquiries, to the correct location for processing. For example, an expense report can be filled out on a computer, which checks the details, alerts the appropriate manager for review, then prints the check and notifies the employee by electronic mail where to pick it up. Workflow automation allows the entire procedure to be completed via computer, without a single employee ever having to handle a paper document. Aetna Life and Casualty Company is using workflow automation to speed the issuance of policies and processing of claims by cutting down the number of employees who must handle documents. Workflow automation also enables small companies to handle paperwork jobs that only firms with large numbers of employees could do in the past.[50]

For management, the rapid advancements in information technology call for new decisions on how it should be used in the organization. AIT makes the organization and the external environment more transparent to top managers. Should they use this power to centralize and tightly control the organization, or should they provide employees with the information needed to act autonomously? AIT can give employees all kinds of data about their customers, market, service, and efficiency. Some organizations use the new technology to simply reinforce rigid hierarchies, centralize decision making, and routinize work. For the most part, however, successful organizations are using this technology to decentralize, and its impact is being felt on management processes, organization design, and workplace culture.

MANAGEMENT PROCESSES

Advanced information technology enables managers to be better connected with the organization, the environment, and each other. Specific improvements in management processes are:

1. *Broader Participation in Decision Making.* Communication among managers takes time and effort, and AIT greatly reduces this effort, especially when managers are physically separated. For example, a product developer sent an elec-

Paradigm Buster

United Parcel Service, Inc.

United Parcel Service went through some serious growing pains, but today, it is once again a tough competitor in the international package distribution business. UPS was a low-tech outfit—and a successful one. The engineering department had perfected its manual packaging system to the point where any new technology just seemed to slow things down. UPS was very well managed—it had the lowest prices in the industry, and its profits kept setting records. But in the 1980s, competitors like Federal Express, which was way ahead in technology, were getting stronger as customers were getting choosier. UPS's management knew that the company could no longer stay ahead just by upgrading its manual system. As Chairman and CEO Kent "Oz" Nelson put it, "We realized that the leader in information management will be the leader in international package distribution—period."

The decade-long transformation cost millions of dollars and tried the patience of employee shareholders and management. To deal with internal resistance, the company sent the top people from each department to school to learn the new technology—a step that quickly turned opponents into supporters of the new plans. Today, United Parcel Service boasts five mainframe computers, a worldwide network, computer-controlled conveyor belts that speed packages along at five hundred feet per minute, and hand-held computers for UPS drivers. The company continues to invest in technology, including efforts to create a machine-readable label that will hold more data than bar codes.

The company that once looked like it might turn into a big brown dinosaur transformed itself to be on the cutting edge in information technology. And despite early fears that technology would just be expensive, inflexible, and prone to failure, rising profits reveal the true story: UPS has attained a new level of productivity, flexibility, and customer service.

Sources: Peter Coy with Chuck Hawkins, "UPS: Up from the Stone Age," *Business Week,* 15 June 1992, 132; and Peter Coy, "The New Realism in Office Systems," *Business Week,* 15 June 1992, 128–33.

tronic message asking for suggestions for a new product feature. He received more than 150 messages from every corner of the organization, almost all from people he did not know.[51] Moreover, research shows that AIT increases contact between the top of the organization and the bottom. Lower-level managers can communicate directly with the CEO, and a vice president can communicate directly with a project engineer. At Mrs. Fields, Inc., the world's largest retailer of cookies, branch employees use electronic mail to communicate directly to CEO Debbi Fields their opinions about products, competitors, and customer reactions. "On-line" at Wright-Patterson Air Force Base in Ohio, enlisted personnel can send messages directly to colonels, a level of communication that would have been unheard of five years ago.[52]

2. *Faster Decision Making.* AIT uses less of the organization's time for decision-related meetings.[53] The technology also reduces the time required to authorize organizational actions. Messages are handled fewer times, and interested parties can communicate directly. For example, Xerox dramatically reduced meeting time with its new computer system. Prior to a presentation, papers are no longer

sent back and forth. Each unit submits a plan electronically five days in advance, which each top executive reads before the meeting. The meeting itself is short because time is spent on substantive issues.

3. *Better Organizational Intelligence, Including More Rapid Identification of Problems and Opportunities.*[54]   With AIT, organizational activities become visible to managers. For example, sales and market research data are now available from grocery store checkout scanners. Organizations can purchase access to hundreds of databases about industry, financial, and demographic patterns in their environments. AIT enables the accumulation of a larger volume as well as a larger range of data. For example, Debbi Fields receives such data as: "I have many customers ask about why we do not have brownies, and I would like to test new brownies in my area." "Hi, Debbi. Customers are asking me what's in the product because some have allergies. How about an ingredient list?"[55]

ORGANIZATION DESIGN

The impact of advanced information technology on the administrative structure of organizations is now being felt. Specific outcomes are:

1. *Flatter Organization Structure.*   AIT has been enabling the lean structures many organizations are adopting. One organization in London that used information technology to empower employees rather than maintain a rigid hierarchy reduced the structure from thirteen to four layers. Hercules, a chemical company, adopted a combination of electronic messaging and groupware, after which the number of management levels between the president and plant foreman was reduced from a dozen to about seven, yet decision speed and effectiveness improved. New information technology has enabled Aetna Life and Casualty Company's sales force to replace its old hierarchy of supervisors and agents with small work teams.[56]

2. *Greater Centralization or Decentralization.*   Depending on manager choices, AIT can either centralize or decentralize the organization. Managers who want to centralize can use the technology to acquire more information and make more decisions, often with greater responsiveness than previously. Likewise, managers can decentralize information to employees and increase participation and autonomy.[57] Management philosophy and corporate culture have substantial bearing on how AIT influences decision making, but enlightened companies seem to use it to empower employees whenever possible.

3. *Improved Coordination.*   Perhaps one of the great outcomes of AIT is the ability to connect managers even when offices or stores are scattered worldwide. At Chase Manhattan Bank, groupware links fifty-two hundred bankers throughout the world. The new technology enables managers to communicate with one another and be aware of organization activities and outcomes. It can help to break down barriers and create a sense of team and organizational identity that was not previously available, especially when people work at different locations.[58]

4. *Fewer Narrow Tasks.*   Fewer administrative tasks under AIT will be subject to narrowly defined policies and job descriptions. Companies using AIT will closely resemble professional service firms. Remaining administrative and clerical tasks will provide intellectual engagement and more challenging work.[59]

5. *Larger Professional Staff Ratio.* The implementation of sophisticated information systems means that employees have to be highly trained and professional to both operate and maintain such systems. For the most part, unskilled employees will be replaced by the new technology, such as when the North American Banking Group installed a customer service information system that shifted the staff mix from 30 percent professionals to 60 percent professionals. Many clerical personnel were replaced by AIT. Fewer employees were needed to type letters, file memos, and fill out forms. Middle- and upper-level managers can use the new technology to type their own memos and send them instantly through electronic mail.

WORKPLACE CULTURE

All these changes in management processes and organization design also mean changes in office life. Corporate culture often changes with the introduction of advanced information technology. Depending on the approach of management, this can lead to a sense of empowerment when employees are given increased access to information previously available only to their bosses or to a loss of privacy for employees whose bosses now keep tabs on their every move. Relationships among workers are also affected when managers decide who within the organization should have access to what information and who should communicate with whom. It is important to remember that advanced information technology affects not just the structure of an organization but the people within it. In the following section, we will examine the impact of advanced information technology on people and jobs.[60]

The Impact of Technology on Job Design

So far, this chapter has described models for analyzing how manufacturing, service, department, and information technologies influence structure and management processes. The relation between a new technology and organization seems to follow a pattern, beginning with immediate effects on the content of jobs followed (after a longer period) by impact on design of the organization. The ultimate impact of technology on employees can be partially understood through the concepts of job design and sociotechnical systems.

JOB DESIGN

Research has studied whether new technologies tend to simplify or enrich jobs. New technologies change how jobs are done and the very nature of jobs.[61] Mass production technologies, for example, produce **job simplification**, meaning the number and difficulty of tasks performed by a single person are reduced. The consequence is boring, repetitive jobs that provide little satisfaction. More advanced technologies have caused **job enrichment**, meaning the jobs are designed to increase responsibility, recognition, and opportunities for growth and achievement.

Recent studies found that the introduction of advanced manufacturing technologies, for example, has had three noticeable results: greater opportunities for intellectual mastery and cognitive skills for workers; more worker responsibility for results; and greater interdependence among workers, enabling more social interaction and the development of teamwork and coordination skills.[62] One large bank that moved from a batch processing system to a fully on-line data entry transaction system found that teller skills became mental rather than manual, workers' increased feelings of responsibility for the whole task caused a sharp decrease in errors, and interdependence among workers resulted in workers helping one another find errors and improve their skills and accuracy.[63] A study of advanced information technology found that employees had to acquire higher-level skills to extract information from data and give it meaning rather than do activities based on physical labor.[64] Research also indicates that workers who are using advanced technologies generally earn 10 percent to 15 percent more than those who don't.[65] Thus, the findings about new technologies are encouraging, suggesting that jobs for workers are enriched rather than simplified, engaging higher mental capacities and providing greater satisfaction and income.

SOCIOTECHNICAL SYSTEMS

The **sociotechnical systems** approach combines the needs of people with the needs of technical efficiency. The *socio* portion of the approach refers to the people and groups who work in organizations. The *technical* portion of the approach refers to the tools and machines used in the work process.[66] The goal of the sociotechnical approach is **joint optimization,** which states that an organization will function best only if its social and technical systems are designed to fit the needs of one another.[67] Designing the structure to meet human needs while ignoring the technical system, or changing technology to improve efficiency while ignoring human needs, may inadvertently cause performance problems.

Sociotechnical principles evolved from work by the Tavistock Institute, a research organization in England, during the 1950s and 1960s.[68] More than 130 examples of organizational changes using sociotechnical principles have been reported around the world.[69] These organizational design changes have occurred in a railway maintenance depot, textile mills, a pet food plant, and new plants using advanced manufacturing technologies.[70] In most of these applications, the joint optimization of changes in technology and structure to meet the needs of people as well as efficiency improves performance, safety, quality, absenteeism, and turnover. In some cases, work design was not the most efficient based on technical and scientific principles, but worker involvement and commitment more than made up for the difference. Thus, once again research shows that new technologies need not have a negative impact on workers, because the technology often requires higher-level mental and social skills and can be organized to encourage the involvement and commitment of employees, thereby benefiting both the employee and the organization.

Summary and Interpretation

This chapter reviewed several frameworks and key research findings on the topic of organizational technology. The potential importance of technology as a factor in organizational structure was discovered during the 1960s. During the 1970s and

1980s, a flurry of research activity was undertaken to understand more precisely the relationship of technology to other characteristics of organizations.

Five ideas in the technology literature stand out. The first is Woodward's research into manufacturing technology. Woodward went into organizations and collected practical data on technology characteristics, organization structure, and management systems. She found clear relationships between technology and structure in high-performing organizations. Her findings are so clear that managers can analyze their own organizations on the same dimensions of technology and structure.

The second important idea is that service technologies differ in a systematic way from manufacturing technologies. Service technologies are characterized by intangible outcomes and direct client involvement in the production process. Service firms do not have the fixed, machine-based technologies that appear in manufacturing organizations; hence, organization design often differs also.

The third significant idea is Perrow's framework applied to department technologies. Understanding the variety and analyzability of a technology tells one about the management style, structure, and process that should characterize that department. Routine technologies are characterized by mechanistic structure and nonroutine technologies by organic structure. Applying the wrong management system to a department will result in dissatisfaction and reduced efficiency.

The fourth important idea is interdependence among departments. The extent to which departments depend on each other for materials, information, or other resources determines the amount of coordination required between them. As interdependence increases, demands on the organization for coordination increase. Organization design must allow for the correct amount of communication and coordination to handle interdependence across departments.

The fifth important idea is that new technologies—advanced manufacturing and advanced information technologies—are being adopted by organizations and having impact on organization design. For the most part, the impact is positive, with shifts toward more organic structures both on the shop floor and in the management hierarchy. These technologies replace routine jobs, give employees more autonomy, produce more challenging jobs, encourage teamwork, and let the organization be more flexible and responsive. The new technologies are enriching jobs to the point where organizations are happier places to work.

KEY CONCEPTS

advanced information technology
advanced manufacturing technology
analyzability
continuous process production
craft technology
engineering technology
executive information system
groupware
intensive technology
interdependence
job enrichment
job simplification
joint optimization
large-batch production

long-linked technology
mediating technology
nonroutine technology
pooled interdependence
reciprocal interdependence
routine technology
sequential interdependence
service technology
small-batch production
sociotechnical systems
technical complexity
technology
variety
workflow automation

DISCUSSION QUESTIONS

1. Where would your university or college department be located on Perrow's technology framework? Look for the underlying variety and analyzability characteristics when making your assessment. Would a department devoted exclusively to teaching be put in a different quadrant from a department devoted exclusively to research?

2. Explain Thompson's levels of interdependence. Identify an example of each level of interdependence in the university or college setting. What kinds of coordination mechanisms should administration develop to handle each level of interdependence?

3. Describe Woodward's classification of organizational technologies. Explain why each of the three technology groups is related differently to organization structure and management processes.

4. What relationships did Woodward discover between supervisor span of control and technological complexity?

5. How do advanced manufacturing technologies differ from other manufacturing technologies? What is the primary advantage of AMT?

6. What is a service technology? Are different types of service technologies likely to be associated with different structures? Explain.

7. Edna Peterson is a colonel in the air force in charge of the finance section of an air base in New Mexico. Financial work in the military involves large amounts of routine matters and paperwork, and Peterson gradually developed a philosophy of management that was fairly mechanistic. She believed that all important decisions should be made by administrators, that elaborate rules and procedures should be developed and followed, and that subordinates should have little discretion and should be tightly controlled. The finance section is about to introduce advanced information technology that will take over most paperwork. Based on what you know about AIT, what advice would you give Edna Peterson?

8. A top executive claimed that top-level management is a craft technology because the work contains intangibles, such as handling personnel, interpreting the environment, and coping with unusual situations that have to be learned through experience. If this is true, is it appropriate to teach management in a business school? Does teaching management from a textbook assume that the manager's job is analyzable, and hence that formal training rather than experience is most important?

9. In which quadrant of Perrow's framework would a mass production technology be placed? Where would small-batch and continuous process technologies be placed? Why? Would Perrow's framework lead to the same recommendation about organic versus mechanistic structures that Woodward made?

10. To what extent does the development of new manufacturing and information technologies simplify and routinize the jobs of employees? Discuss.

GUIDES TO ACTION

As an organization manager, keep these guides in mind:

1. Relate organization structure to technology. Use the two dimensions of variety and analyzability to discover whether the work in a department is routine or nonroutine. If the work in a department is routine, use a mechanistic structure and process. If the work in a department is nonroutine, use an

organic management process. Exhibit 4.10 illustrates this relationship between department technology and organization structure.

2. Use the categories developed by Woodward to diagnose whether the production technology in a manufacturing firm is small-batch, mass production, or continuous process. Use a more organic structure with small-batch or continuous process technologies, and with new advanced manufacturing technology systems. Use a mechanistic structure with mass production technologies.

3. Use the concept of service technology to evaluate the production process in nonmanufacturing firms. Service technologies are intangible and must be located close to the customer. Hence, service organizations may have an organization structure with fewer boundary roles, greater geographical dispersion, decentralization, highly skilled employees in the technical core, and generally less control than in manufacturing organizations.

4. Evaluate the interdependencies among organizational departments. Use the general rule that, as interdependencies increase, mechanisms for coordination must also increase.

5. Analyze organizational and employee requirements when introducing advanced information technologies. Plan for greater participation in decision making, faster decisions, better organizational intelligence, a flatter organization, improved coordination, greater professional staff ratio, and more broadly defined tasks. AIT generally leads to job enrichment in much the same way as advanced manufacturing technologies. With both manufacturing and information technologies, the sociotechnical systems approach can be used to define the optimal fit between the social needs of employees and the technical needs of the organization.

Consider these guides when analyzing the following case.

Olson's Locker Plant*

CASE FOR ANALYSIS

Herb Olson, owner of Olson's Locker Plant, is contemplating the future. He is considering a proposal to acquire, on a trial basis, a Beef-A-Matic to increase plant efficiency.

"I agree that we must increase efficiency," Olson said to his son Jim, assistant plant superintendent, "but if we undertake a full program of automation, we will probably destroy the family atmosphere in the plant. People won't even be able to talk to each other if everyone is hooked up to a machine."

---

*This case is based on materials from Scott Killman, "Power Pork: Corporations Begin To Turn Hog Business Into an Assembly Line," *Wall Street Journal*, 28 March 1994, A1, A10; Horace Thornton and J. F. Gracey, *Textbook of Meat Hygiene*, 6th ed. (London: Bailliere Tindall, 1974), 517–22; John R. Romans and P. Thomas Ziegler, *The Meat We Eat* (Danville, Ill.: Interstate Printers and Publishers, 1977), 94–102; "Pioneer Company (A) and (B)," in Gene W. Dalton, Paul R. Lawrence, and Jay W. Lorsch, eds., *Organization Structure and Design* (Homewood, Ill.: Irwin and Dorsey, 1970), 165–99; "Automated Beef Boning: First Step toward a Totally Robotic System?" *Chilton's Food Engineering* 56 (February 1984): 170.

"Dad, all of the national packers have gone to automation for most jobs. Huge corporations are even getting involved in the pork industry, building fully automated "pig factories" to raise and slaughter hundreds of thousands of hogs a year—that's driving prices way down. And what Tyson did for chicken, they're now planning to do for pork. A program of automation is the only way we can compete."

"We can always sell out to Midwest Packers," Herb Olson responded. "Then they can provide the automation. Midwest would also plug us into their computer technology, voice mail, and the like. That would allow us to go whole hog, so to speak, with respect to new technology."

Jim smiled, "That's an idea, but I think we should try to do it ourselves."

Background

Olson's Locker Plant is located in Grand Island, Nebraska, a city of about fifty thousand people. The locker plant was started in 1972 by Herb Olson. Olson was co-owner and manager of a successful downtown hotel and restaurant with his wife until she died. He sold the hotel business in 1970 at the age of forty. Two years later, he decided to buy a small locker plant as a way to keep busy and increase his knowledge of the meat business.

Olson's reputation for selling good meat at a fair price quickly spread, and his business grew steadily. After ten years, Olson had thirty-two employees, and today he employs 150 people. Ninety percent of the locker plant's business is supplying meat to independent grocery stores, restaurants, and small markets in central Nebraska. Beef products account for 60 percent of the volume, pork the other 40 percent.

Plant and Equipment

As the volume of business increased, the locker plant gradually became more mechanized. The plant is located in a large, single-story building with eleven thousand square feet of work space. The building is divided into two parts. One side is used to kill and dress animals. The other side is used to cut and prepare finished meats for delivery to customers.

Mechanization has developed to the point where carcasses are now transported through the plant entirely by hooks and overhead rails. Workers use mechanical tools for several operations, such as power saws for splitting carcasses and a hydraulic winch to pull the skin from the carcass.

Employees range in age from eighteen to sixty-two. Workers on the shop floor are considered semiskilled and are paid an hourly wage. The company is not unionized. Turnover is low. Many employees have been with the company several years. Few have formal education beyond high school.

Organization

The approximate organization structure for Olson's Locker Plant is shown in Exhibit 4.14. Herb Olson is owner and president. The management team includes a treasurer, sales manager, industrial engineer, plant superintendent, and personnel director. The assistant superintendent is Olson's son, who is twenty-eight years old and has been with the organization five years. Jim Olson has worked at several projects, but this is his first management job and he is considered part of the management team. Jim Olson will take over as plant superintendent when the current

Exhibit 4.14   Organization Chart for Olson's Locker Plant.

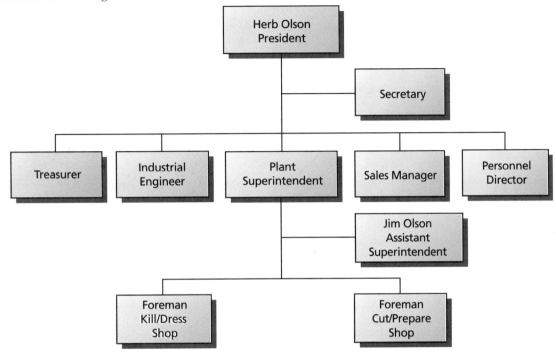

superintendent retires in five years. The sales manager has three sales people reporting to him. The industrial engineer has an assistant to help with job measurement activities. All workers involved in the conversion of live animals to packaged meat report to the plant superintendent.

The managers meet every Thursday evening to review their respective activities and to share information. This meeting is used to coordinate activities and to discuss solutions to unexpected problems.

The management team agrees with the need to increase efficiency. The personnel director is writing policies on such matters as hiring, firing, benefits, absences, and promotions and has requested permission to hire a person to write job descriptions. The industrial engineer is working to systemize jobs and the work flow. The managers believe these moves will improve efficiency in the short term.

The Pork Conversion Process

The process for converting live pigs into bacon and ham normally requires fourteen operations. The dressing sequence begins by stunning the pig electrically. A rear limb is shackled, and the pig is elevated to an overhead rail, where it is stuck and bled. The carcass is then dipped mechanically into a scalding tank for up to five minutes, where the hair is loosened. After scalding, pigs are moved mechanically to the dehairing area, where the carcasses are scraped clean. The scraping process is partly accomplished by hand. After dehairing, the carcass is transferred to the singeing area. Singeing darkens the meat's outer edge and produces skin that has good leather quality. The carcass is then eviscerated. Next, the carcass is skinned and the head is removed. Finally, the carcass is split in half with a handheld electric saw. At this point, the carcass is inspected for disease and sent to the chilling room.

Pig halves are taken from the chilling room as needed by the meat-cutting operation. In this area, meat is thawed; cut into hams, bellies, and shoulders; injected with brine; boned; smoked; packed for sale or shipment; rechilled; and then assembled for customer orders. More detailed descriptions of the brine injection, boning, and order assembly operations follow.

Brine Injection

Brine injection is the third procedure in the meat-cutting operation. After the carcass is warmed and cut into hams and shoulders, brine is injected into the meat. The purpose of the brine injection is to introduce a solution of salt, sugar, and nitrates into the meat. The salt acts as a preservative, and the nitrates are used to retain the reddish color of the meat. The brine is injected by hand using a series of injection needles that are connected to a pumping machine. The brine ensures a more uniform cure and reduces the curing time to two or three days. Bellies are injected twice, once in the morning and again in the evening.

The injection requires modest skill. Operators are responsible for seeing that the quantity of solution does not exceed the limit set by federal law. They must also see that the brine is injected uniformly throughout the meat and that the needles are inserted into the arteries. The rate and pressure of the brine injection are controlled by the pumping machine.

Boning

The boning operation consists of trimming excess fat and cutting out the bones from hams and shoulders. Five employees are assigned to this task. They work around a large rectangular table. Boning the meat typically takes three times as long as trimming the fat and is the most difficult task. The workers along the boning platform are considered to be among the most skilled in the plant. Great dexterity is required to trim the fat and remove the bone with a minimum of waste. It takes a new person at least six months to gain proficiency in this task. Eight different methods of trimming and boning have to be learned to handle the various cuts of meat. Each ham within any category can present specific problems, depending on size and the amount of fat and skin remnants. An experienced operator can tell immediately whether a ham will be difficult to work with. The criteria for assigning people to the boning operation are two years of experience working with meat and excellent manual dexterity.

Order Assembly

The last step in the production sequence is the assembly of customer orders. Three people perform this operation. They assemble items from finished stock, move them to the packing area, check the assembled order against the customer's order, fill cartons with the meat, and arrange shipment.

Other Tasks

Industrial Engineering

Just three years ago, Herb Olson hired an industrial engineer to improve internal efficiency. The industrial engineer is involved with production planning. The work includes studying the production operation throughout the plant, conducting time and motion studies of each task, and suggesting new work procedures. The industrial engineer is also responsible for evaluating new equipment with respect to cost and labor savings. In addition, he plans to start a monthly labor analysis report for Olson and the plant superintendent.

Purchasing and Selling

Herb Olson spends most of his time purchasing live animals. He also visits some area stores because many buyers want to deal directly with him.

Livestock purchasing is tricky because there is no organized commodity market for meat in the area. Meat prices in the major centers (such as Omaha) fluctuate daily. Seventy percent of the cost of the finished product is the value of the livestock, so purchase price directly influences profit margins. Olson usually talks daily with meat brokers, local farmers, sale barns, and other sources of price information. He also negotiates directly with area farmers to buy livestock at a fixed price to reduce the risk for both sides. These purchases require Olson to visit farms and inspect the livestock.

Olson once told an interviewer, "The most difficult part of my job is anticipating meat prices in the future. About 70 percent of the time, I can predict whether prices will increase or decrease and make purchase contracts accordingly."

The Future

Herb Olson is concerned about the future of his meat packing business. He spends most of his time buying rather than planning or learning about new technology. His son Jim champions the Beef-A-Matic because it will replace unskilled workers. With it, two people can produce forty forequarters and fifty hindquarters per hour. New technology is being developed that will handle many tasks, including some in the boning operation, the most difficult to automate.

Herb Olson believes he has three options. First, do not adopt new technology, but continue to tighten up the current operation. Second, start a program of new technology that will eventually automate most tasks and make the plant more efficient. Third, sell out to Midwest Packers, which would introduce new technology for both the plant and administration and agree to leave the current management team in place. Olson is filled with unanswered questions, such as what the correct structure and management systems should be with new technology and whether employees will be happy and motivated.

QUESTIONS

1. How would you classify Olson's Locker Plant in the frameworks for manufacturing technology? Explain.
2. Do the different tasks in the organization reflect different types of department technologies as described by Perrow? How would you classify them?
3. Which of the three alternatives would you recommend that Herb Olson adopt? What advice would you give him concerning the expected impact of new technology on the management of his organization and worker motivation?

NOTES

1. James B. Treece with Patrick Oster, "General Motors: Open All Night," *Business Week,* 1 June 1992, 82–83.

2. Charles Perrow, "A Framework for the Comparative Analysis of Organizations," *American Sociological Review* 32 (1967): 194–208; Denise M. Rosseau, "Assessment of Technology in Organizations: Closed versus Open Systems Approaches," *Academy of Management Review* 4 (1979): 531–42.

3. Linda Argote, "Input Uncertainty and Organizational Coordination in Hospital Emergency Units," *Administrative Science Quarterly* 27 (1982): 420–34; Charles Perrow, *Organizational Analysis: A Sociological Approach* (Belmont, Calif.: Wadsworth, 1970); William Rushing, "Hardness of Material as Related to the Division of Labor in Manufacturing Industries," *Administrative Science Quarterly* 13 (1968): 229–45.

4. Lawrence B. Mohr, "Organizational Technology and Organization Structure," *Administrative Science Quarterly* 16 (1971): 444–59; David Hickson, Derek Pugh, and Diana Pheysey, "Operations Technology and Organization Structure: An Empirical Reappraisal," *Administrative Science Quarterly* 14 (1969): 378–97.

5. Joan Woodward, *Industrial Organization: Theory and Practice* (London: Oxford University Press, 1965); Joan Woodward, *Management and Technology* (London: Her Majesty's Stationery Office, 1958).

6. Hickson, Pugh, and Pheysey, "Operations Technology and Organization Structure"; James D. Thompson, *Organizations in Action* (New York: McGraw-Hill, 1967).

7. Edward Harvey, "Technology and the Structure of Organizations," *American Sociological Review* 33 (1968): 241–59.

8. Wanda J. Orlikowski, "The Duality of Technology: Rethinking the Concept of Technology in Organizations," *Organization Science* 3 (1992): 398–427.

9. Based on Woodward, *Industrial Organization* and *Management and Technology.*

10. Woodward, *Industrial Organization,* vi.

11. William L. Zwerman, *New Perspectives on Organizational Theory* (Westport, Conn.: Greenwood, 1970); Harvey, "Technology and the Structure of Organizations," 241–59.

12. David Wessel, "Pilgrim and Millstone, Two Nuclear Plants, Have Disparate Fates," *Wall Street Journal,* 28 July 1987, 1, 18; Arlen J. Large, "Federal Agency Prods Nuclear-Plant Official to Raise Performance," *Wall Street Journal,* 10 May 1984, 1, 22.

13. Wessel, "Pilgrim and Millstone."

14. Jack R. Meredith, "The Strategic Advantages of the Factory of the Future," *California Management Review* 29 (Spring 1987): 27–41; Jack Meredith, "The Strategic Advantages of the New Manufacturing Technologies for Small Firms," *Strategic Management Journal* 8 (1987): 249–58; Althea Jones and Terry Webb, "Introducing Computer Integrated Manufacturing," *Journal of General Management* 12 (Summer 1987): 60–74.

15. Raymond F. Zammuto and Edward J. O'Connor, "Gaining Advanced Manufacturing Technologies' Benefits: The Roles of Organization Design and Culture," *Academy of Management Review* 17 (1992): 701–28.

16. Paul S. Adler, "Managing Flexible Automation," *California Management Review* (Spring 1988): 34–56.

17. Bela Gold, "Computerization in Domestic and International Manufacturing," *California Management Review* (Winter 1989): 129–43.

18. Graham Dudley and John Hassard, "Design Issues in the Development of Computer Integrated Manufacturing (CIM)," *Journal of General Management* 16 (1990): 43–53.

19. Otis Port, "Smart Factories: America's Turn?" *Business Week,* 8 May 1989, 142–48.

20. Otis Port with John Carey, "This Is What the U.S. Must Do to Stay Competitive," *Business Week,* 16 December 1991, 92–96; Otis Port, "The Responsive Factory," *Business Week/Enterprise,* 1993, 48–52.

21. Meredith, "Strategic Advantages of the Factory of the Future."

22. Patricia L. Nemetz and Louis W. Fry, "Flexible Manufacturing Organizations: Implementations for Strategy Formulation and Organization Design," *Academy of Management Review* 13 (1988): 627–38; Paul S. Adler, "Managing Flexible Automation," *California Management Review* (Spring 1988): 34–56; Jeremy Main, "Manufacturing the Right Way," *Fortune,* 21 May 1990, 54–64; Frank M. Hull and Paul D. Collins, "High-Technology Batch Production Systems: Woodward's Missing Type," *Academy of Management Journal* 30 (1987): 786–97.

23. P. Robert Duimering, Frank Safayeni, and Lyn Purdy, "Integrated Manufacturing: Redesign the

Organization before Implementing Flexible Technology," *Sloan Management Review* (Summer 1993): 47–56; Zammuto and O'Connor, "Gaining Advanced Manufacturing Technologies' Benefits."

24. David E. Bowen, Caren Siehl, and Benjamin Schneider, "A Framework for Analyzing Customer Service Orientations in Manufacturing," *Academy of Management Review* 14 (1989): 79–95; Peter K. Mills and Newton Margulies, "Toward a Core Typology of Service Organizations," *Academy of Management Review* 5 (1980): 255–65; Peter K. Mills and Dennis J. Moberg, "Perspectives on the Technology of Service Operations," *Academy of Management Review* 7 (1982): 467–78; G. Lynn Shostack, "Breaking Free from Product Marketing," *Journal of Marketing* (April 1977): 73–80.

25. Richard B. Chase and David A. Tansik, "The Customer Contact Model for Organization Design," *Management Science* 29 (1983): 1037–50.

26. *Ibid.*

27. David E. Bowen and Edward E. Lawler III, "The Empowerment of Service Workers: What, Why, How, and When," *Sloan Management Review* (Spring 1992): 31–39; Gregory B. Northcraft and Richard B. Chase, "Managing Service Demand at the Point of Delivery," *Academy of Management Review* 10 (1985): 66–75; Roger W. Schmenner, "How Can Service Businesses Survive and Prosper?" *Sloan Management Review* 27 (Spring 1986): 21–32.

28. Minda Zetlin, "When 99 Percent Isn't Enough," *Management Review* (March 1993): 49–52.

29. Perrow, "Framework for Comparative Analysis" and *Organizational Analysis.*

30. Michael Withey, Richard L. Daft, and William C. Cooper, "Measures of Perrow's Work Unit Technology: An Empirical Assessment and a New Scale," *Academy of Management Journal* 25 (1983): 45–63.

31. Christopher Gresov, "Exploring Fit and Misfit with Multiple Contingencies," *Administrative Science Quarterly* 34 (1989): 431–53.

32. Richard Cone, Bruce Snow, and Ricky Waclawcayk, *Datapoint Corporation* (Unpublished manuscript, Texas A&M University, 1981).

33. Gresov, "Exploring Fit and Misfit with Multiple Contingencies"; Charles A. Glisson, "Dependence of Technological Routinization on Structural Variables in Human Service Organizations," *Administrative Science Quarterly* 23 (1978): 383–95; Jerald Hage and Michael Aiken, "Routine Technology, Social Structure and Organizational Goals," *Administrative Science Quarterly* 14 (1969): 368–79.

34. Gresov, "Exploring Fit and Misfit with Multiple Contingencies"; A. J. Grimes and S. M. Kline, "The Technological Imperative: The Relative Impact of Task Unit, Modal Technology, and Hierarchy on Structure," *Academy of Management Journal* 16 (1973): 583–97; Lawrence G. Hrebiniak, "Job Technologies, Supervision and Work Group Structure," *Administrative Science Quarterly* 19 (1974): 395–410; Jeffrey Pfeffer, *Organizational Design* (Arlington Heights, Ill.: AHM, 1978), ch. 1.

35. Patrick E. Connor, *Organizations: Theory and Design* (Chicago: Science Research Associates, 1980); Richard L. Daft and Norman B. Macintosh, "A Tentative Exploration into Amount and Equivocality of Information Processing in Organizational Work Units," *Administrative Science Quarterly* 26 (1981): 207–24.

36. Paul D. Collins and Frank Hull, "Technology and Span of Control: Woodward Revisited," *Journal of Management Studies* 23 (1986): 143–64; Gerald D. Bell, "The Influence of Technological Components of Work upon Management Control," *Academy of Management Journal* 8 (1965): 127–32; Peter M. Blau and Richard A. Schoenherr, *The Structure of Organizations* (New York: Basic Books, 1971).

37. W. Alan Randolph, "Matching Technology and the Design of Organization Units," *California Management Review* 22–23 (1980–81): 39–48; Daft and Macintosh, "Tentative Exploration into Amount and Equivocality of Information Processing"; Michael L. Tushman, "Work Characteristics and Subunit Communication Structure: A Contingency Analysis," *Administrative Science Quarterly* 24 (1979): 82–98.

38. Andrew H. Van de Ven and Diane L. Ferry, *Measuring and Assessing Organizations* (New York: Wiley, 1980); Randolph, "Matching Technology and the Design of Organization Units."

39. Richard L. Daft and Robert H. Lengel, "Information Richness: A New Approach to Managerial Behavior and Organization Design," in Barry Staw and Larry L. Cummings, eds., *Research in Organizational Behavior,* vol. 6 (Greenwich, Conn.: JAI Press, 1984), 191–233; Richard L. Daft and Norman B. Macintosh, "A New Approach into Design and Use of Management Information," *California Management Review* 21 (1978): 82–92; Daft and Macintosh, "Tentative Exploration in Amount and Equivocality of Information Processing"; W. Alan Randolph, "Organizational Technology and the Media and Purpose Dimensions of Organizational Communication," *Journal of Business Research* 6

(1978): 237–59; Linda Argote, "Input Uncertainty and Organizational Coordination in Hospital Emergency Units," *Administrative Science Quarterly* 27 (1982): 420–34; Andrew H. Van de Ven and Andre Delbecq, "A Task Contingent Model of Work Unit Structure," *Administrative Science Quarterly* 19 (1974): 183–97.

40. Peggy Leatt and Rodney Schneck, "Criteria for Grouping Nursing Subunits in Hospitals," *Academy of Management Journal* 27 (1984): 150–65.

41. Gresov, "Exploring Fit and Misfit with Multiple Contingencies"; Michael L. Tushman, "Technological Communication in R&D Laboratories: The Impact of Project Work Characteristics," *Academy of Management Journal* 21 (1978): 624–45.

42. Thanks to Gail Russ for suggesting this example of a technology-structure mismatch.

43. James Thompson, *Organizations in Action* (New York: McGraw-Hill, 1967).

44. *Ibid.*, 40.

45. Christopher Gresov, "Effects of Dependence and Tasks on Unit Design and Efficiency," *Organization Studies* 11 (1990): 503–29; Andrew H. Van de Ven, Andre Delbecq, and Richard Koenig, "Determinants of Coordination Modes within Organizations," *American Sociological Review* 41 (1976): 322–38; Linda Argote, "Input Uncertainty and Organizational Coordination in Hospital Emergency Units"; Jack K. Ito and Richard B. Peterson, "Effects of Task Difficulty and Interdependence on Information Processing Systems," *Academy of Management Journal* 29 (1986): 139–49; Joseph L. C. Cheng, "Interdependence and Coordination in Organizations: A Role-System Analysis," *Academy of Management Journal* 26 (1983): 156–62.

46. Robert W. Keidel, "Team Sports Models as a Generic Organizational Framework," *Human Relations* 40 (1987): 591–612; Robert W. Keidel, "Baseball, Football, and Basketball: Models for Business," *Organizational Dynamics* (Winter 1984): 5–18; Richard L. Daft and Richard M. Steers, *Organizations: A Micro-Macro Approach* (Glenview, Ill.: Scott, Foresman, 1986).

47. Howard Gleckman with John Carey, Russell Mitchell, Tim Smart, and Chris Roush, "The Technology Payoff," *Business Week,* 14 June 1993, 57–68; Michele Liu, Héléné Denis, Harvey Kolodny, and Benjt Stymne, "Organization and Design for Technological Change," *Human Relations* 43 (January 1990): 7–22; George P. Huber, "A Theory of the Effects of Advanced Information Technologies on Organizational Design, Intelligence, and Decision Making," *Academy of Man-*

agement Review 14 (1990): 47–71.

48. Jeremy Main, "At Last, Software CEOs Can Use," *Fortune,* 13 March 1989, 77–82.

49. Richard C. Huseman and Edward W. Miles, "Organizational Communication in the Information Age: Implementations of Computer-Based Systems," *Journal of Management* 14 (1988): 181–204.

50. John W. Verity, "Getting Work to Go with the Flow," *Business Week,* 21 June 1993, 156–61; Gleckman, et al., "The Technology Payoff"; Peter Coy, "Start with Some High-Tech Magic," *Business Week/Enterprise,* 1993, 24–32.

51. Huber, "A Theory of the Effects of Advanced Information Technologies"; Lee Sproull and Sara Keisler, "Reducing Social Context Cues: Electronic Mail in Organizational Communication," *Management Science* 32 (1986): 1492–512.

52. John R. Wilke, "Computer Links Erode Hierarchical Nature of Workplace Culture," *Wall Street Journal,* 9 December 1993, A1, A10; Huber, "A Theory of the Effects of Advanced Information Technologies"; Stephen D. Soloman, "Use Technology to Manage People," *Small Business Report* (September 1990): 46–51.

53. Huber, "A Theory of the Effects of Advanced Information Technologies."

54. *Ibid.*

55. Soloman, "Use Technology to Manage People."

56. Gleckman, et al., "The Technology Payoff"; Shoshanna Zuboff, *In the Age of the Smart Machine* (New York: Basic Books, 1984).

57. Lynda M. Applegate, James I. Cash, Jr., and D. Quinn Mills, "Information Technology and Tomorrow's Manager," *Harvard Business Review* (November–December 1988): 128–36.

58. Wilke, "Computer Links."

59. Applegate, Cash, and Mills, "Information Technology and Tomorrow's Manager."

60. Wilke, "Computer Links."

61. Liu, Denis, Kolodny, and Stymne, "Organization Design for Technological Change."

62. Gerald I. Susman and Richard B. Chase, "A Sociotechnical Analysis of the Integrated Factory," *Journal of Applied Behavioral Science* 22 (1986): 257–70; Paul Adler, "New Technologies, New Skills," *California Management Review* 29 (Fall 1986): 9–28.

63. Adler, "New Technologies, New Skills."

64. Zuboff, *In the Age of the Smart Machine.*

65. Gleckman, et al., "The Technology Payoff."

66. William Passmore, Carol E. Francis, and Jeffrey Haldeman, "Sociotechnical Systems: A North

American Reflection on the Empirical Studies of the 70s," *Human Relations* 35 (1982): 1179–204.

67. F. Emery, "Characteristics of Sociotechnical Systems," Tavistock Institute of Human Relations, document 527, 1959; Passmore, Francis, and Haldeman, "Sociotechnical Systems."

68. Eric Trist and K. Banforth, "Some Social and Psychological Consequences of the Long Wall Method of Coal-Getting," *Human Relations* (1951): 3–38; Eric Trist, C. Higgin, H. Murray,

and A. Pollock, *Organizational Choice* (London: Tavistock Publications, 1963).

69. Passmore, Francis, and Haldeman, "Sociotechnical Systems."

70. Lyman Katchum, "Sociotechnical Design in a Third World Country: The Railway Maintenance Depot at Scennar in the Sudan," *Human Relations* 37 (1984): 135–54; Passmore, Francis, and Haldeman, "Sociotechnical Systems."

CHAPTER

5

Organization Size, Life Cycle, and Decline

Xerox Corporation

Everyone knows Xerox makes copiers. We usually use the trademark "Xeroxing" to talk about copying something, no matter what the name on the machine we're using. But Xerox is trying to transform itself from a company that just sells copiers into one that helps office workers create, use, and share documents and data bases.

Xerox found that it was letting many of its best ideas be stolen away and exploited by outsiders. For example, Xerox researchers developed the software that helped launch such companies as Apple, 3Com, and Sun Microsystems. Now, Xerox is breaking down the bureaucratic walls that kept research and development, marketing, and manufacturing from taking advantage of each other's ideas, thereby allowing valuable technology to leak out of the company.

The giant corporation is trying to think small, emphasizing small management teams running highly decentralized units. Still, new ideas can often be overlooked or ignored in such a large organization, and smaller, more flexible competitors can end up reaping the benefits. So Xerox decided to provide money and resources for employees to start their own small companies, thus making sure the profits from these new technologies benefit Xerox instead.

Xerox Technology Ventures (XTV) provides seed money and helps line up outside investors, with the goal of ultimately taking the new companies public and profiting from the sale of Xerox's stake. So far, well over half of the dozen or so spin-offs are profitable, and only two have failed. XTV not only excites and encourages the creative and entrepreneurial spirit of Xerox scientists, it also makes managers keep a closer eye on internal technologies and employee ideas.

And yes, Xerox is still in the copy machine business. One of its newest start-up companies produces tiny, battery-operated copiers that fit in a briefcase. The concept was rejected by Xerox's operating committee for five years before XTV was instituted and made a Xerox technologist's dream come true. By providing seed money for Quadmark Ltd., XTV prevented the inventor, the technology, and the profits from moving on to a smaller and nimbler competitor.[1]

Xerox Technology Ventures is an example of how companies around the world are combining the advantages of bigness with "the human scale, sharp focus, and fervent entrepreneurship of smallness."[2] Today, many large companies want to minimize size and bureaucracy to be flexible and responsive in a rapidly changing marketplace. As we discussed in Chapter 1, in the 1970s and 1980s, growth and large size were considered natural and desirable; but in the 1990s, small—or at least the ability to behave as a small company—is beautiful.[3]

During the twentieth century, large organizations have become widespread, and over the past thirty years, bureaucracy has been a major topic of study in organization theory.[4] Today, most large organizations have bureaucratic characteristics. They provide us with abundant goods and services, and they surprise us with astonishing feats—astronauts to the moon, thousands of airline flights daily without an accident—that are testimony to their effectiveness. On the other hand, bureaucracy is also accused of many sins, including inefficiency, rigidity, and demeaning, routinized work that alienates both employees and the customers an organization tries to serve.[5]

PURPOSE OF THIS CHAPTER

In this chapter, we will explore the question of large versus small organization and how size is related to structural characteristics. Organization size is a contextual variable that influences organizational design and functioning just as do the contextual variables—technology, environment, goals—discussed in previous chapters. In the first section, we will look at the advantages of large versus small size. Then, we will examine the historical need for bureaucracy as a means to control large organizations and how managers today attack bureaucracy in some large organizations. Next, we will explore what is called an organization's life cycle and the structural characteristics at each stage. Finally, the causes of organizational decline and some methods for dealing with downsizing will be discussed. By the end of this chapter, you should understand the nature of bureaucracy, its strengths and weaknesses, and when to use bureaucratic characteristics to make an organization effective.

Organization Size: Is Bigger Better?

The question of big versus small begins with the notion of growth and the reasons so many organizations feel the need to grow large.

PRESSURES FOR GROWTH

Why do organizations grow? Why should they grow? The following are **reasons organizations grow.**

Organizational Goals   Despite the fact that America's management guru, Peter Drucker, has declared that "the Fortune 500 is over," American companies have a "lingering love affair with big."[6] The dream of practically every businessperson is still to have his or her company become a member of the Fortune 500 list—to grow fast and to grow large. Sometimes, this goal is more urgent than to make the best products or show the greatest profits. As we discussed in Chapter 2, growth is a major goal because it enables the company to provide a complete service or product line, meet new challenges, and become a more complete unit.[7] For example, at Campbell Taggart, a large bakery, top management wants the company to grow in order to move into dinner and sweet rolls, pastries, cookies, and cakes, thereby becoming a well-rounded company poised for future success.[8]

Executive Advancement   Growth is often necessary to attract and keep quality managers. Growing organizations, both public and private, are exciting places to work. There are many challenges and opportunities for advancement when the number of employees is expanding.[9]

Economic Health   Many executives have found that firms must grow to stay economically healthy. To stop growing is to suffocate. To be stable or to relax means customers may not have their demands fully met or that competitors will meet customer needs and increase market share at the expense of your company. Scale is still crucial to economic health in some industries. For example, bigger volumes mean lower unit purchasing costs for food processing companies, such as Kraft General

Foods. Greater size gives marketing-intensive companies, such as beverage distributors Coca-Cola and Anheuser-Busch, power in the marketplace and thus increased revenues.[10]

LARGE VERSUS SMALL

Organizations feel compelled to grow, but how much and how large? What size organization is better poised to compete in a global environment? The arguments are summarized in Exhibit 5.1.

Large Huge resources and economies of scale are needed for many organizations to compete globally. Only large organizations can build a massive pipeline in Alaska. Only a large corporation like Boeing can afford to build a 747, and only a large American Airlines can buy it. Only a large Merck can invest hundreds of millions in new drugs that must be sold worldwide to show a profit. Only a large McDonald's can open a new restaurant somewhere in the world every seventeen hours. Recall from Chapter 3 the Japanese *keiretsu,* a family of interlocking companies whose size gives Japanese competitors enormous scope and global financial power.

Large companies also are standardized, often mechanistically run, and complex. The complexity offers hundreds of functional specialties within the organization to

Exhibit 5.1   Differences between Large and Small Organizations.

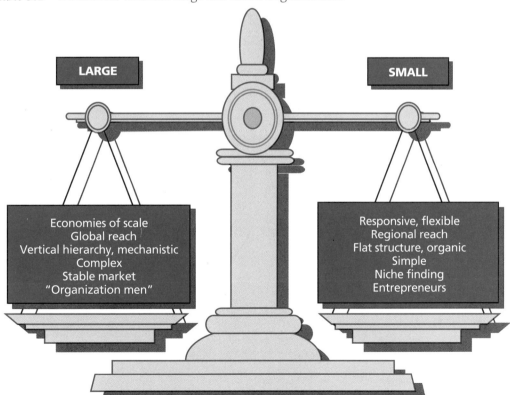

LARGE

Economies of scale
Global reach
Vertical hierarchy, mechanistic
Complex
Stable market
"Organization men"

SMALL

Responsive, flexible
Regional reach
Flat structure, organic
Simple
Niche finding
Entrepreneurs

Source: Based on John A. Byrne, "Is Your Company Too Big?" *Business Week,* 27 March 1989, 84–94.

perform complex tasks and to produce complex products. Moreover, large organizations, once established, can be a presence that stabilizes a market for years. Managers can join the company and expect a career reminiscent of the "organization men" of the 1950s and 1960s. The organization can provide longevity, raises, and promotions.

Small   The competing argument says small is beautiful because the crucial requirements for success in a global economy are responsiveness and flexibility in fast-changing markets. Huge investments are giving way to flexible manufacturing and niche marketing as the ways to succeed.

Recent research shows that the average size of industrial organizations is decreasing, not only in the United States but in Britain and Germany as well. Exhibit 5.2 reflects the decrease in the average number of employees per firm for the three countries. Small organizations have a flat structure and an organic, free-flowing management style that encourages entrepreneurship and innovation. Today's leading biotechnological drugs, for example, were all discovered by small firms, such as Chiron, which developed the hepatitis B vaccines, rather than by huge pharmaceu-

Exhibit 5.2
Average Size of Industrial Firms in Three Countries.

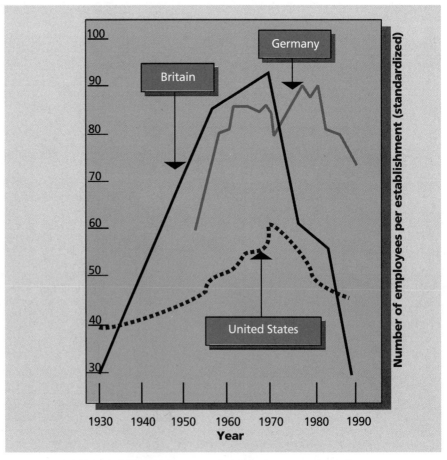

Source: Tom Peters, "Rethinking Scale," *California Management Review* (Fall 1992): 7–29. Used with permission.

tical companies, such as Merck.[11] Moreover, the personal involvement of employees in small firms encourages motivation and commitment because employees personally identify with the company's mission.

Big-Company/Small-Company Hybrid   The paradox is that the advantages of small companies enable them to succeed and, hence, grow large. *Fortune* magazine reported that the fastest growing companies in America are small firms characterized by an emphasis on putting the customer first and being fast and flexible in responding to the environment.[12] But small companies can become victims of their own success as they grow large, shifting to a mechanistic structure emphasizing vertical hierarchies and spawning "organization men" rather than entrepreneurs. The solution is what Jack Welch, chairman of General Electric, calls the "big-company/small-company hybrid" that combines a large corporation's resources and reach with a small company's simplicity and flexibility. This approach is being taken seriously by many large companies, including Johnson & Johnson, Hewlett-Packard, AT&T, and even General Motors. These companies have all undergone massive reorganizations into groups of small companies to capture the mind-set and advantages of smallness. The $14 billion giant Johnson & Johnson is actually a group of 168 separate companies. When a new product is created in one of J&J's fifty-six labs, a new company is created along with it.[13] Microsoft, the software company, was recently split from five units into fifteen, each no larger than two hundred people. Chairman Bill Gates uses electronic mail to allow people throughout the organization to go straight to the top for answers.[14] One of the best examples of the shift to a hybrid form is Carrier Corporation, described in the Paradigm Buster.

A full-service, global firm needs a strong resource base and sufficient complexity and hierarchy to serve clients around the world. A large company can achieve a sense of smallness by reducing the number of middle managers, cutting several layers from the hierarchy, and even reducing size substantially, such as General Electric's reduction in work force by more than 25 percent (150,000 employees).[15]

Organization Size and Bureaucracy

The concept of bureaucracy started out as an extraordinarily successful way to organize. Max Weber, a sociologist who studied government organizations in Europe, developed a framework of administrative characteristics that would make large organizations rational and efficient.[16] Weber wanted to understand how organizations could be designed to play a positive role in the larger society.

WHAT IS BUREAUCRACY?

Weber believed **bureaucracy** could assist organizations. He proposed a set of organizational characteristics that would ensure efficient functioning in both government and business settings. He identified the six characteristics in Exhibit 5.3 that could be found in successful bureaucratic organizations.

Rules and standard procedures enabled organizational activities to be performed in a predictable, routine manner. Specialized duties meant that each employee had a clear task to perform. Hierarchy of authority provided a sensible

Paradigm Buster

Carrier Corporation

Imagine walking into a factory that's as clean and quiet as a research center. Imagine having to complete a tough, six-week training course before even being *considered* for a job there. And then, imagine you actually get a job on the shop floor and you end up interviewing applicants who could be your boss! What's going on here?

As strange as it may seem compared to the mass production factories of the past, the Carrier Corporation plant in Arkadelphia, Arkansas, may be the model for America's future factories. The plant was built because Carrier realized that to stay competitive, it had to make its own compressors for air conditioners. But the company already knew the huge factories it had built in the 1970s and 1980s, with their big costs, layers of management, and inflexible production lines, were money-losers. So it turned in a new direction, and the streamlined Arkadelphia model was born.

The highly automated plant employs only 150 workers, and each is trained in a variety of jobs so they can fill in for one another when necessary. Assembly-line workers have amazing autonomy. They don't punch a time clock, and they don't have to follow strict, inflexible rules regarding sick leave and other matters. One group recently rearranged a series of machines for increased efficiency after clearing it only with their immediate supervisor, rather than having to go through layers of management and then waiting for maintenance staff to do the job. Assembly-line workers can even order needed supplies without management approval.

Getting a job at Carrier's Arkadelphia plant isn't easy, but those who get one exercise a level of authority unheard of in traditional factories. Assembly-line workers even have a chance to influence future hiring decisions—they participate in interviewing all job applicants, even those who could end up being their boss.

Carrier's model plant is making compressors that cost less and are of higher quality than those produced by the old-style mass production factories. Carrier executives are confident that the plant will keep the company competitive in today's global environment.

Source: Erle Norton, "Small, Flexible Plants May Play Crucial Role in U.S. Manufacturing," *Wall Street Journal*, 13 January 1993, A1, A8.

---

mechanism for supervision and control. Technical competence was the basis by which people were hired rather than friendship, family ties, and favoritism that dramatically reduced work performance. The separation of the position from the position holder meant that individuals did not own or have an inherent right to the job, thus promoting efficiency. Written records provided an organizational memory and continuity over time.

Although bureaucratic characteristics carried to an extreme are widely criticized today, the rational control introduced by Weber was a significant idea and a new form of organization. Bureaucracy provided many advantages over organization forms based upon favoritism, social status, family connections, or graft, which are often unfair. For example, in Mexico, a retired American lawyer had to pay a five hundred-dollar bribe to purchase a telephone, then discovered that a government official had sold his telephone number to another family. In China, the tradition of giving government posts to relatives is widespread even under communism. China's emerging class of educated people doesn't like seeing the best jobs going to children and relatives of officials.[17] By comparison, the logical and rational form of organi-

Bureaucracy	Legitimate Bases of Authority
1. Rules and procedures 2. Specialization and division of labor 3. Hierarchy of authority 4. Technically qualified personnel 5. Separate position and incumbent 6. Written communications and records	1. Rational-legal 2. Traditional 3. Charismatic

Exhibit 5.3
Weber's Dimensions of Bureaucracy and Bases of Organizational Authority.

zation described by Weber allows work to be conducted efficiently and in society's best interest.

BASES OF AUTHORITY

The ability of an organization to function efficiently depends upon its authority structure. Proper authority provides managers with the control needed to make the bureaucratic form of organization work. Weber argued that legitimate, rational authority was preferred over other types of control (for example, payoffs or favoritism) as the basis for internal decisions and activities. Within the larger society, however, Weber identified three types of authority that could explain the creation and control of a large organization.[18]

1. **Rational-legal authority** is based on employees' beliefs in the legality of rules and the right of those elevated to authority to issue commands. Rational-legal authority is the basis for both creation and control of most government organizations and is the most common base of control in organizations worldwide.
2. **Traditional authority** is the belief in traditions and in the legitimacy of the status of people exercising authority through those traditions. Traditional authority is the basis for control for monarchies and churches and for some organizations in Latin America and the Persian Gulf.
3. **Charismatic authority** is based upon devotion to the exemplary character or to the heroism of an individual person and the order defined by him or her. Revolutionary military organizations are often based on the leader's charisma, as are North American organizations led by charismatic individuals such as Lee Iacocca or Jack Welch.

   More than one type of authority—such as long tradition and the leader's special charisma—may exist in today's organizations, but *rational-legal authority* is the most widely used form to govern internal work activities and decision making, especially in large organizations.

Size and Structural Characteristics

In the field of organizational theory, organization size has been described as an important variable that influences structural design. Should an organization become more bureaucratic as it grows larger? In what size organizations are bureaucratic characteristics most appropriate? More than one hundred studies have attempted to answer these questions.[19] Most of these studies indicate that large organizations are different from small organizations along several dimensions of bureaucratic structure, including formalization, centralization, complexity, and personnel ratios.

FORMALIZATION

Formalization, as described in Chapter 1, refers to rules, procedures, and written documentation, such as policy manuals and job descriptions, that prescribe the rights and duties of employees.[20] The evidence supports the conclusion that large organizations are more formalized. The reason is that large organizations rely on rules, procedures, and paperwork to achieve standardization and control across their large numbers of employees and departments, whereas top managers can use personal observation to control a small organization.[21] In large firms like US West, Bank of America, and GTE, formal procedures allow top administrators to extend their reach, and rules are established to take the place of personal surveillance for such matters as sexual harassment, smoking bans, and flexible work hours.

DECENTRALIZATION

Centralization refers to the level of hierarchy with authority to make decisions. In centralized organizations, decisions tend to be made at the top. In decentralized organizations, similar decisions would be made at a lower level.

Decentralization represents a paradox because, in the perfect bureaucracy, all decisions would be made by the top administrator, who would have perfect control. However, as an organization grows larger and has more people and departments, decisions cannot be passed to the top, or senior managers would be overloaded. Thus, the research on organization size indicates that larger organizations (for example, Campbell Soup Company and American Airlines) permit greater decentralization.[22] CEO Mike Quinlan of McDonald's pushes decisions as far down the hierarchy as he can; otherwise, McDonald's decision making would be too slow. Moreover, McDonald's has many rules that define boundaries within which decisions can be made, thereby facilitating decentralization.

COMPLEXITY

As discussed in Chapter 1, **complexity** refers to both the number of levels in the hierarchy (vertical complexity) and the number of departments or jobs (horizontal complexity). Large organizations show a definite pattern of greater complexity.[23] The explanation for the relationship between size and complexity is straightforward. First, the need for additional specialties occurs more often in large organizations. For example, a study of new departments reported that new administrative departments were often created in response to problems of large size.[24] A planning department was established in a large organization because a greater need for planning arose after a certain size was reached. Second, as departments within the organization grow in size, pressure to subdivide arises. Departments eventually get so large that managers cannot control them effectively. At this point, subgroups will lobby to be subdivided into separate departments.[25]

Finally, vertical complexity traditionally has been needed to maintain control over a large number of people. As the number of employees increases, additional levels of hierarchy keep spans of control from becoming too large.

As we discussed earlier in this chapter, many large corporations are fighting against the effects of size by simplifying, reducing rules, and pushing decisions to even lower levels. However, bureaucratic characteristics can have positive impact on many firms. One of the most efficient large corporations in the United States and Canada is UPS, often called the Brown Giant for the color of packages it delivers and the trucks that deliver them. In Chapter 4, UPS's paradigm shift into new technology was described. But how did UPS get to that point?

IN PRACTICE ◆ 5.1
United Parcel Service

United Parcel Service took on the U.S. Postal Service at its own game—and won. UPS specializes in the delivery of small packages. It can deliver a package anywhere in the United States for about three dollars. UPS sees itself in competition with the post office, so it sets prices below post office rates and still makes an excellent profit.

Why has the Brown Giant been so successful? Many efficiencies were realized through adoption of the bureaucratic model of organization. UPS was bound up in rules and regulations, and most still apply. There are safety rules for drivers, loaders, clerks, and managers. Strict dress codes are enforced—no beards, hair cannot touch the collar, no sideburns, mustaches must be trimmed evenly and cannot go below the corner of the mouth, and so on. Rules specify the cleanliness of buildings and property. All sixty thousand UPS delivery trucks must be washed inside and out at the end of every day. Each manager is given bound copies of policy books with the expectation that they will be used regularly. Jobs are broken down into a complex division of labor, including those of drivers, loaders, clerks, washers, sorters, and maintenance personnel. Each task is calibrated according to productivity standards. The hierarchy of authority is clearly defined and has eight levels, extending from a washer at the local UPS plant up to the president of the national organization. Drivers often are expected to make fifteen deliveries or pickups an hour, no matter what.

Technical qualification is the criterion for hiring and promotion. The UPS policy book says, "A leader does not have to remind others of authority by use of a title. Knowledge, performance, and capacity should be adequate evidence of position and leadership." Favoritism is forbidden. Moreover, UPS thrives on records. Daily worksheets specify performance goals and work outputs for every employee and department. New technology facilitates record keeping.

Another key to the Brown Giant's success is that, despite its huge size, it has never become impersonal to employees. Everyone is on a first-name basis. No one, not even the chairman, has a private secretary. Top executives started at the bottom, and they still do their own photocopying. The drivers are the real heroes of the company. "Once the employees work into supervisory positions, they receive stock and become owners. Employees care about this company and its customers."[26]

UPS illustrates how bureaucratic characteristics increase with large size. UPS is so productive and dependable that it dominates the small-package delivery market, with more business than even the U.S. Postal Service. Its recent culture change to a more flexible approach has endeared UPS even more to its customers.

PERSONNEL RATIOS

The next characteristic of bureaucracy is **personnel ratios** for administrative, cleri-cal, and professional support staff. The most frequently studied ratio is the adminis-trative ratio. In 1957, C. Northcote Parkinson published *Parkinson's Law,* which argued that work expands to fill the time available for its completion. Parkinson sug-gested that administrators were motivated to add more administrators for a variety of reasons, including the enhancement of their own status through empire building. Parkinson used his argument, called **Parkinson's law,** to make fun of the British Admiralty. During a fourteen-year period from 1914 to 1928, the officer corps increased by 78 percent, although the total navy personnel decreased by 32 percent and the number of warships in use decreased by approximately 68 percent.[27]

In the years since Parkinson's book, the administrative ratio has been studied in school systems, churches, hospitals, employment agencies, and other business and voluntary organizations.[28] Two patterns have emerged.

The first pattern is that the ratio of top administration to total employment is actually smaller in large organizations.[29] This is the opposite of Parkinson's argu-ment and indicates that organizations experience administrative economies as they grow larger. Large organizations have large departments, more regulations, and a greater division of labor. These mechanisms require less supervision from the top. Increasing bureaucratization is a substitute for personal supervision from the admin-istrators.

The second pattern concerns other staff support ratios. Recent studies have subdivided support personnel into subclassifications, such as clerical and profes-sional staff.[30] These support groups tend to increase in proportion to organization size. The clerical ratio increases because of the greater communication (memos, let-ters) and paperwork requirements (policy manuals, job descriptions) in large orga-nizations. The professional staff ratio increases because of the greater need for spe-cialized skills in complex organizations. In a small organization, an individual may be a jack-of-all-trades. In a large organization, people are assigned full time to sup-port activities to help make production employees more efficient.

Exhibit 5.4 illustrates administrative and support ratios for small and large organizations. As organizations increase in size, the administrative ratio declines and the ratios for other support groups increase.[31] The net effect for direct workers is that they decline as a percentage of total employees. Recent studies show that cor-porate America in general needs to reduce its overhead costs to remain competitive. One survey revealed that overhead for U.S. manufacturers equaled 26 percent of sales, compared to 21 percent for Western Europe and only 18 percent for Japan. Yet studies also show that cutting out layers of support staff without first examining and overhauling inefficient processes throughout the organization may be detrimental to the productivity and economic health of the organization.[32]

An interesting pattern emerges from recent research on organizations during periods of growth and decline. In rapidly growing organizations, administrators grow faster than line employees; in declining organizations, they decline more slow-ly. This implies that administrative and staff personnel often are the first hired and last fired.[33] For example, when the University of Michigan was undergoing rapid growth, faculty increased by 7 percent, but professional nonfaculty employees increased by 26 percent, and executive, administrative, and managerial employees increased by 40 percent.[34] If the University of Michigan should suddenly decline

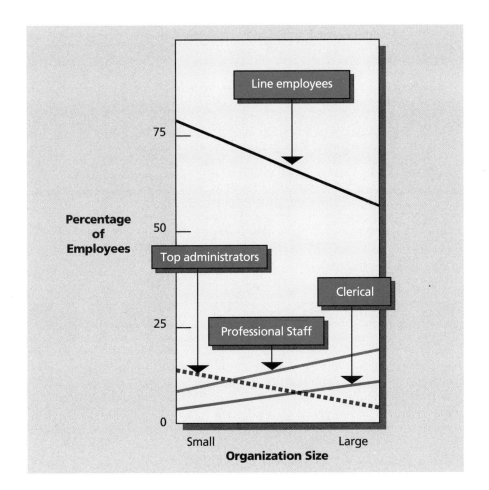

Exhibit 5.4
Percentage of
Personnel
Allocated to
Administrative
and Support
Activities.

rapidly, the administration may decline more slowly than professional and faculty employees.

In summary, top administrators typically do not comprise a disproportionate number of employees in large organizations; in fact, they are a smaller percentage of total employment. However, the idea that proportionately greater overhead is required in large organizations is supported. The number of people in clerical and professional departments increases at a faster rate than does the number of people who work in the technical core of a growing organization.

The differences between small and large organizations are summarized in Exhibit 5.5. Large organizations have many characteristics that distinguish them from small organizations: more rules and regulations; more paperwork, written communication, and documentation; greater specialization; more decentralization; a lower percentage of people devoted to top administration; and a larger percentage of people allocated to clerical, maintenance, and professional support staff.

However, size by itself does not cause these organizational characteristics. Recall from previous chapters that goals, environment, and technology also influence structure. For example, an organization operating in a complex environment will need additional departments, and a changing environment creates the need for

Exhibit 5.5
Relationship
between Size
and Other
Organization
Characteristics.

Greater organization size is associated with:

1. Increased number of management levels (vertical complexity)
2. Greater number of jobs and departments (horizontal complexity)
3. Increased specialization of skills and functions
4. Greater formalization
5. Greater decentralization
6. Smaller percentage of top administrators
7. Greater percentage of technical and professional support staff
8. Greater percentage of clerical and maintenance support staff
9. Greater amount of written communications and documentation

less formalization. Thus, while large organizations will appear different from small organizations, these relationships are not rigid. The impact of other contextual variables can modify bureaucratic structure.

Bureaucracy under Attack

The world is rapidly changing. With global competition and uncertain environments, many organizations are fighting against increasing complexity and professional staff ratios. The problems caused by large bureaucracies have perhaps nowhere been more evident than in the U.S. government. From the bureaucratic obstacles to providing emergency relief following Hurricane Andrew to the bungling by the U.S. Marshal's Service that put a convicted drug kingpin back on the streets, such actions by federal government agencies show how excessive bureaucracy can impede the effectiveness and productivity of organizations.[35] Book Mark 5.0 discusses the problems of the bureaucratic model and describes how organizations can shift to a new paradigm to be more flexible, innovative, and responsive to customers.

Companies like Burlington Northern, Dana, and Hanson Industries have thirty-five to forty thousand employees and fewer than one hundred staff people working at headquarters. Aluminum Company of America (Alcoa) is cutting out two levels of top management, along with about two dozen headquarters staff jobs, giving business-unit managers unprecedented decision-making authority. The point is to not overload headquarters with accountants, lawyers, and financial analysts who will inhibit the autonomy and flexibility of divisions.[36] When Jack Welch laid off more than 100,000 employees during his tenure at General Electric, many of those affected were middle managers, senior managers, and staff professionals. Of course, many companies must be large to have sufficient resources and complexity to produce products for a global environment; but companies such as Johnson & Johnson, Wal-Mart, 3M, Coca-Cola, Emerson Electric, and Heinz are striving toward greater decentralization and leanness.

Another attack on bureaucracy is from the increasing professionalism of employees. Professionalism was defined in Chapter 1 as the length of formal training and experience of employees. More employees need college degrees, MBAs, and other professional degrees to work as attorneys, researchers, or doctors at General Motors, K Mart, and Bristol-Myers Squibb Company. Studies of professionals show that formalization is not needed because professional training regularizes a high

BOOKMARK
5.0

HAVE YOU READ ABOUT THIS?

Busting Bureaucracy
by Kenneth Johnson

- Bureaucracy and communism are two models for organizing enterprises that sound good on paper, but produce really rotten results.
- The single greatest cause for the failure of communism was its organization based on the bureaucratic model, thus creating suffocating and immobilizing bureaucracies.
- Bureaucracy has killed communism, it has socialism in a death grip, and it is suffocating and immobilizing every capitalistic organization that adopts its false promises.

With these three "outrageous statements," Kenneth Johnson contends that the bureaucratic model is the villain that causes organizations to fail to deliver satisfaction to their customers and employees. Bureaucracies stymie action and improvement. Bureaucrats avert accountability. Customers and workers suffer dissatisfaction.

Johnson proposes to replace the bureaucratic paradigm with one called the "mission-driven" organization. Organizations that adopt the new model will be "flexible, responsive, innovative, and have 'customer friendly' policies, practices, and procedures."

The Mission-Driven Model

Johnson recommends replacing the bureaucratic form with the mission-driven model. The characteristics of a mission-driven organization are:

- A customer focused mission (e.g. providing a first quality product or an extraordinary service).
- Performance measurements based on customer satisfaction.
- A reoriented hierarchy in which: Senior management articulates vision and strategy, middle managers empower teams and remove obstacles, and everyone else is organized into cross-functional teams.
- Decision making is devolved to those with appropriate skills and training, not by management rank.
- Attention is paid to the individual needs of customers and employees.
- Hiring is based on human as well as technical and business skills.

- Job security depends on mission achievement.

Over time, the teams will evolve into completely self-directed groups, responsible for their own goals, strategies, and vision. When that happens, the traditional bureaucracy will be displaced.

However, replacing bureaucracy with a mission-driven organization should be viewed as a never-ending process. A firm does not simply get rid of the bureaucratic form. Customer satisfaction is an ever-shifting target. The mission-driven firm will follow a strategy of continuous improvement to replace bureaucracy.

Getting There

Johnson describes the change process. He recommends assigning people to a "shadow organization" to spearhead and manage the changes. The shadow organization provides planning and goal definition, continuous customer feedback, assistance from outside experts, and extensive training of all personnel. Among the most important things to teach all workers is what Johnson calls the new "social compact":

> In a service economy, we take turns serving each other. When it's our turn to serve, we give the customer the deference, the respect and the dignity that customers deserve. When it's our turn to be served, we can then expect, and even insist on, the deference, the respect and the dignity that we deserve.

Conclusion

Busting Bureaucracy is a simple but compelling guide to the nature and deficiencies of the bureaucratic model and to the benefits of and transition to the new mission-driven model. The book hammers home the essence of successful businesses in a world of intense global competition: Unrestrained commitment to customers and employees.

Busting Bureaucracy by Kenneth Johnson is published by Business One Irwin.

standard of behavior for employees that acts as a substitute for bureaucracy.[37] Professional employees should not be overwhelmed with bureaucracy, which will constrain their creativity to solve problems independently.

In addition, a form of organization called the *professional partnership* has emerged that is made up completely of professionals.[38] These organizations include medical practices, law firms, and consulting firms, such as Touche Ross and Price Waterhouse. The general findings concerning professional partnerships is that branches have substantial autonomy and decentralized authority to make necessary decisions. They work with a consensus orientation rather than top-down direction typical of traditional business and government organizations. Thus, the trend of increasing professionalism combined with rapidly changing environments is leading to less bureaucracy in corporate North America.

Organizational Life Cycle

STAGES OF LIFE CYCLE DEVELOPMENT

A useful way to think about organizational growth and change is provided by the concept of a **life cycle**,[39] which suggests that organizations are born, grow older, and eventually die. Organization structure, leadership style, and administrative systems follow a fairly predictable pattern through stages in the life cycle. Stages are sequential in nature and follow a natural progression.

Recent work on organizational life cycle suggests that four major stages characterize organizational development.[40] These stages are illustrated in Exhibit 5.6 along with the problems associated with transition to each stage. Growth is not easy. Each time an organization enters a new stage in the life cycle, it enters a whole new ballgame with a new set of rules for how the organization functions internally and how it relates to the external environment.[41]

1. Entrepreneurial Stage   When an organization is born, the emphasis is on creating a product and surviving in the marketplace. The founders are entrepreneurs, and they devote their full energies to the technical activities of production and marketing. The organization is informal and nonbureaucratic. The hours of work are long. Control is based on the owners' personal supervision. Growth is from a creative new product or service. Apple Computer was in the **entrepreneurial stage** when it was created by Steven Jobs and Stephen Wozniak in Wozniak's parents' garage. Software companies like Microsoft and Lotus Development were in the entrepreneurial stage when their original software programs were written and marketed.

> Crisis: Need for Leadership. As the organization starts to grow, the larger number of employees causes problems. The creative and technically oriented owners are confronted with management issues, but they may prefer to focus their energies on making and selling the product or inventing new products and services. At this time of crisis, entrepreneurs must either adjust the structure of the organization to accommodate continued growth or else bring in strong managers who can do so. When Apple began a period of rapid growth, A. C. Markkula was brought in as a leader because neither Jobs nor Wozniak was qualified or cared to manage the expanding company.

Exhibit 5.6   Organizational Life Cycle.

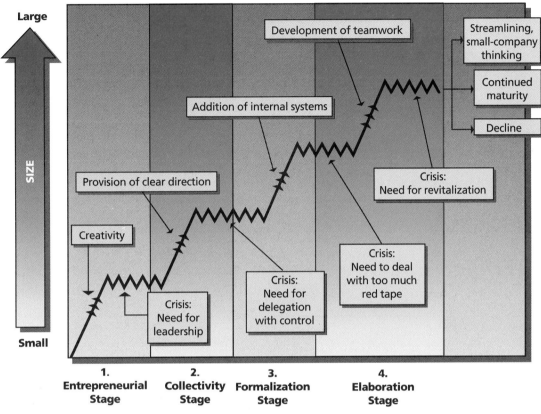

ORGANIZATION STAGES OF DEVELOPMENT

Source: Adapted from Robert E. Quinn and Kim Cameron, "Organizational Life Cycles and Shifting Criteria of Effectiveness: Some Preliminary Evidence," *Management Science* 29 (1983): 33–51; and Larry E. Greiner, "Evolution and Revolution as Organizations Grow," *Harvard Business Review* 50 (July–August 1972): 37–46.

2. Collectivity Stage   If the leadership crisis is resolved, strong leadership is obtained and the organization begins to develop clear goals and direction. Departments are established along with a hierarchy of authority, job assignments, and a beginning division of labor. Employees identify with the mission of the organization and spend long hours helping the organization succeed. Members feel part of a collective, and communication and control are mostly informal although a few formal systems begin to appear. Apple Computer was in the **collectivity stage** during the rapid growth years from 1978 to 1981. Employees threw themselves into the business as the major product line was established and more than two thousand dealers signed on.

> Crisis: Need for Delegation. If the new management has been successful, lower-level employees gradually find themselves restricted by the strong top-down leadership. Lower-level managers begin to acquire confidence in their own functional areas and want more discretion. An autonomy crisis occurs when top managers, who were successful because of their strong leadership and vision, do not want to give up responsibility. Top managers want to

make sure that all parts of the organization are coordinated and pulling together. The organization needs to find mechanisms to control and coordinate departments without direct supervision from the top.

3. Formalization Stage   The **formalization stage** involves the installation and use of rules, procedures, and control systems. Communication is less frequent and more formal. Engineers, personnel specialists, and other staff may be added. Top management becomes concerned with issues such as strategy and planning, and leaves the operations of the firm to middle management. Product groups or other decentralized units may be formed to improve coordination. Incentive systems based upon profits may be implemented to ensure that managers work toward what is best for the overall company. When effective, the new coordination and control systems enable the organization to continue growing by establishing linkage mechanisms between top management and field units. Apple Computer was in the formalization stage in the mid-1980s.

> Crisis: Too Much Red Tape. At this point in the organization's development, the proliferation of systems and programs may begin to strangle middle-level executives. The organization seems bureaucratized. Middle management may resent the intrusion of staff people. Innovation may be restricted. The organization seems too large and complex to be managed through formal programs. It was at this stage of Apple's growth that Jobs resigned from the company and CEO John Sculley took full control to face his own management challenges.[42]

4. Elaboration Stage   The solution to the red tape crisis is a new sense of collaboration and teamwork. Throughout the organization, managers develop skills for confronting problems and working together. Bureaucracy may have reached its limit. Social control and self-discipline reduce the need for additional formal controls. Managers learn to work within the bureaucracy without adding to it. Formal systems may be simplified and replaced by manager teams and task forces. To achieve collaboration, teams are often formed across functions or divisions of the company. The organization may also be split into multiple divisions to maintain a small-company philosophy. As described earlier in the chapter, Bill Gates divided Microsoft into divisions of no more than two hundred people. Apple Computer is currently in the **elaboration stage** of the life cycle, as are such large companies as Caterpillar and Motorola.

> Crisis: Need for Revitalization. After the organization reaches maturity, it may enter periods of temporary decline.[43] A need for renewal may occur every ten to twenty years. The organization shifts out of alignment with the environment or perhaps becomes slow moving and overbureaucratized and must go through a stage of streamlining and innovation. Top managers are often replaced during this period. At Apple, CEO Sculley recently resigned and turned over the reins to Michael Spindler.

Apple went through a needed streamlining in 1985 and further reorganization in 1990, but Spindler will be leading the company through its most difficult transition yet, as Apple faces the simultaneous needs for innovative new products and major cost-cutting to remain competitive. Organizations need bold leadership to face the crisis at this stage of the life cycle and move forward into a new era. If mature organizations do not go through periodic revitalizations, they will decline, as shown in the last stage of Exhibit 5.6.

Summary Eighty-four percent of businesses that make it past the first year still fail within five years because they can't make the transition from the entrepreneurial stage.[44] And the transitions become even more difficult as organizations progress through future stages of the life cycle. Organizations that do not successfully resolve the problems associated with these transitions are restricted in their growth and may even fail. From within an organization, the life cycle crises are very real, as illustrated by RailTex Service Company.

IN PRACTICE ◆ 5.2
RailTex Service Company

In the late 1970s, Bruce Flohr raised $500,000 and started RailTex Service Company, leasing open-top freight cars to quarry operators to haul rock, sand, and gravel for construction sites. When recession hit in 1982, Flohr and his ten employees survived by serving as consultants for short-line railroads. This proved to be a turning point for RailTex, and by 1989, the company owned or leased nine of these "feeder" lines around the country.

As hundreds of these lines came on the market, Bruce Flohr bet the company's future entirely on the short-line business. Financially, there was no doubt he'd done the right thing; revenues surged from $16.5 million to $38 million in three years. The company moved from its cramped start-up quarters into larger and fancier offices. But Flohr was smart enough to see that the enormous growth of RailTex could outdistance his ability to manage the company. So he set up each RailTex short line as a separately incorporated entity much like a franchise, giving total authority to line managers for everything from local personnel decisions to setting shipping prices. The role of headquarters is not to manage the lines, but to set direction within which local decisions can be made, enabling RailTex to move through a potential leadership crisis.

Unlike many entrepreneurs, Bruce Flohr realizes that the people and procedures needed to start and manage a small company have to grow as the company grows. He has created a decentralized structure for RailTex to avoid creating a cumbersome bureaucracy.

RailTex has successfully made it through the first two stages to the formalization stage in its life cycle. It was recently voted "Short Line Railroad of the Year" by *Railway Age* magazine. But the company continues to grow, and Bruce Flohr will face new challenges. The management system he has instituted should ensure that RailTex can keep rolling for a long time.[45]

ORGANIZATIONAL CHARACTERISTICS DURING THE LIFE CYCLE

As organizations evolve through the four stages of the life cycle, changes take place in structure, control systems, innovation, and goals. The organizational characteristics associated with each stage are summarized in Exhibit 5.7.

Exhibit 5.7   Organization Characteristics during Four Stages of Life Cycle.

Characteristic	1. Entrepreneurial Nonbureaucratic	2. Collectivity Prebureaucratic	3. Formalization Bureaucratic	4. Elaboration Very Bureaucratic
Structure	Informal, one-person show	Mostly informal, some procedures	Formal procedures, division of labor, new specialties added	Teamwork within bureaucracy, small-company thinking
Products or services	Single product or service	Major product or service, with variations	Line of products or services	Multiple product or service lines
Reward and control systems	Personal, paternalistic	Personal, contribution to success	Impersonal, formalized systems	Extensive, tailored to product and department
Innovation	By owner-manager	By employees and managers	By separate innovation group	By institutionalized R&D
Goal	Survival	Growth	Internal stability, market expansion	Reputation, complete organization
Top management style	Individualistic, entrepreneurial	Charismatic, direction-giving	Delegation with control	Team approach, attack bureaucracy

Source: Adapted from Larry E. Greiner, "Evolution and Revolution as Organizations Grow," *Harvard Business Review* 50 (July–August 1972): 37–46; G. L. Lippitt and W. H. Schmidt, "Crises in a Developing Organization," *Harvard Business Review* 45 (November–December 1967): 102–12; B. R. Scott, "The Industrial State: Old Myths and New Realities," *Harvard Business Review* 51 (March–April 1973): 133–48; Robert E. Quinn and Kim Cameron, "Organizational Life Cycles and Shifting Criteria of Effectiveness," *Management Science* 29 (1983): 33–51.

Entrepreneurial   Initially, the organization is small, nonbureaucratic, and a one-person show. The top manager provides the structure and control system. Organizational energy is devoted toward survival and the production of a single product or service.

Collectivity   This is the organization's youth. Growth is rapid, and employees are excited and committed to the organization's mission. The structure is still mostly informal, although some procedures are emerging. Strong charismatic leaders like Bill Gates of Microsoft or Michael Dell of Dell Computer Corporation provide direction and goals for the organization. Continued growth is a major goal.

Formalization   At this point, the organization is entering midlife. Bureaucratic characteristics emerge. The organization adds staff support groups, formalizes procedures, and establishes a clear hierarchy and division of labor. Innovation may be achieved by establishing a separate research and development department. Major goals are internal stability and market expansion. Top management has to delegate, but it also implements formal control systems. The organization may develop complementary products to offer a complete product line.

Elaboration The mature organization is large and bureaucratic, with extensive control systems, rules, and procedures. Organization managers attempt to develop a team orientation within the bureaucracy to prevent further bureaucratization. Top managers are concerned with establishing a complete organization. Organizational stature and reputation are important. Innovation is institutionalized through an R&D department. Management may attack the bureaucracy and streamline it.

Summary Growing organizations move through stages of a life cycle, and each stage is associated with specific characteristics of structure, control systems, goals, and innovation. The life cycle phenomenon is a powerful concept used for understanding problems facing organizations and how managers can respond in a positive way to move an organization to the next stage.

Organizational Decline and Downsizing

One reality facing leaders of today's organizations is that continual growth and expansion may not be possible. All around us we see evidence that some organizations have had to stop growing, and many are declining. Schools have decreasing enrollments, churches have closed their doors, municipal services have been curtailed, and industries have closed plants and laid off employees.[46]

In this section, we will examine the causes of decline and how leaders can effectively manage the downsizing associated with it.

DEFINITION AND CAUSES

The term **organizational decline** is defined as a condition in which a substantial, absolute decrease in an organization's resource base occurs over a period of time.[47] Organizational decline is often associated with environmental decline in the sense that an organizational domain experiences either a reduction in size (such as shrinkage in customer demand or erosion of a city's tax base) or a reduction in shape (for example, shift in consumer demand). In general, three factors are considered to cause organization decline:

1. *Organizational Atrophy.* Atrophy occurs when organizations grow older, become inefficient and overly bureaucratic, and lose muscle tone. The organization's ability to adapt to its environment deteriorates. Often atrophy follows success because an organization takes success for granted and no longer has a sharp edge. Warning signals for organizational atrophy include excess staff personnel, cumbersome administrative procedures, lack of effective communication and coordination, and outdated organization structure.[48]

2. *Vulnerability.* Vulnerability reflects an organization's strategic inability to prosper in its environment. This often happens to small organizations that are not yet fully established. They are vulnerable to shifts in consumer tastes or in the economic health of the larger community. Some organizations are vulnerable because they are unable to define the correct strategy to fit the environment. Vulnerable

organizations typically need to redefine their environmental domain to enter new industries and markets.

3. *Environmental Decline.*   Environmental decline refers to reduced energy and resources available to support an organization. When the environment has less capacity to support organizations, the organization has to either scale down operations or shift to another domain.[49] This circumstance is faced by organizations in a stagnating economy. For example, banks, real estate firms, oil service firms, and many other organizations found the total resource base in the Southwest declining after oil prices dropped. Companies had to divide up a shrinking pie, so several of them inevitably declined.

A MODEL OF DECLINE STAGES

Based on an extensive review of organizational decline research, a model of decline stages has been proposed and is summarized in Exhibit 5.8. This model suggests that decline, if not managed properly, can move through five stages resulting in organizational dissolution.[50]

1. *Blinded Stage.*   The first stage of decline is the internal and external changes that threaten long-term survival and may require the organization to tighten up. The organization may have excess personnel, cumbersome procedures, or lack of har-

Exhibit 5.8
Stages of Decline and the Widening Performance Gap.

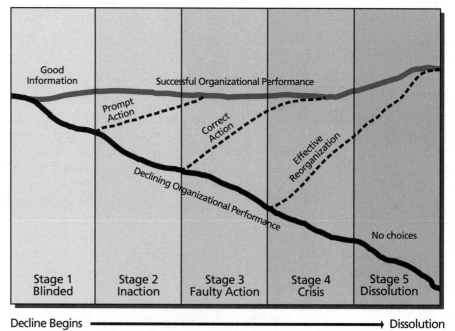

Source: Reprinted from "Decline in Organizations: A Literature Integration and Extension," by William Weitzel and Ellen Jonsson, published in *Administrative Science Quarterly,* Vol. 34 (1), March 1989, by permission of *Administrative Science Quarterly.*

mony with customers. Leaders often miss the signals of decline at this point, and the solution is to develop effective scanning and control systems that indicate when something is wrong. With timely information, alert leaders can bring the organization back to top performance.

2. *Inaction Stage.* The second stage of decline is called inaction, in which denial occurs despite signs of deteriorating performance. Leaders may try to persuade employees that all is well. Creative accounting may make things look well during this period. The solution is for leaders to recognize decline and take prompt action to realign the organization with the environment. Leadership actions can include new problem-solving approaches, increasing decision-making participation, and encouraging expression of dissatisfaction to learn what is wrong.

3. *Faulty Action.* In the third stage, the organization is facing serious problems, and indicators of poor performance cannot be ignored. Failure to adjust to the declining spiral at this point can lead to organizational failure. Leaders are forced by severe circumstances to consider major changes. Actions may involve retrenchment, including downsizing personnel. Leaders should reduce employee uncertainty by clarifying values and providing information. A major mistake at this stage decreases the organization's chance for a turnaround.

4. *The Crisis Stage.* In stage four, the organization still has not been able to deal with decline effectively and is facing a panic. The organization may experience chaos, efforts to go back to basics, sharp changes, and anger. It is best for an organization to prevent a stage-four crisis, and the only solution is major reorganization. The social fabric of the organization is eroding, and dramatic action, such as replacing top administrators, and revolutionary changes in structure, strategy, and culture, are necessary. Work force downsizing may be severe.

5. *Dissolution.* This stage of decline is irreversible. The organization is suffering loss of markets and reputation, the loss of its best personnel, and capital depletion. The only available strategy is to close down the organization in orderly fashion and reduce the separation trauma of employees.

The responsibility of alert leadership is to detect the signs of decline, acknowledge them, implement necessary action, and reverse course. Some of the most difficult decisions pertain to **downsizing**—laying off employees to whom commitments have been made.

DOWNSIZING IMPLEMENTATION

Downsizing has become a common practice in America's organizations and has affected hundreds of companies and millions of workers. For example, General Electric has cut its labor force by more than 150,000 since the early 1980s, and DuPont recently cut two layers of management and up to 25 percent of the employees in every department.[51] Downsizing has become such a part of the revitalization cycle of modern organizations that it is no longer considered only in connection with the decline and failure of organizations but as a routine part of management.[52]

When jobs are cut, managers must be prepared for conflict and decreased trust and morale. The following techniques can help smooth the downsizing process and ease the tensions for employees who leave as well as those who remain.[53]

1. *Communicate and overcommunicate.* Provide advance notice of layoffs with as much detailed information as possible. Even when managers are not certain about what's going to happen, they need to give employees periodic reports on

the company's standing. Otherwise, employees assume the worst, and morale decreases as stress increases. At the Kansas City drug company Marion Merrell Dow, managers held frequent "town meetings" following the layoff of 13 percent of the work force to explain the company's plan for fueling new growth.

2. *Allow employees to leave with dignity.* It is important that layoffs be handled appropriately and humanely; otherwise, employees sense that management does not value them as human beings. One communications company leaked the news of layoffs to the media before employees were told; thus, some people learned they were losing their jobs over the radio. This approach damaged the dignity of workers who left and the trust and morale of those who stayed. Employees should be allowed to say good-bye to coworkers and to express their sadness and anger. At Josten's Learning, maker of class rings and yearbooks, employees were urged on the day of layoffs to help dismissed colleagues clean out their desks and leave with dignity.[54]

3. *Provide assistance to displaced workers.* Workers who lose their jobs can be given severance pay and extended benefits. Outplacement assistance and additional training eases the trauma of layoffs and helps workers find new jobs. Raychem, a California plastics and electronics company, offers career development programs not only to those who have been laid off but also to employees who stay, reasoning that if the company can't guarantee its workers employment, it should at least help them become more employable.

4. *Use ceremonies to reduce anger and confusion.* Important changes in people's lives are usually marked by rites and ceremonies to recognize the transition from one stage to another. Ceremonies connected with layoffs allow employees who are leaving as well as those remaining to acknowledge their feelings of grief, anxiety, guilt, or anger and thus better cope with this major transition. When layoffs at R. R. Donnelley, the world's largest printing company, broke the company's long tradition of lifetime employment, one manager likened the process to experiencing a death. Donnelley now offers off-site training courses and lectures that are designed partially to let employees vent their emotions.

Even the best managed companies may face the need to lay off workers in today's volatile environment. For organizations in decline, layoffs are often a first step toward turnaround and rejuvenation. Positive results can be obtained only if downsizing is handled in a way that enables remaining organization members to increase productivity and efficiency.

Summary and Interpretation

The material covered in this chapter contains several important ideas about organizations. One is that bureaucratic characteristics, such as rules, division of labor, written records, hierarchy of authority, and impersonal procedures, become important as organizations grow large and complex. Bureaucracy is a logical form of organizing that lets firms use resources efficiently. However, in many large corporate and government organizations, bureaucracy has come under attack with attempts to decentralize authority, flatten organization structure, reduce rules and written records, and create a small-company mind-set. These companies are willing to trade economies of scale for responsive, adaptive organizations. Many companies are subdividing into small divisions to gain small-company advantages.

In large organizations, Parkinson's notion that top administrators build empires is not found. Greater support is required, however, from clerical and professional staff specialists in large organizations. This is a logical outcome of employee specialization and the division of labor. By dividing an organization's tasks and having specialists perform each part, the organization can become more efficient. Many organizations today need to reduce their overhead costs by cutting support personnel.

Organizations evolve through distinct life cycle stages as they grow and mature. Organization structure, internal systems, and management issues are different for each stage of development. Growth creates crises and revolutions along the way toward large size. A major task of managers is to guide the organization through the entrepreneurial, collectivity, formalization, and elaboration stages of development.

Organizations today are facing the reality that they cannot always continue to grow. Many organizations have stopped growing, and many are declining. One of the most difficult aspects is downsizing, or laying off employees. To smooth the downsizing process, managers can keep employees informed, allow those who are laid off to leave with dignity, provide assistance to displaced workers, and use ceremonies to reduce feelings of anger and grief during the transition.

In the final analysis, large organization size and accompanying bureaucracy have many advantages, but they also have shortcomings. Large size and bureaucratic characteristics are important but can impede an organization that must act as if it is small, is a professional partnership, or needs to survive in a rapidly changing environment.

KEY CONCEPTS

bureaucracy
charismatic authority
centralization
collectivity stage
complexity
downsizing
elaboration stage
entrepreneurial stage
formalization

formalization stage
life cycle
organizational decline
Parkinson's law
personnel ratios
rational-legal authority
reasons organizations grow
traditional authority

DISCUSSION QUESTIONS

1. Describe the three bases of authority identified by Weber. Is it possible for each of these types of authority to function at the same time within an organization?

2. Discuss the key differences between large and small organizations. Which kinds of organizations would be better off acting as large organizations, and which are best trying to act as big-company/small-company hybrids?

3. How would you define organization size? What problems can you identify with using number of employees as a measure of size?

4. The manager of a medium-sized manufacturing plant once said, "We can't compete on price with the small organizations because they have lower overhead costs." Based upon the discussion in this chapter, would you agree or disagree with that manager? Why?

5. Why do large organizations tend to be more formalized?

6. If you were managing a department of college professors, how might you structure the department differently than if you were managing a department of bookkeepers? Why?

7. Do you think everyone would like to work in the new Carrier Corporation Arkadelphia factory (discussed in the Paradigm Buster)? Would you? What type of employee would be best suited to a new factory like this versus a traditional mass production factory?

8. Apply the concept of life cycle to an organization with which you are familiar, such as a university or a local business. What stage is the organization in now? How did the organization handle or pass through its life cycle crises?

9. Discuss advantages and disadvantages of rules and regulations.

10. Should a "no-growth" philosophy of management be taught in business schools? Is a no-growth philosophy more realistic for today's economic conditions?

GUIDES TO ACTION

As an organization designer, keep these guides in mind:

1. Decide whether your organization should act like a large or small company. To the extent that economies of scale, global reach, and complexity are important, introduce greater bureaucratization as the organization increases in size. As it becomes necessary, add rules and regulations, written documentation, job specialization, technical competence in hiring and promotion, and decentralization.

2. If responsiveness, flexibility, simplicity, and niche finding are important, subdivide the organization into simple, autonomous divisions that have freedom and a small-company approach.

3. Grow when possible. With growth, you can provide opportunities for employee advancement and greater profitability and effectiveness. Apply new management systems and structural configurations at each stage of an organization's development. Interpret the needs of the growing organization and respond with the management and internal systems that will carry the organization through to the next stage of development.

4. Don't cut support personnel to reduce overhead without first examining inefficient processes throughout the organization. Unless tasks assigned to support personnel can be handled in other ways, cutting support staff can seriously damage the health of the organization.

5. When layoffs are necessary, handle them with care. Treat departing employees humanely. Give them plenty of notice, allow them to leave with dignity, and offer assistance, such as severance pay and job leads.

Consider these guides when analyzing the following cases.

Sunoco, Inc.*

CASE FOR ANALYSIS

Collin Swift was a maintenance worker in the Pine River Baker Industries' division of Sunoco. Swift, who serves as a volunteer emergency medical technician, was fired for leaving his maintenance job in response to an emergency call to help two victims of heart attack.

Swift left his job at 11:20 A.M. He did not tell a company supervisor or get a written slip acknowledging his sudden departure, as company rules require. As Swift explained, "When you're talking about a heart attack victim, you have four to six minutes to respond. I knew what I had to do." An elderly couple were having simultaneous heart attacks. "I thought someone's life was worth more than going through the ritual of hunting up a supervisor." Both heart attack victims survived.

Swift returned to work at 1 P.M. that day, and signed a return-to-work form. Three days later, he was dismissed. He had held the job for nearly eighteen years.

The dismissal of Swift is being challenged through a union grievance procedure. The industrial relations manager for Sunoco said in a statement:

". . .We do want to make it clear that our corporate and local practices are to encourage employees to be involved in civic activities. In fact, many of our employees are able to engage in such volunteer services and still abide by the plant rules that have been established."

QUESTIONS

1. Take Sunoco's point of view and explain why it is correct to apply bureaucratic regulations in this instance.
2. Take Swift's point of view and explain why this application of bureaucratic regulations is not a good thing for Sunoco.
3. How might Sunoco use rules and regulations to handle employees fairly and uniformly without creating this kind of incident?

Sears Roebuck & Company*

Many people believe large size is an advantage in the retail industry because of economies in purchasing and distribution; but look at the problems facing Sears, a retailer now considered bloated and elephantine.

Sears grew up in a stable retail environment and at one time was bigger in merchandise sales than its next four competitors combined. But Sears failed to

*Based on an Associated Press dispatch reported in *Inc.,* July 1986, 22.

*This case was based on Carol J. Loomis, "Dinosaurs?" *Fortune,* 3 May 1993, 36–42; William Weitzel and Ellen Jonsson, "Reversing the Downward Spiral: Lessons from W. T. Grant and Sears Roebuck," *Academy of Management Executive* 5 (1991): 7–22; Susan Caminiti, "Sears' Need: More Speed," *Fortune,* 15 July 1991, 86–90; Francine Schwadle, "Sears's Brennan Faces Facts about Costs," *Wall Street Journal,* 10 August 1990, B1; Kevin Kelly, "Can Ed Brennan Salvage the Sears He Designed?" *Business Week,* 27 August 1990, 34; Patricia Sellers, "Why Bigger Is Badder at Sears," *Fortune,* 5 December 1988, 79–84.

adapt as the environment changed. The giant retailer didn't take discounters like Wal-Mart and K Mart seriously, and the discount chains stole customers right out from under Sears's turned-up nose.

On Sears's other flank are trendy specialist stores such as Circuit City for electronics, Toys 'R' Us for children, Home Depot for hardware and appliances, the Limited and Gap for clothing, and discount warehouses such as Sam's and Price Costco. Within the whirlwind of this competition, Sears sits with 526,000 employees, a superb reputation as reflected in a survey of Americans, and sales that declined for several years while costs increased. Sears merchandising sales for 1992 were $32 billion, compared to $55 billion for Wal-Mart.

What's the problem? Most observers say bureaucracy. Sears has six thousand headquarters employees, compared with twenty-five hundred at Wal-Mart. Selling and administrative expenses take thirty cents of the sales dollar at Sears, compared with twenty-four cents at K Mart, twenty cents at Home Depot, and a mere seventeen cents at Wal-Mart. Sears is burdened with a labor-intensive, archaic distribution and warehousing system that alone soaks up 8 percent of the sales dollar, compared with 3 percent at Wal-Mart and K Mart. Despite the huge cost, Sears can't even track what is selling so slow-moving items can be replaced, as is done at Wal-Mart.

Even worse is the bureaucratic tar pit within which change gets mired. When Sears decided to reduce inventories on men's apparel from a twenty-two to an eight weeks' supply, items were boxed up but never returned to suppliers. Disagreement over who did what meant that the apparel sat in boxes until the next selling season. Or consider the power battles between headquarters buyers and store managers. Store managers may simply ignore new merchandise or a new promotion if it doesn't suit them. One senior executive tried to institute a bedding department with flashy quilts and sheets for yuppie tastes. The plan stalled through several layers of approval. Twelve stores agreed to participate as a test, but after huge delays, only four stores were left. Now the bedding idea is collecting dust along with the boxed men's apparel. As a former senior executive pointed out, the processes of how decisions were made took up so much time at Sears that there was little time to focus on what—or if—decisions were ever actually made.

Sears, now operating under Chairman Edward A. Brennan, is determined to change. Brennan has cut management positions, frozen the salaries of about twenty thousand other managers, and generally begun chopping away at the number of employees with a hatchet rather than a scalpel. He's brought Sears's retailing business back under the control of headquarters by creating closely controlled "superstores." Sears Superstores will have six central areas specializing in electronics, children's clothing, and so on, with the individual department managers reporting directly to headquarters rather than to the superstore manager. One important thing this has done is to give Sears something it amazingly never had before: a way to accurately measure the costs and profits for each store department.

Another Brennan idea is to close the fourteen regional offices to reduce bureaucracy and a layer of approval and thereby improve communication between headquarters and the stores.

Brennan hopes these steps, combined with recent innovations, such as everyday low pricing and the inclusion of name brands along with Kenmore and Craftsman, will attract a broader customer base and get Sears back on the right track.

An ironic event in this industry was the turnaround orchestrated at Montgomery Ward & Company by Bernard Brennan, Edward Brennan's brother, who slashed unproductive stores along with 20 percent of employees and dumped unprofitable merchandise lines. Ward's now acts responsively and efficiently to compete with discount stores and specialists. Can big brother Edward Brennan do the same for big brother Sears?

QUESTIONS

1. To what extent do you think the ideas proposed for change by Edward Brennan make sense? Discuss.
2. Is part of Sears's problem the life cycle? Are Sears and its new competitors in different stages of the life cycle? Is it inevitable that Sears be sluggish and slow-moving at this size and age? Discuss.
3. What ideas would you propose for making Sears more responsive and quick-footed? Where would you start to battle the bureaucracy?

NOTES

1. Larry Armstrong, "Nurturing an Employee's Brainchild," *Business Week/Enterprise,* 1993, 196; Brian Dumaine, "Bureaucracy Busters," *Fortune,* 17 June 1991, 36–50.
2. Richard A. Melcher, "How Goliaths Can Act Like Davids," *Business Week/Enterprise,* 1993, 192–201.
3. Kim S. Cameron, "Organizational Downsizing," in George P. Huber and William H. Glick, eds., *Organizational Change and Redesign* (New York: Oxford University Press, 1992).
4. James Q. Wilson, *Bureaucracy* (Basic Books: 1989).
5. Charles Perrow, *Complex Organizations: A Critical Essay* (Glenview, Ill.: Scott, Foresman, 1979), 4.
6. Tom Peters, "Rethinking Scale," *California Management Review* (Fall 1992): 7–29.
7. William H. Starbuck, "Organizational Growth and Development," in James March, ed., *Handbook of Organizations* (New York: Rand McNally, 1965), 451–522.
8. Ann M. Morrison, "A Big Baker That Won't Live by Bread Alone," *Fortune,* 7 September 1981, 70–76.
9. Starbuck, "Organizational Growth and Development"; John Child, *Organizations* (New York: Harper & Row, 1977), ch. 7.
10. James B. Treece, "Sometimes, You've Still Gotta Have Size," *Business Week/Enterprise,* 1993, 200–201.
11. Alan Deutschman, "America's Fastest Risers," *Fortune,* 7 October 1991, 46–57.
12. *Ibid.*
13. Melcher, "How Goliaths Can Act Like Davids."
14. Brian Dumaine, "Is Big Still Good?" *Fortune,* 20 April 1992, 50–60.
15. Wayne F. Cascio, "Downsizing: What Do We Know? What Have We Learned?" Academy of Management Executive 7 (1993): 95–104.
16. Max Weber, *The Theory of Social and Economic Organizations,* translated by A. M. Henderson and T. Parsons (New York: Free Press, 1947).
17. John Crewdson, "Corruption Viewed as a Way of Life," *Bryan-College Station Eagle,* 28 November 1982, 13A; Barry Kramer, "Chinese Officials Still Give Preference to Kin, Despite Peking Policies," *Wall Street Journal,* 29 October 1985, 1, 21.
18. Weber, *Theory of Social and Economic Organizations,* 328–40.
19. Allen C. Bluedorn, "Pilgrim's Progress: Trends and Convergence in Research on Organizational Size and Environment," *Journal of Management Studies* 19 (Summer 1993): 163–91; John R. Kimberly, "Organizational Size and the Structuralist Perspective: A Review, Critique, and Proposal," *Administrative Science Quarterly* (1976): 571–97; Richard L. Daft and Selwyn W. Becker, "Managerial, Institutional, and Technical Influences on Administration: A Longitudinal Analysis," *Social Forces* 59 (1980): 392–413.

20. James P. Walsh and Robert D. Dewar, "Formalization and the Organizational Life Cycle," *Journal of Management Studies* 24 (May 1987): 215–31.

21. Nancy M. Carter and Thomas L. Keon, "Specialization as a Multidimensional Construct," *Journal of Management Studies* 26 (1989): 11–28; Cheng-Kuang Hsu, Robert M. March, and Hiroshi Mannari, "An Examination of the Determinants of Organizational Structure," *American Journal of Sociology* 88 (1983): 975–96; Guy Geeraerts, "The Effect of Ownership on the Organization Structure in Small Firms," *Administrative Science Quarterly* 29 (1984): 232–37; Bernard Reimann, "On the Dimensions of Bureaucratic Structure: An Empirical Reappraisal," *Administrative Science Quarterly* 18 (1973): 462–76; Richard H. Hall, "The Concept of Bureaucracy: An Empirical Assessment," *American Journal of Sociology* 69 (1963): 32–40; William A. Rushing, "Organizational Rules and Surveillance: A Proposition in Comparative Organizational Analysis," *Administrative Science Quarterly* 10 (1966): 423–43.

22. Jerald Hage and Michael Aiken, "Relationship of Centralization to Other Structural Properties," *Administrative Science Quarterly* 12 (1967): 72–91.

23. Guy Geeraerts, "The Effect of Ownership on the Organization Structure in Small Firms"; Hsu, Marsh, and Mannari, "An Examination of the Determinants of Organizational Structure"; Robert Dewar and Jerald Hage, "Size, Technology, Complexity, and Structural Differentiation: Toward a Theoretical Synthesis," *Administrative Science Quarterly* 23 (1978): 111–36.

24. Richard L. Daft and Patricia J. Bradshaw, "The Process of Horizontal Differentiation: Two Models," *Administrative Science Quarterly* 25 (1980): 441–56.

25. Peter M. Blau, *The Organization of Academic Work* (New York: Wiley Interscience, 1973).

26. Kathy Goode, Betty Hahn, and Cindy Seibert, *United Parcel Service: The Brown Giant* (Unpublished manuscript, Texas A&M University, 1981); Kenneth Labich, "Big Changes at Big Brown," *Fortune*, 18 January 1988, 56–64; Chuck Hawkins with Patrick Oster, "After a U-Turn, UPS Really Delivers," *Business Week*, 31 May 1993, 92–93.

27. Peter Brimelow, "How Do You Cure Injelitance?" *Forbes*, 7 August 1989, 42–44.

28. Jeffrey D. Ford and John W. Slocum, Jr., "Size, Technology, Environment and the Structure of Organizations," *Academy of Management Review* 2 (1977): 561–75; John D. Kasarda, "The Structural Implications of Social System Size: A Three-Level Analysis," *American Sociological Review* 39 (1974): 19–28.

29. Graham Astley, "Organizational Size and Bureaucratic Structure," *Organization Studies* 6 (1985): 201–28; Spyros K. Lioukas and Demitris A. Xerokostas, "Size and Administrative Intensity in Organizational Divisions," *Management Science* 28 (1982): 854–68; Peter M. Blau, "Interdependence and Hierarchy in Organizations," *Social Science Research* 1 (1972): 1–24; Peter M. Blau and R. A. Schoenherr, *The Structure of Organizations* (New York: Basic Books, 1971); A. Hawley, W. Boland, and M. Boland, "Population Size and Administration in Institutions of Higher Education," *American Sociological Review* 30 (1965): 252–55; Richard L. Daft, "System Influence on Organization Decision-Making: The Case of Resource Allocation," *Academy of Management Journal* 21 (1978): 6–22; B. P. Indik, "The Relationship between Organization Size and the Supervisory Ratio," *Administrative Science Quarterly* 9 (1964): 301–12.

30. T. F. James, "The Administrative Component in Complex Organizations," *Sociological Quarterly* 13 (1972): 533–39; Daft, "System Influence on Organization Decision-Making"; E. A. Holdaway and E. A. Blowers, "Administrative Ratios and Organization Size: A Longitudinal Examination," *American Sociological Review* 36 (1971): 278–86; John Child, "Parkinson's Progress: Accounting for the Number of Specialists in Organizations," *Administrative Science Quarterly* 18 (1973): 328–48.

31. Richard L. Daft and Selwyn Becker, "School District Size and the Development of Personnel Resources," *Alberta Journal of Educational Research* 24 (1978): 173–87.

32. Thane Peterson, "Can Corporate America Get out from under Its Overhead?" *Business Week*, 18 May 1992, 102; Mark F. Blaxill and Thomas M. Hout, "The Fallacy of the Overhead Quick Fix," *Harvard Business Review* (July–August 1991): 93–101.

33. Robert M. Marsh and Hiroshi Mannari, "The Size Imperative? Longitudinal Tests," *Organization Studies* 10 (1989): 83–95.

34. Karen Grassmuck, "U-M's Work Force: A Growth Industry," *Ann Arbor (Mich.) News* 17 April 1989, A1, A4.

35. Bob Davis, "Federal Relief Agency Is Slowed by Infighting, Patronage, Regulations," *Wall Street Journal*, 31 August 1992, A1, A12; Paul M. Barrett, "Bureaucratic Bungling Helps Fugitives

Evade Capture by Feds," *Wall Street Journal, 7* August 1991, A1, A6.

36. Michael Schroder, "The Recasting of Alcoa," *Business Week,* 9 September 1991, 62–64; Thomas Moore, "Goodbye Corporate Staff," *Fortune,* 21 December 1987, 65–76.

37. Philip M. Padsakoff, Larry J. Williams, and William D. Todor, "Effects of Organizational Formalization on Alienation among Professionals and Nonprofessionals," *Academy of Management Journal* 29 (1986): 820–31.

38. Royston Greenwood, C. R. Hinings, and John Brown, "'P² Form' Strategic Management: Corporate Practices in Professional Partnerships," *Academy of Management Journal* 33 (1990): 725–55; Royston Greenwood and C. R. Hinings, "Understanding Strategic Change: The Contribution of Archtypes," *Academy of Management Journal* 36 (1993): 1052–81.

39. John R. Kimberly, Robert H. Miles, and Associates, *The Organizational Life Cycle* (San Francisco: Jossey-Bass, 1980); Ichak Adices, "Organizational Passages—Diagnosing and Treating Lifecycle Problems of Organizations," *Organizational Dynamics* (Summer 1979): 3–25; Danny Miller and Peter H. Friesen, "A Longitudinal Study of the Corporate Life Cycle," *Management Science* 30 (October 1984): 1161–83; Neil C. Churchill and Virginia L. Lewis, "The Five Stages of Small Business Growth," *Harvard Business Review* 61 (May–June 1983): 30–50.

40. Larry E. Greiner, "Evolution and Revolution as Organizations Grow," *Harvard Business Review* 50 (July–August 1972): 37–46; Robert E. Quinn and Kim Cameron, "Organizational Life Cycles and Shifting Criteria of Effectiveness: Some Preliminary Evidence," *Management Science* 29 (1983): 33–51.

41. George Land and Beth Jarman, "Moving beyond Breakpoint," in Michael Ray and Alan Rinzler, eds., *The New Paradigm* (New York: Jeremy P. Tarcher/Perigee Books, 1993), 250–66; Michael L. Tushman, William H. Newman, and Elaine Romanelli, "Convergence and Upheaval: Managing the Unsteady Pace of Organizational Evolution," *California Management Review* 29 (1987): 1–16.

42. Kathy Rebello with Russell Mitchell and Evan I. Schwartz, "Apple's Future," *Business Week,* 5 July 1993, 22–28.

43. David A. Whetten, "Sources, Responses, and Effects of Organizational Decline," in John R. Kimberly, Robert H. Miles, and Associates, *The*

Organizational Life Cycle (San Francisco: Jossey-Bass, 1980), 342–74.

44. George Land and Beth Jarman, "Moving Beyond Breakpoint."

45. Jay Finegan, "The Continuously Improving CEO," *Inc.*, February 1993, 72–81.

46. Whetten, "Sources, Responses, and Effects of Organizational Decline"; David A. Whetten, "Organizational Decline: A Neglected Topic in Organizational Science," *Academy of Management Review* 5 (1980): 577–88.

47. Kim S. Cameron, Myung Kim, and David A. Whetten, "Organizational Effects of Decline and Turbulence," *Administrative Science Quarterly* 32 (1987): 222–40.

48. Leonard Greenhalgh, "Organizational Decline," in Samuel B. Bacharach, ed., *Research in the Sociology of Organizations* 2 (Greenwich, Conn.: JAI Press, 1983), 231–76; Peter Lorange and Robert T. Nelson, "How to Recognize—and Avoid—Organizational Decline," *Sloan Management Review* (Spring 1987): 41–48.

49. Kim S. Cameron and Raymond Zammuto, "Matching Managerial Strategies to Conditions of Decline," *Human Resources Management* 22 (1983): 359–75; Leonard Greenhalgh, Anne T. Lawrence, and Robert I. Sutton, "Determinants of Workforce Reduction Strategies in Declining Organizations," *Academy of Management Review* 13 (1988): 241–54.

50. William Weitzel and Ellen Jonsson, "Reversing the Downward Spiral: Lessons from W. T. Grant and Sears Roebuck," *Academy of Management Executive* 5 (1991): 7–21; William Weitzel and Ellen Jonsson, "Decline in Organizations: A Literature Integration and Extension," *Administrative Science Quarterly* 34 (1989): 91–109.

51. Cascio, "Downsizing: What Do We Know? What Have We Learned?"; John A. Byrne, "Belt Tightening the Smart Way," *Business Week/Enterprise,* 1993, 34–38.

52. Sarah J. Freeman and Kim S. Cameron, "Organizational Downsizing: A Convergence and Reorientation Framework," *Organization Science* 4 (1993): 10–29.

53. Based on Joel Brockner, "Managing the Effects of Layoffs on Survivors," *California Management Review* (Winter 1992): 9–28; Ronald Henkoff, "Getting beyond Downsizing," *Fortune,* 10 January 1994, 58–64.

54. Joann S. Lublin, "Survivors of Layoffs Battle Angst, Anger, Hurting Productivity," *Wall Street Journal,* 6 December 1993, A1, A16.

CHAPTER

6

Designing Organization Structures

190

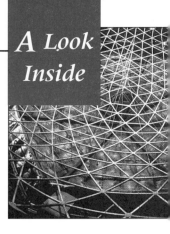
Chrysler Corporation

Within two years, Chrysler came back from near-insolvency to become the world's most successful automaker. The company recorded 1993 profits of about $2 billion, earning more from the auto business than Ford and GM combined. A large part of Chrysler's success is due to a change in organization structure.

It is the least bureaucratic and the least vertically integrated of the Big Three U.S. automakers. The layers of management hierarchy cut out in the early 1980s haven't been rebuilt. In addition, Chrysler's "platform teams," autonomous groups made up of all the professionals needed to design and produce a new car, may become a model for other automakers.

The standard practice in the auto industry has been for designers, engineers, and manufacturers to work in isolation—the design for a new car advances from one department to the next with little or no communication and coordination among departments. But Chrysler puts everyone who's working on a specific project together on a single floor and then throws in representatives from marketing, finance, purchasing, and even outside suppliers. By 1991, Chrysler had dissolved most of its functional departments in favor of platform teams.

Platform teams promote informal communication internally as well as with outside suppliers. Industry expert Martin Anderson commented that "Chrysler is behaving more like Hewlett-Packard than a traditional auto company." He thinks Chrysler's teams can serve as a model for companies in many fast-moving consumer-focused industries.[1]

Although Chrysler is still the smallest and financially weakest of the Big Three, the company's new structure is helping it outpace the others in the fast-changing auto industry. New CEO Robert Eaton, who was recruited from GM to succeed Lee Iacocca, continues to fine-tune the team structure as he emphasizes a new commitment to quality.

Nearly every firm undergoes reorganization at some point. Structural changes are needed every few years as the environment, technology, size, or competitive strategy changes. The challenge for managers is to understand how to design organization structure to achieve their company's goals.

PURPOSE OF THIS CHAPTER

The general concept of organization structure has been discussed in previous chapters. Structure includes such things as the number of departments in an organization, the span of control, and the extent to which the organization is formalized or centralized. The purpose of this chapter is to bring together these ideas to show how to design structure as it appears on the organization chart.

The material on structure is presented in the following sequence. First, structure is defined. Second, an information-processing perspective on structure explains how vertical and horizontal linkages are designed to provide needed information capacity. Third, basic organization design options are presented. Fourth, strategies for grouping organizational activities into functional, product, hybrid, or matrix structures are discussed. By the end of this chapter, you will understand how organization structure can help companies like Chrysler achieve their goals.

Definition of Structure

Organization **structure** is reflected in the organization chart. The organization chart is the visible representation for a whole set of underlying activities and processes in an organization. The three key components in the definition of organization structure are:

1. Organization structure designates formal reporting relationships, including the number of levels in the hierarchy and the span of control of managers and supervisors.
2. Organization structure identifies the grouping together of individuals into departments and of departments into the total organization.
3. Organization structure includes the design of systems to ensure effective communication, coordination, and integration of effort across departments.[2]

These three elements of structure pertain to both vertical and horizontal aspects of organizing. For example, the first two elements are the structural *framework,* which is the vertical hierarchy drawn on the organization chart.[3] The third element pertains to the pattern of *interactions* among organizational employees. An ideal structure encourages employees to provide horizontal information and coordination where and when it is needed.

Exhibit 6.1 illustrates that structural design is influenced by the environment, goals, technology, and size. Each of these key contextual variables was discussed at length in a previous chapter. Recall that an environment can be stable or unstable; management's goals and strategies may stress internal efficiency or adaptation to external markets; production technologies can be routine or nonroutine; and an

Exhibit 6.1
Organization Contextual Variables That Influence Structure.

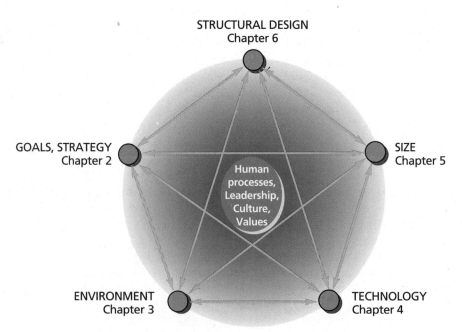

Source: Adapted from Jay R. Galbraith, *Organization Design* (Reading, Mass.: Addison-Wesley, 1977), ch. 1.

organization's size may be large or small. Each variable influences the correct structural design. Moreover, environment, technology, goals, and size may also influence one another, as illustrated by the connecting lines among these contextual variables in Exhibit 6.1. Human processes (such as leadership and culture) within the organization also influence structure as indicated in the center of Exhibit 6.1. These processes will be discussed in later chapters.

Information-Processing Perspective on Structure

The concepts in previous chapters—technology, environment, size—impose different information-processing requirements on organizations. A nonroutine technology or an uncertain environment, for example, requires employees to process more information to understand and respond to unexpected events. Reciprocal interdependence between departments requires substantially more communication and coordination than is needed for pooled interdependence. Thus, the organization must be designed to encourage information flow in both vertical and horizontal directions necessary to achieve the organization's overall task.[4] Exhibit 6.2 illustrates how structure should fit the information requirements of the organization. If it does not, people will either have too little information or will spend time processing information not vital to their tasks, thus reducing effectiveness.[5]

VERTICAL INFORMATION LINKAGES

Organization design should facilitate the communication among employees and departments that is necessary to accomplish the organization's overall task. *Linkage* is defined as the extent of communication and coordination among organizational elements. **Vertical linkages** are used to coordinate activities between the top and bottom of an organization. Employees at lower levels should carry out activities

Exhibit 6.2   Information-Processing Approach to Structural Design.

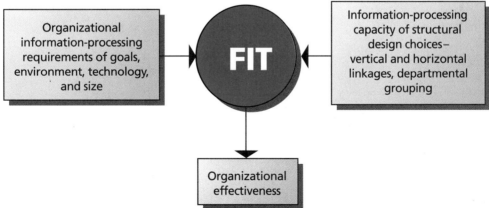

Source: Based on Richard L. Daft and Robert H. Lengel, "Organizational Information Requirements, Media Richness and Structural Design," *Management Science* 32 (1986): 554–71; and David Nadler and Michael Tushman, *Strategic Organization Design* (Glenview, Ill.: Scott Foresman, 1988).

consistent with top-level goals, and top executives must be informed of activities and accomplishments at the lower levels. Organizations may use any of a variety of structural devices to achieve vertical linkage, including hierarchical referral, rules and procedures, plans and schedules, positions or levels added to the hierarchy, and formal management information systems.[6]

Hierarchical Referral   The first vertical device is the hierarchy, or chain of command, which is illustrated by the vertical lines in Exhibit 6.3. If a problem arises that employees don't know how to solve, it can be referred up to the next level in the hierarchy. When a camera operator in the printing company encounters an unusual situation, the correct response is to refer it to the supervisor. When the problem is solved, the answer is passed back down to the operator. The lines of the organization chart act as communication channels.

Rules and Plans   The next linkage device is the use of rules and plans. To the extent that problems and decisions are repetitious, a rule or procedure can be established so employees know how to respond without communicating directly with their manager. Rules provide a standard information source enabling compositors and operators in the printing company to be coordinated without actually communicating about every job. A plan also provides standing information for employees. The most widely used plan is the budget. With carefully designed budget plans, employees at lower levels can be left on their own to perform activities within their resource allotment.

Add Positions to Hierarchy   When many problems occur, planning and hierarchical referral may overload managers. In growing or changing organizations, additional vertical linkages may be required. One technique is to add positions to the vertical hierarchy. In some cases, an assistant will be assigned to help an overloaded manager. In other cases, positions in the direct line of authority may be added. Such positions reduce the span of control and allow closer communication and control.

Exhibit 6.3
Organization Chart for the Manufacturing Department of a Printing Company.

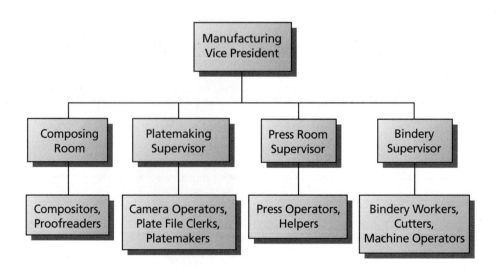

Vertical Information Systems   Vertical information systems are another strategy for increasing vertical information capacity. **Vertical information systems** include the periodic reports, written information, and computer-based communications distributed to managers. Information systems make communication up and down the hierarchy more efficient. For example, Chairman Bill Gates of Microsoft communicates regularly with employees through his company's electronic mail system. He responds to a dozen individual messages each day. At Xerox, some 40,000 customers are polled each month, and this data is aggregated, summarized, and transferred up the hierarchy to managers.

Summary   Structural mechanisms that can be used to achieve vertical linkage and coordination are summarized in Exhibit 6.4. These structural mechanisms represent alternatives managers can use in designing an organization. Depending upon the amount of coordination needed in the organization, several of the linkage mechanisms in Exhibit 6.4 may be used. For example, Ford developed a vertical information system based upon surveys of dealer service. Ford uses the information as a management tool to pinpoint problems, devise solutions, and ultimately win steady customers through better dealer service.

HORIZONTAL INFORMATION LINKAGES

Horizontal communication overcomes barriers between departments and provides opportunities for coordination among employees to achieve unity of effort and organizational objectives. **Horizontal linkage** refers to the amount of communication and coordination horizontally across organizational departments. Its importance was discovered by Lee Iacocca when he took over Chrysler Corporation.

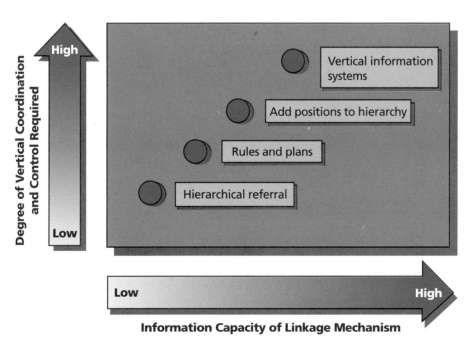

Exhibit 6.4
Ladder of Mechanisms for Vertical Linkage and Control.

What I found at Chrysler were thirty-five vice presidents, each with his own turf. . . . I couldn't believe, for example, that the guy running engineering departments wasn't in constant touch with his counterpart in manufacturing. But that's how it was. Everybody worked independently. I took one look at that system and I almost threw up. That's when I knew I was in really deep trouble.

. . . Nobody at Chrysler seemed to understand that interaction among the different functions in a company is absolutely critical. People in engineering and manufacturing almost have to be sleeping together. These guys weren't even flirting![7]

As we saw at the beginning of the chapter, horizontal communication has evolved to a high level at Chrysler and has had a significant positive impact.

The need for horizontal coordination increases as the amount of uncertainty increases, such as when the environment is changing, the technology is nonroutine and interdependent, and goals stress innovation and flexibility. Horizontal linkage mechanisms often are not drawn on the organization chart, but nevertheless are part of organization structure. The following devices are structural alternatives that can improve horizontal coordination and information flow.[8] Each device enables people to exchange information.

Paperwork—Memos, Reports   One form of horizontal linkage is simply to exchange paperwork about a problem or decision or to put other departments on a mailing list so they will be informed about activities. Other departments may be sent copies of correspondence or may have reports forwarded to them.

Direct Contact   A somewhat higher level of horizontal linkage is direct contact between managers affected by a problem. To revive customer loyalty by improving service and quality, CEO Louis Morris began encouraging communication across department lines at Simplicity Pattern Company, so that creative design managers were talking with managers in sales and financing. Direct contact is very effective for coordination.[9]

Liaison Roles   Creating a special **liaison role** is the next alternative. A liaison person is located in one department but has the responsibility for communicating and achieving coordination with another department. Liaison roles often exist between engineering and manufacturing departments because engineering has to develop and test products to fit the limitations of manufacturing facilities. A computer department or transportation department may assign a liaison person to work with other departments that use its services.

Task Forces   Direct contact and liaison roles usually link only two departments. When linkage involves several departments, a more complex device such as a task force is required. A **task force** is a temporary committee composed of representatives from each department affected by a problem.[10] Each member represents the interest of a department and can carry information from the meeting back to that department.

Task forces are an effective horizontal linkage device for temporary issues. They solve problems by direct horizontal coordination and reduce the information load on the vertical hierarchy. Typically, they are disbanded after their tasks are accomplished.

Xerox used a task force of twenty hand-picked members to develop its application for the Malcolm Baldrige National Quality Award. Book publishers coordinate the editing, production, advertising, and distribution of a special book with a temporary task force.

Full-time Integrator   A stronger horizontal linkage device is to create a full-time position or department solely for the purpose of coordination. A full-time **integrator** frequently has a title, such as product manager, project manager, program manager, or brand manager. Unlike the liaison person described earlier, the integrator does not report to one of the functional departments being coordinated. He or she is located outside the departments and has the responsibility for coordinating several departments.

The brand manager for Planters Peanuts, for example, coordinates the sales, distribution, and advertising for that product. Gillette Company created product line managers for multinational coordination. A product line manager coordinates marketing and sales strategies for Trac II across fifteen countries, achieving savings by using similar advertising and marketing techniques in each country.

The integrator also can be responsible for an entire project. An organization chart that illustrates the location of full-time project coordinators is shown in Exhibit 6.5.

Exhibit 6.5   Project Manager Location in the Structure.

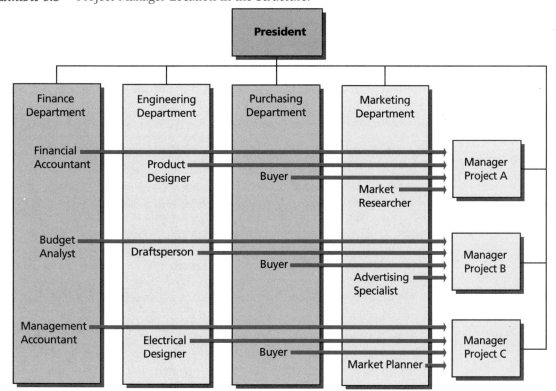

The project managers are drawn to the side to indicate their separation from other departments. The arrows indicate project members assigned to the projects. Project A, for example, has a financial accountant assigned to keep track of costs and budgets. The engineering member provides design advice, and purchasing and manufacturing members represent their areas. The project manager is responsible for the entire project. He or she sees that the project is completed on time, makes a profit, or achieves other project goals. The horizontal lines in Exhibit 6.5 indicate that project managers do not have formal authority over team members with respect to giving pay raises, hiring, or firing. Formal authority rests with the managers of the functional departments, who have formal authority over subordinates.

Integrating roles require excellent people skills. Integrators in most companies have a lot of responsibility but little authority. The integrator has to use expertise and persuasion to achieve coordination. He or she spans the boundary between departments and must be able to get people together, maintain their trust, confront problems, and resolve conflicts and disputes in the interest of the organization.[11] The integrator must be forceful in order to achieve coordination, but must stop short of alienating people in the line departments. Some organizations, such as General Mills, have several integrators working simultaneously.

IN PRACTICE ◆ 6.1

General Mills

"When General Mills completed a ten-story tower at its suburban Minneapolis headquarters last summer, the company discovered that not all the telephones could be installed at once. 'Hook up the product managers' first,' the senior executive ordered. 'The business can't run without them.' "[12]

General Mills assigns a product manager to each of the more than twenty-five products in its line, including Cheerios, Wheaties, Bisquick, Softasilk Cake Mix, Stir-n-Frost Icing, Hamburger Helper, and Gold Medal Flour. Brand managers are also assigned to develop new products, name them, and test them in the marketplace.

Product managers at General Mills act as if they are running their own businesses. They set marketing goals and plot strategies to achieve those goals. They are responsible for product success, but they have no authority. Product management is management by persuasion. A good product manager is vibrant, challenging, and a little abrasive. He or she has to be to get things done without the aid of formal authority.

If the product manager for Cocoa Puffs needs special support from the sales force and additional output from the plant for a big advertising campaign, she has to sell the idea to people who report to managers in charge of sales and manufacturing. Product managers work laterally across the organization rather than within the vertical structure. When the product manager for Crispy Wheats 'n Raisins decides the product needs different packaging, a new recipe, a more focused commercial, or new ingredients, he must convince the departments to pay attention to his brand. The product manager can also expect to work with the procurement department, a controller, and the research lab at some point during the year.[13]

The product managers at General Mills are full-time integrators. They coordinate marketing, manufacturing, purchasing, research, and other functions relevant to their product lines. They provide horizontal linkages by persuading diverse departments to focus on the needs of their products. General Mills has been very profitable in a highly competitive industry, and one reason is the role played by product managers.

Teams   Project teams tend to be the strongest horizontal linkage mechanism. **Teams** are permanent task forces and are often used in conjunction with a full-time integrator. When activities between departments require strong coordination over a long period of time, a cross-functional team is often the solution. Special project teams may be used when organizations have a large-scale project, a major innovation, or a new product line, such as Chrysler's Nova.

Hallmark Cards lives or dies on new products, producing some forty thousand new cards and other items a year. The company has been reorganized into teams to cut the cycle time required for new product development and to be more responsive to changing consumer tastes. For example, a team of writers, artists, lithographers, and merchandisers is assigned to work on cards for each particular holiday. The company thinks cross-functional teams can cut in half the time it takes to create new products.[14]

The Rodney Hunt Company develops, manufactures, and markets heavy industrial equipment and uses teams to coordinate each product line across the manufacturing, engineering, and marketing departments. These teams are illustrated by the dashed lines and shaded areas in Exhibit 6.6. Members from each team meet the first thing each day as needed to resolve problems concerning customer needs, backlogs, engineering changes, scheduling conflicts, and any other problem with the product line.

A more intense use of teams was adopted by Florida Power & Light Company, one of the best-managed utilities in North America, to build nuclear power plants. Permanent teams were combined with full-time team leaders (integrators) to achieve remarkable coordination.

IN PRACTICE ◆ 6.2
Florida Power & Light Company

Building a nuclear power plant can take as long as fifteen years, and the costs are enormous. However, long delays did not happen when Florida Power built St. Lucie No. 2, which went into commercial operation only six years after construction started. The credit goes to Bill Derrickson, manager of the project, who overcame a hurricane, two strikes, and hundreds of federally required design changes.

Derrickson's solution was to develop fifteen teams to handle critical parts of the project. Each team was headed by what Derrickson called a mother, because, he says "If you want something to happen, it has to have a mother." One such team presided over a computerized list of twenty-five thousand tasks needed to finish the plant. The mother was Steve Reuwer, and daily team meetings were intense. Anyone who couldn't answer questions was asked to leave and return with the answer. Supervisors who fell behind either quit or were replaced. Reuwer's job was to keep the pressure on.

The teams were able to assimilate and coordinate design changes and were responsible for developing innovative construction techniques. A slipforming technique was developed for pouring concrete around the clock, allowing the three-foot-thick, 190-foot-tall concrete shell to be finished in just seventeen days, compared with a year for other power companies. The teams also worked face-to-face with government regulators and suppliers to get things done on schedule.

Florida Power's use of teams to handle urgent problems was so effective that other companies are adopting the idea. Derrickson's role was also recognized. He was hired from Florida Power to become senior vice-president of Public Service Company of New Hampshire, where he was asked to create a similar organization structure to speed construction of Public Service's Seabrook nuclear plant.[15]

Summary   The mechanisms for achieving horizontal linkages in organizations are summarized in Exhibit 6.7. These devices represent alternatives that managers can select to achieve horizontal coordination in any organization. The higher-level devices provide more horizontal information capacity. If communication is insufficient, departments will find themselves out of synchronization, and they will not contribute to the overall goals of the organization.

Organization Design Alternatives

The overall design of organization structure indicates three things—needed work activities, reporting relationships, and departmental groupings.

DEFINE WORK ACTIVITIES

Departments are created to perform tasks considered strategically important to the company. For example, when moving huge quantities of supplies in the Persian Gulf, the U.S. Army's logistics commander created a squad of fifteen soldiers called Ghostbusters who were charged with getting out among the troops, identifying logistics problems, and seeing that the problems got fixed. The fiberglass group at Manville set a priority on growth and, hence, created a department that was simply called Growth Department. Defining a specific department is a way to accomplish tasks deemed valuable by the organization to accomplish its goals.

REPORTING RELATIONSHIPS

Reporting relationships, often called the chain of command, are represented by vertical lines on an organization chart. The chain of command should be an unbroken line of authority that links all persons in an organization and shows who reports to whom. In a large organization like Standard Oil Company, one hundred or more charts are required to identify reporting relationships among thousands of employees. The definition of departments and the drawing of reporting relationships defines how employees are to be grouped into departments.

DEPARTMENTAL GROUPING OPTIONS

Options for departmental grouping are illustrated in Exhibit 6.8. Employees can be grouped by activity, output, user or customer, or some combination. **Departmental grouping** has impact on employees because they share a common supervisor and common resources, are jointly responsible for performance, and tend to identify and

Exhibit 6.6 Teams Used for Horizontal Coordination at Rodney Hunt Company.

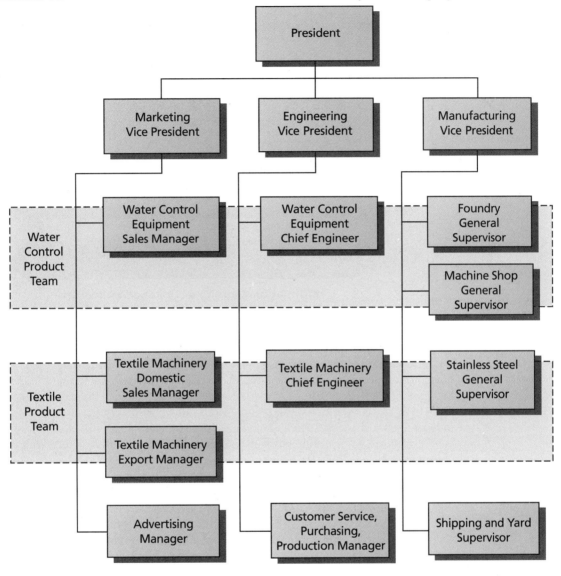

collaborate with one another.[16] For example, at Albany Ladder Company, the credit manager was shifted from the finance department to the marketing department.
By being grouped with marketing, the credit manager started working with sales
people to increase sales, thus becoming more liberal with credit than when he was
located in the finance department.

Grouping by activity places employees together who perform similar functions or work processes or who bring similar knowledge and skills to bear. For
example, all marketing people would work together under the same supervisor, as
would manufacturing and engineering people. All people associated with the assembly process for generators would be grouped together in one department. All

Exhibit 6.7
Ladder of
Mechanisms for
Horizontal
Linkage and
Coordination.

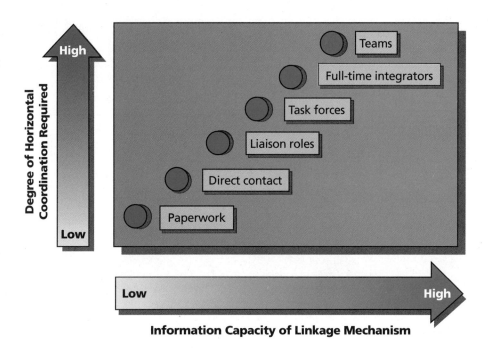

Information Capacity of Linkage Mechanism

chemists may be grouped in a department different from biologists because they represent different disciplines.

Grouping by output means people are organized according to what the organization produces. All people required to produce toothpaste—including the marketing, manufacturing, and sales people—are grouped together under one executive. In huge corporations such as PepsiCo, the product lines may represent independent businesses, such as Taco Bell, Frito Lay, and Pepsi Cola.

Grouping by users or customers means resources are organized to serve a customer or client. Thus, the activities required to serve a large government account may all be grouped together under one supervisor. All the activities required to serve the eastern United States or Canada or Latin America might be grouped together, or managers may deem it strategically advantageous to organize their resources to serve specific market segments, such as business customers and residential customers.

Multifocused grouping means an organization embraces two structural grouping alternatives simultaneously. These structural forms are often called matrix or hybrid and will be discussed in more detail later in this chapter. An organization may need to group by function and product simultaneously or perhaps by product and geography.

The organizational forms described in Exhibit 6.8 provide the overall options within which the organization chart is drawn and the detailed structure is designed. Each structural design alternative has significant strengths and weaknesses, to which we now turn.

Functional, Product, and Geographical Designs

Activity grouping and output grouping are the two most common approaches to structural design. In the business world, these two approaches are typically called functional and product structures.

Exhibit 6.8   Structural Design Options for Grouping Employees into Departments.

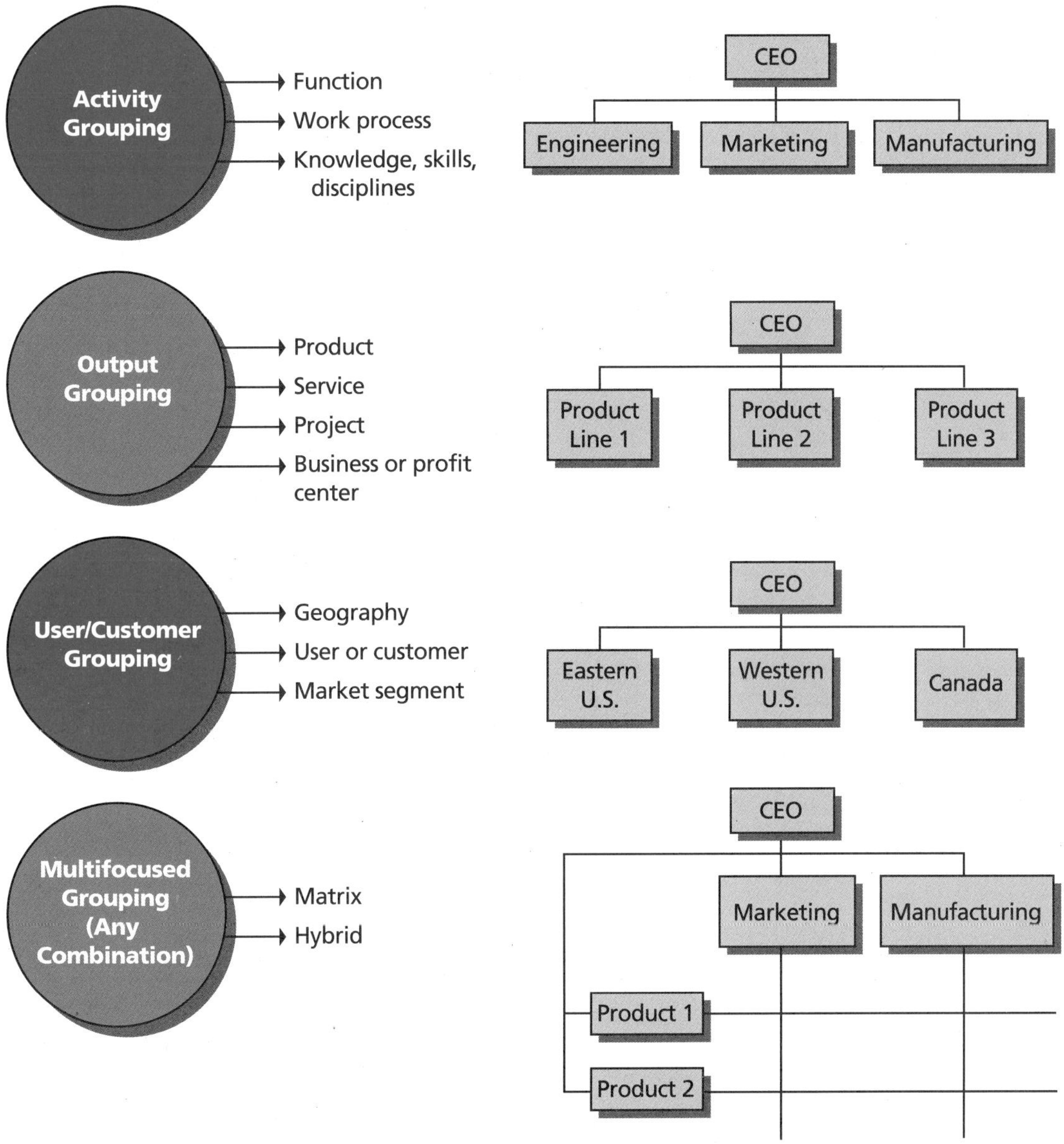

Source: Adapted from David Nadler and Michael Tushman, *Strategic Organization Design* (Glenview, Ill.: Scott Foresman, 1988), 68.

FUNCTIONAL STRUCTURE

In a **functional structure,** activities are grouped together by common function from the bottom to the top of the organization. All engineers are located in the engineering department, and the vice president of engineering is responsible for all engineering activities. The same is true in marketing, research and development, and manufacturing. An example of the functional organization structure is the printing company shown in Exhibit 6.3.

Exhibit 6.9 summarizes the organizational characteristics typically associated with the functional structure. This structure is most effective when the environment is stable and the technology is relatively routine with low interdependence across functional departments. Organizational goals pertain to internal efficiency and technical specialization. Size is small to medium. Each of these characteristics is associated with a low need for horizontal coordination. The stable environment, routine technology, internal efficiency, and small size mean the organization can be controlled and coordinated primarily through the vertical hierarchy. Within the organization, employees are committed to achieving the operative goals of their respective functional departments. Planning and budgeting is by function and reflects the cost of resources used in each department. Formal authority and influence within the organization rests with upper managers in the functional departments.

One strength of the functional structure is that it promotes economy of scale within functions. Economy of scale means all employees are located in the same place and can share facilities. Producing all products in a single plant, for example, enables the plant to acquire the latest machinery. Constructing only one facility instead of separate facilities for each product line reduces duplication and waste. The functional structure also promotes in-depth skill development of employees. Employees are exposed to a range of functional activities within their own depart-

Exhibit 6.9
Summary of
Functional
Organization
Characteristics.

Context
Structure: Functional Environment: Low uncertainty, stable Technology: Routine, low interdependence Size: Small to medium Goals: Internal efficiency, technical quality
Internal Systems
Operative goals: Functional goal emphasis Planning and budgeting: Cost basis—budget, statistical reports Formal authority: Functional managers
Strengths
1. Allows economies of scale within functional departments 2. Enables in-depth skill development 3. Enables organization to accomplish functional goals 4. Is best in small to medium-sized organizations 5. Is best with only one or a few products
Weaknesses
1. Slow response time to environmental changes 2. May cause decisions to pile on top, hierarchy overload 3. Leads to poor horizontal coordination among departments 4. Results in less innovation 5. Involves restricted view of organizational goals

Source: Adapted from Robert Duncan, "What Is the Right Organization Structure? Decision Tree Analysis Provides the Answer," *Organizational Dynamics* (Winter 1979): 429.

ment. The functional form of structure is best for small to medium-sized organizations when only one or a few products are produced.[17]

The main weakness of the functional structure is a slow response to environmental changes that require coordination across departments. If the environment is changing or the technology is nonroutine and interdependent, the vertical hierarchy becomes overloaded. Decisions pile up, and top managers do not respond fast enough. Other disadvantages of the functional structure are that innovation is slow because of poor coordination, and each employee has a restricted view of overall goals.

The functional organization structure is just right for Blue Bell Creameries, where the primary goal is quality ice cream. Consider how the functional structure provides the coordination Blue Bell needs.

IN PRACTICE ♦ 6.3

Blue Bell Creameries, Inc.

Within seconds, the old-timer on the radio had taken listeners out of their bumper-to-bumper Houston world and placed them gently in Brenham, Texas, with its rolling hills and country air, in the era when the town got its first traffic light.

"You know," he said, "that's how Blue Bell Ice Cream is. Old-fashioned, uncomplicated, homemade good." He paused. "It's all made in that little creamery in Brenham."

That little creamery isn't little anymore, but the desire for first-quality homemade ice cream is stronger than when Blue Bell started in 1907. Today, Blue Bell has more than eight hundred employees and will sell over $160 million in ice cream. The company has an unbelievable 60 percent share of the ice cream market in Houston, Dallas, and San Antonio—Texas's three largest cities.

The company cannot meet the demand for Blue Bell Ice Cream. It doesn't even try. Top managers recently decided to expand slowly into Louisiana and Oklahoma. Management refuses to compromise quality by expanding into regions that cannot be adequately serviced or by growing so fast that it can't adequately train employees in the art of making ice cream.

Blue Bell's major departments are sales, quality control, production, maintenance, and distribution. There is also an accounting department and a small research and development group. Product changes are infrequent because the orientation is toward tried-and-true products. The environment is stable. The customer base is well established. The only change has been the increase in demand for Blue Bell Ice Cream.

Blue Bell's quality control department tests all incoming ingredients and ensures that only the best products go into its ice cream. Quality control also tests outgoing ice cream products. After years of experience, quality inspectors can taste the slightest deviation from expected quality. It's no wonder Blue Bell has successfully maintained the image of a small-town creamery making homemade ice cream.[18]

In the case of Blue Bell Creameries, the functional structure works just fine; but as the company expands, it may have difficulty coordinating across departments.

FUNCTIONAL STRUCTURE WITH HORIZONTAL LINKAGES

Today, there is a shift toward flatter, more horizontal structures because of the uncertain environment. Very few of today's successful companies can maintain a strictly functional structure. Organizations compensate for the vertical functional hierarchy by installing horizontal linkages, as described earlier in this chapter. Managers improve horizontal coordination by using liaisons, project or brand managers, task forces, or teams. Nonprofit organizations are also recognizing the importance of horizontal linkages. Consider how the San Diego Zoo uses horizontal linkages to coordinate a nonroutine technology and hold its own among stiff competition.

IN PRACTICE ◆ 6.4
San Diego Zoo

Once upon a time, a groundskeeper at the San Diego Zoo might have swept cigarette butts under a bush if he was tired or rushed—that made it the gardener's problem, not his. And the gardener would have tended to the plants, but as far as she was concerned, it was someone else's job to deal with the visitors. Such attitudes are gone now, replaced by a desire to make sure visitors enjoy their visit from beginning to end. Zoo attendance has increased, despite a decline in southern California tourism and competition from Sea World and Disneyland. The zoo director credits the employees' new sense of ownership for that success.

Traditionally, the San Diego Zoo was managed through its fifty functional departments—animal keeping, horticulture, maintenance, education, and so on. Today, cross-functional teams are jointly responsible for the success of specific parts of the zoo. Team members like the groundskeeper and the gardener now work together to get the job done, and a horticulturalist may double as groundskeeper or construction worker if that's what it takes. Teams manage their own budgets and schedule their own vacations. And cross-training makes all team members knowledgeable enough to answer visitors' questions.[19]

The San Diego Zoo is using horizontal linkages to overcome some of the disadvantages of the functional structure. The team concept has led employees to take a broad view of the organization's goals and work for a common purpose. We will talk more about this trend toward horizontal organizing in Chapter 7.

PRODUCT STRUCTURE

The term **product structure** is used here as the generic term for what is sometimes called a *divisional structure* or *self-contained units*. With this structure, divisions can be organized according to individual products, services, product groups, major projects or programs, divisions, businesses, or profit centers. The distinctive feature of a product structure is that grouping is based on organizational outputs.

The difference between a product structure and a functional structure is illustrated in Exhibit 6.10. The functional structure can be redesigned into separate product groups, and each group contains the functional departments of R&D, manufacturing, accounting, and marketing. Coordination across functional departments within each product group is maximized. The product structure promotes flexibility and change because each unit is smaller and can adapt to the needs of its environment. Moreover, the product structure decentralizes decision making, because the lines of authority converge at a lower level in the hierarchy. The functional struc-

Exhibit 6.10 Reorganization from Functional Structure to Product Structure at Info-Tech.

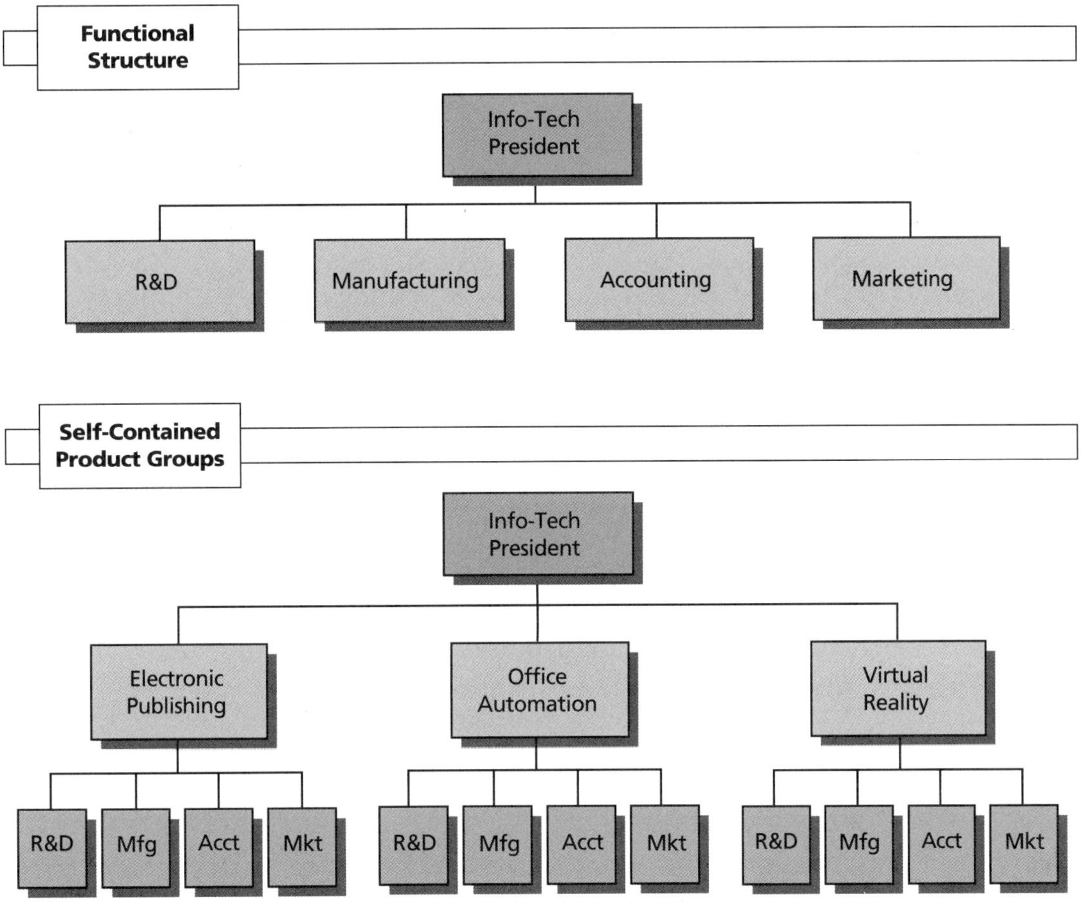

ture, by contrast, forces decisions all the way to the top before a problem affecting several functions can be resolved.

The product structure fits the context summarized in Exhibit 6.11.[20] This form of structure is excellent for achieving coordination across functional departments. When the environment is uncertain, the technology is nonroutine and interdependent across departments, and goals are external effectiveness and adaptation, then a product structure is appropriate.

Large size is also associated with product structure. Giant, complex organizations such as General Electric, PepsiCo, and Johnson & Johnson are subdivided into a series of smaller, self-contained organizations for better control and coordination. In these large companies, the units are sometimes called divisions, businesses, or strategic business units. The structure at Johnson & Johnson includes 168 separate operating units, including McNeil Consumer Products, makers of Tylenol; Ortho Pharmaceuticals, which makes Retin-A and birth control pills; Vistakon, which holds a huge share of the market for disposable contact lenses; and J & J Consumer Products, the company that brings us Johnson's Baby Shampoo and Band-Aids. Each division is a separately chartered, autonomous company operating under the guidance of Johnson & Johnson's corporate headquarters.[21]

Exhibit 6.11
Summary of
Product Organi-
zation Charac-
teristics.

Context
Structure: Product Environment: Moderate to high uncertainty, changing Technology: Nonroutine, high interdependence among departments Size: Large Goals: External effectiveness, adaptation, client satisfaction
Internal Systems
Operative goals: Product line emphasis Planning and budgeting: Profit center basis—cost and income Formal authority: Product managers
Strengths
1. Suited to fast change in unstable environment 2. Leads to client satisfaction because product responsibility and contact points are clear 3. Involves high coordination across functions 4. Allows units to adapt to differences in products, regions, clients 5. Best in large organizations with several products 6. Decentralizes decision making
Weaknesses
1. Eliminates economies of scale in functional departments 2. Leads to poor coordination across product lines 3. Eliminates in-depth competence and technical specialization 4. Makes integration and standardization across product lines difficult

Source: Adapted from Robert Duncan, "What Is the Right Organization Structure? Decision Tree Analysis Provides the Answer," *Organizational Dynamics* (Winter 1979): 431.

The product structure has several strengths. It is suited to fast change in an unstable environment and provides high product visibility. Since each product is a separate division, clients are able to contact the correct division and achieve satisfaction. Coordination across functions is excellent. Each product can adapt to requirements of individual customers or regions. The product structure typically works best in organizations that have multiple products or services and enough personnel to staff separate functional units. At corporations like Johnson & Johnson and PepsiCo, decision making is pushed down to the lowest levels. Each division is small enough to be quick on its feet, responding rapidly to changes in the market.

One disadvantage of using product structuring is that the organization loses economies of scale. Instead of fifty research engineers sharing a common facility in a functional structure, ten engineers may be assigned to each of five product divisions. The critical mass required for in-depth research is lost, and physical facilities have to be duplicated for each product line. Another problem is that product lines become separate from each other, and coordination across product lines can be difficult. As one Johnson & Johnson executive said, "We have to keep reminding ourselves that we work for the same corporation"[22]

Companies such as Hewlett-Packard, Xerox, and Digital Equipment have a large number of divisions and have had real problems with horizontal coordination.

The software division may produce programs that are incompatible with business computers sold by another division. Customers are frustrated when a sales representative from one division is unaware of developments in other divisions. Task forces and other linkage devices are needed to coordinate across divisions. A lack of technical specialization is also a problem in a product structure. Employees identify with the product line rather than with a functional specialty. R&D personnel, for example, tend to do applied research to benefit the product line rather than basic research to benefit the entire organization.

GEOGRAPHICAL STRUCTURE

Another basis for structural grouping is the organization's users or customers. The most common structure in this category is geography. Each region of the country may have distinct tastes and needs. Each geographic unit includes all functions required to produce and market products in that region. For multinational corporations, self-contained units are created for different countries and parts of the world.

A few years ago, Apple Computer reorganized from a functional to a geographical structure to facilitate manufacture and delivery of Apple computers to customers around the world. Exhibit 6.12 contains a partial organization structure illustrating the geographical thrust. Apple used this structure to focus managers and employees on specific geographical customers and sales targets. In Canada, department stores frequently use a geographical structure with a separate entity for Quebec because customers there are physically smaller, use a different language, and have different tastes than those in Ontario or the Maritime Provinces. The regional structure allows Apple or a Canadian department store chain to focus on the needs of customers in a geographical area.

The strengths and weaknesses of a geographic divisional structure are similar to the product organization characteristics listed in Exhibit 6.11. The organization can adapt to specific needs of its own region, and employees identify with regional goals rather than with national goals. Horizontal coordination within a region is emphasized rather than linkages across regions or to the national office.

Hybrid Structure

As a practical matter, many structures in the real world do not exist in the pure form of functional, product, or geographic. An organization's structure may be multifocused in that both product and function, or product and geography, are emphasized at the same time. One type of structure that combines characteristics of both is called the **hybrid structure.**

CHARACTERISTICS

When a corporation grows large and has several products or markets, it typically is organized into self-contained units of some type. Functions that are important to each product or market are decentralized to the self-contained units. However, some functions are also centralized and located at headquarters. Headquarters's functions are relatively stable and require economies of scale and in-depth specialization. By combining characteristics of product and functional or product and geographical

Exhibit 6.12   Geographical Structure for Apple Computer.

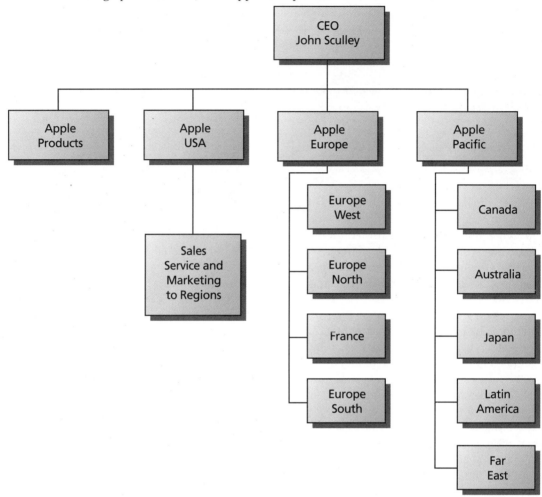

Source: Based on John Markoff, "John Sculley's Biggest Test," *New York Times,* 26 February 1989, sec. 3, pp. 1, 26.

structures, corporations can take advantage of the strengths of each and avoid some of the weaknesses. Xerox Corporation recently reorganized into a hybrid structure, with nine nearly independent product divisions and three geographical sales divisions. CEO Paul Allaire thinks the hybrid structure can provide the coordination and flexibility needed to help Xerox get products to market faster and thrive in a competitive environment.[23]

Sun Petroleum Products restructured from a functional to a hybrid structure by combining three product divisions with several functional departments.

IN PRACTICE ◆ 6.5

Sun Petroleum Products Company

Sun Petroleum Products Company (SPPC) had sales of approximately $7 billion in the early 1980s and a work force of 5,400 people. Its refineries produced about 500,000 barrels of products per day. The six refineries manufactured fuels, lubricants, and chemicals that were marketed by Sun's sales force.

SPPC was traditionally organized by function with each functional head reporting directly to the president or to the vice president of operations. Then a study revealed that Sun should be more responsive to changing markets. It recommended a reorganization into three major product lines of fuels, lubricants, and chemicals. Each product line served a different market and required a different strategy and management style.

The new hybrid organization structure adopted by SPPC is illustrated in Exhibit 6.13. Each product line vice president is now in charge of both marketing and manufacturing for that product, so coordination is easy to achieve. Each product line vice president also has planning, supply, and manufacturing departments reporting to him or her. The vice president in charge of refinery facilities is in charge of a functional department because there are major economies of scale by having all refineries work together. The output of these refineries becomes the input to the fuels, lubricants, and chemicals divisions. Other departments centralized as functional departments to achieve economies of scale are human resources, technology, financial services, and resources and strategy. Each of these departments provides services for the entire organization. The new structure is just right for SPPC because of the company's large size, moderate environmental change, interdependence, and goal of adapting to the environment.[24]

STRENGTHS AND WEAKNESSES

The hybrid structure typically appears in a context similar to that of the product structure. Hybrid structures tend to be used in an uncertain environment because product divisions are designed for innovation and external effectiveness. Technologies may be both routine and nonroutine, and interdependencies exist across the functions in product groupings. Size is typically large to provide sufficient resources for duplication of resources across product divisions. The organization has goals of client satisfaction and innovation, as well as goals of efficiency with respect to functional departments.

As summarized in Exhibit 6.14, a major strength of the hybrid structure is that it enables the organization to pursue adaptability and effectiveness within the product divisions simultaneously with efficiency in the functional departments. Thus, the organization can attain the best of both worlds. This structure also provides alignment between product division and corporate goals. The product groupings provide effective coordination within divisions, and the central functional departments provide coordination across divisions.

One weakness of the hybrid structure is administrative overhead. Some organizations experience a buildup of corporate staffs to oversee divisions. Some corporate functions duplicate activities undertaken within product divisions. If uncontrolled, administrative overhead can increase as the headquarters staff grows large. Decisions then become more centralized, and the product divisions lose the ability to respond quickly to market changes. As described in Chapter 5 on size, companies such as Nucor, Hanson Industries, and Burlington Northern have resisted administrative overhead by keeping headquarters staffs at fewer than one hundred people despite having as many as thirty-three thousand employees in product divisions. Managers in these companies minimize headquarters staffs to reduce bureaucracy and encourage division flexibility.[25]

Exhibit 6.13   Sun Petroleum Products Company's Hybrid Organization.

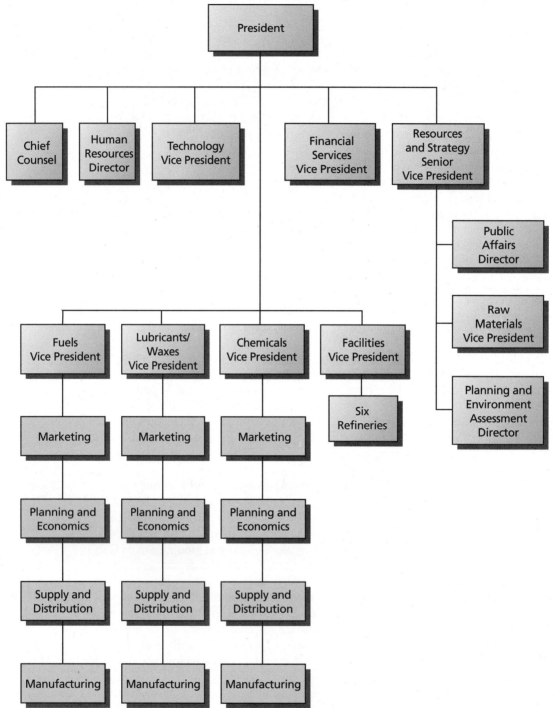

Source: Linda S. Ackerman, "Transition Management: An In-depth Look at Managing Complex Change," *Organizational Dynamics* (Summer 1982): 46–66. Reprinted with permission of the publisher, © 1982, American Management Association, New York. All rights reserved.

Context
Structure: Hybrid
Environment: Moderate to high uncertainty, changing customer demands
Technology: Routine or nonroutine, with some interdependencies between functions
Size: Large
Goals: External effectiveness and adaptation plus efficiency within some functions

Internal Systems
Operative goals: Product line emphasis, some functional emphasis
Planning and budgeting: Profit center basis for divisions; cost basis for central functions
Formal authority: Product managers; coordination responsibility resting with functional managers

Strengths
1. Allows organization to achieve adaptability and coordination in product divisions and efficiency in centralized functional departments
2. Results in better alignment between corporate and division-level goals
3. Achieves coordination both within and between product lines

Weaknesses
1. Has potential for excessive administrative overhead
2. Leads to conflict between division and corporate departments

Exhibit 6.14
Summary of Hybrid Organization Characteristics.

An associated weakness is the conflict between corporate and divisional personnel. Headquarters functions typically do not have line authority over divisional activities. Division managers may resent headquarters's intrusions, and headquarters managers may resent the desire of divisions to go their own way. Headquarters executives often do not understand the unique needs of the individual divisions that are trying to satisfy different markets.

The hybrid structure is often preferred to either the pure functional or pure product structure. It overcomes many of the weaknesses of these other structures and provides some advantages of both.

Matrix Structure

Another way to achieve focus on multiple outcomes is with the **matrix structure.** The matrix can be used when one sector of the environment requires technological expertise, for example, and another sector requires rapid change within each product line. The matrix structure often is the answer when organizations find that neither the functional, product, geographical, nor hybrid structures combined with horizontal linkage mechanisms will work.

The matrix is a strong form of horizontal linkage. The unique characteristic of the matrix organization is that both product and functional structures (horizontal and vertical) are implemented simultaneously, as shown in Exhibit 6.15. Rather than divide the organization into separate parts as in the hybrid structure, the product managers and functional managers have equal authority within the organization, and employees report to both of them. The matrix structure is similar to the use of full-time integrators or product managers described earlier in this chapter (Exhibit 6.5), except that in the matrix structure the product managers (horizontal) are given formal authority equal to that of the functional managers (vertical).

CONDITIONS FOR THE MATRIX

A dual hierarchy may seem an unusual way to design an organization, but the matrix is the correct structure when the following conditions are met.[26]

- *Condition 1.*   Pressure exists to share scarce resources across product lines. The organization is typically medium-sized and has a moderate number of product lines. It feels pressure for the shared and flexible use of people and equipment across those products. For example, the organization is not large enough to assign

Exhibit 6.15   Dual-Authority Structure in a Matrix Organization.

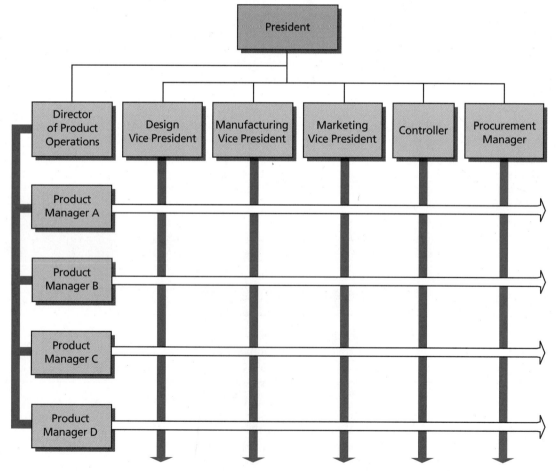

engineers full-time to each product line, so engineers are assigned part-time to several products or projects.

- *Condition 2.* Environmental pressure exists for two or more critical outputs, such as for technical quality (functional structure) and frequent new products (product structure). This dual pressure means a balance of power is needed between the functional and product sides of the organization, and a dual-authority structure is needed to maintain that balance.
- *Condition 3.* The environmental domain of the organization is both complex and uncertain. Frequent external changes and high interdependence between departments require a large amount of coordination and information processing in both vertical and horizontal directions.

Under these three conditions, the vertical and horizontal lines of authority must be given equal recognition. A dual-authority structure is thereby created so the balance of power between them is equal.

Referring again to Exhibit 6.15, assume the matrix structure is for a clothing manufacturer. Product A is footwear, product B is outerwear, product C is sleepwear, and so on. Each product line serves a different market and customers. As a medium-size organization, the company must effectively use people from manufacturing, design, and marketing to work on each product line. There are not enough designers to warrant a separate design department for each product line, so the designers are shared across product lines. Moreover, by keeping the manufacturing, design, and marketing functions intact, employees can develop the in-depth expertise to serve all product lines efficiently.

KEY MATRIX ROLES

The unique aspect of matrix structure as reflected in Exhibit 6.15 is that some employees have two bosses. Working within a matrix structure is difficult for most managers because it requires a new set of skills compared with those required for a single-authority structure. For the matrix to succeed, managers in key roles have specific responsibilities. The key roles are top leaders, matrix bosses, and two-boss employees. These roles are illustrated in the College of Business matrix in Exhibit 6.16. In this matrix, the functional departments are the academic departments of management, marketing, finance, and accounting, which represent the vertical hierarchy. The horizontal reporting relationships are to the program directors for the undergraduate, MBA, and doctoral programs.

Top Leader The dean is the **top leader,** who is the head of both command structures. The primary responsibility for this person is to maintain a power balance between the functional managers (department heads) and product managers (program directors). The top leader must also be willing to delegate decisions and encourage direct contact and group problem solving between department heads and program directors, which will encourage information sharing and coordination.

Matrix Boss The problem for **matrix bosses**—department heads and program directors in Exhibit 6.16—is that they do not have complete control over their subordinates. Matrix bosses must work with each other to delineate activities over which they are responsible. The department head's responsibilities pertain to functional

Exhibit 6.16   Key Positions in a College of Business Matrix Structure.

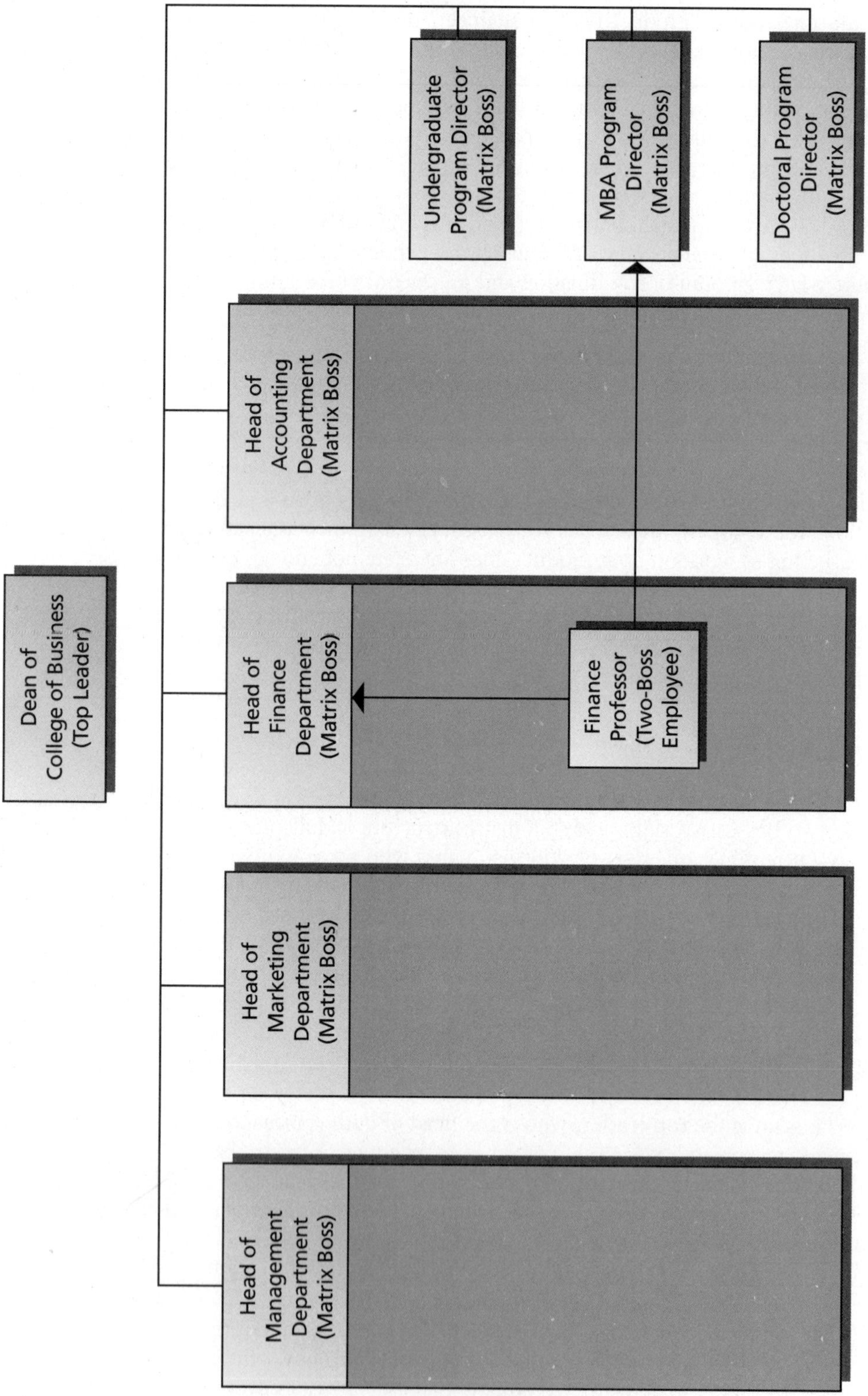

expertise, rules, and teaching standards. The program director is responsible for coordinating the whole program. This person has authority over subordinates for such activities as class scheduling, exams, and preventing overlapping of course content. Matrix bosses must be willing to confront one another on disagreements and conflicts. They must also collaborate on such things as performance reviews, promotions, and salary increases, since professors report to both of them. These activities require a great deal of time, communication, patience, and skill at working with people, which are all part of matrix management.

Two-Boss Employees   The **two-boss employee** often experiences anxiety and stress. Conflicting demands are imposed by the matrix bosses. The finance professor in Exhibit 6.16, for example, must cope with conflicting demands imposed by the finance department head and the MBA program director. The department head's demand to do research is in direct conflict with the MBA program director's demand that time be spent reading and developing teaching materials for use in the MBA program. The two-boss employee must confront both the department head and the MBA program director on these demands and reach a joint decision about how to spend his or her time. Two-boss employees must maintain an effective relationship with both managers, and they should display a dual loyalty toward both their departments and their programs.

STRENGTHS AND WEAKNESSES

The matrix structure is best when environmental uncertainty is high and when goals reflect a dual requirement, such as for both product and functional goals. The dual-authority structure facilitates communication and coordination to cope with rapid environmental change and enables an equal balance between product and functional bosses. The matrix is also good for nonroutine technologies that have interdependencies both within and across functions. The matrix is an organic structure that facilitates discussion and adaptation to unexpected problems. It tends to work best in organizations of moderate size with a few product lines. The matrix is not needed for only a single-product line, and too many product lines make it difficult to coordinate both directions at once.

The matrix structure has been used in organizations for more than thirty years. Although horizontal linkages are increasingly popular, empirical evidence of specific advantages is still relatively sparse. Exhibit 6.17 summarizes the strengths and weaknesses of the matrix structure based on what we know of organizations that use it.[27]

Internal systems reflect the dual organization structure. Two-boss employees are aware of and adopt subgoals for both their functions and their products. Dual planning and budgeting systems should be designed, one for the functional hierarchy and one for the product line hierarchy. Power and influence are shared equally by functional and product heads.

The strength of the matrix is that it enables an organization to meet dual demands from the environment. Resources (people, equipment) can be flexibly allocated across different products, and the organization can adapt to changing external requirements.[28] This structure also provides an opportunity for employees to acquire either functional or general management skills, depending on their interests.

One disadvantage of the matrix is that some employees experience dual authority, which is frustrating and confusing. They need excellent interpersonal and

Context
Structure: Matrix Environment: High uncertainty Technology: Nonroutine, many interdependencies Size: Moderate, a few product lines Goals: Dual—product innovation and technical specialization
Internal Systems
Operative goals: Equal product and functional emphasis Planning and budgeting: Dual systems—by function and by product line Formal authority: Joint between functional and product heads
Strengths
1. Achieves coordination necessary to meet dual demands from environment 2. Flexible sharing of human resources across products 3. Suited to complex decisions and frequent changes in unstable environment 4. Provides opportunity for functional and product skill development 5. Best in medium-sized organizations with multiple products
Weaknesses
1. Causes participants to experience dual authority, which can be frustrating and confusing 2. Means participants need good interpersonal skills and extensive training 3. Is time-consuming; involves frequent meetings and conflict resolution sessions 4. Will not work unless participants understand it and adopt collegial rather than vertical-type relationships. 5. Requires dual pressure from environment to maintain power balance

Source: Adapted from Robert Duncan, "What Is the Right Organization Structure? Decision Tree Analysis Provides the Answer," *Organizational Dynamics* (Winter 1979): 429.

conflict-resolution skills, which may require special training in human relations. The matrix also forces managers to spend a great deal of time in meetings.[29] If managers do not adapt to the information and power sharing required by the matrix, the system will not work. Managers must collaborate with one another rather than rely on vertical authority in decision making. The successful implementation of one matrix structure occurred at a steel company in Pittsburgh.

IN PRACTICE ◆ 6.6
Pittsburgh Steel Company

As far back as anyone can remember, the steel industry in the United States was stable and certain. If steel manufacturers could produce quality steel at a reasonable price, that steel would be sold. No more. Inflation, a national economic downturn, reduced consumption of autos, and competition from steelmakers in Germany and Japan forever changed the steel industry. Today, steelmakers have shifted to specialized steel products. They must market aggressively, make efficient use of internal resources, and adapt to rapid-fire changes.

Pittsburgh Steel employs 2,500 people, makes 300,000 tons of steel a year, and is 170 years old. For 160 of those years, functional structure worked fine. As the environment became more turbulent and competitive, however, Pittsburgh Steel managers discovered they were not keeping up. Fifty percent of Pittsburgh's orders were behind schedule. Profits were eroded by labor, material, and energy cost increases. Market share declined.

In consultation with outside experts, the president of Pittsburgh Steel saw that the company had to walk a tightrope. Pittsburgh Steel had to specialize in a few high-value-added products tailored for separate markets, while maintaining economies of scale and sophisticated technology within functional departments. The dual pressure led to an unusual solution for a steel company: a matrix structure.

Pittsburgh Steel had four product lines: open-die forgings, ring-mill products, wheels and axles, and steelmaking. A business manager was given responsibility and authority of each line, which included preparing a business plan for each product line and developing targets for production costs, product inventory, shipping dates, and gross profit. They were given authority to meet those targets and to make their lines profitable. Functional vice presidents were responsible for technical decisions relating to their function. Functional managers were expected to stay abreast of the latest techniques in their areas and to keep personnel trained in new technologies that could apply to product lines. With twenty thousand recipes for specialty steels and several hundred new recipes ordered each month, functional personnel had to stay current. Two functional departments—field sales and industrial relations—were not included in the matrix because they worked independently. The final design was a hybrid matrix structure with both matrix and functional relationships, as illustrated in Exhibit 6.18.

Implementation of the matrix was slow. Middle managers were confused. Meetings to coordinate across functional departments seemed to be held every day. One manager said, "How can we have time for our normal responsibilities and still have meetings all the time? These procedures are disturbing everything we've always done."

After about a year of training by external consultants, Pittsburgh Steel is on track. Ninety percent of the orders are now delivered on time. Market share has recovered. Both productivity and profitability are increasing steadily. The managers thrive on matrix involvement. Meetings to coordinate product and functional decisions have provided a growth experience. Middle managers now want to include younger managers in the matrix discussions as training for future management responsibility.[30]

Pittsburgh Steel Company illustrates the correct use of a matrix structure. The dual pressure to maintain economies of scale and to market four product lines gave equal emphasis to the functional and product hierarchies. Through continuous meetings for coordination, Pittsburgh Steel achieved both economies of scale and flexibility.

All kinds of organizations have experimented with the matrix, including consulting firms, hospitals, banks, insurance companies, government, and many types of industrial firms.[31] Although it has been widely adopted, the matrix is not a cure-all for structural problems. Many organizations have found the matrix described here, sometimes called a balanced matrix, difficult to install and maintain because one side of the authority structure often dominates. Recognizing this tendency, two variations of matrix structure have evolved—the **functional matrix** and the **project matrix.** In a functional matrix, the functional bosses have primary authority, and project or product managers simply coordinate product activities. In a project matrix, by contrast, the project or product manager has primary responsibility, and

Exhibit 6.18 Matrix Structure for Pittsburgh Steel Company.

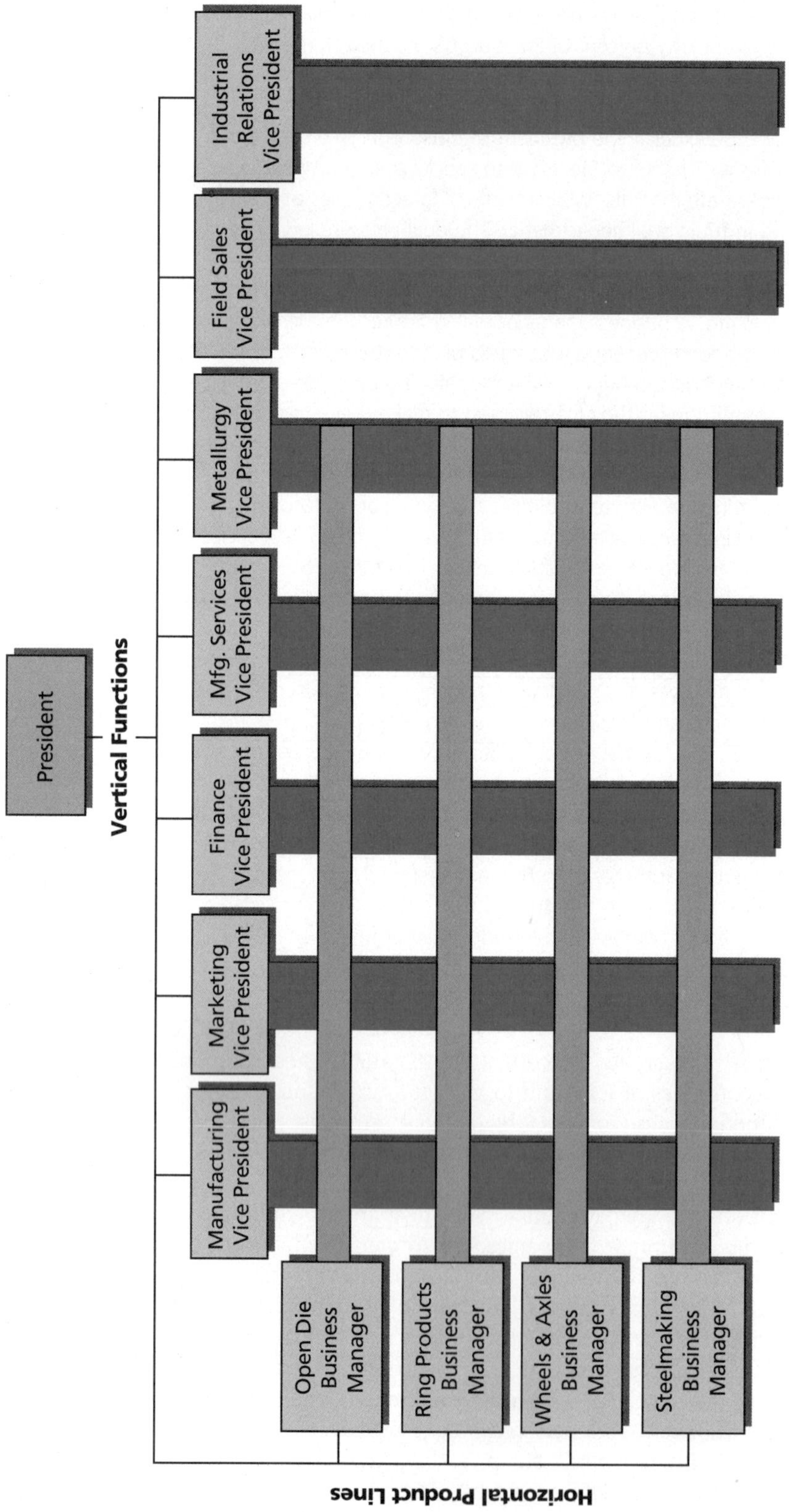

functional managers simply assign technical personnel to projects and provide advisory expertise as needed. For many organizations, one of these approaches works better than the balanced matrix and dual lines of authority.[32]

Symptoms of Structural Deficiency

Each form of structure—functional, product, hybrid, matrix—represents a tool that can help managers make an organization more effective depending on the demands of its situation. Senior managers periodically evaluate organization structure to determine whether it is appropriate to changing organization needs. Many organizations try one organization structure, then reorganize to another structure in an effort to find the right fit between internal reporting relationships and the needs of the external environment. Compaq Computer Corporation, for example, switched from a functional structure to a product structure for about a year to develop new products and then switched back to a functional structure to reduce competition among its product lines.[33]

As a general rule, when organization structure is out of alignment with organization needs, one or more of the following **symptoms of structural deficiency** appear.[34]

- *Decision making is delayed or lacking in quality.* Decision makers may be overloaded because the hierarchy funnels too many problems and decisions to them. Delegation to lower levels may be insufficient. Another cause of poor-quality decisions is that information may not reach the correct people. Information linkages in either the vertical or horizontal direction may be inadequate to ensure decision quality.
- *The organization does not respond innovatively to a changing environment.* One reason for lack of innovation is that departments are not coordinated horizontally. The identification of customer needs by the marketing department and the identification of technological developments in the research department must be coordinated. Organization structure also has to specify departmental responsibilities that include environmental scanning and innovation.
- *Too much conflict is evident.* Organization structure should allow conflicting departmental goals to combine into a single set of objectives for the entire organization. When departments act at cross purposes or are under pressure to achieve departmental goals at the expense of organizational goals, the structure is often at fault. Horizontal linkage mechanisms are not adequate.

Summary and Interpretation

Organization structure must accomplish two things for the organization. It must provide a framework of responsibilities, reporting relationships, and groupings, and it must provide mechanisms for linking and coordinating organizational elements into a coherent whole. The structure is reflected on the organization chart. Linking the organization into a coherent whole requires the use of information systems and linkage devices in addition to the organization chart.

It is important to understand the information-processing perspective on structure. Organization structure can be designed to provide vertical and horizontal information linkages based upon the information processing required because of an uncertain environment, technology, size, or goals. Early organization theorists stressed vertical design and relied on vertical linkages, such as the hierarchy, planning, and new positions, to provide coordination. Vertical linkages are not sufficient for most organizations in today's complex and rapidly changing world.

The trend is toward flatter, more horizontal structures. Many organizations are breaking down the vertical hierarchy in favor of cross-functional teams. Other ways organizations provide horizontal linkages are through temporary task forces; regular, direct contact between managers across department lines; and through full-time integrators, such as product managers.

Alternatives for grouping employees and departments into overall structural design include activity (functional) grouping, output (product) grouping, user or customer (geographic) grouping, and multifocused (hybrid, matrix) grouping. The best organization design achieves the correct balance between vertical and horizontal coordination. The choice between functional, product and hybrid structures determines vertical priority and, hence, where coordination and integration will be greatest. Horizontal linkage mechanisms complement the vertical dimension to achieve the integration of departments and levels into an organizational whole. The matrix organization implements an equal balance between the vertical and horizontal dimensions of structure.

Finally, an organization chart is only so many lines and boxes on a piece of paper. A new organization structure will not necessarily solve an organization's problems. The organization chart simply reflects what people should do and what their responsibilities are. The purpose of the organization chart is to encourage and direct employees into activities and communications that enable the organization to achieve its goals. The organization chart provides the structure, but employees provide the behavior. The chart is a guideline to encourage people to work together, but management must implement the structure and carry it out.

KEY CONCEPTS

activity grouping
departmental grouping
functional matrix
functional structure
horizontal linkage
hybrid structure
integrator
liaison role
matrix bosses
matrix structure
multifocused grouping
output grouping

product structure
project matrix
structure
symptoms of structural deficiency
task force
teams
top leader
two-boss employee
user or customer grouping
vertical information system
vertical linkages

DISCUSSION QUESTIONS

1. What is the definition of *organization structure*? Does organization structure appear on the organization chart? Explain.

2. How do rules and plans help an organization achieve vertical integration?

3. When is a functional structure preferable to a product structure?

4. Large corporations tend to use hybrid structures. Why?

5. How does organizational context influence the choice of structure? Are some contextual variables more important than others? Discuss.

6. What is the difference between a task force and a team? Between liaison role and integrating role? Which of these provides the greatest amount of horizontal coordination?

7. What conditions usually have to be present before an organization should adopt a matrix structure?

8. The manager of a consumer products firm said, "We use the brand manager position to train future executives." Do you think the brand manager position is a good training ground? Discuss.

9. In a matrix organization, how do the role requirements of the top leader differ from the role requirements of the matrix bosses?

10. In your opinion, what is the value of an information-processing perspective on structure?

 GUIDES TO ACTION

As an organization designer, keep these guides in mind:

1. Develop organization charts that describe task responsibilities, vertical reporting relationships, and the grouping of individuals into departments. Provide sufficient documentation so that all people within the organization know to whom they report and how they fit into the total organization picture.

2. Provide vertical and horizontal information linkages to integrate diverse departments into a coherent whole. Achieve vertical linkage through hierarchy referral, rules and plans, new positions, and vertical information systems. Achieve horizontal linkage through paperwork, direct contact, liaison roles, task forces, full-time integrators, and teams.

3. Choose between functional or product structures when designing overall organization structure. Use a functional structure in a small or medium-sized organization that has a stable environment. Use a product structure in a large organization that has multiple product lines and when you wish to give priority to product goals and to coordination across functions.

4. Implement hybrid structures, when needed, in large corporations by dividing the organization into self-contained product divisions and assigning to the product division each function needed for the product line. If a function serves the entire organization rather than a specific product line, structure that function as a central functional department. Use a hybrid structure to gain the advantages of both functional and product design while eliminating some of the disadvantages.

5. Consider a matrix structure in certain organization settings if neither the product nor the functional structure meets coordination needs. For best results with a matrix structure, use it in a medium-sized organization with

a small number of products that has a changing environment and needs to give equal priority to both products and functions because of dual pressures from the environment. Do not use the matrix structure unless there is truly a need for a dual hierarchy and employees are well trained in its purpose and operation.

6. Consider a structural reorganization whenever the symptoms of structural deficiency are observed. Use organization structure to solve the problems of poor-quality decision making, slow response to the external environment, and too much conflict between departments.

Consider these guides when analyzing the following case.

CASE FOR ANALYSIS

Aquarius Advertising Agency*

The Aquarius Advertising Agency is a middle-sized firm that offered two basic services to its clients: (1) customized plans for the content of an advertising campaign (for example, slogans, layouts) and (2) complete plans for media (such as radio, TV, newspapers, billboards, and magazines). Additional services included aid in marketing and distribution of products and marketing research to test advertising effectiveness.

Its activities were organized in a traditional manner. The formal organization is shown in Exhibit 6.19. Each department included similar functions.

Each client account was coordinated by an account executive who acted as a liaison between the client and the various specialists on the professional staff of the operations and marketing divisions. The number of direct communications and contacts between clients and Aquarius specialists, clients and account executives, and Aquarius specialists and account executives is indicated in Exhibit 6.20. These sociometric data were gathered by a consultant who conducted a study of the patterns of formal and informal communication. Each intersecting cell of Aquarius personnel and the clients contains an index of the direct contacts between them.

Although an account executive was designated to be the liaison between the client and specialists within the agency, communications frequently occurred directly between clients and specialists and bypassed the account executive. These direct contacts involved a wide range of interactions, such as meetings, telephone calls, letters, and so on. A large number of direct communications occurred between agency specialists and their counterparts in the client organization. For example, an art specialist working as one member of a team on a particular client account would often be contacted directly by the client's in-house art specialist, and agency research personnel had direct communication with research people of the client firm. Also, some of the unstructured contacts often led to more formal meetings with clients in which agency personnel made presentations, interpreted

*Adapted from John F. Veiga and John N. Yanouzas, "Aquarius Advertising Agency," *The Dynamics of Organization Theory* (St. Paul, Minn.: West, 1984), 212–17, with permission.

Exhibit 6.19   Aquarius Advertising Agency Organization Chart.

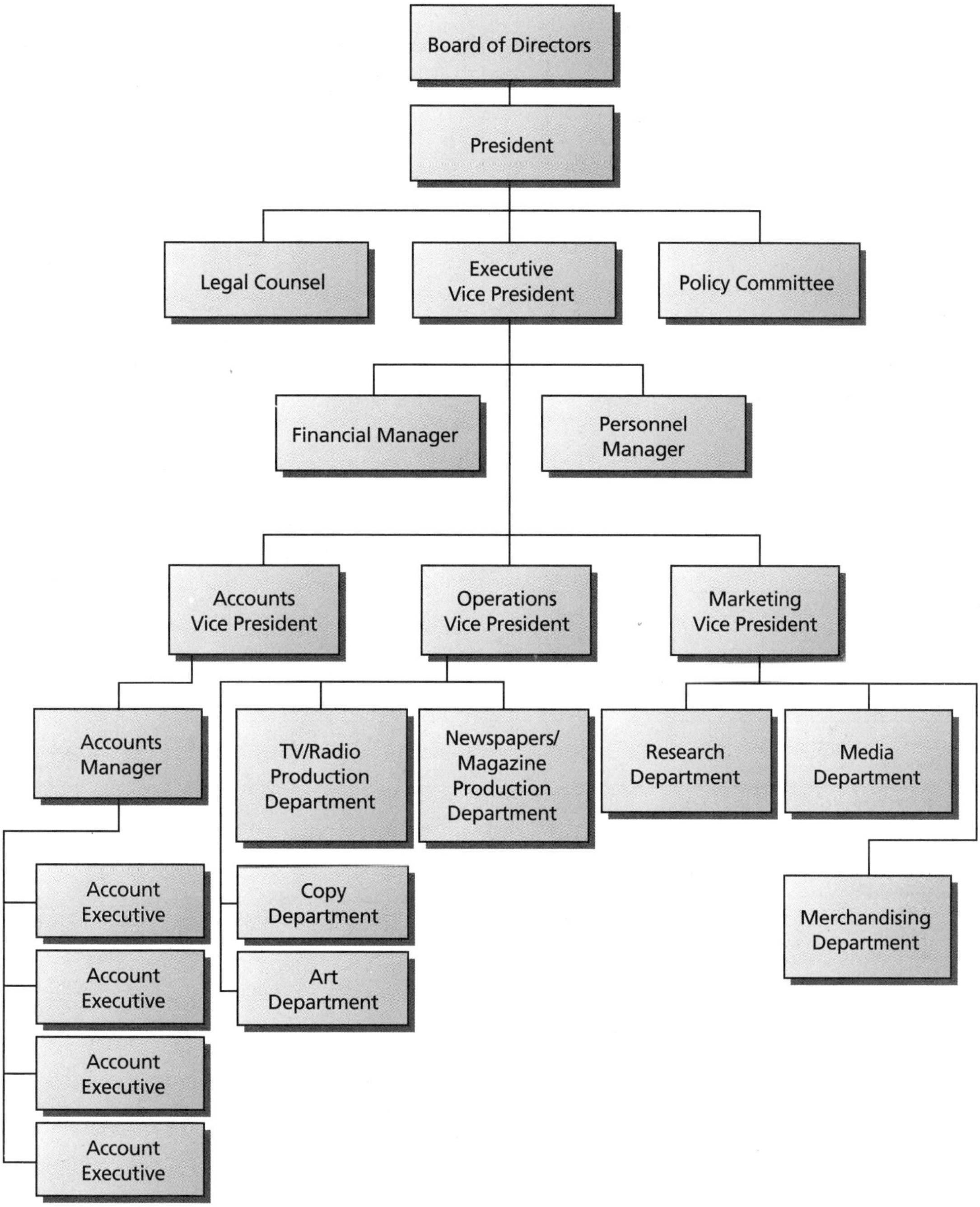

and defended agency policy, and committed the agency to certain courses of action.

Both hierarchical and professional systems operated within the departments of the operations and marketing divisions. Each department was organized hierarchically

Exhibit 6.20   Sociometric Index of Contacts of Aquarius Personnel and Clients.

	Clients	Account Manager	Account Executives	TV/Radio Specialists	Newspaper/Magazine Specialists	Copy Specialists	Art Specialists	Merchandising Specialists	Media Specialists	Research Specialists
Clients	X	F	F	N	N	O	O	O	O	O
Account Manager		X	F	N	N	N	N	N	N	N
Account Executives			X	F	F	F	F	F	F	F
TV/Radio Specialists				X	N	O	O	N	N	O
Newspaper/Magazine Specialists					X	O	O	N	O	O
Copy Specialists						X	N	O	O	O
Art Specialists							X	O	O	O
Merchandising Specialists								X	F	F
Media Specialists									X	F
Research Specialists										X

F = Frequent – daily
O = Occasional – once or twice per project
N = None

with a director, an assistant director, and several levels of authority. Professional communications were widespread and mainly concerned with sharing knowledge and techniques, technical evaluation of work, and development of professional interests. Control in each department was exercised mainly through control of promotions and supervision of work done by subordinates. Many account executives, however, felt the need for more influence, and one commented:

Creativity and art. That's all I hear around here. It is hard as hell to effectively manage six or seven hotshots who claim they have to do their own thing.
Each of them tries to sell his or her idea to the client, and most of the time I
don't know what has happened until a week later. If I were a despot, I
would make all of them check with me first to get approval. Things would
sure change around here.

The need for reorganization was made more acute by changes in the environment. Within a short period of time, there was a rapid turnover in the major
accounts handled by the agency. It was typical for advertising agencies to gain or
lose clients quickly, often with no advance warning as consumer behavior and life-
style changes emerged and product innovations occurred.

An agency reorganization was one solution proposed by top management to
increase flexibility in this unpredictable environment. The reorganization was
aimed at reducing the agency's response time to environmental changes and at
increasing cooperation and communication among specialists from different
departments. The top managers are not sure what type of reorganization is appropriate. They would like your help analyzing their context and current structure
and welcome your advice on proposing a new structure.

QUESTIONS

1. Analyze Aquarius with respect to the five contextual variables in Exhibit 6.1.
   How would you describe the environment, goals, technology, size, and structure
   for Aquarius?
2. Design an organization structure that takes into consideration the contextual variables and the information flows in Exhibit 6.2. (Hint: One approach would be to
   treat account managers as project managers. Another approach would be to design
   a product structure with departments reporting to each account executive.)
3. Would a matrix structure be feasible for Aquarius? Why or why not?

NOTES

1. Alex Taylor III, "Will Success Spoil Chrysler?" *Fortune,* 10 January 1994, 88–92.
2. John Child, *Organization* (New York: Harper & Row, 1984).
3. Stuart Ranson, Bob Hinings, and Royston Green-wood, "The Structuring of Organizational Struc-tures," *Administrative Science Quarterly* 25 (1980): 1–17; Hugh Willmott, "The Structuring of Orga-nizational Structure: A Note," *Administrative Sci-ence Quarterly* 26 (1981): 470–74.
4. David Nadler and Michael Tushman, *Strategic Organization Design* (Glenview, Ill.: Scott Fores-man, 1988).
5. *Ibid.*
6. Based on Jay R. Galbraith, *Designing Complex Organizations* (Reading, Mass.: Addison-Wesley, 1973) and *Organization Design* (Reading, Mass.: Addison-Wesley, 1977), 81–127.
7. Lee Iacocca with William Novak, *Iacocca: An Autobiography* (New York: Phantom Books, 1984), 152–53.
8. Based on Galbraith, *Designing Complex Organiza-tions.*
9. Barbara Ettorre, "Simplicity Cuts a New Pattern," *Management Review* (December 1993): 25–29.
10. Walter Kiechel III, "The Art of the Corporate Task Force," *Fortune,* 28 January 1991, 104–5; William J. Altier, "Task Forces: An Effective Management Tool," *Management Review* (February 1987): 52–57.
11. Paul R. Lawrence and Jay W. Lorsch, "New Man-agerial Job: The Integrator," *Harvard Business Review* (November-December 1967): 142–51.
12. Ann M. Morrison, "The General Mills Brand of Managers," *Fortune,* 12 January 1982, 99–107.
13. *Ibid.;* Daniel Rosenheim, "The Metamorphosis of

General Mills," *Houston Chronicle*, 1 April 1982, sec. 3, p. 4.

14. Thomas A. Stewart, "The Search for the Organization of Tomorrow," *Fortune*, 18 May 1992, 92–98.

15. Ron Winslow, "Utility Cuts Red Tape, Builds Nuclear Plant Almost on Schedule," *Wall Street Journal*, 22 February 1984, 1, 18.

16. Henry Mintzberg, *The Structuring of Organizations* (Englewood Cliffs, N.J.: Prentice-Hall, 1979).

17. Based on Robert Duncan, "What Is the Right Organization Structure?" *Organizational Dynamics* (Winter 1979): 59–80; W. Alan Randolph and Gregory G. Dess, "The Congruence Perspective of Organization Design: A Conceptual Model and Multivariate Research Approach," *Academy of Management Review* 9 (1984): 114–27.

18. Toni Mack, "The Ice Cream Man Cometh," *Forbes*, 22 January 1990, 52–56; David Abdalla, J. Doehring, and Ann Windhager, "Blue Bell Creameries, Inc.: Case and Analysis" (Unpublished manuscript, Texas A&M University, 1981); Jorjanna Price, "Creamery Churns Its Ice Cream into Cool Millions," *Parade*, 21 February 1982, 18–22.

19. Thomas A. Stewart, "The Search for the Organization of Tomorrow," *Fortune*, 18 May 1992, 92–98; and Rahul Jacob, "Absence of Management," *American Way*, 15 February 1993, 38–41.

20. Based on Duncan, "What Is the Right Organization Structure?"

21. Joseph Weber, "A Big Company That Works," *Business Week*, 4 May 1992, 124–132; and Elyse Tanouye, "Johnson & Johnson Stays Fit by Shuffling Its Mix of Businesses," *Wall Street Journal*, 22 December 1992, A1, A4.

22. Weber, "A Big Company That Works."

23. Lisa Driscoll, "The New, New Thinking at Xerox," *Business Week*, 22 June 1992, 120–21.

24. Adapted from Linda S. Ackerman, "Transition Management: An In-depth Look at Managing Complex Change," *Organizational Dynamics* (Summer 1982): 46–66.

25. Terrence P. Pare, "How to Cut the Cost of Headquarters," *Fortune*, 11 September 1989, 189–96; Thomas Moore, "Goodbye, Corporate Staff," *Fortune*, 21 December 1987, 65–76.

26. Stanley M. Davis and Paul R. Lawrence, *Matrix* (Reading, Mass.: Addison-Wesley, 1977), 11–24.

27. Robert C. Ford and W. Alan Randolph, "Cross-Functional Structures: A Review and Integration of Matrix Organizations and Project Management," *Journal of Management* 18 (June 1992): 267–94; Duncan, "What Is the Right Organization Structure?"

28. Lawton R. Burns, "Matrix Management in Hospitals: Testing Theories of Matrix Structure and Development," *Administrative Science Quarterly* 34 (1989): 349–68.

29. Christopher A. Bartlett and Sumantra Ghoshal, "Matrix Management: Not a Structure, a Frame of Mind," *Harvard Business Review* (July-August 1990): 138–45.

30. This case was inspired by John E. Fogerty, "Integrative Management at Standard Steel" (Unpublished manuscript, Latrobe, Pennsylvania, 1980); Bill Saporito, "Allegheny Ludlum has Steel Figured Out," *Fortune*, 25 June 1984, 40–44; John M. Starrels, "Steel's Stiff Competition," *Wall Street Journal*, 9 July 1982, 12; "The Worldwide Steel Industry: Reshaping to Survive," *Business Week*, 20 August 1984, 150–54.

31. Davis and Lawrence, *Matrix*, 155–80.

32. Erik W. Larson and David H. Gobeli, "Matrix Management: Contradictions and Insight," *California Management Review* 29 (Summer 1987): 126–38.

33. Jo Ellen Davis, "Who's Afraid of IBM?" *Business Week*, 29 June 1987, 68–74.

34. Based on Child, *Organization*, ch. 1.

CHAPTER

7

Contemporary Designs for Global Competition

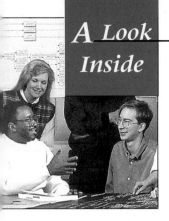

General Electric

General Electric is a leader among global technology organizations, but like all businesses today it feels increasing competition in the world marketplace. GE remains competitive by staying in touch with the rapidly changing global scene and reorganizing to meet new challenges.

Several years ago, the company's $3 billion lighting division scrapped its traditional vertical hierarchy for an organization design in which a team of only nine to twelve senior executives oversees about one hundred processes or programs worldwide. Cross-functional teams work together on virtually all division processes, from designing new products to improving the yield on production machinery. Day-to-day activities are managed by the teams themselves. The role of senior executives is to allocate resources and ensure coordination among the numerous programs and processes, not to supervise the work teams.

The shift to a horizontal organization has led to significant gains for GE. It has reduced costs and shortened product development time, enabling the company to get products to market faster. It has also allowed the giant company to be as responsive to its worldwide customers as if it were a small, local organization. GE knows that staying in tune with customers will be increasingly important in a world of heightened global competition.

And changes in GE's training and evaluation processes keep the company innovative and responsive. GE's team workers are evaluated—and compensated—based not just on the individual work they do but, more important, on the new cross-functional skills they learn. By encouraging and nurturing the desire and ability of the workers to improve and innovate, GE's systems help keep the company competitive domestically and able to face increasing global competition.[1]

General Electric is not the only large corporation looking for new ways to fight on the increasingly competitive global battleground. Dozens of America's top manufacturers, including Gillette, Xerox, Hewlett-Packard, Dow Chemical, 3M, and DuPont, sell more of their products outside of the United States than they do at home. In terms of profits, Coca-Cola made more money in both the Pacific and western Europe than it did in the United States, and nearly 70 percent of General Motors's profit in recent years has been from non-U.S. operations.

Even more ominous for North American companies is the arrival on North American shores of foreign competitors in enormous numbers and strength. Companies such as Nestle (Switzerland), Philips (Netherlands), Michelin (France), Sony and Honda (Japan), Bayer (Germany), Northern Telecom (Canada), and Unilever (United Kingdom) all receive more than 40 percent of annual sales from foreign countries.[2] They are in North America competing vigorously for markets.

No company is safe. Japanese, Canadian, and British businesses acquire hundreds of U.S. companies each year.[3] North American companies simply have no choice about global competition. If companies decide not to sell overseas, overseas competitors will come here and compete with them or buy them out. No company is isolated from global influence. No employee is immune. A small company, Florod Corporation, made a laser eraser that had a market of no more than forty companies. Giant NEC from Japan pushed its way in with a better product, practically destroying Florod, which had to scramble for other products to survive.

PURPOSE OF THIS CHAPTER

This chapter will introduce new approaches to organization design that enable organizations to compete effectively in a global environment. First, we will discuss the grim reality of worldwide competition. Then we will examine new designs for domestic advantage, including a shift from vertical to horizontal management, the radical redesign of business processes known as *reengineering,* and the use of network structures. Finally, we will discuss how companies can best organize for worldwide advantage, ranging from adding an export department to establishing a worldwide matrix or heterarchy structure. By the end of the chapter, you will understand how to apply organization design innovations to a variety of domestic and international situations.

Global Forces at Work

It is hard to deny the impact of globalization on each of us. We buy goods and services from around the world. Many U.S. workers are already working for foreign bosses. Even if you live and work in a small city, an international thrust for your company may be just around the corner, with rewards going to employees who can speak a foreign language or who have international abilities.

Globalization is so pervasive that it is hard to sort out, but the boxes in Exhibit 7.1 identify some of the key elements.[4] International forces at work today include the dominant economies of Japan and Germany, which sponsor powerhouse international companies and have huge positive trade balances with the United States. This means the end of U.S. company dominance and the onset of intense competition among high-wage nations. Newly industrialized countries such as Korea, Taiwan, and Spain are fast-growing and rapidly becoming industrialized. Their companies produce low-cost, high-quality commodities and are moving into high-value items, such as automobiles and high-technology electronic goods. The shift toward market economies in eastern Europe and the former Soviet republics is rapidly producing more sources of goods, potential new markets, and, to some extent, an unpredictable future about how these countries will affect globalization.

More uncertainty will be caused by international blocs, including: the European Economic Community agreement to drop internal trade barriers during 1992 and beyond, spawning even larger, more competitive international companies and erecting barriers to outsiders; the "yen bloc" that includes Asian powerhouse nations; and the North American Free Trade Agreement. These power blocs will shape the world economy into the twenty-first century and will certainly mean the end of U.S. domination of international trade policy.

What are the outcomes for individuals and businesses within the United States and Canada—or any other country, for that matter? One outcome is economic volatility: No one knows whether oil will cost fifteen or twenty dollars a barrel next year. Likewise, currency values fluctuate based on inflation, trade balances, and capital investments over which no single country has control. Products we buy today, such as an IBM PC or a Black & Decker appliance, may include components from a dozen nations. No company or country can provide global economic leadership; every company and country is subordinate to larger economic forces.

Exhibit 7.1   Global Forces Influencing Domestic Organizations.

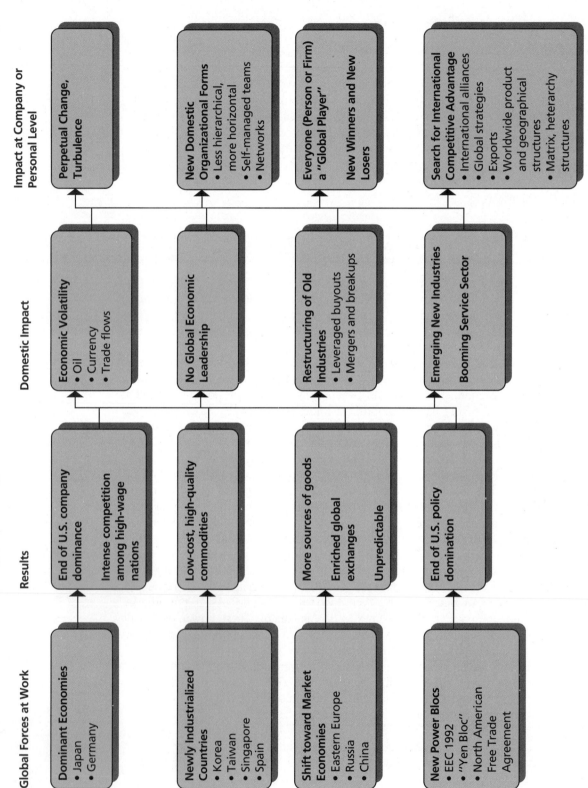

Source: Adapted from Tom Peters, "Prometheus Barely Unbound," *Academy of Management Executive* 4 (1990): 71.

No wonder we've seen the dramatic restructuring of traditional industries in the United States through leveraged buyouts, mergers, and breakups. These companies were striving for greater efficiency within an increasingly turbulent and competitive international environment. Indeed, the spinoffs and breakups of previous mergers may turn out to be a bigger story than the mergers, because the smaller players are efficient and well managed. Also, expect new and rapidly emerging industries—such as information technology, that already contributes 20 percent directly to gross national product. Biotechnology is just underway and may foster its own industrial revolution. People who grew up feeling comfortable and secure working for a manufacturing firm appreciate just how elusive stability and security are in the new world order.

The impact at a personal level is illustrated in the righthand column of Exhibit 7.1. Companies operating nationally, such as Wal-Mart or Quad/Graphics, are adopting new organizational forms that include less hierarchy and more self-managed teams and dynamic network structures that provide autonomy to clusters of people and activities. These organizational forms utilize human resources better than ever before and enable companies to fend off international competition. One example of this shift is Ciba-Geigy Canada, described in the Paradigm Buster.

Another outcome is perpetual change—enduring turbulence that organizations must learn to accept as the norm. Everyone—employees, organizations—needs to begin thinking of themselves as global players; they must try to use global alliances to advantage, sell to global markets, and be ready to meet global competition. This is

 Paradigm Buster

Ciba-Geigy Canada, Ltd.

By getting rid of the bosses, Ciba-Geigy's agricultural chemicals plant in Ontario has boosted productivity by up to 30 percent. Plant workers set schedules, manage jobs, create job descriptions, interview new job applicants, and handle numerous decisions and tasks once handled by their supervisors. For Director of Production Gerry Rich and his team of workers, the post-boss paradigm is a dream come true.

When Rich first came to Ciba-Geigy, he found twelve managers and supervisors watching over ninety employees who "seemed to be leaving their ability to think at the factory gate." Productivity was low, and standards of quality were slipping. Rich decided to throw out the management rulebook in a daring effort to turn the plant around. Production workers served on the design team along with representatives from management, the warehouse, the administrative office, and the chemical lab. Ultimately, the plant was redesigned for participative management, with production, warehouse, and maintenance at the center of the new organization. The structure looks something like the rings on a dartboard, with administration and support services, such as the lab, forming layers surrounding the center. On the very outside are the managers—now called advisers—whose primary job is to facilitate teamwork and act as liaison between teams. Many of the old-style managers couldn't adapt; by the end of the reorganization, two of the plant's three foremen and half of the management staff had left the company. As Rich put it, "People who can't change, you have to ask to work in an authoritarian environment—somewhere else."

Clearly, the loss of the bosses hasn't hurt at Ciba-Geigy.

Source: John Southerst, "First, We Dump the Bosses," *Canadian Business,* April 1992, 46–51.

especially true for Americans, who grew up believing in the superiority and invincibility of the U.S. economy.

All of this turbulence creates new winners and new losers. New winners are companies thriving under the new rules of the game—Nucor in steel, Dell in computers, MCI in telecommunications—companies not even in existence twenty-five years ago. Moreover, companies are learning to search for international competitive advantage through international alliances and joint ventures. Even small companies are learning to produce quality products that can compete overseas and, hence, are adding export departments. Larger companies have learned to organize themselves into worldwide product or geographical structures. A few global firms have attained a quality of being transnational—almost without a home country—and are held together through complex international matrix or heterarchy structures that allow them to be global and local in fifty or more countries at the same time.

These international forces and the impact on individuals and companies mean that things must be done faster, organizations must be flexible, and innovation and improvement are paramount. Companies must be designed for maximum domestic or worldwide advantage.

In the next section, we will discuss some new organizational designs for domestic advantage, and then we will look at worldwide organization designs.

New Designs for Domestic Advantage

The functional organization structure described in Chapter 6 was the first to be used by large firms and eventually became associated with bureaucracy. The product or divisional structure was the next innovation in structure and provided a way to subdivide huge firms like General Motors and Sears Roebuck into more manageable profit centers. Then came the notion of cross-functional teams that worked horizontally to coordinate across departments. Horizontal teams evolved into the matrix structure that has two hierarchies simultaneously.

The most recent organization design innovations are a significant shift toward horizontal rather than vertical management, the radical redesign of business processes referred to as reenginnering, and the use of dynamic network structures. These approaches harness human resources in new ways to give companies a competitive advantage.

THE HORIZONTAL CORPORATION

Many of today's corporations are shifting away from the top-heavy functionally organized structures of the past to a form that virtually eliminates both the vertical hierarchy and old departmental boundaries. The newly emerging **horizontal corporation** is illustrated in Exhibit 7.2 and has the following characteristics:

1. Structure is created around work flows or processes rather than departmental functions. Boundaries between traditional departments are obliterated. At Chrysler, for example, the structure is designed around the core processes of new car development.
2. The vertical hierarchy is flattened, with perhaps only a few senior executives in traditional support functions, such as finance and human resources.

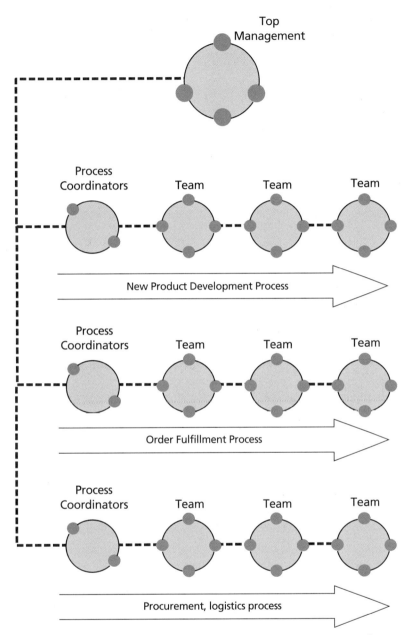

Exhibit 7.2
The Horizontal
Corporation.

Source: Based on John A. Byrne, "The Horizontal Corporation," *Business Week,* 20 December 1993, 76–81; and Thomas A. Stewart, "The Search for the Organization of Tomorrow," *Fortune,* 18 May 1992, 92–98.

3. Management tasks are delegated to the lowest level. Most employees work in multidisciplinary, self-managed teams organized around a process, such as new product development. Kodak, for example, did away with its senior vice presidents in charge of such functions as administration, manufacturing, and R&D and replaced them with self-directed teams. The company has over one thousand such teams working on various processes and programs.

4. Customers drive the horizontal corporation. For the horizontal design to work, processes must be based on meeting customer needs. Employees are brought into direct, regular contact with customers as well as suppliers. Sometimes, representatives of these outside organizations serve as full-fledged team members.[5]

Self-Managed Teams   Self-managed teams are the building blocks of the new horizontal organization. A **self-managed team** is an outgrowth of earlier team approaches.[6] For example, many companies have used cross-functional teams to achieve coordination across departments and task forces to accomplish temporary projects. Other companies have experimented with problem-solving teams of voluntary hourly employees who meet to discuss ways to improve quality, efficiency, and work environment.

Self-managed teams, also called self-directed teams, typically consist of five to thirty workers with different skills who rotate jobs and produce an entire product or service and who take over managerial duties, such as work and vacation scheduling, ordering materials, and hiring new members. To date, several hundred companies in Canada and the United States have experimented with a self-managed team design.[7] These companies include AT&T, Xerox, General Mills, Federal Express, Ryder Systems and Motorola.

The self-managed team design consists of permanent teams that include the following three elements:

1. The team is given access to resources, such as materials, information, equipment, machinery, and supplies, needed to perform a complete task.
2. The team includes a range of employee skills, such as engineering, manufacturing, finance, and marketing. The team eliminates barriers between departments, functions, disciplines, or specialties. Team members are cross-trained to perform one another's jobs, and the combined skills are sufficient to perform a major organizational task.
3. The team is empowered with decision-making authority, which means members have the freedom to plan, solve problems, set priorities, spend money, monitor results, and coordinate activities with other departments or teams. The team must have autonomy to do what is necessary to accomplish the task.[8]

Volvo uses self-managed teams of seven to ten hourly workers, with each team assembling four cars per shift. Members are trained to handle all assembly jobs, creating greater employee motivation and decreased absenteeism.[9] In Canada, Campbell Soup Company Ltd. designed self-managed teams to make its operations competitive with U.S. operations, achieving an "impossible" assignment of finding $700,000 of savings in three months.[10] At a General Mills cereal plant, teams of hourly workers designed the work process and purchased the machinery. Team members schedule, operate, and maintain the machinery, and do it all so well that the factory runs without managers during the night shift.[11]

From Vertical to Horizontal   So far, most of the experimentation with teams and horizontal structures has been at the lower levels of organizations, but today, more companies are shifting their entire structure to a horizontal mode. Some start-up companies, such as Astra-Merck Group, a stand-alone company created to market anti-ulcer and blood-pressure medicine from Sweden's Astra, are structuring themselves as horizontal organizations from the beginning. Astra-Merck is organized around processes, such as drug development and product distribution, rather than divided into functional departments.

Eastman Chemical Company, a $3.5 billion stand-alone unit of Eastman-Kodak, replaced several of its senior vice presidents with self-managed teams. The company calls its new organization chart "the pizza chart," because it looks like a round pizza with several slices of pepperoni on top. Each slice of pepperoni (small circles) on the pizza represents a self-managed team that is responsible for a work flow, such as cellulose technology. The president of the company is in the center of the pizza. Surrounding him are the self-managed teams, with the white space in between reflecting where the interaction among teams should take place. As Ernest W. Deavenport, Jr., the "head pepperoni," says, "We did it in circular form to show that everyone is equal in the organization. No one dominates the other."[12]

Similarly, at FourGen Technologies Software, Inc., there are no bosses. The employees run the company.

IN PRACTICE ◆ 7.1
FourGen Technologies Software, Inc.

In six years, Seattle-based FourGen Technologies has grown into a $10 million company and become a key player in its market niche, accounting software for the Unix operating system.

FourGen's eighty-five employees work in cross-functional teams of three or four people and manage themselves. They learn each other's jobs. They work directly with customers. There are no bosses, no job descriptions, and no doors—everyone, including the president of the company, works in accessible cubicles rather than offices. The self-managed teams are held accountable for contributing to the value of the company, which is measured strictly in terms of customer satisfaction. Managers serve as facilitators, not directors. All team decisions are reached through consensus.

While large corporations are struggling to break down vertical hierarchies, small companies like FourGen face the challenge of keeping such hierarchies from developing as they grow. So far, FourGen is doing it by continuing to create new teams. If an employee isn't able to grow along with the company, the team members have to come up with solutions, which may mean shifting that person to another team or trying to help him or her find a better-suited position somewhere else.

In addition, all employees are encouraged to continually examine and question the company's structure and operations. As president Gary Gagliardi says, "You constantly have to reinvent the organization if it's going to work."[13]

Advantages and Disadvantages   The horizontal structure with self-managed teams has yielded excellent results in many organizations. But, as with all structures, it has disadvantages as well as advantages. The most significant advantage is that it delivers dramatic improvements in speed and efficiency. Rapid response time and quicker decisions mean greater customer satisfaction. Second, there are reduced, practically nonexistent barriers among departments, which means achieving cooperation with the total task in mind. Third, there is better morale because employees are enthused about their involvement and participation. Finally, administrative overhead is reduced because teams take on the administrative tasks.

But shifting to a horizontal structure can be a lengthy and difficult process. For example, simply defining the processes around which teams are to be organized can be mind-boggling. AT&T's sixteen thousand employee Network Systems Division eventually counted up 130 processes, then began working to pare them down to thirteen core ones.[14] Another major difficulty is acceptance by middle managers, who may fear the loss of their jobs or their status in the functional hierarchy. The shift to horizontal structures and self-managed teams also means that employees spend a lot of time in meetings to coordinate and to reach consensual decisions. In addition, there is a danger that the company will organize around processes without analyzing and linking processes to its key goals, in which case the new structure may bring about more negative than positive results. In the next section, we discuss *reengineering,* which can prevent this from happening.

REENGINEERING

One popular management concept sweeping through corporate America is **reengineering,** the radical redesign of business processes to achieve dramatic improvements in cost, quality, service, and speed. Taco Bell, Union Carbide, Eastman Kodak, and American Express are among the dozens of companies that have used reengineering to reap extraordinary gains in productivity and profitability. After reengineering, Union Carbide cut $400 million out of fixed costs in just three years. Taco Bell was able to lower its prices and still boost peak serving capacity from four hundred to fifteen hundred dollars per hour at its average restaurant.[15]

Reengineering basically means starting over, pushing aside all the notions of how work *was* done and then deciding how it can best be done now. The idea is to squeeze out the dead space and time lags in work flows. This almost always means rethinking organization structure and is often the first step in a shift to a more horizontal structure. For example, reengineering almost always leads to organizing work around process rather than function. When reengineering is implemented, companies are more likely to organize around processes that are closely tied to their key goals. As described in Book Mark 7.0, reengineering can lead to stunning results, but, as with all business ideas, it has its drawbacks. Because reengineering is expensive, time-consuming, and usually painful, it seems best suited to corporations that are facing major shifts in the nature of competition, such as in the field of telecommunications.

DYNAMIC NETWORK DESIGN

Another major trend of the 1990s is the choice companies are making to limit themselves to only a few activities that they do extremely well and let outside specialists handle the rest. These network organizations, sometimes also called *modular corporations,* are flourishing particularly in fast-moving industries, such as apparel and electronics, but even companies in such industries as steel and chemicals are shifting toward this type of structure.[16]

The **dynamic network** structure incorporates a free market style to replace the traditional vertical hierarchy. A company keeps key activities in-house and then outsources other functions, such as sales, accounting, and manufacturing, to separate companies or individuals who are coordinated or brokered by a small headquarters. In most cases, these separate organizations are connected electronically to a central office.[17] An illustration of how this organization might look is in Exhibit 7.3.

 BOOKMARK 7.0

HAVE YOU READ ABOUT THIS?

Reengineering the Corporation
by Michael Hammer and James Champy

One of the most memorable moments in baseball history occurred during Game 3 of the 1932 World Series when Babe Ruth pointed at a spot in the outfield bleachers, then hit a home run there. American business, like baseball fans, has long been enamored of the home run.

Although many U.S. companies have been successful with incremental approaches like total quality management, Michael Hammer and James Champy argue that most firms are better off eschewing incrementalism, which means trying to do worthless tasks more efficiently. Corporations can seek quantum leaps. Old ways of doing business no longer work. Reengineering, their solution to poor business performance, promises huge benefits—home runs instead of singles, walks, and sacrifices.

The Old Way

The typical modern business is organized on Adam Smith's principle of the division of labor and task specialization. The resulting work fragmentation makes coordination within the organization extremely difficult. This old way now confronts a powerful force with which it is ill-suited to deal—demanding, expectant customers. Today's customers "expect products that are configured to their needs, delivery schedules that match their manufacturing plans or work hours, and payment terms that are convenient for them."

The Reengineering Process

Hammer and Champy define reengineering as "fundamental rethinking and radical redesign of processes to achieve dramatic improvements in critical contemporary measures of performance, such as cost, service, or speed." Meeting customer demands for ever more customized goods and services requires a process focus: "It is not products but the processes that create products that bring companies long-term success. Good products don't make winners; winners make good products."

Reengineering the corporation involves several steps. First, top management adopts "discontinuous thinking" by which managers find and drop "outdated rules and fundamental assumptions that underlie current business operations." Second, top executives make an unwavering commitment to radical change, set ambitious goals, and initiate the reengineering process. Third, they must enlist the support of their organization by presenting a factual, lengthy "case for action."

Hammer and Champy identify several recurring characteristics of successful reengineering projects, including:

- The combination of several jobs into one
- Workers empowered to make decisions
- Process steps performed in "natural order"
- Process teams replace functional teams
- Focus of performance measures and compensation shifts from activity to results
- Managers become coaches, not supervisors
- Executives become leaders

Conclusion

Reengineering the Corporation argues for a new approach to organize a business. It outlines the way to implement the new approach, using many examples, including Ford, IBM Credit, Taco Bell, and Bell Atlantic. It presents a strong case for a recommitment by business to swing for the home run.

Reengineering the Corporation by Michael Hammer and James Champy is published by HarperCollins.

For example, Lewis Galoob Toys, Inc., sold $58 million worth of toys with only 115 employees. Galoob contracts out manufacturing and packaging to contractors in Hong Kong, toy design to independent inventors, and sales to independent distribution representatives. Galoob never touches a product and does not even collect the money. The company is held together with phones, telexes, and other electronic technology.[18]

The free market aspect means subcontractors flow in and out of the system as needed. Subcontractors may be autonomous teams but are not part of the hierarchy,

Exhibit 7.3
Dynamic Net-
work Structure.

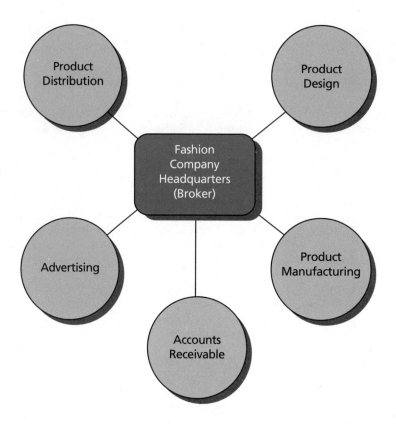

perhaps being hired only temporarily to do a specific task. For example, a buyer with J. C. Penney stores may see a beautiful sweater at Dillard's. She buys it and faxes photographs of it to contractors around the globe. In a day or two, a contractor finds a factory in Kuala Lumpur or Bangkok that can copy it. In a matter of two weeks, thousands of replicas are headed toward Penney stores. Then that part of the network structure is disbanded until the next time design, purchase, and delivery tasks are needed.

One company, the FI Group, a large software system developer in Britain, took a serious look at subcontracting possibilities and decided that everything could be farmed out "except for the chief executive officer and his car phone."[19]

IN PRACTICE ◆ 7.2
FI Group

Most of FI's eleven hundred technical employees are free-lancers who work about twenty hours a week, none of them on-site. Employees work at home and are linked to FI electronically. When required, they can meet face-to-face in meeting rooms in their locale. This flexible configuration provides many advantages to employees and to the firm, which has become one of the largest software houses in the United Kingdom. The organization is loosely connected because people are contracted and paid for the work perfomed, hence are free to act on their own. Only a small core of central staff sets strategic direction and provides operational support necessary to sustain the network.[20]

The network structure is especially valuable to information-intensive service firms like FI because the weblike structure keeps information free-flowing more than the traditional pyramid. Rogers Communications, Inc., in Toronto, Canada, uses a work-group software program called "The Coordinator" and personal computers to connect employees in a network-like structure.[21] Many firms such as FI and Rogers are succeeding with aspects of the dynamic network structure.

Advantages and Disadvantages   The advantages of the dynamic network structure are several. The structure is unbelievably lean, with almost no administrative overhead because work activities are contracted and coordination is electronic.

The approach can help new entrepreneurs get products to market quickly without having to incur huge start-up costs.[22] In mature industries that are beginning to stagnate, the network structure can reinvigorate companies by enabling them to develop new products without huge investments. Work force flexibility is high in network organizations because employees are subcontractors who respond to changing tasks and new demands. In addition, the network preserves highly specialized business units, teams, or individuals who can retain separate cultures and still be linked together.

The disadvantages are related to the unusual nature of this organization design. For one thing, there is little hands-on control. Operations are not under one roof, and managers must adjust to relying on independent subcontractors to do the work. Companies can experience problems with quality control when many different subcontractors are involved. In addition, some companies have found that subcontractors tend to dramatically raise prices once the company becomes hooked on their products or services.[23] Moreover, it can be difficult with a network structure to define the organization, since it may change from week to week as the set of subcontractors changes. Likewise, the organization can occasionally lose a part if a subcontractor defects or goes out of business and can't be replaced. A final disadvantage is weakened employee loyalty. A cohesive corporate culture for the larger organization is difficult to establish. Turnover tends to be high because employees are committed only to their own task or subcontractor, and they may be dismissed at any time in favor of a new contractor.

Organizational Designs for Global Advantage

Companies in the 1990s must think globally to remain competitive. At least 70 to 85 percent of the U.S. economy is feeling the impact of foreign competition.[24] The global environment is a huge potential market. International expansion can lead to greater profits, efficiency, and responsiveness. Of course, no company can become a global giant overnight. The change from domestic to international usually occurs through stages of development, similar to the life cycle described in Chapter 5.

STAGES OF INTERNATIONAL DEVELOPMENT

Exhibit 7.4 summarizes the four stages many companies go through as they evolve toward full-fledged global operations.[25] In stage one, the **domestic stage,** the

Exhibit 7.4   Four Stages of International Evolution.

	I. Domestic	II. International	III. Multinational	IV. Global
Strategic Orientation	Domestically oriented	Export-oriented, multidomestic	Multinational	Global
Stage of Development	Initial foreign involvement	Competitive positioning	Explosion	Global
Structure	Domestic structure, plus export department	Domestic structure, plus international division	Worldwide geographic, product	Matrix, heterarchy
Market Potential	Moderate, mostly domestic	Large, multidomestic	Very large, multinational	Whole world

Source: Based on Nancy J. Adler, *International Dimensions of Organizational Behavior* (Boston: PWS-Kent, 1991), 7–8; and Theodore T. Herbert, "Strategy and Multinational Organization Structure: An Interorganizational Relationships Perspective," *Academy of Management Review* 9 (1984): 259–71.

company is domestically oriented, but managers are aware of the global environment and may want to consider initial foreign involvement to expand production volume. Market potential is limited and is primarily in the home country. The structure of the company is domestic, typically functional or divisional, and initial foreign sales are handled through an export department. The details of freight forwarding, customs problems, and foreign exchange are handled by outsiders.

In stage two, the **international stage**, the company takes exports seriously and begins to think multidomestically. **Multidomestic** means competitive issues in each country are independent of other countries; the company deals with each country individually. The concern is with international competitive positioning compared with other firms in the industry. At this point, an international division has replaced the export department, and specialists are hired to handle sales, service, and warehousing abroad. Multiple countries are identified as a potential market.

In stage three, the **multinational stage**, the company is becoming a truly multinational company, which means it has marketing and production facilities in many countries and has more than one-third of its sales outside the home country. Explosion occurs as international operations take off, and the company has business units scattered around the world along with suppliers, manufacturers, and distributors.

The fourth and ultimate stage is the **global stage,** which means the company transcends any single country. The business is not merely a collection of domestic industries; rather, subsidiaries are interlinked to the point where competitive position in one country significantly influences activities in other countries.[26] Truly **global companies** are transnational and no longer think of themselves as having a single home country, and, indeed, have been called "stateless" corporations.[27] This represents a new and dramatic evolution from the multinational company of the 1960s and 1970s.

Global companies operate in truly global fashion, and the entire world is their marketplace. Organization structure at this stage can be extremely complex and often evolves into an international matrix or heterarchy, which will be discussed later in this chapter.

Global companies such as Procter and Gamble, Unilever, and Matsushita Electric may operate in forty to seventy-five countries. The structural problem of holding together this huge complex of subsidiaries scattered thousands of miles apart is immense. Before turning to a discussion of specific structures, let's briefly consider another approach to international activity, which is international alliances.

INTERNATIONAL STRATEGIC ALLIANCES

Strategic alliances are perhaps the hottest way to get involved in international operations. Typical alliances include licensing, joint ventures, and consortia.[28] Licensing agreements are frequently entered into by manufacturing firms to capitalize on the diffusion of new technology quickly and inexpensively while getting the advantage of lucrative worldwide sales. For example, Merck, Eli Lilly, and Bayer cross-license their newest drugs to one another to support industrywide innovation and advertising and offset the high fixed costs of research and distribution.[29] **Joint ventures** are separate entities created with two or more active firms as sponsors. This is another approach to sharing development and production costs and penetrating new markets. It is estimated that the rate of joint venture formation between U.S. and international companies has been growing by 27 percent annually since 1985. Joint ventures may be with either customers or competitors. Merck has put together major ventures with such competitors as Johnson & Johnson and AB Astra of Sweden.[30] A manufacturer may seek a joint venture to distribute its new technology and products through another country's distribution channels and markets.

The agreement between Toyota and General Motors to construct a Chevrolet Nova plant in California was Toyota's way of distributing its technology to the United States. Texas Instruments sought long-term alliances with its biggest customers in Japan, including Sony, to gain subsidiaries in Japan. Over time, TI bought out Sony's share and ended up with four major plants in Japan producing semiconductors for the rest of TI's worldwide operations.[31]

Given the expense of new technology, **consortia** of organizations are likely to be the wave of the future. Rather than one-on-one competition among individual firms, groups of firms will venture into new products and technologies together. This means managers must learn to cooperate as well as compete.[32] For example, Airbus Industrie is a European consortium of businesses backed by the governments of Germany, France, the United Kingdom, and Spain to produce commercial aircraft. Airbus is slowly gaining market share and is successfully selling aircraft worldwide. Consortia are often used in other parts of the world, such as the *keiretsu* families of corporations in Japan described in Chapter 3. In Korea, these interlocking company arrangements are called *choebol*. Cross-industry consortia in the United States are just underway and offer a promising avenue for worldwide competition in the future. Some U.S. executives believe shifting to a more *keiretsu*-like approach is the only way U.S. companies can compete in the global marketplace.[33]

International Strategy and Organization Design Fit

As we discussed in Chapter 6, an organization's structure must fit its situation by providing sufficient information processing for coordination and control while focusing employees on specific functions, products, or geographic regions. Organization design for international structure follows a similar logic, with special interest on global versus local strategic opportunities.

MODEL FOR GLOBAL VERSUS LOCAL OPPORTUNITIES

A major strategic issue for firms venturing into the international domain is whether (and when) to use a globalization rather than a multidomestic strategy. The **globalization strategy** means that product design and advertising strategy are standardized throughout the world.[34] For example, the Japanese took business away from Canadian and American companies by developing similar high-quality, low-cost products for all countries. The Canadian and American companies incurred higher costs by tailoring products to specific countries. Black & Decker became much more competitive internationally when it standardized its line of power hand tools. Other products, such as Coca-Cola and Levi blue jeans, are naturals for globalization, because only advertising and marketing need to be tailored for different regions.

A **multidomestic strategy** means that competition in each country is handled independently of competition in other countries. Thus, a multidomestic strategy would encourage product design, assembly, and marketing tailored to the specific needs of each country. Some companies have found that their products do not thrive in a single global market. The French do not drink orange juice for breakfast, and laundry detergent is used to wash dishes, not clothes, in parts of Mexico. Parker Pen experienced a disaster when it reduced from five hundred to one hundred pen styles because the different styles were valued in different countries.

The model in Exhibit 7.5 illustrates how organization design and international strategy fit.[35] Companies can be characterized by whether their product and service lines have potential for globalization, which means advantages through worldwide standardization. Companies that sell diverse products or services across many countries have a globalization strategy. On the other hand, some companies have products and services appropriate for a multidomestic strategy, which means local-country advantages through differentiation and customization.

As indicated in Exhibit 7.5, when a company is low with respect to developing either a globalization or multidomestic strategy, simply using an international division with the domestic structure is an appropriate way to handle international business. For some businesses, however, the basis for advantage may be a globalization strategy—selling the same products worldwide—in which case a global product structure is appropriate. This structure will provide product managers with authority to handle their product lines worldwide. When a company's strategy is multidomestic through locally based customization, then a worldwide geographical structure is appropriate, with each country or region having subsidiaries modifying products and services to fit that locale.

In many instances, companies will have both global and local opportunities simultaneously, in which case the matrix structure or heterarchy can be used. Part of the product line may need to be standardized globally, and other parts tailored to the needs of local countries, in which case the matrix structure may work. When the company achieves truly global size and scope beyond what can be handled by the matrix, the heterarchy may be used. Next, we will discuss each of the structures in Exhibit 7.5 in more detail.

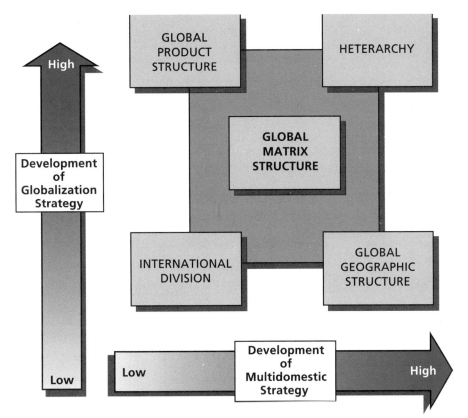

Source: Roderick E. White and Thomas A. Poynter, "Organizing for Worldwide Advantage," *Business Quarterly* (Summer 1989): 84–89. Adapted by permission of *Business Quarterly*, published by the Western Business School, the University of Western Ontario, London, Ontario, Canada.

INTERNATIONAL DIVISION

As companies begin to explore international opportunities, they typically start with an export department that grows into an **international division.** The international division has a status equal to the other major departments or divisions within the company and is illustrated in Exhibit 7.6. The international division has its own hierarchy to handle business (licensing, joint ventures) in various countries, selling the products and services created by the domestic divisions, opening subsidiary plants, and in general moving the organization into more sophisticated international operations.

Although functional structures are often used domestically, they are less frequently used to manage a worldwide business.[36] Lines of functional hierarchy running around the world would extend too long, so some form of product or geographical structure is used to subdivide the organization into smaller units. Firms typically start with an international department and, depending on their strategy, later use product or geographic structures, to which we will now turn.

Exhibit 7.6
Domestic
Hybrid Structure
with Interna-
tional Division.

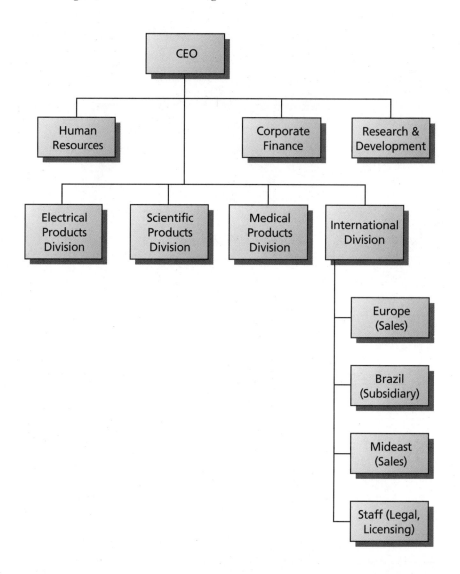

Structural Designs for Global Operations

The international arena produces complex structures because of defined national boundaries and great distances. The structures most typically used by international firms are the global product structure and global geographic structure.

GLOBAL PRODUCT DIVISION STRUCTURE

In a **global product structure**, the product divisions take responsibility for global operations in their specific product area. Each product division can organize for international operations as it sees fit. Each division manager is responsible for planning, organizing, and controlling all functions for the production and distribution of its products for any market around the world. The product-based structure works best when a division handles products that are technologically similar and can be standardized for marketing worldwide. As we saw in Exhibit 7.5, the global product structure works best when the company has opportunities for worldwide production and sale of standard products for all markets, thus providing economies of scale and standardization of production, marketing, and advertising.

Eaton Corporation has used a form of worldwide product structure, as illustrated in Exhibit 7.7. In this structure, the automotive components group, industrial group, and so on are responsible for manufacture and sale of products worldwide. The vice president of international is responsible for coordinators in each region, including a coordinator for Japan, Australia, South America, and northern Europe. The coordinators find ways to share facilities and improve production and delivery across all product lines sold in their region. These coordinators provide the same function as integrators described in Chapter 6.

The product structure is great for standardizing production and sales around the globe, but it also has problems. Often the product divisions do not work well together, competing instead of cooperating in some countries; and some countries may be ignored by product managers. The solution adopted by Eaton Corporation

Exhibit 7.7   Partial Global Product Structure Used by Eaton Corporation.

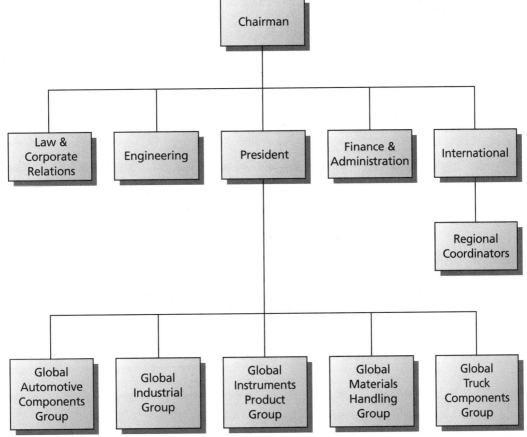

Source: Based on *New Directions in Multinational Corporate Organization* (New York: Business International Corp., 1981).

of using country coordinators who have a clearly defined role is a superb way to overcome these problems.

GLOBAL GEOGRAPHIC DIVISION STRUCTURE

A worldwide regional organization divides the world into regions, each of which reports to the CEO. Each region has full control of functional activities in its geographical area. Companies that use this **global geographic structure** tend to have mature product lines and stable technologies. They find low-cost manufacturing within countries as well as different needs across countries for marketing and sales. Strategically, this structure can exploit many opportunities for regional or locally based competitive advantages.[37]

The problems encountered by senior management using a global geographic structure result from the autonomy of each regional division. For example, it is difficult to do planning on a global scale—such as new product R&D—because each division acts to meet only the needs of its region. New domestic technologies and products can be difficult to transfer to international markets because each division feels it will develop what it needs. Likewise, it is difficult to rapidly introduce products developed offshore into domestic markets; and there is often duplication of line and staff managers across regions. Companies such as Dow Chemical find ways to take advantage of the geographic structure while overcoming these problems.

IN PRACTICE ◆ 7.3
Dow Chemical

For several years, Dow Chemical used a geographic structure of the form illustrated in Exhibit 7.8. First, Dow Europe developed its own manufacturing, sales, and technical services that became an autonomous division. Subsequently the Pacific and Latin American areas developed as regional entities, also, as did Canadian operations. Dow handled the problems of coordination across regions by creating a corporate-level product department to provide long-term planning and worldwide product coordination and communication. It used six corporate product directors, each of whom had been a line manager with overseas experience. The product directors are essentially staff coordinators, but they have authority to approve large capital investments and to move manufacturing of a product from one geographic location to another to best serve corporate needs. With this structure, Dow maintains its focus on each region and achieves coordination for overall planning, savings in administrative staff, and manufacturing and sales efficiency.[38]

GLOBAL MATRIX STRUCTURE

We've discussed how Eaton used a global product division structure and found ways to coordinate across worldwide divisions. Dow Chemical used a global geographic division structure and found ways to coordinate across geographical regions. Each of these companies emphasized a single dimension. Recall from Chapter 6 that a matrix structure provides a way to achieve vertical and horizontal coordination simultaneously along two dimensions. Matrix structures used by multinational cor-

Exhibit 7.8   Global Geographic Division Structure.

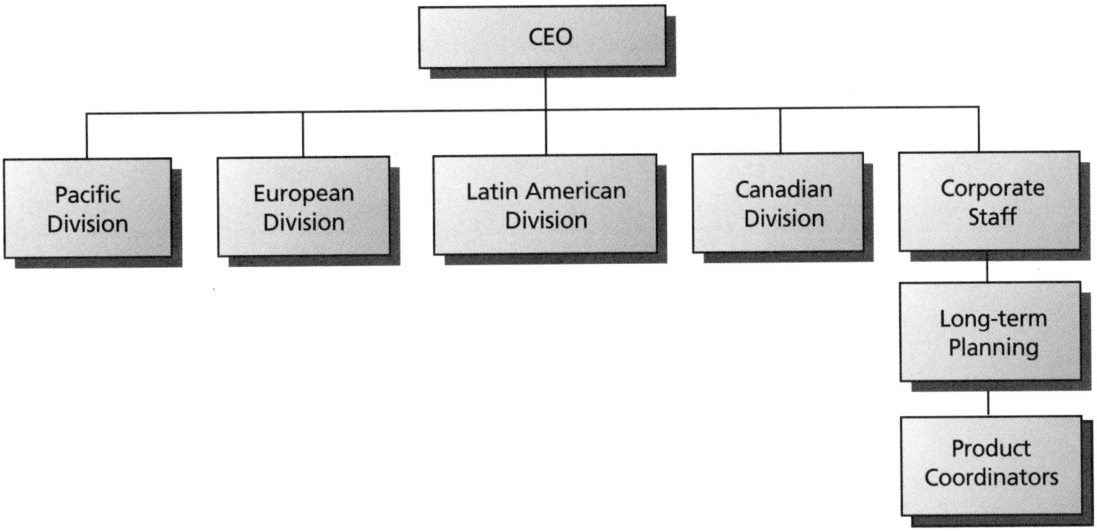

porations are similar to those described in Chapter 6, except that geographical distances for communication are greater and coordination is more complex.

The matrix works best when pressure for decision making balances the interests of both product standardization and geographical localization and when coordination to share resources is important. An excellent example of a **global matrix structure** that works extremely well is ABB, an electrical equipment corporation headquartered in Zurich.

IN PRACTICE ♦ 7.4
Asea Brown Boveri (ABB)

ABB employs 210,000 people worldwide and has annual revenues of more than $29 billion. It owns some twelve hundred subsidiary companies around the globe and uses a matrix structure similar to Exhibit 7.9 to achieve worldwide economies of scale combined with local flexibility and responsiveness.

At the top are the chief executive officer and an international committee of thirteen top managers. These managers hold frequent meetings around the world; since they share no common first language, they speak only English, which is foreign to all but one of them. Along one side of the matrix are sixty-five or so business sectors located worldwide, into which ABB's products and services are grouped. Each business sector leader is responsible for handling business on a global scale, allocating export markets, establishing cost and quality standards, and creating mixed-nationality teams to solve problems. For example, the leader for power transformers is responsible for twenty-five factories in sixteen countries.

Along the other side of the matrix is a country structure; ABB has about one hundred country managers, most of them citizens of the country in which they work. They run national companies and are responsible for local balance sheets, income statements, and career ladders. The German president, for example, is responsible for thirty-six thousand people across several business sectors that generate annual revenues in Germany of more than $4 billion.

The matrix structure converges at the level of the eleven hundred local companies. The presidents of local companies report to two bosses—the business sector leader, who is usually located outside the country, and the country president who runs the company of which the local organization is a subsidiary.

ABB's philosophy is to decentralize things to the lowest levels. Global managers are generous, patient, and multilingual. They must work with teams made up of different nationalities and be culturally sensitive. They craft strategy and evaluate performance for people and subsidiaries around the world. Country managers, by contrast, are regional line managers responsible for several country subsidiaries. They must cooperate with business sector managers to achieve worldwide efficiencies and the introduction of new products. Finally, the presidents of local companies have both a global boss—the business sector manager—and a country boss, and they learn to coordinate the needs of both.[39]

In the language of Chapter 6, the CEO is the "top leader," the business sector and country managers are "matrix bosses," and the presidents of local company affiliates are "two-boss employees." ABB is a large, successful company that manages to achieve the benefits of both product and geographic organizations through this matrix structure.

GLOBAL HETERARCHY

The **global heterarchy structure** occurs for huge multinational firms with subsidiaries in many countries that try to exploit both global and local advantages, and perhaps technological superiority, rapid innovation, and functional control. The matrix is effective for handling two issues (product and geographic), but more than two competitive issues requires a more complex form of structure, such as the heterarchy. The heterarchy is not possible to draw, but it would be used by a complex organization such as N. V. Phillips, illustrated in Exhibit 7.10. Phillips is a global company headquartered in the Netherlands. It has operating units in sixty countries and is typical of global companies, such as Heinz, Unilever, or Procter and Gamble.[40]

The units in Exhibit 7.10 are far-flung. Achieving coordination, a sense of participation and involvement by subsidiaries, and a sharing of information, new technologies, and customers requires a complex and multidimensional form of structure. For example, a global corporation like Phillips is so large that size itself is a problem when coordinating global operations. In addition, some subsidiaries may become so large that they no longer fit a narrow strategic role assigned to them by headquarters. While being part of a large organization, they also need autonomy for themselves and need to have impact on other parts of the organization.

The heterarchy is more than just a structure drawn on an organization chart. It is a state of mind, a set of values, and a desire to make a worldwide system work. The heterarchy cannot be given a precise definition, but the following characteristics distinguish heterarchy from and move it beyond a matrix structure.[41]

1. *The heterarchy has many centers of different kinds.*   The matrix structure had a single headquarters, a single center of control for each country, and a single center for each product line. In the heterarchy, headquarters functions are diffused geographically. An R&D center may be in Holland with global responsibilities for developing certain products, a financial center in Brussels, a large division head-

Exhibit 7.9   Global Matrix Structure.

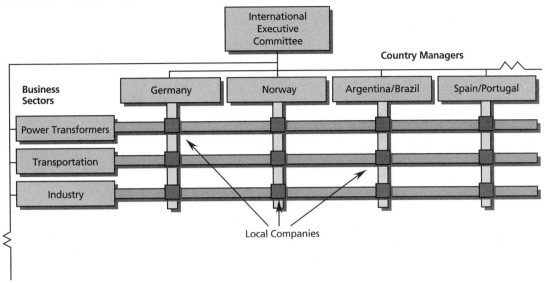

quarters in London, a unit in Hong Kong responsible for coordinating activities in Asia, a marketing center in Germany, and a center for dealing with global purchases in Sweden. These centers in some cases relate to the size of the subsidiary, as illustrated in Exhibit 7.10.

2. *Subsidiary managers initiate strategy for the corporation as a whole.*   In traditional structures, managers have a strategic role only for their division. In a heterarchy, various centers and subsidiaries can shape the company from the bottom up because there is no notion of a single headquarters, no clear top-down corporate level responsibility. R&D managers, country managers, and product managers may all initiate strategy based new opportunities and what they have to offer.

3. *Coordination and integration are achieved through corporate culture, shared values, and management style rather than through the vertical hierarchy.*   The heterarchy is essentially a horizontal structure. It is diverse, extended, and exists in a fluctuating environment so that standard rules, procedures, and close supervision are not appropriate. To achieve control and coordination, leaders stress company values, vision, and culture. People are promoted mainly by rotation into different jobs and countries. Moreover, the heterarchy requires that employees have long experience. Experience plus rotation through different regions means that people share corporate culture and values sufficient for unity of purpose.

4. *Alliances are established with other company parts and with other companies.*   Each part of the company can serve as an independent catalyst, bringing together unique elements with synergistic potential, perhaps firms or subsidiaries from different continents previously not known to one another. These alliances may include joint ventures, cooperation with governments, and licensing arrangements.

5. *Strategy often grows from radical problem orientation and action programs.*   Managers at all levels have authority to initiate programs to achieve better synergy and competitive advantage and to solve problems from their competitive positions.

Exhibit 7.10   International Organizational Units and Interlinkages within N.V. Philips.

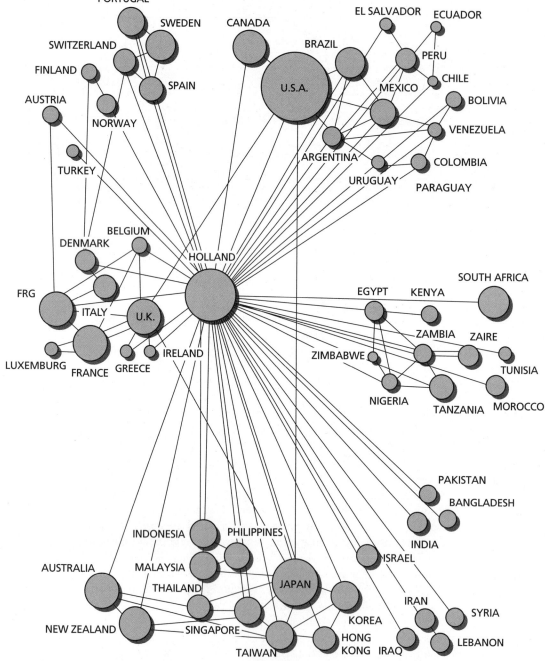

Source: Sumantra Ghoshal and Christopher A. Bartlett, "The Multinational Corporation as an Interorganizational Network," *Academy of Management Review* 15 (1990): 605. Used by permission.

Action programs may create new markets, seek new coordination of activities, or seize a previously unseen possibility. Managers are not expected to rely on existing resources or corporate policy.

The heterarchy is truly a "messy" structure, but it is becoming relevant for large, transnational firms that treat the whole world as their playing field and do not have a single country base. The autonomy of organizational parts gives strength to smaller units and allows the firm to take advantage of rapid change and competitive opportunities. To achieve this end, a broad range of people throughout the global firm must develop capacity for strategic thinking and strategic action. Managers must follow their own instincts, using worldwide resources to achieve their local objectives. Strategy is the result of action in the sense that company parts seek to improve on their own rather than waiting for a strategy from the top. Indeed, each part of the heterarchy must be aware of the whole organization so its local actions will complement and enhance other company parts.

Summary and Interpretation

The concepts about organization design in this chapter build upon the approaches to organizational structure and design described in Chapter 6. Significant global forces are causing American companies to find innovative designs and to extend operations overseas. The international forces include the dominant economies of Japan and Germany, newly industrialized countries, a shift toward market economies in Eastern Europe, and new power blocs. One response to these pressures is for domestic organizations to become more competitive. One significant innovation is the shift away from top-heavy, functionally organized structures toward horizontal structures. With a horizontal structure, the focus is on processes rather than function, the hierarchy is flattened, and self-managed teams are empowered to make the decisions necessary to satisfy the customer.

Sometimes the first step in shifting to a horizontal structure is *reengineering,* one of the hottest concepts in management today. Reengineering basically means throwing out old ideas and looking at how work can best be done in today's circumstances.

Another innovation is the dynamic network structure, which uses a free market approach rather than a vertical hierarchy. Separate companies or individuals are coordinated through contracts with a small headquarters organization. New contractors can be added as needed to respond immediately to changes in the environment.

Many companies are developing overseas operations to take advantage of world markets. These companies typically evolve through four stages, beginning with a domestic orientation, shifting to an international orientation, then a multinational orientation, finally to a global orientation that sees the whole world as a potential market. Organizations initially use an export department, then an international division, and finally develop into a worldwide geographic or product structure. Huge global companies may use a matrix or a heterarchy form of structure.

A global product structure is typically best when a company has many opportunities for globalization, which means products can be standardized and sold worldwide. A global geographic structure is typically used when a company's products and services have local country advantages, which means they do best when tailored to local needs and cultures. When an international company must succeed on two dimensions—global and local—simultaneously, the matrix structure is appropriate. When global companies must compete on multiple dimensions simultaneously, a new form of structure called the heterarchy, which is a form of horizontal organization, may be used. A heterarchy has multiple centers; subsidiary managers initiate strategy for the company as a whole; and coordination and control is achieved through corporate culture and shared values.

KEY CONCEPTS

consortia
domestic stage
dynamic network
global company
global geographic structure
global heterarchy structure
global matrix structure
global product structure
global stage
globalization strategy

horizontal corporation
international division
international stage
joint venture
multidomestic company
multidomestic strategy
multinational stage
reengineering
self-managed team

DISCUSSION QUESTIONS

1. What do you see as the primary differences between horizontal corporations and traditional, functionally organized corporations?

2. What are the consequences to organizations of no single company or country being able to dominate global commerce?

3. How do self-managed teams differ from the cross-functional teams described in Chapter 6?

4. Would you like to work on a self-managed team where decisions are made by the team rather than by individuals and individual rewards are subordinated to team rewards? Discuss.

5. How does the dynamic network structure enable an organization to respond rapidly in a changing, competitive environment?

6. Under what conditions should an organization consider a global product structure as opposed to a global geographic structure?

7. How does an international matrix structure differ from the domestic matrix structure described in Chapter 6?

8. Why do you think firms should join strategic alliances? Would they be better served to go it alone in international operations? Explain.

9. What problems might arise with the global geographic structure, and how might a company overcome them?

10. Describe the heterarchy. Does this structure seem workable in a huge global firm? Discuss.

 GUIDES TO ACTION

As an organization designer, keep these guides in mind:

1. Analyze the global forces at work that influence your company, and respond by designing new domestic or international structures that enable international competitive advantage.

2. Move the organization through the four stages of international evolution, including domestic, international, multinational, and global. Maintain con-

gruence between stage of development, strategic orientation, resource flow, structure, market potential, and facilities location.

3. Shift to a horizontal structure with self-managed teams or a dynamic network structure to maintain domestic competitiveness in the face of global competitive forces. Use self-managed teams to gain motivation and commitment of employees and a dynamic network structure to maintain a fluid responsiveness to the changing international environment.

4. Choose a global product structure when the organization can gain advantages with a globalization strategy. Choose a global geographic structure when the company has advantages with a multidomestic strategy. Choose an international division when the company is primarily domestic and has only a few international opportunities.

5. Develop international strategic alliances, such as licensing, joint ventures, and consortia, as fast and less expensive ways to become involved in international sales and operations.

6. Implement a matrix structure when the opportunities for globalization and multidomestic opportunities are about equal. Implement a heterarchy when the organization is truly global and is responding to many global forces simultaneously.

Keep these guides in mind when analyzing the following cases.

CASE FOR ANALYSIS

Saint-Gobain-Pont-a-Mousson*

Saint-Gobain-Pont-a-Mousson (SGPM) is a worldwide manufacturer of glass, paper, pipe, and related products. The corporate headquarters is in Paris. Over 50 percent of its Fr 50 billion in sales is from international business.

SGPM is organized into a three-tiered structure, as illustrated in Exhibit 7.11. The structure consists of five corporate functional vice presidents at headquarters, nine worldwide product group presidents, and seven "general delegates" or country managers.

Manufacturing operations exist in several countries and report to their respective product groups headquartered in France and to the country manager. Each product group has its own marketing staff and has more influence over country subsidiaries than do country managers, who are responsible for the finance, tax, and legal functions within their countries. The country manager is the political knowledge center for the country, having an understanding of the environment, government regulations, pricing, labor negotiations, and the like. The worldwide product manager does the business planning, which reflects business and product goals rather than country-by-country requirements. Profit and loss responsibility is at the product manager level.

New Directions in Multinational Corporate Organization (New York: Business International Corporation, 1981), 44–45. Used by permission.

Exhibit 7.11   International Organization Structure for Saint-Gobain-Pont-a-Mousson.

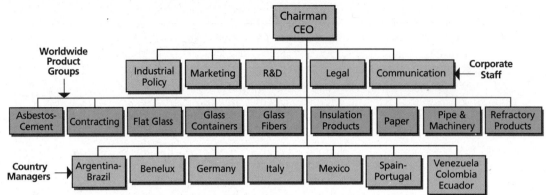

Source: New Directions in Multinational Corporate Organization (New York: Business International Corporation, 1981), 44–45. Used by permission.

Most senior line and staff managers possess significant international experience—business, cultural, linguistic—although virtually all are French nationals, including the country managers. This broad scope arises from assignment rotation and from exposure to international situations.

QUESTIONS

1. What type of structure does SGPM have? Does it contain elements of more than one structure?
2. Based on your analysis of structure, what stategic opportunities do you think SGPM has?
3. What problems do you think SGPM encounters with this structure?

Company Y*

Company Y is a U.S.-based company that sells in excess of $2 billion annually in products and services for a variety of industrial applications. It has facilities and offices in dozens of locations throughout the world. The organization has a strong domestic product structure that has been in place for ten years. An international division exists that has responsibility for the company's international operations.

A consulting study of the international division suggested that the division develop country specialists who are well-regarded and helpful to product division managers; the study further suggested that the specialists be given some authority to influence international decisions made by product managers.

The international division vice president reports directly to the CEO and has veto power over international acquisitions and international capital appropriations.

---

* Based on *New Directions in Multinational Corporate Organization* (New York: Business International Corporation, 1981).

Product line managers often work with international managers to gain acceptance of their proposed international actions.

The international vice president has set up a new structure with four regional managers reporting to him. The regional managers are stationed in the United States and travel about 50 percent of the time to provide regional and country information to product line managers. Field managers eventually will be stationed in every country with multiple operations; they will support marketing and business development efforts of the local business units. Current field managers report to one of the four regional managers.

The international vice president believes the success of the international division comes from maintaining quality working relationships with the product divisions. The company is considering three possibilities for the future direction of the international division. The first is to continue to grow in influence and to continue adding regional and country managers. The second is to help each product group develop its own in-house capacity to conduct effective international operations; this could eventually mean the demise of the international division as now defined. The third idea is to develop in-house expertise within each division and to maintain strong international expertise at the corporate level. This would enable the corporate international division to act as an independent international agent and provide advice to divisions on such matters as finance, countertrade, and marketing.

QUESTIONS

1. At what stage of international evolution (Exhibit 7.4) is Company Y? Explain.
2. What problems do you think Company Y is experiencing with its present structure?
3. Which of the three alternatives do you think should be adopted for the future international structure at Company Y? Consider advantages and disadvantages of each.

NOTES

1. John A. Bryne, "The Horizontal Corporation," *Business Week,* 20 December 1993, 76–81; Noel M. Tichy and Stratford Sherman, *Control Your Destiny or Someone Else Will* (New York: Currency Doubleday, 1993).
2. William J. Holstein. "The Stateless Corporation," *Business Week,* 14 May 1990, 98–105.
3. Jonathan P. Hicks, "The Takeover of American Industry," *New York Times,* 28 May 1989, sec. 3, 1, 8.
4. Based on Tom Peters, "Prometheus Barely Unbound," *Academy of Management Executive* 4 (November 1990): 70–84.
5. Byrne, "The Horizontal Corporation"; Thomas A. Stewart, "The Search for the Organization of Tomorrow," *Fortune,* 18 May 1992, 92–98.
6. Jack D. Orsburn, Linda Moran, Ed Musselwhite, and John H. Zenger, *Self-Directed Work Teams: The New American Challenge* (Homewood, Ill.: Business One Irwin, 1990).
7. Charles C. Mainz, David E. Keating, and Anne Donnellon, "Preparing for an Organizational Change to Employee Self-Managed Teams: The Managerial Transition," *Organizational Dynamics* (Autumn 1990): 15–26.
8. Thomas Owens, "The Self-Managing Work Team," *Small Business Reports* (February 1991): 53–65.
9. Jonathan Kapstein, "Volvo's Radical New Plant: 'The Death of the Assembly Line'?" *Business Week,* 28 August 1989, 92–93.
10. Wendy Trueman, "Alternate Visions," *Canadian Business,* March 1991, 29–33.

11. Brian Dumaine, "Who Needs a Boss?" *Fortune,* 7 May 1990, 52–60.

12. Byrne, "The Horizontal Corporation."

13. Jenny C. McCune, "More Power to Them," *Small Business Reports* (November 1992): 51–59.

14. Byrne, "The Horizontal Corporation."

15. Thomas A. Stewart, "Reengineering: The Hot New Managing Tool," *Fortune,* 23 August 1993, 41–48; John Hillkirk, "More Companies Reenginnering: Challenging Status Quo Now in Vogue," *USA Today,* 9 November 1993, Money sec., p. 1.

16. Charles C. Snow, Raymond E. Miles, and Henry J. Coleman, Jr., "Managing 21st Century Network Organizations," *Organizational Dynamics* 20 (Winter 1992): 5–19; Shawn Tully, "The Modular Corporation," *Fortune,* 8 February 1993, 106–14.

17. Raymond E. Miles and Charles C. Snow, "Fit, Failure and the Hall of Fame," *California Management Review* 26 (Spring 1984): 10–28.

18. Richard L. Daft, *Management* 2d ed. (Chicago: Dryden Press, 1991).

19. Peters, "Prometheus Barely Unbound."

20. Gareth Morgan, *Creative Organization Theory: A Resource Book* (Newbury Park, Calif: Sage 1989), 64–67.

21. Harry S. Dent, Jr., "Organizing for the Productivity Leap," *Small Business Reports* (September 1990): 31–44.

22. Jenny C. McCune, "Thin Is in," *Small Business Reports* (May 1993): 30–40.

23. Donna Brown, "Outsourcing: How Corporations Take Their Business Elsewhere," *Management Review* (February 1992): 16–19.

24. Snow, Miles, and Coleman, "Managing 21st Century Network Organizations."

25. Based heavily on Nancy J. Adler, *International Dimensions of Organizational Behavior,* 2d ed. (Boston: PWS-Kent, 1991); Theodore T. Herbert, "Strategy and Multinational Organizational Structure: An Interorganizational Relationships Perspective," *Academy of Management Review* 9 (1984): 259–71; Laura K. Rickey, "International Expansion—U.S. Corporations: Strategy, Stages of Development and Structure," (Unpublished manuscript, Vanderbilt University, 1991.)

26. Michael E. Porter, "Changing Patterns of International Competition," *California Management Review* 28 (Winter 1986): 9–40.

27. Holstein, "The Stateless Corporation."

28. David Lei and John W. Slocum, Jr., "Global Strategic Alliances: Payoffs and Pitfalls," *Organizational Dynamics* (Winter 1991): 17–29.

29. *Ibid.*

30. Stratford Sherman, "Are Strategic Alliances Working?" *Fortune,* 21 September 1992, 77–78; David Lei, "Strategies for Global Competition," *Long-Range Planning* 22 (1989): 102–09.

31. Lei, "Strategies For Global Competition."

32. Kathryn Rudie Harrigan, "Managing Joint Ventures: Part I," *Management Review* (February 1987): 24–41.

33. Kevin Kelly and Otis Port, with James Treece, Gail DeGeorge, and Zachary Schiller, "Learning from Japan," *Business Week,* 27 January 1992, 52–60.

34. Kenichi Ohmae, "Managing in a Borderless World," *Harvard Business Review* (May-June 1989): 152–61.

35. Sumantra Ghoshal and Nitin Nohria, "Horses for Courses: Organizational Forms for Multinational Corporations," *Sloan Management Review* (Winter 1993): 23–35; Roderick E. White and Thomas A. Poynter, "Organizing for Worldwide Advantage," *Business Quarterly* (Summer 1989): 84–89.

36. John D. Daniels, Robert A. Pitts, and Marietta J. Tretter, "Strategy and Structure of U.S. Multinationals: An Exploratory Study," *Academy of Management Journal* 27 (1984): 292–307.

37. *New Directions in Multinational Corporate Organization* (New York: Business International Corporation, 1981).

38. *Ibid.*

39. William Taylor, "The Logic of Global Business: An Interview with ABB's Percy Barnevik," *Harvard Business Review* (March-April 1991): 91–105; Carla Rappaport, "A Tough Swede Invades the U.S.," *Fortune,* 29 January 1992, 76–79.

40. Sumantra Ghoshal and Christopher A. Bartlett, "The Multinational Corporation as an Interorganizational Network," *Academy of Management Review* 15 (1990): 603–25.

41. Gunnar Hedlund and Dag Rolander, "Action in Heterarchies: New Approaches to Managing the MNC," in Christopher A. Bartlett, Yves Doz, and Gunnar Hedlund, eds., *Managing the Global Firm* (New York: Routledge, 1990), 15–46; Gunnar Hedlund, "The Hypermodern MNC—A Heterarchy?" *Human Resource Management* 25 (Spring 1986): 9–35.

4

Organization Design Process

CHAPTER
8

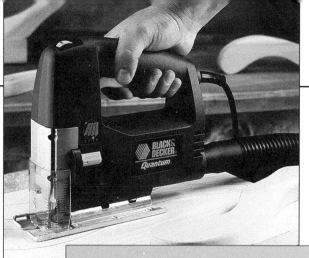

Innovation and Change

261

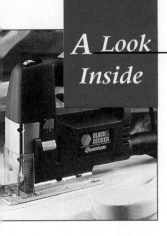

Black & Decker

Black & Decker is a powerful name in the power tool business. But recently, the company was seeing a growing share of the power tool market going to competitors like Japan's Makita and the Sears Craftsman line. Then Black & Decker stumbled across an interesting fact: One of the fastest-growing segments of the tool market was the serious do-it-your-selfer (known in the trade as the DIYer), who was purchasing products other than Black & Decker's.

This discovery called for quick action. Whereas in the old days, the company might have simply tried to come out with Black & Decker versions of competitor's products, CEO Nolan Archibald knew that approach wouldn't work today—things are moving too fast. "You're always two steps behind," he said, unless you go straight to your customers to find out what they want.

That's just what Black & Decker did, practically moving in with fifty DIYers selected by an independent research firm. Black & Decker researchers hung out with the do-it-your-selfers in their homes and workshops, went shopping with them, and asked lots of questions about what they liked and didn't like about the tools they were using and how the tools felt in their hands. This research was fortified by interviewing hundreds of additional Black & Decker customers.

The next step was to turn ideas and suggestions into new products—fast. Black & Decker had already shifted its manufacturing process to cross-functional teams. So the company unleashed these "fusion teams," made up of engineers, finance people, design-ers, marketers, and others, to create the new product line. In almost no time, the teams were designing and building new products that would answer customer complaints, such as creating a cordless drill that wouldn't run out of power before the job was done and building in a safety feature that stops a saw blade within two seconds. Even the color of the tools and the name of the line—Quantum—was based on customer preferences. Says CEO Archibald, "The whole point of this product line was to have it driven to market by what the consumers really wanted."

The strategy worked. The new Quantum line earned a prestigious Retailers' Choice award in 1993, and one market analyst predicted sales of $30 to $40 million by the end of 1994. Black & Decker has succeeded in taking market share away from rival companies by getting to know what do-it-yourself customers want and giving it to them fast.[1]

Black & Decker saw an opportunity and took advantage of it by developing a new line of products to meet the needs of a specific, growing market segment. At Black & Decker, innovation is a top goal preached by management, and management realizes that product innovations have to meet customer needs to be success-ful. The company's cross-functional teams help speed new products to market.

Innovation is not limited to Black & Decker. Every organization in the 1990s must change to survive. New discoveries and inventions quickly replace standard ways of doing things. The pace of change is revealed in the fact that the parents of today's college-age students grew up without cable television, VCRs, crease-resistant clothing, personal computers, compact disc players, video games, and talking checkout machines in supermarkets.

PURPOSE OF THIS CHAPTER

This chapter will explore how organizations change and how managers direct the innovation and change process. The next section describes the difference between incremental and radical change, the four types of change—technology, product, structure, people—occurring in organizations, and how to manage change successfully. The organization structure and management approach for facilitating each type of change is then discussed. Management techniques for influencing both the creation and implementation of change are also covered.

Innovate or Perish: The Strategic Role of Change

If there is one theme or lesson that emerges from previous chapters, it is that organizations must run fast to keep up with changes taking place all around them. Organizations must modify themselves not just from time to time, but all of the time. Large organizations must find ways to act like small, flexible organizations. Manufacturing firms need to reach out for new advanced manufacturing technology and service firms for new information technology. As we saw in Chapter 7, international competition can create the need for structural innovations such as self-managed teams, network structure, and ways to extend markets into other countries. One Silicon Valley firm changed its structure twenty-four times in four years to keep up with changes in the environment. Today's powerful managed-health care networks are shunning drug company sales representatives—and their free offers—in an effort to hold down pharmaceutical costs. A top challenge for today's drug companies is to find new marketing structures to survive.[2] Organizations simply must poise themselves to innovate, to change, or they risk decline and death.[3]

By innovating, Black & Decker remains competitive in the tool business. Some of today's most successful companies thrive on change. Companies ranked in a recent *Fortune* survey as the most innovative are also some of today's most successful, such as Microsoft, General Electric, AT&T, and Wal-Mart.[4] Another company that has learned to thrive on change is PepsiCo.

IN PRACTICE ◆ 8.1

PepsiCo

PepsiCo CEO Wayne Calloway insists the company's goal is simply "to be the best consumer products company in the world." PepsiCo and its divisions—Frito-Lay, Pizza Hut, Taco Bell, and KFC—have been awesome in recent years.

Probably the key element in PepsiCo's success is its passion for change. Calloway and top executives of PepsiCo's divisions realize they're in the risk business as much as the consumer products business. PepsiCola North American, for example, recently stuck its neck out on a number of new products, such as Crystal Pepsi, All Sport, and H2OH!, in its efforts to transform itself into a "total beverage company." Other divisions of the company also follow PepsiCo's risk-taking tradition.

Calloway insists the worst rule of management is "if it ain't broke, don't fix it. In today's economy, if it ain't broke, you might as well break it yourself, because it soon will be." One way he enforces this policy is to force change by moving managers back and forth among PepsiCo divisions. A former soft drink executive may be assigned to KFC to see problems through a different lens and initiate new improvements. Senior executives are sent on field trips to observe companies renowned for innovation and customer service. PepsiCo, as much as any North American company, has learned to thrive on continuous change.[5]

INCREMENTAL VERSUS RADICAL CHANGE

The changes used to adapt to the environment can be evaluated according to scope—that is, the extent to which changes are incremental or radical for the organization.[6] As summarized in Exhibit 8.1, **incremental change** represents a series of continual progressions that maintain the organization's general equilibrium and often affect only one organizational part. **Radical change,** by contrast, breaks the frame of reference for the organization, often creating new equilibrium because the entire organization is transformed. For example, an incremental change is the implementation of sales teams in the marketing department, while a radical change is reengineering the organization to develop new products in only one year instead of four and maintaining one year as the new equilibrium.

For the most part, incremental change occurs through the established structure and management processes, and it may include new technologies—such as advanced manufacturing technologies—and product improvements such as those at PepsiCo. Radical change involves the creation of a new structure and management processes. The technology is likely to be breakthrough, and new products thereby created will establish new markets.

Although most change is incremental, there is a growing emphasis on the need for radical change because of today's turbulent, unpredictable environment.[7] Indeed, some experts argue that firms must be constantly changing their structures and management processes in response to changing demands, as discussed in Book Mark 8.0. As mentioned earlier in this chapter, the health care industry is facing tremendous upheaval, and companies likely will have to implement radical change to survive. Corporate transformations and turnarounds are considered radical change. Another example of radical change was the revolution at Motorola that achieved an astounding six sigma quality (only 3.4 mistakes per million parts produced). This previously considered impossible level of quality became the new norm.

An example of a radical corporate transformation is Globe Metallurgical, Inc., which was a typical Rust Belt company in the early 1980s: old-fashioned, bureaucratic, slow-moving, and unresponsive to customers. Costs were high and quality was low. When Arden Sims took over as chief executive in 1984, the company was in a death spiral, sure to be run out of business by foreign competition. Over a period of eight years, Sims transformed Globe into today's top source for specialty metals for the chemical and foundry industries worldwide. The transformation involved fundamental changes in management systems, work structures, products, technology, and worker attitudes. In 1988, Globe became the first small company to win a Malcolm Baldrige National Quality Award.[8]

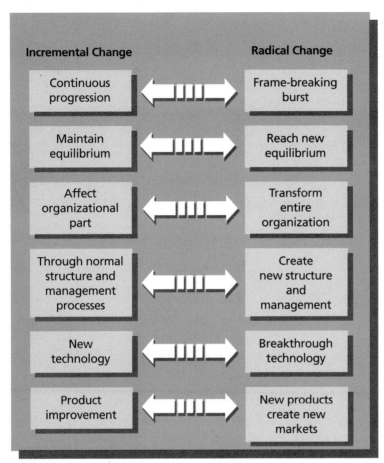

Exhibit 8.1
Incremental versus Radical Change.

Source: Based on Alan D. Meyer, James B. Goes, and Geoffrey R. Brooks, "Organizations in Disequilibrium: Environmental Jolts and Industry Revolutions," in George Huber and William H. Glick, eds., *Organizational Change and Redesign* (New York: Oxford University Press, 1992), 66–111; and Harry S. Dent, Jr., "Growth through New Product Development," *Small Business Reports* (November 1990): 30–40.

STRATEGIC TYPES OF CHANGE

Given that most planned changes are incremental, managers can focus on four types within organizations to achieve strategic advantage. These four types of changes are summarized in Exhibit 8.2 as products and services, strategy and structure, people and culture, and technology. We touched on overall leadership and organizational strategy in Chapter 2, and we will touch these topics again along with corporate culture in Chapter 10. These factors provide an overall context within which the four types of change serve as a competitive wedge to achieve an advantage in the international environment. Each company has a unique configuration of products and services, strategy and structure, people and culture, and technologies that can be focused for maximum impact upon the company's chosen markets.[9]

Technology changes are changes in an organization's production process, including its knowledge and skill base, that enable distinctive competence. These

BOOKMARK
8.0

HAVE YOU READ ABOUT THIS?

The Virtual Corporation
by William H. Davidow and Michael S. Malone

Virtual reality is one of the hottest electronic technologies of our time. A person wearing a special headset and glove can enter a computer-created world that looks and feels much like the real world outside. Virtual reality pioneers envision many entertainment applications, including virtual vacations, virtual video games, and even virtual sex.

In *The Virtual Corporation*, William H. Davidow and Michael S. Malone propose an entirely new organizational reality for America's businesses. They argue that unless American businesses become "virtual" corporations, the United States "will be a post-industrial version of a developing country" by the year 2015. Davidow and Malone define virtual to mean "elastic." The virtual corporation is fast and flexible in responding to rapidly-changing customer expectations.

Nothing Stays the Same

Virtual enterprises will notice "formerly well-defined structures beginning to lose their edges, seemingly permanent things starting to continuously change, and products and services adapting to match our desires." Customer demands dictate structure in the virtual corporation, so structure is constantly changing. Boundaries between the corporation and its customers and suppliers are soft and permeable; indeed, "some customers and suppliers begin to spend more time in the company than some of the firm's own workers." Internal structures, job responsibilities, and lines of authority shift as needed.

In addition to constantly recreating structures to meet variable demands, the virtual corporation reflects several other characteristics:

- It masters new manufacturing and information technologies that speed the production process and the flow of information through the corporation.
- It responds to changing customer demands with ever more customized products and services—available at any time and in any place.
- The corporation, its people, and its processes are interdependent and symbiotic. The entire work force is capable of taking initiative in pursuit of the corporate goal.
- Management delegates control while infusing workers with a clear vision.

Conclusion

Davidow and Malone cite numerous examples of firms that are leading the way into the 21st century, such as Boeing, Beretta, and Lenscrafters. These companies use advanced technologies and cooperative work forces to be fast and flexible in producing new and highly customized products. Time may be running out for other companies to follow suit.

The Virtual Corporation by William H. Davidow and Michael S. Malone is published by HarperCollins.

---

changes are designed to make production more efficient or to produce greater volume. Changes in technology involve the techniques for making products or services. They include work methods, equipment, and work flow. For example, in a university, technology changes are changes in techniques for teaching courses. As another example, Globe Metallurgical changed its production process using breakthrough furnace technology.

Product and service changes pertain to the product or service outputs of an organization. New products include small adaptations of existing products or entirely new product lines. New products are normally designed to increase the market share or to develop new markets, customers, or clients. Globe Metallurgical shifted its product line to high-margin specialty metals, which helped take the company global and into highly profitable niche markets. The Saturn automobile developed by General Motors is a product change.

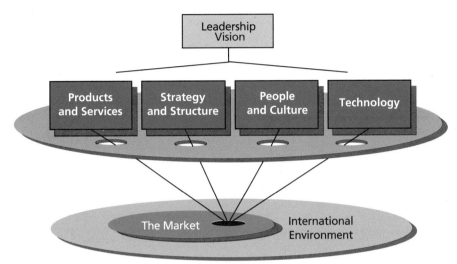

Exhibit 8.2
The Four Types of Change Provide a Strategic Competitive Wedge.

Source: Joseph E. McCann, "Design Principles for an Innovating Company," *Academy of Management Executive* 5 (May 1991): 76–93. Used by permission.

Strategy and structure changes pertain to the administrative domain in an organization. The administrative domain involves the supervision and management of the organization. These changes include changes in organization structure, strategic management, policies, reward systems, labor relations, coordination devices, management information and control systems, and accounting and budgeting systems. Structure and system changes are usually top-down, that is, mandated by top management, whereas product and technology changes may often come from the bottom up. The structure at Globe Metallurgical was changed after managers discovered the power of flexible work teams when they were forced to run the furnaces during a year-long strike. When workers came back on the job, management instituted a new team structure. A system change instituted by management in a university might be a new merit pay plan. Corporate downsizing is another example of top-down structure change.

People and culture changes refer to changes in the values, attitudes, expectations, beliefs, abilities, and behavior of employees. An organization may wish to hire only the best people or to upgrade the leadership ability of key managers. Changes in communication networks and improved problem-solving and planning skills of employees are people changes. In transformations and turnarounds, the entire culture of the organization is changed. In the old days at Globe Metallurgical, employees were suspicious of management, who dictated new policies without consulting workers. One of the results of Globe's transformation is a new culture that values employee empowerment and involvement, a new respect for management, and a new commitment to quality.

Change Interdependence The four types of changes in Exhibit 8.2 are interdependent—a change in one often means a change in another. A new product may require changes in the production technology, or a change in structure may require new employee skills. For example, when Shenandoah Life Insurance Company acquired new computer technology to process claims, the technology was not fully utilized until clerks were restructured into teams of five to seven members that were compatible with the technology. The structural change was an outgrowth of the technology change. In a manufacturing company, engineers introduced robots and advanced manufacturing technologies, only to find that the technology placed greater demands on employees. Upgrading employee skills required a change in wage systems. Organizations are interdependent systems, and changing one part often has implications for other organization elements.

ELEMENTS FOR SUCCESSFUL CHANGE

Regardless of the scope or type of change, most innovations and changes are adopted through a sequence of events. In the research literature on innovation, **organizational change** is considered the adoption of a new idea or behavior by an organization.[10] **Organizational innovation**, in contrast, is the adoption of an idea or behavior that is new to the organization's industry, market, or general environment.[11] The first organization to introduce a new product is considered the innovator, and organizations that copy are considered to adopt changes. For purposes of managing change, however, the terms *innovation* and *change* will be used interchangeably because the **change process** within organizations tends to be identical whether a change is early or late with respect to other organizations in the environment.

Innovations typically are assimilated into an organization through a series of steps or elements. Organization members first become aware of a possible innovation, evaluate its appropriateness, and then evaluate and choose the idea.[12] The required elements of successful change are summarized in Exhibit 8.3. For a change to be successfully implemented, managers must make sure each element occurs in the organization. If one of the elements is missing, the change process will fail.

1. *Ideas.*   Although creativity is a dramatic element of organizational change, creativity within organizations has not been widely and systematically studied. No company can remain competitive without new ideas; change is the outward expression of those ideas.[13] An idea is a new way of doing things. It may be a new product or service, a new management concept, or a new procedure for working together in the organization. Ideas can come from within or from outside the organization.
2. *Need.*   Ideas are generally not seriously considered unless there is a perceived need for change. A perceived need for change occurs when managers see a gap between actual performance and desired performance in the organization. For example, IBM executives perceived a strong need for structural change after the company posted operating losses for two consecutive years. Sometimes, ideas are generated to meet a perceived need; other times, a new idea occurs first and will stimulate consideration of problems it will solve or opportunities it provides.
3. *Adoption.*   Adoption occurs when decision makers choose to go ahead with a proposed idea. Key managers and employees need to be in agreement to support the change. For a major organizational change, the decision might require the signing of a legal document by the board of directors. For a small change, adoption might occur with informal approval by a middle manager. When Ray Kroc was CEO of McDonald's, he made the adoption decision about innovations such as the Big Mac and Egg McMuffin.
4. *Implementation.*   Implementation occurs when organization members actually use a new idea, technique, or behavior. Materials and equipment may have to be

Exhibit 8.3   Sequence of Elements for Successful Change.

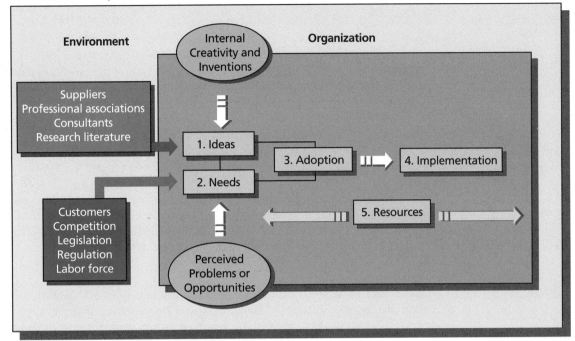

acquired, and workers may have to be trained to use the new idea. Implementation is a very important step because without it, previous steps are to no avail. Implementation of change is often the most difficult part of the change process. Until people use the new idea, no change has actually taken place.

5. *Resources.*   Human energy and activity are required to bring about change. Change does not happen on its own; it requires time and resources, for both creating and implementing a new idea. Employees have to provide energy to see both the need and the idea to meet that need. Someone must develop a proposal and provide the time and effort to implement it. Most innovations go beyond ordinary budget allocations and require special funding. At Teleflex, an engineering and manufacturing company near Philadelphia, employees can acquire from $1,000 to $200,000 to develop and implement new ideas. At S. C. Johnson & Son, a $250,000 seed fund has been set up for anyone with a promising new product idea. Other companies use committees and task forces, as described in Chapter 6, to focus resources on a change.

One point about Exhibit 8.3 is especially important. Needs and ideas are listed simultaneously at the beginning of the change sequence. Either may occur first. Many organizations adopted the computer, for example, because it seemed a promising way to improve efficiency. The search for a polio vaccine, on the other hand, was stimulated by a severe need. Whether the need or the idea occurs first, for the change to be accomplished, each of the steps in Exhibit 8.3 must be completed. Frito-Lay uses this change process to facilitate frequent innovations to stay ahead of its competition.

IN PRACTICE ◆ 8.2
Frito-Lay, Inc.

Frito-Lay plants make more than ten thousand packages of snacks per minute. Frito-Lay uses about 5 percent of all potatoes grown in the United States. Claiming about half of the salty snack food market, Frito-Lay has been called the Mozart of the industry because of its ability to produce themes and variations on established product lines.

Committees and researchers generate hundreds of new ideas each year, of which maybe one hundred will receive serious study. Product ideas are tested on some one hundred people each night, five nights a week, who sample from five to ten different products. Some of the recent successful innovations were Cool Ranch Doritos and a new line of low-oil, lower-fat snacks, including low-oil Ruffles potato chips and Nacho Cheese Dorito Light chips.

Many product ideas are developed to meet specific competitive threats. Other products are dreamed up by employees simply in the hope of selling more snacks. Frito-Lay has tried carrot chips, plantain chips, and apple chips, which never made it to market. It takes about a year for an idea to go from product concept to test market, and it can be killed at any stage—from test kitchen through consumer taste-testing, package design, or manufacturing.

Teams and committees are an important part of Frito-Lay's success. They share ideas and make decisions. Each year the industry may introduce some thirteen hundred new snack and candy products, but Frito-Lay has more than its share of successful and enduring ones.[14]

Frito-Lay is designed to facilitate each of the five change elements. The competition from other chip manufacturers and internal ideas trigger a perceived need for innovation. Many ideas are generated, although only a few ideas are adopted and implemented. Frito-Lay is a continual innovator and, hence, devotes many resources to the change process. Special departments are established for making, testing, advertising, and marketing new products, and committees with broad representation are involved in the decision process. The allocation of so many resources has paid off, because Frito-Lay continues to be the innovation leader in its industry.

Technology Change

In today's rapidly changing world, any company that isn't constantly developing, acquiring, or adapting new technology will likely be out of business in a few years. However, organizations face a contradiction when it comes to technology change, for the conditions that promote new ideas are not generally the best for implementing those ideas for routine production. An innovative organization is characterized by flexibility, empowered employees, and the absence of rigid work rules.[15] As discussed earlier in this book, an organic, free-flowing organization is typically associated with change and is considered the best organization form for adapting to a chaotic environment.

The flexibility of an organic organization is attributed to people's freedom to create and introduce new ideas. Organic organizations encourage a bottom-up innovation process. Ideas bubble up from middle- and lower-level employees because they have the freedom to propose ideas and to experiment. A mechanistic structure, on the other hand, stifles innovation with its emphasis on rules and regulations, but it is often the best structure for efficiently producing routine products. The challenge for organizations is to create both organic and mechanistic conditions within organizations to achieve both innovation and efficiency. To achieve both aspects of technological change, many organizations use the ambidextrous approach.

THE AMBIDEXTROUS APPROACH

Recent thinking has refined the idea of organic versus mechanistic structures with respect to innovation creation versus innovation utilization. For example, sometimes an organic structure generates innovative ideas but is not the best structure for using those ideas.[16] In other words, the initiation and the utilization of change are two distinct processes. Organic characteristics such as decentralization and employee freedom are excellent for initiating ideas; but these same conditions often make it hard to use a change because employees are less likely to comply. Employees can ignore the innovation because of decentralization and a generally loose structure.

How does an organization solve this dilemma? One approach is for the organization to be **ambidextrous**—to incorporate structures that are appropriate to both the creation and use of innovation.[17] The organization can behave in an organic way when the situation calls for the initiation of new ideas and in a mechanistic way to implement and use the ideas.

An example of the ambidextrous approach is the Freudenberg-NOK auto-parts factory in Ligonier, Indiana. Shifting teams of twelve, including plant workers, managers, and outsiders, each spend three days creating ideas to cut costs and boost productivity in various sections of the plant. At the end of the three days, team members go back to their regular jobs, and a new team comes in to look for even more improvements. Over a year's time, there are approximately forty of these GROWTTH (Get Rid of Waste Through Team Harmony) teams roaming through the sprawling factory. Management has promised that no one will be laid off as a result of suggestions from GROWTTH teams, which further encourages employees to both create and use innovations.[18]

TECHNIQUES FOR ENCOURAGING TECHNOLOGY CHANGE

Freudenberg-NOK has created both organic and mechanistic conditions in the factory. Some of the techniques used by many companies to maintain an ambidextrous approach are switching structures, separate creative departments, venture teams, and corporate entrepreneurship.

Switching Structures   **Switching structures** means an organization creates an organic structure when such a structure is needed for the initiation of new ideas.[19] Some of the ways organizations have switched structures to achieve the ambidextrous approach are as follows.

- Philips Corporation, a building materials producer in Ohio, each year creates groups of five employees from various departments—up to 150 teams—to work together for five days to improve Philips products. After the five days of organic brainstorming and problem solving, the company switches back to running things on a more mechanistic basis as the improvements are implemented into the system.[20]

- Lockheed's famous Skunk Works, a secret research and development subsidiary, was purposely isolated from the corporation's sprawling bureaucracy. Staffed with creative mavericks not afraid to break conventions, Skunk Works has been responsible for some of Lockheed's greatest innovations. Chief Executive Daniel M. Tellup counts on the innovators at Skunk Works to help Lockheed maintain its technological edge as the defense industry shrinks and becomes more competitive.[21]
- Apple Computer designates highly paid Apple Fellows who are free to brainstorm for new ideas as they please. One fellow is studying how children learn to create artificial intelligence, and another is looking for ways to combine video devices and computers.[22] As these ideas take shape, they are gradually taken over for implementation by Apple's traditional structure.
- Westinghouse has more than one hundred quality circles, one of which saved the company $2.4 million. Members are volunteers who meet regularly to create solutions to problems affecting their work. Quality circles provide organic conditions to allow brainstorming for improved production. Then employees return to their jobs to implement approved suggestions.

Each of these organizations found creative ways to be ambidextrous, establishing organic conditions for developing new ideas in the midst of more mechanistic conditions for implementing and using those ideas.

Creative Departments   In many large organizations the initiation of innovation is assigned to separate **creative departments**.[23] Staff departments, such as research and development, engineering, design, and systems analysis, create changes for adoption in other departments. Departments that initiate change are organically structured to facilitate the generation of new ideas and techniques. Departments that use those innovations tend to have a mechanistic structure more suitable for efficient production. Exhibit 8.4 indicates how one department is responsible for creation and another department implements the innovation.

Raytheon's New Products Center, in operation for twenty-five years, illustrates how creativity and entrepreneurial spirit can coexist with discipline and controls. The center has been responsible for many technical innovations, including industry-leading combination ovens, which added microwave capabilities to conventional stoves. The New Products Center provides autonomy and freedom for staff to explore new ideas, yet staff must also establish a working relationship with other departments so that innovations meet a genuine need for Raytheon departments.[24]

Exhibit 8.4
Division of Labor between Departments to Achieve Changes in Technology.

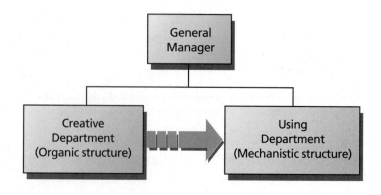

Venture Teams **Venture teams** are a recent technique used to give free reign to creativity within organizations. Venture teams are often given a separate location and facilities so they are not constrained by organizational procedures. Dow Chemical created an innovation department that has virtually total license to establish new venture projects for any department in the company. Convergent Technologies uses the name "strike force" for a separate team that will develop a new computer. The team is cut loose to set up its own company and pursue members' ideas. The venture groups are kept small so they have autonomy and no bureaucracy emerges.

A new venture team is a small company within a large company. To giant companies like Eastman Kodak and AT&T, new venture teams are essential to free creative people from the bureaucracy. Eastman Kodak has launched fourteen new ventures since 1984. Each is like a company-within-a-company that explores such ideas as computerized photo imaging, lithium batteries, or technology to project computer images on a large screen. AT&T has created eleven venture companies, one of which developed Pixel Machines, which offer striking capability to produce sharp pictures on a computer terminal. These venture companies are carefully nurtured and are given freedom from the AT&T bureaucracy.[25]

Corporate Entrepreneurship Corporate entrepreneurship attempts to develop an internal entrepreneurial spirit, philosophy, and structure that will produce a higher than average number of innovations.[26] Corporate entrepreneurship may involve the use of creative departments and new venture teams as described above, but it also attempts to release the creative energy of all employees in the organization. The most important outcome is to facilitate **idea champions** which go by a variety of names, including advocate, intrapreneur, or change agent. Idea champions provide the time and energy to make things happen. They fight to overcome natural resistance to change and to convince others of the merit of a new idea.[27] For example, when Texas Instruments reviewed fifty successful and unsuccessful technical projects, one fascinating finding emerged. Every failure was characterized by the absence of a volunteer champion. There was no one who passionately believed in the idea, who pushed the idea through all the necessary obstacles to make it work. Texas Instruments took this finding so seriously that now its number one criterion for approving new technical projects is the presence of a zealous champion.[28]

Companies encourage idea champions by providing freedom and slack time to creative people. 3M encourages researchers to spend up to 15 percent of their time thinking about ideas that might lead to new products. Companies such as IBM and General Electric allow employees to develop new technologies without company approval. Known as "bootlegging," the unauthorized research often pays big dividends. As one IBM executive said, "We wink at it. It pays off. It's just amazing what a handful of dedicated people can do when they are really turned on."[29]

Idea champions usually come in two types. The **technical or product champion** is the person who generates or adopts and develops an idea for a technological innovation and is devoted to it, even to the extent of risking position or prestige. The **management champion** acts as a supporter and sponsor to shield and promote an idea within the organization.[30] The management champion sees the potential application and has the prestige and authority to get it a fair hearing and to allocate resources to it. Technical and management champions often work together because a technical idea will have a greater chance of success if a manager can be found to sponsor it. At Black & Decker, Peter Chaconas is a technical champion. He invented the

Piranha circular saw blade, which is a best-selling tool accessory. Next, he invented the Bullet, which is a bit for home power drills and is the first major innovation in this product in almost one hundred years. Chaconas works full-time designing products and promoting their acceptance. Randy Blevins, his boss, acts as management champion for Chaconas's ideas.[31]

The following example illustrates the integral roles of technical and management champions and the obstacles they often face, even in companies that are supportive of innovation.

IN PRACTICE ◆ 8.3
Hewlett-Packard

As a young engineer at Hewlett-Packard, Chuck House helped develop oscilloscope technology for use in an improved airport control tower monitor for the Federal Aviation Administration. Although the HP monitor ultimately lost out to competitors, House saw some features of the prototype that deserved further investigation. For example, the Hewlett-Packard monitor was smaller and lighter in weight than its competitors; it was twenty times as fast; and it provided a brighter, energy-efficient picture. In his efforts to demonstrate the value of the prototype, House broke a number of organization rules and boundaries. In conducting his own market research on potential applications, he violated functional boundaries by bypassing HP's marketing department, and he breached company security, which forbade the showing of prototypes to customers. House's enthusiasm was not shared by company founder David Packard, who said: "When I come back next year, I don't want to see that project in the lab!"

With the clandestine support of his boss, Das Howard, House managed to get the time and resources to complete the project within a year, and when Packard returned for the next annual review, the monitor was in the marketplace. Packard, rather than firing House and Howard for insubordination, revealed his own maverick tendencies by supporting the project and giving the team permission to develop further applications. Eventually, the Hewlett-Packard monitor was used for the National Aeronautics and Space Administration's moon mission and was the medical monitor used during the first artificial heart transplant. Without the dedication of technical champion Chuck House and the support and sponsorship of management champion Das Howard, these landmark innovations would probably never have come about.[32]

The development of the NASA moon mission monitor illustrates how technical and management champions work together and how they sometimes break the rules to support and develop technological innovations. Champions who are willing to risk their jobs and their prestige are crucial for technology change.

New Products and Services

Many of the concepts described for technology change are also relevant to the creation of new products and services. However, in many ways, new products and services are a special case of innovation because they are used by customers outside the organization. Since new products are designed for sale in the environment, uncertainty about the suitability and success of an innovation is very high.

NEW PRODUCT SUCCESS RATE

Research has explored the enormous uncertainty associated with the development and sale of new products.[33] To understand what this uncertainty can mean to organizations, just consider such flops as RCA's VideoDisc player, which lost an estimated $500 million, or Time Incorporated's *TV-Cable Week,* which lost $47 million. Producing new products that fail is a part of business in all industries. One survey examined two hundred projects in nineteen chemical, drug, electronics, and petroleum laboratories to learn about success rates. To be successful, the new product had to pass three stages of development: technical completion, commercialization, and market success. The findings about success rates are given in Exhibit 8.5.

On the average, only 57 percent of all projects undertaken in the R&D laboratories achieved technical objectives, which means all technical problems were solved and the projects moved on to production. Of all projects that were started, however, less than one-third (31 percent) were fully marketed and commercialized. Several projects failed at this stage because production estimates or test market results were unfavorable.

Finally, only 12 percent of all projects originally undertaken achieved economic success. Most of the commercialized products did not earn sufficient returns to cover the cost of development and production. This means that only about one project in eight returns a profit to the company. New product development is thus very risky.

REASONS FOR NEW PRODUCT SUCCESS

The next question to be answered by research was, "Why are some products more successful than others?" Further studies indicated that innovation success was related to collaboration between technical and marketing departments. Successful new products and services seemed to be technologically sound and also carefully tailored to customer needs.[34] A study called Project SAPPHO examined seventeen pairs of new product innovations, with one success and one failure in each pair, and concluded the following.

1. Successful innovating companies had a much better understanding of customer needs and paid much more attention to marketing.
2. Successful innovating companies made more effective use of outside technology and outside advice, even though they did more work in-house.
3. Top management support in the successful innovating companies was from people who were more senior and had greater authority.

	Probability
Technical completion (technical objectives achieved)	.57
Commercialization (full-scale marketing)	.31
Market success (earns economic returns)	.12

Exhibit 8.5
Probability of New Product Success.

Source: Based on Edwin Mansfield, J. Rapaport, J. Schnee, S. Wagner, and M. Hamburger, *Research and Innovation in Modern Corporations* (New York: Norton, 1971), 57.

Thus, there is a distinct pattern of tailoring innovations to customer needs, making effective use of technology, and having influential top managers support the project. These ideas taken together indicate that the effective design for new product innovation is associated with horizontal linkage across departments.

HORIZONTAL LINKAGE MODEL

The organization design for achieving new product innovation involves three components—departmental specialization, boundary spanning, and horizontal linkages. These components are similar to the differentiation and integration ideas in Chapter 3 and the information linkage mechanisms in Chapter 6. Exhibit 8.6 illustrates these components in the **horizontal linkage model.**

Specialization   The key departments in new product development are R&D, marketing, and production. The specialization component means that the personnel in all three of these departments are highly competent at their own tasks. The three departments are differentiated from each other and have skills, goals, and attitudes appropriate for their specialized functions.

Boundary Spanning   This component means each department involved with new products has excellent linkage with relevant sectors in the external environment. R&D personnel are linked to professional associations and to colleagues in other R&D departments. They are aware of recent scientific developments. Marketing personnel are closely linked to customer needs. They listen to what customers have to say, and they analyze competitor products and suggestions by distributors. For example, Worlds of Wonder had astonishing success with its Teddy Ruxpin and Laser Tag toys because of market research, which meant working with some one thousand families chosen at random to learn their needs.[35]

Exhibit 8.6   Horizontal Linkage Model for New Product Innovations.

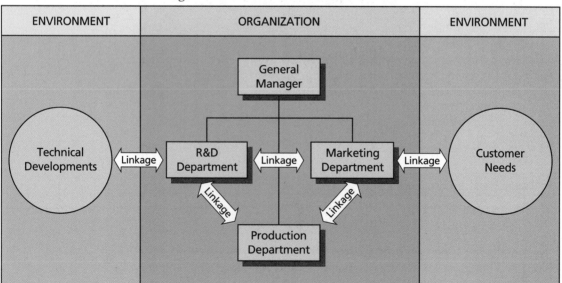

Horizontal Linkages   This component means that technical, marketing, and production people share ideas and information. Research people inform marketing of new technical developments to learn whether the developments are applicable to customers. Marketing people provide customer complaints and information to R&D to use in the design of new products. People from both R&D and marketing coordinate with production because new products have to fit within production capabilities so costs are not exorbitant. The decision to launch a new product is ultimately a joint decision among all three departments.

At General Electric, members of the R&D department have a great deal of freedom to imagine and invent, and then they have to shop their ideas around other departments and divisions, sometimes finding applications for new technologies that are far from their original intentions. As a result, one study shows that of 250 technology products GE undertook to develop over a four-year period, 150 of them produced major applications, far above the U.S. average of about one success out of ten. Boeing's engineers and manufacturers worked side-by-side on the new 777 project, sometimes bringing in representatives from outside suppliers, airline customers, maintenance, and finance.[36] Famous innovation failures—such as Weyerhaeuser's UltraSoft diapers, General Mills's Benefit cereal, Anheuser-Busch's LA Beer, and RJR Nabisco's Premier smokeless cigarettes—usually violate the horizontal linkage model. Employees fail to connect with customer needs, or internal departments fail to adequately share needs and coordinate with one another. Perhaps the most successful company of all in new product development is Rubbermaid, a maker of simple, low-tech products.

IN PRACTICE ◆ 8.4
Rubbermaid

Rubbermaid's unusual single-minded focus on successful innovation has paid off. Not only does the company generate 30 percent of sales from products no more than five years old, but it launches about one hundred new products annually and is rated fifth on *Fortune's* list of most admired corporations.

The most astonishing feat is that almost all new products are a hit—Rubbermaid claims a new product success rate of 90 percent. One-third of these products are new from the ground up, such as the recently introduced molded-plastic items for home offices.

Rubbermaid accounts for its success through a fetish of staying in touch with potential customers. It uses focus groups year-round in five cities to test color preferences. It quizzes people in shopping malls, and most of its executives read customer letters to learn what consumers are thinking. These sources led to the idea for a one-piece dish drainer designed for people in small households.

Rubbermaid also maintains a competitive edge by avoiding test marketing, a staple in many organizations. The reason is to keep from tipping off competitors. Rubbermaid prefers instead to use panels, brand awareness studies, and consumer diaries about product use to judge whether a product will succeed.

What about the 10 percent of products that fail? Sometimes product research doesn't help. A line of garden accessories sold okay, but not well enough to be kept in production. However, the few product failures are more than made up through employee innovations for internal efficiency. Last year, employees generated 12,600 suggestions.

> With that kind of innovation focus, it's no wonder the company's production process is so efficient and most new products succeed.[37]

Companies such as Rubbermaid, 3M, General Electric, N. V. Phillips, and Xerox have all learned another application for the horizontal linkage model—speeding new products to market.

SPEED AND PRODUCT INNOVATION

One of the most practical ways for organizations to gain an advantage in today's rapidly changing world is to get new products or services to the market faster than the competition does. Fast product development is becoming a way of life at companies like Xerox, Hewlett-Packard, and Chrysler. One authority on time-based competition has said that the old paradigm for success—"provide the most value for the least cost"—has been updated to "provide the most value for the least cost in the least elapsed time."[38]

To gain business, companies are learning to develop new products and services incredibly fast. Whether the approach is called the horizontal linkage model, concurrent engineering, companies without walls, the parallel approach, or simultaneous coupling of departments, the point is the same—get people working together simultaneously on a project rather than in sequence. Many companies are learning to sprint to market with new products. Chrysler chopped 40 percent off the time it took to develop its new line of LH sedans and delivered the Neon in a speedy forty-two months, at a fraction of what any recent small car has cost. Hewlett-Packard has made speed a top priority, getting products out the door twice as fast and urging employees to rethink every process in terms of speed. A printer that once took fifty-four months to develop is now on the market in twenty-two. Speed is becoming the major competitive issue in the 1990s and requires the use of cross-functional teams and other horizontal linkages.[39]

Strategy and Structure Change

The preceding discussion focused on new production processes and products, which are based in the technology of an organization. The expertise for such innovation lies within the technical core and professional staff groups, such as research and engineering. This section turns to an examination of structural and strategy changes. These changes are the responsibility of upper managers in organizations. The overall process of these changes is typically different from the process for innovations in technology or new products.

THE DUAL-CORE APPROACH

The dual-core approach compares administrative and technical changes. Administrative changes pertain to the design and structure of the organization itself, including restructuring, downsizing, teams, control systems, information systems, and departmental grouping. Research into administrative change suggests two things. First, administrative changes occur less frequently than do technical changes. Second, administrative changes occur in response to different environmental sectors and follow a different internal process than do technology-based changes.[40] The

dual-core approach to organizational change identifies the unique processes associated with administrative change.[41]

Organizations—schools, hospitals, city governments, welfare agencies, government bureaucracies, and many business firms—can be conceptualized as having two cores: a technical core and an administrative core. Each core has its own employees, tasks, and environmental domain. Innovation can originate in either core.

The administrative core is above the technical core in the hierarchy. The responsibility of the administrative core includes the structure, control, and coordination of the organization itself and concerns the environmental sectors of government, financial resources, economic conditions, human resources, and competitors. The technical core is concerned with the transformation of raw materials into organizational products and services and involves the environmental sector of customers and technology.[42]

The findings from research comparing administrative and technical change suggest that a mechanistic organization structure is appropriate for frequent administrative changes, including changes in goals, strategy, structure, control systems, and personnel.[43] For example, administrative changes in policy, regulations, or control systems are more critical than technical changes in many government organizations that are bureaucratically structured. Organizations that successfully adopt many administrative changes often have a larger administrative ratio, are larger in size, and are centralized and formalized compared with organizations that adopt many technical changes.[44] The reason is the top-down implementation of changes in response to changes in the government, financial, or legal sectors of the environment. In contrast, if an organization has an organic structure, lower-level employees have more freedom and autonomy and, hence, may resist top-down initiatives. An organic structure is more often used when changes in organizational technology or products are important to the organization.

The innovation approaches associated with administrative versus technical change are summarized in Exhibit 8.7. Technical change, such as changes in production techniques and innovation technology for new products, is facilitated by an

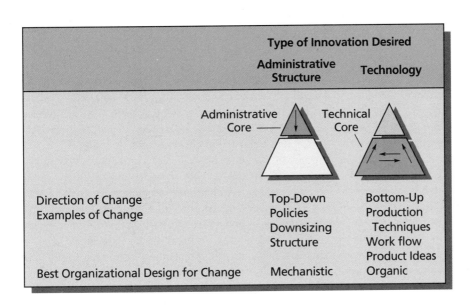

Exhibit 8.7 Dual-Core Approach to Organization Change.

organic structure, which allows ideas to bubble upward from lower- and middle-level employees. Organizations that must adopt frequent administrative changes tend to use a top-down process and a mechanistic structure. For example, policy changes, such as the adoption of tough no-smoking policies by companies like Park Nicollet Medical Center in Minnesota, are facilitated by a top-down approach. Downsizing and restructuring are nearly always managed top-down, such as when Ronald E. Compton, CEO of Aetna Life and Casualty Company, recently announced plans to slash over four thousand jobs and drop two of the company's product lines.[45]

The point of the dual-core approach is that many organizations—especially not-for-profit and government organizations—must adopt frequent administrative changes, so a mechanistic structure may be appropriate. For example, research into civil service reform found that the implementation of administrative innovation was extremely difficult in organizations that had an organic technical core. The professional employees in a decentralized agency could resist civil service changes. By contrast, organizations that were considered more bureaucratic in the sense of high formalization and centralization adopted administrative changes readily.[46]

What about business organizations that normally are technologically innovative in bottom-up fashion but suddenly face a crisis and need to reorganize? Or consider a technically innovative, high-tech firm that must reorganize frequently or must suddenly cut back to accommodate changes in production technology or the environment. Technically innovative firms may suddenly have to restructure, reduce the number of employees, alter pay systems, disband teams, or form a new division.[47] The answer is to use a top-down change process. The authority for strategy and structure change lies with top management, who should initiate and implement the new strategy and structure to meet environmental circumstances. Employee input may be sought, but top managers have the responsibility to direct the change. *Downsizing, restructuring,* and *reorganizing* are common terms for what happens in times of rapid change and global competition. Often, strong top-down changes follow the installation of new top management. Consider what's happening at Autodesk, Inc.

IN PRACTICE ◆ 8.5
Autodesk, Inc.

When Carol Bartz left Sun Microsystems, Inc. to run Autodesk, the world's sixth largest PC software company and a leader in sales of computer-aided design software, she introduced a first for the company: a management hierarchy. For the freethinkers at Autodesk, who brought their dogs to work and sent endless memos through e-mail trying to reach consensus on strategy decisions, it was a shock that has sent them reeling.

But when Bartz was hired, profits were falling, Autodesk's growth was continuing to slow, and stock prices were declining sharply. Something had to be done. Bartz came in with a mandate for change and is taking a strong top-down approach to try to build a billion-dollar company in a highly competitive industry. While the company's programmers are not happy with the new hierarchy, sales and marketing are pleased to have someone setting priorities to get the company back on track as far as sales are concerned.

Bartz knows any change, particularly one this momentous, is stressful, so she's instituted a series of "brown-bag chats" with employees to hear their side of things and try to build faith in the new structure as one that will have a positive outcome. As Bartz put it, "It's safe to say there are good ways to manage change and bad ways to manage change, and we have to get on the right side of that paradigm."[48]

Carol Bartz knows that while it is important to communicate with employees, top management is responsible for firmly directing restructuring changes. Fortunately, at this point, Autodesk has not had to lay off employees. Restructuring and especially downsizing can be painful and difficult, so top managers should move quickly and authoritatively to make both as humane as possible.[49]

People and Culture Change

The target of people change is the values, attitudes, and skills of individual employees. In a world where any organization can purchase new technology, the motivation, skill, and commitment of employees can provide the competitive edge. Human resource systems can be designed to attract, develop, and maintain an efficient force of employees.

Sometimes achieving a new way of thinking requires a focused change on the underlying corporate culture values and norms. In the last decade, numerous large corporations, including DuPont, Rockwell, and Amoco, have undertaken some type of culture change initiative. Changing corporate culture fundamentally shifts how work is done in an organization and generally leads to renewed commitment and empowerment of employees and a stronger bond between the company and its customers.[50]

Changing corporate culture is a key aspect of total quality management programs, because TQM requires all employees to think in new ways about how work is done. Organizational development programs also focus on changing old culture values to new ways of thinking, including greater employee participation and empowerment and developing a shared companywide vision.

TOTAL QUALITY MANAGEMENT

About ten years ago, three-fourths of all Americans considered foreign-made products equal or superior in quality to products made in the United States. Over the last decade, the quality revolution has spread throughout North American companies.[51]

The approach known as **total quality management** infuses quality values throughout every activity within a company. The concept is simple: workers, not managers, are handed the responsibility for achieving standards of quality. No longer are quality control departments and other formal control systems in charge of checking parts and improving quality. Companies are training their workers and then trusting them to infuse quality into everything they do. The results of TQM programs can be staggering. After noticing that Ford Motor Company cut $40 billion out of its operating budget by adopting quality principles and changing corporate culture, the Henry Ford Health System recently instituted a quality program. CEO Gail Warden says of quality programs at Henry Ford and other U.S. health care institutions, "We have to change the way we practice medicine" to get health care costs down and remain competitive in the rapidly changing health care industry.[52]

By requiring organizationwide participation in quality control, TQM requires a major shift in mind-set for both managers and workers. In TQM, workers must be trained, involved, and empowered in a way that many managers at first find frightening. One way in which workers are involved in through **quality circles,** groups of six to twelve volunteer workers who meet to analyze and solve problems. A quality circle at Henry Ford Hospital came up with the suggestion that patients could be given detailed instructions before admission for a specific form of chemotherapy that would cut down their stay in the hospital by at least a day.[53]

Another technique of total quality management is known as **benchmarking,** a process whereby companies find out how others do something better than they do and then try to imitate or improve on it. Through research and field trips by small teams of workers, companies compare their products, services, and business practices with those of their competitors and other companies. AT&T, Xerox, DuPont, Eastman Kodak, and Motorola are constantly benchmarking. Ford Motor Company shamelessly benchmarked more than two hundred features of the Ford Taurus against seven competitors, including the Honda Accord, Chevy Lumina, and Nissan Maxima, helping to make the Taurus one of the top-selling cars.[54]

While the focus of total quality programs is generally on improving quality and productivity, it always involves a significant people and culture change. Managers must be prepared for this aspect before undertaking quality programs.

ORGANIZATIONAL DEVELOPMENT

Another concept that is concerned primarily with improved performance but focuses largely on the development and fulfillment of people is known as organizational development. During the 1970s, **organizational development** (OD) evolved as a separate field in the behavioral sciences, one devoted to a special kind of organizational change.[55] OD uses knowledge and techniques from the behavioral sciences to improve performance through trust, open confrontation of problems, employee empowerment and participation, the design of meaningful work, cooperation between groups, and the full use of human potential. OD practitioners believe the best performance occurs by breaking down hierarchical and authoritarian approaches to management. In terms of the competing values effectiveness model described in Chapter 2, OD places high value on internal processes and human relationships. However, consistent with the arguments in the environment and technology chapters, research has shown that the OD approach may not enhance performance or satisfaction in stable business environments and for routine tasks.[56]

The spirit of the people change OD tries to accomplish is illustrated by efforts at DuPont to move to a participative management style. When Jack Kane began working at a DuPont plant in the mid-1950s, a supervisor answered one of his questions by saying, "You don't need to know that." Today, Kane is manager of one of DuPont's most efficient plants, and he says most of his factory's productivity gains have come from involving workers in the process. He'll "give cost figures on any of our operations down to the newest guy on a maintenance team," he says. Plant workers also get bonuses for actions that save the factory money. One such worker got one thousand dollars for rejecting a contractor's bid to paint the plant's building and equipment. Management admits that couldn't have happened even a couple of years ago. Today, it ended up saving DuPont plenty—the contractor came back in with a bid 20 percent lower.[57]

The implementation of more participative management is not easy. Managers and employees have to think in new ways about human relationships. But the rewards can be tremendous. Spurred by pleas from new staffers, self-confessed "authoritarian" manager Sharon Jacobs at Hewlett-Packard's direct marketing organization is doing her best to "let go," to ask her telemarketers for solutions, to listen to the ideas of even lowest-level staff members. Despite the difficulties in the beginning, the new style has resulted in a 40 percent increase in productivity, a rise in employee morale significant enough to warrant a note from HP's president, and a 44 percent decline in the unit's annual attrition rate.[58] By using organizational development to create a higher quality of working life and participation for employees, managers like Sharon Jacobs and Jack Kane are helping their organizations improve performance and save money.

ORGANIZATIONAL DEVELOPMENT INTERVENTIONS

OD interventions involve training of specific groups or of everyone in the organization. For OD intervention to be successful, senior management in the organization must see the need for OD and must provide enthusiastic support for the change. Techniques used by many organizations for improving people skills through OD include the following.

Survey Feedback   Organizational personnel are surveyed about their job satisfaction, attitudes, performance, leader behavior, climate, and quality of work relationships. A consultant feeds back the data to stimulate a discussion of organizational problems. Plans are then made for organizational change.[59]

Team Building   **Team building** activities promote the idea that people who work together can work as a team. A work team can be brought together to discuss conflicts, goals, the decision-making process, communication, creativity, and leadership. The team can then plan to overcome problems and improve results.[60] Team building activities are also used in many companies to train task forces, committees, and new product development groups.

Intergroup Activities   Representatives from different groups are brought together in a mutual location to surface conflict, diagnose its causes, and plan improvement in communication and coordination. This type of intervention has been applied to union-management conflict, headquarters-field office conflict, interdepartmental conflict, and mergers.[61]

In today's world, the work force is becoming more and more diverse, and organizations are constantly changing in response to environmental uncertainty and increasing international competition. As the 1990s progress, OD interventions can respond to these new realities in organizations.[62] One example of an effective OD implementation is described in the Paradigm Buster.

Strategies for Implementing Change

This chapter began by looking at incremental versus radical change, the four types of changes managers can use to gain a competitive edge, and the five elements that must be present for any change to succeed—idea, need, adoption, implementation, and resources. In this final section, we are going to briefly discuss resistance to

---

Paradigm Buster

Amoco Corporation

Amoco Corporation has been a leading world-wide petroleum and chemical company for more than a hundred years and did things much the same way for most of those hundred years. But after the oil price collapse of the mid-1980s and subsequent environmental changes, Amoco had to step back and rethink the ways it had always done things. This rethinking ultimately led to a culture change process affecting fifty-five thousand employees worldwide, from executives at the corporate level to pumpers and pipe fitters in the oil fields and refineries.

In the late 1980s, Amoco asked all its employees to start discussing such questions as "What do we believe in and how do we want to behave as a company?" These discussions created a shared mind-set among Amoco employees from top to bottom that was critical for the success of change efforts. These questions also expanded Amoco's concept of strategy beyond financial and operational interests to one integrating people issues into the whole process. A related phase of the change process was a survey that revealed that employees thought Amoco fell short in the area of human resources.

Renewal at Amoco began with making sure every single employee understood the company's mission, vision, and values. Amoco realized that all employees needed to share a sense of identification with the company's mission and understand how their jobs fit into the bigger picture. Once this was done, senior management began to focus specifically on people systems, redesigning performance management procedures, overhauling recruiting practices, and working on processes for managing the diversity of a changing work force. In addition, employee involvement processes were examined, and structures were studied to see if decision-making was being handled at the appropriate level.

A number of important elements helped smooth the culture change process at Amoco. Executives recognized that change in any one area of the organization affects all the other areas. They also learned that rapid change can cause confusion among employees, so timing and explanation of changes were critical. Constant communication was necessary about the company's strategic direction and how employees were to be involved. And finally, Amoco executives learned that they had to continually explain and reinforce the need for change in the first place. By providing on-going information and feedback, executives headed off questions and concerns that can impede the change process.

Source: Benson L. Porter and Warrington S. Parker, Jr., "Culture Change," *Human Resource Management,* 31 (Spring-Summer 1992): 45–67.

---

change and the resources managers can use to implement change. These ideas are summarized in Exhibit 8.8.

BARRIERS TO CHANGE

Many barriers to change exist at the organizational level.[63] Management may possess the mind-set that costs are all-important and may fail to see the importance of a change for employee motivation or customer satisfaction. Failure to perceive benefits usually means education is needed. If managers feel the risk is too high, the reward system may discourage risk-taking. Organizational fragmentation and conflict often mean too little coordination and cooperation for change implementation. Moreover, in the case of new technology, the old and new systems must be compatible.

Exhibit 8.8   Implementation Barriers and Techniques.

Barriers to Change	Techniques for Change Implementation

Organizational:
1. Excessive focus on costs
2. Failure to perceive benefits
3. Risk too high
4. Lack of coordination and cooperation
5. Incompatible systems
Personal:
1. Uncertainty avoidance
2. Fear of loss
	1. Diagnose a true need for change
	2. Find an idea that fits the need
	3. Get top management support
	4. Design change for incremental implementation
	5. Plan to overcome resistance to change
	  • Alignment with needs and goals of users
	  • Communication and education
	  • Participation and involvement
	  • Forcing and coercion
	6. Create change teams
	7. Foster idea champions

At a personal level, many individuals fear the uncertainty associated with change, or they fear potential loss of power and status. In these cases, employees should be involved and implementation should be careful and incremental. Implementation can typically be designed to overcome these organizational and personal barriers.

TECHNIQUES FOR IMPLEMENTATION

1. *Diagnose a true need for change.*   A careful diagnosis of the existing situation is necessary to determine the extent of the problem or opportunity. If the people affected by the change do not agree with a problem, the change process should stop right there. Chrysler may run into problems with its $30 million plans to reeducate 100,000 employees in its dealerships because some of them don't perceive a true need for change. Chrysler wants to change the entire way in which dealers relate to customers. But some dealers think the corporation doesn't understand the retail business and therefore shouldn't be trying to make changes in it.[64] A perceived problem is necessary to unfreeze participants and make them willing to invest time and energy to adopt new techniques and procedures.[65]

2. *Find an idea that fits the need.*   Finding the right idea often involves search procedures—talking with other managers, assigning a task force to investigate the problem, sending out a request to suppliers, or asking creative people within the organization to develop a solution. The creation of a new idea requires organic conditions. This is a good opportunity to encourage employee participation, because they need the freedom to think about and explore new options.[66]

3. *Get top management support.*   Successful change requires the support of top management. Top managers should articulate clear innovation goals. For a single large change, such as a structural reorganization, the president and vice presidents must give their blessing and support. For smaller changes, the support of influential managers in relevant departments is required. The lack of top management support is one of the most frequent causes of implementation failure.[67] For that reason, when USF&G introduced new pricing and underwriting guidelines, President Paul Scheel and other top executives visited branch offices to communicate the changes to every single employee.

4. *Design the change for incremental implementation.*   When a large bank in South Carolina installed a complete new $6 million system to computerize processing, it was stunned that the system didn't work very well. The prospect for success of such a large change is improved if the change can be broken into subparts and each part adopted sequentially. Then designers can make adjustments to improve the innovation, and hesitant users who see success can throw support behind the rest of the change program. An incremental approach also reduces the cost of failure because only a few resources are lost on a bad idea.

5. *Develop plans to overcome resistance to change.*   Many good ideas are never used because managers failed to anticipate or prepare for resistance to change by consumers, employees, or other managers. No matter how impressive the performance characteristics of an innovation, its implementation will conflict with some interests and jeopardize some alliances in the organization. To increase the chance of successful implementation, management must acknowledge the conflict, threats, and potential losses perceived by employees. Several strategies can be used by managers to overcome the resistance problem:

- *Alignment with needs and goals of users.*   The best strategy for overcoming resistance is to make sure change meets a real need. Employees in R&D often come up with great ideas that solve nonexistent problems. This happens because initiators fail to consult with the people who use a change. Resistance can be frustrating for managers, but moderate resistance to change is good for an organization. If users believe that a change has no value or if top management does not support it, the organization is probably not served by the change. Resistance to change provides a barrier to frivolous changes or to change for the sake of change. The process of overcoming resistance to change normally requires that the change be good for its users.

- *Communication and education.*   Communication informs users about the need for change and about the consequences of a proposed change. Educational efforts prevent false rumors, misunderstanding, and resentment. Open communication often gives management an opportunity to explain what steps will be taken to ensure that the change will have no adverse consequences for employees.[68] Management should provide far more information and education than it thinks is necessary to be sure users are properly informed.

- *Participation and involvement.*   Early and extensive participation in a change should be part of implementation. Participation gives those involved a sense of control over the change activity. They understand it better, and they become committed to successful implementation. One recent study of the implementation and adoption of computer technology at two companies showed a much smoother implementation process at the company that introduced the new technology using a participatory approach. B. F. Goodrich successfully implemented a new maintenance management system in four plants in about two years by letting employees be heavily involved in design and implementation.[69]

- *Forcing and coercion.*   As a last resort, managers may overcome resistance by threatening employees with loss of jobs or promotions or by firing or transferring them. In other words, management power is used to overwhelm resistance. In most cases, this approach is not advisable because it leaves people angry at change managers, and the change may be sabotaged. However, this technique may be needed when speed is essential, such as when the organization faces a crisis. It may also be required for needed administrative changes that flow from the top down, such as downsizing the work force.[70]

6. *Creating change teams.*   Throughout, this chapter has discussed the need for resources and energy to make change happen. Separate creative departments, new venture groups, or an ad hoc team or task force are ways to focus energy on both creation and implementation. A separate department has the freedom to create a new technology that fits a genuine need. A task force can be created to see that implementation is completed. The task force can be responsible for communication, involvement of users, training, and other activities needed for change.

7. *Foster idea champions.*   One of the most effective weapons in the battle for change is the idea champion. The most effective champion is a volunteer champion who is deeply committed to a new idea. The idea champion sees that all technical activities are correct and complete. An additional champion, such as a manager sponsor, may also be needed to persuade people about implementation, even using coercion if necessary. For example, John Cunningham was the idea champion at Cheseborough-Ponds who developed the polishing pen, through which nail polish is applied. Management supporters at Cheseborough-Ponds then solved the implementation problems of manufacturing, packaging, and marketing.[71] Both technical and management champions may break the rules and push ahead even when others are nonbelieving, but the enthusiasm pays off.[72]

Summary and Interpretation

Organizations face a dilemma. Managers prefer to organize day-to-day activities in a predictable, routine manner. However, change—not stability—is the natural order of things in the global environment of the 1990s. Thus, organizations need to build in change as well as stability, to facilitate innovation as well as efficiency.

The models and ideas described in this chapter can be thought of as ways to encourage incremental change within current management structures. Four types of change—products and services, strategy and structure, people and culture, and technology—may give an organization a competitive edge, and managers can make certain each of the necessary ingredients for change is present.

For technical innovation, which is of concern to most organizations, an organic structure that encourages employee autonomy works best because it encourages a bottom-up flow of ideas. Other approaches are to establish a separate department charged with creating new technical ideas, establish venture teams, and encourage idea champions. New products and services generally require cooperation among several departments, so horizontal linkage is an essential part of the innovation process.

For changes in strategy and structure, a top-down approach is typically best. These innovations are in the domain of top administrators who take responsibility for restructuring, for downsizing, and for changes in policies, goals, and control systems.

People changes are also generally the responsibility of top management. Sometimes, the entire corporate culture must change. Total quality management programs can help all employees from top to bottom think in new ways to improve quality and enhance productivity. Organization development also focuses on worker fulfillment, favoring organic conditions that lead to employee participation in decisions, interesting work, and the freedom to initiate ideas to improve their jobs.

Finally, the implementation of change can be difficult. There are organizational barriers, such as excessive focus on cost, failure to perceive benefits, and lack of coordination, along with such personal barriers as uncertainty avoidance and fear of loss. Managers must thoughtfully plan how to deal with resistance to increase the likelihood of success. Techniques that will facilitate implementation are to obtain top management support, implement the change incrementally, align change with the needs and goals of users, include users in the change process through communication and participation, and, in some cases, to force the innovation, if necessary. Change teams and idea champions are also effective.

KEY CONCEPTS

ambidextrous approach	people and culture changes
benchmarking	product and service changes
change process	quality circles
creative departments	radical change
dual-core approach	strategy and structure changes
horizontal linkage model	switching structures
idea champion	team building
incremental change	technical or product champion
management champion	technology changes
organizational change	total quality management
organizational development	venture teams
organizational innovation	

DISCUSSION QUESTIONS

1. How is the management of radical change likely to differ from the management of incremental change?
2. How are organic characteristics related to changes in technology? To administrative changes?
3. Describe the dual-core approach. How does administrative change normally differ from technology change? Discuss.
4. How might organizations manage the dilemma of needing both stability and change? Discuss.
5. Why do organizations experience resistance to change? What steps can managers take to overcome this resistance?
6. "Bureaucracies are not innovative." Discuss.
7. A noted organization theorist said, "Pressure for change originates in the environment; pressure for stability originates within the organization." Do you agree? Discuss.
8. Of the five elements required for successful change, which element do you think managers are most likely to overlook? Discuss.
9. Why do total quality management programs lead to significant culture changes when these programs are aimed at improving quality and productivity? Discuss.
10. The manager of R&D for a drug company said only 5 percent of the company's new projects ever achieve market success. He also said the industry average is 10 percent and wondered how his organization might increase its success rate. If you were acting as a consultant, what advice would you give him concerning organization structure?

GUIDES TO ACTION

As an organization designer, keep these guides in mind:

1. Facilitate frequent changes in internal technology by adopting an organic organizational structure. Give technical personnel freedom to analyze problems and develop solutions or create a separate organically structured department or venture group to conceive and propose new ideas.
2. Facilitate changes in strategy and structure by adopting a top-down approach. Use a mechanistic structure when the organization needs to adopt frequent administrative changes in a top-down fashion.
3. Work with organization development consultants for large-scale changes in the attitudes, values, or skills of employees. Adopt total quality management programs to facilitate change in company culture toward greater quality and productivity.
4. Encourage marketing and research departments to develop linkages to each other and to their environments when new products or services are needed.
5. Make sure every change undertaken has a definite need, idea, adoption, decision, implementation strategy, and resources. Avoid failure by not proceeding until each element is accounted for.
6. Use techniques to achieve successful implementation, including obtaining top management support, implementing the change in a series of steps, assigning an idea champion, and overcoming resistance to change by actively communicating with users and encouraging their participation.

Consider these guides when analyzing the following cases.

Information Reports, Inc.

CASE FOR ANALYSIS

Jane Haynes was recently promoted to sales manager for Information Reports, Inc. Information Reports gathers data from huge business data bases and formulates it into reports that are sold to business firms. Reports include everything from credit reports to airline schedules to market research. Information Reports' major competitor is Dun & Bradstreet, a large firm that is considered agile and innovative. Information Reports' growth has been rapid; about the time Haynes was promoted, eight new sales persons were added to her staff. They were recent college graduates and eager to make a mark with the company.

Within a few months, one of the new staffers approached Haynes with an idea for a new product. A customer needed specialized data and, if the price was right, this report could be a profitable new area for Information Reports to enter. Haynes helped the new employee develop a proposal for the executive vice president, seeking permission to develop the new product. Three weeks passed, and permission was not yet granted.

Haynes decided to go ahead and establish a product design team on a trial basis that would consist of one person each from the sales, administrative services, and information analysis departments. Haynes later received an okay from the executive vice president and talked to other department heads about the change.

The design team produced the new report in just three weeks. The customer was very satisfied, and several other customers were excellent prospects as buyers for the new report.

Seeing the success of the new report, other new sales people began to suggest new product possibilities. Some older sales people were skeptical because the new products changed the products they were used to. They gradually agreed to go along if an idea worked out but were reluctant to make suggestions of their own.

Soon Haynes had several design teams coordinating work on new information products. She even recommended that the teams do special "upset" analyses to look for unusual product variations of existing reports.

Things were going well except for the long-term employees. They seemed to be fearful about the rapid changes and the direction sales was heading. Four senior sales people came to Haynes's office to protest the pace at which new reports were generated. They pointed out how one idea hadn't worked at all and that the effort lost developing it had been equivalent to five employees for six weeks. The failure had set everyone behind because several customers were interested, and then Information Reports was unable to deliver. Haynes admitted that she had made a serious mistake in judgment in accepting the design team's recommendation.

The older workers preferred the slower method of passing a new idea from one department to the next and getting top management approval before starting. This gave the sales people a chance to learn about the data content of a new report and to update the catalogs they used to sell reports to customers. "We don't want to stifle change," said one of the senior workers. "We just want to do a good job with the products we have. We don't see why you should force change through these design teams, and we would like to see them disbanded."

Haynes wasn't sure what to do. She believed the product design teams gave Information Reports a fast response that would meet customer needs faster than major competitors such as D&B. She also felt the design team success would give her a good shot at promotion to the position of marketing vice president, which would be open with the retirement of her boss next year. If the established workers were unhappy, however, her promotion was not ensured. If she disbanded the design teams, new product innovation would slow down, and the younger sales people would be frustrated and would consider leaving the company. Haynes saw that resentment was growing between the two groups, and she wondered what could be done that would satisfy everyone. To make matters worse, at a recent executive committee meeting, the president stressed the importance of creating a corporate culture in which all employees felt involved and committed to the organization and satisfied with their work.

QUESTIONS

1. What is the problem in this case? How could Haynes get the older workers to go along with design team development of new products?
2. Is Haynes using the right techniques for developing new products? For implementing change? If so, why are the older workers unhappy? How can she satisfy both groups of workers?

Ward Metal Products Ltd. (Quebec)*

Ward Metal Products Ltd. was a large manufacturer of light- and medium-weight metal products, such as metal frames, vestibule intercom panels, assorted metal containers, boxes, and cabinets. Its primary customers were contractors and hardware wholesalers. From rather modest beginnings in 1925, the company had steadily expanded, with few exceptions, and by 1989, it enjoyed a large volume of sales in eastern Canada. The company, located in Montreal, Quebec, employed three hundred persons.

The Ward Family and Employee Relations

Over the years, the ownership and senior managerial control of the company had remained in the hands of the Ward family. Dexter Ward, the founder and president, had become wealthy as a result of his activity and investment in this company and elsewhere. Largely through their aggressive support of and involvement in civic projects and welfare drives, Dexter Ward and other members of the family had become well known to both the French- and English-speaking segments of Montreal's population.

Nearly two-thirds of the company's personnel worked in the production department. A large majority of the jobs in this area were held by French Canadians, many of whom had considerable seniority with the company. Service history records of fifteen and twenty years were quite common. The French Canadian employees in the production department seemed especially to cherish the freedom they enjoyed under their French Canadian supervisors.

Study of Operations

In 1986, Donald Chapman, general manager of the Ward company, conducted a review of all the firm's operations. The company had been facing keener price competition since 1983; although sales had continued at their higher level, profits had begun to drop off noticeably because of reduced margins. The president and other senior company officials had become most anxious to improve the profitability of the company, but they were unsure as to how this might be done. Chapman, who had joined the company some ten years earlier, concluded as a result of the study that cost and procedural controls throughout the organization were lacking. He also believed the rapid growth of the company in recent years had created a need for additional specialized staff personnel in accounting, marketing, and related areas. Accordingly, he made it generally known that if the company was to maintain its market position and improve its profits, some of the organizational "vacuums" would have to be filled.

Organization and Procedural Changes

In the early part of 1987, Chapman appointed Jack Sillman as the first comptroller and manager of the company's new administrative services department. As a chartered accountant, Sillman had previously served as a chief officer in the revenue

---

*Prepared by Professor P. E. Pitsiladis, April 1968, Sir George Williams University, Montreal. Use or reproduction of any portion of this case is prohibited, except with written permission. Reprinted by permission. The case was prepared as the basis for class discussion rather than to illustrate either effective or ineffective handling of administrative situations.

department of the provincial government. According to organizational plans, the administrative services department was to include, as a start, all the existing accounting functions, such as accounts payable and accounts receivable. The primary function of the department was to tighten up controls throughout the company but, more particularly, in "those areas where the potential for new economies was greatest."

In addition to the accounting functions, two new sections would eventually be established within the administrative services department. First, a budgeting section would be needed to install and administer a more sophisticated company-wide budgeting program. Budgeting, as it had existed up until that time, was informal and for the most part consisted simply of each department manager submitting to the company treasurer for approval an annual estimate of expenditures for the coming year. Secondly, a systems section would be needed to conduct a procedures program involving the study and write-up of interdepartmental administrative practices.

Implementation of New Program

By the summer of 1987, both section heads had been appointed. George Finch, the new supervisor of the budgeting section, was to devote his time to developing the framework and details of the budgetary control program. Charles Bond, formerly a branch manager of a systems service organization, was to begin, as supervisor of the systems section, the study and write-up of interdepartmental procedures.

George Finch, in the meantime, had worked out what he thought would be an acceptable budgetary control program. After Sillman had examined and approved the new program, Finch suggested a meeting be arranged with the other department managers at which time they could outline the new program.

The meeting that followed was attended by the staff of the administrative services department and all of the departmental managers except "Rollie" Cloutier, manager of production. Chapman and other senior management officials had previously declined to attend, indicating that they preferred not to "interfere." Sillman was surprised by Cloutier's absence, however, inasmuch as he had been ensured by Cloutier that the date and time of the meeting were perfectly acceptable. Finch described the new budgetary program to those present; no major objections were raised, but the reception was hardly more than lukewarm. Nonetheless, the department managers did agree to Sillman's suggestion that a task force be established to assist Finch in implementing the program and working out any of the problems that might arise. The task force was to consist of department representatives to be appointed by each of the managers.

Interdepartmental Difficulties

In the months that followed, Sillman kept receiving unfavorable progress reports from both Finch and Bond. Bond complained:

> My boys can't seem to make any headway in their procedure work; the biggest problem is the production department; those people never have the time for us. Whenever we do manage to nail them down to a time and a place, they don't bother to show up anyway. We are generally left standing around sucking our thumbs. To top it all off, we've found that those procedure instructions which we have managed to issue over your signature are being ignored by the production people altogether. I'm fed up with the

whole thing. So are the boys. We're not getting the support of the management and the people we are supposed to be working with won't cooperate.

From the reports he received and from his own personal feelings on the matter, Sillman believed that the situation had become acute. However, as a start, he thought a heart-to-heart talk with Rollie Cloutier might be helpful. Early one morning, Sillman called Cloutier and suggested they get together to discuss the situation. "There is no point in it, Jack," Cloutier replied. "I may just as well be sincere. We are busy people here in production, and we do not have a lot of time to play around. Our problems are a helluva lot more complicated than anything you'll find in bookkeeping. We'll work with you, but it will have to be in our spare time."

Sillman decided to refer the entire matter to Chapman, the general manager.

QUESTIONS

1. What approach to change describes the change process attempted at Ward Metal Products? Will the change be successful? Discuss.
2. What is the problem with the implementation techniques used in the case? What recommendations would you make to help implement the proposed changes?

NOTES

1. Susan Caminiti, "A Star Is Born," *Fortune,* 29 November 1993, 44–47.
2. George Anders, "Managed Health Care Jeopardizes Outlook for Drug 'Detailers,'" *Wall Street Journal,* 10 September 1993, A1, A6.
3. Tom Peters, "Get Innovative or Get Dead," *California Management Review* (Fall 1990): 9–26.
4. Jacqueline Graves, "Most Innovative Companies," *Fortune,* 13 December 1993, 11.
5. Laura Zinn, "Pepsi's Future Becomes Clearer," *Business Week,* 1 February 1993, 74–75; Patricia Sellers, "Pepsi Keeps on Going after No. 1," *Fortune,* 11 March 1991, 61–70.
6. David A. Nadler and Michael L. Tushman, "Organizational Frame Bending: Principles for Managing Reorientation," *Academy of Management Executive* 3 (1989): 194–204.
7. Connie J. G. Gersick, "Revolutionary Change Theories: A Multilevel Exploration of the Punctuated Equilibrium Paradigm," *Academy of Management Review* 16 (1991): 10–36; Dexter Dunphy and Doug Stace, "The Strategic Management of Corporate Change," *Human Relations* 46 (1993): 905–20.
8. Bruce Rayner, "Trial-by-Fire Transformation: An Interview with Globe Metallurgical's Arden C.

9. Sims," *Harvard Business Review* (May–June 1992): 117–29.
9. Joseph E. McCann, "Design Principles for an Innovating Company," *Academy of Management Executive* 5 (May 1991): 76–93.
10. John L. Pierce and Andre L. Delbecq, "Organization Structure, Individual Attitudes and Innovation," *Academy of Management Review* 2 (1977): 27–37; Michael Aiken and Jerald Hage, "The Organic Organization and Innovation," *Sociology* 5 (1971): 63–82.
11. Richard L. Daft, "Bureaucratic versus Nonbureaucratic Structure in the Process of Innovation and Change," in Samuel B. Bacharach, ed., *Perspectives in Organizational Sociology: Theory and Research* (Greenwich, Conn.: JAI Press, 1982), 129–66.
12. Alan D. Meyer and James B. Goes, "Organizational Assimilation of Innovations: A Multilevel Contextual Analysis," *Academy of Management Journal* 31 (1988): 897–923.
13. Richard W. Woodman, John E. Sawyer, and Ricky W. Griffin, "Toward a Theory of Organizational Creativity," *Academy of Management Review* 18 (1993): 293–321; Alan Farnham, "How to Nurture Creative Sparks," *Fortune,* 10 January 1994, 94–100.

14. Gary Jacobson, "How Frito-Lay Stays in the Chips," *Management Review* (December 1989): 11–13; "Frito-Lay Successfully Uses Work Teams at Manufacturing Plant," *Industry Week,* 23 February 1987, 15.

15. D. Bruce Merrifield, "Intrapreneurial Corporate Renewal," *Journal of Business Venturing* 8 (September 1993): 383–89; Linsu Kim, "Organizational Innovation and Structure," *Journal of Business Research* 8 (1980): 225–45; Tom Burns and G. M. Stalker, *The Management of Innovation* (London: Tavistock Publications, 1961).

16. James Q. Wilson, "Innovation in Organization: Notes toward a Theory," in James D. Thompson, ed., *Approaches to Organizational Design* (Pittsburgh: University of Pittsburgh Press, 1966), 193–218.

17. Robert B. Duncan, "The Ambidextrous Organization: Designing Dual Structures for Innovation," in Ralph H. Killman, Louis R. Pondy, and Dennis Slevin, eds., *The Management of Organization,* vol. 1 (New York: North-Holland, 1976), 167–88.

18. James B. Treece, "Improving the Soul of an Old Machine," *Business Week,* 25 October 1993, 134–36.

19. Edward F. McDonough III and Richard Leifer, "Using Simultaneous Structures to Cope with Uncertainty," *Academy of Management Journal* 26 (1983): 727–35.

20. John McCormick and Bill Powell, "Management for the 1990s," *Newsweek,* 25 April 1988, 47–48.

21. Eric Schine, "Out at the Skunk Works, the Sweet Smell of Success," *Business Week,* 26 April 1993, 101.

22. Brenton R. Schlender, "Apple Computer Tries to Achieve Stability by Remaining Creative," *Wall Street Journal,* 16 July 1987, 1, 21.

23. Judith R. Blau and William McKinley, "Ideas, Complexity, and Innovation," *Administrative Science Quarterly* 24 (1979): 200–19.

24. Rosabeth Moss Kanter, Jeffrey North, Lisa Richardson, Cynthia Ingols, and Joseph Zolner, "Engines of Progress: Designing and Running Entrepreneurial Vehicles in Established Companies: Raytheon's New Product Center, 1969–1989," *Journal of Business Venturing* 6 (March 1991): 145–63.

25. Rosabeth Moss Kanter, Lisa Richardson, Jeffrey North, and Erika Morgan, "Engines of Progress: Designing and Running Entrepreneurial Vehicles in Established Companies: The New Venture Process at Eastman Kodak, 1983–1989," *Journal of Business Venturing* 6 (January 1991): 63–82; Gene Bylinsky, "The New Look at America's Top

Lab," *Fortune,* 1 February 1988, 60–64.

26. Daniel F. Jennings and James R. Lumpkin, "Functioning Modeling Corporate Entrepreneur-ship: An Empirical Integrative Analysis," *Journal of Management* 15 (1989): 485–502.

27. Jane M. Howell and Christopher A. Higgins, "Champions of Technology Innovation," *Administrative Science Quarterly* 35 (1990): 317–41; Jane M. Howell and Christopher A. Higgins, "Champions of Change: Identifying, Understanding, and Supporting Champions of Technology Innovations," *Organizational Dynamics* (Summer 1990): 40–55.

28. Thomas J. Peters and Robert H. Waterman, Jr., *In Search of Excellence* (New York: Harper & Row, 1982).

29. Ibid., p. 205.

30. Peter J. Frost and Carolyn P. Egri, "The Political Process of Innovation," in L. L. Cummings and Barry M. Straw, eds., *Research in Organizational Behavior,* vol. 13 (New York: JAI Press, 1991), 229–95; Jay R. Galbraith, "Designing the Innovating Organization," *Organizational Dynamics* (Winter 1982): 5–25; Marsha Sinatar, "Entrepreneurs, Chaos, and Creativity—Can Creative People Really Survive Large Company Structure?" *Sloan Management Review* (Winter 1985): 57–62.

31. "Black & Decker Inventory Makes Money for Firm by Just Not 'Doing the Neat Stuff,'" *Houston Chronicle,* 25 December 1987, sec. 3, p. 2.

32. Frost and Egri, "The Political Process of Innovation."

33. Christopher Power with Kathleen Kerwyn, Ronald Grover, Keith Alexander, and Robert D. Hof, "Flops," *Business Week,* 16 August 1993, 76–82; Modesto A. Maidique and Billie Jo Zirger, "A Study of Success and Failure in Product Innovation: The Case of the U.S. Electronics Industry," *IEEE Transactions in Engineering Management* 31 (November 1984): 192–203; Edwin Mansfield, J. Rapaport, J. Schnee, S. Wagner, and M. Hamburger, *Research and Innovation in Modern Corporations* (New York: Norton, 1971).

34. Robert G. Cooper and Ulricke de Brentani, "New Industrial Financial Services: What Distinguishes the Winners," *Journal of Productive Innovation Management* 8 (1991): 75–90; F. Axel Johne and Patricia A. Snelson, "Success Factors in Product Innovation: A Selective Review of the Literature," *Journal of Product Innovation Management* 5 (1988): 114–28; Science Policy Research Unit, University of Sussex, *Success and Failure in Industrial Innovation* (London: Centre for the Study of

Industrial Innovation, 1972).

35. Jerry Jakubobics, "Rising Stars in Toys and Togs," *Management Review* (May 1987): 19–21.

36. Amal Kumar Naj, "GE's Latest Invention: A Way to Move Ideas from Lab to Market," *Wall Street Journal,* 14 June 1990, A1, A9; Dora Jones Yang, "Boeing Knocks Down the Walls between the Dreamers and the Doers," *Business Week,* 28 October 1991, 120–21.

37. Alex Taylor III, "Why the Bounce at Rubbermaid?" *Fortune,* 13 April 1987, 77–78; "Rubbermaid Projects Growth from Core Lines of Domestic Business," *Wall Street Today,* 23 March 1987, 1, 12.

38. George Stalk, Jr., "Time and Innovation," *Canadian Business Review,* Autumn 1993, 15–18.

39. David Woodruff with Karen Lowry Miller, "Chrysler's Neon: Is This the Small Car Detroit Couldn't Build?" *Business Week,* 3 May 1993, 116–26; Robert D. Hof, "From Dinosaur to Gazelle: HP's Evolution Was Painful but Necessary," *Business Week/Reinventing America,* 1992, 65; Karne Bronikowski, "Speeding New Products to Market," *Journal of Business Strategy* (September–October 1990): 34–37; Brian Dumaine, "How Managers Can Succeed through Speed," *Fortune,* 13 February 1989, 54–59; Otis Port, Zachary Schiller, and Resa W. King, "A Smarter Way to Manufacture," *Business Week,* 30 April 1990, 110–17; Tom Peters, "Time-Obsessed Competition," *Management Review* (September 1990): 16–20.

40. Fariborz Damanpour and William M. Evan, "Organizational Innovation and Performance: The Problem of 'Organizational Lag,'" *Administrative Science Quarterly,* 29 (1984): 392–409; David J. Teece, "The Diffusion of an Administrative Innovation," *Management Science* 26 (1980): 464–70; John R. Kimberly and Michael J. Evaniski, "Organizational Innovation: The Influence of Individual, Organizational and Contextual Factors on Hospital Adoption of Technological and Administrative Innovation," *Academy of Management Journal* 24 (1981): 689–713; Michael K. Moch and Edward V. Morse, "Size, Centralization, and Organizational Adoption of Innovations," *American Sociological Review* 42 (1977): 716–25; Mary L. Fennell, "Synergy, Influence, and Information in the Adoption of Administrative Innovation," *Academy of Management Journal* 27 (1984): 113–29.

41. Richard L. Daft, "A Dual-Core Model of Organizational Innovation," *Academy of Management*

Journal 21 (1978): 193–210.

42. Daft, "Bureaucratic versus Nonbureaucratic Structure"; Robert W. Zmud, "Diffusion of Modern Software Practices: Influence of Centralization and Formalization," *Management Science* 28 (1982): 1421–31.

43. Daft, "A Dual-Core Model of Organizational Innovation"; Zmud, "Diffusion of Modern Software Practices."

44. Fariborz Damanpour, "The Adoption of Technological, Administrative, and Ancillary Innovations: Impact of Organizational Factors," *Journal of Management* 13 (1987): 675–88.

45. Mark Landler with Ronald Grover, "Aetna's Heavy Ax," *Business Week,* 14 February 1994, 32.

46. Gregory H. Gaertner, Karen N. Gaertner, and David M. Akinnusi, "Environment, Strategy, and the Implementation of Administrative Change: The Case of Civil Service Reform," *Academy of Management Journal* 27 (1984): 525–43.

47. Claudia Bird Schoonhoven and Mariann Jelinek, "Dynamic Tension in Innovative, High Technology Firms: Managing Rapid Technology Change through Organization Structure," in Mary Ann Von Glinow and Susan Albers Mohrman, eds., *Managing Complexity in High Technology Organizations* (New York: Oxford University Press, 1990), 90–118.

48. Lawrence M. Fisher, "Imposing a Hierarchy on a Gaggle of Techies," *New York Times,* 29 November 1992, F4.

49. David Ulm and James K. Hickel, "What Happens after Restructuring?" *Journal of Business Strategy* (July–August 1990): 37–41; John L. Sprague, "Restructuring and Corporate Renewal: A Manager's Guide," *Management Review* (March 1989): 34–36.

50. Benson L. Porter and Warrington S. Parker, Jr., "Culture Change," *Human Resource Management* 31 (Spring–Summer 1992): 45–67.

51. This section is adapted from Richard L. Daft, *Management* (Fort Worth: Dryden Press, 1994), ch. 18.

52. Ron Winslow, "Healthcare Providers Try Industrial Tactics to Reduce Their Costs," *Wall Street Journal,* 3 November 1993, A1, A16.

53. Ibid.

54. Jeremy Main, "How to Steal the Best Ideas Around," *Fortune,* 19 October 1992, 102–06.

55. Michael Beer and Elisa Walton, "Developing the Competitive Organization: Interventions and Strategies," *American Psychologist* 45 (February 1990): 154–61; Marshall Sashkin and W. Warner

Burke, "Organization Development in the 1980s," *Journal of Management* 13 (1987): 393–417.

56. Beer and Walton, "Developing the Competitive Organization."

57. Scott McMurray, "DuPont Tries to Make Its Research Wizardry Serve the Bottom Line," *Wall Street Journal,* 27 March 1992, A1, A5.

58. Joseph Weber, "Letting Go Is Hard to Do," *Business Week/Enterprise,* 1993, 218–19.

59. David A. Nadler, *Feedback and Organizational Development: Using Data-based Methods* (Reading, Mass.: Addison-Wesley, 1977), 5–8.

60. Wendell L. French and Cecil H. Bell, Jr., *Organization Development* (Englewood Cliffs, N.J.: Prentice-Hall, 1978), 117–29.

61. Paul F. Buller, "For Successful Strategic Change: Blend OD Practices with Strategic Management," *Organizational Dynamics* (Winter 1988): 42–55.

62. Jyotsna Sanzgiri and Jonathan Z. Gottlieb, "Philosophic and Pragmatic Influences on the Practice of Organization Development, 1950–2000," *Organizational Dynamics* (Autumn 1992): 57–69.

63. Based on Carol A. Beatty and John R. M. Gordon, "Barriers to the Implementation of CAD/CAM Systems," *Sloan Management Review* (Summer 1988): 25–33.

64. Bradley A. Steartz, "For LH Models, Chrysler Maps New Way to Sell," *Wall Street Journal,* 30 June 1992, B6, B9.

65. Michael Aiken, Samuel B. Bacharach, and Lawrence J. French, "Organizational Structure, Work Process and Proposal-Making in Administrative Bureaucracies," *Academy of Management Journal* 23 (1980): 631–52; Gerald Zaltman, Robert Duncan, and Jonny Holbek, *Innovations and Organizations* (New York: Wiley, 1973), 55–58.

66. Richard L. Daft and Selwyn W. Becker, *Innovation in Organizations* (New York: Elsevier, 1978); John P. Kotter and Leonard A. Schlesinger, "Choosing Strategies for Change," *Harvard Business Review* 57 (1979): 106–14.

67. Everett M. Rogers and Floyd Shoemaker, *Communication of Innovations: A Cross Cultural Approach,* 2d ed. (New York: Free Press, 1971); Stratford P. Sherman, "Eight Big Masters of Innovation," *Fortune,* 15 October 1984, 66–84.

68. Kotter and Schlesinger, "Choosing Strategies for Change."

69. Philip H. Mirvis, Amy L. Sales, and Edward J. Hackett, "The Implementation and Adoption of New Technology in Organizations: The Impact on Work, People, and Culture," *Human Resource Management* 30 (Spring 1991): 113–39; Arthur E. Wallach, "System Changes Begin in the Training Department," *Personnel Journal* 58 (1979): 846–48, 872; Paul R. Lawrence, "How to Deal with Resistance to Change," *Harvard Business Review* 47 (January–February 1969): 4–12, 166–76.

70. Dexter C. Dunphy and Doug A. Stace, "Transformational and Coercive Strategies for Planned Organizational Change: Beyond the O. D. Model," *Organizational Studies* 9 (1988): 317–34; Kotter and Schlesinger, "Choosing Strategies for Change."

71. "How Cheseborough-Ponds Put Nail Polish in a Pen," *Business Week,* 8 October 1984: 196–200.

72. Richard L. Daft and Patricia J. Bradshaw, "The Process of Horizontal Differentiation: Two Models," *Administrative Science Quarterly* 25 (1980): 441–56; Alok K. Chakrabrati, "The Role of Champion in Product Innovation," *California Management Review* 17 (1974): 58–62.

CHAPTER

9

*I*nformation Technology and Organizational Control

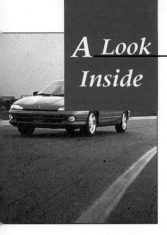

A Look Inside

Connor Formed Metal Products

Like many manufacturing companies, Connor Formed Metal Products processed information with techniques from the 1950s. Engineers figured cost estimates by hand, scribbling down figures for raw materials, machine speeds, and labor costs, then starting over from scratch when the bottom line seemed too high or low. Clerical workers typed out detailed shop orders ten carbons deep, using White-Out to correct errors, while supervisors in the shop struggled to decipher specifications from smudged copies. Salespeople kept written records of sales trips and carried copies of letters in cumbersome loose-leaf notebooks.

Connor is a job-shop manufacturer of springs and other components made to customer specifications. When Bob Sloss inherited the family business, he invested heavily in state-of-the-art machinery and instituted changes in structure and strategy that brought the old-line, low-tech business into the modern era. But despite all that, Sloss noticed the company wasn't making decent money. So he took another step forward, one that is not only dramatically reducing costs and increasing sales but transforming the company's entire culture. The step he took was to hire a programmer to computerize the company's information flow. Today, engineers use an estimating program that calculates quotes in minutes instead of hours. Customer-service reps prepare shop orders on PCs linked by a network, and every worker in the shop has instant access to complete data about the jobs he or she is working on. Any employee—not just the supervisor—who spots a problem can put a "shop hold" on a job. Problems get nipped in the bud, with the direct result that rejects and rework time have decreased from 4.28 percent of sales to only 0.5 percent.

Other payoffs from the introduction of information technology have also been tremendous. Though the plant's head count dropped by fifteen through attrition, sales rose by 28 percent. Late jobs have declined from 10 percent of backlog to less than 1 percent, and customer satisfaction scores have climbed to near-perfection. The company's quality and service record commands a premium in the marketplace. "We're competing with the best house in Japan, and the best in Germany, and the best in Korea," Sloss says. "And we're still in the game."[1]

onnor's new information technology has given it a competitive edge by enabling the company to respond to customers quickly and guarantee near-flawless quality. Information technology has become an important component of Connor's organization design because it is used for responsiveness, decision making, and organizational control. It has empowered employees by giving them the complete information they need to do their jobs well and opportunities to propose new ways of doing things. The use of information technology frees employees to do thoughtful work and enables Connor and other companies to serve their customers better.

PURPOSE OF THIS CHAPTER

Information and control are essential components of organizations. Managers spend 80 percent of their time actively exchanging information.[2] They need this information to hold the organization together. For example, the vertical and horizontal information linkages described in Chapter 6 are designed to provide managers with relevant data for decision making and evaluation. Moreover, control systems depend on information. The first part of this chapter examines information processing requirements in organizations and then evaluates how technology helps meet the requirements and provides a strategic advantage. Then we will examine mechanisms of organizational control and how information technology assists in management control.

Information Requirements

Information is the lifeblood of organizations because information feeds decision making about such things as structure, technology, and innovation and because information is the lifeline to suppliers and customers. Organizations should be designed to provide both the correct amount and richness of information to managers. Before moving into information technology and design, however, one must understand what is information.

Information is that which alters or reinforces understanding, while **data** is the input of a communication channel.[3] Data is tangible and includes the number of words, telephone calls, or pages of computer printout sent or received. Data does not become information unless people use it to improve their understanding. Managers want information, not data. Organizational information systems should provide information rather than data to managers.

INFORMATION AMOUNT AND RICHNESS

The factors that shape organizational information processing are summarized in Exhibit 9.1. Changes in the environment, large size, and nonroutine or interdependent technologies may create both higher uncertainty and higher ambiguity for managers in organizations.[4] **Uncertainty** is the absence of information; when uncertainty is high, a greater amount of information has to be acquired and processed.[5] **Information amount** is the volume of data about organizational activities that is gathered and interpreted by organization participants. Under conditions of high uncertainty, data can be gathered that will answer questions and reduce uncertainty. Often this data can be provided by technology-based information systems, called **high tech** for short.

Information ambiguity means issues cannot be objectively analyzed and understood, and additional data cannot be gathered that will resolve an issue. Encountering an ambiguous situation means managers process richer information and discuss the situation with each other to create a solution, since external data does not provide an answer. Face-to-face discussion is **high touch** and enables managers to understand ill-defined issues and reach agreement to the best of their ability about how to respond.

The formal definition of **information richness** is the information carrying capacity of data.[6] Some data is highly informative and provides deeper, richer understanding to managers, especially for ambiguous issues. The communication channels used in organizations can be roughly organized into a continuum of four categories ranging from highest to lowest in richness. Channels low in richness are considered lean because they are effective for conveying a large amount of data and facts.

1. Face-to-face is the richest medium. It provides many cues, such as body language and facial expression. Immediate feedback allows understanding to be checked

Exhibit 9.1
Uncertainty and
Ambiguity Influ-
ence Informa-
tion Processing
Amount and
Channels.

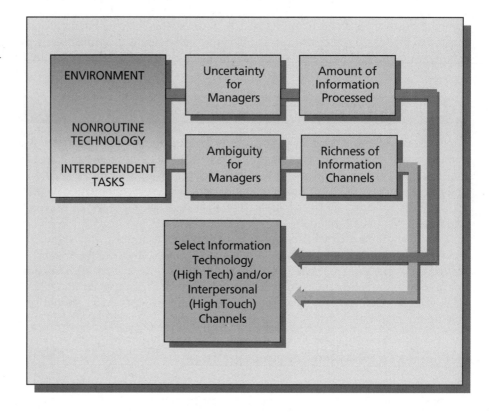

and corrected. This channel is best for mitigating ambiguity, enabling managers to create a shared understanding.
2. Telephone and other personal electronic media such as voice mail are next in richness, representing a relatively rich channel because feedback is fast and messages are personally focused, although visual cues are missing.
3. Written, addressed documents—such as letters, memos, notes, and faxes—are lower still in richness. Feedback is slow compared with richer media, and visual cues are minimal.
4. Written, impersonally addressed documents—including bulletins, standard computer reports, computer data bases, and printouts—are the leanest channels. These documents are not amenable to feedback and are often quantitative in nature. This channel is best for conveying a large amount of precise data to numerous people.

When a customer calls Connor with a new order, uncertainty is high and a substantial amount of data will be processed by computers to figure price, production, and delivery answers. A lean channel such as impersonal computer technology is effective for this application because it can *calculate* an answer. However, when a managerial problem is ambiguous, computer technology is not as effective as face-to-face communication. For example, a company wanted to develop a new concept for a restaurant and there was no data base that would tell it which concept would succeed. The response was to pick a date or a place as a restaurant theme and to form a team of experts to *create* a solution. The team included chefs, architects, designers, and artists. The group stayed focused on this issue and brainstormed for several days until they created all of the details for the restaurant. The result, Ed Debevic's, has been a smashing success in Beverly Hills and Chicago.[7]

Information Technology and the Organizational Hierarchy

Recall from Chapter 4 that advanced information technology—including executive information systems, groupware, and work flow automation—has impact by making organization structure leaner and with fewer levels. Information systems have gradually evolved toward a variety of applications at all levels in organizations, to which we now turn.

INFORMATION TECHNOLOGY EVOLUTION

The evolution of information technology is illustrated in Exhibit 9.2. First-line management is typically characterized with well-defined, programmed problems about operational issues and past events. Top management, by contrast, is concerned with uncertain, ambiguous issues, such as strategy, planning, and other nonprogrammed events, about which decisions must be made. As the complexity of computer-based information technology has increased, applications have grown

Exhibit 9.2   Evolution of Organizational Applications of Information Technology.

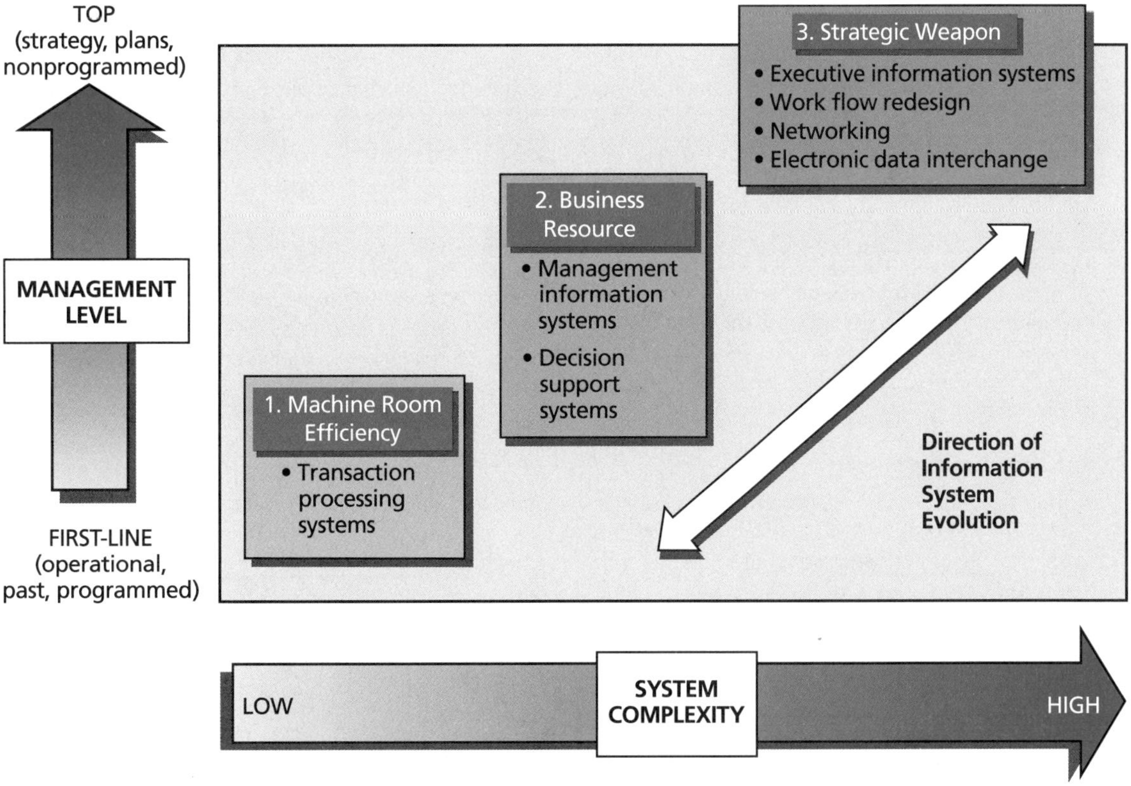

to include nonprogrammed issues at top management levels.[8] However, as described in Book Mark 9.0, the evolving technology has sometimes been misapplied by top management.

The initial applications were based on the notion of machine room efficiency—that is, current tasks could be performed more efficiently with the use of computer technology. The goal was to reduce labor cost by having computers take over some tasks. These systems became known as **transaction processing systems** (TPS), which automate the organization's routine, day-to-day business transactions. Routine transactions include sending bills to customers, depositing checks in the bank, or placing orders. For example, American Airlines introduced Sabre in the 1960s to keep track of customer reservations, by far its biggest set of daily transactions.

In the next stage, technology became a business resource. Through the application of management information systems and decision support systems, managers

---

HAVE YOU READ ABOUT THIS?

In the Age of the Smart Machine: The Future of Work and Power
by Shoshana Zuboff

Shoshana Zuboff, a faculty member of the Harvard Business School, has written an important book for anyone interested in the impact of information technology (IT) on business performance. Zuboff defines IT as "the convergence of several streams of technical developments . . . that dramatically increase the ability to record, store, analyze, and transmit information in ways that permit flexibility, accuracy, immediacy, geographic independence, volume, and complexity." She holds that IT has the potential to change the ways we do our jobs and interact with our colleagues. Zuboff maintains that new technology used incorrectly will not be the miracle it is often thought to be. Information technology can easily be misapplied "by managers who use the technology to mask themselves in an opaque cloak of 'knowledge' which they conceal from their workers in order to control them."

Informating Employees

Zuboff coined the term **informating** to mean providing the new streams of data from technology to employees, empowering them to interpret and translate information into action. The creation of new information from IT provides the basis for transforming the old workplace into a highly participative, informated workplace within which workers themselves can solve problems to improve product quality and service delivery. If used correctly, IT enables employees throughout the organization to respond immediately to emerging situations.

Zuboff's many case studies demonstrate how managers are reluctant to accept these changes. They often want to keep the output of their new "smart machines" for themselves, reducing the potential of technology to benefit the organization. To succeed with IT, management must be willing to empower the work force.

Conclusion

Zuboff recognizes the many difficulties and dangers arising from the full use of information technology, but she is enthusiastic about its potential in most organizations. At the end of the book, she offers her vision of the new egalitarian workplace in which managers and employees are equal, each using information as needed to perform his or her job. "The informative workplace, which may no longer be a place at all, is an arena through which information circulates, information to which intellective effort is applied. The quality, rather than the quantity, of effort will be the source from which added value is derived. . . . Jobs are comprehensive . . . and power is a roving force that comes to rest as dictated by function and need."

In the Age of the Smart Machine: The Future of Work and Power by Shoshana Zuboff is published by Basic Books.

had tools to improve performance of departments and the organization as a whole. As data bases accumulated from transaction processing systems, managers began envisioning ways the computer could help them make important decisions by using data in summary form.

A **management information system** (MIS) is a system that generally contains comprehensive data about all transactions within an organization. MISs can provide data to help managers make decisions and perform their management functions. However, while these vast, comprehensive data bases are vital to businesses, they do not present information in the fast and flexible ways most managers regularly need. An **executive information system** (EIS) is a higher-level application because it focuses on information as opposed to data: this interactive system helps top managers monitor and control organizational operations by processing and presenting data in usable form. A **decision support system** (DSS) provides specific benefits to managers at all levels of the organization because it enables them to retrieve, manipulate, and display information from integrated data bases for making specific decisions.[9] For example, Frito-Lay, Inc. was described in Chapter 8 as an innovative firm, and one area of innovation has been the use of information technology to develop decision support systems.

IN PRACTICE ◆ 9.1

Frito-Lay, Inc.

Frito-Lay has developed a huge data base that draws upon information fed into it by ten thousand sales people reporting each day with hand-held computers on about one hundred product lines selling in 400,000 stores. This enormous data base builds a powerful decision support system for Frito-Lay executives. For example, sales were observed to be slumping in San Antonio and Houston. Analyzing the data for south Texas, it became clear something was wrong. Executives discovered a regional competitor introduced a white-corn tortilla chip called El Galindo that was receiving good word-of-mouth publicity. Supermarkets were allocating more shelf space to it and customers were buying. Having identified the problem with the decision support system, Frito-Lay introduced within three months a white-corn version of Tostitos and soon won back its market share.

Frito-Lay uses its decision support system so effectively that it continues to improve local promotions and expand its share of shelf space. Since the introduction of Frito-Lay's decision support systems, one competitor, Tri-Sum Potato Chip Company, said it is much tougher to compete.[10]

Frito-Lay uses information technology so well that the DSS has become a strategic weapon, enabling the company to gain market share.

Using information technology, such as executive information systems, as a strategic weapon is the highest level of application (Exhibit 9.2). Work flow redesign, networks, and electronic data interchange systems are other ways organizations use information technology in their strategy. **Networking**, which links computers within or between organizations and enables coworkers within a business or even in separate companies to share information and cooperate on projects, is rapidly becoming a primary strategic weapon for many companies. When GE's medical division put maintenance and repair records on a wide-area network spanning North America, Europe, and Asia, maintenance engineers were able to solve problems within hours rather than the days it used to take.[11] Networks enable companies like Texas Instruments, described in the Paradigm Buster, to operate globally and speed new products to market. Before turning to a further discussion of the strategic use of information technology, let's explore a model for tailoring information support systems to organizational needs.

A Model for Designing Information Support Systems

Organizations can be designed to provide the right kind of information to managers. So can information support systems. Frito-Lay enjoys success with its decision support system because it applied technology to measurable, analyzable problems. Some problems, especially at the top management level, are handled by face-to-face discussions. The application of MIS, EIS, and DSS to the right task is essential for its successful application.

A framework for applying information concepts to organizational departments is given in Exhibit 9.3. This framework is based upon Perrow's concept of department technology, which was discussed in Chapter 4. Technology represents the pattern of issues and tasks performed in different parts of the organization. Exhibit 9.3 identifies the two relationships that determine information requirements based upon the type of task performed by a department.

 Paradigm Buster

Texas Instruments

When Texas Instruments decides to design a new calculator, it puts designers and engineers around the world to work on it. That's nothing new—TI has long used its worldwide resources to develop new products. But today, thanks to the revolution in information technology, TI employees no longer have to spend days sending drawings back and forth or piecing together and trying to decipher blurry faxes of blueprints. TI's worldwide computer network enables far-flung designers and engineers to work on new products simultaneously and, in the process, cut more than 35 percent off development time.

The new technology seems to make time and distance disappear. Through the network, an engineer in Dallas can examine process data from TI's assembly and test plant in Kuala Lumpur, spotting any disturbing trends the staff there needs to correct. Consequently, the Malaysian plant doesn't need high-priced engineers and can be staffed with relatively low-cost labor. TI's Tiris unit, which makes small James Bond-type communication devices for security and identification purposes, is managed from England, develops products in Germany and the Netherlands, and manufactures and assembles products in Japan and Malaysia. Staff at these sites, as well as those at the nine centers that design new applications, send information, diagrams, and drawings to one another continuously over the network. Tiris North American general manager David Slinger estimates that the company is eighteen to twenty four months ahead of everyone else because of this communications expertise.

Texas Instruments has advanced to the cutting edge of the information revolution and in the process has gained a significant competitive advantage.

Source: Myron Magnet, "Who's Winning the Information Revolution," *Fortune,* 30 November 1992, 110–17.

Exhibit 9.3 Task Characteristics and Information-Processing Requirements.

ANALYZABILITY:
Greater ambiguity increases need for richer information

Unanalyzable

Analyzable

Craft Technology
Small amount of rich information, personal observation, occasional face-to-face and group meetings. Little MIS, DSS support. High touch. For example, **fine furniture making.**

Nonroutine Technology
Large amount of rich information — frequent face-to-face and group meetings, unscheduled discussions, substantial MIS, DSS support. High tech and high touch. For example, **strategy formulation.**

Routine Technology
Small amounts of clear, often quantitative information — written reports, procedures, schedules, some MIS and data base support. For example, **credit checking.**

Engineering Technology
Large amounts of primarily quantitative information — large computer data bases, written and technical materials, reliance on MIS, DSS support, high tech. For example, **architectural engineering.**

Low   High

TASK VARIETY:
Greater uncertainty increases need for more information

Source: Adapted from Richard L. Daft and Norman B. Macintosh, "A New Approach to Design and Use of Management Information," *California Management Review* 21 (1978): 82–92. Copyright © 1978 by the Regents of the University of California. Reprinted by permission of the Regents.

1. When task variety is high, problems are frequent, wide ranging, and unpredictable. Uncertainty is greater, so the amount of information needed also will be greater. Employees spend more time processing information, and they need access to high tech sources and large data bases. When variety is low, the amount of information processed is less.[12]
2. When tasks are unanalyzable and hence lead to ambiguous problems, employees need rich, high touch information.[13] Face-to-face discussions and telephone

conversations transmit multiple information cues in a short time. When tasks are simple, managers will use lean media. Then the underlying problem is clear, so only simple, written or computer-based information is needed.

The implication of these relationships is reflected in the framework in Exhibit 9.3. Organization structure and information support systems should be designed to provide department managers and employees with the appropriate amount and richness of information. *Routine* activities have only a few problems, which are well understood. For such activities, the amount of information can be small and directed toward clear applications. Written procedures and economic order quantity (EOQ) reorder systems for inventory control are examples of information support used for a routine task.

Engineering tasks have high variety, which increases the demand for information. With these tasks, managers and employees typically need access to large data bases and high tech decision support systems. A large information base is appropriate. The huge number of engineering blueprints that support an engineering project is an example of a large data base that can be stored on a computer. So is the large data base made available to airline reservation agents.

Craft departments require a different form of information. Here, task variety is not high, but problems are ambiguous and hard to analyze. Problems are handled on the basis of high touch experience and judgment. There are many intangibles, so managers need rich information. An example of a craft organization is a psychiatric care unit. The process of therapeutic change is not well understood. MIS information about costs and benefits cannot be directly related to the healing process. When psychiatrists are unclear about an issue, they discuss it face-to-face among themselves to reach a solution.

Nonroutine departments are characterized by many problems that are ambiguous. Large amounts of rich information have to be accessible or gathered. Managers spend time in both scheduled and unscheduled meetings. For technical problems in these departments, management information and decision support systems are valuable. Managers may need to interact directly with data bases to ask "what if" questions. Strategic planning units and basic research departments are examples of nonroutine tasks that use both high tech and high touch information.

The underlying tasks determine the pattern of issues and information needs confronting managers. The information support systems and organization structure should provide information to managers based upon the pattern of decisions to be made. More information should be available when tasks have many problems, and richer information should be provided when tasks are poorly defined and unanalyzable. When information systems are poorly designed, problem solving and decision processes will be ineffective, and managers may not understand why.

The following case illustrates how an organization can be designed to provide the correct information for engineering tasks.

IN PRACTICE ◆ 9.2
Ingersoll Milling Machine Co.

Ingersoll Milling is an extraordinarily successful machine tool builder. It makes large-scale custom machines and machining systems for special applications, such as a $50 million system for computer-controlled auto assembly recently ordered by General Motors.

Ingersoll is the only company in the industry that eschews government protection. The boss believes companies that can't handle foreign competition should be allowed to go under.

The company's success is due to supersophisticated planning and information systems that are nearly paperless. Ingersoll was first in the industry to use computers. Designers draw blueprints on computer screens rather than on drafting tables. Programmers write instructions to accompany a blueprint, and the computer generates a tape with those instructions. The tape is used to control machinery that shapes the metal to build the machine. Ingersoll builds some of the most sophisticated production lines in the world, including highly computerized systems for GE and Ford.

Ingersoll's smart move was to get rid of drafting tables and everything else that could be computerized. Everyone at Ingersoll speaks the same computer language. All three U.S. divisions are linked to a common computer data base. Every department—accounting, engineering, shipping, purchasing—in each division exchanges design, product, and financial information. When an engineer designs a cutting tool, the computer generates a list of materials needed, which goes to purchasing. The next step is to computerize Ingersoll's tool sales force. Sales people will use briefcase terminals to call in specifications from the field. The central computer will then instruct the machinery to turn out an order.

Ingersoll's computer technology is so sophisticated that other machine tool builders are barely able to compete. Boeing and other aerospace companies prefer Ingersoll because the company is efficient and accurate. The specialty orders that carry big profits come Ingersoll's way. Ingersoll's huge but highly quantified information system is perfectly tailored to the very complicated yet analyzable task of designing sophisticated machine tool systems.[14]

Large data bases are appropriate when a task is well understood but is complex and has to answer many questions. For Ingersoll, a huge amount of computer-based data was just right. Competitors in the machine tool industry that used seat-of-the-pants guesswork never achieved the same efficiency. Quantitative computer-based information is not suitable for many ambiguous tasks, however, such as those associated with top management. However, information technology in recent years has been adapted to a strategic role at the top of organizations as illustrated in Exhibit 9.2.

The Strategic Advantage of Information Technology

Managers are increasingly considering the role of information management in their constant search for the right combination of strategy, motivation, technology, and business design to maintain a competitive edge in today's rapidly changing world.[15]

Recall from Chapter 2 that two of the competitive strategies firms can adopt are *low-cost leadership* and *differentiation*. The low-cost leader incurs low production costs and can price its product or service offerings low enough so it makes a profit while rival firms are sustaining losses. Differentiation means a firm offers a unique product or service based on product features, superb service, or rapid delivery. An important question for top managers is whether information technology can be used to achieve cost leadership or differentiation. Information technology might be used to create barriers to entry for new firms, high product switching costs for competitors, or efficient relationships with suppliers that can alter competitive balance with respect to cost leadership or differentiation.[16]

The American Airlines Sabre system, originally installed to keep track of reservations, evolved into a strategic weapon. More than 85,000 Sabre terminals have been installed at travel agencies in 47 countries, keeping track of fares and schedules for 665 airlines, 20,000 hotels, and 52 rental car companies. This information service differentiates American and is an enormous profit maker. It has also increased American's efficiency by enabling it to load as many as 1.5 million new fares daily to meet competition and to make precise calculations for flight plans, aircraft weight, fuel requirements, and takeoff power settings for 2,300 American flights each day.[17] Other organizations find other ways of using information technology for strategic advantage. Wal-Mart recognized the importance of information about sales and inventories for remaining competitive and invested heavily in information systems. Today, Wal-Mart converts information into action almost immediately: managers gather information from Monday through Thursday, exchange ideas face-to-face on Friday and Saturday, then implement decisions in Wal-Mart's stores on Monday morning.[18] Exhibit 9.4 lists a few ways information technology can be used to give companies a strategic edge over competitors.

LOW-COST LEADERSHIP

Perhaps the most obvious way information technology can lower cost is through *operational efficiency;* but this means more than simply doing the same work faster. One element of operational efficiency has been the development of *executive information systems,* as discussed earlier in this chapter. Executive information systems use computer technology to facilitate the highest levels of strategic decision making, helping senior managers diagnose problems and develop solutions. Executive information systems can shape masses of numbers into simple, colorful charts and can be operated without in-depth computer skills. For example, the CEO of Duracell used EIS to compare the performance of hourly and salaried work forces in the United States and overseas. Within seconds, he had a crisp color table showing that U.S. workers produced more sales. Asking for more data, he discovered that sales people overseas spent too much time calling on small stores. The EIS provided sufficient information to diagnose and solve this problem.[19]

Another way to improve efficiency is **work flow redesign,** which means reengineering (described in Chapter 7) work processes to fit new information technology rather than simply layering new systems on top of the old work processes.

For example, the number of people "pushing paper" in the insurance industry barely declined within a decade—from 49 percent to 47 percent. At Cigna Systems Corporation, the reengineering team found that workers in the computer unit were

Exhibit 9.4 Strategic Advantages from Information Technology.

Low-Cost Leadership	Differentiation
Operational efficiency	Lock in customers
Interdepartmental coordination	Customer service
Rapid resupply	Product development, market niches

merely doing again by computer the work that had been done by independent agents or other employees on paper. Reengineering in the company's reinsurance unit cut the 225-person payroll in half while dramatically speeding document handling. Ford Motor Company discovered that Mazda handled accounts payable with only five people compared to Ford's five hundred. Reengineering revealed that Ford had a cumbersome system of workers matching forms, sending paper copies of purchase orders, and tracking paper invoices. When Ford shifted to a completely paperless electronic system, the company was able to save costs by cutting nearly four hundred employees from its payroll.[20]

Advances in information technology are also leading to greater interdepartmental coordination as well as growing linkages between organizations. Thanks to *networks* of computers, boundaries between departments within organizations as well as between organizations seem to dissolve, making a division or company across the world seem as close as one down the hall. Networks allow computers to talk to one another about all aspects of business, such as customer orders, parts requirements, invoices, manufacturing dates, and market share slippage.[21]

One specific type of interorganizational linkage, **electronic data interchange** (EDI), ties businesses with suppliers. EDI, which links a computer at one company to a computer at another for the transmission of business data, such as sales statistics, without human interference, can enable businesses to achieve low-cost leadership through *rapid resupply*. For example, Dillard's department stores have negotiated electronic linkages with suppliers of men's clothing so that when the computer detects low inventory, additional clothes are ordered automatically. The computer even alerts employees as to when the clothes will arrive. No orders have to be handwritten, no data is keypunched into order entry systems, and no time is lost waiting for orders to arrive through the mail. In the retail industry, this allows stores to cut several days from resupply, lowering costs and maintaining inventories of hot-selling products.[22] Dillard's, as well as other powerhouse retailers like Wal-Mart, charges a penalty for the extra paperwork caused by any manufacturer not equipped to receive orders electronically.

DIFFERENTIATION

A way to differentiate a company is to *lock in customers* with information technology. The innovator of this strategy was American Hospital Supply Corporation. Senior executives decided to give computer terminals free to hospitals around the country, linking hospital purchasers directly with AHS, enabling customers to directly place orders for any of more than 100,000 products. AHS immediately gained sales and market share at competitors' expense.[23]

This approach can be upgraded to electronic data interchange so supplies are reordered automatically. EDI is gradually replacing traditional paper document flows. It is estimated that by the end of the decade, at least 75 percent of all interorganization transactions will be over EDI networks.[24]

Exhibit 9.5 shows how EDI can be used to connect several organizations to facilitate trade on both domestic and international levels. Companies that are not plugged into this technology will be at a competitive disadvantage.

Improving customer service can differentiate a company from competitors. For example, automating the sales force can dramatically reduce the time it takes to close an order as well as increase the rate of successful closes. Deere Power Systems,

Exhibit 9.5
Electronic Data
Interchange for
International
Transactions.

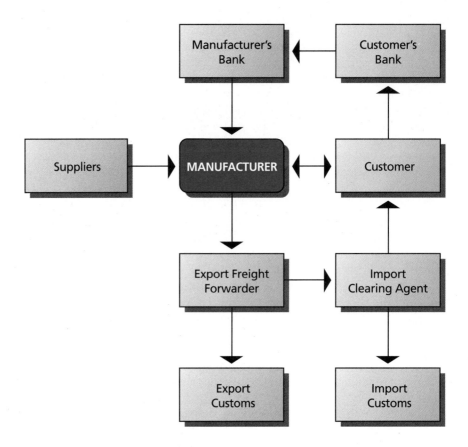

a division of John Deere that makes diesel engines and other heavy equipment, found that its sales people might spend a full day logging into various computer systems and calling different departments for information before going on a call. In the meantime, competitors would step in and beat Deere to the deal. With new information technology, departments that once kept information to themselves are sharing it on a network, and a sales person is generally able to get all the information needed for a call in half a day or less.[25] Connor Formed Metal Products, described at the beginning of the chapter, used networking to dramatically improve response time and customer satisfaction. The speed and flexibility of information technology achieves a dramatic advantage over firms that continue to deal with customers the old way.

A third dimension of differentiation is *new product development for specialized market niches.* Coleco, for example, used computers to design millions of its wildly successful Cabbage Patch dolls, each of which was unique. Moreover, a rapidly growing web of twenty-five thousand corporate, educational, and research computer networks around the world, known as *Internet,* has essentially become the world's largest public library, enabling companies to spot unutilized niches, detect needs for new products or services, learn about their competitors, and stay up-to-date on the latest technological advances. Users can find information on anything from semiconductor manufacturing to the Boy Scouts. Financial firms like J.P. Morgan, for example, use Internet to examine Security and Exchange Commission filings, Commerce Department data (including requests for bids), Census Bureau information, new patent titles, and stock market updates. Companies like J.P. Morgan, General Electric, and Xerox are using the resources of Internet to differentiate themselves from their competitors.[26]

Companies constantly try to find new ways to use information technology to gain a step on competitors. A recent contender in this category is Walgreen Company.

IN PRACTICE ◆ 9.3

Walgreen Company

Computerized systems have made Walgreen Company one of the most profitable retailers in the country. Computers are used for marketing strategy, efficiency, and customer satisfaction. By using computers to analyze prescription order zip codes, executives discover areas where customers are not served and target new stores in those areas. Moreover, all fifteen hundred Walgreen stores are networked so a customer can refill a prescription at any other Walgreen in the country.

Walgreen fills 300,000 prescriptions a day, and the computer provides data to bill insurers and update customers' records. Moreover, the computer enables Walgreen to corner business from insurance companies, group medical plans, and health maintenance organizations. Walgreen typically offers these payers a discount on prescriptions filled in its stores. Walgreen can even provide information back to payers to control costs. By culling prescription records, Walgreen identifies physicians who refuse to prescribe lower-cost generic drugs and provides the names to health plans that use its service.

Walgreen believes that, to survive in the 1990s, the store has to be a superefficient operator that offers a high level of service to customers.[27]

Strategic Control

A large part of organizational information processing pertains to control, which is a major responsibility of management. **Strategic control** is the overall evaluation of the strategic plan, organizational activities, and results that provides information for future action.[28] Exhibit 9.6 illustrates a simplified model of strategic control. The cycle of control includes the strategic plan, measuring production activities to determine whether they are on target, and assuring control by correcting or changing activities as needed. Note in Exhibit 9.6 that strategic control also includes the measurement of inputs to the production activity, as well as outputs, and continuous information about the external environment to determine whether the strategic plan is responding to emerging developments.

Strategic control differs from **operational control,** which is a short-term cycle that includes the four stages of target-setting, measurement of performance, comparison of performance against standards, and feedback.[29] Operational control tends to focus on a specific department or activity and to be short-term.

Strategic control typically uses both feedback and "feedforward" information. Feedback control measures outputs, and control information is fed back and compared to targets to make required changes. Feedforward control measures inputs on the front end of the process, both with respect to production activities and environmental changes that may affect strategic plans. Feedforward control enables the organization to be proactive and change plans earlier than would be possible with

Exhibit 9.6   A Simplified Model of Strategic Control.

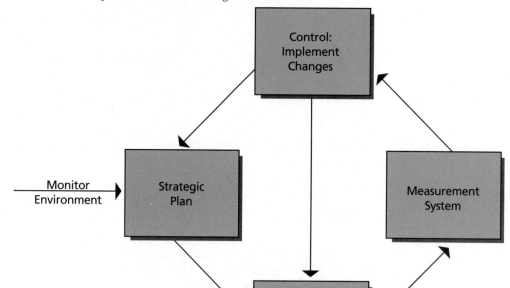

Source: Adapted from David Asch, "Strategic Control: A Problem Looking for a Solution," *Long Range Planning* 25 (1992): 105–10.

output data alone and before the organization gets out of alignment with external needs. Strategic control is an ongoing process that requires monitoring not only conditions within the organization but also in the external environment.

Strategic control directs the activities of the firm toward strategic objectives. For example, Frito-Lay uses the information system described earlier for strategic control. Frito-Lay establishes targets in each region of the country for snack food sales. The hand-held computers used by ten thousand sales people provide daily information on actual sales levels. This data is compared, and feedback is used to change strategies, products, or marketing approaches to improve sales as needed. The control system reflects the strategic direction of the firm.[30]

Major Control Approaches

Managers at the top and middle levels of an organization can choose among three overall approaches for control. These approaches come from a framework for organizational control proposed by William Ouchi of the University of California at Los Angeles. Ouchi suggested three control strategies that organizations could adopt— market, bureaucratic, and clan.[31] Each form of control uses different types of information. However, all three types may appear simultaneously in an organization. The requirements for each control strategy are given in Exhibit 9.7.

Type	Requirements
Market	Prices, competition, exchange relationship
Bureaucracy	Rules, standards, hierarchy, legitimate authority
Clan	Tradition, shared values and beliefs, trust

Source: Based upon William G. Ouchi, "A Conceptual Framework for the Design of Organizational Control Mechanisms," *Management Science* 25 (1979): 833–48.

Exhibit 9.7
Three Organizational Control Strategies.

MARKET CONTROL

Market control occurs when price competition is used to evaluate the output and productivity of an organization. The idea of market control originated in economics.[32] A dollar price is an efficient form of control because managers can compare prices and profits to evaluate the efficiency of their corporation. Top managers nearly always use the price mechanism to evaluate performance in corporations. Corporate sales and costs are summarized in a profit-and-loss statement that can be compared against performance in previous years or with that of other corporations.

The use of market control requires that outputs be sufficiently explicit for a price to be assigned and that competition exist. Without competition, the price will not be an accurate reflection of internal efficiency. A few traditionally not-for-profit organizations are turning to market control. Phoenix requires its Public Works Department to bid against private garbage haulers. At first, DPW lost out, but after becoming more efficient by automating and trimming staff, the department won back the business, and solid waste removal costs have dropped 4 percent a year.[33]

Market control is used primarily at the level of the entire organization, but it also can be used in product divisions. Profit centers are self-contained product divisions, such as those described in Chapter 6. Each division contains resource inputs needed to produce a product. Each division can be evaluated on the basis of profit or loss compared with other divisions. For example, S.I. Newhouse and Sons owns several newspapers (*Newark Star-Ledger* and *Cleveland Plain Dealer*), magazines (*Vogue, House & Garden*), and television stations. The performance of each newspaper, magazine, and television station is evaluated with market control. Each is a profit center, and top managers need only a few key profit figures to evaluate performance across all of their businesses.

Market control can be used only when the output of a division or company can be assigned a dollar price and when there is competition. One of the most competitive businesses around today is the outsourcing business, which is part of the trend toward network structures described in Chapter 7. Companies such as Electronic Data Systems and Computer Sciences Corporation are taking over running the computers and communications systems for thousands of companies that prefer to focus their energies on their core business and outsource the data processing to others. Outsourcers are able to assign their task a dollar price and submit competitive bids for contracts. EDS recently submitted a competitive bid and won a $4 billion contract to provide worldwide data processing services to Xerox Corporation.[34]

However, market control is generally not appropriate for the control of functional departments, such as a personnel department, where the organization has no means of putting an accurate price on such services or of comparing prices with those of competitive services in the marketplace. Thus, market control typically fails in functional departments, as it did in the following case.

IN PRACTICE ◆ 9.4
Bakerstown University

After successfully organizing its various colleges into profit centers, a private university in Bakerstown, California, decided to extend the profit center approach to functional services. But where the process of turning the business college, engineering college, and arts and sciences college into profit centers had been smooth, Bakerstown found itself in the midst of chaos when it tried to extend the approach to computer services.

The president of Bakerstown decided the computer center was to become self-sufficient by selling its services to the colleges within the university. Each user was given a code that indicated the college to be billed, and all computer transactions were automatically recorded and billed to colleges by the computer.

Within two years, the colleges were in an uproar. The computer center had steadily increased its prices, and the teaching and research budgets of the colleges were being drained to cover the cost of computer services. The colleges joined forces and insisted that the computer center be brought back under the central administration.

A university committee analyzed the computer situation. It discovered that users of computer services were being charged a price nearly three times the actual cost to the computer center. Computer center managers used the revenue to hire additional staff and to finance their own research. They were able to increase the price because no competitive computer services were available. Each college had to buy services from the computer center or use no service at all. The price did not reflect the true value of computer services.

The university committee recommended that the computer department once again be made a part of administration and that services be provided free of charge. The colleges were in unanimous agreement. They even agreed to increase the overhead payment to the university administration to cover computer costs.

The decision by administrators at Bakerstown University to use market control for a functional department did not work because competitive services were not available. Market control is effective only when the price is set in competition with the prices of other suppliers so that it represents the true value of services provided.

BUREAUCRATIC CONTROL

Bureaucratic control is the use of rules, policies, hierarchy of authority, written documentation, standardization, and other bureaucratic mechanisms to standardize behavior and assess performance. Bureaucratic control uses the bureaucratic characteristics defined by Weber and discussed in Chapter 5 on bureaucracy. The primary purpose of bureaucratic rules and procedures is to standardize and control employee behavior.

Within a large organization, thousands of work behaviors and information exchanges take place both vertically and horizontally. Rules and policies evolve through a process of trial and error to regulate these behaviors. Bureaucratic control mechanisms are used when behavior and methods of processing information are too complex or ill-defined to be controlled with a price mechanism. For example, when

Bakerstown University decided to make the computer center a part of administration, it used bureaucratic control. The provision of services to the various colleges was then controlled by rules and policies rather than by price.

Some degree of bureaucratic control is used in virtually every organization. Rules, regulations, and directives contain information about a range of behaviors. Bureaucratic mechanisms are especially valuable in not-for-profit organizations for which prices and competitive markets often do not exist.

Management Control Systems   **Management control systems** are broadly defined as the formalized routines, reports, and procedures that use information to maintain or alter patterns in organizational activity.[35] The management information and strategic control systems discussed earlier in this chapter are critical tools to help managers control organizational operations. Control systems include the formalized information-based activities for planning, budgeting, performance evaluation, resource allocation, and employee rewards. These systems operate as feedback systems, with the targets set in advance, outcomes compared with targets, and variance reported to managers for remedial actions.[36]

In the past, most organizations relied largely on financial accounting measures as the basis for measuring organization performance, but today's companies realize that a balanced view of both financial and operational measures is needed for successful organization control in a competitive and rapidly changing environment.[37] The four control system elements listed in Exhibit 9.8 are often considered the core of management control systems. These four elements include the budget, periodic nonfinancial statistical reports, performance appraisal systems, and standard operating procedures.[38] The management control system elements enable middle and upper management to both monitor and influence major departments.

The operating budget is used to set financial targets and record costs during the year. Periodic statistical reports are used to evaluate and monitor nonfinancial performance. These reports typically are computer-based and may be available daily, weekly, or monthly. Performance evaluation systems are mechanisms for evaluating managers and their departments. Managers and superiors may sit down and set goals for the year and evaluate how well previous goals were met. Standard

Subsystem	Content and Frequency
Budget	Financial, resource expenditures, monthly
Statistical reports	Nonfinancial outputs, weekly or monthly, often computer-based
Performance appraisal	Evaluation of department managers based on department goals and performance, annually
Standard operating procedures	Rules and regulations, policies that prescribe correct behavior, continuous

Exhibit 9.8
Management Control Systems Used as Part of Bureaucratic Control.

Source: Based on Richard L. Daft and Norman B. Macintosh, "The Nature and Use of Formal Control Systems for Management Control and Strategy Implementation," *Journal of Management* 10 (1984): 43–66.

operating procedures are traditional rules and regulations. Managers use all of these systems to correct variances and bring activities back into line.

One finding from research into management control systems is that each of the four control systems focuses on a different aspect of the production process. These four systems thus form an overall management control system that provides middle managers with control information about resource inputs, process efficiency, and output.[39] Moreover, the use of and reliance on control systems depend on the strategic targets set by top management. The relationship of strategy, management control systems, and departmental activities is illustrated in Exhibit 9.9.

The budget is used primarily to allocate resource inputs. Managers use the budget for planning the future and reducing uncertainty about the availability of human and material resources needed to perform department tasks. Computer-based statistical reports, by contrast, are used to control outputs. These reports contain data about output volume and quality and other indicators that provide feedback to middle management about departmental results. The performance appraisal system and the policies and procedures are directed at the production process. Performance appraisals evaluate and correct employee work activities. Standard operat-

Exhibit 9.9
Four Management Control Subsystems and Focus of Control.

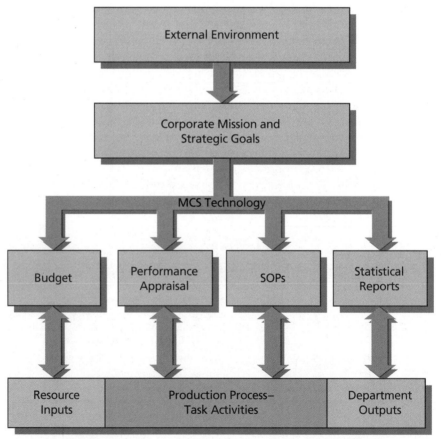

Source: Adapted from Richard L. Daft and Norman B. Macintosh, "The Nature and Use of Formal Control Systems for Management Control and Strategy Implementation," *Journal of Management* 10 (1984): 43–66.

ing procedures (SOPs) give explicit guidelines about appropriate behaviors. Managers also use direct supervision in conjunction with performance appraisal and procedures to keep departmental work activities within desired limits.

Technology Overcontrol   Taken together, the management control subsystems described in Exhibit 9.9 provide important information within the overall bureaucratic control framework used to monitor and influence departmental performance. However, the information technology described earlier in this chapter can be used to increase the speed and intensity of control over employees. As businesses continue to try to squeeze out more productivity in today's competitive environment, they sometimes turn to electronic technology to track workers' every move. In the retail industry, Safeway Stores, Inc., installed dashboard computers to monitor driving speed, engine RPMs, and idling time, believing drivers would be more careful.[40] In the belief that carefully monitored employees will perform more efficiently, some organizations have taken the use of computer control to the point of overkill. Organizations count the number of elapsed seconds per phone call, the number of keystrokes per minute, and every other measurable behavior related to the job, creating stress for employees.

Unions and employee associations are fighting back, and several organizations have reduced control and discovered that performance actually improved.[41] Canada Bell started monitoring employees in groups rather than individually, responding only if the group average fell below target levels. This has not been needed, however, because overall performance increased. Northwestern Bell and Federal Express decreased monitoring and found that productivity remained high and employee satisfaction increased. In one study, "monitored" service workers reported that production quantity was high but work quality was poor. "Unmonitored" employees reported that work quality, service, accuracy, and teamwork were more important than work quantity. On average, the unmonitored workers provided better customer service, taking more time to do the job right rather than trying to save seconds at the expense of customers or fellow employees.[42]

Cypress Semiconductor uses technology-based management control systems that are extremely powerful, but it uses them in concert with employee needs, not against them.

IN PRACTICE ◆ 9.5

Cypress Semiconductor Corporation

T.J. Rogers, president and CEO of Cypress, says Cypress's management control systems track corporate, departmental, and individual performance so regularly and in such detail that no manager can possibly claim to be in the dark about critical problems. Things are monitored so closely that "no surprises" is a way of life. Strategic managers cannot see five years, or even one year, into the future, but revenue and profit budgets and sales production targets for each quarter must be met. Product shipments and revenues are tracked on a daily basis and compared with targets, enabling managers to identify adjustments to make.

The system is anything but an "electronic treadmill," because it is designed to encourage collective thinking and problem solving. For example, one system is designed to encourage everyone in the organization to set challenging goals and then measure and meet them. Each of the fourteen hundred employees sets his or her own goals every week and commits to achieving them by a specific date. These goals and ways of measuring them are all entered into a data base. Employees help each other achieve goals.

The budget system allocates key resources—people, capital, operating expenses—for maximum productivity. Departments can obtain additional resources as the company grows, but top management expects ever-increasing revenue per employee, higher productivity ratios, and ever-lower expense ratios.

The employee performance appraisal system rank-orders employees according to performance. A committee is formed to rank all shipping clerks, circuit designers, or vice presidents. Using a committee takes the pressure off the immediate manager and provides a broader perspective. Then salary increases are allocated according to rank-order performance.

All of these control systems are computerized. The president can review the raises of every employee in two hours. Top managers can review recent trends—such as quality level—in each product line. The trends enable stategic adjustments in data bases or work procedures in the next quarter.

The control systems have enabled Cypress to become large without waste or bureaucracy. The control system is rigorous, but it works.[43]

CLAN CONTROL

Clan control is the use of social characteristics, such as corporate culture, shared values, commitment, traditions, and beliefs, to control behavior. Organizations that use clan control require shared values and trust among employees.[44] Clan control is important when ambiguity and uncertainty are high. High uncertainty means the organization cannot put a price on its services, and things change so fast that rules and regulations are not able to specify every correct behavior. Under clan control, people may be hired because they are committed to the organization's purpose, such as in a religious organization. New employees may be subjected to a long period of socialization to gain acceptance by colleagues. Clan control is most often used in small, informal organizations or in organizations with a strong culture, because of personal involvement in and commitment to the organization's purpose. In addition, the increasing use of computer networks, which can lead to a democratic spread of information throughout the organization, may force many companies to depend less on bureaucratic control and more on shared values that guide individual actions for the corporate good.[45] Clan control is used by companies that shift to the new management paradigm of decentralization, horizontal teams, and employee participation.

Clan control was used along with market control at S.I. Newhouse and Sons. S.I. Newhouse and Sons hired family members in the upper echelons of the organization. The family members trusted each other and shared common beliefs and traditions. With clan control, S.I. Newhouse and Sons did not need as many bureaucratic controls to regulate the behavior of its executives.

Clan control may also be used in certain departments, such as research and development, where uncertainty is high and performance is difficult to measure. Managers of departments that rely on clan control must not assume that the absence of written, bureaucratic control means no control is present. Clan control is invisible yet very powerful. One recent study found that the actions of employees were controlled even more powerfully and completely with clan control than with a bureaucratic hierarchy.[46] When clan control works, bureaucratic control is not needed, as in the following case.

IN PRACTICE ◆ 9.6
Metallic, Inc.

Stuart Tubbs came up through the manufacturing ranks at Metallic, Inc., a producer of chrome finishes and specialty metals. He was accustomed to the use of lengthy budgets and statistical reports, in which almost every manufacturing activity was counted and evaluated weekly. When Tubbs was promoted to executive vice president, one of the first things he wanted to do was get the research and development department "under control." He'd noticed the department was run very loosely, and people had the freedom to do as they pleased, even working at night instead of during regular business hours if they preferred.

Tubbs's first step was to install a detailed budget system. A budget was established for each research project. Even minor expenditures had to be budgeted. The research and development director was expected to keep each expense category on target. Statistical reports were implemented to keep track of all nonfinancial items, such as how employees spent their time and the productivity level for each research project. Number of technical papers written, conferences attended, and use of equipment were all measured and monitored.

As the detail and intensity of the bureaucratic control system increased, satisfaction and productivity within research and development decreased. At least once a week the executive vice president and the R&D director battled over differences between actual expenditures and budget or over the interpretation of activity reports. After about a year, the R&D director resigned. This was followed by the resignations of several key researchers.

The board of directors asked that a management consultant examine problems in R&D. She found that the control procedures were not appropriate in an R&D department characterized by a long time horizon, technical change, and uncertainty. Precise, detailed reports may work for a stable manufacturing department, but they do not capture the uncertain nature of R&D activities. Minor deviations from budget are the rule rather than the exception. A less precise control system used just to plan future projects and to keep research output consistent with company goals would be more effective. The consultant recommended that the bureaucratic system be reduced so that the shared values and commitment of professional employees regulate behavior.

Stuart Tubbs had failed to recognize and understand the strong system of clan control that was operating in the R&D department at Metallic. Employees were socialized into professional norms and practices and shared a strong departmental culture. Most researchers worked extra hours at night to finish projects because they were deeply committed. The lack of bureaucratic control mechanisms did not mean lack of control.

Contingency Control Model

A question for organization designers is when to emphasize each control strategy. A **contingency control model** that describes contingencies associated with market, bureaucratic, and clan control is shown in Exhibit 9.10. Each type of control often appears in the same organization, but one form of control will usually dominate.[47]

Bureaucratic control mechanisms are by far the most widely used control strategy. Some form of bureaucratic control combined with internal management control systems is almost always necessary. Bureaucratic control is used more exclusively when organizations are large and when the environment and technology are certain, stable, and routine. It is also associated with the functional structure described in Chapter 6. Bureaucratic control emphasizes a vertical information and control process.

Clan control is almost the opposite of bureaucratic control. When organizations are small and when the environment and technology are uncertain, unstable, and nonroutine, then trust, tradition, and shared culture and values are important sources of control. Clan control is best when horizontal information sharing and coordination are needed, as they are with a matrix, team-based, or horizontal organization structure. Rules and budgets will be used, of course, but trust, values, and commitment will be the primary reasons for employee compliance.

Exhibit 9.10   Contingency Model for Organizational Control Strategies.

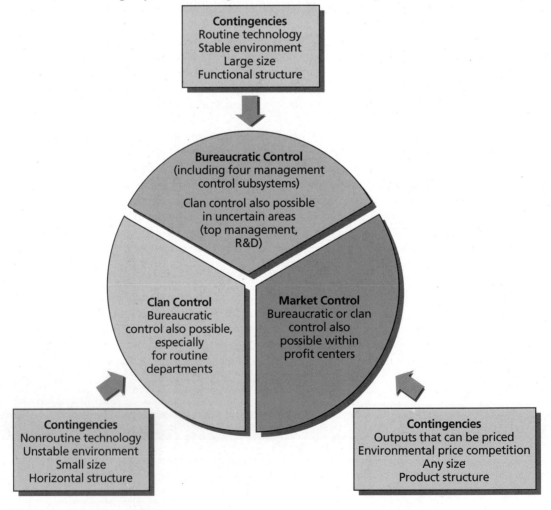

Market control has limited applications. It is used when costs and outputs can be priced and a market is available for price competition. The technology must produce outputs that can be defined and priced, and competition must exist in the environment. Market control can be used in organizations of any size so long as costs can be identified and outputs are competitively priced. It is frequently used in the self-contained product divisions of a business corporation, as described in Chapter 6. Each such division is a profit center. When applicable, market control is efficient because performance information is summarized in a profit-and-loss statement.

The balance among control strategies may differ from organization to organization. The use of each strategy reflects the structure, technology, and environment, as well as the ability to price output. When managers emphasize the correct type of control, the outcome can be very positive, as it has been at Allegheny Ludlum Steel.

IN PRACTICE ◆ 9.7
Allegheny Ludlum Steel Corporation

Unlike most steel companies, Allegheny Ludlum makes a profit. One reason is that chief executive Richard Simmons has installed an information system that borders on the fanatic. Simmons believes, "if you can't measure it, you can't manage it." The system counts every nickel's worth of metal that goes into the furnace. The cost information is tourniquet-tight, and Simmons believes this keeps his high-volume business competitive. Steelmaking is complex, with thousands of recipes for specialty steels and hundreds of new recipes monthly. Allegheny makes steel by the numbers. The information system categorizes more than fifty possible blemishes a coil can have, for example. Production managers get weekly control reports that allow them to adjust production quickly. Precise information has enabled them to improve quality by 30 percent.

Every order received at Allegheny is analyzed by size, profit margin, and the demand it makes on production time. Some orders are rejected if they are inefficient. The information system schedules production. A computer tracks each order through the system.

During the toughest years the steel industry has ever known, Allegheny Steel is riding a crest of profitability. The computer has memorized an engineering model of the production process. Scheduling, cost control, and problems are compared against the model, and the managers are quickly informed. The data base is huge but efficient. A large but number-based bureaucratic control system is just right for Allegheny's highly complex but analyzable organization tasks.[48]

Allegheny Ludlum uses both market and bureaucratic control. Outputs can be priced, and the industry is very competitive, so bottom-line profit is the important criterion for company success. Moreover, internal rules, budget, and statistical reports are used ruthlessly to monitor all activities. This, too, is appropriate because the technology is well defined and measurable. Clan control is not used. There is little shared value or tradition. Cost efficiency is the dominant issue in the control strategy.

Supervisory Control Strategies

The control strategies described so far apply to the top and middle levels of an organization where the concern is for the entire organization or major departments. Control is also an issue at the lower, operational level in organizations where supervisors must directly control employee subordinates, which is called supervisory control. **Supervisory control** focuses on the performance of individual employees. Three types of supervisory control available to managers are output control, behavior control, and input control.[49]

Output control is based upon written records that measure employee outputs and productivity. It is used when the outputs of individual workers can be easily measured, such as for piece-rate jobs where the number of units per hour can be easily calculated. Many sales jobs can be handled with output control because measurement of performance is reflected in the number of sales, the amount of sales, or commissions earned.

The research productivity of university professors is normally evaluated by output control. The process of creative research is not well understood, so bureaucratic procedures for researchers cannot be prescribed. The test of good research is whether the output is accepted for publication in books and journals. Research activity is thus normally measured by the number and quality of publication outputs.

Behavior control is based on personal observation of employee behavior to see whether an employee follows correct procedures. Behavioral control usually takes more time than output control because it requires personal surveillance. Managers must observe employees at work. Behavior control is used when outputs are not easily measured. High school and college teaching is often monitored and influenced through behavior control. The outputs of teaching are the amount of student learning, which is very difficult to measure. Consequently, teachers are usually evaluated on the procedures or behavior they use in teaching. A high school principal may personally observe teachers to learn whether they follow accepted practices. Student evaluations are often used at universities to provide information to managers about the classroom behavior of teachers. Teaching and research activities are thus controlled in different ways.

Input control uses employee selection and training to regulate the knowledge, skills, abilities, values, and motives of employees. This type of control attempts to align the goals of individual employees with those of the company. Input control is used when neither procedures nor outcomes are easily measurable. Some not-for-profit service organizations, such as welfare departments, use input control as a primary means of control because the helping professions cannot be perfectly programmed and their outcomes are not measurable. Managers therefore socialize employees into correct knowledge and values. Input control involves rigorous staff selection and ongoing training and development programs.[50]

The choice of supervisory control depends upon the nature of employee tasks. A simple model of when each control approach can be used is shown in Exhibit 9.11. The two dimensions are the extent to which task outcomes are measurable and the extent to which task procedures are programmable.[51] When tasks are programmable and outcomes are measurable, as in quadrant 1, then managers can use behavior control, output control, or both. Piece-rate work in a manufacturing plant is often of this variety, and managers typically choose output control because output is easier to measure than is behavior. In quadrant 2, when outcomes are measurable and the tasks are not programmable—such as in research or strategic planning—then output control has to be used. The outcomes of a research project or a strategic plan are measured, not the techniques used to develop them.

In quadrant 3, outcomes are difficult to measure, but the task is programmable. This occurs in university teaching, for example, and behavior control has to be

Exhibit 9.11   Relationship of Supervisory Control to Employee Task Characteristics.

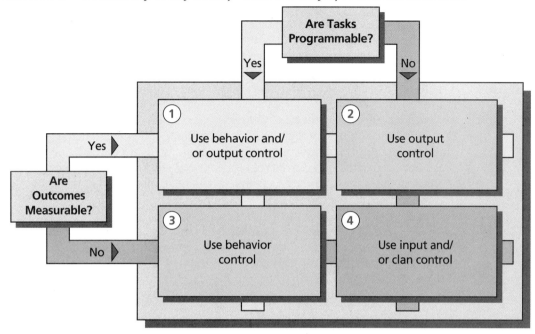

Source: Based on William Ouchi, "A Conceptual Framework for Design of Organization Control Mechanisms," *Management Science* 25 (1979): 833–48; and Kathleen M. Eisenhardt, "Control: Organizational and Economic Approaches," *Management Science* 31 (1985): 134–49.

used. Customer satisfaction from service in a department store is another hard-to-measure output. Many stores use behavior control by prescribing explicit procedures for how employees are to deal with customers, stock shelves, and keep things clean and tidy.

In quadrant 4 of Exhibit 9.11, neither procedures nor outcomes are measurable. This situation is fairly rare at the operational level, but when it occurs, managers must rely on input control, clan control, or both to regulate employee performance. Some not-for-profit service organizations must rely totally on input control procedures. In addition, organizations may emphasize clan control by building a strong culture with shared performance values.

Summary and Interpretation

An organization's situation creates uncertainty and ambiguity for managers, which translates into requirements for information amount and richness. Determining how manager and department information needs differ along these two dimensions and how to design information support systems are key problems for organizations to solve. Generally, as ambiguity of managerial tasks increases, more rich, personal information is required. Well-defined tasks that are complex and of high variety require a large amount of precise, quantitative data.

The evolution of information technology in organizations reflects these information needs. Initial transaction processing systems were applied to well-defined tasks at lower levels, and they increased efficiency. Then management information systems and decision support systems were developed as business resources at the middle- and upper-management levels. Finally, executive information systems are being used at top levels of management as a strategic weapon. Advances in networking technology are leading to greater cooperation between departments as well as between organizations. Interorganization linkages, such as electronic data interchange, also provide strategic advantages.

Information technology plays an important role in helping organizations achieve a competitive advantage through low-cost leadership or differentiation. Information technology can increase operational efficiency, coordination, and the speed of resupply, and can lock in customers, improve customer service, and enhance product development.

A large part of information processing pertains to control. The concepts of market, bureaucratic, clan, output, behavior, and input control help explain how control is exercised in organizations. Market control is used where product or service outputs can be priced and competition exists. Clan control is associated with uncertain and rapidly changing organizational processes and relies on commitment, tradition, and shared values for control. Bureaucratic control relies on the bureaucratic characteristics of organizations described in Chapter 5, as well as on the four internal management control systems of budgets, statistical reports, standard operating procedures, and performance appraisal systems. At the supervisory level, managers use output, behavior, clan, or input control or some combination to control the performance of individual employees.

KEY CONCEPTS

ambiguity
behavior control
bureaucratic control
clan control
contingency control model
data
decision support system
electronic data interchange
executive information system
high tech
high touch
informating
information
information amount

information richness
input control
management control systems
management information system
market control
networking
operational control
output control
supervisory control
strategic control
transaction processing systems
uncertainty
work flow redesign

DISCUSSION QUESTIONS

1. How do uncertainty and ambiguity affect information processing requirements and the design of information support systems?

2. To what extend can technology meet the needs of top managers for rich information? Do you think technology will ever enable top managers to do their job without face-to-face communication? Discuss.

3. How might electronic data interchange provide a competitive advantage to a company?

4. The manager of a computer processing department told his employees: "Top managers need the same control data everyone else needs, except that we'll aggregate it for the company as a whole." Agree or disagree with the manager's philosophy, and explain why.

5. An organization consultant argued that managers need information that is independent of computers. Explain why you agree or disagree with her point of view.

6. In writing about types of control, William Ouchi said, "The Market is like the trout and the Clan like the salmon, each a beautiful highly specialized species which requires uncommon conditions for its survival. In comparison, the bureaucratic method of control is the catfish—clumsy, ugly, but able to live in the widest range of environments and ultimately, the dominant species." Discuss what Ouchi meant with that analogy.

7. What type of controls do most professors use to control students—output, input, behavior, or all of these?

8. Government organizations often seem more bureaucratic than for-profit organizations. Could this partly be the result of the type of control used in government organizations? Explain.

9. Discuss the following statements: "Things under tight control are better than things under loose control." "The more data managers have, the better decisions they make."

10. Discuss how the spread of computer networking may affect the control processes used in organizations.

 ## GUIDES TO ACTION

As an organization designer, keep these guides in mind:

1. Provide managers and employees with information support that reflects the frequency and type of the problems with which they deal. Design both the amount and the richness of information to meet the problem-solving needs of managers.

2. Use information technology as a strategic weapon. Use technology to achieve differentiation or low-cost leadership by becoming more efficient, locking in customers and suppliers, and developing new products.

3. Implement one of the three basic choices—bureaucratic, clan, market—as the primary means of organizational control. Use bureaucratic control when organizations are large, have a stable environment, and use routine technology. Use clan control in small, uncertain departments. Use market control when outputs can be priced, and when competitive bidding is available.

4. Use management control systems to monitor and influence department-level activities. The budget controls resources into the department, and statistical reports control the product and service outcomes of the department. Performance appraisal and standard operating procedures can be used to control work activities within departments.

Consider these guides when analyzing the following case.

Sunflower Incorporated*

Sunflower Incorporated is a large distribution company with more than five thousand employees and gross sales of more than $550 million (1992). The company purchases salty snack foods and liquor and distributes them to independent retail stores throughout the United States and Canada. Salty snack foods include corn chips, potato chips, cheese curls, tortilla chips, and peanuts. The United States and Canada are divided into twenty-two regions, each with its own central warehouse, sales people, finance department, and purchasing department. The company distributes national as well as local brands, and packages some items under private labels. Competition in this industry is intense. The demand for liquor has been declining, and competitors like Procter & Gamble and Frito-Lay develop new snack foods to gain market share from smaller companies like Sunflower. The head office encourages each region to be autonomous because of local tastes and practices. In the northeast United States, for example, people consume a greater percentage of Canadian whisky and American bourbon, while in the West, they consume more light liquors, such as vodka, gin, and rum. Snack foods in the Southwest are often seasoned to reflect Mexican tastes.

Early in 1988, Sunflower began using a financial reporting system that compared sales, costs, and profits across company regions. Each region was a profit center, and top management was surprised to learn that profits varied widely. By 1990, the differences were so great that management decided some standardization was necessary. Managers believed highly profitable regions were sometimes using lower-quality items, even seconds, to boost profit margins. This practice could hurt Sunflower's image. Most regions were facing cutthroat price competition to hold market share. Triggered by price cuts by Anheuser-Busch Company's Eagle Snacks division, national distributors, such as Frito-Lay, Borden, Nabisco, Procter & Gamble (Pringles), and Standard Brands (Planters Peanuts), were pushing to hold or increase market share by cutting prices and launching new products.

As these problems accumulated, Joe Steelman, president of Sunflower, decided to create a new position to monitor pricing and purchasing practices. Loretta Williams was hired from the finance department of a competing organization. Her new title was director of pricing and purchasing, and she reported to the vice president of finance, Peter Langly. Langly gave Williams great latitude in organizing her job and encouraged her to establish whatever rules and procedures were necessary. She was also encouraged to gather information from each region. Each region was notified of her appointment by an official memo sent to the twenty-two regional directors. A copy of the memo was posted on each warehouse bulletin board. The announcement was also made in the company newspaper.

After three weeks on the job, Williams decided two problems needed her attention. Over the long term, Sunflower should make better use of information

---

*This case was inspired by "Frito-Lay May Find Itself in a Competition Crunch," *Business Week,* 19 July 1982, 186; "Dashman Company," in Paul R. Lawrence and John A. Seiler, *Organizational Behavior and Administration: Cases, Concepts, and Research Findings* (Homewood, Ill: Irwin and Dorsey, 1965), 16–17; and Laurie M. Grossman, "Price Wars Bring Flavor to Once-Quiet Snack Market," *Wall Street Journal,* 23 May 1991, B1, B3.

technology. Williams believed information technology could provide more information to headquarters for decision making. Top managers in the divisions were connected to headquarters by an electronic messaging system, but lower employees and sales people were not connected. Only a few senior managers in about half the divisions used the system regularly.

In the short term, Williams decided fragmented pricing and purchasing decisions were a problem and these decisions should be standardized across regions. This should be undertaken immediately. As a first step, she wanted the financial executive in each region to notify her of any change in local prices of more than 3 percent. She also decided that all new contracts for local purchases of more than five thousand dollars should be cleared through her office. (Approximately 60 percent of items distributed in the regions were purchased in large quantities and supplied from the home office. The other 40 percent were purchased and distributed within the region). Williams believed the only way to standardize operations was for each region to notify the home office in advance of any change in prices or purchases. She discussed the proposed policy with Langly. He agreed, so they submitted a formal proposal to the president and board of directors, who approved the plan. The changes represented a complicated shift in policy procedures, and Sunflower was moving into peak holiday season, so Williams wanted to implement the new procedures right away. She decided to send an electronic mail message followed by a fax to the financial and purchasing executives in each region notifying them of the new procedures. The change would be inserted in all policy and procedure manuals throughout Sunflower within four months.

Williams showed a draft of the message to Langly and invited his comments. Langly said the message was a good idea but wondered if it was sufficient. The regions handled hundreds of items and were used to decentralized decision making. Langly suggested that Williams ought to visit the regions and discuss purchasing and pricing policies with the executives. Williams refused, saying that such trips would be expensive and time-consuming. She had so many things to do at headquarters that trips were impossible. Langly also suggested waiting to implement the procedures until after the annual company meeting in three months, when Williams could meet the regional directors personally. Williams said this would take too long, because the procedures would then not take effect until after the peak sales season. She believed the procedures were needed now. The messages went out the next day.

During the next few days, electronic mail replies came in from seven regions. The managers said they were in agreement and said they would be happy to cooperate.

Eight weeks later, Williams had not received notices from any regions about local price or purchase changes. Other executives who had visited regional warehouses indicated to her that the regions were busy as usual. Regional executives seemed to be following usual procedures for that time of year. She telephoned one of the regional managers and discovered that he did not know who she was and had never heard of the position called director of pricing and purchasing. Besides, he said, "we have enough to worry about reaching profit goals without additional procedures from headquarters." Williams was chagrined that her position and her suggested changes in procedure had no impact. She wondered whether field managers were disobedient or whether she should have used another communication strategy.

QUESTIONS

1. What is the problem with Williams's approach? What types of control were used at Sunflower? By Williams?
2. What information medium would you consider appropriate for communicating new procedures on pricing and purchasing to employees? For announcing and providing authority to a new person occupying a new position? Why?
3. What advice would you give Williams about the potential use of information technology for strategic advantage? About how to implement change?

NOTES

1. John Case, "The Knowledge Factory," *Inc.,* October 1991, 54–59.
2. Henry Mintzberg, *The Nature of Managerial Work* (New York: Harper & Row, 1972), 39.
3. Richard L. Daft and Norman B. Macintosh, "A Tentative Exploration into the Amount and Equivocality of Information Processing in Organizational Work Units," *Administrative Science Quarterly* 26 (1981): 207–24.
4. Michael L. Tushman and David A. Nadler, "Information Processing as an Integrating Concept in Organization Design," *Academy of Management Review* 3 (1978): 613–24; Samuel B. Bacharach and Michael Aiken, "Communication in Administrative Bureaucracies," *Academy of Management Journal* 20 (1977): 365–77.
5. Jay R. Galbraith, *Organization Design* (Reading, Mass.: Addison-Wesley, 1977), 35–36; William E. Souder and Ruby K. Moenaert, "Integrating Marketing and R&D Project Personnel within Innovation Projects: An Information Uncertainty Model," *Journal of Management Studies* 29 (July 1992): 485–512.
6. Richard L. Daft, Robert H. Lengel, and Linda Klebe Trevino, "Message Equivocality, Media Selection, and Manager Performance: Implications for Information Systems," *MIS Quarterly* 11 (1987): 355–66; Richard L. Daft and Robert H. Lengel, "Information Richness: A New Approach to Managerial Behavior and Organization Design," in Barry Staw and Larry L. Cummings, eds., *Research in Organizational Behavior,* vol. 6 (Greenwich, Conn.: JAI Press, 1984), 191–233; Robert H. Lengel, "Managerial Information Processing and Communication-Media Source Selection Behavior" (Unpublished Ph.D. dissertation, Texas A&M University, 1982).
7. Erik Larson, "The Man with the Golden Touch," *Inc.,* October 1988, 67–77.
8. David W. L. Wightman, "Competitive Advantage through Information Technology," *Journal of General Management* 12 (Summer 1987): 36–45; M. J. Bissett, "Competitive Advantage—through Controlling the Middle Ground," (Paper presented at Southcourt Conference: Improving Business-Based IT Strategy, October 1986).
9. Robin Matthews and Anthony Shoebridge, "EIS: A Guide for Executives," *Long Range Planning* 25, no. 6 (1992): 94–101; Jeffrey P. Stamen, "Decision Support Systems Help Planners Hit Their Targets," *Journal of Business Strategy,* March/April 1990, 30–33.
10. Jeffrey Rothfeder, Jim Bartimo and Lois Therrien, "How Software Is Making Food Sales a Piece of Cake," *Business Week,* 2 July 1990, 54–55.
11. Peter Nulty, "When to Murder Your Mainframe," *Fortune,* 1 November 1993, 109–20.
12. Richard L. Daft and Robert H. Lengel, "Organizational Information Requirements, Media Richness and Structural Design," *Management Science* 32 (1986): 554–71; Daft and Macintosh, "A Tentative Exploration," W. Alan Randolph, "Matching Technology and the Design of Organization Units," *California Management Review* 22–23 (1980–81): 39–48; Michael L. Tushman "Technical Communications in R&D Laboratories: The Impact of Project Work Characteristics," *Academy of Management Journal* 21 (1978): 624–45.
13. Robert H. Lengel and Richard L. Daft, "The Selection of Communication Media as an Executive Skill," *Academy of Management Executive* 2 (August 1988): 225–32.
14. Michael McFadden, "The Master Builder of Mammoth Tools," *Fortune,* 3 September 1984, 58–64.
15. Renae Broderick and John W. Boudreau, "Human Resource Management, Information Technology and the Competitive Edge," *Academy of Management Executive* 6, no. 2 (1992): 7–17.

16. Mark C.S. Lee and Dennis A. Adams, "A Manager's Guide to the Strategic Potential of Information Systems," *Information and Management* (1990): 169–82; Wightman, "Competitive Advantage through Information Technology."

17. Kenneth Lebich, "America Takes on the World," *Fortune,* 24 September 1990, 40–48.

18. Bill Saporito, "What Sam Walton Taught America," *Fortune,* 4 May 1992, 104–105.

19. Fess Crockett, "Revitalizing Executive Information Systems," *Sloan Management Review* (Summer 1992): 39–47; Jeremy Main, "At Last, Software CEOs Can Use," *Fortune,* 13 March 1989, 77–81.

20. Peter Coy, "The New Realism in Office Systems," *Business Week,* 15 June 1992, 128–33; Michael Hammer, "Reengineering Work: Don't Automate, Obliterate," *Harvard Business Review* (July-August 1990): 104–12.

21. Myron Magnet, "Who's Winning the Information Revolution," *Fortune,* 30 November 1992, 110–17; Jeremy Main, "Computers of the World, Unite!" *Fortune,* 24 September 1990, 114–22.

22. Brian Dearing, "The Strategic Benefits of EDI," *Journal of Business Strategy* (January-February, 1990): 4–6; Benn R. Konsynski and F. Warren McFarlan, "Information Partnerships—Shared Data, Shared Scale," *Harvard Business Review* (September-October 1990): 114–20; Robert I. Benjamin, David W. de Long and Michael S. Scott Morton, "Electronic Data Interchange: How Much Competitive Advantage?" *Long Range Planning* 23 (1990): 29–40.

23. Robert I. Benjamin, John F. Rockart, Michael S. Scott Morton, and John Wyman, "Information Technology: A Strategic Opportunity," *Sloan Management Review* 25 (Spring 1984): 3–10.

24. N. Venketraman, "IT-Enabled Business Transformation: From Automation to Business Scope Redefinition," *Sloan Management Review* (Winter 1994): 73–87.

25. John W. Verity, "Taking a Laptop on a Call," *Business Week,* 25 October 1993, 124–25.

26. Rick Tetzeili, "The Internet and Your Business," *Fortune,* 7 March 1994, 86–96.

27. Rick Reiff, "Convenience with a Difference," *Forbes,* 11 July 1990, 184–86.

28. John F. Preble, "Towards a Comprehensive System of Strategic Control," *Journal of Management Studies* 29 (July 1992): 391–409; David Asch, "Strategic Control: A Problem Looking for a Solution," *Long Range Planning* 25, no. 2 (1992): 105–10.

29. T. K. Das, "Organizational Control: An Evolutionary Perspective," *Journal of Management Studies* 26

(1989): 459–75; Kenneth A. Merchant, *Control in Business Organizations* (Marshfield, Mass: Pitman, 1985); William G. Ouchi, "The Relationship between Organizational Structure and Organizational Control," *Administrative Science Quarterly* 22 (1977): 95–113.

30. Michael Goold, "Strategic Control in the Decentralized Firm," *Sloan Management Review* (Winter 1991): 69–81: Robert Simons, "Strategic Orientation and Top Management Attention to Control Systems," *Strategic Management Journal* 12 (1991): 49–62.

31. William G. Ouchi, "Markets, Bureaucracies, and Clans," *Administrative Science Quarterly* 25 (1980): 129–41;—idem, "A Conceptual Framework for the Design of Organizational Control Mechanisms," *Management Science* 25 (1979): 833–48.

32. Oliver A. Williamson, *Markets and Hierarchies: Analyses and Antitrust Implications* (New York: Free Press, 1975).

33. Paula Dwyer, "The New Gospel of Good Government," *Business Week,* 20 January 1992, 66–70.

34. Donna Brown, "Outsourcing: How Corporations Take Their Business Elsewhere," *Management Review* (February 1992): 16–19; "Xerox Awards Huge Contract," *Tennessean,* 22 March 1994, E1.

35. Simons, "Strategic Organizations and Top Management Attention to Control Systems."

36. Stephen G. Green and M. Ann Welsh, "Cybernetics and Dependents: Reframing the Control Concept," *Academy of Management Review* 13 (1988): 287–301.

37. Robert S. Kaplan and David P. Norton, "The Balanced Scorecard—Measures That Drive Performance," *Harvard Business Review* (January-February 1992): 71–79; Robert G. Eccles, "The Performance Measurement Manifesto," *Harvard Business Review,* (January-February 1991): 131–37.

38. Richard L. Daft and Norman B. Macintosh, "The Nature and Use of Formal Control Systems for Management Control and Strategy Implementation," *Journal of Management* 10 (1984): 43–66.

39. Ibid.; Scott S.Cowen and J. Kendall Middaugh II, "Matching an Organization's Planning and Control System to Its Environment," *Journal of General Management* 16 (1990): 69–84.

40. Lee Smith, "What the Boss Knows about You," *Fortune,* 9 August 1993, 88–93; Jeffrey Rothfeder, Michele Galen, and Lisa Driscoll, "Is Your Boss Spying on You?" *Business Week,* 15 January 1990, 74–75.

41. Marlene C. Piturro, "Employee Performance Monitoring . . . or Meddling?" *Management Review*

(May 1989): 31–33.

42. Rebecca A. Grant, Christopher A. Higgins, and Richard H. Irving, "Computerized Performance Monitors: Are They Costing You Customers?" *Sloan Management Review* (Spring 1988): 39–45.

43. T. J. Rodgers, "No Excuses Management," *Harvard Business Review* (July-August 1990): 84–98.

44. Ouchi, "Markets, Bureaucracies, and Clans."

45. Stratford Sherman, "The New Computer Revolution," *Fortune,* 14 June 1993, 56–80.

46. James R. Barker, "Tightening the Iron Cage: Concertive Control in Self-Managing Teams," *Administrative Science Quarterly* 38 (1993): 408–37.

47. Carol R. Snodgrass and Edward J. Szewczak, "The Substitutability of Strategic Control Choices: An Empirical Study," *Journal of Management Studies* 27 (1990): 535–53.

48. Bill Saporito, "Allegheny Ludlum Has Steel Figured Out," *Fortune,* 25 June 1984, 40–44.

49. Scott A. Snell, "Control Theory in Strategic Human Resource Management: The Mediating Effect of Administrative Information," *Academy of Management Journal* 35 (1992): 292–327; Ouchi, "Relationship between Organizational Structure and Organizational Control," William G. Ouchi and Mary Ann McGuire, "Organizational Control: Two Functions," *Administrative Science Quarterly* 20 (1975): 559–69.

50. Snell, "Control Theory in Strategic Human Resource Management."

51. Kathleen M. Eisenhardt, "Control: Organizational and Economic Approaches," *Management Science* 31 (1985): 134–49; Ouchi and McGuire, "Organizational Control."

Organizational Culture and Ethical Values

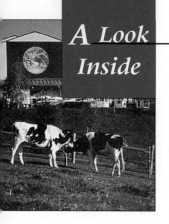
Ben & Jerry's Homemade, Inc.

Ben Cohen and Jerry Greenfield never intended to become businessmen. When they opened an ice cream parlor in a renovated gas station, their underlying vision was, according to Jerry, "to spread joy and not to make money." But spreading joy quickly led to prosperity as Ben & Jerry's surpassed $50 million in sales. Uncomfortable with the starchiness and cash-based morality of large corporations, Ben and Jerry started concentrating on enhancing and protecting their company's unique culture values.

Above all, Ben & Jerry's is a happy family, more concerned with fun, charity, and goodwill toward workers than with profit. Every employee is a shareholder, and the top salary in the company is limited to seven times that of the lowest-paid employee (compared with an average eighty-five times greater in other major corporations). The company gives 7.5 percent of pretax profits to the Ben & Jerry Foundation, which supports a variety of community projects. Such products as Peace Pops and Rain Forest Crunch were created to benefit specific social causes.

All employees are invited to the monthly staff meeting. Here, they sit around in casual slacks and T–shirts, munching on doughnuts and coffee, while Jerry, self-appointed "Undersecretary of Joy," proposes appointing a Joy Committee charged with infusing more joy into the workplace. People have to work very hard, he points out, and are under a lot of stress, so it would be a good idea to bring more joy to each workday. The crowd shows its agreement with applause. They then discuss whether the Ben & Jerry Foundation should give money to rehabilitate a subway station in New York or buy large cardboard boxes printed with the Ben & Jerry's logo to distribute to the homeless.

During a subsequent crisis, all hands rush to the production line to generate a needed three hundred pallets of ice cream. The company hires a masseuse to give workers massages during breaks. Other staffers cook dinner for the overworked production crew.

Ben & Jerry's has become one of the top superpremium ice cream companies, competing with the likes of Haagen-Dazs, Frusen Gladje, and Steve's Homemade. But the company has maintained its unique culture. The company is succeeding, its stock price continues to go up, and the employees like one another and like going to work.[1]

Ben & Jerry's Homemade, Inc., has definite values that make it unique. Ben and Jerry have established a corporate culture, which is one of the most talked about organizational characteristics in business today. Organizational success or failure is often attributed to culture. The new CEO at Black & Decker was credited with transforming an entire corporate culture, replacing the complacent manufacturing mentality with an almost manic market-driven way of doing things. Food-Lion's success as a food market chain is attributed to a culture that emphasizes hard work, simplicity, and frugality. Firms such as 3M and Johnson & Johnson have been praised for their innovative cultures. Corporate culture also has been implicated in problems faced by IBM, Sears, Bank of America, and General Motors, where changing their cultures is considered essential for ultimate success.[2]

PURPOSE OF THIS CHAPTER

This chapter explores ideas about corporate culture and associated ethical values and how these are influenced by organizations. The first section will describe the nature of corporate culture, its origins and purpose, and how to identify and interpret culture through ceremonies, stories, and symbols. Then we turn to ethical values in organizations and how managers can implement ethical structures that will shape employee behavior. In the last section, we will discuss how leaders shape cultural and ethical values in a direction suitable for strategy and performance outcomes.

Organizational Culture

The popularity of the organizational culture topic raises a number of questions. Can we identify cultures? Can culture be aligned with strategy? How can cultures be managed or changed? The best place to start is by defining culture and explaining how it can be identified in organizations.

WHAT IS CULTURE?

Culture is the set of values, guiding beliefs, understandings, and ways of thinking that is shared by members of an organization and is taught to new members as correct.[3] It represents the unwritten, feeling part of the organization. Everyone participates in culture, but culture generally goes unnoticed. It is only when organizations try to implement new strategies or programs that go against basic culture norms and values that they come face to face with the power of culture.

Organizational culture exists at two levels, as illustrated in Exhibit 10.1. On the surface are visible artifacts and observable behaviors—the ways people dress and act, the symbols, stories, and ceremonies that are shared among organization members. But the visible elements of culture reflect deeper values in the minds of organization members. These underlying values, assumptions, beliefs, and thought processes are the true culture.[4] For example, at Ben & Jerry's the observable behavior is Jerry's effort to make employees more joyful, and the underlying belief and assumption is that "we are one family of people who care about each other." The attributes of culture display themselves in many ways but typically evolve into a patterned set of activities carried out through social interactions.[5] Those patterns can be used to interpret culture.

EMERGENCE AND PURPOSE OF CULTURE

Culture provides members with a sense of organizational identity and generates a commitment to beliefs and values that are larger than themselves. Though ideas that become part of culture can come from anywhere within the organization, an organization's culture generally begins with a founder or early leader who articulates and implements particular ideas and values as a vision, philosophy, or business strategy. When these ideas and values lead to success, they become institutionalized, and an organizational culture emerges that reflects the vision and strategy of the founder or leader, as it did at Ben & Jerry's.[6]

Cultures serve two critical functions in organizations: (1) to integrate members so that they know how to relate to one another, and (2) to help the organization adapt to the external environment. **Internal integration** means that members develop a collective identity and know how to work together effectively. It is culture that guides day-to-day working relationships and determines how people communicate

Exhibit 10.1
Levels of Corpo-
rate Culture.

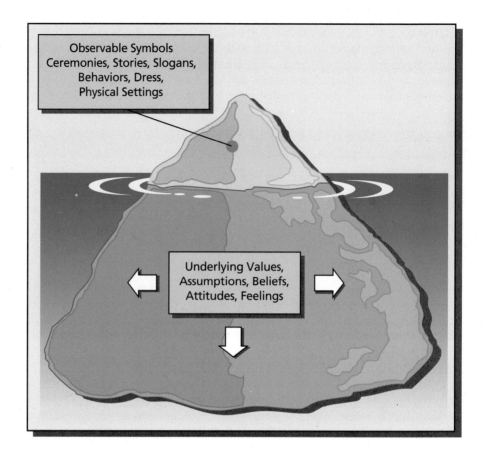

within the organization, what behavior is acceptable or not acceptable, and how power and status is allocated. **External adaptation** refers to how the organization meets goals and deals with outsiders. Culture helps guide the daily activities of workers to meet certain goals. It can help the organization respond rapidly to customer needs or the moves of a competitor. Ben & Jerry's was able to react quickly to customer demand for three hundred pallets of ice cream largely because its culture values workers helping one another. We will discuss culture and adaptation in more detail later in the chapter.

INTERPRETING CULTURE

To identify and interpret the content of culture requires that people make inferences based on observable artifacts. Artifacts can be studied but are hard to decipher accurately. An award ceremony in one company may have a different meaning than in another company. To decipher what is really going on in an organization requires detective work and probably some experience as an insider. Some of the typical and important observable aspects of culture are rites and ceremonies, stories, symbols, and language.

Rites and Ceremonies   Important artifacts for culture are **rites and ceremonies,** the elaborate, planned activities that make up a special event and are often conducted for the benefit of an audience. Managers can hold rites and ceremonies to provide dramatic examples of what a company values. These are special occasions that reinforce specific values, create a bond among people for sharing an important understanding, and can anoint and celebrate heroes and heroines who symbolize important beliefs and activities.[7]

Four types of rites that appear in organizations are summarized in Exhibit 10.2. *Rites of passage* facilitate the transition of employees into new social roles. *Rites of enhancement* create stronger social identities and increase the status of employees. *Rites of renewal* reflect training and development activities that improve organization functioning. *Rites of integration* create common bonds and good feelings among employees and increase commitment to the organization. The following examples illustrate how these rites and ceremonies are used by top managers to reinforce important cultural values.

- In a major bank, election as an officer was seen as the key event in a successful career. A series of activities accompanied every promotion to bank officer, including a special method of notification, taking the new officer to the officers' dining room for the first time, and the new officer buying drinks on Friday after his or her notification.[8] This is a rite of passage.
- Tupperware sales people hold a weekly rally at which sales people are recognized in reverse order of sales volume. The event is associated with celebration and hoopla. The ceremony reinforces the goal of sales volume held by the company.[9] This is a rite of enhancement.
- An important annual event at McDonald's is the nationwide contest to determine the best hamburger cooking team in the country. The contest encourages all stores to reexamine the details of how they cook hamburgers. The ceremony is highly visible and communicates to all employees the McDonald's value of hamburger quality.[10] This is a rite of renewal.

Type of Rite	Example	Social Consequences
Passage	Induction and basic training, U.S. Army	Facilitate transition of persons into social roles and statuses that are new for them
Enhancement	Annual awards night	Enhance social identities and increase status of employees
Renewal	Organizational development activities	Refurbish social structures and improve organization functioning
Integration	Office Christmas party	Encourage and revive common feelings that bind members together and commit them to the organization

Exhibit 10.2
A Typology of Organizational Rites and Their Social Consequences.

Source: Adapted from Harrison M. Trice and Janice M. Beyer, "Studying Organizational Cultures through Rites and Ceremonials," *Academy of Management Review* 9 (1984): 653–59. Used with permission.

- In a major midwestern firm, every Christmas the chairman of the board comes down from his office on the top floor to walk through every department, shaking hands with each employee. His appearance serves as a ceremony to communicate concern for the organizational "family."[11] This is a rite of integration.

Stories   **Stories** are narratives based on true events that are frequently shared among organizational employees and told to new employees to inform them about an organization. Many stories are about company **heroes** who serve as models or ideals for serving cultural norms and values. Some stories are considered **legends** because the events are historic and may have been embellished with fictional details. Other stories are **myths**, which are consistent with the values and beliefs of the organization but are not supported by facts.[12] Stories keep alive the primary values of the organization and provide a shared understanding among all employees. Examples of how stories shape culture are as follows:

- At 3M, top managers keep alive stories that describe innovative projects that were killed by top management. The hero of the stories worked on a project in secret and eventually proved management wrong by developing a successful new product. These stories are repeated by top managers to enhance the entrepreneurial spirit at 3M and to let employees know that if they feel frustrated and discouraged, they are not the first ones to overcome considerable odds in the process of innovation.[13]
- Two stories that symbolize the "HP way" at Hewlett–Packard involve the hero founders, David Packard and Bill Hewlett. After work hours one evening, Packard was wandering around the Palo Alto lab. He discovered a prototype constructed of inferior materials. Packard destroyed the model and left a note saying, "That's not the HP way. Dave." Similarly, Bill Hewlett is said to have gone to a plant on Saturday and found the lab stockroom door locked. He cut the padlock and left a note saying, "Don't ever lock this door again. Thanks, Bill." Hewlett wanted the engineers to have free access to components, and even to take them home, to stimulate the creativity that is part of the HP way.[14]

Symbols   Another tool for interpreting culture is the symbol. A **symbol** is something that represents another thing. In one sense, ceremonies, stories, slogans, and rites are all symbols. They symbolize deeper values of an organization. Another symbol is a physical artifact of the organization. Physical symbols are powerful because they focus attention on a specific item. Examples of physical symbols are as follows:

- Nordstrom department store symbolizes the importance of supporting lower-level employees with the organization chart in Exhibit 10.3. Nordstrom's is known for its extraordinary customer service, and the organization chart symbolizes that managers are to support the employees who *give* the service rather than be managers who control them.[15]
- President Bill Arnold of Nashville's Centennial Medical Center symbolized his commitment to an open door policy by ripping his office door from its hinges and suspending it from the ceiling where all employees could see it. At Sequint Computer Systems, all employees are expected to pitch in and help anyone wearing a red button. The red button symbolizes that a critical project is behind schedule.[16]

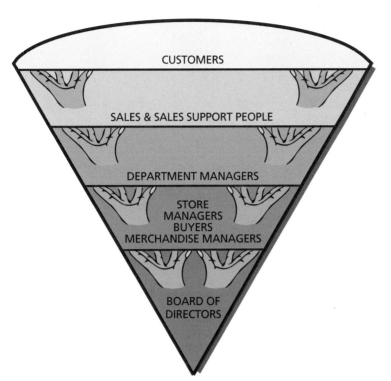

Exhibit 10.3
Organization
Chart for Nord-
strom, Inc.

Source: Used with permission of Nordstrom, Inc.

Language   The final technique for influencing culture is **language**. Many companies use a specific saying, slogan, metaphor, or other form of language to convey special meaning to employees. Slogans can be readily picked up and repeated by employees as well as customers of the company. At Speedy Muffler in Canada, the saying "At Speedy you're somebody" applies to employees and customers alike. Other significant uses of language to shape culture are as follows:

- T. J. Watson, Jr., son of the founder of International Business Machines, used the metaphor "wild ducks" to describe the type of employees needed by IBM. His point was, "You can make wild ducks tame, but you can never make tame ducks wild again."[17] Wild ducks symbolized the freedom and opportunity that must be available to keep from taming creative employees at IBM.
- Satisfaction Guaranteed Eateries, Inc., uses a slogan as the key value for employee action: "Your Enjoyment Guaranteed. Always." The acronym YEGA is printed on every menu, check, report form, and training manual and is on letterhead, wall signs, pins, name tags, and shirts. Each of six hundred employees signs a contract pledging YEGA follow-through.[18]

Recall that culture exists at two levels—the underlying values and assumptions and the visible artifacts and observable behaviors. The slogans, symbols, and ceremonies described above are artifacts that reflect underlying company values. These visible artifacts and behaviors can be used by managers to shape company values and to strengthen organizational culture. Now we will discuss how a strong corporate culture can have either positive or negative outcomes.

CULTURE STRENGTH AND ADAPTATION

When an organizational culture is strong, it can have a powerful impact, though not necessarily always a positive one. **Culture strength** refers to the degree of agreement among members of an organization about the importance of specific values. If widespread consensus exists about the importance of those values, the culture is cohesive and strong; if little agreement exists, the culture is weak.[19]

A strong culture is typically associated with the frequent use of ceremonies, symbols, stories, heroes, and slogans. These elements increase employee commitment to the values and strategy of a company.

However, research into some two hundred corporate cultures found that a strong culture does not ensure success unless the culture is one that encourages a healthy adaptation to the external environment.[20] A strong culture that does not encourage adaptation can be more damaging to an organization's success than having a weak culture. Consider the case of IBM in Chapter 1, where a strong corporate culture actually precluded adaptation.

As illustrated in Exhibit 10.4, adaptive corporate cultures have different values and behavior patterns than unadaptive cultures. In adaptive cultures, managers are concerned about customers and employees, and they strongly value processes that contribute to useful change. Behavior is flexible; managers initiate change when needed, even if it involves risk. In an unadaptive corporate culture, on the other hand, managers are more concerned about themselves or some pet project. Their

Exhibit 10.4   Adaptive versus Nonadaptive Corporate Cultures.

	Adaptive Corporate Cultures	Unadaptive Corporate Cultures
Core Values	Managers care deeply about customers, stockholders, and employees. They also strongly value people and processes that can create useful change (for example, leadership initiatives up and down the management hierarchy).	Managers care mainly about themselves, their immediate work group, or some product (or technology) associated with that work group. They value the orderly and risk-reducing management process much more highly than leadership initiatives.
Common Behavior	Managers pay close attention to all their constituencies, especially customers, and initiate change when needed to serve their legitimate interests, even if it entails taking some risks.	Managers tend to be somewhat isolated, political, and bureaucratic. As a result, they do not change their strategies quickly to adjust to or take advantage of changes in their business environments.

Source: Adapted and reprinted with the permission of The Free Press, an imprint of Simon & Schuster, from *Corporate Culture and Performance* by John P. Kotter and James L. Heskett. Copyright © 1992 by Kotter Associates, Inc. and James L. Heskett.

values discourage risk-taking and change. Thus, while strong, healthy cultures help organizations adapt to the external environment, strong, unhealthy cultures can encourage an organization to march resolutely in the wrong direction.

The stories at Hewlett-Packard described above reinforced an adaptive internal culture consistent with the "HP way." Insistence on product quality, recognition of employee achievement, and respect for individual employees are the values responsible for HP's success. Another strong adaptive culture exists at Southwest Airlines.

IN PRACTICE ◆ 10.1
Southwest Airlines

Success in the intensely competitive airline industry seems nearly impossible. A number of once-major airlines, such as Eastern and Braniff, have fallen by the wayside, and most of the rest have lost money for several years.

Southwest Airlines has found a vital niche in this competitive field and managed to maintain an enviable record of profitability and quality. One of the reasons for this success is a strong culture that knits Southwest employees together and enables them to face extreme challenges.

"We tell our people all the time, 'You have to be ready for change,'" says co-founder Herb Kelleher. "In fact, only in change is there security." Kelleher has developed a culture in which change is embraced rather than feared. Southwest's dominant culture values focus on employee and customer satisfaction. Southwest's guiding principle that people want better service at a lower price, provided by people who love what they're doing, has inspired intense loyalty from customers and employees alike.

Every employee is treated as an individual—Kelleher has been known to visit sick workers from the lowest levels of the company. Every Southwest manager, including Kelleher, spends at least one day per quarter doing some other job, such as a gate agent or baggage handler. Every employee is encouraged to accept responsibility for decision making and to be a leader. A baggage handler who does his job well and sets an example for others is recognized as a leader just as much as a manager would be.

Southwest hires people who understand that the company's mission is to work hard and have fun and who feel that by joining Southwest, they're joining an extended family. Customers are included in the family, too. Each month, Southwest's frequent fliers are invited to interview prospective employees. By hiring people who match the company's customers in personality, Southwest reinforces the culture. As a result, the company has the lowest annual turnover in the industry, and customer satisfaction continues to climb.

Southwest has created a strong, adaptive corporate culture, which has helped to build a continuously profitable $1.2 billion company that thrives in a brutally competitive industry.[21]

CREATING THE CULTURE

How do managers infuse and maintain strong, adaptive corporate cultures at companies like Southwest, J. C. Penney, or Morgan Guaranty Trust?[22] The techniques described earlier of using symbols, stories, language, and ceremonies are important. In addition, emphasis can be given to the selection and socialization of new employees. For example, at Southwest, prospective employees are subjected to rigorous interviewing, sometimes even by Southwest's regular customers, so that only those who fit the culture are hired. In a company such as Procter and Gamble, new employees are assigned minor tasks while they learn to question their prior behaviors, beliefs, and values. Then they have room to assimilate the beliefs and values of P&G. Through extensive training, new recruits constantly hear about the company's transcendent values and overarching purposes, about watershed events in the company's history, and about exemplary individuals—the heroes. These procedures enable organizations to develop strong cultures and use them as a strategic weapon.

Strategy and Culture

Strategy and the external environment are big influences on corporate culture. Corporate culture should embody what the organization needs to be effective within its environment. For example, if the external environment requires flexibility and responsiveness, the culture should encourage adaptability. The correct relationship between cultural values and beliefs, organizational strategy, and the business environment can enhance organizational performance.

Professor Dan Denison conducted a study of culture and effectiveness and proposed that the fit among strategy, environment, and culture is associated with four categories of culture, which are illustrated in Exhibit 10.5.[23] These categories are based on two factors: (1) the extent to which the competitive environment requires change or stability and (2) the extent to which the strategic focus and strength is

Exhibit 10.5
Relationship of Environment and Strategy to Corporate Culture.

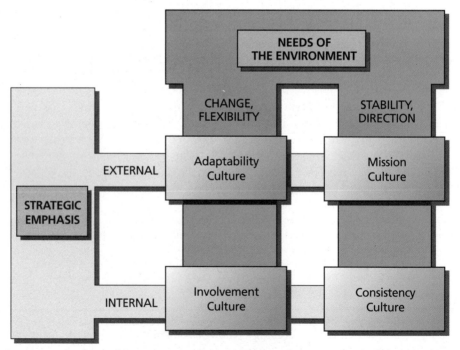

Source: Based on Daniel R. Denison, *Corporate Culture and Organizational Effectiveness* (New York: John Wiley & Sons, 1990). Copyright © 1990. Reprinted by permission of John Wiley and Sons, Inc.

internal or external. The four categories associated with these differences are adaptability, mission, involvement, and consistency.

THE ADAPTABILITY CULTURE

The **adaptability culture** is characterized by strategic focus on the external environment through flexibility and change to meet customer needs. The culture encourages norms and beliefs that support the capacity of the organization to detect, interpret, and translate signals from the environment into new behavior responses. This type of company may need to react quickly to bid on major new projects and have the capacity to restructure or adopt a new set of behaviors and processes for a new task. Marketing, electronics, and cosmetic companies may use this culture because they must move quickly to satisfy customers.

Another example is Detroit Edison, which experienced years of predictable growth and suddenly found itself in a decade of rapid change and external demand. The energy crisis, nuclear power, affirmative action, and the abrupt end of energy growth required a corporate culture that encouraged adaptation to these demands. The organization changed from a focus on technical quality to a focus linking itself to a diverse set of constituents.

THE MISSION CULTURE

An organization concerned with serving the external environment, but without the need for rapid change, is suited to the mission culture. The **mission culture** places major importance on a shared vision of organization purpose. The vision provides members' work activities with meaning that goes beyond typically defined jobs and roles. Organizational leaders shape behavior by envisioning a desired future state that is important to everyone.

One example is Medtronic, the premier manufacturer of cardiac pacemakers. Its mission is to "contribute to human welfare by application of biomedical engineering." Company employees believe the organization is on a mission to serve people, to make a difference in the medical field. Over the years the environment has changed with respect to government regulation, competition, and health care reimbursement, but the organization's mission remains essentially the same.[24]

THE INVOLVEMENT CULTURE

The **involvement culture** has a primary focus on the involvement and participation of the organization's members and on rapidly changing expectations from the external environment. The high-involvement culture is similar to the clan form of control described in Chapter 9. More than any other, this culture focuses on the needs of employees as the route to high performance. Involvement and participation create a sense of responsibility and ownership and, hence, greater commitment to the organization.

Ben & Jerry's Homemade, Inc., described at the beginning of this chapter, is an example of an involvement culture. The most important value is taking care of employees. In so doing, the organization is able to adapt to competition and changing markets. Companies in the fashion and retail industries also use this culture because it releases the creativity of employees to respond to rapidly changing tastes.

THE CONSISTENCY CULTURE

The **consistency culture** has an internal focus and a consistency orientation for a stable environment. This organization has a culture that supports a methodical approach to doing business. Symbols, heroes, and ceremonies support cooperation, tradition, and following established policies and practices as a way to achieve goals. Personal involvement is somewhat lower here, but that is outweighed by a high level of consistency, conformity, and collaboration among members. This organization succeeds by being highly integrated and efficient.

One example of a consistency culture is Safeco Insurance Company, considered by some to be stuffy and regimented. Employees take their coffee breaks at an assigned time, and the dress codes specify white shirts and suits for men and no beards. However, employees like this culture. Reliability counts. Extra work is not required. The culture is appropriate for the insurance company, which succeeds because it can be trusted to deliver on insurance policies as agreed.[25]

Ethical Values in Organizations

Of the values that make up an organization's culture, ethical values are now considered among the most important. Ethical standards are becoming part of the formal policies and informal cultures of many organizations, and courses in ethics are taught in many business schools. **Ethics** is the code of moral principles and values that governs the behaviors of a person or group with respect to what is right or wrong. Ethical values set standards as to what is good or bad in conduct and decision making.[26]

Ethics is distinct from behaviors governed by law. The **rule of law** arises from a set of codified principles and regulations that describe how people are required to act, are generally accepted in society, and are enforceable in the courts.[27]

The relationship between ethical standards and legal requirements is illustrated in Exhibit 10.6. Ethical standards for the most part apply to behavior not covered

Exhibit 10.6
Relationship between the Rule of Law and Ethical Standards.

Source: LaRue Tone Hosmer, *The Ethics of Management,* 2d ed. (Homewood, Ill.: Irwin, 1991).

by the law, and the rule of law covers behaviors not necessarily covered by ethical standards. Current laws often reflect combined moral judgments, but not all moral judgments are codified into law. The morality of aiding a drowning person, for example, is not specified by law, and driving on the righthand side of the road has no moral basis; but in areas such as robbery or murder, rules and moral standards overlap.

Ethical behavior does not mean simply following the law. Many behaviors have not been codified, and managers must be sensitive to emerging norms and values about those issues. **Managerial ethics** are principles that guide the decisions and behaviors of managers with regard to whether they are right or wrong in a moral sense. The notion of **social responsibility** is an extension of this idea and refers to management's obligation to make choices and take action so that the organization contributes to the welfare and interest of society as well as to itself.[28]

Examples of the need for managerial ethics are as follows:[29]

- The supervisor of a travel agency was aware that her agents and she could receive large bonuses for booking one hundred or more clients each month with an auto rental firm, although clients typically wanted the rental agency selected on the basis of lowest cost.
- The executive in charge of a parts distribution facility told employees to tell phone customers that inventory was in stock even if it was not. Replenishing the item only took one to two days, no one was hurt by the delay, and the business was kept from competitors.
- The project manager for a consulting project wondered whether some facts should be left out of a report because the marketing executives paying for the report would look bad if the facts were reported.
- A North American manufacturer operating abroad was asked to make cash payments (a bribe) to government officials and was told it was consistent with local customs, despite being illegal in North America.

These issues are exceedingly difficult to resolve and often represent dilemmas. An **ethical dilemma** arises when each alternative choice or behavior seems undesirable because of a potentially negative ethical consequence. Right or wrong cannot be clearly identified. These choices can be aided by establishing ethical values within the organization as part of corporate culture. Corporate culture can embrace the ethical values needed for business success.

Sources of Ethical Values in Organizations

The standards for ethical or socially responsible conduct are embodied within each employee as well as within the organization itself. The immediate forces that impinge on ethical decisions are summarized in Exhibit 10.7. Individual beliefs and values, a person's ethical decision framework, and moral development influence personal ethics. Organization culture, as we have already discussed, shapes the overall framework of values within the organization. Moreover, formal organization systems influence values and behaviors according to the organization's policy framework and reward systems. All of these factors can be explored to understand ethical decisions in organizations.[30]

Exhibit 10.7
Forces That
Shape Manageri-
al Ethics.

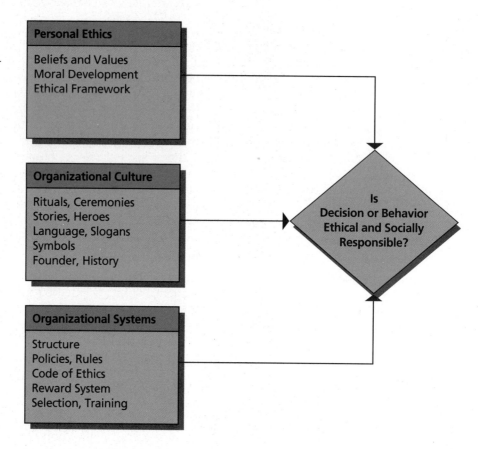

PERSONAL ETHICS

Every individual brings a set of personal beliefs and values into the workplace. Personal values and the moral reasoning that translates these values into behavior are an important aspect of ethical decision making in organizations.[31]

The family backgrounds and spiritual values of managers provide principles by which they carry out business. In addition, people go through stages of moral development that affect their ability to translate values into behavior. For example, children have a low level of moral development, making decisions and behaving to obtain rewards and avoid physical punishment. At an intermediate level of development, people learn to conform to expectations of good behavior as defined by colleagues and society. Most managers are at this level, willingly upholding the law and responding to societal expectations. At the highest level of moral development are people who develop an internal set of standards. These are self-chosen ethical principles that are more important to decisions than external expectations. Only a few people reach this high level, which can mean breaking laws if necessary to sustain higher moral principles.[32]

The other personal factor is whether managers have developed an *ethical framework* that guides their decisions. *Utilitarian theory,* for example, argues that ethical decisions should be made to generate the greatest benefits for the largest number of people. This framework is often consistent with business decisions because costs and benefits can be calculated in dollars. The *personal liberty* framework argues that decisions should be made to ensure the greatest possible freedom of choice and liberty for individuals. Liberties include freedom to act on one's conscience, free speech, due process, and the right to privacy. The *distributive justice* framework holds that moral decisions are those that promote equity, fairness, and impartiality with respect to the distribution of rewards and the administration of rules, which are essential for social cooperation.[33]

ORGANIZATIONAL CULTURE

Rarely can ethical or unethical business practices be attributed entirely to the personal ethics of a single individual. Since business practices reflect the values, attitudes, and behavior patterns of an organization's culture, ethics is as much an organizational issue as a personal one. Though Johnson & Johnson's handling of the Tylenol-poisoning crisis has sometimes been attributed to the ethical standards of then-CEO James Burke, the decisions in connection with that crisis actually reflected a shared set of values and guiding principles that have been deeply ingrained throughout the company since its early days. In 1989, Johnson & Johnson won a Business Ethics Award for sustaining ethical decision making over four decades.[34]

General Mills is another company whose ethical standards have been maintained from its beginning through seven CEOs, multiple acquisitions, and geographical expansion. The legal department always advises managers not to enter into a proposed move if there is any question about legality. Investments in equipment to ensure environmental safety are considered less expensive than risking contamination. A toy called Riviton was pulled from the market because of two children's deaths in one year, although obvious misuse by the customers was the cause and there was no request for a recall. These decisions are part of the General Mills ethical culture.[35]

ORGANIZATIONAL SYSTEMS

The third category of influences that shape managerial ethics is formal organizational systems. This includes the basic architecture of the organization, such as whether ethical values are incorporated in policies and rules; whether an explicit code of ethics is available and issued to members; whether organizational rewards, including praise, attention, and promotions, are linked to ethical behavior; and whether ethics is a consideration in the selection and training of employees. These formal efforts can reinforce ethical values that exist in the informal culture.

Today, more and more companies are establishing formal ethics programs. Hewlett-Packard works hard to familiarize all employees with its high standards for business practice, which cover everything from conflicts of interest to accepting gratuities. HP salespeople are instructed to refrain from commenting on a competitor's character or business practices. At Northrup, managers are rated on their ethical behavior by peers and subordinates through anonymous questionnaires. General Mills has explicit policy statements regarding corporate ethical values and expected employee conduct.[36] Inland Steel Industries is another example of an organization that combines ethics and organizational factors to reach ethically and socially responsible decisions.

IN PRACTICE ◆ 10.2
Inland Steel Industries

Inland Steel Industries' president Bob Darnall was called "Rev" during college because of his strong sense of right and wrong. His religious background shaped these values, which are still present today in his job as head of Inland.

When Inland went through a difficult contraction in the early 1980s—losing money, closing plants, and laying people off—ethical values were challenged. Inland's corporate culture had always valued employees, and some managers wanted to keep everyone on board as long as possible. However, the greatest good for Inland and its employees required Darnall to run the organization with economic integrity, which meant keeping it alive as a place where a smaller number of employees could have productive careers. Once the decision was made to reduce staff by 18 percent, the cultural values helped the implementation. The tradition of openness meant information was provided to employees and the news media far in advance so everyone could prepare. The cutbacks were implemented ethically by providing months of financial assistance, continued insurance coverage, and a job placement program.

Ethics has been a long tradition at Inland and is integrated into the organization's mission statement, making it a formal part of policies and procedures. With its reputation for high ethical standards, Inland attracts ethical people who themselves build on the culture and tradition of Inland, leading to decisions that are both ethical and socially responsible.[37]

How Leaders Shape Culture and Ethics

A report issued by the Business Roundtable—an association of chief executives from 250 large corporations—discussed ethics, policy, and practice in one hundred member companies, including GTE, Xerox, Johnson & Johnson, Boeing, and Hewlett-Packard.[38] In the experience of the surveyed companies, the single most important factor in ethical decision making was the role of top management in providing commitment, leadership, and example for ethical values. The CEO and other top managers must be committed to specific values and must give constant leadership in tending and renewing those values. Values can be communicated in a number of ways—speeches, company publications, policy statements, and, especially, personal actions. Top leaders are responsible for creating and sustaining a culture that emphasizes the importance of ethical behavior for all employees every day. When the CEO engages in unethical practices or fails to take firm and decisive action in response to the unethical practices of others, this attitude filters down through the organization. Formal ethics codes and training programs are worthless if leaders do not set and live up to high standards of ethical conduct.[39]

The following sections examine how managers signal and implement values through symbolic management as well as through the formal systems of the organization. The impact of a leader on the Body Shop's ethical values is illustrated in the Paradigm Buster.

SYMBOLIC LEADERSHIP

The underlying value system of an organization cannot be managed in the traditional way. Issuing an authoritative directive, for example, has little or no impact on

Paradigm Buster

Body Shop

Anita Roddick has built a highly successful global cosmetics company based on strong ethics and a sense of social responsibility. Roddick started Body Shop in 1976 with a $6,500 loan, fifteen products with handwritten labels, and a set of principles and values based on caring about others and the environment. Today, Roddick's company has hundreds of products and franchises in over forty countries, but the values are the same.

Each Body Shop store has a community project that employees do on company time. The company's Third World trade department is charged with going into Third World areas and "creating trade in an ethical way, paying First World prices, making sure the environment is protected, and making sure that the social fabric of that environment is protected." Body Shop raises large amounts of money to help people in rain forest areas. The company gave 25 percent of the profits from a soap production plant in a poor area of Glasgow back to the community.

Roddick insists that every aspect of her company's business be carried out with an attitude of care. There is strictly no animal testing of cosmetics products; natural ingredients from around the world are used; packaging is kept to a minimum and recycled materials are used when possible; the stores display explanations of the cultural backgrounds of the products and photos of the people living in the areas where product ingredients originated. Honesty and integrity are important values. For example, while most "henna" shampoos do not actually contain henna because it smells like horse manure, Body Shop's henna shampoo *does* contain henna—along with the smell, which is clearly explained on the bottle.

The caring attitude of the Body Shop comes through not only in its relationship to the environment and the community but in the way it treats employees as well. Roddick doesn't accept the claim that executives are doing good for their companies through such "immoral" acts as corporate raiding and "firing five hundred people at the stroke of a pen." Roddick's way of doing business is not only moral but good for the company, the employees, and the world.

Source: "Exemplar: The Body Shop," in Michael Ray and Alan Rinzler, eds., *The New Paradigm in Business* (Los Angeles: Jeremy P. Tarcher/Perigee Books, 1993), 222; and John R. Schermerhorn, Jr., James G. Hunt, and Richard N. Osborn, *Managing Organizational Behavior* (New York: John Wiley & Sons, 1994), 443.

an organization's value system. Most of us are unaware that we use symbols every day of our lives, but it is critical that managers recognize the power and significance of symbolism, for they must learn to communicate and signal actions in ways that will be accepted by employees. A **symbolic leader** defines and uses signals and symbols to influence corporate cultures and ethical value systems. For example, the director of a business school who wanted to create a more research-oriented culture moved his computer to the foyer of the school where he could be seen working on his own research as staff came in and out.[40] Symbolic leaders influence cultural and ethical values by articulating a vision for organizational values that employees can believe and by engaging in day-to-day activities that reinforce these values. The symbolic leader makes sure symbols, ceremonies, speeches, and slogans match the values. Most important, actions speak louder than words, so symbolic leaders "walk their talk."[41]

Leaders must remember that every statement and action has impact on culture and values, perhaps without their realizing it. Employees learn about values, beliefs, and goals from watching managers, just as students learn which topics are important for an exam, what professors like, and how to get a good grade from watching professors. In the world of business and government, the ceremonial and symbolic activities of executives are used to signal cultural and ethical values to large numbers of employees.

To be effective managing values, executives may need to learn symbolic and ceremonial skills, and how to use speech, writing, and gestures. Symbols, stories, and ceremonies are used because they provide information about what really counts in an organization and where people fit into the organization.[42] As one writer in organization theory, Karl Weick, expressed it, "Managerial work can be viewed as managing myth, symbols, and labels . . . ; because managers traffic so often in images, the appropriate role for the manager may be evangelist rather than accountant."[43]

Symbolic leaders search for opportunities to communicate values. They make public statements to groups or to the organization as a whole. They undertake the many small deeds, actions, and ceremonies to infuse values widely. For example, Roy Ash signaled the new culture for AM International by removing copying machines, making his own calls, and encouraging people to drop by and discuss problems face-to-face. His symbolic behavior broke the pattern of bureaucracy and centralized decision making that previously had been valued in the organization.[44] Consider the many symbols used by Jim Treybig, founder of Tandem Computers.

IN PRACTICE ◆ 10.3
Tandem Computers

At Tandem Computers, Jim Treybig created a culture to fit his vision. At four o'clock every Friday afternoon, employee beer busts were in full swing at Tandem Computers' offices around the country. Every week, 60 percent of the company dropped in at the beer busts for an hour, joined by visiting customers and suppliers. Employees at Tandem had neither time clocks nor name tags, but they did have flexible hours, a swimming pool, a volleyball court, and locker room and showers.

Despite all the fun, Treybig was serious about his five cardinal points for running a company, which defined the Tandem culture:

1. All people are good.
2. People, workers, management, and company are all the same thing.
3. Every single person in a company must understand the essence of the business.
4. Every employee must benefit from the company's success.
5. You must create an environment where all of the above can happen.

Treybig was a hero. He symbolized hard work and concern for people. Without question, his culture worked.

Then suddenly, the party at Tandem was over. Growth slowed, profits went flat, and the stock price dropped. The creator of culture had to find a new strategy and change the culture to fit it.

At Treybig's behest, Tandem developed a new line of products. Even more important, Treybig had to change his style. He symbolized the seriousness of the situation by asking salaried workers to put in 10 percent overtime without pay, stopped all hiring, froze salary increases, and required a vice president's approval for travel. Treybig also became more authoritative and no longer acted like one of the gang. His new style sent signals to tighten up internal controls yet get new products into the marketplace.

It worked. New products now account for 75 percent of sales, and administrative procedures are more systematic and suited to a large corporation. Tandem still has the swimming pool and Friday beer busts to encourage informal communications among people from different departments, as well as other significant elements from the previous culture; but its new culture also fits its new strategy and competitive environment.[45]

At Tandem Computers, Jim Treybig used symbols both to create an organizational culture and then to change the culture to fit a new competitive environment. Fitting Tandem's culture to its strategy has allowed the company to be extraordinarily successful.

FORMAL STRUCTURE AND SYSTEMS

Another set of tools leaders can use to shape cultural and ethical values is the formal structure and systems of the organization. These systems have been especially effective in recent years for influencing managerial ethics. Book Mark 10.0 discusses how leaders can use formal systems to promote cultural diversity in today's workplace.

Structure   Managers can assign responsibility for ethical values to a specific position. This not only allocates organization time and energy to the problem but symbolizes to everyone the importance of ethics. One example is an **ethics committee,** which is a group of executives appointed to oversee company ethics. The committee provides rulings on questionable ethical issues and assumes responsibility for disciplining wrongdoers. At Boeing, an ethics committee of senior managers reports directly to the board of directors.

Another example is an **ethics ombudsperson,** who is a single manager, perhaps with a staff, who serves as the corporate conscience. As work forces become more diverse and organizations continue to emphasize greater employee involvement, it is likely that more and more companies will assign ombudspersons to listen to grievances, investigate ethical complaints, and point out employee concerns and possible ethical abuses to top management. For the system to work, it is necessary for the person in this position to have direct access to the chairman or CEO, as does the corporate ombudsman for Pitney Bowes.[46]

Disclosure Mechanisms   The ethics committee or ombudsperson provide mechanisms for employees to voice concerns about ethical practices. One important function is to establish supportive policies and procedures about whistle-blowing. **Whistle-blowing** is employee disclosure of illegal, immoral, or illegitimate practices on the part of the organization.[47] One value of corporate policy is to protect whistle-blowers so they will not be transferred to lower-level positions or fired because of their ethical concerns. A policy can also encourage whistle-blowers to stay within the organization—for instance, to quietly blow the whistle to responsible managers.[48] Whistle-blowers have the option to stop organizational activities by going to newspaper or television reporters, but as a last resort.

Although whistle-blowing has become widespread in recent years, it is still risky for employees, who can lose their jobs or be ostracized by coworkers. Sometimes managers believe a whistle-blower is out of line and think they are acting correctly to fire or sabotage that employee. As ethical problems in the corporate world increase, many companies are looking for ways to protect whistle-blowers.

BOOKMARK 10.0

HAVE YOU READ ABOUT THIS?

The New Leaders: Guidelines on Leadership Diversity in America
by Ann M. Morrison

Ann Morrison, author of *The New Leaders* acknowledges that promoting cultural diversity is a "difficult and risky challenge." But leaders who rise to the challenge will find real rewards in better quality management, improved productivity and cost performance, and a substantial head start in developing the worldwide business perspective essential to global companies. Socially–conscious corporate leaders realize that by the year 2000, white males will comprise only about one-third of new entrants to the work force. Developing a culturally diverse workforce today—especially integrating women and minorities at the top level—makes ethical and business sense for the corporation of tomorrow.

Barriers to Nontraditional Worker Advancement

Morrison cites six conditions as primary barriers to the advancement of nontraditional workers: prejudice and the equation of difference with deficiency; poor career planning; hostile and unsupportive work environments; lack of organizational savvy on the part of nontraditional managers; greater comfort dealing with "one's own kind"; and difficulty in balancing family and career.

The Five Step Process

Morrison's five step process for developing and carrying out successful diversity programs incorporates basic principles of organizational change and emphasizes developing plans that will work within the culture of the specific organization.

Step 1. Discover and rediscover problems in the organization. Top managers can stop assuming they know the problems before studying the data on diversity within the firm.

Step 2. Strengthen top management commitment. Personal, informal intervention by top managers will help foster diversity. Diversity goals can be incorporated into the firm's evaluation and compensation systems for the long–term success of diversity programs.

Step 3. Select diversity practices to fit a balanced strategy. Some effective practices are targeted recruitment, internal advocacy groups, training programs, and changes in reward systems.

Step 4. Demand results and revisit goals. Management can track nontraditional employees' satisfaction with work environment, supervision, and career development. Look for nontraditional representation in key functional areas that serve as feeder pools for senior manager positions.

Step 5. Use building blocks to maintain momentum. Publicize the successes of diversity efforts to motivate employees to continue investing in those efforts.

Conclusion

Ann Morrison based *The New Leaders* on four years of research about the diversity practices of 16 successful companies. She is cautiously optimistic about the progress of women and minorities in U.S. organizations, and her book offers many lessons on how to make diversity efforts more successful. As companies strive to gain a competitive edge in today's changing world, their ability to foster diversity will become an increasingly important asset.

The New Leaders by Ann M. Morrison is published by Jossey–Bass.

In addition, calls are increasing for legal protection for those who report illegal or unethical business activities.[49]

One example of whistle-blowing involved Stephen Hayes, who designed an amusement park ride in Canada. The park's owner substituted a light-gauge metal culvert for reinforced concrete in order to have the ride ready by the Labor Day weekend. Hayes called the Association of Professional Engineers of Toronto, and that group informed local authorities. The ride was closed, and Hayes lost the business of the park's owner.[50]

Although many whistle-blowers are prepared to suffer financial loss to maintain ethical standards, many companies have created a climate in which employees feel free to point out problems. A growing number of corporations, including Texas Instruments, Nynex, Raytheon, Pacific Bell, and General Dynamics, are setting up ethics offices, usually with hot lines that give employees a confidential way to report misconduct. At General Dynamics, more than thirty thousand employee contacts with the ethics office since 1985 have led to almost fifteen hundred sanctions, ranging from demotion to referral for criminal action.[51]

Code of Ethics   Recent surveys show that 90 percent of Fortune 500 companies have a corporate *code of ethics*, a formal statement of the company's ethical guidelines.[52] The code clarifies company expectations of employee conduct and makes clear that the company expects its personnel to recognize the ethical dimensions of corporate behavior.

Some companies use broader mission statements within which ethics is a part. These statements define ethical values as well as corporate culture and contain language about company responsibility, quality of product, and treatment of employees. GTE, Norton, and Chemical Bank all have established statements of cultural and ethical values.[53]

A code of ethics states the values or behaviors that are expected as well as those that will not be tolerated or backed up by management's action. A code of ethics or larger mission statement is an important tool in the management of organizational values.

Training Programs   To ensure that ethical issues are considered in daily decision making, companies can supplement a written code of ethics with employee training programs.[54] A recent survey showed that 45 percent of responding companies were including ethics training in employee seminars. McDonnell Douglas has a corporatewide ethics training program that all management and nonmanagement employees attend.[55] These training programs include case examples to give employees a chance to wrestle with ethical dilemmas. Training also provides rules or guidelines for decision making, and it discusses codes of ethics and mission statements. Citicorp has developed an ethics board game, which teams of employees use to solve hypothetical ethical problems.[56]

In an important step, ethics programs also include frameworks for ethical decision making, such as the utilitarian approach described earlier in this chapter. Learning frameworks like this helps managers act autonomously and still think their way through a difficult decision. In a few companies, managers are also taught about the stages of moral development, helping bring them to a high stage of ethical decision making. This training has been an important catalyst for establishing ethical behavior and integrity as critical components of strategic competitiveness.[57]

Summary and Interpretation

This chapter covered a range of material on corporate culture, the importance of cultural and ethical values, and techniques managers can use to influence these values.

Culture is the set of key values, beliefs, and understandings shared by members of an organization. Organizational cultures serve two critically important functions—to integrate members so that they know how to relate to one another and to help the organization adapt to the external environment. Culture can be observed and interpreted through rites and ceremonies, stories and heroes, symbols, and language. Strong corporate cultures can be either adaptive or unadaptive. Adaptive cultures have different values and different behavior patterns than unadaptive cultures. Strong but unhealthy cultures can be detrimental to a company's chances for success. Four types of cultures that may exist in organizations are adaptability culture, mission culture, involvement culture, and consistency culture.

An important aspect of organizational values is management ethics, which is the set of values governing behavior with respect to what is right or wrong. Ethical decision making in organizations is shaped by many factors: personal characteristics, including personal beliefs, moral development, and the adoption of ethical frameworks for decision making; organizational culture, which is the extent to which values, heroes, traditions, and symbols reinforce ethical decision making; and organizational systems, which pertain to the formal structure, policies, codes of ethics, and reward systems that reinforce ethical or unethical choices.

Finally, the chapter discussed how leaders can shape culture and ethics. One important idea is symbolic leadership, which means managers define a vision of proper values and then use symbolic tools to implement that vision. We also discussed formal systems that are important for shaping ethical values. Formal systems include an ethics committee, an ethics ombudsperson, disclosure mechanisms for whistle-blowing, ethics training programs, and a code of ethics or mission statement that specifies ethical values.

KEY CONCEPTS

adaptability culture	language
consistency culture	legends
culture	managerial ethics
culture strength	mission culture
ethical dilemma	myths
ethics	rites and ceremonies
ethics committee	rule of law
ethics ombudsperson	social responsibility
external adaptation	stories
heroes	symbol
involvement culture	symbolic leader
internal integration	whistle-blowing

DISCUSSION QUESTIONS

1. Describe observable symbols, ceremonies, dress, or other aspects of culture and the underlying values they represent for an organization where you have worked.

2. Discuss how a strong corporate culture could be negative as well as positive for an organization.

3. Do you think a consistency culture would be less employee-oriented than an involvement culture? Discuss.

4. Discuss the differences between rites of enhancement, renewal, and integration.

5. Why is symbolic leadership so important to the influence of culture? Does a symbolic act communicate more about company values than an explicit statement? Discuss.

6. Are you aware of a situation where either you or someone you know was confronted by an ethical dilemma, such as being encouraged to inflate an expense account? Do you think the person's decision was affected by individual moral development or by the accepted values within the company? Explain.

7. From where do managers derive ethical values? From where have you derived your ethical values? Do you think managers use ethical decision frameworks as a part of their decision making? Why?

8. What importance would you attribute to leadership statements and actions for influencing ethical values and decision making in an organization?

9. Codes of ethics have been criticized for transferring responsibility for ethical behavior from the organization to the individual employee. Do you agree? Do you think a code of ethics is valuable for an organization?

 GUIDES TO ACTION

As an organization's top manager, keep these guides in mind:

1. Pay attention to corporate culture. Understand the underlying values, assumptions, and beliefs on which culture is based as well as its observable manifestations. Evaluate corporate culture based on rites and ceremonies, stories and heroes, symbols, and language.

2. Make sure corporate culture is consistent with strategy and environment. Culture can be shaped to fit the needs of both. Four types are adaptability culture, mission culture, involvement culture, and consistency culture.

3. Take control of ethical values in the organization. Ethics is not the same as following the law. Ethical decisions are influenced by management's personal background, by organizational culture, and by organizational systems.

4. Act as a leader for the internal culture and ethical values that are important to the organization. Influence the value system through symbolic leadership, including the use of ceremonies, slogans, symbols, and stories. Communicate important values to employees to enhance organizational effectiveness.

5. Use the formal systems of the organization to implement desired cultural and ethical values. These systems include an ethics committee, ethics ombudsperson, disclosure mechanisms, a code of ethics, a mission statement, and training in ethical decision-making frameworks.

Consider these guides when analyzing the following cases.

CASE FOR ANALYSIS

Stride Rite Corporation*

Lining the walls of Stride Rite's corporate headquarters in Cambridge, Massachusetts, are plaques honoring the shoe company for its good deeds. In the first three years of the 1990s alone, Stride Rite received fourteen public service awards, including ones praising the company for "improving the quality of life" in its community and the nation. Stride Rite's good deeds are matched by its success, as sales, profits, and stock prices continue to rise.

Everyone agrees that this company has done good things. It has contributed 5 percent of pretax profits to the Stride Rite Charitable Foundation, sent 100,000 pairs of sneakers to Mozambique, given scholarships to inner-city youths, and allowed employees to tutor disadvantaged children on company time. Stride Rite was a pioneer in establishing on-site child- and elder-care facilities.

But there's another side to the Stride Rite story. The company has prospered in the past decade partly by closing fifteen factories and moving most production to Asia, where the search for low-cost labor continues. In recent years, Stride Rite closed factories in South Korea as wages rose and moved to lower-cost areas in Indonesia and China.

Many of the lost Stride Rite jobs in the United States were held by workers living in depressed areas with high unemployment rates. In Boston's rough inner-city neighborhood of Roxbury, where local unemployment is nearly 30 percent, and in nearby New Bedford, where unemployment is 14 percent, Stride Rite is closing facilities and moving operations to Kentucky, where labor and transportation costs will be much lower. The company estimates these closings will save millions of dollars.

The moves also leave a lot of low-skilled workers, many of whom hardly speak English and were already just barely hanging on, out of work and out of hope. The decisions have caused soul-searching among Stride Rite's top management, but they ultimately agreed that their primary responsibility is to the stockholders.

One Roxbury worker encapsulated what the closing means to those who'll soon be out of work. A 70-year-old Irish immigrant who rented a room from the worker recently died and left behind a 32-year-old mentally retarded son. The Stride Rite worker reflected, "I don't have the heart to ask him to leave. If I did, I would be doing to him what my company is doing to me."

QUESTIONS

1. The executive director of Boston's Economic Development and Industrial Corporation tried to persuade Stride Rite not to close the Roxbury and New Bedford operations, saying, "The most socially responsible thing a company can do is give a person a job." Discuss this statement. What ethical framework is implied by this statement? By Stride Rite's plant closings?

---

*Based on Joseph Pereira, "Split Personality: Social Responsibility and Need for Low Cost Clash at Stride Rite," *Wall Street Journal*, 28 May 1993, A1.

2. How would you describe the corporate culture at Stride Rite, and what are some of the values operating at the company? Are the values in conflict?
3. Do you consider Stride Rite's practice of moving to lower-cost locations ethical? Explain.

Traffic Technology, Inc. (Canada)*

Part I

Guillaume Delacroix, vice president of sales for Traffic Technology, Inc. (TTI), headquartered in Ontario, was on his first sales trip to the Middle East. TTI designs computerized traffic flow management systems for large cities, and the Middle East was a potentially rich market for the company. The specific deal he was negotiating was worth $3.5 million.

On Thursday afternoon, Delacroix met with technical advisors, who were impressed with his plans. The final negotiating session with the minister's advisor also went well, and they decided to reach the final deal in the evening over dinner.

The dinner went flawlessly, with the advisor and Delacroix reaching an agreement on price and establishing a common bond from their collegiate past. As the minister's limo dropped Delacroix at his hotel about 2 A.M., the minister said, "Did you include the normal commission for government personnel in your price? The German and Italian bids did."

After a sleepless night, Delacroix called TTI's local agent, who said, "It is standard procedure, and ten thousand dollars is about right for a contract this size. You can funnel it through our legal fee if you want."

Delacroix was horrified. This went against the corporate culture of TTI; but he didn't want to lose a lucrative contract, and ten grand was a small price to pay.

QUESTIONS

1. Should Delacroix take the moral high road and refuse to pay the bribe?
2. Is there a way he can avoid paying the bribe and still manage to salvage this deal?

Part II

After much soul-searching and a telephone call with TTI's president, Delacroix and the president decided the contract was too lucrative to pass up and TTI would pay the commission through the legal fee. Both were uncomfortable with the bribe but felt they must pay since their competitors paid. They vowed to establish a new procedure in the future that would help them eliminate bribes from their contracts.

TTI won the contract and has since sold its system to cities in three other foreign countries. One thing Delacroix learned was to hire a reputable agent, someone who knows the power brokers and the ins and outs of the country's

*Based on Vaune Davis, "Grappling with Graft," *Canadian Business,* September 1990, 103–105.

government. The agent can help TTI avoid paying bribes if at all possible. However, the company has since then had to pay one more commission.

QUESTIONS

1. Can you justify TTI paying two bribes?
2. What long-term implications might this practice have for TTI, especially its culture and values? Discuss.

NOTES

1. Erik Larson, "Forever Young," *Inc.,* July 1988, 50–56; "Exemplar: Ben & Jerry's Homemade Ice Cream, Inc.," in Michael Ray and Alan Rinzler, eds., *The New Paradigm in Business* (Los Angeles: Jeremy P. Tarcher/Perigree Books, 1993), 138.

2. Charles O'Reilly, "Corporations, Culture, and Commitment: Motivation and Social Control in Organizations," *California Management Review* 31 (Summer 1989): 9–25.

3. W. Jack Duncan, "Organizational Culture: 'Getting a Fix' on an Elusive Concept," *Academy of Management Executive* 3 (1989): 229–36; Linda Smircich, "Concepts of Culture and Organizational Analysis," *Administrative Science Quarterly* 28 (1983): 339–58; Vijay Sathe, "Implications of Corporate Culture: A Manager's Guide to Action," *Organizational Dynamics* (Autumn 1983): 5–23.

4. Edgar H. Schein, "Organizational Culture," *American Psychologist* 45 (February 1990): 109–19.

5. Harrison M. Trice and Janice M. Beyer, "Studying Organizational Cultures through Rites and Ceremonials," *Academy of Management Review* 9 (1984): 653–69; Janice M. Beyer and Harrison M. Trice, "How an Organization's Rites Reveal Its Culture," *Organizational Dynamics* 15 (Spring 1987): 5–24; Steven P. Feldman, "Management in Context: An Essay on the Relevance of Culture to the Understanding of Organizational Change," *Journal of Management Studies* 23 (1986): 589–607; Mary Jo Hatch, "The Dynamics of Organizational Culture," *Academy of Management Review* 18 (1993): 657–93.

6. This discussion is based on Edgar H. Schein, *Organizational Culture and Leadership,* 2d ed. (Homewood, Ill.: Richard D. Irwin, 1992); John P. Kotter and James L. Heskett, *Corporate Culture and Performance* (New York: Free Press, 1992).

7. Charlotte B. Sutton, "Richness Hierarchy of the Cultural Network: The Communication of Corporate Values" (Unpublished manuscript, Texas A & M University, 1985); Terrence E. Deal and Allan A. Kennedy, "Culture: A New Look through Old Lenses," *Journal of Applied Behavioral Science* 19 (1983): 498–505.

8. Thomas C. Dandridge, "Symbols at Work" (Working paper, School of Business, State University of New York at Albany, 1978), 1.

9. Thomas J. Peters and Robert H. Waterman, Jr., *In Search of Excellence* (New York: Harper & Row, 1982).

10. Ibid.

11. Dandridge, "Symbols at Work."

12. Trice and Beyer, "Studying Organizational Cultures through Rites and Ceremonials."

13. Sutton, "Richness Hierarchy of the Cultural Network"; L. W. Lehr, "How 3M Develops Entrepreneurial Spirit throughout the Organization," *Management Review* 69, no. 10 (1980): 31.

14. Sutton, "Richness Hierarchy of the Cultural Network"; Deal and Kennedy, *Corporate Cultures.*

15. "FYI," *Inc.,* April 1991, 14.

16. Nancy K. Austin, "Wacky Management Ideas That Work," *Working Woman,* November 1991, 42–44; Susan Benner, "Culture Shock," *Inc.,* August 1985, 73–82.

17. Richard Ott, "Are Wild Ducks Really Wild: Symbolism and Behavior in the Corporate Environment" (Paper presented at the Northeastern Anthropological Association, March 1979).

18. Timothy W. Firnstahl, "My Employees Are My Service Guarantee," *Harvard Business Review* (July–August 1989): 28–32.

19. Bernard Arogyaswamy and Charles M. Byles, "Organizational Culture: Internal and External Fits," *Journal of Management* 13 (1987): 647–59.

20. Kotter and Heskett, *Corporate Culture and Performance.*

21. James Campbell Quick, "Crafting an Organizational Culture: Herb's Hand at Southwest Airlines," *Organizational Dynamics* (Autumn 1992):

45–56; Edward O. Welles, "Captain Marvel," *Inc.,* January 1992, 44–47.

22. Based on Richard Pascale, "Fitting New Employees into the Company Culture," *Fortune,* 28 May 1984, 28–39; and Richard Pascale, "The Paradox of 'Corporate Culture': Reconciling Ourselves to Socialization," *California Management Review* 27 (Winter 1985): 26–41.

23. Based on Daniel R. Denison, *Corporate Culture and Organizational Effectiveness* (New York: John Wiley & Sons, 1990), 11–15.

24. Ibid.

25. Carey Quan Jelernter, "Safeco: Success Depends Partly on Fitting the Mold," *Seattle Times,* 5 June 1986, D8.

26. Gordon F. Shea, *Practical Ethics* (New York: American Management Association, 1988); Linda K. Trevino, "Ethical Decision Making in Organizations: A Person–Situation Interactionist Model," *Academy of Management Review* 11 (1986): 601–17.

27. LaRue Tone Hosmer, *The Ethics of Management,* 2d ed., (Homewood, Ill.: Irwin, 1991).

28. Eugene W. Szwajkowski, "The Myths and Realities of Research on Organizational Misconduct," in James E. Post, ed., *Research and Corporate Social Performance and Policy,* vol. 9 (Greenwich, Conn.: JAI Press, 1986), 103–22.

29. These incidents are from Hosmer, *The Ethics of Management.*

30. Linda Klebe Trevino, "A Cultural Perspective on Changing and Developing Organizational Ethics," in Richard Woodman and William Pasmore, eds., *Research and Organizational Change and Development,* vol. 4 (Greenwich, Conn.: JAI Press, 1990).

31. James Weber, "Exploring the Relationship between Personal Values and Moral Reasoning," *Human Relations* 46 (1993): 435–63.

32. L. Kohlberg, "Moral Stages and Moralization: The Cognitive–Developmental Approach," in T. Likona, ed., *Moral Development and Behavior: Theory, Research, and Social Issues* (New York: Holt, Rinehart & Winston, 1976).

33. Hosmer, *The Ethics of Management.*

34. Lynn Sharp Paine, "Managing for Organizational Integrity," *Harvard Business Review* (March–April 1994): 106–17; Margaret Kaeter, "The 5th Annual Business Ethics Awards for Excellence in Ethics," *Business Ethics,* November–December 1993, 26–29.

35. *Corporate Ethics: A Prime Business Asset* (New York: The Business Roundtable, February 1988).

36. Ibid.; Kenneth Labich, "The New Crisis in Business Ethics," *Fortune,* 20 April 1992, 167–76.

37. "Principles and Profit: Can They Exist Together?" *Inland* (A publication of Inland Steel Industries), Winter 1989, 10–13.

38. *Corporate Ethics: A Prime Business Asset.*

39. Andrew W. Singer, "The Ultimate Ethics Test," *Across the Board,* March 1992, 19–22.

40. Gerry Johnson, "Managing Strategic Change: The Role of Symbolic Action," *British Journal of Management* 1 (1990): 183–200.

41. Peters and Waterman, *In Search of Excellence.*

42. Jeffrey Pfeffer, "Management as Symbolic Action: The Creation and Maintenance of Organizational Paradigms," in L. L. Cummings and Barry M. Staw, eds., *Research in Organizational Behavior,* vol. 3 (Greenwich, Conn.: JAI Press, 1981), 1–52; Thomas C. Dandridge, Ian I. Mitroff, and William F. Joyce, "Organizational Symbolism: A Topic to Expand Organizational Analysis," *Academy of Management Review* 5 (1980): 77–82.

43. Karl E. Weick, "Cognitive Processes in Organizations," in B. M. Staw, ed., *Research in Organizations,* vol. 1 (Greenwich, Conn.: JAI Press, 1979), 42.

44. Louis Kraar, "Roy Ash Is Having Fun at Addressogrief–Multigrief," *Fortune,* 27 February 1978, 47–52; Thomas J. Peters, "Symbols, Patterns, and Settings: An Optimistic Case for Getting Things Done," *Organizational Dynamics* 7 (1978): 2–23.

45. Jonathan B. Levine, "How Jim Treybig Whipped Tandem Back into Shape," *Business Week,* 23 February 1987, 124–26; Brian O'Reilly, "How Jimmy Treybig Turned Tough," *Fortune,* 25 May 1987, 102–104; Myron Magnet, "Managing by Mystique at Tandem Computers," *Fortune,* 28 June 1982, 84–91.

46. Justin Martin, "New Tricks for an Old Trade," *Across the Board,* June 1992, 40–44.

47. Marcia Parmarlee Miceli and Janet P. Near, "The Relationship among Beliefs, Organizational Positions and Whistle-Blowing Status: A Discriminate Analysis," *Academy of Management Journal* 27 (1984): 687–705.

48. Richard P. Nielsen, "Changing Unethical Organizational Behavior," *Academy of Management Executive* 3 (1989): 123–30.

49. Jene G. James, "Whistle–Blowing: Its Moral Justification," in Peter Madsen and Jay M. Shafritz, eds., *Essentials of Business Ethics* (New York: Meridian Books, 1990), 160–90; Janet P. Near, Terry Morehead Dworkin, and Marcia P. Miceli, "Explaining the Whistle–Blowing Process: Suggestions from Power Theory and Justice Theory,"

Organization Science 4 (1993): 393–411.

50. Lawrence Archer, "The Moral Minority," *Canadian Business,* January 1986, 56–59.

51. Barnaby J. Feder, "Helping Corporate America Hew to the Straight and Narrow," *New York Times,* 3 November 1991, F5.

52. Michael Matzger, Dan R. Dalton, and John W. Hill, "The Organization of Ethics and the Ethics of Organizations: The Case for Expanded Organizational Ethics Audits," *Business Ethics Quarterly* 3 (1991): 27–43.

53. Saul W. Gellerman, "Managing Ethics from the Top Down," *Sloan Management Review* (Winter 1989): 73–79; Donald Robin, Michael Giallourakis, Fred R. David, and Thomas E. Moritz, "A Different Look at Codes of Ethics," *Business Horizons* (January–February 1989): 66–71.

54. James Weber, "Institutionalizing Ethics into Business Organizations: A Model and Research Agenda," *Business Ethics Quarterly* 3 (1993): 419–36.

55. Susan J. Harrington, "What Corporate America Is Teaching about Ethics," *Academy of Management Executive* 5 (1991): 21–30.

56. Labich, "The New Crisis in Business Ethics."

57. Harrington, "What Corporate America Is Teaching about Ethics."

PART
5

*M*anaging Dynamic Processes

359

Decision-Making Processes

CHAPTER TOPICS

Pepsi-Cola

When claims began surfacing across the country that syringes and hypodermic needles had been found in cans of Pepsi, Pepsi-Cola Company made the choice to not close plants or conduct a recall. Instead, the company mounted a major public relations campaign.

Pepsi-Cola's CEO Craig Weatherup and his staff prepared video footage demonstrating the tamperproof features of Pepsi's canning process and sent the footage by satellite to television stations across the nation. Weatherup himself took to the airwaves, appearing on "Nightline," "The McNeil-Lehrer Newshour," and "Larry King Live," to explain how implausible it was for syringes to have been put into Pepsi cans at the canning plants. At one point, Weatherup appeared on "Nightline" together with Food and Drug Administration Commissioner David Kessler. Though the FDA was cautioning consumers to pour Pepsi into a glass before drinking, the agency did not feel that consumers were in danger, nor was there evidence of nationwide tampering. The evidence that Pepsi, and separately, the FDA presented went a long way toward quelling public fears.

Explaining the decision not to issue a product recall, Weatherup said, a recall would be "dishonest" since there had been no injuries and not a single confirmed case of a syringe found in an unopened can of Pepsi. A recall would also have been extremely expensive for the company—but then, loss of consumer trust could have been even more expensive in the long run. At Pepsi-Cola's headquarters, a twelve member crisis management team was working nearly around the clock. At least two dozen employees staffed phone lines to take calls from worried customers and bottlers. Some bottlers took their own steps to quiet local fears. "Hell, we opened up our plant to everybody," said James C. Lee, Jr., chairman of Buffalo Rock Bottling Company in Birmingham, Alabama. "The TV stations came over, and we showed 'em we got 28 people doing quality control 'round the clock."

Pepsi managers made the right choice, believing that syringes couldn't appear in unopened cans of Pepsi. By allying itself with the FDA and responding quickly and openly to consumer fears, Pepsi weathered the syringe-scare crisis with little damage. In fact, all the publicity associated with the hoax, and the extra publicity Pepsi received in response to it, may have benefited the company in the long run.[1]

The syringe scare at Pepsi-Cola provides several insights into organizational decision making. First, managers must sometimes make decisions very quickly in response to circumstances out of the control of the organization. Second, decisions can be risky and uncertain, without any guarantee of success. Weatherup knew his decision not to conduct a recall could backfire if the company were unable to convince consumers that Pepsi products were truly safe. Third, major decisions are not made all at once. After Pepsi decided not to recall their product and instead mount a massive public relations campaign, subsequent decisions had to be made about how to do it. Decision implementation is crucial. Pepsi-Cola set up a crisis management team, provided constant updates to bottlers and customers nationwide, set up consumer phone lines, ran ads, and decided that Weatherup was the best person to appear publicly. The Pepsi-Cola example also shows that major organizational decisions are usually not made by a single manager. Though Craig Weatherup was at the forefront, he was talking daily with other managers and with his boss, Pepsi-Co Chairman Wayne Calloway.

PURPOSE OF THIS CHAPTER

Decision-making processes can be thought of as the brain and nervous system of an organization. Decision making is the end use of the information and control systems described in Chapter 9. Decisions are made about organization strategy, structure, innovation, and acquisitions. This chapter explores how organizations can and should make decisions about these issues.

Although Pepsi's decision worked well, many organizational decisions are complete failures. RCA intended to capture the video recorder market with its Videodisc but instead lost nearly $500 million because the machine couldn't tape television shows. The successful bike maker Huffy made a $5 million mistake by assuming its traditional sales outlets, such as K Mart and Toys 'R' Us, were appropriate for its new "Cross Sport" bike, priced 15 percent higher than other Huffy models and aimed at adults looking for a specialty bike. Miller Brewing decided to construct a $412 million, fully equipped brewery in Trenton, Ohio, which never opened because the demand for Miller beer did not increase as managers expected.[2]

At any time, an organization may be identifying problems and implementing alternatives for hundreds of decisions. Organizations somehow muddle through these processes.[3] The purpose here is to analyze these processes to learn what decision making is actually like in organizational settings.

The first section of this chapter defines decision making. The next section examines how individual managers make decisions. Then several models of organizational decision making are explored. Each model is used in a different organizational situation. The final section in this chapter combines the models into a single framework that describes when and how they should be used and discusses special issues, such as decision mistakes.

DEFINITIONS

Organizational decision making is formally defined as the process of identifying and solving problems. The process contains two major stages. The **problem identification** stage is where information about environmental and organizational conditions is monitored to determine if performance is satisfactory and to diagnose the cause of shortcomings. The **problem solution** stage is where alternative courses of action are considered and one alternative is selected and implemented. At Pepsi-Cola, problem identification was easy—Craig Weatherup realized the claims that syringes had been found in cans of Pepsi could potentially devastate the company's sales. The problem solution stage involved examining various courses of action, deciding to launch a massive public relations campaign, and making subsequent decisions about implementation.

Organizational decisions vary in complexity and can be categorized as programmed or nonprogrammed.[4] **Programmed decisions** are repetitive and well defined, and procedures exist for resolving the problem. They are well structured because criteria of performance are normally clear, good information is available about current performance, alternatives are easily specified, and there is relative certainty that the chosen alternative will be successful. Examples of programmed decisions include decision rules, such as when to replace an office copy machine, when to reimburse managers for travel expenses, or whether an applicant has sufficient qualifications for an assembly-line job. Many companies adopt rules based on experience with programmed decisions. For example, general pricing rules in the restaurant industry are that food is marked up three times direct cost, beer four times, and liquor six times. A rule for large hotels staffing banquets is to allow one server per thirty guests for a sit-down function and one server per forty guests for a buffet.[5]

Nonprogrammed decisions are novel and poorly defined, and no procedure exists for solving the problem. They are used when an organization has not seen a problem before and may not know how to respond, as happened with the Pepsi-Cola syringe scare. Clear-cut decision criteria do not exist. Alternatives are fuzzy. There is uncertainty about whether a proposed solution will solve the problem. The decision at Pepsi-Cola against a recall and in favor of a campaign to calm consumer fears was clearly a nonprogrammed decision. Pepsi Cola executives faced a dilemma: clear evidence of danger, such as the traces of poisonous benzine found in unopened Perrier several years earlier, would have required a recall, but such evidence didn't exist. Typically, few alternatives can be developed for a nonprogrammed decision, so a single solution is custom-tailored to the problem.

Individual Decision Making

Individual decision making by managers can be described in two ways. First is the **rational approach,** which suggests how managers should try to make decisions. Second is the **bounded rationality perspective,** which describes how decisions actually have to be made under severe time and resource constraints. The rational approach is an ideal managers may work toward but never reach.

RATIONAL APPROACH

The rational approach to individual decision making stresses the need for systematic analysis of a problem followed by choice and implementation in a logical step-by-step sequence. The rational approach was developed to guide individual decision making because many managers were observed to be unsystematic and arbitrary in their approach to organizational decisions. According to the rational approach, the decision process can be broken down into the following eight steps.[6]

1. *Monitor the decision environment.*   In the first step, a manager monitors internal and external information that will indicate deviations from planned or acceptable behavior. He or she talks to colleagues and reviews financial statements, performance evaluations, industry indices, competitors' activities, and so forth. For example, during the pressure-packed five-week Christmas season, Linda Koslow, general manager of Marshall Fields's Oakbrook, Illinois, store, checks out competitors around the mall, eyeing whether they are marking down merchandise. She also scans printouts of her store's previous day's sales to learn what is or is not moving.[7]

2. *Define the decision problem.*   The manager responds to deviations by identifying essential details of the problem: where, when, who was involved, who was affected, and how current activities are influenced. For Koslow, this means defining

whether store profits are low because overall sales are less than expected or because certain lines of merchandise are not moving as expected.

3. *Specify decision objectives.*   The manager determines what performance outcomes should be achieved by a decision.

4. *Diagnose the problem.*   In this step, the manager digs below the surface to analyze the cause of the problem. Additional data may be gathered to facilitate this diagnosis. Understanding the cause enables appropriate treatment. For Koslow at Marshall Fields, the cause of slow sales may be competitors' marking down of merchandise or Marshall Fields's failure to display hot-selling items in a visible location.

5. *Develop alternative solutions.*   Before a manager can move ahead with a decisive action plan, he or she must have a clear understanding of the various options available to achieve desired objectives. The manager may seek ideas and suggestions from other people. Koslow's alternatives for increasing profits could include buying fresh merchandise, running a sale, or reducing the number of employees.

6. *Evaluate alternatives.*   This step may involve the use of statistical techniques or personal experience to assess the probability of success. The merits of each alternative are assessed as well as the probability that it will reach the desired objectives.

7. *Choose the best alternative.*   This step is the core of the decision process. The manager uses his or her analysis of the problem, objectives, and alternatives to select a single alternative that has the best chance for success. At Marshall Fields, Koslow may choose to reduce the number of staff as a way to meet the profit goals rather than increase advertising or markdowns.

8. *Implement the chosen alternative.*   Finally, the manager uses managerial, administrative and persuasive abilities and gives directions to ensure that the decision is carried out. The monitoring activity (step 1) begins again as soon as the solution is implemented. For Linda Koslow, the decision cycle is a continuous process, with new decisions made daily based on monitoring her environment for problems and opportunities.

The first four steps in this sequence are the problem identification stage, and the next four are the problem solution stage of decision making, as indicated in Exhibit 11.1. All eight steps normally appear in a manager's decision, although each step may not be a distinct element. Managers may know from experience exactly what to do in a situation, so one or more steps will be minimized. The following case illustrates how the rational approach is used to make a decision about a personnel problem.

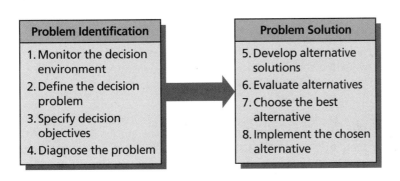

Problem Identification	Problem Solution
1. Monitor the decision environment 2. Define the decision problem 3. Specify decision objectives 4. Diagnose the problem	5. Develop alternative solutions 6. Evaluate alternatives 7. Choose the best alternative 8. Implement the chosen alternative

Exhibit 11.1
Steps in Rational Approach to Decision Making.

<u>**IN PRACTICE**</u> ◆ 11.1

Alberta Manufacturing

1. *Monitor the decision environment.*   It is Monday morning, and Joe DeFoe, one of Alberta's most skilled cutters, is absent again.
2. *Define the decision problem.*   This is the sixth consecutive Monday DeFoe has been absent. Company policy forbids unexcused absenteeism, and DeFoe has been warned about his excessive absenteeism on the last three occasions. A final warning is in order but can be delayed, if warranted.
3. *Specify decision objectives.*   DeFoe should attend work regularly and establish the production and quality levels of which he is capable. The time period for solving the problem is two weeks.
4. *Diagnose the problem.*   Discreet discussions with DeFoe's co-workers and information gleaned from DeFoe indicate that DeFoe has a drinking problem. He apparently uses Mondays to dry out from weekend benders. Discussion with other company sources confirms that DeFoe is a problem drinker.
5. *Develop alternative solutions.*   (1) Fire DeFoe. (2) Issue a final warning without comment. (3) Issue a warning and accuse DeFoe of being alcoholic to let him know you are aware of his problem. (4) Talk with DeFoe to see if he will discuss his drinking. If he admits he has a drinking problem, delay the final warning and suggest that he enroll in Alberta's new employee assistance program for helping with personal problems, including alcoholism. (5) Talk with DeFoe to see if he will discuss his drinking. If he does not admit he has a drinking problem, let him know that the next absence will cost him his job.
6. *Evaluate alternatives.*   The cost of training a replacement is the same for each alternative. Alternative 1 ignores cost and other criteria. Alternatives 2 and 3 do not adhere to company policy, which advocates counseling where appropriate. Alternative 4 is designed for the benefit of both DeFoe and the company. It might save a good employee if DeFoe is willing to seek assistance. Alternative 5 is primarily for the benefit of the company. A final warning might provide some initiative for DeFoe to admit he has a drinking problem. If so, dismissal might be avoided, but further absences will no longer be tolerated.
7. *Choose the best alternative.*   DeFoe does not admit that he has a drinking problem. Choose alternative 5.
8. *Implement the chosen alternative.*   Write up the case and issue the final warning.[8]

In the preceding case, issuing the final warning to Joe DeFoe was a programmable decision. The standard of expected behavior was clearly defined, information on the frequency and cause of DeFoe's absence was readily available, and acceptable alternatives and procedures were described. The rational procedure works best in such cases, when the decision maker has sufficient time for an orderly, thoughtful process. Moreover, Alberta Manufacturing had mechanisms in place to implement the decision, once made.

When decisions are nonprogrammed, ill defined, and piling on top of one another, the individual manager should still try to use the steps in the rational approach, but he or she often will have to take short cuts by relying on intuition and experience. Deviations from the rational approach are explained by the bounded rationality perspective.

BOUNDED RATIONALITY PERSPECTIVE

The point of the rational approach is that managers should try to use systematic procedures to arrive at good decisions. When organizations are facing little competition and are dealing with well-understood issues, managers generally use rational procedures to make decisions.[9] Yet research into managerial decision making shows managers often are unable to follow an ideal procedure. In today's competitive environment, decisions often must be made very quickly. Time pressure, a large number of internal and external factors affecting a decision, and the ill-defined nature of many problems make systematic analysis virtually impossible. Managers have only so much time and mental capacity and, hence, cannot evaluate every goal, problem, and alternative. The attempt to be rational is bounded (limited) by the enormous complexity of many problems. There is a limit to how rational managers can be. For example, an executive in a hurry may have a choice of fifty ties on a rack but will take the first or second one that matches his suit. The executive doesn't carefully weigh all fifty alternatives because the short amount of time and the large number of plausible alternatives would be overwhelming. The manager simply selects the first tie that solves the problem and moves on to the next task.

Large organizational decisions are not only too complex to fully comprehend, but many other constraints impinge upon the decision maker, as illustrated in Exhibit 11.2. The circumstances are ambiguous, requiring social support, a shared perspective on what happens, and acceptance and agreement. For example, in a study of the decision making surrounding the Cuban missile crisis, the executive committee in the White House knew a problem existed but was unable to specify

Exhibit 11.2 Constraints and Trade-offs during Nonprogrammed Decision Making.

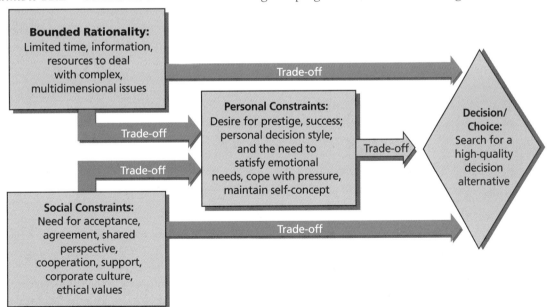

Source: Adapted from Irving L. Janis, *Crucial Decisions* (New York: Free Press, 1989); and A. L. George, *Presidential Decision Making in Foreign Policy: The Effective Use of Information and Advice* (Boulder, Colo.: Westview Press, 1980).

exact goals and objectives. The act of discussing the decision led to personal objections and finally to the discovery of desired objectives that helped clarify the desired course of action and possible consequences.[10] In addition, personal constraints—such as decision style, work pressure, desire for prestige, or simple feelings of insecurity—may constrain either the search for alternatives or the acceptability of an alternative. All of these factors constrain a perfectly rational approach that should lead to an obviously ideal choice.[11] Recent research on the importance of personal decision style is discussed in Book Mark 11.0. Even seemingly simple decisions, such as selecting a job upon graduation from college, can quickly become so complex that a bounded rationality approach is used. Graduating students have been known to search for a job until they have two or three acceptable job offers, at which point their search activity rapidly diminishes. Hundreds of firms may be available for interviews, and two or three job offers are far short of the maximum number that would be possible if students made the decision based on perfect rationality.

The bounded rationality perspective is often associated with intuitive decision processes. In **intuitive decision making**, experience and judgment rather than sequential logic or explicit reasoning are used to make decisions.[12] Intuition is not arbitrary or irrational because it is based on years of practice and hands-on experience, often stored in the subconscious.[13] Long experience with organizational issues provides managers with a gut feeling or hunch about which alternative will solve a problem. Indeed, many universities are offering courses in creativity and intuition so business students can learn to understand and rely on these processes.

In a situation of great complexity or ambiguity, previous experience and judgment are needed to incorporate intangible elements.[14] The intuitive processes may be associated with both the problem identification and problem solution stages of a decision. A study of manager problem finding showed that thirty of thirty-three problems were ambiguous and ill defined.[15] Bits and scraps of unrelated information from informal sources resulted in a pattern in the manager's mind. The manager could not "prove" a problem existed but knew intuitively that a certain area needed attention. A too simple view of a complex problem is often associated with decision failure,[16] and research shows managers are more likely to respond intuitively to a perceived threat to the organization than to an opportunity.[17]

Although IDS Financial Services was very profitable and grew rapidly in the early 1990s, a manager perceived a high turnover rate among the company's financial planners. He interpreted this as a weakness that could seriously threaten IDS's position in the increasingly competitive financial services industry. Other examples of problems that might be discovered through informal, intuitive processes are the possibility of impending legislation against the company, the need for a new product, customer dissatisfaction, and a need for reorganization by creating new departments.[18]

Intuitive processes are also used in the problem solution stage. A survey found that executives frequently made decisions without explicit reference to the impact on profits or to other measurable outcomes.[19] As we saw in Exhibit 11.2, many intangible factors—such as a person's concern about the support of other executives, fear of failure, and social attitudes—influence selection of the best alternative. These factors cannot be quantified in a systematic way, so intuition guided the choice of a solution. Managers may make a decision based upon what they sense to be right rather than upon what they can document with hard data.

A number of important decisions, some quite famous, have been based on hunch and intuition. One was film director George Lucas's choice of *Star Wars* as the

BOOKMARK
11.0

HAVE YOU READ ABOUT THIS?

The Dynamic Decisionmaker
by Michael J. Driver, Kenneth R. Brousseau, and Philip L. Hunsaker

The Dynamic Decisionmaker discusses the thought processes and decision styles managers use when making decisions. The authors develop a model based on two decision factors that combine into five decision styles.

Two Key Factors

The basic decision style model presented by the authors is based on two decision elements—the amount of information used in making a decision (called information use) and the number of alternatives considered (called focus). With respect to information use, managers may be maximizers or satisficers. The maximizer wants as much relevant information as possible before making a decision; the satisficer, in contrast, is a fast-action person who wants just enough information to get on with the decision.

Moreover, some decision makers are unifocused, which means they look at the problem with the idea of coming up with a single solution. Others are multifocused, wanting to develop a variety of options and related pros and cons before deciding.

Five Decision Styles

The underlying elements can appear in various combinations to form five decision making styles.

The **decisive style** is satisficing and unifocused. This style uses minimum information and perhaps a single alternative to solve a problem quickly. Attention quickly shifts to the next problem.

The **flexible style** is satisficing and multifocused. This style moves fast also but often changes focus, interpreting information to see multiple alternatives.

The **hierarchic style** is maximizing and unifocused. This style uses lots of information and analysis to create a detailed, specific solution to a problem. This style exerts control with emphasis on quality and perfection to reach the "best" solution.

The **integrative style** is maximizing and multifocused. Lots of information is collected but is used to develop many possible solutions. Emphasis is on creativity and exploration and on openness to new options.

The **systemic style** is the most complex of all. This style is both multifocused and unifocused and prefers maximum information while looking at different perspectives and alternative solutions. This style sees the big picture and handles complex decisions well.

Conclusion

Learning one's personal style and the style of co-workers will increase a manager's effectiveness as a leader and in interpersonal relationships. For example, a supervisor and employee may have a "style clash." A multifocused manager is seen by a unifocused subordinate as wishy-washy, and the unifocused subordinate is seen by the manager as having tunnel vision.

While the authors suggest there is no best style, people should adapt their style to the decision. Managers fail not because they make wrong decisions but because they use the wrong style for the situation—deciding too quickly and impulsively, gathering too much information, or postponing action too long.

The Dynamic Decisionmaker by Michael J. Driver, Kenneth R. Brousseau, and Phillip L. Hunsaker is published by Ballinger.

---

title of his film. Researchers who analyzed hard data warned him that the title would turn away crowds at the box office.[20] In another example, Ray Kroc felt that purchasing the McDonald name for $2.7 million was highway robbery, but he knew intuitively that he should pay whatever price was demanded, and he did.[21]

Remember that the bounded rationality perspective applies mostly to nonprogrammed decisions. The novel, unclear, complex aspects of nonprogrammed decisions mean hard data and logical procedures are not available. A study of executive decision making found that managers simply could not use the rational approach for nonprogrammed decisions, such as when to buy a CT scanner for an osteopathic hospital or whether a city had a need for and could reasonably adopt a data processing system.[22] In those cases, managers had limited time and resources, and some factors simply couldn't be measured and analyzed. Trying to quantify such information could cause mistakes because it may oversimplify decision criteria. When Michael Eisner was president of Paramount Pictures, he learned to rely on intuition for making nonprogrammed decisions. His decision approach was astonishingly successful at Paramount and, more recently, at Disney.

IN PRACTICE ◆ 11.2
Paramount Pictures Corporation

When Barry Diller and Michael Eisner went to the movies, it wasn't for entertainment. They were checking audience reaction on one of their new movies. Barry Diller was chairman and Michael Eisner was president of Paramount Pictures Corporation.

   Some of Paramount's successes under their leadership were *Indiana Jones and the Temple of Doom, Raiders of the Lost Ark, An Officer and a Gentleman, Trading Places, 48 Hours, Flashdance,* and *Terms of Endearment.* A major reason for the string of hits was the excellent choice of films. Paramount decision makers were attuned to the tastes of eighteen- to twenty-four-year olds, who count most. Paramount had also gotten into other ventures, such as selling its films to Showtime. And "Entertainment Tonight," Paramount's entertainment-news TV show, was also hugely successful.

   Why was Paramount so successful at selecting films? Diller and Eisner claim they relied on gut reaction when picking films or other projects. Their tastes were shaped while they were executives at ABC, where they were responsible for the "Movie of the Week." Their experience paid off. Columbia Pictures, then a division of Coca-Cola, used market research to identify what people want to see. "We don't use Coca-Cola type research. We think it's junk," said Eisner. He thinks about what he likes, not what the public likes. "If I ask Miss Middle America if she wants to see a movie about religion, she'll say yes. If I say, 'Do you want to see a movie about sex,' she'll say no. But she'll be lying."

   Experience is so important, Eisner said, because "you tend not to make the same mistakes twice." Eisner and Diller made their share of mistakes, and they frequently disagreed about the right path. They hammered out the best decision and combined their intuition through intense arguments. One bomb was *The Keep,* which ran for only three weeks. *Flashdance* went the other way because no one realized it would be a smash. The experience of both successes and failures helped Diller and Eisner develop an intuition for projects the public wanted.

   Eisner's remarkable success led to his selection as president of Disney. After he took over, Disney's studio, Touchstone, moved from last place to being a top studio in the industry. Eisner's intuitive decision skills have made two studios successful, an incredible record in an unpredictable business.[23]

Organizational Decision Making

Organizations are composed of managers who make decisions using both rational and intuitive processes; but organization-level decisions are not usually made by a single manager. Many organizational decisions involve several managers. Problem identification and problem solution involve many departments, multiple viewpoints, and even other organizations, which are beyond the scope of an individual manager.

The processes by which decisions are made in organizations are influenced by a number of factors, particularly the organization's own internal structures as well as the degree of stability or instability of the external environment.[24] Research into organization-level decision making has identified four types of organizational decision-making processes: the management science approach, the Carnegie model, the incremental decision process model, and the garbage can model.

MANAGEMENT SCIENCE APPROACH

The **management science approach** to organizational decision making is the analog to the rational approach by individual managers. Management science came into being during World War II.[25] At that time, mathematical and statistical techniques were applied to urgent, large-scale military problems that were beyond the ability of individual decision makers. Mathematicians, physicists, and operations researchers used systems analysis to develop artillery trajectories, antisubmarine strategies, and bombing strategies such as salvoing (discharging multiple shells simultaneously). Consider the problem of a battleship trying to sink an enemy ship several miles away. The calculation for aiming the battleship's guns should consider distance, wind speed, shell size, speed and direction of both ships, pitch and roll of the firing ship, and curvature of the earth. Methods for performing such calculations using trial and error and intuition are not accurate, take far too long, and may never achieve success.

This is where management science came in. Analysts were able to identify the relevant variables involved in aiming a ship's guns and could model them with the use of mathematical equations. Distance, speed, pitch, roll, shell size, and so on could be calculated and entered into the equations. The answer was immediate, and the guns could begin firing. Factors such as pitch and roll were soon measured mechanically and fed directly into the targeting mechanism. Today, the human element is completely removed from the targeting process. Radar picks up the target, and the entire sequence is computed automatically.

Management science yielded astonishing success for many military problems. This approach to decision making diffused into corporations and business schools, where techniques were studied and elaborated. Today, many corporations have assigned departments to use these techniques. The computer department develops quantitative data for analysis. Operations research departments use mathematical models to quantify relevant variables and develop a quantitative representation of alternative solutions and the probability of each one solving the problem. These departments also use such devices as linear programming, Bayesian statistics, PERT charts, and computer simulations.

Management science is an excellent device for organizational decision making when problems are analyzable and when the variables can be identified and measured. Mathematical models can contain a thousand or more variables, each one relevant in some way to the ultimate outcome. Management science techniques have been used to correctly solve problems as diverse as finding the right spot for a church camp, test marketing the first of a new family of products, drilling for oil, and radically altering the distribution of telecommunications services.[26] Other problems amenable to management science techniques are the scheduling of airline employees, telephone operators, and turnpike toll collectors.[27] As illustrated in the following case, management science techniques can also be applied to a situation as complicated as scheduling ambulance technicians.

IN PRACTICE ◆ 11.3

Urgences Santé

Urgences Santé, the public agency responsible for coordinating ambulance service in the Montréal area, schedules vehicle time and working hours for approximately 80 ambulances and 700 technicians. The agency does not own any of the vehicles or directly employ any technicians, but rents these services from 15 private companies. Urgences Santé wanted to optimize the schedule to keep costs as low as possible, realizing that, with ambulance rental fees at $55 an hour, a daily excess of 10 hours represents more than $200,000 a year.

Two types of calls require ambulance service—emergency calls from the public, which occur randomly throughout the day and require immediate attention, and calls from hospitals, which are concentrated in specific time periods and are generally not urgent. In addition, demand for ambulance service is generally higher in the winter, but with more emergency calls on weekends during the summer months. Besides meeting shifting demand, a number of other constraints governed the design of a new schedule, for example, the fair distribution of work hours among the 15 service companies; the provisions of the union contract; the number of ambulances available; and the quality and consistency of work schedules for technicians.

Urgences Santé applied mathematical formulations and techniques to first build workday schedules for each type of day (weekday or weekend) for each season, then equitably assign workdays to the 15 service companies, and finally to build individual schedules for the 700 service technicians. The agency is able to create at least 85 percent of the individual schedules automatically. Implementing the new system has had two positive effects. First, Urgences Santé was able to meet ambulance demand while cutting rental hours per week by up to 110 hours, thus saving approximately $250,000 a year. Second, the quality of the ambulance technicians' schedules has been vastly improved. This has led to an increase in the number of full-time rather than part-time technicians and a decrease in turnover for the service companies. Impressed with these results, Urgences Santé continues to use management science techniques to adapt to new demands and shifts in operational methods.[28]

Management science can accurately and quickly solve problems that have too many explicit variables for human processing. This system is at its best when applied to problems that are analyzable, are measurable, and can be structured in a logical way.

Management science has also produced many failures.[29] Part of the reason, as discussed in Chapter 9, is that quantitative data are not rich. Informal cues that indicate the existence of problems have to be sensed on a more personal basis by managers.[30] The most sophisticated mathematical analyses are of no value if the important factors cannot be quantified and included in the model. Such things as competitor reactions, consumer "tastes," and product "warmth" are qualitative dimensions. In these situations, the role of management science is to supplement manager decision making. Quantitative results can be given to managers for discussion and interpretation along with their informal opinions, judgment, and intuition. The final decision can include qualitative factors as well as quantitative calculations.

CARNEGIE MODEL

The **Carnegie model** of organizational decision making is based upon the work of Richard Cyert, James March, and Herbert Simon, who were all associated with Carnegie-Mellon University.[31] Their research helped formulate the bounded rationality approach to individual decision making as well as provide new insights about organization decisions. Until their work, research in economics assumed that business firms made decisions as a single entity, as if all relevant information were funneled to the top decision maker for a choice. Research by the Carnegie group indicated that organization-level decisions involved many managers and that a final choice was based on a coalition among those managers. A **coalition** is an alliance among several managers who agree about organizational goals and problem priorities.[32] It could include managers from line departments, staff specialists, and even external groups, such as powerful customers, bankers, or union representatives.

Management coalitions are needed during decision making for two reasons. First, organizational goals are often ambiguous, and operative goals of departments are often inconsistent. When goals are ambiguous and inconsistent, managers disagree about problem priorities. They must bargain about problems and build a coalition around the question of which problems to solve. For example, months of discussion, bargaining, and planning took place before Chrysler decided not to abandon small-car production and began working on the new Neon.[33]

The second reason for coalitions is that individual managers intend to be rational but function with human cognitive limitations and other constraints, as described earlier. Managers do not have the time, resources, or mental capacity to identify all dimensions and to process all information relevant to a decision. These limitations lead to coalition-building behavior. Managers talk to each other and exchange points of view to gather information and reduce ambiguity. People who have relevant information or a stake in a decision outcome are consulted. Building a coalition will lead to a decision that is supported by interested parties.

The process of coalition formation has several implications for organizational decision behavior. First, as discussed in Chapter 2 on goals, decisions are made to satisfice rather than to optimize problem solutions. The coalition will accept a solution that is perceived as satisfactory to all coalition members. Second, managers are concerned with immediate problems and short-run solutions. They engage in what Cyert and March called problemistic search.[34] **Problemistic search** means managers look around in the immediate environment for a solution to quickly resolve a problem. Managers don't expect a perfect solution when the situation is ill defined and conflict-laden. This contrasts with the management science approach, which assumes that analysis can uncover every reasonable alternative. The Carnegie model says search behavior is just sufficient to produce a satisfactory solution and that managers typically adopt the first satisfactory solution that emerges. Third, discussion and bargaining are especially important in the problem identification stage of decision making. Unless coalition members perceive a problem, action will not be taken. The decision process described in the Carnegie model is summarized in Exhibit 11.3.

The Carnegie model points out that building agreement through a managerial coalition is a major part of organizational decision making. This is especially true at upper management levels. Discussion and bargaining are time-consuming, so search procedures are usually simple and the selected alternative satisfices rather than optimizes problem solution. When problems are programmed—are clear and

Exhibit 11.3   Choice Processes in the Carnegie Model.

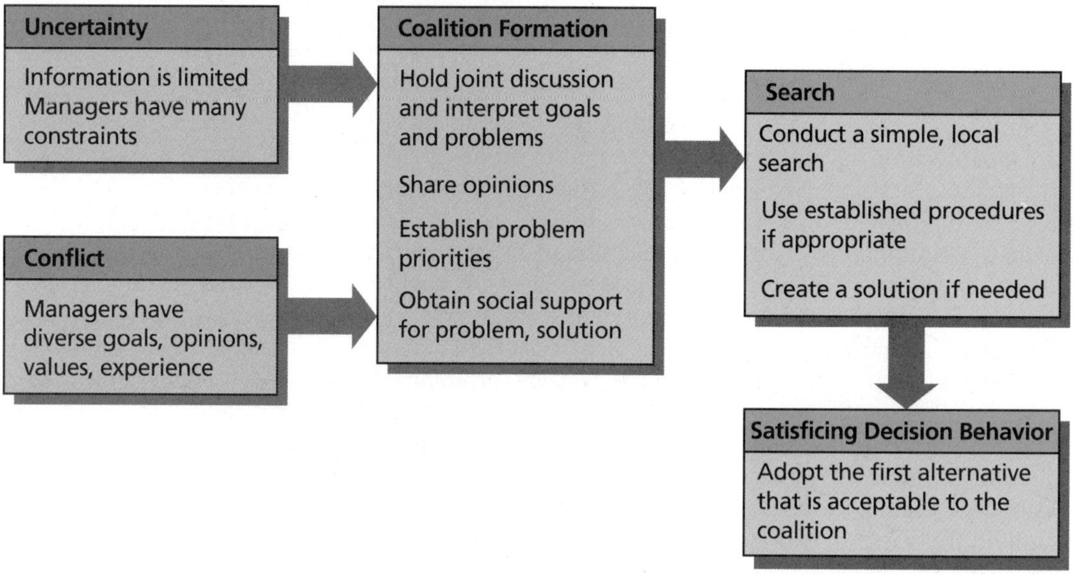

Uncertainty

Information is limited
Managers have many
constraints

Conflict

Managers have
diverse goals, opinions,
values, experience

Coalition Formation

Hold joint discussion
and interpret goals
and problems

Share opinions

Establish problem
priorities

Obtain social support
for problem, solution

Search

Conduct a simple, local
search

Use established procedures
if appropriate

Create a solution if needed

Satisficing Decision Behavior

Adopt the first alternative
that is acceptable to the
coalition

have been seen before—the organization will rely on previous procedures and routines. Rules and procedures prevent the need for renewed coalition formation and political bargaining. Nonprogrammed decisions, however, require bargaining and conflict resolution.

One of the best and most visible coalition builders of recent years was former President George Bush, who would seek a broad-based coalition at the start of an important decision process. During the decision process regarding the Persian Gulf War, President Bush kept up a barrage of personal calls and visits to world leaders to gain agreement for his vision of forcing Saddam Hussein from Kuwait and for shaping a "new world order."[35]

When senior managers are unable to build a coalition around goals and problem priorities, the results can be a disaster, as illustrated by the case of Arp Instruments.

IN PRACTICE ◆ 11.4
Arp Instruments, Inc.

When Arp Instruments was founded by Alan Pearlman in the late 1960s, it quickly became the premier manufacturer of musical synthesizers (instruments that produce electronic music). Arp provided synthesizers to the stars, including Stevie Wonder, Paul McCartney, Elton John, The Bee Gees, Kiss, and The Who. By the mid-1970s, Arp had 40 percent of the market, ahead of Moog synthesizers, and enjoyed preeminence in the marketplace. By the early 1980s, Arp Instruments was dead, the victim of management disagreement and infighting.

Arp was shaped by three individuals: Pearlman, chairman of the board; Louis G. Pollock, legal counsel and chairman of the executive committee; and David Friend, president. Each individual brought distinct goals and backgrounds to the company. Pearlman was concerned with new technology and planning, Pollock was an entrepreneur who pushed new products, and Friend was a technical and musical whiz. The egos and goals of the three frequently clashed. The men disagreed about which products to invest in, whether the disco market would change the demand for synthesizers, and expense budgets.

As time passed, the division among the three intensified. Each man pursued his own vision and would align himself with whoever would support his own ideas. Pearlman became increasingly alienated from his own company. The three managers kept one another in the dark about their own plans.

The problem crystallized when Arp embarked on the development of a guitar synthesizer despite an uncertain demand and having only skills accumulated on keyboard synthesizers. Friend pushed the idea, and Pearlman couldn't stop it, having lost his voice at Arp. The infighting continued, and the guitar synthesizer, called the Avatar, was marketed. The Avatar was an excellent product, but it flopped for lack of demand.

The disagreements among executives led to bitter compromises and more product failures. Lower-level managers and employees experienced chaos and conflicting signals. The company could not focus itself sufficiently to adapt to the changing music world. The lack of agreement translated into lousy management. A management consultant who also served as a director knew where the blame should rest: "It's a sin. It's a tragedy to see a beautiful little company, and two hundred jobs, go under because of bad management. . . . All three of them—honest to God—they should physically have to go to jail and serve six months for screwing up a beautiful thing like that."[36]

The point of the Carnegie model and the Arp case is that coalitions are needed for strong performance. When top managers perceive a problem or want to make a major decision, they need to reach agreement with other managers to support the decision.[37]

INCREMENTAL DECISION PROCESS MODEL

Henry Mintzberg and his associates at McGill University in Montreal approached organizational decision making from a different perspective. They identified twenty-five decisions made in organizations and traced the events associated with these decisions from beginning to end.[38] Their research identified each step in the decision sequence. This approach to decision making, called the **incremental decision process model**, places less emphasis on the political and social factors described in the Carnegie model, but tells more about the structured sequence of activities undertaken from the discovery of a problem to its solution.[39]

Sample decisions in Mintzberg's research included choosing which jet aircraft to acquire for a regional airline, developing a new supper club, developing a new container terminal in a harbor, identifying a new market for a deodorant, installing a controversial new medical treatment in a hospital, and firing a star announcer.[40] The scope and importance of these decisions are revealed in the length of time taken to complete them. Most of these decisions took more than a year, and one-third of them took more than two years. Most of these decisions were nonprogrammed and required custom-designed solutions.

One discovery from this research is that major organization choices are usually a series of small choices that combine to produce the major decision. Thus, many organizational decisions are a series of nibbles rather than a big bite. Organizations move through several decision points and may hit barriers along the way. Mintzberg called these barriers *decision interrupts*. An interrupt may mean an organization has to cycle back through a previous decision and try something new. Decision loops or cycles are one way the organization learns which alternatives will work. The ultimate solution may be very different from what was initially anticipated.

The pattern of decision stages discovered by Mintzberg and his associates is shown in Exhibit 11.4. Each box indicates a possible step in the decision sequence. The steps take place in three major decision phases: identification, development, and selection.

Identification Phase   The identification phase begins with *recognition*. Recognition means one or more managers become aware of a problem and the need to make a decision. Recognition is usually stimulated by a problem or an opportunity. A problem exists when elements in the external environment change or when internal performance is perceived to be below standard. In the case of firing a radio announcer, comments about the announcer came from listeners, other announcers, and advertisers. Managers interpreted these cues until a pattern emerged that indicated a problem had to be dealt with.

The second step is *diagnosis,* which is where more information is gathered if needed to define the problem situation. Diagnosis may be systematic or informal, depending upon the severity of the problem. Severe problems do not have time for extensive diagnosis; the response must be immediate. Mild problems are usually diagnosed in a more systematic manner.

Development Phase   The development phase is when a solution is shaped to solve the problem defined in the identification phase. The development of a solution takes one of two directions. First, *search* procedures may be used to seek out alternatives within the organization's repertoire of solutions. For example, in the case of firing a star announcer, managers asked what the radio station had done the last time an announcer had to be let go. To conduct the search, organization participants may look into their own memories, talk to other managers, or examine the formal procedures of the organization.

The second direction of development is to *design* a custom solution. This happens when the problem is novel so that previous experience has no value. Mintzberg found that in these cases, key decision makers have only a vague idea of the ideal solution. Gradually, through a trial-and-error process, a custom-designed alternative will emerge. Development of the solution is a groping, incremental procedure, building a solution brick by brick.

Selection Phase   The selection phase is when the solution is chosen. This phase is not always a matter of making a clear choice among alternatives. In the case of custom-made solutions, selection is more an evaluation of the single alternative that seems feasible.

Evaluation and choice may be accomplished in three ways. The *judgment* form of selection is used when a final choice falls upon a single decision maker, and the choice involves judgment based upon experience. In *analysis,* alternatives are evaluated on a more systematic basis, such as with management science techniques. Mintzberg found that most decisions did not involve systematic analysis and evaluation of alternatives. *Bargaining* occurs when selection involves a group of decision makers. Each decision maker may have a different stake in the outcome, so conflict

Exhibit 11.4 The Incremental Decision Process Model.

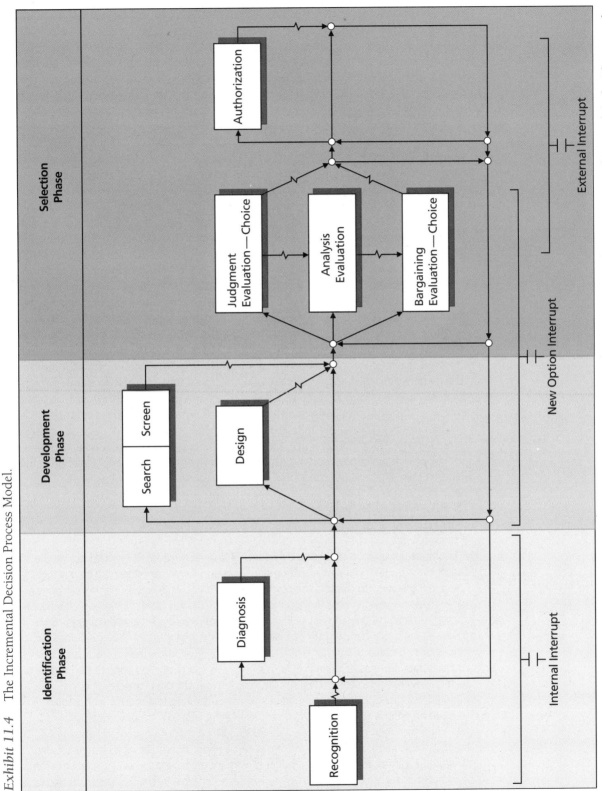

Source: Adapted and reprinted from "The Structure of Unstructured Decision Processes" by Henry Mintzberg, Duru Raisinghani, and André Théorêt, published in *Administrative Science Quarterly* 21, no. 2 (1976), 266, by permission of *The Administrative Science Quarterly*. Copyright © 1976 Cornell University.

emerges. Discussion and bargaining occur until a coalition is formed, as in the Carnegie model described earlier.

When a decision is formally accepted by the organization, *authorization* takes place. The decision may be passed up the hierarchy to the responsible hierarchical level. Authorization is often routine because the expertise and knowledge rest with the lower decision makers who identified the problem and developed the solution. A few decisions are rejected because of implications not anticipated by lower-level managers.

Dynamic Factors   The lower part of the chart in Exhibit 11.4 shows lines running back toward the beginning of the decision process. These lines represent loops or cycles that take place in the decision process. Organizational decisions do not follow an orderly progression from recognition through authorization. Minor problems arise that force a loop back to an earlier stage. These are decision interrupts. If a custom-designed solution is perceived as unsatisfactory, the organization may have to go back to the very beginning and reconsider whether the problem is truly worth solving. Feedback loops can be caused by problems of timing, politics, disagreement among managers, inability to identify a feasible solution, turnover of managers, or the sudden appearance of a new alternative. For example, when a small Canadian airline made the decision to acquire jet aircraft, the board authorized the decision, but shortly after, a new chief executive was brought in and he canceled the contract, recycling the decision back to the identification phase. He accepted the diagnosis of the problem, but insisted upon a new search for alternatives. Then a foreign airline went out of business and two used aircraft became available at a bargain price. This presented an unexpected option, and the chief executive used his own judgment to authorize the purchase of the aircraft.[41]

Since most decisions take place over an extended period of time, circumstances change. Decision making is a dynamic process that may require a number of cycles before a problem is solved. An example of the incremental process and cycling that can take place is illustrated in Gillette's decision to create a new razor.

IN PRACTICE ◆ 11.5
Gillette Company

A bright idea developed at Gillette Company's British research facility finally became the Sensor razor thirteen years later, after more twists and turns than shaving a craggy face. The bright idea was to create a thinner razor blade that would make Gillette's cartridges easier to clean (recognition). The technical development cost for the idea ran $200 million.

The technical demands of building a razor with thin blades and floating parts to follow a man's face had several blind alleys. Engineers first tried to find established techniques (search, screen), but none fit the bill. One idea called for the blades to sit on tiny rubber tubes, perhaps filled with fluid, but that was too costly and complicated to manufacture (new option interrupt). Eventually, a prototype was built (design), and five hundred men liked it. The next problem was manufacturing (diagnosis), which again required an entirely new process to laser weld each blade to a support (design).

Top management gave the go-ahead to develop manufacturing equipment (judgment, authorization). Then a conflict broke out among two groups of Gillette executives. One group wanted to orient the product toward inexpensive disposables, while the other group fought for a heavier, more permanent razor (internal interrupt). Then Gillette was threatened with an outside takeover, reducing resources allocated to the project (external interrupt). A new executive vice president made the choice to deemphasize disposables (judgment). A nine-member task force was then authorized to live with the razor for fifteen months to get it to market (authorization). Another $100 million was authorized for advertising and marketing promotions.

The razor has been a smashing success, smoothly sliding off shelves, and Gillette expects to recover its huge investment in record time. Now Gillette is starting the process over again, experimenting with a curved blade and perhaps a new ceramic blade, moving ahead in increments until the new razors are ready, probably not before the turn of the century.[42]

At Gillette, the identification phase occurred because executives were aware of the need for a new razor and became aware of the idea for floating, thin blades. The development phase was characterized by the trial-and-error custom design leading to the Sensor. During the selection phase, certain approaches were found unacceptable, causing Gillette to recycle back, redesign the razor, and reappraise whether it should be a permanent or disposable razor. Advancing once again to the selection phase, the Sensor passed the judgment of executives, and manufacturing and marketing budgets were quickly authorized. This decision took thirteen years, reaching completion in January 1990.

INTEGRATING THE INCREMENTAL PROCESS AND CARNEGIE MODELS

At the beginning of this chapter, decision making was defined as occurring in two stages: problem identification and problem solution. The Carnegie description of coalition building is especially relevant for the problem identification stage. When issues are ambiguous, or if managers disagree about problem severity, discussion, negotiation, and coalition building are needed. Once agreement is reached about the problem to be tackled, the organization can move toward a solution.

The incremental process model tends to emphasize the steps used to reach a solution. After managers agree upon a problem, the step-by-step process is a way of trying various solutions to see what will work. When problem solution is unclear, a trial-and-error solution may be designed.

The two models do not disagree with one another. They describe how organizations make decisions when either problem identification or solution is uncertain. The application of these two models to the stages in the decision process is illustrated in Exhibit 11.5. When both parts of the decision process are highly uncertain simultaneously, the organization is in an extremely difficult position. Decision processes in that situation may be a combination of Carnegie and incremental process models, and this combination may evolve into a situation described in the garbage can model.

GARBAGE CAN MODEL

The **garbage can model** is one of the most recent and interesting descriptions of organizational decision processes. It is not directly comparable to the earlier models, because the garbage can model deals with the pattern or flow of multiple decisions within organizations, while the incremental and Carnegie models focus upon how a

Exhibit 11.5   Organizational Decision Process When Either Problem Identification or Problem Solution Is Uncertain.

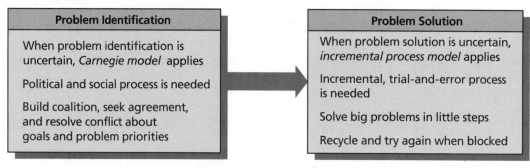

Problem Identification	Problem Solution
When problem identification is uncertain, *Carnegie model* applies	When problem solution is uncertain, *incremental process model* applies
Political and social process is needed	Incremental, trial-and-error process is needed
Build coalition, seek agreement, and resolve conflict about goals and problem priorities	Solve big problems in little steps
	Recycle and try again when blocked

single decision is made. The garbage can model helps you think of the whole organization and the frequent decisions being made by managers throughout.

Organized Anarchy   The garbage can model was developed to explain the pattern of decision making in organizations that experience extremely high uncertainty. Michael Cohen, James March, and Johan Olsen, the originators of the model, called the highly uncertain conditions an **organized anarchy**, which is an extremely organic organization.[43] Organized anarchies do not rely on the normal vertical hierarchy of authority and bureaucratic decision rules. They are caused by three characteristics:

1. *Problematic preferences.*   Goals, problems, alternatives, and solutions are ill defined. Ambiguity characterizes each step of a decision process.
2. *Unclear, poorly understood technology.*   Cause-and-effect relationships within the organization are difficult to identify. An explicit data base that applies to decisions is not available.
3. *Turnover.*   Organizational positions experience turnover of participants. In addition, employees are busy and have only limited time to allocate to any one problem or decision. Participation in any given decision will be fluid and limited.

The organized anarchy describes organizations characterized by rapid change and a collegial, nonbureaucratic environment. No organization fits this extremely organic circumstance all the time. Many organizations will occasionally find themselves in positions of making decisions under unclear, problematic circumstances. The garbage can model is useful for understanding the pattern of these decisions.

Streams of Events   The unique characteristic of the garbage can model is that the decision process is not seen as a sequence of steps that begins with a problem and ends with a solution. Indeed, problem identification and problem solution may not be connected to each other. An idea may be proposed as a solution when no problem is specified. A problem may exist and never generate a solution. Decisions are the outcome of independent streams of events within the organization. The four streams relevant to organizational decision making are as follows:

1. *Problems.*   Problems are points of dissatisfaction with current activities and performance. They represent a gap between desired performance and current activ-

ities. Problems are perceived to require attention. However, they are distinct from solutions and choices. A problem may lead to a proposed solution or it may not. Problems may not be solved when solutions are adopted.

2. *Potential solutions.* A solution is an idea somebody proposes for adoption. Such ideas form a flow of alternative solutions through the organization. Ideas may be brought into the organization by new personnel or may be invented by existing personnel. Participants may simply be attracted to certain ideas and push them as logical choices regardless of problems. Attraction to an idea may cause an employee to look for a problem to which the idea can be attached and, hence, justified. The point is that solutions exist independent of problems.

3. *Participants.* Organization participants are employees who come and go throughout the organization. People are hired, reassigned, and fired. Participants vary widely in their ideas, perception of problems, experience, values, and training. The problems and solutions recognized by one manager will differ from those recognized by another manager.

4. *Choice opportunities.* Choice opportunities are occasions when an organization usually makes a decision. They occur when contracts are signed, people are hired, or a new product is authorized. They also occur when the right mix of participants, solutions, and problems exists. Thus, a manager who happened to learn of a good idea may suddenly become aware of a problem to which it applies and, hence, can provide the organization with a choice opportunity. Match-ups of problems and solutions often result in decisions.

With the concept of four streams, the overall pattern of organizational decision making takes on a random quality. Problems, solutions, participants, and choices all flow through the organization. In one sense, the organization is a large garbage can in which these streams are being stirred, as illustrated in Exhibit 11.6. When a problem, solution, and participant happen to connect at one point, a decision may be made and the problem may be solved; but if the solution does not fit the problem, the problem may not be solved. Thus, when viewing the organization as a whole and considering its high level of uncertainty, one sees problems arise that are not solved and solutions tried that do not work. Organization decisions are disorderly and not the result of a logical, step-by-step sequence. Events may be so ill defined and complex that decisions, problems, and solutions act as independent events. When they connect, some problems are solved, but many are not.[44]

Consequences   Four consequences of the garbage can decision process for organizational decision making are as follows:

1. *Solutions may be proposed even when problems do not exist.* An employee may be sold on an idea and may try to sell it to the rest of the organization. An example was the adoption of computers by many organizations during the 1970s. The computer was an exciting solution and was pushed by both computer manufacturers and systems analysts within organizations. The computer did not solve any problems in those initial applications. Indeed, some computers caused more problems than they solved.

2. *Choices are made without solving problems.* A choice such as creating a new department may be made with the intention of solving a problem; but, under conditions of high uncertainty, the choice may be incorrect. Moreover, many choices just seem to happen. People decide to quit, the organization's budget is

Exhibit 11.6
Illustration of
Independent
Streams of
Events in the
Garbage Can
Model of Deci-
sion Making.

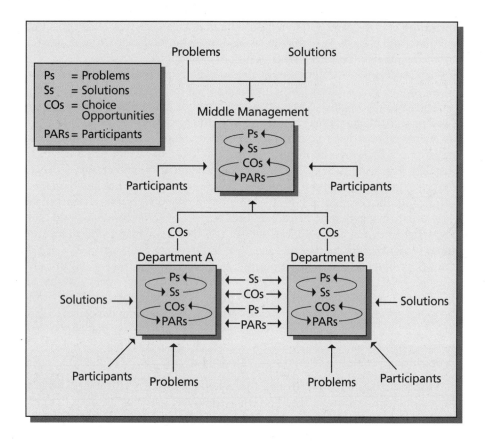

cut, or a new policy bulletin is issued. These choices may be oriented toward problems but do not necessarily solve them.

3. *Problems may persist without being solved.* Organization participants get used to certain problems and give up trying to solve them; or participants may not know how to solve certain problems because the technology is unclear. A university in Canada was placed on probation by the American Association of University Professors because a professor had been denied tenure without due process. The probation was a nagging annoyance that the administrators wanted to remove. Fifteen years later, the nontenured professor died. The probation continues because the university did not acquiesce to the demands of the heirs of the association to reevaluate the case. The university would like to solve the problem, but administrators are not sure how, and they do not have the resources to allocate to it. The probation problem persists without a solution.

4. *A few problems are solved.* The decision process does work in the aggregate. In computer simulation models of the garbage can model, important problems were often resolved. Solutions do connect with appropriate problems and participants so that a good choice is made. Of course, not all problems are resolved when choices are made, but the organization does move in the direction of problem reduction.

The effects of independent streams and the rather chaotic decision processes of the garbage can model can be seen in the production of the classic film *Casablanca*.

IN PRACTICE ◆ 11.6
Casablanca

The public flocked to see *Casablanca* when it opened in 1942. The film won Academy awards for best picture, best screenplay, and best director, and is recognized today by film historians and the public alike as a classic. But up until the filming of the final scene, no one involved in the production of the now-famous story even knew how it was going to end.

Everybody Comes to Rick's wasn't a very good play, but when it landed on Hal Wallis's desk at Warner Brothers, Wallis spotted some hot-from-the-headlines potential, purchased the rights, and changed the name to *Casablanca* to capitalize on the geographical mystique the story offered. A series of negotiations led to casting Humphrey Bogart as Rick, even though studio chief Jack Warner questioned his romantic appeal. The casting of Ingrid Bergman as Ilsa was largely by accident. A fluke had left an opening in her usually booked schedule. The screenplay still wasn't written.

Filming was chaotic. Writers made script changes and plot revisions daily. Actors were unsure of how to develop their characterizations, so they just did whatever seemed right at the time. For example, when Ingrid Bergman wanted to know which man should get most of her on-screen attention, she was told, "We don't know yet—just play it, well . . . in between." Scenes were often filmed blindly with no idea of how they were supposed to fit in the overall story. Amazingly, even when it came time to shoot the climactic final scene, no one involved in the production seemed to know who would "get the girl"; a legend still persists that two versions were written. During filming, Bogart disagreed with director Michael Curtiz's view that Rick should kiss Ilsa good-bye, and Hal Wallis was summoned to mediate. Since the cast received their scripts only hours before filming began, they couldn't remember their lines, causing continual delays.

Some industry analysts predicted disaster, but the haphazard process worked. Ingrid Bergman plays it "in between" just right. Bogart's characterization of Rick is perfect. The tale of love and glory and heartbreaking romance couldn't have been told better than it was in *Casablanca*. In addition, fortuitous circumstances outside the studio contributed to the film's commercial success. Just eighteen days before the premiere on Thanksgiving Day, 1942, the Allies invaded North Africa and fought the Battle of Casablanca. Then, when the film opened nationwide, President Franklin D. Roosevelt and Prime Minister Winston Churchill presided over the Casablanca Conference, a historical coincidence that was clearly a boon to the film, helping to push its initial gross to $3.7 million.[45]

The production of *Casablanca* was not a rational process that started with a clear problem and ended with a logical solution. Many events occured by chance and were intertwined, which characterizes the garbage can model. Everyone from the director to the actors continuously added to the stream of new ideas to the story. Some solutions were connected to emerging problems: the original script arrived just when Hal Wallis was looking for topical stories; and Bergman was surprisingly available to be cast in the role of Ilsa. The actors (participants) daily made personal choices regarding characterization that proved to be perfect for the story line. Other events that contributed to *Casablanca's* success were not even connected to the film—for example, the invasion of North Africa only eighteen days before the premiere. Overall, the production of *Casablanca* had a random, chancy flavor that is characteristic of the garbage can model. As evidenced by the film's huge success and continuing popularity after more than fifty years, the random, garbage can decision process did not hurt the film or the studio.

Contingency Decision-Making Framework

This chapter has covered several approaches to organizational decision making, including management science, the Carnegie model, the incremental decision process model, and the garbage can model. It has also discussed rational and intuitive decision processes used by individual managers. Each decision approach is a relatively accurate description of the actual decision process, yet all differ from each other. Management science, for example, reflects a different set of decision assumptions and procedures than does the garbage can model.

One reason for having different approaches is that they appear in different organizational situations. The use of an approach is contingent on the organization setting. Two characteristics of organizations that determine the use of decision approaches are (1) goal consensus and (2) technical knowledge about the means to achieve those goals.[46] Analyzing organizations along these two dimensions suggests which approach will be used to make decisions.

GOAL CONSENSUS

Goal consensus refers to the agreement among managers about which organizational goals and outcomes to pursue. This variable ranges from complete agreement to complete disagreement. When managers agree, the goals of the organization are clear and so are standards of performance. When managers disagree, organization direction and performance expectations are in dispute. One example of goal uncertainty occurred among cabinet members and presidential advisors during the Cuban missile crisis. Participants fought intensely over what goals should be pursued.[47] Another example of goal uncertainty occurred within the Penn Central Railroad after it went bankrupt. Some managers wanted to adopt the goal of becoming more efficient and profitable as a railroad. Other managers wanted to diversify into other businesses. Eventually, a strong coalition formed in favor of diversification, and that goal was adopted.

Goal consensus tends to be low when organizations are differentiated, as described in Chapter 3. Recall that uncertain environments cause organizational departments to differentiate from one another in goals and attitudes to specialize in specific environmental sectors. This differentiation leads to disagreement and conflict about organizational goals. When differentiation among departments or divisions is high, managers must make a special effort to build coalitions during decision making.

Goal consensus is especially important for the problem identification stage of decision making. When goals are clear and agreed upon, they provide clear standards and expectations for performance. When goals are not agreed upon, problem identification is uncertain and management attention must be focused on gaining agreement about goals and problem priorities.

TECHNICAL KNOWLEDGE

Technical knowledge refers to understanding and agreement about how to reach organizational goals. This variable can range from complete agreement and certainty to complete disagreement and uncertainty about cause-effect relationships leading to goal attainment. An example of low technical knowledge was reflected in market strategies at 7-Up. The goal was clear and agreed upon—increase market share from 6 percent to 7 percent, but the means for achieving this increase in market share were not known or agreed upon. A few managers wanted to use discount pricing in supermarkets. Other managers believed they should increase the number of soda fountain outlets in restaurants and fast-food chains. A few other managers insisted that the best approach was to increase advertising through radio and television. Managers did not know what would cause an increase in market share. Eventually, the advertising judgment prevailed at 7-Up, but it did not work very well. The failure of its decision reflected 7-Up's low technical knowledge about how to achieve its goal.

Technical knowledge is especially important to the problem-solution stage of decision making. When means are well understood, the appropriate alternatives can be identified and calculated with some degree of certainty. When means are poorly understood, potential solutions are ill defined and uncertain. Intuition, judgment, and trial and error become the basis for decisions.

CONTINGENCY FRAMEWORK

The **contingency decision-making framework** brings together the two organizational dimensions of goal consensus and technical knowledge. Exhibit 11.7 shows how these two variables influence the decision situation. Goals and technical knowledge determine the extent to which problem identification and solution stages are uncertain. Depending on the situation, an organization may have to focus on gaining goal consensus, increasing technical knowledge, or both. Low uncertainty means that rational, analytical procedures can be used. High uncertainty leads to greater use of judgment, bargaining, and other less systematic procedures.

Exhibit 11.8 describes the contingency decision framework. Each cell represents an organizational situation that is appropriate for the decision making approaches described in this chapter.

Cell 1   In cell 1 of Exhibit 11.8, rational decision procedures are used because goals are agreed upon and cause-effect relationships are well understood. Decisions can be made in a computational manner. Alternatives can be identified and the best solution adopted through analysis and calculations. The rational models described earlier in this chapter, both for individuals and for the organization, are appropriate when goals and technical means are well defined. When problems occur, a logical process can be used to decide upon the solutions.

Cell 2   In cell 2, bargaining and compromise are used to reach consensus about goals and priorities. Diverse opinions are present in this situation. Achieving one goal would mean the exclusion of another goal. The priorities given to respective goals are decided through discussion, debate, and coalition building.

Exhibit 11.7
Contingency
Decision
Situations.

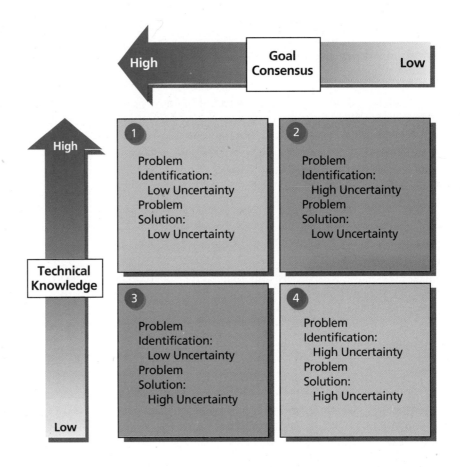

Managers in this situation should use broad participation to achieve goal consensus in the decision process. Opinions should be surfaced and discussed until compromise is reached. The organization will not otherwise move forward as an integrated unit. In the case of Penn Central Railroad, the diversification strategy was eventually adopted, but only after much bargaining. During the Cuban missile crisis, debate finally led to the goal of establishing a blockade to prevent Soviet ships from reaching Cuba. At Gillette, much debate surrounded the struggle between executives favoring disposable versus permanent Sensor razors, eventually consolidating toward the permanent.

The Carnegie model applies when there is dissension about organizational goals. When groups within the organization disagree, or when the organization is in conflict with constituencies (government regulators, suppliers, unions), bargaining and negotiation are required. The bargaining strategy is especially relevant to the problem identification stage of the decision process. Once bargaining and negotiation are completed, the organization will have support for one direction.

Cell 3   In a cell 3 situation, goals and standards of performance are certain, but alternative technical solutions are vague and uncertain. Techniques to solve a problem are ill defined and poorly understood. When an individual manager faces this situation, intuition will be the decision guideline. The manager will rely on past experience and judgment to make a decision. Rational, analytical approaches are not

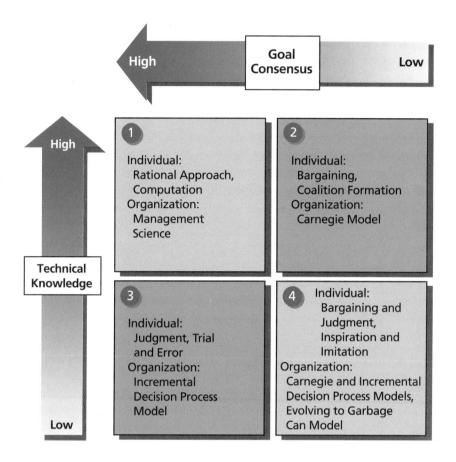

Exhibit 11.8
Contingency
Framework for
Using Decision
Models.

effective because the alternatives cannot be identified and calculated. Hard facts and accurate information are not available.

The incremental decision process model reflects trial and error on the part of the organization. Once a problem is identified, a sequence of small steps enables the organization to learn a solution. As new problems arise, the organization may recycle back to an earlier point and start over. Eventually, over a period of months or years, the organization will acquire sufficient experience to solve the problem in a satisfactory way. Solving the engineering and manufacturing problems for the Sensor razor, described earlier, is an example of a cell 3 situation. Gillette engineers had to use trial and error to develop an efficient manufacturing process.

The situation in cell 3, of senior managers agreeing about goals but not knowing how to achieve them, occurs frequently in business organizations. If managers use incremental decisions in such situations, they will eventually acquire the technical knowledge to accomplish goals and solve problems.

Cell 4   The situation in cell 4, characterized by low consensus and low technical knowledge, occurs infrequently but is difficult for decision making. An individual manager making a decision under this high level of uncertainty can employ techniques from both cell 2 and cell 3. The manager can attempt to build a coalition to establish goals and priorities, and use judgment or trial and error to solve problems. Additional techniques, such as inspiration and imitation, also may be required.

Inspiration refers to an innovative, creative solution that is not reached by logical means. **Imitation** means adopting a decision tried elsewhere in the hope that it will work in this situation.

For example, in one university, accounting department faculty were unhappy with their current circumstances but could not decide upon the direction the department should go. Some faculty members wanted a greater research orientation, while others wanted greater orientation toward business firms and accounting applications. The disagreement about goals was compounded because neither group was sure about the best technique for achieving their goals. The ultimate solution was inspirational on the part of the dean. An accounting research center was established with funding from Big Eight accounting firms. The funding was used to finance research activities for faculty interested in basic research and to provide contact with business firms for other faculty. The solution provided a common goal and unified people within the department to work toward that goal.

When an entire organization is characterized by low goal consensus and low technical knowledge and many decisions are characterized by a high level of uncertainty, elements of the garbage can model will appear. Managers may first try techniques from both cells 2 and 3, but logical decision sequences starting with problem identification and ending with problem solution will not occur. Potential solutions will precede problems as often as problems precede solutions. In this situation, managers should encourage widespread discussion of problems and idea proposals to facilitate the opportunity to make choices. Eventually, through trial and error, the organization will solve some problems.

Special Decision Circumstances

In a highly competitive world beset by global competition and rapid change, decision making seldom fits the traditional rational, analytical model. To cope in today's world, managers must learn to make decisions fast, especially in high-velocity environments, to learn from decision mistakes, and to avoid escalating commitment to an unsatisfactory course of action.

HIGH-VELOCITY ENVIRONMENTS

In some industries today, the rate of competitive and technological change is so extreme that market data is either unavailable or obsolete, strategic windows open and shut quickly, perhaps within a few months, and the cost of a decision error is company failure. Recent research has examined how successful companies make decisions in these **high-velocity environments,** especially to understand whether organizations abandon rational approaches or have time for incremental implementation.[48]

Comparing successful with unsuccessful decisions in high-velocity environments suggests the following guidelines.

- Successful decision makers track information in real time to develop a deep and intuitive grasp of the business. Two to three intense meetings per week with all key players are usual. Decision makers track operating statistics about cash, scrap, backlog, work in process, and shipments to constantly feel the pulse of what is happening. Unsuccessful firms were more concerned with future planning and forward-looking information, with only a loose grip on immediate happenings.

- During a major decision, successful companies began immediately to build multiple alternatives. Implementation may run in parallel before finally settling on a final choice. Slow-decision companies developed only a single alternative, moving to another only after the first one failed.
- Fast, successful decision makers sought advice from everyone and depended heavily on one or two savvy, trusted colleagues as counselors. Slow companies were unable to build trust and agreement among the best people.
- Fast companies involved everyone in the decision and tried for consensus; but if consensus did not emerge, the top manager made the choice and moved ahead. Waiting for everyone to be on board created more delays than warranted. Slow companies delayed decisions to achieve a uniform consensus.
- Fast, successful choices were well integrated with other decisions and the overall strategic direction of the company. Less successful choices considered the decision in isolation from other decisions; the decision was made in the abstract.[49]

When speed matters, a slow decision is as ineffective as the wrong decision. As we discussed in Chapter 8, speed is a crucial competitive weapon in a growing number of industries, and companies can learn to make decisions fast. Managers must be plugged into the pulse of the company, must seek consensus and advice, and then be ready to take the risk and move ahead.

DECISION MISTAKES AND LEARNING

Organizational decisions produce many errors, especially when made under high uncertainty. Managers simply cannot determine or predict which alternative will solve a problem. In these cases, the organization must make the decision—and take the risk—often in the spirit of trial and error. If an alternative fails, the organization can learn from it and try another alternative that better fits the situation. Each failure provides new information and learning. The point for managers is to move ahead with the decision process despite the potential for mistakes. "Chaotic action is preferable to orderly inaction."[50]

In many cases, managers have been encouraged to instill a climate of experimentation, even foolishness, to facilitate creative decision making. If one idea fails, another idea should be tried. For example, Tandy Corporation was disappointed in sales through its 386 computer centers, which were set up to sell computers directly to businesses. However, Tandy learned what it had done wrong—retail stores did not provide entry into the business market. Tandy is now experimenting in Dallas with a direct-sales force that is headquartered at Infomart, the company's computer merchandise outlet. Past mistakes are allowing Tandy to gradually encroach on IBM and Apple as a major player in the business computer market. Failure often lays the groundwork for success, as when technicians at 3M developed Post-it Notes based on a failed product—a not-very-sticky glue. Companies like Pepsi-Cola believe that if all their new products succeed, they're doing something wrong, not taking the necessary risks to develop new markets.[51]

Only by making mistakes can managers and organizations go through the process of **decision learning** and acquire sufficient experience and knowledge to perform more effectively in the future. Robert Townsend, who was president at Avis Corporation, gives the following advice:

> Admit your mistakes openly, maybe even joyfully. Encourage your associates to do likewise by commiserating with them. Never castigate. Babies learn to walk by falling down. If you beat a baby every time he falls down, he'll never care much for walking.
>
> My batting average on decisions at Avis was no better than a .333. Two out of every three decisions I made were wrong. But my mistakes were discussed openly and most of them corrected with a little help from my friends.[52]

ESCALATING COMMITMENT

A much more dangerous mistake is to persist in a course of action when it is failing. Research suggests that organizations often continue to invest time and money in a solution despite strong evidence that it is not working. Two explanations are given for why managers **escalate commitment** to a failing decision. The first is that managers block or distort negative information when they are personally responsible for a negative decision. They simply don't know when to pull the plug. In some cases, they continue to throw good money after bad even when a strategy seems incorrect.[53] An example of this distortion is the reaction at Borden when the company began losing customers following its refusal to lower prices on dairy products. When the cost of raw milk dropped, Borden hoped to boost the profit margins of its dairy products, convinced that customers would pay a premium for the brand name. Borden's sales plummeted as low-priced competitors mopped up, but top executives stuck with their premium pricing policy for almost a year. By then, the company's dairy division was operating at a severe loss. Other companies have done the same, such as when Emery Air Freight Corporation acquired Consolidated Freightways, Inc. In the year since acquiring Consolidated, Emery lost $100 million on it, but executives were reluctant to admit it was a bad choice, believing things were about to get better.[54] Negative information often doesn't sink in.

As another example, consider the increasing investment of the Canadian Imperial Bank of Commerce in the ill-fated Canary Wharf project, an $8 billion development in London's remote Docklands area. CIBC had already lent over $1 billion for Canary Wharf to the now-failed Olympia & York Developments Ltd. and its subsidiaries. Despite loads of negative information that led CEO Al Flood to pronounce Canary Wharf a project that "would not meet our lending criteria today," CIBC turned around and invested an additional $36 million in the project. Flood said the move was designed to "protect our investment . . . and try to make the project work."[55] These additional millions now seem like a terrible choice.

A second explanation for escalating commitment to a failing decision is that consistency and persistence are valued in contemporary society. Consistent managers are considered better leaders than those who switch around from one course of action to another. Even though organizations learn through trial and error, organizational norms value consistency. These norms may result in a course of action being maintained, resources being squandered, and learning being inhibited. Emphasis on consistent leadership was partly responsible for the Long Island Lighting Company's refusal to change course in the construction of the Shoreham Nuclear Power Plant, which was eventually abandoned—after an investment of more than $5 billion—without ever having begun operation. Shoreham's cost was estimated at $75 million when the project was announced in 1966, but by the time a construction permit was granted, LILCO had already spent $77 million. Opposition to nuclear power was growing. Critics continued to decry the huge sums of money being pumped into Shoreham. Customers complained that LILCO was cutting back on customer service and maintenance of current operations. But Shoreham officials seemed convinced that they would triumph in the end; their response to criticism was, "If people will just wait until the end, they are going to realize that this is a hell of an investment."

The end came in 1989, when a negotiated agreement with New York led LILCO to abandon the $5.5 billion plant in return for rate increases and a $2.5 billion tax write-off. By the time Governor Mario Cuomo signed an agreement with the company, LILCO had remained firmly committed to a losing course of action for more than twenty three years.[56]

Failure to admit a mistake and adopt a new course of action is far worse than an attitude that encourages mistakes and learning. Based upon what has been said about decision making in this chapter, one can expect companies to be ultimately successful in their decision making by adopting a learning approach toward solutions. They will make mistakes along the way, but they will resolve uncertainty through the trial-and-error process.

Summary and Interpretation

The single most important idea in this chapter is that most organizational decisions are not made in a logical, rational manner. Most decisions do not begin with the careful analysis of a problem, followed by systematic analysis of alternatives, and finally implementation of a solution. On the contrary, decision processes are characterized by conflict, coalition building, trial and error, speed, and mistakes. Managers operate under many constraints that limit rationality; hence, intuition and hunch often are the criteria for choice.

Another important idea is that individuals make decisions, but organizational decisions are not made by a single individual. Organizational decision making is a social process. Only in rare circumstances do managers analyze problems and find solutions by themselves. Many problems are not clear, so widespread discussion and coalition building take place. Once goals and priorities are set, alternatives to achieve those goals can be tried. When a manager does make an individual decision, it is often a small part of a larger decision process. Organizations solve big problems through a series of small steps. A single manager may initiate one step but should be aware of the larger decision process in which it is embedded.

The greatest amount of conflict and coalition building occurs when goals are not agreed upon. Priorities must be established to indicate which goals are important and what problems should be solved first. If a manager attacks a problem other people do not agree with, the manager will lose support for the solution to be implemented. Thus, time and activity should be spent building a coalition in the problem identification stage of decision making. Then the organization can move toward solutions. Under conditions of low technical knowledge, the solution unfolds as a series of incremental trials that will gradually lead to an overall solution.

The most novel description of decision making is the garbage can model. This model describes how decision processes can almost seem random in highly organic organizations. Decisions, problems, ideas, and people flow through organizations and mix together in various combinations. Through this process, the organization gradually learns. Some problems may never be solved, but many are, and the organization will move toward maintaining and improving its level of performance.

Finally, many organizations must make decisions with speed, which means staying in immediate touch with operations and the environment. Moreover, in an uncertain world, organizations will make mistakes, and mistakes made through trial and error should be encouraged. Encouraging trial-and-error increments facilitates organizational learning. On the other hand, an unwillingness to change from a failing course of action can have serious negative consequences for an organization. Norms for consistency and the desire to prove one's decision correct can lead to continued investment in a useless course of action.

KEY CONCEPTS

bounded rationality perspective	inspiration
Carnegie model	intuitive decision making
coalition	management science approach
contingency decision-making	nonprogrammed decisions
framework	organizational decision making
decision learning	organized anarchy
escalating commitment	problem identification
garbage can model	problem solution
goal consensus	problemistic search
high velocity environment	programmed decisions
imitation	rational approach
incremental decision process model	technical knowledge

DISCUSSION QUESTIONS

1. A professional economist once told his class, "An individual decision maker should process all relevant information and select the economically rational alternative." Do you agree? Why or why not?

2. Why is intuition used in decision making?

3. The Carnegie model emphasizes the need for a political coalition in the decision making process. When and why are coalitions necessary?

4. What are the three major phases in Mintzberg's incremental decision process model? Why might an organization recycle through one or more phases of the model?

5. An organization theorist once told her class, "Organizations never make big decisions. They make small decisions that eventually add up to a big decision." Explain the logic behind this statement.

6. Why would managers in high-velocity environments worry more about the present than the future? Discuss.

7. How does goal consensus influence problem identification in an organization?

8. Describe the four streams of events in the garbage can model of decision making. Why are they considered to be independent?

9. Are there decision-making situations in which managers should be expected to make the "correct" decision? Are there situations in which decision makers should be expected to make mistakes? Discuss.

10. Why are decision mistakes usually accepted in organizations but penalized in college courses and exams that are designed to train managers?

GUIDES TO ACTION

As an organization manager, keep these guides in mind:

1. Adopt decision processes to fit the organizational situation.
2. Use a rational decision approach—computation, management science—when a problem situation is well understood.
3. Use a coalition-building approach when organizational goals and problem priorities are in conflict. When managers disagree about priorities or the true nature of the problem, they should discuss and seek agreement about priorities. The Carnegie model emphasizes the need for building a coalition and maintaining agreement about goals and problems.
4. Take risks and move the company ahead by increments when a problem is defined but solutions are uncertain. Try solutions step-by-step to learn whether they work.
5. Apply both the Carnegie model and the incremental process model in a situation with low goal consensus and low technical knowledge. Decision making may also employ garbage can procedures. Move the organization toward better performance by proposing new ideas, spending time working in important areas, and persisting with potential solutions.
6. Track real-time information, build multiple alternatives simultaneously, and try to involve everyone—but move ahead anyway when making decisions in a high-velocity environment.
7. Do not persist in a course of action that is failing. Some actions will not work out if uncertainty is high, so encourage organizational learning by readily trying new alternatives. Seek information and evidence that indicates when a course of action is failing, and allocate resources to new choices rather than to unsuccessful ventures.

Consider these guidelines when analyzing the following case.

The New Library*

CASE FOR ANALYSIS

Jefferson University is a sizable and complex institution with an enrollment of more than ten thousand students in a number of undergraduate, graduate, and professional programs. The formal organization of the senior administration is shown in Exhibit 11.9.

Ralph White, the executive vice president, had called the meeting. "I've asked each of you to look at the proposal for the new library for our health sciences campus from your own points of view," he said. "I have to make my recommendation to the president and the board tomorrow. What position should we take?" Having posed the question, he sat back and listened.

*Excerpted from John A. Dunn, Jr., "Organizational Decision Making," in Walter C. Swap and Associates, eds., *Group Decision Making* (Beverly Hills: Sage, 1984), pp. 280–310. Used with permission.

Exhibit 11.9 Administrative Organization Chart for Jefferson University.

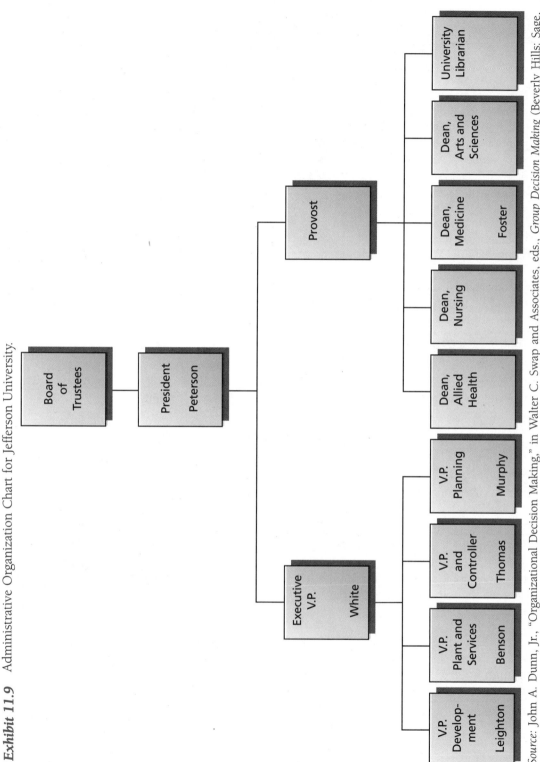

Source: John A. Dunn, Jr., "Organizational Decision Making," in Walter C. Swap and Associates, eds., *Group Decision Making* (Beverly Hills: Sage, 1984), 282. Used with permission.

When the vice president for development came in, the rest of the group was sitting around the big table on the fourth floor of Jefferson Hall. "Evelyn," said Al Benson, the vice president for plant and services, "we've already set your target for you." Evelyn grinned; somehow, lately, all the big decisions seemed to rest on the ability of her shop to find new money. This time, however, she wasn't sure she could deliver.

The problem was the size of the project. Conversations about the need for a major library and learning resources center on the health sciences campus had been going on for years. A fund-raising campaign had been started four years before but, aside from about $3 million in major gifts, had not produced anything like the funds needed to cover the project. Changes in the medical school's leadership and in faculty ideas about the sort of facility needed had muddied the water.

During those four years, a good deal of money had been spent on the project. An architectural programmer had been hired to work with faculty members and administrators in clarifying specifically of what the building should consist. Schematic designs had been prepared. Fund-raising staff had been hired and paid; lots of proposals had been written, brochures prepared, prospects identified and solicited, trips made. The net result was that the expenses of the campaign had eaten up a great deal of what had been raised; about a million was still due to be collected in the future.

Mike Thomas, vice president and comptroller, did not let Evelyn forget the cash-flow problem either. The bills had to be paid as they were incurred; much of the fund-raising progress was in pledges; payments were dribbling in over a number of years. That meant Mike had to use other money to pay the bills, to be refunded when and if the pledges were paid. The payment record was good; these were major donors who honored their commitments. Mike could be pretty sure of his repayments. There remained a related problem, however. Time was going by, and inflation was a major factor. He was paying bills in current dollars; the pledges, when they were paid, would be worth less, but the costs of the building would be going up—potentially leaving a gap in the financing.

There didn't seem to be much doubt about the need for the building. The present library conditions were less than marginal. The accreditation team for the American Medical Association gave the school its accreditation, to be sure, but only on the clear understanding that the new facility would be complete by time of its next visit. The accreditation teams for the nursing and allied health schools had also criticized the inadequacy of the facility and scope of the collection. Working with expert consultants, the university librarian had developed a detailed program for the needed facility.

The medical school also had an image problem. The allied health school had its own new building, constructed about ten years ago. The nursing school was building superb new facilities. The medical school, the "flagship" of the complex, had never in its eighty years of existence had a new building. It was housed in converted manufacturing buildings. These made good laboratories, because they were constructed to support sizable machinery; but the close columns and relatively low ceilings made for terrible classrooms. The recent advent of the nursing school had required shoehorning additional faculty members into already crowded quarters. In an era when all three schools were trying to increase research activity, there was a critical shortage of research lab space. Some of the functions that could be moved from present quarters into the new building would free space that could be converted to lab use (at additional capital cost, of course).

So the needs were clear, but the financing wasn't. Early cost estimates ranged from $9 million to $15 million, depending on the size of the building and the mix of components proposed for it. A site was acquired in a good central location. Cost estimates kept rising as people got more and more enthusiastic about the possibilities and as construction costs rose with inflation. Evelyn Leighton took over the development division after the campaign had started, reviewed the discouraging progress to date, changed the fund-raising staff, and set to work. Not much happened. There was an acting dean of the medical school at the time who, despite his best efforts, could not be as effective as a permanent dean could be; and there was still some general skepticism about the university's ability to raise that kind of money. Some of the alumni remembered the strenuous efforts that had been made to raise funds for the new allied health tower and the disappointment when the campaign fell far short. The building plans had to be cut back; and for years, the allied health students have had to carry an extra eight hundred dollars per student per year on their tuition to pay the mortgages on the building.

This year, Dr. Peter Q. Foster was appointed dean of the medical school. He had been the director of a major medically oriented foundation. A nationally known researcher, he also brought strong administrative skills and high aspirations to the city campus. He quickly realized the need for the new facility but added an even more urgent dimension to its importance. He and many of his health science colleagues realized that the ways in which future health practitioners and others needed to have access to information was radically different from the past. They should not be looking through card indices or thumbing through past issues of periodicals; they should be inquiring directly from data bases by computer. Nothing of that sort existed at the university, though there were, of course, computer terminals in the library for accessing Medlines and other search services.

For the health schools, such developments had particular urgency. Each of the schools is linked for educational purposes with many associated institutions. The medical school has more than a dozen major teaching hospitals and an additional thirty hospitals with specialized programs. The health sciences schools could and should provide core information access services to all these institutions, tying them together into an even more effective teaching patient care network. The development of the new library would provide that possibility. Unfortunately, money doesn't come just because you need it.

Dr. Foster promptly undertook a serious study of the possibilities. An outside consulting group worked with a core group of medical school and central administrative people in a financial feasibility study. Cost estimates for various building sizes and configurations were prepared, starting at about $20 million and going up to $35 million. Estimates of the incremental costs of operating the building were worked out; the added costs would raise the tuitions of all three of the health sciences schools from eight hundred to thirteen hundred dollars per student per year. The consultant, acknowledging the importance of the project, recommended downsizing the building as much as possible, so as to bring it within the capacity of Jefferson University to afford.

Then came an almost incredible break. President Peterson and Evelyn Leighton had over the course of two years been working quietly in Mexico with an elderly, very wealthy medical school alumna. With long and patient work, she was persuaded to grant the school a total of $15 million through a private foundation. Suddenly everyone's mood brightened.

It was now clearly possible to build the building. The question of total size remained. The huge grant was not enough. Would $23 million be adequate? $25 million? $30 million? How much more could the university raise? What would the operating costs be, and who was going to pay them?

"Damn it, Evelyn, I think we ought to be going," said Al, after reviewing the fact sheets White had distributed. ""The old gal gave us enough to get started; but we have to go through a formal application process to her foundation, and the deadline for that is a month from now. It will take my people that long to get the application done, once we've made our decision to go ahead. Our present estimate is $23 million. There's some room for slack in that, because we can always leave a couple of administrative office floors unfinished if we have to, and we can save the cost of the furnishings on those floors. Can't we raise the $8 million?"

"What about the operating costs of the new building?" asked Ralph White.

"They are going to be high," said Jerry Murphy, the vice president for planning. "That building will add about $1.5 million to the budgets of the schools every year. With six hundred medical students, six hundred allied health students, and two hundred nursing students, that means more than one thousand dollars per student per year. Maybe the medical students can stand it. The tuition is very high there, but there are still a lot of people who want to get into medical school; and the earning potential of the graduates is high. But interest in allied health is slowing down, and their earnings aren't as high; I don't want to see us sock another thousand dollars on top of the eight hundred they are already paying for their own building. And as for the nursing school, those tuitions are already incredibly high; I'd hate to see us load anything more there. It's going to be hard enough to get the nursing school onto a balanced budget under the best of circumstances."

Mike Thomas took out his calculator. "Since we can only count on about 5 percent or 6 percent as a long-run payout rate on endowment, it would take an endowment of $30 million to generate that $1.5 million annual income, if the students aren't going to pay for it. Can you raise $38 million, Evelyn?"

"Come on, you guys," replied Leighton. "We got you the $15 million. Give us a little time and I think we can probably raise at least enough to cover the balance of the cost of the building. Psychologically, having the grant money in hand helps us, because it gives a sense of reality to the whole project. This is the biggest project we're going to have on the health sciences campus for many years. We can do it. It may take some time, that's all."

"Let me add one complexity," said Murphy. "If all we were doing was to build a conventional library building, we'd know how to do it. The building itself will not be complicated; Al and his crew have a good handle on those costs. What about the new technology? We're going to try communications and computer linkages that haven't been tried anywhere else. That means that there's going to be added systems development expense and some rather unusual equipment costs, right? And we can pretty well bet that there are going to be some mistakes made; we're not perfect; we don't have all the answers going in. My own guess is that we could easily add $1 million to $1.5 million in unanticipated systems development costs to the project. When can we have any better handle on those costs?"

"Dr. Foster has several committees working on the program right now," said Al. "The problem is that they may take some months thinking through all the pieces of this puzzle, and we have to make a decision very quickly. I can pretty well specify the cash payment schedule for the building right now, though. Figure about $100,000 per month starting in April when the project gets board approval, and then after a year, figure $1 million per month for the twenty-three months of construction."

Evelyn piped in, "Some of my staff has been working with the National Library of Medicine to see if we can get systems development support. They don't have any money right now, but it's possible that something may come through on that in the future. We may also be able to get some support from computer manufacturers who'd like to be involved in the development so they could use the technology elsewhere."

"Evelyn, let's come back to the fund-raising for a minute," said White. "How sure are you?"

My best guess is as follows: I can be 90 percent sure of raising $4 million; for $6 million, I guess about 70 percent sure; for $8 million, about 50 percent sure. I think there is a chance we can go even higher—maybe $10 million, but that's very risky. We should be able to get pledges in the next three years; most of those pledges will be payable over three years. And just to anticipate Mike's next question, you should deduct about 8 percent to 15 percent from the total for fund-raising costs."

"You guys are all forgetting the problem of how we get from here to there," added Mike. "Al, you're going to be spending money on the building design and then on the construction. We can draw down on the foundation grant pretty quickly, but what do we do for the rest of the money? Evelyn can't guarantee that she can raise it. And even if she does, you heard how long it's going to take. That means I may not get some of my cash for six or seven years. We're awfully tight for working capital now. We financed the classroom renovation project out of working capital and the hockey rink as well. And we haven't yet raised the funds to pay for those. There's just so far I can stretch. I can borrow some from the banks, of course, but that will cost us at least one point over prime. Who's going to be paying those interest charges? They should be charged to the project, but that just raises the total cost; the medical school operating budget is already tight and probably can't afford to absorb them."

"Look, we're not getting anywhere," said Murphy. "Al, you want to build the building, and you've got time constraints. We need a decision now. Mike, you've got real cash flow problems, and you're worried about whether or not we'll ever raise the construction money. I'm concerned about the operating costs and the unknowns in the systems development. Evelyn's a born optimist, but even she can't guarantee how much she and the president and Dr. Foster can raise, or when."

Al boomed in: "Come on. I say we go ask the board for approval of the $23 million project. That's what Dr. Foster wants. We've got some flexibility within that total to cut back if we need to—maybe $2 million. That gives Evelyn her fund-raising target. And it gets us the building we've all been talking about, the best thing that's happened to this place in years."

"Okay," said Ralph White. "You've brought out the important factors. I think we've chewed on this enough. I understand the various concerns around the table. Now here's what I think I'll recommend to the president and the board: can you all support a recommendation to. . . ."

QUESTIONS

1. What is the problem in this case? What would you recommend to the president and the board?
2. Which decision models from this chapter can be used to explain the decision processes in this case?
3. Can anything be done to improve the decision-making process about the new library?

NOTES

1. Laura Zinn with Mary Beth Regan, "The Right Moves, Baby," *Business Week,* 5 July 1993, 30–31; Michael J. McCarthy, "Pepsi Faces Problems in Trying to Contain Syringe Scare," *Wall Street Journal,* 17 June 1993, B1.

2. Christopher Power with Kathleen Kerwin, Ronald Grover, Keith Alexander, and Robert D. Hof, "Flops," *Business Week,* 16 August 1993, 76–82; John Merwin, "A Billion in Blunders," *Forbes,* 1 December 1986, 97–111.

3. Charles Lindblom, "The Science of 'Muddling Through,'" *Public Administration Review* 29 (1954): 79–88.

4. Herbert A. Simon, *The New Science of Management Decision* (Englewood Cliffs, N.J.: Prentice-Hall, 1960), 1–8.

5. Paul J. H. Schoemaker and J. Edward Russo, "A Pyramid of Decision Approaches," *California Management Review* (Fall 1993): 9–31.

6. Earnest R. Archer, "How to Make a Business Decision: An Analysis of Theory and Practice," *Management Review* 69 (February 1980): 54–61; Boris Blai, "Eight Steps to Successful Problem Solving," *Supervisory Management* (January 1986): 7–9.

7. Francine Schwadel, "Christmas Sales' Lack of Momentum Test Store Managers' Mettle," *Wall Street Journal,* 16 December 1987, 1.

8. Adapted from Archer, "How to Make a Business Decision," 59–61.

9. James W. Dean, Jr., and Mark P. Sharfman, "Procedural Rationality in the Strategic Decision-Making Process," *Journal of Management Studies* 30 (1993): 587–610.

10. Paul A. Anderson, "Decision Making by Objection and the Cuban Missile Crisis," *Administrative Science Quarterly* 28 (1983): 201–22.

11. Irving L. Janis, *Crucial Decisions: Leadership in Policymaking and Crisis Management* (New York: Free Press, 1989); Paul C. Nutt, "Flexible Decision Styles and the Choices of Top Executives," *Journal of Management Studies* 30 (1993): 695–721.

12. Herbert A. Simon, "Making Management Decisions: The Role of Intuition and Emotion," *Academy of Management Executive* 1 (February 1987): 57–64; Daniel J. Eisenberg, "How Senior Managers Think," *Harvard Business Review* 62 (November-December 1984): 80–90.

13. Orlando Behling and Norman L. Eckel, "Making Sense Out of Intuition," *Academy of Management Executive* 5, no. 1 (1991): 46–54.

14. Thomas F. Issack, "Intuition: An Ignored Dimension of Management," *Academy of Management Review* 3 (1978): 917–22.

15. Marjorie A. Lyles, "Defining Strategic Problems: Subjective Criteria of Executives," *Organizational Studies* 8 (1987): 263–80; Marjorie A. Lyles and Ian I. Mitroff, "Organizational Problem Formulation: An Empirical Study," *Administrative Science Quarterly* 25 (1980): 102–19.

16. Marjorie A. Lyles and Howard Thomas, "Strategic Problem Formulation: Biases and Assumptions Embedded in Alternative Decision-Making Models," *Journal of Management Studies* 25 (1988): 131–45.

17. Susan E. Jackson and Jane E. Dutton, "Discerning Threats and Opportunities," *Administrative Science Quarterly* 33 (1988): 370–87.

18. David A. Cowan, "Developing a Classification Structure of Organizational Problems: An Empirical Investigation," *Academy of Management Journal* 33 (1990): 366–90; David Greising, "Rethinking IDS from the Bottom Up, *Business Week,* 8 February 1993, 110–12.

19. Ross Stagner, "Corporate Decision-Making: An Empirical Study," *Journal of Applied Psychology* 53 (1969): 1–13.

20. Annetta Miller and Dody Tsintar, "A Test for Market Research," *Newsweek,* 28 December 1987, 32–33.

21. Trish H. Hall, "For a Company Chief, Where There's a Whimm, There's Often a Way," *Wall Street Journal,* 1 October 1984, 1; Roy Rowan,

"Those Business Hunches Are More Than Blind Faith," *Fortune,* 25 April 1979, 110–14.

22. Paul C. Nutt, "Types of Organizational Decision Processes," *Administrative Science Quarterly* 29 (1984): 414–50.

23. "How Paramount Keeps Turning Out Winners," *Business Week,* 11 June 1984, 148–151; Ron Grover, "Michael Eisner's Hit Parade," *Business Week,* 1 February 1988, 27.

24. Nandini Rajagopalan, Abdul M. A. Rasheed, and Deepak K. Datta, "Strategic Decision Processes: Critical Review and Future Decisions," *Journal of Management* 19 (1993): 349–84; Paul J. H. Schoemaker, "Strategic Decisions in Organizations: Rational and Behavioral Views," *Journal of Management Studies* 30 (1993): 107–29; Charles J. McMillan, "Qualitative Models of Organizational Decision Making," *Journal of Management Studies* 5 (1980): 22–39; Paul C. Nutt, "Models for Decision Making in Organizations and Some Contextual Variables Which Stimulate Optimal Use," *Academy of Management Review* 1 (1976): 84–98.

25. Hugh J. Miser, "Operations Analysis in the Army Air Forces in World War II: Some Reminiscences," *Interfaces* 23 (September-October 1993): 47–49; Harold J. Leavitt, William R. Dill, and Henry B. Eyring, *The Organizational World* (New York: Harcourt Brace Jovanovich, 1973), chap. 6.

26. Stephen J. Huxley, "Finding the Right Spot for a Church Camp in Spain," *Interfaces* 12 (October 1982): 108–14; James E. Hodder and Henry E. Riggs, "Pitfalls in Evaluating Risky Projects," *Harvard Business Review* (January-February 1985): 128–35.

27. Edward Baker and Michael Fisher, "Computational Results for Very Large Air Crew Scheduling Problems," *Omega* 9 (1981): 613–18; Jean Aubin, "Scheduling Ambulances," *Interfaces* 22 (March-April, 1992): 1–10.

28. Jean Aubin, "Scheduling Ambulances."

29. Harold J. Leavitt, "Beyond the Analytic Manager," *California Management Review* 17 (1975): 5–12; C. Jackson Grayson, Jr., "Management Science and Business Practice," *Harvard Business Review* 51 (July-August 1973): 41–48.

30. Richard L. Daft and John C. Wiginton, "Language and Organization," *Academy of Management Review* (1979): 179–91.

31. Based on Richard M. Cyert and James G. March, *A Behavioral Theory of the Firm* (Englewood Cliffs, N.J.: Prentice-Hall, 1963); and James G. March and Herbert A. Simon, *Organizations* (New York: Wiley, 1958).

32. William B. Stevenson, Joan L. Pearce, and Lyman W. Porter, "The Concept of 'Coalition' in Organization Theory and Research," *Academy of Management Review* 10 (1985): 256–68.

33. David Woodruff with Karen Lowry Miller, "Chrysler's Neon," *Business Week,* 3 May 1993, 116–26.

34. Cyert and March, *Behavioral Theory of the Firm,* 120–22.

35. Ann Reilly Dowd, "How Bush Decided," *Fortune,* 11 February 1991, 45–46.

36. Craig R. Waters, "Raiders of the Lost Arp," *Inc.,* November 1982, 39–44; Tom Richman, "What America Needs is a Few Good Failures," *Inc.,* September 1983, 63–72.

37. Lawrence G. Hrebiniak, "Top-Management Agreement and Organizational Performance," *Human Relations* 35 (1982): 1139–58; Richard P. Nielsen, "Toward a Method for Building Consensus during Strategic Planning," *Sloan Management Review* (Summer 1981): 29–40.

38. Based on Henry Mintzberg, Duru Raisinghani, and André Théorêt, "The Structure of 'Unstructured' Decision Processes," *Administrative Science Quarterly* 21 (1976): 246–75.

39. Lawrence T. Pinfield, "A Field Evaluation of Perspectives on Organizational Decision Making," *Administrative Science Quarterly* 31 (1986): 365–88.

40. Mintzberg, et al, "The Structure of 'Unstructured' Decision Processes."

41. Ibid., 270.

42. Keith H. Hammonds, "How a $4 Razor Ends up Costing $300 Million," *Business Week,* 29 January 1990, 62–63.

43. Michael D. Cohen, James G. March, and Johan P. Olsen, "A Garbage Can Model of Organizational Choice," *Administrative Science Quarterly* 17 (March 1972): 1–25; Michael D. Cohen and James G. March, *Leadership and Ambiguity: The American College President* (New York: McGraw-Hill, 1974).

44. Michael Masuch and Perry LaPotin, "Beyond Garbage Cans: An AI Model of Organizational Choice," *Administrative Science Quarterly* 34 (1989): 38–67.

45. David Krouss, "Casablanca," *Sky,* November 1992, 82–91

46. Adapted from James D. Thompson, *Organizations in Action* (New York: McGraw-Hill, 1967), chap. 10; and McMillan, "Qualitative Models of Organizational Decision Making," 25.

47. Anderson, "Decision Making by Objection and

the Cuban Missile Crisis."

48. L. J. Bourgeois III and Kathleen M. Eisenhardt, "Strategic Decision Processes in High Velocity Environments: Four Cases in the Microcomputer Industry," *Management Science* 34 (1988): 816–35.

49. Kathleen M. Eisenhardt, "Speed and Strategic Course: How Managers Accelerate Decision Making," *California Management Review* (Spring 1990): 39–54.

50. Karl Weick, *The Social Psychology of Organizing,* 2d ed. (Reading, Mass.: Addison-Wesley, 1979), 243.

51. Power, et al., "Flops"; Todd Mason, "Tandy Finds a Cold Hard World Outside the Radio Shack," *Business Week,* 31 August 1987, 68–70.

52. Robert Townsend, *Up the Organization* (New York: Knopf, 1974), 115.

53. Joel Brockner, "The Escalation of Commitment to a Failing Course of Action: Toward Theoretical Progress," *Academy of Management Review* 17 (1992): 39–61; Barry M. Staw and Jerry Ross, "Knowing When to Pull the Plug," *Harvard Business Review* 65 (March-April 1987): 68–74: Barry M. Staw, "The Escalation of Commitment to a Course of Action," *Academy of Management Review* 6 (1981): 577–87; Barry M. Staw, "Knee-Deep in the Big Muddy: A Study of Escalating Commitment to a Chosen Course of Action," *Organizational Behavior and Human Performance* 16 (1976): 27–45.

54. Elizabeth Lesly, "Why Things Are So Sour at Borden," *Business Week,* 22 November 1993, 78–85; Joan O' C. Hamilton, "Emery Is One Heavy Load for Consolidated Freightways," *Business Week,* 26 March 1990, 62–64.

55. Shona McKay, "When Good People Make Bad Choices," *Canadian Business,* February 1994, 52–55.

56. Jerry Ross and Barry M. Staw, "Organizational Escalation and Exit: Lessons from the Shoreham Nuclear Power Plant," *Academy of Management Journal* 36 (1993): 701–32.

CHAPTER 12

Power and Politics

Semco S/A (Brazil)

Ricardo Semler, president of Semco—Brazil's largest manufacturer of marine and food-processing machinery—has turned the organization on its head, diffusing power among its eight hundred employees in a country where fiefdoms and hierarchies flourish. Workers at Semco set their own production quotas and working hours, even coming in on their own time to meet quotas. They help redesign the products they make, formulate marketing plans, evaluate their bosses, and even set their own salaries. Everyone has access to the company's finances. No one is hired or promoted until interviewed and accepted by his or her new coworkers.

Big decisions are made by companywide vote. Workers decided to acquire and move into an abandoned factory, overriding Semler's reluctance. Employees outvoted him again with their refusal to acquire a company because they didn't feel ready to digest it.

Semler believes democratic power sharing is fundamental to making organizations productive. The traditional organizational pyramid emphasizes power at the top, the single biggest obstacle to participatory management. At Semco, the hierarchy has been shrunk to three layers, drawn as three concentric circles. Five counselors are in the center circle, eight division heads called partners are in the second circle, and all the other employees—called associates—are in the outer circle. Team and task force leaders are called coordinators. That's it: three management layers, four titles.

Incidentally, the factory that workers voted to purchase over Semler's objection has been outfitted with the most sophisticated computer-integrated technology and was painted by an artist so that Semler feels like a guest every time he walks in. Semco has been repeatedly named the best company to work for in Brazil. Productivity isn't bad either, with employee output tripling in three years.[1]

Semco S/A represents a trend that is starting to take place both in North America and in other parts of the world—turning power over to workers. Rather than top managers taking responsibility for making the company work, using power and authority to the fullest, many managers are giving power away as fast as they can, with astonishing results. Sometimes it's done by creating a high-involvement corporate culture, or perhaps through self-managed teams, or by using clan control, all of which have been discussed in previous chapters. The implications are enormous because if this trend continues, managers will have to learn power sharing rather than power grabbing, a new way to manage effectively in today's world.

PURPOSE OF THIS CHAPTER

Most organizations still operate under the old rules of power and politics. This chapter will explore power in organizations as a way to get things done. The following sections examine sources of power in organizations and the way power is used to attain organizational goals. Vertical and horizontal power are quite different, so these are discussed separately. We will also explore the new trend of worker empowerment to understand how it works. The latter part of the chapter looks at politics, which is the application of power and authority to achieve desired outcomes.

The study of power and politics is a natural extension of the previous chapter on decision making. Like decision making, power involves the development of coalitions among executives. The dynamic processes associated with power and politics are thus similar in some respects to the processes associated with decision making.

Individual versus Organizational Power

In popular literature, power is often described as a personal characteristic, and a frequent topic is how one person can influence or dominate another person.[2] You probably recall from an earlier management or organizational behavior course that managers have five sources of personal power.[3] *Legitimate power* is the authority granted by the organization to the formal management position a manager holds. *Reward power* stems from the ability to bestow rewards—promotion, raise, pat on the back—to other people. The authority to punish or recommend punishment is called *coercive power. Expert power* derives from a person's higher skill or knowledge about the tasks being performed. The last one, *referent power,* derives from personal characteristics such that people admire the manager and want to be like or identify with the manager out of respect and admiration. Each of these sources may be used by individuals within organizations.

Power in organizations, however, is often the result of structural characteristics.[4] Organizations are large, complex systems that contain hundreds, even thousands, of people. These systems have a formal hierarchy in which some tasks are more important regardless of who performs them. In addition, some positions have access to greater resources, or their contribution to the organization is more critical. Thus, the important power processes in organizations reflect larger organizational relationships, both horizontal and vertical, and organizational power usually is vested in the position, not in the person.

Power versus Authority

Power is an intangible force in organizations. It cannot be seen, but its effect can be felt. Power is often defined as the potential ability of one person (or department) to influence other persons (or departments) to carry out orders[5] or to do something they would not otherwise have done.[6] Other definitions stress that power is the ability to achieve goals or outcomes that power holders desire.[7] The achievement of desired outcomes is the basis of the definition used here: **Power** is the ability of one person or department in an organization to influence other people to bring about desired outcomes. It is the potential to influence others within the organization, but with the goal of attaining desired outcomes for power holders.

Power exists only in a relationship between two or more people, and it can be exercised in either vertical or horizontal directions. The source of power often derives from an exchange relationship in which one position or department provides scarce or valued resources to other departments. When one person is dependent on another person, a power relationship emerges in which the person with the resources has greater power.[8] When power exists in a relationship, the power holders can achieve compliance with their requests. For example, the following outcomes are indicators of power in an organization:

- Obtain a larger increase in budget than other departments
- Obtain above-average salary increases for subordinates

- Obtain production schedules that are favorable to your department
- Get items on the agenda at policy meetings[9]

The inability to achieve a desired outcome came as a shock to Steve Jobs when he tried to oust John Sculley from Apple Computer. Sculley wrested control from Jobs after Jobs tried to fire him. The board of directors and senior managers supported Sculley, so Sculley, not Jobs, effectively had power.[10] Shortly after, Jobs, who had created Apple Computer, was forced from the company.

The concept of formal authority is related to power but is narrower in scope. **Authority** is also a force for achieving desired outcomes, but only as prescribed by the formal hierarchy and reporting relationships. Three properties identify authority:

1. *Authority is vested in organizational positions.*   People have authority because of the positions they hold, not because of personal characteristics or resources.
2. *Authority is accepted by subordinates.*   Subordinates comply because they believe position holders have a legitimate right to exercise authority.[11] Richard Ferris resigned as chairman of Allegis Corporation (now UAL, Inc.) because few people accepted his strategy of making Allegis a travel empire. Other senior managers, airline pilots, and board members preferred to see the company concentrate on its major business, United Airlines, and didn't accept Ferris's authority to implement his strategy.
3. *Authority flows down the vertical hierarchy.*[12]   Authority exists along the formal chain of command, and positions at the top of the hierarchy are vested with more formal authority than are positions at the bottom.

Organizational power can be exercised upward, downward, and horizontally in organizations. Formal authority is exercised downward along the hierarchy and is the same as vertical power and legitimate power. The next section examines the use of vertical power as well as sources of power for lower participants. A later section examines the use of horizontal power in organizations, which is not defined by the vertical hierarchy and is determined by power relationships across departments.

Vertical Power

All employees along the vertical hierarchy have access to some sources of power. Although any person may have access to almost any source of power, each level in the hierarchy tends to be concerned with different power issues and to rely on somewhat different power sources.

POWER SOURCES FOR TOP MANAGEMENT

The formal pyramid of authority provides power and authority to top management. Top management is responsible for a great number of people and many resources, and its authority is equal to those responsibilities. The chain of command converges at the top of the organization, so authority is great for top offices. The authority to govern granted to top management is reflected in both the formal organization structure and the decision authority defined by that structure.

> The design of an organization, its structure, is first and foremost the system of control and authority by which the organization is governed. In

the organizational structure, decision discretion is allocated to various positions and the distribution of formal authority is established. Furthermore, by establishing the pattern of prescribed communication and reporting requirements, the structure provides some participants with more and better information and more central locations in the communication network. . . . Thus, organizational structures create formal power and authority by designating certain persons to do certain tasks and make certain decisions, and create informal power through the effect on information and communication structures within the organization. Organizational structure is a picture of the governance of the organization and a determinant of who controls and decides organizational activities.[13]

A large amount of power is allocated to senior management positions by the traditional organizational structure. The power of top management comes from four major sources: formal position, resources, control of decision premises and information, and network centrality.[14]

Formal Position   Certain rights, responsibilities, and prerogatives accrue to top positions. People throughout the organization accept the legitimate right of top managers to set goals, make decisions, and direct activities. Thus, the power from formal position is sometimes called legitimate power.

Senior managers often use symbols and language to perpetuate their legitimate power. Reserving the top floor for senior executives and giving them wood-paneled offices are ways to communicate legitimate authority to others in the organization. When James Dutt was chairman of Beatrice, he had his picture hung in every facility worldwide. Such symbols reinforce the legitimacy of top management's authority.

Most Americans accept the legitimate right of top managers to direct an organization. They believe that "those in authority have the right to expect compliance; those subject to authority have the duty to obey."[15]

Resources   Organizations allocate huge amounts of resources. Buildings are constructed, salaries are paid, and equipment and supplies are purchased. Each year, new resources are allocated in the form of budgets. These resources are allocated downward from top managers. In many companies, top managers own stock, which gives them property rights over resource allocation. A senior vice president with large shareholdings may sometimes be more powerful than the CEO.[16]

Top managers control the resources and, hence, can determine their distribution. Resources can be used as rewards and punishments, which are also sources of power. Resource allocation also creates a dependency relationship. Lower-level participants depend upon top managers for the financial and physical resources needed to perform their tasks. Top management can exchange resources in the form of salaries, personnel, promotion, and physical facilities for compliance with the outcomes they desire.

Control of Decision Premises and Information   Control of **decision premises** means that top managers place constraints on decisions made at lower levels by specifying a decision frame of reference and guidelines. For example, President Sandy McDonnell at McDonnell Douglas prescribed a value of participative management, which was a frame of reference for the decisions of other managers. In one sense, top managers make big decisions, while lower-level participants make small decisions. Top management decides which goal an organization will try to achieve, such as increased market share. Lower-level participants then decide how the goal is to be reached. In one company, top management appointed a committee to select a new marketing vice president. The CEO provided the committee with detailed qualifications that the new vice president should have. He also selected people to serve on the committee. In this way, the CEO shaped the decision premises within which the marketing vice president would be chosen. Top manager actions and decisions such as these place limits on the decisions of lower-level managers and thereby influence their behavior.[17]

The control of information can also be a source of power. Managers in today's organizations recognize that information is a primary business resource and that by controlling what information is collected, how it is interpreted, and how it is shared, they can influence how decisions are made.[18] Top managers often have access to more information than do other managers. This information can be released as needed to shape the decision outcomes of other people. For example, during the bidding war between Viacom Inc. and QVC Network Inc. to acquire Paramount Communications Inc., Paramount chairman Martin S. Davis was determined to accept the friendly Viacom offer and reject QVC's offer. Speaking to the board of directors, Davis attacked the QVC bid and had investment advisors provide a positive written opinion about Viacom's offer. Directors felt they weren't given the full story because Davis wanted Viacom to win.[19]

In another organization, Clark, Ltd., the senior manager controlled information given to the board of directors and thereby influenced the board's decision to purchase a large computer system.[20] The board of directors had formal authority to decide from which company the computer would be purchased. The management services group was asked to recommend which of six computer manufacturers should receive the order. Jim Kenny was in charge of the management services group, and Kenny disagreed with other managers about which computer to purchase. As shown in Exhibit 12.1, other managers had to go through Kenny to have their viewpoints heard by the board. Kenny shaped the decision premises of the board by discussing his preferred computer manufacturer more often than other manufacturers. His comments about other manufacturers tended to be negative. He shaped the board's thinking to select the computer he preferred by controlling information given to them.

Network Centrality   Top managers can locate themselves centrally in an organization. They can surround themselves with a network of loyal subordinates and use their networks to learn about events throughout the organization.[21] By placing managers whom they know in critical positions, top managers increase their power. They gain power by being well informed, having access to other people in the network, and having multiple people dependent upon them. They can use their central positions to build alliances and loyalty and, hence, be in a position to wield substantial power in the organization.

When Harvey Golub was named chief executive officer of American Express, the board of directors put him on a short leash, naming a board member as chairman and assigning a committee to keep tabs on the new CEO. But Golub moved quickly to put his imprint on the company and establish friendships and support among board members. He was named chairman within five months and then

Exhibit 12.1
Information
Flow for Com-
puter Decision
at Clark Ltd.

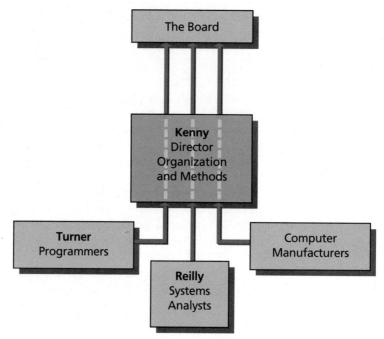

Source: Andrew M. Pettigrew, *The Politics of Organizational Decision-Making* (London: Tavistock, 1973), 235, with permission.

moved to surround himself with hand-picked top managers he trusted to be loyal and supportive.[22]

The following example illustrates a successful power play at Time Warner, where president and co-CEO Nicholas J. Nicholas, Jr., was ousted and replaced by a long-time rival.

IN PRACTICE ♦ 12.1

Time Warner

The board meeting that changed the line of succession at the world's largest media and entertainment company lasted less than an hour. But the internal conflicts and struggles for power that led to that meeting had been building up since the merger of Time, Inc. and Warner Communications in 1990. At that time, Steven J. Ross, the Warner chairman, and Nicholas J. Nicholas, Jr., who had been designated heir by Time's chairman, were put in a rather awkward position of being co-CEOs. As a part of the merger negotiation, Nicholas was to become sole CEO in August 1994, on the eve of Ross's sixty-seventh birthday. But while Nicholas was enjoying a family skiing trip in early 1992, the directors at a specially called meeting moved to oust him as president and co-CEO and replace him with vice chairman and chief operating officer Gerald M. Levin, a supporter of Ross.

Nicholas had complained that Ross controlled most of the directors, but the extent of Ross's power was never more clear than when Nicholas was given the sad and shocking news that his twenty-eight year career at Time and Time Warner had come to an end. Ross and Levin had moved quickly, building support among executives and board members, so that by the time Levin approached retired Time chairman J. Richard Munro, the move to oust Munro's named successor had already gained so much momentum that a pragmatic Munro agreed to support Levin in the move.

Levin and Ross first contacted the directors they knew they could rely on, then gradually expanded the network so that those who were reluctant felt they had little choice but to go along. By the time of the fateful meeting, only one director voted against the ouster.[23]

Though at least one board member felt that the evidence produced to remove Nicholas didn't constitute cause, Ross and Levin had developed sufficient **network centrality** to push the co-CEO out. Moreover, once things were set in motion, they moved quickly, not allowing Nicholas time to mount a defense and gain his own support among directors.

POWER SOURCES FOR MIDDLE MANAGERS

The distribution of power down the hierarchy is influenced by organization design factors. Top managers will almost always have more power than middle managers, but the amount of power provided to any given position or organizational group can be built into the organization's structural design.

The allocation of power to middle managers and staff is important because power enables employees to be productive. Managers need sufficient power and latitude to perform their jobs well. When positions are powerless, middle managers may seem ineffective and may become petty, dictatorial, and rules-minded.[24] Several factors that influence the amount of power along the hierarchy are shown in Exhibit 12.2. Power is the result of both task activities and network interactions. When a position is nonroutine, it encourages discretion, flexibility, and creativity. When a job pertains to pressing organizational problems, power is more easily accumulated. Power is also increased when a position encourages contact with high-level people, brings visibility and recognition to employees, and facilitates peer networks both inside and outside the organization.

The variables in Exhibit 12.2 can be designed into specific roles or departments. For example, funds can be allocated to a department so members can attend professional meetings, thereby increasing their visibility and stature. Allowing people to approve their own decisions gives more discretion, reduces dependence on others, and increases power.

The logic of designing positions for more power assumes an organization does not have a limited amount of power to be allocated among high-level and low-level employees. The total amount of power in an organization can be increased by designing tasks and network interactions along the hierarchy so everyone has more influence. If the distribution of power is too heavily skewed toward the top so middle managers are powerless, research suggests the organization will be less effective. A study by Rosabeth Moss Kanter showed that design factors prevented some middle managers and staff personnel from having enough power to accomplish their jobs.

Decision factors can leave an entire level of the hierarchy, such as first line supervisors, in a position of powerlessness. Their jobs may be overwhelmed with rules and precedents, and they may have little opportunity to develop an interaction network in the organization. Minority group members often have little power because management is overprotective,

Exhibit 12.2   Ways in Which Vertical Design Contributes to Power at Middle-Manager Levels.

Design Factor	Generates Power When Factor Is	Generates Powerlessness When Factor Is
Task Activities		
Rules, precedents, and established routines in the job	Few	Many
Task variety and flexibility	High	Low
Rewards for unusual performance and innovation	Many	Few
Approvals needed for nonroutine decisions	Few	Many
Relation of tasks to current problem areas	Central	Peripheral
Network Interactions		
Physical location	Central	Distant
Publicity about job activities and contact with senior officials	High	Low
Participation in programs, conferences, meetings	High	Low
Participation in problem-solving task forces	High	Low

Source: Based on Rosabeth Moss Kanter, "Power Failure in Management Circuits," *Harvard Business Review* 57 (July–August 1979): 65–75.

and thereby precludes opportunities for initiative and exposure needed for power accumulation. The same fate can befall staff specialists.

As advisors behind the scenes, staff people must sell their programs and bargain for resources, but unless they get themselves entrenched in organizational power networks, they have little in the way of favors to exchange. They are not seen as useful to the primary tasks of the organization. . . . Lacking growth prospects themselves and working alone or in very small teams, they are not in a position to develop others or pass on power to them. They miss out on an important way in which power can be accumulated.[25]

Without sufficient power, middle-level people cannot be productive. Power can be built into positions and departments through the design of task activities and interaction opportunities.

POWER SOURCES FOR LOWER-LEVEL PARTICIPANTS

Positions at the bottom of an organization have less power than positions at higher levels. Often, however, people at the bottom levels obtain power disproportionate to their positions and are able to exert influence in an upward direction. Secretaries, maintenance people, word processors, computer programmers, and others find themselves being consulted in decisions or having great latitude and discretion in the performance of their jobs. The power of lower-level employees often surprises managers. The vice president of a university may be more reluctant to fire a secretary than to fire an academic department head. Why does this happen?

People at lower levels obtain power from several sources. Some of these sources are individual because they reflect the personality and skill of employees.[26] Other power sources are position based, as indicated in Exhibit 12.3. One study found that unexpectedly high levels of power came from expertise, physical location, information, and personal effort.[27] When lower-level participants become knowledgeable and expert about certain activities, they are in a position to influence decisions. Sometimes individuals take on difficult tasks and acquire specialized knowledge, and then become indispensable to managers above them. Power accumulation is also associated with the amount of effort and interest displayed. People who have initiative and work beyond what is expected often find themselves with influence. Physical location also helps because some locations are in the center of things. Central location lets a person be visible to key people and become part of interaction networks. Likewise, certain positions are in the flow of organizational information. One example is the secretary to a senior executive. He or she can control information that other people want and will be able to influence those people.

Additional personal sources of upward influence are persuasion and manipulation.[28] Persuasion is a direct appeal to upper management and is the most frequent type of successful upward influence.[29] Manipulation means arranging information to achieve the outcome desired by the employee. It differs from persuasion because, with manipulation, the true objective for using influence is concealed. The final source of power is a position that provides access to other important people.[30] Access to powerful people and the development of a relationship with them provide a strong base of influence. However, access, persuasion, and manipulation only work as sources of power if employees are willing to make influence attempts that will provide desired outcomes.

The Trend Toward Empowerment

A vertical hierarchy with greater power centralized at the top has been a distinctive feature of organizations almost since the appearance of the first large organization. Now we see a major shift away from this approach. Whether we are talking about organic structures, self-managed teams, or high-involvement cultures, the attempts to diffuse and share power are widespread. The notion of encouraging employees to participate fully in the organization is called empowerment. **Empowerment** is power sharing, the delegation of power or authority to subordinates in the organization.[31] It means giving power to others in the organization so they can act more freely to accomplish their jobs.

Personal Sources	Position Sources
Expertise	Physical Location
Effort	Information Flow
Persuasion	Access
Manipulation	

Exhibit 12.3
Power Sources
for Lower-Level
Participants.

In an environment characterized by intense global competition and new technology, many top managers believe giving up centralized control will promote speed, flexibility, and decisiveness. Indeed, fully 74 percent of CEOs reported in a recent survey that they are more participatory, more consensus-oriented, and now rely more on communication than on command. They are finding less value in being dictatorial, autocratic, or imperial.[32] The trend is clearly toward moving power out of the executive suite and into the hands of employees. This trend can be seen in a variety of manufacturing and service industries, including some of the best known companies in the world, such as Chrysler, IDS, Honeywell, Cummins Engine, Boeing, General Electric, and Caterpillar.[33]

REASONS FOR EMPOWERMENT

How can empowerment make an organization more flexible or more effective? There are two answers. The first is that empowerment *increases* the total amount of power in the organization. Many managers mistakenly believe power is a zero-sum game, which means they must give up power in order for someone else to have more. Not true. Both research and the experience of managers indicates that delegating power from the top creates a bigger power pie, so that everyone has more power.[34] Ralph Stayer, CEO of Johnsonville Foods, has given away practically all of his power. Before he did so, he realized central power was an illusion because employees wandered around not caring about doing a good job. "Real power is getting people committed. Real power comes from giving it up to others who are in a better position to do things than you are."[35] In a sense, the executive who gives away power receives a price for it in commitment and creativity. When employees have power, they find ways to use their abilities to make good things happen. Management's fear of power loss is the biggest barrier to empowerment of employees; but by understanding they will actually gain power, delegation should be easy.

Empowerment also increases employee motivation. Research indicates that individuals have a need for *self-efficacy,* which is the capacity to produce results or outcomes, to feel they are effective. Increasing employee power heightens motivation for task accomplishment because people improve their own effectiveness, choosing how to do the task and using their creativity.[36] Most people come into the organization with the desire to do a good job, and empowerment enables them to release the motivation already there. Their reward is a sense of personal mastery and competence.

ELEMENTS OF EMPOWERMENT

Empowering employees means giving them four elements that enable them to act more freely to accomplish their jobs: information, knowledge, power, and rewards.[37]

1. *Employees receive information about company performance.* In companies where employees are fully empowered, such as Semco S/A (described at the beginning of this chapter), no information is secret. At Semco, every employee has access to the books and any other information, including executive salaries. To show they're serious about sharing information, Semco management works with the labor union that represents its workers to train employees—even messengers and cleaning people—to read balance sheets and cash flow statements.

2. *Employees have knowledge and skills to contribute to company goals.* Companies use training programs to give employees the knowledge and skills they need to personally contribute to company performance. For example, regular quality awareness workshops are held at Chrysler Canada's assembly plant in Bramalea, Ontario, so that employees can initiate quality improvements on their own.[38]

3. *Employees have the power to make substantive decisions.* Many of today's most competitive companies are giving workers the power to influence work procedures and organizational direction through quality circles and self-managed work teams. At Prudential Insurance Company's Northeastern Group Operations, teams made up of clerical, processing, technical, and quality control specialists are empowered to approve claims of a certain type or for a certain customer up to a dollar amount representing 95 percent of all claim submissions. Another team decided employees could save the company money by processing claims from home. Workers, free to set their own hours, are setting new records for productivity.[39]

4. *Employees are rewarded based on company performance.* Two of the ways in which organizations can reward employees financially based on company performance are through profit sharing and employee stock ownership plans (ESOPs). At W. L. Gore & Associates, makers of Gore-Tex, compensation takes three forms—salary, profit sharing, and an associates stock ownership program.[40] Reflexite Corporation, a growing and profitable technology-based business described in the Paradigm Buster, is taking the concept of employee empowerment to new levels with its ESOP.

THE EMPOWERMENT PROCESS

When managers decide that delegation of power is important, the process can be accomplished in three stages. The first stage is to diagnose conditions within the organization that cause powerlessness for subordinates. The second stage is to engage in empowerment practices that will increase power at lower levels. Stage three involves feedback to employees that reinforces their success and feelings of effectiveness.

The first stage of diagnosis means looking carefully at organizational and job design elements at the middle and lower levels that reduce power. Recall from Exhibit 12.2 that such factors as too many rules, little task variety, being stuck in a remote location, rewards for routine output rather than innovation, and no opportunity for participating in task forces all reduce power. By analyzing these factors within organizations, the necessary changes for empowerment can be identified.

In stage two of empowerment, the old factors that generate powerlessness are changed, and employees are given access to the elements described in the previous section: information; knowledge and skills; power to make decisions; and rewards based on company performance. This stage usually starts with a clear goal or vision, from the top, publicly stated. Top managers make clear their desire for empowerment, and they articulate clear organizational goals. Employees no longer need to walk in step, but they should all head in the same direction. Next is widespread communication and information sharing. Employees must understand what's going on, otherwise they will not use power.

Employees must also be educated in the knowledge and skills they need to contribute to meeting organizational performance goals. In addition, a systematic

Paradigm Buster

Reflexite Corporation

Once or twice a month, Cecil Ursprung gets a call from someone who wants to buy Reflexite Corporation. Ursprung tells them the company's already been sold—to its employees. Reflexite employees own 59 percent of the company's stock. Reflexite pushes employee ownership to the limit, unlike big-company ESOPs, in which employees hold only 5 to 10 percent of company stock.

And at Reflexite, stock ownership allows workers to behave like owners instead of wage earners. Reflexite manufactures retroreflective material (which coats highway signs and barricades). The technology is extremely complex—the tooling, machinery, and chemicals have to work together just right. As one manager said, "There are so many little things to pay attention to. We've got to have the hearts of the employees to make this thing run." The company has created a "culture of ownership," where employees truly feel a sense of proprietorship and long-term stake in the company. Reflexite employees aren't likely to forget the stake they own—it's reflected in a supplementary paycheck, which may be several hundred dollars a month for an experienced employee. In addition, every letter-

head reads, "An ESOP company . . . where employees are owners." Regular meetings provide information about the company's performance and priorities. At the annual meeting, employees vote for the board of directors.

The structure and culture of ownership helps the company retain experienced employees, a critical asset for a company dependent on complex technology. When the company was facing a financial crisis and potential layoffs because of an economic downturn, the employee-owners devised a voluntary leave-of-absence plan, combined with a pay cut for top and middle management and a cut in manufacturing costs that saved the company more than $200,000. The year ended with profitability intact. When the company comes back strong, everyone will share in the rewards.

Back in the mid-1980s, Cecil Ursprung believed giving employees "some power" made good business sense. Time is proving him right. Though Reflexite competes with the giant 3M Company, which once tried to buy it out, the smaller company has more than doubled its sales, tripled its work force, and increased its profits sixfold.

Source: John Case, "Collective Effort," *Inc.,* January 1992, 32–43.

change in structure is needed to increase employee power. This means jobs will be given more variety, rules will be withdrawn, high-level approvals will no longer be needed, physical locations can be consolidated, levels of the hierarchy can be eliminated, and employees can participate in teams and task forces as they see fit. These structural changes provide the basis for enlarged jobs and enlarged decision making. Recall that at Semco S/A, the employees outvoted the president to acquire a factory building and to shun a possible merger. With clarity on overall company direction and goals, complete information, and a structure that provides latitude, employees can make decisions that use their power to enact task accomplishment.

In the third stage, which is feedback, employees learn how they are doing. Many companies place new emphasis on pay for performance, so employees' success is immediately rewarded. Career advancement is also encouraged as another way to reward excellence. At Prudential's Northeastern Group Operations, workers who take the initiative to solve problems are recognized by awards presented by top managers at company programs. Positive feedback reinforces employee feelings of self-efficacy, so they become comfortable and prosper under empowerment. The organization that has empowered employees will look and act differently from before, with major changes in structure, information sharing, and decision making responsibility.

More organizations can be expected to push power down the vertical hierarchy in the future.

Horizontal Power

Horizontal power pertains to relationships across departments. All vice presidents are usually at the same level on the organization chart. Does this mean each department has the same amount of power? No. Horizontal power is not defined by the formal hierarchy or the organization chart. Each department makes a unique contribution to organizational success. Some departments will have greater say and will achieve their desired outcomes, while others will not. For example, Charles Perrow surveyed managers in several industrial firms.[41] He bluntly asked, "Which department has the most power?" among four major departments: production, sales and marketing, research and development, and finance and accounting. Partial survey results are given in Exhibit 12.4. In most firms, sales had the greatest power. In a few firms, production was also quite powerful. On average, the sales and production

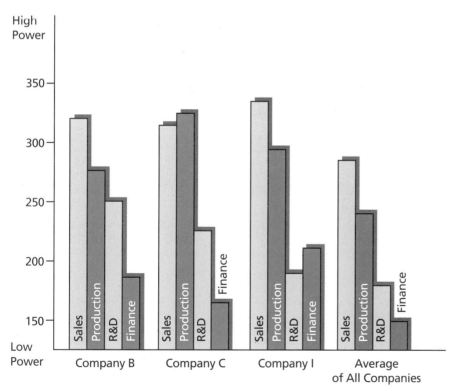

Exhibit 12.4
Ratings of Power among Departments in Industrial Firms.

Source: Charles Perrow, "Departmental Power and Perspective in Industrial Firms," in Mayer N. Zald, ed., *Power in Organizations* (Nashville, Tenn.: Vanderbilt University Press, 1970), 64.

departments were more powerful than R&D and finance, although substantial variation existed. Differences in the amount of horizontal power clearly occurred in those firms.

Horizontal power is difficult to measure because power differences are not defined on the organization chart. However, some initial explanations for departmental power differences, such as those shown in Exhibit 12.4, have been found. The theoretical concept that explains relative power is called strategic contingencies.[42]

STRATEGIC CONTINGENCIES

Strategic contingencies are events and activities both inside and outside an organization that are essential for attaining organizational goals. Departments involved with strategic contingencies for the organization tend to have greater power. Departmental activities are important when they provide strategic value by solving problems or crises for the organization. For example, if an organization faces an intense threat from lawsuits and regulations, the legal department will gain power and influence over organizational decisions because it copes with such a threat. If product innovation is the key strategic issue, the power of R&D can be expected to be high.

The strategic contingency approach to power is similar to the interorganizational power relationships described in Chapter 3. Recall that organizations try to reduce dependency on the external environment. The strategic contingency approach to power suggests that the departments most responsible for dealing with key issues and dependencies in the environment will become most powerful.

POWER SOURCES

Jeffrey Pfeffer and Gerald Salancik, among others, have been instrumental in conducting research on the strategic contingency theory.[43] Their findings indicate that a department rated as powerful may possess one or more of the characteristics illustrated in Exhibit 12.5.[44] In some organizations these five **power sources** overlap, but each provides a useful way to evaluate sources of horizontal power.

Dependency   Interdepartmental dependency is a key element underlying relative power. Power is derived from having something someone else wants. The power of department A over department B is greater when department B depends upon A.[45]

Many dependencies exist in organizations. Materials, information, and resources may flow between departments in one direction, such as in the case of sequential task interdependence (Chapter 4). In such cases, the department receiving resources is in a lower power position than the department providing them. The number and strength of dependencies are also important. When seven or eight departments must come for help to the engineering department, for example, engineering is in a strong power position. In contrast, a department that depends upon many other departments is in a low power position.

In a cigarette factory, one might expect that the production department would be more powerful than the maintenance department, but this was not the case in a cigarette plant near Paris.[46] The production of cigarettes was a routine process. The machinery was automated and production jobs were small in scope. Production workers were not highly skilled and were paid on a piece-rate basis to encourage high production. On the other hand, the maintenance department required skilled

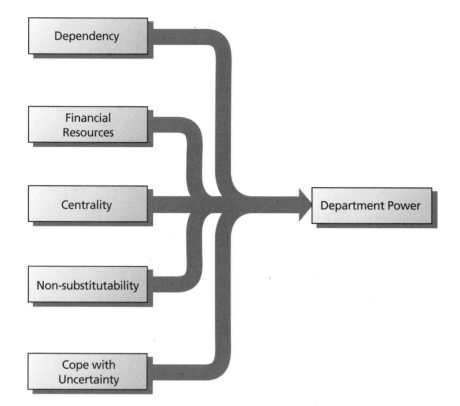

Exhibit 12.5
Strategic Contingencies That Influence Horizontal Power among Departments.

workers. These workers were responsible for repair of the automated machinery, which was a complex task. They had many years of experience. Maintenance was a craft because vital knowledge to fix machines was stored in the minds of maintenance personnel.

Dependency between the two groups was caused by unpredictable assembly line breakdowns. Managers could not remove the breakdown problem; consequently, maintenance was the vital cog in the production process. Maintenance workers had the knowledge and ability to fix the machines, so production managers became dependent upon them. The reason for this dependence was that maintenance managers had control over a strategic contingency—they had the knowledge and ability to prevent or resolve work stoppages.

Financial Resources   There's a new golden rule in the business world: "The person with the gold makes the rules."[47] Control over various kinds of resources, and particularly financial resources, is an important source of power in organizations. Money can be converted into other kinds of resources that are needed by other departments. Money generates dependency; departments that provide financial resources have something other departments want. Departments that generate income for an organization have greater power. The survey of industrial firms reported in Exhibit 12.4 showed sales as the most powerful unit in most of those firms. Sales had power because sales people find customers and sell the product, thereby removing an important problem for the organization. The sales department ensures the inflow of money. An ability to provide financial resources also explains why certain departments are powerful in other organizations, such as universities.

IN PRACTICE ◆ 12.2
University of Illinois

You might expect budget allocation in a state university to be a straightforward process. The need for financial resources can be determined by such things as the number of undergraduate students, the number of graduate students, and the number of faculty in each department.

In fact, resource allocation at the University of Illinois is not clear-cut. The University of Illinois has a relatively fixed resource inflow from state government. Beyond that, important resources come from research grants and the quality of students and faculty. University departments that provide the most resources to the university are rated as having the most power. Some departments have more power because of their resource contribution to the university. Departments that generate large research grants are more powerful because research grants contain a sizable overhead payment to university administration. This overhead money pays for a large share of the university's personnel and facilities. The size of a department's graduate student body and the national prestige of the department also add to power. Graduate students and national prestige are nonfinancial resources that add to the reputation and effectiveness of the university.

How do university departments use their power? Generally, to obtain even more resources from the rest of the university. Very powerful departments receive university resources, such as graduate student fellowships, internal research support, and summer faculty salaries, far in excess of their needs based on the number of students and faculty.[48]

As shown in the example of the University of Illinois, power accrues to departments that bring in or provide resources that are highly valued by an organization. Power enables those departments to obtain more of the scarce resources allocated within the organization. "Power derived from acquiring resources is used to obtain more resources, which in turn can be employed to produce more power—the rich get richer."[49]

Centrality   **Centrality** reflects a department's role in the primary activity of an organization.[50] One measure of centrality is the extent to which the work of the department affects the final output of the organization. For example, the production department is more central and usually has more power than staff groups (assuming no other critical contingencies). Centrality is associated with power because it reflects the contribution made to the organization. The corporate finance department of an investment bank generally has more power than the stock research department. At Morgan Stanley Group, research analysts say they've been pressured to alter negative research reports on the stocks of the firm's corporate clients. "We were held accountable to corporate finance," a former Morgan Stanley analyst said, "playing the game the way corporate finance dictated."[51] By contrast, in the manufacturing firms described in Exhibit 12.4, finance tends to be low in power. When the finance department has the limited task of recording money and expenditures, it is not responsible for obtaining critical resources or for producing the products of the organization.

Nonsubstitutability   Power is also determined by **nonsubstitutability**, which means that a department's function cannot be performed by other readily available resources. Nonsubstitutability increases power. If an employee cannot be easily replaced, his or her power is greater. If an organization has no alternative sources of skill and information, a department's power will be greater. This can be the case when management uses outside consultants. Consultants might be used as substitutes for staff people to reduce the power of staff groups.

The impact of substitutability on power was studied for programmers in computer departments.[52] When computers were first introduced, programming was a rare and specialized occupation. People had to be highly qualified to enter the profession. Programmers controlled the use of organizational computers because they alone possessed the knowledge to program them. Over a period of about ten years, computer programming became a more common activity. People could be substituted easily, and the power of programming departments dropped.

Coping with Uncertainty The chapters on environment and decision making described how elements in the environment can change swiftly and can be unpredictable and complex. In the face of uncertainty, little information is available to managers on appropriate courses of action. Departments that cope with this uncertainty will increase their power.[53] Just the presence of uncertainty does not provide power, but reducing the uncertainty on behalf of other departments will. When market research personnel accurately predict changes in demand for new products, they gain power and prestige because they have reduced a critical uncertainty. Forecasting is only one technique for **coping with uncertainty.** Sometimes uncertainty can be reduced by taking quick and appropriate action after an unpredictable event occurs.

Three techniques departments can use to cope with critical uncertainties are (1) obtaining prior information, (2) prevention, and (3) absorption.[54] *Obtaining prior information* means a department can reduce an organization's uncertainty by forecasting an event. Departments increase their power through *prevention* by predicting and forestalling negative events. *Absorption* occurs when a department takes action after an event to reduce its negative consequences. In the following case, the industrial relations department increased its power by absorbing a critical uncertainty. It took action after the event to reduce uncertainty for the organization.

IN PRACTICE ◆ 12.3
Crystal Manufacturing

Although union influence has been declining in recent years, unions are still actively seeking to extend their membership to new organizations. A new union is a crucial source of uncertainty for many manufacturing firms. It can be a countervailing power to management in decisions concerning wages and working conditions.

In 1990, the workers in Crystal Manufacturing Company voted to become part of the Glassmakers Craft Union. Management had been aware of union organizing activities, but it had not taken the threat seriously. No one had acted to forecast or prevent the formation of a union.

The presence of the union had potentially serious consequences for Crystal. Glassmaking is a delicate and expensive manufacturing process. The float-glass process cannot be shut down even temporarily except at great expense. A strike or walkout would mean financial disaster. Therefore, top management decided that establishing a good working relationship with the union was critically important.

The industrial relations department was assigned to deal with the union. This department was responsible for coping with the uncertainties created by the new union. The industrial relations group quickly developed expertise in union relationships. It became the contact point on industrial relations matters for managers throughout the organization. Industrial relations members developed a network throughout the organization and could bypass the normal chain of command on issues they considered important. Industrial relations had nearly absolute knowledge and control over union relations.

In Crystal Manufacturing Company, the industrial relations unit coped with the critical uncertainty by absorption. It took action to reduce the uncertainty after it appeared. This action gave the unit increased power.

Horizontal power relationships in organizations change as strategic contingencies change. For example, in recent years, a few unions have increased their power by involving themselves in companies' strategic contingencies. In addition to the normal activities of work stoppages and strikes, these unions have become involved in pressuring companies' banks and creditors, challenging applications for financing and industrial revenue bonds, and using boycotts of products, banks, and health insurance companies. Unions have gone so far as to embarrass directors and executives by picketing their homes, opposing management in proxy battles, and communicating directly with stockholders.[55] These activities create new uncertainties and strategic issues for an organization, which can be reduced with the union's cooperation—thereby increasing union influence.

Political Processes in Organizations

Politics, like power, is intangible and difficult to measure. It is hidden from view and is hard to observe in a systematic way. Two recent surveys uncovered the following reactions of managers toward political behavior.[56]

1. Most managers have a negative view towards politics and believe that politics will more often hurt than help an organization in achieving its goals.
2. Managers believe political behavior is common to practically all organizations.
3. Most managers think political behavior occurs more often at upper rather than lower levels in organizations.
4. Political behavior arises in certain decision domains, such as structural change, but is absent from other decisions, such as handling employee grievances.

Based upon these surveys, politics seems more likely to occur at the top levels of an organization and around certain issues and decisions. Moreover, managers do not approve of political behavior. The remainder of this chapter explores more fully what is political behavior, when it should be used, the type of issues and decisions most likely to be associated with politics, and some political tactics that may be effective.

DEFINITION

Power has been described as the available force or potential for achieving desired outcomes. *Politics* is the use of power to influence decisions in order to achieve those outcomes. The exercise of power and influence has led to two ways to define politics—as self-serving behavior or as a natural organizational decision process. The first definition emphasizes that politics is self-serving and involves activities that are not sanctioned by the organization.[57] In this view, politics involves deception and dishonesty for purposes of individual self-interest. This dark view of politics is widely held by laypeople. Recent studies have shown that workers who perceive politics at work within their organization often have related feelings of anxiety and job dissatisfaction. This view explains why managers in the surveys described above did not approve of political behavior.

The second view sees politics as a natural organizational process for resolving differences among organizational interest groups.[58] Politics is the process of bargaining and negotiation that is used to overcome conflicts and differences of opinion. In this view, politics is very similar to the coalition-building decision processes defined in Chapter 11 on decision making. As you read Book Mark 12.0, decide whether the author believes in politics as selfish behavior or as a natural organizational process.

The organization theory perspective views politics as described in the second definition—as a normal decision-making process. Politics is simply the activity through which power is exercised in the resolution of conflicts and uncertainty. Politics is neutral and is not necessarily harmful to the organization. The formal definition of organizational politics is as follows: **Organizational politics** involves activities to acquire, develop, and use power and other resources to obtain one's preferred outcome when there is uncertainty or disagreement about choices.[59] Recall from earlier in the chapter how Steve Ross and Gerald Levin used organizational politics to achieve their desired outcome at Time Warner.

Political behavior can be either a positive or a negative force. Politics is the use of power to get things accomplished—good things as well as bad. Uncertainty and conflict are natural and inevitable, and politics is the mechanism for reaching agreement. Politics includes informal discussions that enable participants to arrive at consensus and make decisions that otherwise might be stalemated or unsolvable.

One reason for a negative view of politics is that political behavior is compared with more rational procedures in organizations. Rational procedures are considered by many managers to be more objective and reliable and to lead to better decisions than political behavior. Rational approaches are effective, but only in certain situations. Both rational and political processes are normally used in organizations.

RATIONAL CHOICE VERSUS POLITICAL BEHAVIOR

Rational Model   The **rational model** of organization is an outgrowth of the rational approach to decision making described in Chapter 11. It describes a number of activities beyond decision making, as summarized in Exhibit 12.6. Behavior in the rational organization is not random or accidental. Goals are clear and choices are made in a logical way. When a decision is needed, the goal is defined, alternatives are identified, and the choice with the highest probability of achieving the desired outcome is selected. The rational model of organization is also characterized by extensive, reliable information systems, central power, a norm of optimization, uniform values across groups, little conflict, and an efficiency orientation.[60]

Political Model   The opposite view of organizational processes within organizations is the **political model,** outlined in Exhibit 12.6. This model assumes organizations

HAVE YOU READ ABOUT THIS?

Managing With Power: Politics and Influence in Organizations
by Jeffrey Pfeffer

Our mental images of power-hungry politicians and ruthless corporate executives have given power and politics a bad name. But Jeffrey Pfeffer argues in his book, *Managing With Power,* that to be effective and successful as individuals and organizations, we must learn how to get power and how to use it. The skills of using power and political influence to get things done are essential to keep organizations from falling further behind in the rapidly changing and increasingly competitive world.

The Sources of Power

Why do some people have power and others do not? Three primary sources of power, according to Pfeffer, are control over resources, the ties one has to other powerful individuals, and the formal authority that comes from one's place in the hierarchy. One of the most important ways an organizational member can increase his or her power base and get things accomplished is by developing allies and building coalitions. "Failures in implementation," Pfeffer points out, "are almost invariably failures to build successful coalitions." Power comes primarily through interactions with others.

The Bottom Line—Political Tactics for Using Power

What good is having power if you never use it? Unless organizational members learn political tactics and strategies for using power, promising projects never get off the ground, new products sit on the drawing board, and organizations suffer. Pfeffer describes a number of tactics for using power to get things accomplished, including:

- Proper framing. The framing of an issue can often decide its outcome, and it's important to lay the groundwork early for a positive discussion. Proper framing means presenting an idea or decision so that it is seen in the most favorable light.

- Proper timing. Determining when to do something is almost as important as determining what to do. It is essential to understand the benefits and costs of taking early action, the strategies of delay, and how deadlines affect decisions and implementation.

- Proper procedures. To make the use of power more easily accepted, follow an organizational pattern that is familiar and comfortable to everyone involved. Consult with those who have a stake in the final outcome or create task forces to share the responsibility.

Keeping Power and Coping with its Loss

According to Pfeffer, there may be a greater sin than making mistakes when using power—the sin of doing nothing, of remaining passive in the face of great challenges, opportunities, or problems. Ironically, the fear of losing power often causes people to behave in ways that virtually guarantee its loss. A defensive management style that avoids confronting changes and problems leads to sluggish or even stagnant organizations. Yet managers can recognize that people and positions lose power eventually in a shifting world, and organizations can smooth these changes.

Conclusion

Organizational decisions are worthless unless they are implemented. For organizations and organizational members to succeed, they can recognize that implementation comes about only through the effective use of power. At its best, politics is a skillful, shrewd, and sensitive use of power to bring about positive results for our organizations and our world.

Managing With Power: Politics and Influence in Organizations by Jeffrey Pfeffer is published by Harvard Business School Press.

are made up of coalitions that disagree about goals and have poor information about alternatives. The political model defines the organization as made up of groups that have separate interests, goals, and values. Disagreement and conflict are normal, so power and influence are needed to reach decisions. Groups will engage in the push

Exhibit 12.6   Rational versus Political Models of Organization.

Organizational Characteristic	Rational Model	Political Model
Goals, preference	Consistent across participants	Inconsistent, pluralistic within the organization
Power and control	Centralized	Decentralized, shifting coalitions and interest groups
Decision process	Orderly, logical, rational	Disorderly, characterized by push and pull of interests
Rules and norms	Norm of optimization	Free play of market forces; conflict is legitimate and expected
Information	Extensive, systematic, accurate	Ambiguous; information used and withheld strategically
Beliefs about cause-effect relationships	Known, at least to a probability estimate	Disagreements about causes and effects
Decisions	Based on outcome-maximizing choice	Result of bargaining and interplay among interests
Ideology	Efficiency and effectiveness	Struggle, conflict, winners and losers

Source: Based on Jeffrey Pfeffer, *Power in Organizations* (Marshfield, Mass.: Pitman, 1981), 31.

and pull of debate to decide goals and to reach decisions. Decisions are disorderly. Information is ambiguous and incomplete. Bargaining and conflict are the norm. The political model applies to organizations that strive for democracy and participation in decision making by empowering workers. Purely rational procedures do not work in democratic organizations.

Mixed Model   In many organizations neither the rational model nor the political model characterizes things fully, but each will be observed some of the time. This might be called a **mixed model.** One model may dominate, depending on organizational environment and context. The important thing is that both models apply to organizational processes. Managers may strive to adopt rational processes, but it is wishful thinking to assume an organization can be run without politics. Bargaining and negotiation should not be avoided for fear they are improper. The political model is an effective mechanism for reaching decisions under conditions of uncertainty and disagreement.

The rational model applies best to organizations in stable environments with well-understood technologies. It is inadequate when there is uncertainty and conflict, as illustrated in the following case.

IN PRACTICE ◆ 12.4

Britt Technologies, Inc.

Britt Technologies was a new manufacturer of computer peripheral equipment, including tape and disk drives. The company's target was to sell equipment to manufacturers of complete computer systems. The strategy was working and the company was initially quite successful, but a problem emerged.

The problem pertained to the extent to which products should be custom-designed for customers. A manufacturer might be interested in a tape or disk product, but only if it could be reengineered to change some operating characteristics. This reengineering was expensive and time-consuming, and some managers felt it would be better to sell only what had already been designed. Indeed, almost every customer would ask for some modifications rather than accept the standard models that were available.

The design problem led to disagreement among executives. The marketing vice president believed engineering and production should produce whatever the market demanded. The vice president of production disagreed, saying that efficiencies would never be achieved unless the company developed a standard product line. The controller agreed with the production vice president, because profit margins would be reduced if redesigned units were continually produced. The engineering vice president was willing to redesign products so long as doing so didn't result in engineering overload.

Rather than hammer out this problem among themselves, Britt's executives decided to retain an outside consultant. They believed an outside consultant with experience in these matters would know how to rationally arrive at the correct answer, which each manager would accept. The consultant did some market research, competitive analysis, and strategic planning. Another consultant was hired to examine manufacturing operations.

Unfortunately, the company was left in a state of drift while the consultants did their research. Without a clear strategy, Britt Technologies was not excelling at either standard products or custom-designed peripherals. Marketing would sometimes accept custom orders, but manufacturing would refuse to produce them. The consultants' reports arrived in due course and were very logical, but Britt executives still disagreed among themselves. A clear strategy was delayed. In this highly competitive industry, once the company fell behind the competition, bankruptcy was inevitable.[61]

Britt Technologies was searching for a logical, correct answer through an orderly decision process that used precise data. Executives tried to apply the rational model to a situation that required a political model. The managers had to bargain and negotiate, use whatever information was available, and build a coalition among themselves. They couldn't do it. The search for rational answers was a time-consuming process that caused the company's failure.

DOMAINS OF POLITICAL ACTIVITY

Politics is a mechanism for arriving at consensus when uncertainty is high. Managers at the top of an organization face greater uncertainty than those at lower levels, so more political activity will appear. Moreover, some issues are associated with inherent disagreement. Resources, for example, are critical for the survival and effectiveness of departments, so resource allocation often becomes a political issue. "Rational" methods of allocation do not satisfy participants. Four **domains of political activity** (areas in which politics plays a role) in most organizations are structural change, interdepartmental coordination, management succession, and resource allocation.

Structural Change   Structural reorganizations strike at the heart of power and authority relationships. Reorganizations such as those discussed in Chapter 6 change responsibilities and tasks, which also affects the underlying power base from strategic contingencies. For these reasons, a major reorganization can lead to an explosion of political activity.[62] Managers will actively bargain and negotiate to maintain the responsibilities and power bases they have. Without the commitment of top management, the implementation of a new structure would be difficult because of resistance and political disagreements. The effective use of top manager politics was demonstrated by Don Keith at Phillips Electrical.

IN PRACTICE ◆ 12.5
Phillips Electrical, Ltd.

Phillips Electrical is a huge Canadian electronics manufacturer based in Toronto. The president of the radio group, Don Keith, wanted to reorganize from a functional structure to a product structure. His group had forty-two hundred employees and manufactured four types of sophisticated radio equipment for airlines and air forces around the world. Keith knew the proposed reorganization would generate resistance because the functional managers (for example, the manager of engineering) would lose power and stature. They would manage service groups to the major product lines rather than be dominant managers in the organization.

Keith's first step was to get top management support from headquarters for the reorganization. The next step was to sell the change within his radio group. Keith knew he could impose reorganization unilaterally, but the cost would be great. He would lose the cooperation of some managers, especially those in the functional areas that stood to lose stature. Keith held a series of meetings to explain the problems being faced by the company and the potential benefits of reorganization. He spent time teaching what product management was all about, especially to the functional managers. He also spent time talking to individual managers, thereby building a coalition in favor of the reorganization. Keith kept the allegiance of one key functional manager by agreeing to reassign him as a product manager to maintain his power base in the organization. For two other managers, Keith had to rely heavily on his formal authority to impose the new structure despite resistance.

The entire process of persuasion and negotiation took fourteen months. Once the organization structure was in place, weekly meetings of functional and product managers were continued, chaired by Don Keith, so managers could see each other's problems and gain confidence in the new structure.

The effective use of politics by Don Keith early in the development of the product structure at Phillips made the ultimate outcome successful. Obtaining headquarters's support and building a coalition in his radio group were critical. After the functional managers adapted to the changes, they became more cooperative and played an important support role to the product lines. The new structure enabled Phillips to attain a higher level of performance.

Interdepartmental Coordination Relationships between major organizational departments typically are not well defined. When joint issues arise, managers have to meet and work out solutions on an ad hoc basis. The ability of one department to achieve its goal often involves the cooperation of other departments. Interdepartmental coordination lacks rules and precedents to guide it. Uncertainty and conflict are common, especially when the issues are departmental territory and responsibility. Political processes help define respective authority and task boundaries.[63]

For example, a marketing department decided to hire its own computer people because it could not get sufficient help from the management information systems department to do marketing projects. The marketing vice president argued that poor service from the MIS department justified hiring his own people. The vice president of MIS rallied the rest of the organization in arguing that the marketing department was now getting additional services at the expense of the other departments. Top management agreed, and the data processing people hired by marketing were transferred to the MIS department.[64] The MIS department preserved its boundaries through political influence.

Management Succession   Management succession involves hiring new executives, promotions, and transfers.[65] These changes have great political significance at top organizational levels where uncertainty is high and networks of trust, cooperation, and communication among executives are important. A new manager with a new set of alliances or values can upset stable working relationships and previous agreements. Hiring decisions can generate uncertainty, discussion, and disagreement. Managers can use hiring and promotion to strengthen network alliances and coalitions by putting their own people in prominent positions. Subordinates often feel obligated and will go along with their benefactor in critical decisions.

At General Motors, Fred Donner often promoted people within the finance group who were generally not even considered contenders for the position. This earned Donner the undying loyalty of these managers, who in a sense owned their corporate life to him.[66]

Resource Allocation   Resource allocation decisions encompass all resources required for organizational performance, including salaries, operating budgets, employees, office facilities, equipment, use of the company airplane, and so forth. Resource allocation is something of a puzzle because these decisions can be accomplished by either the rational model or the political model. The value of resources is easy to compute, so the calculations should be straightforward. Allocation of a travel budget could be based upon the number of employees in a department, for example, but the political model is often used. Resources are so vital that disagreement about priorities exists, and political processes help resolve the dilemmas: For example, the new dean of one engineering department computed his budget request based on the number of students, not realizing that many precedents, allowances, and special considerations were involved in the budget allocation. His department's budget was reduced to benefit the powerful business department, which was responsible for most student enrollment and for the university's reputation.

PROCESS FRAMEWORK

The framework in Exhibit 12.7 summarizes the political processes described so far. Uncertainty and disagreement are the antecedent conditions that influence whether the political model is used. The political approach typically will be used in specific areas, such as structural change, interdepartmental coordination, management succession, and resource allocation. Political behavior is often used for reaching decisions in these areas because the areas are uncertain and are associated with conflict. Managers who ignore political processes in these situations will have little influence over final outcomes.

Exhibit 12.7   A Process Framework of Organizational Politics.

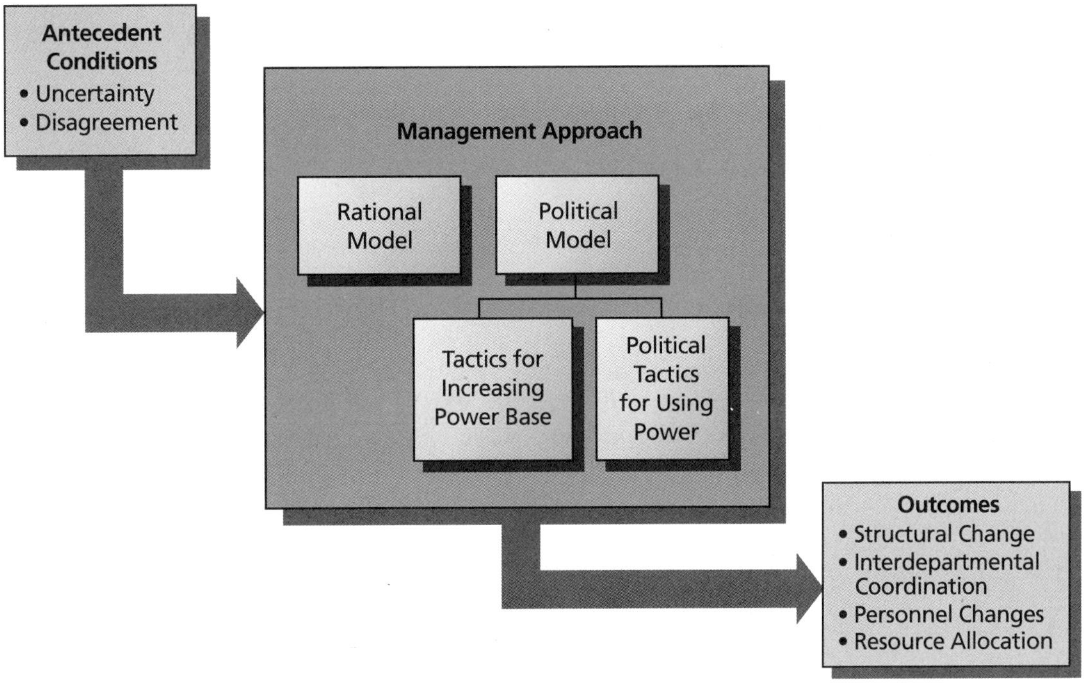

Source: Adapted from Donald J. Vredenburgh and John G. Maurer, "A Process Framework of Organizational Politics," *Human Relations* 37 (1984): 47–66.

Exhibit 12.7 also illustrates that when the political model is used, managers may wish to adopt specific tactics for increasing power or for using their power politically. The next section examines specific factors that managers can adopt to increase or use power.

Power and Political Tactics

One theme in this chapter has been that power in organizations is not primarily a phenomenon of the individual. It is related to the resources departments command, the role departments play in an organization, and the environmental contingencies with which departments cope. Position and responsibility more than personality and style determine a manager's influence on outcomes in the organization.

Power is used through individual political behavior, however. Individual managers seek agreement about a strategy to achieve their departments' desired outcomes. Individual managers negotiate decisions and adopt tactics that enable them to acquire and use power.

Thus, to fully understand the use of power within organizations, it is important to look at both structural components and individual behavior.[67] While the power base comes from larger organizational forms and processes, the political use of power involves individual-level activities. This section briefly summarizes tactics managers can use to increase the power base of their departments and political tactics they can use to achieve desired outcomes. These tactics are summarized in Exhibit 12.8

TACTICS FOR INCREASING THE POWER BASE

Four **tactics for increasing the power base** are:

1. *Enter areas of high uncertainty.*   One source of departmental power is to cope with critical uncertainties.[68] If department managers can identify key uncertainties and take steps to remove those uncertainties, the department's power base will be enhanced. Uncertainties could arise from stoppages on an assembly line, from the needed quality of a new product, or from the inability to predict a demand for new services. Once an uncertainty is identified, the department can take action to cope with it. By their very nature, uncertain tasks will not be solved immediately. Trial and error will be needed, which is to the advantage of the department. The trial-and-error process provides experience and expertise that cannot easily be duplicated by other departments.

2. *Create dependencies.*   Dependencies are another source of power.[69] When the organization depends upon a department for information, materials, knowledge, or skills, that department will hold power over the others. This power can be increased by incurring obligations. Doing additional work that helps out other departments will obligate the other departments to respond at a future date. The power accumulated by creating a dependency can be used to resolve future disagreements in the department's favor. An equally effective and related strategy is to reduce dependency on other departments by acquiring necessary information or skills. For example, data processing departments have created dependencies in many health care organizations because of the enormous amount of paperwork. Doing paperwork fast and efficiently has created a dependency, giving data processing more power.

3. *Provide resources.*   Resources are always important to organizational survival. Departments that accumulate resources and provide them to an organization in the form of money, information, or facilities will be powerful. For example, In Practice 12.2 described how university departments with the greatest power are those that obtain external research funds for contributions to university overhead. Likewise, marketing departments are powerful in industrial firms because

Exhibit 12.8
Power and Political Tactics in Organizations.

Tactics for Increasing the Power Base	Political Tactics for Using Power
1. Enter areas of high uncertainty 2. Create dependencies 3. Provide resources 4. Satisfy strategic contingencies	1. Build coalitions 2. Expand networks 3. Control decision premises 4. Enhance legitimacy and expertise 5. Make preferences explicit, but keep power implicit

they bring in financial resources. As mentioned earlier, "The person with the gold makes the rules."

4. *Satisfy strategic contingencies.*   The theory of strategic contingencies says that some elements in the external environment and within the organization are especially important for organizational success. A contingency could be a critical event, a task for which there are no substitutes, or a central task that is interdependent with many others in the organization. An analysis of the organization and its changing environment will reveal strategic contingencies. To the extent that contingencies are new or are not being satisfied, there is room for a department to move into those critical areas and increase its importance and power.

In summary, the allocation of power in an organization is not random. Power is the result of organizational processes that can be understood and predicted. The abilities to reduce uncertainty, increase dependency on one's own department, obtain resources, and cope with strategic contingencies will all enhance a department's power. Once power is available, the next challenge is to use it to attain helpful outcomes.

POLITICAL TACTICS FOR USING POWER

The use of power in organizations requires both skill and willingness. Many decisions are made through political processes because rational decision processes do not fit. Uncertainty or disagreement is too high. **Political tactics for using power** to influence decision outcomes were discussed briefly in Book Mark 12.0 and are described in more detail as follows:

1. *Build coalitions.*   Coalition building means taking the time to talk with other managers to persuade them to your point of view.[70] Most important decisions are made outside formal meetings. Managers discuss issues with each other and reach agreements on a one-to-one basis. Effective managers are those who huddle, meeting in groups of twos and threes to resolve key issues.[71] An important aspect of coalition building is to build good relationships. Good interpersonal relationships are built on liking, trust, and respect. Reliability and the motivation to work with others rather than exploit others are part of coalition building.[72]

2. *Expand networks.*   Networks can be expanded (1) by reaching out to establish contact with additional managers and (2) by co-opting dissenters. The first approach is to build new alliances through the hiring, transfer, and promotion process. Placing in key positions people who are sympathetic to the outcomes of the department can help achieve departmental goals.[73] On the other hand, the second approach, co-optation, is the act of bringing a dissenter into one's network. One example of co-optation involved a university committee whose membership was based on promotion and tenure. Several female professors who were critical of the tenure and promotion process were appointed to the committee. Once a part of the administrative process, they could see the administrative point of view and learned that administrators were not as evil as suspected. Co-optation effectively brought them into the administrative network.[74]

3. *Control decision premises.*   To control decision premises means to constrain the boundaries of a decision. One technique is to choose or limit information provided to other managers. A common method is simply to put your department's

best foot forward, such as selectively presenting favorable criteria. A variety of statistics can be assembled to support the departmental point of view. A university department that is growing rapidly and has a large number of students can make claims for additional resources by emphasizing its growth and large size. Such objective criteria do not always work, but they are a valuable step.

Decision premises can be further influenced by limiting the decision process. Decisions can be influenced by the items put on an agenda for an important meeting or even by the sequence in which items are discussed.[75] Items discussed last, when time is short and people want to leave, will receive less attention than those discussed early. Calling attention to specific problems and suggesting alternatives also will affect outcomes. Stressing a specific problem to get it—rather than problems not relevant to your department—on the agenda is an example of agenda setting.

4. *Enhance legitimacy and expertise.*   Managers can exert the greatest influence in areas in which they have recognized legitimacy and expertise. If a request is within the task domain of a department and is consistent with the department's vested interest, other departments will tend to comply. Members can also identify external consultants or other experts within the organization to support their cause.[76] For example, a financial vice president in a large retail firm wanted to fire the director of human resource management. She hired a consultant to evaluate the human resource management projects undertaken to date. A negative report from the consultant provided sufficient legitimacy to fire the director, who was replaced with a director loyal to the financial vice president.

5. *Make preferences explicit, but keep power implicit.*   If managers do not ask, they seldom receive. Political activity is effective only when goals and needs are made explicit so the organization can respond. Managers should bargain aggressively and be persuasive. An assertive proposal may be accepted because other managers have no better alternatives. Moreover, an explicit proposal will often receive favorable treatment because other alternatives are ambiguous and less well defined. Effective political behavior requires sufficient forcefulness and risk taking to at least try to achieve desired outcomes.

The use of power, however, should not be obvious.[77] If one formally draws upon his or her power base in a meeting by saying, "My department has more power, so the rest of you have to do it my way," the power will be diminished. Power works best when it is used quietly. To call attention to power is to lose it. Explicit claims for power are made by the powerless, not by the powerful. People know who has power. There is substantial agreement on which departments are more powerful. Explicit claims to power are not necessary and can even harm the department's cause.

When using any of the preceding tactics, recall that most people feel self-serving behavior hurts rather than helps an organization. If managers are perceived to be throwing their weight around or are perceived to be after things that are self-serving rather than beneficial to the organization, they will lose respect. On the other hand, managers must recognize the relational and political aspect of their work. It is not sufficient to be rational and technically competent. Politics is a way to reach agreement. When managers ignore political tactics, they may find themselves failing without understanding why. This happened to Jeff Glover, a new manager with a firm in California's Silicon Valley.

IN PRACTICE ◆ 12.6
Halifax Business Machines

Jeff Glover was promoted to group leader at Halifax Business Machines because of his reputation as a well-respected technical specialist. Glover was interested in medical applications of the electronic business machines manufactured by his company. After visiting a hospital several times during his wife's illness, he developed specifications for a new piece of medical equipment. It was a clever modification of one of Monarch's existing products, and Glover's bosses were enthusiastic. They gave him permission to work half time on the new product and asked for cooperation from appropriate people in engineering, marketing, and manufacturing to develop a prototype.

A month after the project began, Glover was told that the engineer assigned to the project had to reduce his time to only five hours a week. Then Glover discovered that the manufacturing engineer who was supposed to do cost estimates was temporarily reassigned to a small crisis in a New York plant. Three days later, Glover was hit with the most damaging blow. His boss said that marketing had redone the market potential analysis and found the projected market was only one-fifth the size originally forecast. The project would have to be stopped immediately. Glover was furious. He resigned at the end of the day.

A few weeks later, Glover learned from a friend that the sales manager had immediately disliked Glover's idea when it was proposed. He didn't want his people to develop new knowledge about hospitals and medical purchasing practices. He had gotten one of his people to develop pessimistic numbers about market potential and had suggested to top management that time not be wasted on Glover's project.[78]

Glover's problem was that he naively assumed the logic and technical merits of his proposed machine would carry the day. He ignored political relationships, especially with the sales manager. He did not take the time to build a network of support for the project among key managers. He should have devoted more time to building a coalition and enhancing the legitimacy of his proposal, perhaps with his own market research.

Summary and Interpretation

This chapter presented two views of organization. One view, covered only briefly, is the rational model of organization. This view assumes that organizations have specific goals and that problems can be logically solved. The other view, discussed throughout most of the chapter, is based upon a power and political model of organization. This view assumes the goals of an organization are not specific or agreed upon. Organizational departments have different values and interests, so managers come into conflict. Decisions are made on the basis of power and political influence. Bargaining, negotiation, persuasion, and coalition building decide outcomes.

The most important idea from this chapter is the reality of power and political processes in organizations. Differences in departmental tasks and responsibilities inevitably lead to differences in power and influence. Power differences determine decision outcomes. Uncertainty and disagreement lead to political behavior.

Understanding sources of power and how to use politics to achieve outcomes for the organization are requirements for effective management.

Many managers prefer the rational model of decision making. This model is clean and objective. Rational thinking is effective when decision factors are sharply specified because of manager agreement and good information. Political processes, however, should not be ignored. Political decision processes are used in situations of uncertainty, disagreement, and poor information. Decisions are reached through the clash of values and preferences, and by the influence of dominant departments.

Other important ideas in this chapter pertain to power in organizations. The traditional view of vertical power, with power centralized at the top, still applies to most organizations. However, as today's organizations face increasing global competition and environmental uncertainty, top managers are finding that empowering lower-level employees helps their organizations run leaner and more profitably, fight off competition, and move rapidly into new markets.

Research into horizontal power processes has uncovered characteristics that make some departments more powerful than others. Such factors as dependency, resources, and the removal of strategic contingencies determine the influence of departments. Political strategies, such as coalition building, expanded networks, and control of decision premises, help departments achieve desired outcomes. Organizations can be more effective when managers appreciate the realities of power and politics.

Finally, despite its widespread use in organizations, many people distrust political behavior. They fear political behavior may be used for selfish ends that benefit the individual but not the organization. If politics is used for personal gain, other managers will become suspicious and will withdraw their support. Politics will be accepted when it is used to achieve the legitimate goal of a department or an organization.

KEY CONCEPTS

authority	organizational politics
centrality	political model
coping with uncertainty	power
decision premises	power sources
domains of political activity	rational model
empowerment	strategic contingencies
mixed model	tactics for increasing the power base
nonsubstitutability	tactics for using power
network centrality	

DISCUSSION QUESTIONS

1. If an organization decides to empower lower-level workers, are future decisions more likely to be made using the rational or political model of organization? Discuss.

2. Explain how control over decision premises gives power to a person.

3. In Exhibit 12.4, research and development has greater power in company B than in the other firms. Discuss possible strategic contingencies that give R&D greater power in this firm.

4. If you are a lower-level employee in an organization, how might you increase your power base?

5. Some positions are practically powerless in an organization. Why would this be? How could those positions be redesigned to have greater power?

6. State University X receives 90 percent of its financial resources from the state and is overcrowded with students. It is trying to pass regulations to limit student enrollment. Private University Y receives 90 percent of its income from student tuition and has barely enough students to make ends meet. It is actively recruiting students for next year. In which university will students have greater power? What implications will this have for professors and administrators? Discuss.

7. Do you believe it is possible to increase the total amount of power in an organization by delegating power to employees? Explain.

8. Why do you think most managers have a negative view of politics?

9. The engineering college at a major university brings in three times as many government research dollars as does the rest of the university combined. Engineering appears wealthy and has many professors on full-time research status. Yet, when internal research funds are allocated, engineering gets a larger share of the money, even though it already has substantial external research funds. Why would this happen?

10. Would the rational model, political model, or mixed model be used in each of the following decision situations: quality-control testing in a production department, resource allocation in an executive suite, and deciding which division will be in charge of a recently built plant.

GUIDES TO ACTION

As an organization manager, keep these guides in mind:

1. Do not leave lower organization levels powerless. If vertical power is too heavy in favor of top management, empower lower levels by giving them the tools they need to perform better: information about the company's performance; knowledge and skills that help them contribute to company goals; the power to make decisions; and rewards based on company performance.

2. Be aware of the less visible, but equally important, horizontal power relationships that come from the ability of a department to deal with strategic contingencies that confront the organization. Increase the horizontal power of a department by increasing involvement in strategic contingencies.

3. Expect and allow for political behavior in organizations. Politics provides the discussion and clash of interests needed to crystallize points of view and to reach a decision. Build coalitions, expand networks, control decision premises, enhance legitimacy, and make preferences explicit to attain desired outcomes.

4. Use the rational model of organization when alternatives are clear, when goals are defined, and when managers can estimate the outcomes accurately. In these circumstances, coalition building, cooptation, or other political tactics are not needed and will not lead to effective decisions.

Consider these guides when analyzing the following cases.

Diamy Corporation (Canada)

Diamy Corporation is the second largest producer of household appliances in Canada. Three-quarters of Diamy's production is sold wholesale to retail chains that put their own brand on the product. Diamy also exports to the United States and Europe.

Len Sullivan became transportation director seven years ago. He has spent his entire career with Diamy. In the early days, his job was to trace shipments and check freight rates in huge catalogs. Sometimes he did other transportation jobs, such as chauffeuring VIPs or giving bus tours to groups of foreign visitors.

Times have changed in the transportation department. The director is a senior executive, and his staff spends time negotiating with hundreds of carriers to reduce freight rates and improve service.

Freight rates have gradually increased to almost 10 percent of the wholesale price of appliances. Getting a good deal can make a real difference to Diamy's profit margin. Provincial regulations have been reduced in response to deregulation in the United States and to the federal government in Ottawa. Freight haulers used to set their rates by gentleman's agreement, and they were all but identical. Now both truck and rail carriers are in head-to-head price competition to win the business of Diamy and other manufacturers.

The transportation department uses a computer to calculate the best freight rates. The cost of shipping a truckload of washing machines from Ottawa to Toronto could vary from four hundred to eight hundred dollars. The computer keeps track of the dizzying array of changing freight rates and helps calculate the most economical mode of transportation.

Sullivan recently met with Elizabeth Dee from InterCanada Lines, Inc. Dee explained that several trucks were returning from the Maritimes half empty. She proposed that if Diamy would rent space on the half-empty trailers, InterCanada would give it full-truckload rates. This would save Diamy 10 percent to 15 percent on hauls from its plant in New Brunswick.

Sullivan was noncommittal and offered to have his team look over the details and calculate competitive rates. At a departmental meeting a few days later, Sullivan was surprised by intense disagreement within his group about whether Diamy should make a deal with InterCanada. One manager felt Diamy could do as well using the lowest rates available at the time of haul. Another believed Diamy should pressure InterCanada into an even better deal because Diamy was a major customer. This manager believed Diamy could play InterCanada off against Montreal Freight for a low bid to become one of Diamy's two major carriers (a major carrier was guaranteed a large amount of freight business for an agreed-upon rate).

The next day, Diamy's president mentioned to Sullivan that the idea of using InterCanada as a major carrier seemed like a good one. He hoped Sullivan would be able to strike a deal with InterCanada that would save Diamy money on freight costs.

Sullivan was stunned that the president was aware of the debate in the transportation department and wanted an agreement with InterCanada. He wondered what he should do next.

QUESTIONS

1. What is the problem within the transportation department? Is Sullivan an effective politician?
2. Why have the stature and influence of the transportation department increased at Diamy over the last few years? Explain.
3. Is Diamy a strategic contingency for freight companies? Would it be in Sullivan's interest to use just a few trucking lines and have them dependent upon Diamy for most of their business? Discuss.

The Air Force A-7D Brake Problem

From the hearing before the Subcommittee on Economy in Government of the Joint Economic Committee of the Congress of the United States, 91st Congress, August 13, 1969:

Mr. Vandivier: In the early part of 1967, the B. F. Goodrich Wheel & Brake Plant at Troy, Ohio, received an order from the Ling-Temco-Vought Company of Dallas, Texas, to supply wheels and brakes for the A-7D aircraft, built by LTV for the Air Force.

The tests on the wheels and brakes were to be conducted in accordance with the requirements of military specification Mil-W-5013G as prepared and issued by the U.S. Air Force and to the requirements set forth by LTV Specification Document 204-16-37D.

The wheels were successfully tested to the specified requirements, but the brake, manufactured by Goodrich under BEG part No. 2-1162-3, was unable to meet the required tests.

The laboratory tests specified for the brake were divided into two categories: dynamic brake tests and static brake tests. . . .

Generally speaking, the brake passed all the static brake tests, but the brake could not and did not pass any of the dynamic tests I have just described with the exception of the new brake maximum energy stop.

During the first few attempts to qualify the brake to the dynamic tests, the brake ran out of lining material after a few stops had been completed and the tests were terminated. Attempts were made to secure a lining material that would hold up during the grueling fifty-one-stop test, but to no avail. Although I have been aware for several months that great difficulty was being experienced with the A-7D brake, it was not until April 11, 1968, almost a full year after qualification testing had begun, that I became aware of how these tests were being conducted.

The thirteenth attempt at qualification was being conducted under B.F. Goodrich internal Test No. T-1867.

On the morning of April 11, Richard Gloor, who was the test engineer assigned to the A-7D project, came to me and told me he had discovered that some time during the previous twenty-four hours, instrumentation used to record brake pressure had been miscalibrated deliberately so that while the instrumentation showed that a pressure of 1,000 pounds per square inch had been used to conduct brake stop numbers 46 and 47 (two overload energy stops) 1,100 p.s.i.

had actually been applied to the brakes. Maximum pressure available on the A-7D is 1,000 p.s.i.

Mr. Gloor further told me he had questioned instrumentation personnel about the miscalibration and had been told they were asked to do so by Searle Lawson, a design engineer on the A-7D.

Chairman Proxmire: Is this the gentleman who is with you now, Mr. Vandivier?

Mr. Vandivier: That is correct. I subsequently questioned Lawson who admitted he had ordered the instruments miscalibrated at the direction of a superior.

Upon examining the log sheets kept by laboratory personnel, I found that other violations of the test specifications had occurred.

For example, after some of the overload stops, the brake had been disassembled and the three stators or stationary members of the brake had been taken to the plant toolroom for rework and, during an earlier part of the test, the position of elements within the brake had been reversed to distribute the lining wear more evenly.

Additionally, instead of braking the dynamometer to a complete stop as required by military specifications, pressure was released when the wheel and brake speed had decelerated to 10 miles per hour.

The reason for this, I was later told, was that the brakes were experiencing severe vibrations near the end of the stops, causing excessive lining wear and general deterioration of the brake.

All these incidents were in clear violation of military specifications and general industry practice.

I reported these violations to the test lab supervisor, Mr. Ralph Gretzinger, who reprimanded instrumentation personnel and stated that under no circumstance would intentional miscalibration of instruments be tolerated.

As for the other discrepancies noted in test procedures, he said that he was aware that they were happening but that as far as he was concerned the tests could not, in view of the way they were being conducted, be classified as qualification tests.

Later that same day, the worn-brake, maximum energy stop was conducted on the brake. The brake was landed at a speed of 161 m.p.h. and the pressure was applied. The dynamometer rolled a distance of 16,800 feet before coming to rest. The elapsed stopping time was 141 seconds. By computation, this stop time shows the aircraft would have traveled over three miles before stopping.

Within a few days, a typewritten copy of the test logs of test T-1867 was sent to LTV to assure LTV that a qualified brake was almost ready for delivery.

Virtually every entry in this so-called copy of the test logs was drastically altered. As an example, the stop time for the worn-brake maximum energy stop was changed from 141 seconds to a mere 46.8 seconds.

On May 2, 1968, the fourteenth attempt to qualify the brakes was begun, and Mr. Lawson told me that he had been informed by both Mr. Robert Sink, project manager at Goodrich—I am sorry, Mr. Sink is project manager—and Mr. Russell Van Horn, project manager at Goodrich, that "regardless of what the brake does on test, we're going to qualify it."

Chairman Proxmire: What was that?

Mr. Vandivier: The statement was, "Regardless of what the brake does on test, we're going to qualify it."

He also said that the latest instructions he had received were to the effect that if the data from this latest test turned out worse than did test T-1867, then we would write our report based on T-1867.

Chairman Proxmire: The statement was made by whom?

Mr. Vandivier: Mr. Lawson told me this statement was made to him by Mr. Robert Sink, project manager, and Mr. Russell Van Horn, project manager.

During this latest and final attempt to qualify the four-rotor brake, the same illegal procedures were used as had been used on attempt number thirteen. Again after thirty stops had been completed, the positions of the friction members of the brake were reversed to distribute wear more evenly. After each stop, the wheel was removed from the brake and the accumulated dust was blown out. During each stop, pressure was released when the deceleration had reached 10 m.p.h. . . .

After stop number 48—the third overlap stop—temperatures in the brake were so high that the fuse plug, a safety device that allows air to escape from the tire to prevent blowout, melted and allowed the tire to deflate.

The same thing happened after stop number 49—the fourth overload stop. Both these occurrences were highly irregular and in direct conflict with the performance criteria of the military requirements.

Chairman Proxmire: I understand you have a picture of this that might help us see it.

Mr. Vandivier: Yes.

Chairman Proxmire: Do you want to show that to us now?

Mr. Vandivier: I was going to show it here just a little bit later.

Chairman Proxmire: Go ahead. . . .

Mr. Vandivier: All right.

In addition to these highly questionable practices, a turnaround capability test, or simulated mission test, was conducted incorrectly due to a human error. When the error was later discovered, no corrections were made.

While these tests were being conducted, I was asked by Mr. Lawson to begin writing a qualification report for the brake. I flatly refused and told Mr. Gretzinger, the lab supervisor, who was my superior, that I could not write such a report because the brake had not been qualified.

He agreed and he said that no one in the laboratory was going to issue such a report unless a brake was actually qualified in accordance with the specification and using standard operating procedures.

He said that he would speak to his own supervisor, the manager of the technical services section, Mr. Russell Line, and get the matter settled at once.

He consulted Mr. Line and assured me that both had concurred in the decision not to write a qualification report.

I explained to Lawson that I had been told not to write the report and that the only way such a report could be written was to falsify test data.

Mr. Lawson said that he was well aware of what was required but that he had been ordered to get a report written, regardless of how or what had to be done.

He stated that, if I would not write the report, he would have to, and he asked if I would help him gather the test data and draw up the various engineering curves and graphic displays that are normally included in a report.

I asked Mr. Gretzinger, my superior, if this was all right and he agreed. As long as I was only assisting in the preparation of the data, it would be permissible.

Both Lawson and I worked on the elaborate curves and logs in the report for nearly a month. During this time, we both frankly discussed the moral aspects of what we were doing, and we agreed that our actions were unethical and probably illegal.

Several times during that month I discussed the A-7D testing with Mr. Line and asked him to consult his superiors in Akron to prevent a false qualification report from being issued. Mr. Line declined to do so and advised me that it would be wise to just do my work and keep quiet.

I told him of the extensive irregularities during testing and suggested that the brake was actually dangerous and, if allowed to be installed on an aircraft, might cause an accident.

Mr. Line said he thought I was worrying too much about things that did not really concern me and advised me to just "do what you're told."

About the first of June. . . .

Chairman Proxmire: You skipped one line here.

Mr. Vandivier: Yes.

Chairman Proxmire: You said "I asked him". . . .

Mr. Vandivier: Yes. I asked Mr. Line if his conscience would hurt him if such a thing caused the death of a pilot and this is when he replied that I was worrying about too many things that did not concern me and advised me to "do what you're told."

About the first of June 1968, Mr. Gretzinger asked if I was finished with the graphic data and said he had been advised by the chief engineer, Mr. H. C. Sunderman, that when the data were finished they were to be delivered to him—Sunderman—and he would instruct someone in the engineering department to actually write the report. Accordingly, when I had finished with the data, I gave it to Mr. Gretzinger, who immediately took it from the room. Within a few minutes, he was back and was obviously angry.

He said that Mr. Sunderman had told him no one in the engineering department had time to write the report and that we would have to do it ourselves.

At this point, Mr. Line came into the room demanding to know "What the hell is going on." Mr. Gretzinger explained the situation again and said he would not allow such a report to be issued by the lab.

Mr. Line then turned to me and said he was "sick of hearing about this damned report. Write the———————thing and shut up about it." . . .

Many, many of the elaborate engineering curves attached to the report were complete and total fabrications, based not on what had actually occurred, but on information that would fool both LTV and the Air Force.

I have mentioned already that the turnaround capability test that was supposed to determine what temperatures might be experienced by the brake during a typical flight mission had been misconducted through a human error on the part of the test lab operator.

Rather than rerun this very important test, which would have taken only some six hours to complete, it was decided to manufacture the data.

This we did, and the result was some very convincing graphic curves. These curves were supposed to demonstrate to LTV and the Air Force exactly what the temperatures in the brakes had been during each minute of the simulated mission.

They were completely false and based only on data that would be acceptable to the customers.

I could spend the entire day here discussing the various elaborate falsifications that went into this report but I feel that, by now, the picture is clear.

The report was finally issued on June 5, 1968, and almost immediately, flight tests on the brake were begun at Edwards Air Force Base in California.

Mr. Lawson was sent to Goodrich to witness these tests, and when he returned, he described various mishaps that had occurred during the flight tests and he expressed the opinion to me that the brake was dangerous.

That same afternoon, I contacted my attorney and after describing the situation to him, asked for his advice. . . .

About this time the Air Force demanded that Goodrich produce its raw data from the tests. This Goodrich refused to do, claiming that the raw data was proprietary information.

Goodrich management decided that, since pressure was being applied by the Air Force, a conference should be arranged with LTV management and engineering staff. A preconference meeting was set for Goodrich personnel to go over the questionable points in the report.

On Saturday, July 27, 1968, Mr. Robert Sink, Mr. Lawson, Mr. John Warren—A-7D project engineer—and I met and went over the discrepant items contained in the qualification report. Each point was discussed at great length and a list of approximately forty separate discrepancies was compiled. These, we were told by Mr. Sink, would be revealed to LTV personnel the following week.

However, by the time of the meeting with LTV, only a few days later, the list of discrepancies had been cut by Mr. Sink from forty-three items to a mere three.

Mr. Chairman, during this meeting, Mr. Lawson took from the blackboard at the Goodrich conference room word for word listing of all these discrepancies. This contains the forty-three items I have just mentioned. I would like to enter this into the record and also enter the subsequent list of three major discrepancies that later came out of this meeting.

Chairman Proxmire: Do you have copies of those documents?

Mr. Vandivier: Yes, I do have.

Mr. Vandivier: The following two-month period was one of a constant running battle with LTV and the Air Force, during which time the Air Force refused final approval of the qualification report and demanded a confrontation with Goodrich about supplying raw data.

On October 8, another meeting was held, again with Mr. Sink, Mr. Lawson, Mr. Warren, and myself present.

This was only one day prior to a meeting with Air Force personnel, and Mr. Sink said that he had called the meeting "so that we are all coordinated and tell the same story." Mr. Sink said that LTV personnel would be present at the meeting with the Air Force and our policy would be to "Let LTV carry the ball." Mr. Sink appeared to be especially concerned because Mr.. Bruce Tremblay, the Air Force engineer most intimate with A-7D brake, would be present at the meeting, and it was felt at B.F. Goodrich that Mr. Tremblay was already suspicious.

Mr. Sink warned us that "Mr. Tremblay will probably be at his antagonistic best." He added that the Air Force had wanted to meet at the Goodrich plant, but that we—Goodrich—couldn't risk having them that close to the raw data. "We don't want those guys in the plant," Mr. Sink said.

What happened at the meeting with the Air Force, I do not know, I did not attend.

On October 18, I submitted my resignation to Goodrich effective November 1.

Chairman Proxmire: Thank you, Mr. Vandivier.

Mr. Lawson, . . . the statement you have just heard read by Mr. Vandivier, do you agree with it fully or in part or do you disagree and can you tell us your reaction to it?

Mr. Lawson: The factual data that Mr. Vandivier has presented is correct, to the best of my knowledge. . . .

Chairman Proxmire: How long did you work as a technical writer?

Mr. Vandivier: Approximately three years. . . .

Chairman Proxmire: In your statement, you say "Accordingly I wrote the report but in the conclusion I stated that the brake had 'not' met either the intent or the requirement of the specification and therefore was 'not' qualified." Then you said, "When the final report was typewritten and ready for publication the two 'nots' in the conclusion had been eliminated, thereby changing the entire meaning of the conclusion." . . .

Was this the only time in the three years you worked as a technical writer with Goodrich; the only time that you made false entries into a report of manufacture?

Mr. Vandivier: Yes it was.

Chairman Proxmire: I cannot understand what was going through the minds of Goodrich's management the way you have told the story. . . .

Mr. Vandivier: I cannot tell you what their motivation is. I can tell you what I feel was behind this.

Chairman Proxmire: All right.

Mr. Vandivier: I feel in the beginning stages of this program someone made a mistake and refused to admit that mistake, and to hide his stupidity or his ignorance, or his pride, or whatever it was, he simply covered up, you know, with more false statements, false information, and at the time it came time to deliver this brake, Goodrich was so far down the road that there was nothing else to do.

They had no time to start over; I think it was a matter not of company policy but of company politics. I think that probably three or four persons within the Goodrich organization at Troy were responsible for this. I do not believe for a moment that the corporate officials in Akron knew that this was going on.

QUESTIONS

1. What is the underlying problem at B.F. Goodrich?
2. Analyze the sources of vertical and horizontal power within the B.F. Goodrich Wheel & Brake Plant. Compare the power of project managers versus the power of technical specialists. Is this the type of situation in which politics can be expected to appear? Discuss.
3. Why do you think the company got to the point of needing to falsify data? Why did employees yield to pressures to falsify data? What were the costs to B.F. Goodrich? To the whistle-blower?

NOTES

1. Ricardo Semler, *Maverick: The Success Story Behind the World's Most Unusual Workplace* (New York: Warner Books, 1993); Ricardo Semler, "All for One, One for All," *Harvard Business Review* (September-October, 1989): 76–84.

2. Examples are Michael Korda, *Power: How to Get It, How To Use It* (New York: Random House, 1975), and Robert J. Ringer, *Winning through Intimidation* (Los Angeles: Los Angeles Book Publishing, 1973).

3. John R. P. French, Jr., and Bertram Raven, "The Bases of Social Power," *Group Dynamics,* in D. Cartwright and A.F. Zander, eds. (Evanston, Ill.: Row Peterson, 1960), 607–23.

4. Ran Lachman, "Power from What? A Reexamination of Its Relationships with Structural Conditions," *Administrative Science Quarterly* 34 (1989): 231–51; Daniel J. Brass, "Being in the Right Place: A Structural Analysis of Individual Influence in an Organization," *Administrative Science Quarterly* 29 (1984): 518–39.

5. Robert A. Dahl, "The Concept of Power," *Behavioral Science* 2 (1957): 201–15.

6. W. Graham Astley and Paramijit S. Sachdeva, "Structural Sources of Intraorganizational Power: A Theoretical Synthesis," *Academy of Management Review* 9 (1984): 104–13; Abraham Kaplan, "Power in Perspective," in Robert L. Kahn and Elise Boulding, eds., *Power and Conflict in Organizations* (London: Tavistock, 1964), 11–32.

7. Gerald R. Salancik and Jeffrey Pfeffer, "The Bases and Use of Power in Organizational Decision-Making: The Case of the University," *Administrative Science Quarterly* 19 (1974): 453–73.

8. Richard M. Emerson, "Power-Dependence Relations," *American Sociological Review* 27 (1962): 31–41.

9. Rosabeth Moss Kanter, "Power Failure in Management Circuits," *Harvard Business Review* (July-August 1979): 65–75.

10. Bro Uttal, "Behind the Fall of Steve Jobs," *Fortune,* 5 August 1985, 20–24; Deborah C. Weise, "Steve Jobs versus Apple: What Caused the Final Split," *Business Week,* 30 September 1985, 48.

11. A. J. Grimes, "Authority, Power, Influence, and Social Control: A Theoretical Synthesis," *Academy of Management Review* 3 (1978): 724–35.

12. Astley and Sachdeva, "Structural Sources of Intraorganizational Power."

13. Jeffrey Pfeffer, "The Micropolitics of Organizations," in Marshall W. Meyer, et al., *Environments and Organizations* (San Francisco: Jossey-Bass, 1978): 29–50.

14. Jeffrey Pfeffer, *Managing with Power: Politics and Influence in Organizations* (Boston: Harvard Business School Press, 1992).

15. Robert L. Peabody, "Perceptions of Organizational Authority," *Administrative Science Quarterly* 6 (1962): 479.

16. Sydney Finkelstein, "Power in Top Management Teams: Dimensions, Measurement, and Validation," *Academy of Management Journal* 35 (1992): 505–38.

17. Jeffrey Pfeffer, *Power in Organizations* (Marshfield, Mass.: Pitman, 1981).

18. Thomas H. Davenport, Robert G. Eccles, and Lawrence Prusak, "Information Politics," *Sloan Management Review* (Fall 1992): 53–65.

19. Johnnie L. Roberts and Randall Smith, "Who Gets the Blame for Paramount Gaffes: Big Cast of Characters," *Wall Street Journal,* 13 December 1993, A1.

20. Andrew M. Pettigrew, *The Politics of Organizational Decision-Making* (London: Tavistock, 1973).

21. Astley and Sachdeva, "Structural Sources of Intraorganizational Power"; Noel M. Tichy and Charles Fombrun, "Network Analysis in Organizational Settings," *Human Relations* 32 (1979): 923–65.

22. Steven Lipin, "Golub Solidifies Hold at American Express, Begins to Change Firm," *Wall Street Journal,* 30 June 1993, A1.

23. Ann M. Morrison, "After the Coup at Time Warner," *Fortune,* 23 March 1992, 82–89.

24. Kanter, "Power Failure in Management Circuits."

25. Ibid., p. 70.

26. David C. Wilson and Graham K. Kenny, "Managerially Perceived Influence over Intradepartmental Decisions," *Journal of Management Studies* 22 (1985): 155–73; Warren Keith Schilit, "An Examination of Individual Differences as Moderators of Upward Influence Activity in Strategic Decisions," *Human Relations* 39 (1986): 933–53.

27. David Mechanic, "Source of Power in Lower Participants in Complex Organizations," *Administrative Science Quarterly* 7 (1962): 349–64.

28. Richard T. Mowday, "The Exercise of Upward Influence in Organizations," *Administrative Science Quarterly* 23 (1978): 137–56.

29. Warren K. Schilit and Edwin A. Locke, "A Study of Upward Influence in Organizations," *Administrative Science Quarterly* 27 (1982): 304–16.

30. Richard S. Blackburn, "Lower Participant Power: Toward a Conceptual Integration," *Academy of*

Management Review 6 (1981): 127–31.

31. Edwin P. Hollander and Lynn R. Offermann, "Power and Leadership in Organizations," *American Psychologist* 45 (February 1990): 179–89.

32. Thomas A. Stewart, "New Ways to Exercise Power," *Fortune,* 6 November 1989, 52–64; Thomas A. Stewart, "CEOs See Clout Shifting," *Fortune,* 6 November 1989, 66.

33. Frank Shipper and Charles C. Manz, "Employee Self-Management without Formally Designated Teams: An Alternative Road to Empowerment," *Organizational Dynamics* (Winter 1992): 48–61; Bob Filipczak, "Ericsson General Electric: The Evolution of Empowerment," *Training,* September 1993, 21–27.

34. Arnold S. Tannenbaum and Robert S. Cooke, "Organizational Control: A Review of Studies Employing the Control Graph Method," in Cornelius J. Lamners and David J. Hickson, eds., *Organizations Alike and Unlike* (Boston: Rutledge and Keegan Paul, 1980), 183–210.

35. Stewart, "New Ways to Exercise Power."

36. Jay A. Conger and Rabindra N. Kanungo, "The Empowerment Process: Integrating Theory and Practice," *Academy of Management Review* 13 (1988): 471–82.

37. David E. Bowen and Edward E. Lawler III, "The Empowerment of Service Workers: What, Why, How, and When," *Sloan Management Review* (Spring 1992): 31–39.

38. Gordon Brockhouse, "Can This Marriage Succeed?" *Canadian Business,* October 1992, 128–35.

39. Peter C. Fleming, "Empowerment Strengthens the Rock," *Management Review* (December 1991): 34–37.

40. Shipper and Manz, "An Alternative Road to Empowerment."

41. Charles Perrow, "Departmental Power and Perspective in Industrial Firms," in Mayer N. Zald, ed., *Power in Organizations* (Nashville, Tenn.: Vanderbilt University Press, 1970), 59–89.

42. D. J. Hickson, C. R. Hinings, C. A. Lee, R. E. Schneck, and J. M. Pennings, "A Strategic Contingencies Theory of Intraorganizational Power," *Administrative Science Quarterly* 16 (1971): 216–29; Gerald R. Salancik and Jeffrey Pfeffer, "Who Gets Power—and How They Hold onto It: A Strategic-Contingency Model of Power," *Organizational Dynamics* (Winter 1977): 3–21.

43. Pfeffer, *Managing with Power;* Salancik and Pfeffer, "Who Gets Power"; C. R. Hinings, D. J. Hickson, J. M. Pennings, and R. E. Schneck, "Structural Conditions of Intraorganizational Power,"

Administrative Science Quarterly 19 (1974): 22–44.

44. Carol Stoak Saunders, "The Strategic Contingencies Theory of Power: Multiple Perspectives," *Journal of Management Studies* 27 (1990): 1–18; Warren Boeker, "The Development and Institutionalization of Sub-Unit Power in Organizations," *Administrative Science Quarterly* 34 (1989): 388–510; Irit Cohen and Ran Lachman, "The Generality of the Strategic Contingencies Approach to Sub-Unit Power," *Organizational Studies* 9 (1988): 371–91.

45. Emerson, "Power-Dependence Relations."

46. Michel Crozier, *The Bureaucratic Phenomenon* (Chicago: University of Chicago Press, 1964).

47. Pfeffer, *Managing with Power.*

48. Jeffrey Pfeffer and Gerald Salancik, "Organizational Decision-Making as a Political Process: The Case of a University Budget," *Administrative Science Quarterly* (1974): 135–51.

49. Salancik and Pfeffer, "Basis and Use of Power in Organizational Decision-Making," 470.

50. Hickson, et al., "Strategic Contingencies Theory."

51. Michael Siconolfi, "At Morgan Stanley, Analysts Were Urged to Soften Harsh Views," *Wall Street Journal,* 14 July 1992, A1.

52. Pettigrew, *Politics of Organizational Decision-Making.*

53. Hickson, et al., "Strategic Contingencies Theory."

54. Ibid.

55. Aaron Bernstein, "The Unions Are Learning to Hit Where It Hurts," *Business Week,* 17 March 1986, 112–14.

56. Jeffrey Gantz and Victor V. Murray, "Experience of Workplace Politics," *Academy of Management Journal* 23 (1980): 237–51; Dan L. Madison, Robert W. Allen, Lyman W. Porter, Patricia A. Renwick, and Bronston T. Mayes, "Organizational Politics: An Exploration of Managers' Perception," *Human Relations* 33 (1980): 79–100.

57. Gerald R. Ferris and K. Michele Kacmar, "Perceptions of Organizational Politics," *Journal of Management* 18 (1992): 93–116; Parmod Kumar and Rehana Ghadially, "Organizational Politics and its Effects on Members of Organizations," *Human Relations* 42 (1989): 305–14; Donald J. Vredenburgh and John G. Maurer, "A Process Framework of Organizational Politics," *Human Relations* 37 (1984): 47–66; Bronston T. Mayes and Robert W. Allen, "Toward a Definition of Organizational Politics," *Academy of Management Review* 2 (1977): 675; Gantz and Murray, "Experience of Workplace Politics," 248.

58. Amos Drory and Tsilia Romm, "The Definition of Organizational Politics: A Review," *Human Relations* 43 (1990): 1133–54; Vredenburgh and Maurer, "A Process Framework of Organizational Politics."

59. Pfeffer, *Power in Organizations,* p. 70.

60. Ibid.

61. Adapted from Don Hellriegel, John W. Slocum, Jr., and Richard W. Woodman, *Organizational Behavior* (St. Paul: West, 1986); and Pfeffer, *Power in Organizations,* 339–41.

62. Madison, et al., "Organizational Politics;" Jay R. Galbraith, *Organizational Design* (Reading, Mass.: Addison-Wesley, 1977).

63. Gantz and Murray, "Experience of Workplace Politics," 248.

64. Victor Murray and Jeffrey Gantz, "Games Executives Play: Politics at Work," *Business Horizons,* December 1980, 14.

65. Gantz and Murray, "Experience of Workplace Politics"; Pfeffer, *Power in Organizations.*

66. J. Patrick Wright, *On a Clear Day You Can See General Motors: John D. DeLorean's Look inside the Automotive Giant* (Grosse Point, Mich.: Wright Enterprises, 1979), 41.

67. Daniel J. Brass and Marlene E. Burkhardt, "Potential Power and Power Use: An Investigation of Structure and Behavior," *Academy of Management Journal* 38 (1993): 441–70.

68. Hickson, et al., "A Strategic Contingencies Theory."

69. Pfeffer, *Power in Organizations.*

70. Ibid.

71. V. Dallas Merrell, *Huddling: The Informal Way to Management Success* (New York: AMACON, 1979).

72. Vredenburgh and Maurer, "A Process Framework of Organizational Politics."

73. Ibid.

74. Pfeffer, *Power in Organizations.*

75. Ibid.

76. Ibid.

77. Kanter, "Power Failure in Management Circuits"; Pfeffer, *Power in Organizations.*

78. Based on John P. Kotter, "How to Win Friends and Influence Comanagers," *Canadian Business,* October 1985, 29–30, 100–107.

CHAPTER

13

Intergroup Relations and Conflict

CHAPTER TOPICS

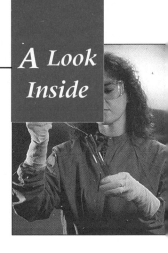

Centers for Disease Control

When the Centers for Disease Control set up the AIDS (acquired immunodeficiency syndrome) laboratory in Atlanta with new funding, hopes were high about discovering new information on the disease. The AIDS lab hired several well-known scientists who were to undertake several lines of research. However, because of emerging conflicts, research was slowed, and some experiments were sabotaged.

One conflict was between administrators and research scientists. Most of the administrators were epidemiologists, who used statistical surveys to investigate diseases; most of the researchers considered themselves laboratory researchers. The difference led to disagreements about the types of data to be collected and the publication of research papers. Another conflict was between M.D. and Ph.D. researchers. M.D. researchers had a little knowledge across several areas; Ph.D. researchers specialized in one area, perhaps spending several years on one research project. These contrasting philosophies led to conflicts about the types of research to be undertaken. In one confrontation, a noted virologist ordered another researcher's experiments thrown away. In yet another dispute, a conservative administrator did not support a research project sponsored by a homosexual rights activist.

The consequence of these rivalries led to the resignations of five of the six senior scientists. Distrust among scientific subgroups also led to some projects being abandoned. Moreover, a few scientists claimed tampering, such as cultures being rearranged at night or on weekends.

Because of conflicts, the AIDS lab was judged a failure, so the CDC sought new management. The hope was that a strong manager could correct the rivalries and distrust, and use the AIDS laboratory's resources to further the battle against this horrifying disease.[1]

T he AIDS laboratory is a dramatic illustration of how conflict can thwart the mission of even a professional organization. Scientists fought petty battles and even sabotaged one another's experiments. Intergroup jealousy and rivalry colored decision making on nearly every issue, delaying the publication of key results and slowing the more important battle against AIDS. Conflict within the CDC produced no winners.

A question for managers is whether conflict or collaboration should be encouraged across departments. Will people be more highly motivated when they are urged to cooperate with one another or when they compete? How can managers get the most out of people, enhance job satisfaction and team identification, and realize high organizational performance?

PURPOSE OF THIS CHAPTER

This chapter will discuss the nature of conflict among groups—similar to what occurred in the CDC's AIDS laboratory—and whether conflict is healthy or unhealthy for organizations. The notion of conflict has appeared in previous chapters. In Chapter 6, we talked about horizontal linkages, such as teams and task forces, that encourage coordination among functional departments. Chapter 7 examined the trend in today's globally competitive companies toward flatter, more horizontal structures that emphasize cooperation rather than competition among employees in self-managed teams. In Chapter 11 on decision making, coalition building was proposed as one way to resolve disagreements among departments. Chapter 12 examined power and political processes for managing competing claims on scarce resources. The very nature of organizations invites conflict, because organizations are composed of departmental groupings that have diverse and conflicting interests.

This chapter examines the nature and resolution of conflict more closely. Organizational conflict comes in many forms. Departments differ in goals, work activities, and prestige, and their members differ in age, education, and experience. The seeds of conflict are sown in these differences. As in the AIDS lab, conflict has to be effectively managed or an organization may fail completely to achieve its goals.

In the first sections of this chapter, intergroup conflict is defined, and the consequences of conflict are identified. Then the causes of horizontal conflict in organizations are analyzed, followed by a detailed discussion of techniques for preventing and reducing horizontal conflict. The final sections turn to vertical conflict, such as between management and unions, and consider techniques for controlling and resolving this conflict.

What Is Intergroup Conflict?

Intergroup conflict requires three ingredients: group identification, observable group differences, and frustration. First, employees have to perceive themselves as part of an identifiable group or department.[2] Second, there has to be an observable group difference of some form. Groups may be located on different floors of the building, members may have gone to different schools, or members may work in different departments. The ability to identify oneself as a part of one group and to observe differences in comparison with other groups is necessary for conflict.[3]

The third ingredient is frustration. Frustration means that if one group achieves its goal, the other will not; it will be blocked. Frustration need not be severe and only needs to be anticipated to set off intergroup conflict. Intergroup conflict will appear when one group tries to advance its position in relation to other groups. **Intergroup conflict** can be defined as the behavior that occurs between organizational groups when participants identify with one group and perceive that other groups may block their group's goal achievement or expectations.[4] Conflict means that groups clash directly, that they are in fundamental opposition. Conflict is similar to competition but more severe. **Competition** means rivalry between groups in the pursuit of a common prize, while *conflict* presumes direct interference with goal achievement. Intergroup conflict within organizations can occur in both horizontal and vertical directions.

HORIZONTAL CONFLICT

As shown in Exhibit 13.1, **horizontal conflict** occurs between groups or departments at the same level in the hierarchy, such as between line and staff.[5] Production may have a dispute with quality control because new quality procedures reduce production efficiency. The sales department may disagree with finance about credit policies that make it difficult to win new customers. R&D and sales may fight over the design for a new product.[6] In the AIDS lab described at the beginning of this chapter, the

Exhibit 13.1 Types of Intergroup Conflict.

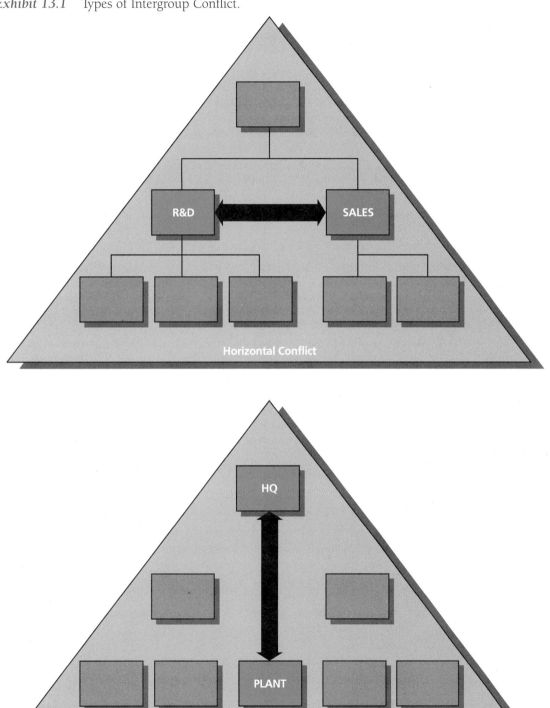

fight between M.D. and Ph.D. researchers would be considered horizontal. Horizontal coordination of some sort is needed to reduce conflict and achieve collaboration.

VERTICAL CONFLICT

Conflict also arises vertically between hierarchical levels.[7] **Vertical conflict** arises over issues of control, power, goals, and wages and benefits. A typical source of vertical conflict is between headquarters executives and regional plants or franchises. For example, one study found conflict between a local television station and its New York headquarters. As another example, franchise owners for Taco Bell, Burger King, and KFC are in conflict with headquarters because of the rapid increase of company-owned stores, often in neighborhoods where they compete directly with franchisees. Some franchisees have gone so far as to take headquarters to court over this issue.[8] Vertical conflict can occur among any levels of the hierarchy, such as between crew leaders and supervisors. The most visible form of vertical conflict occurs between management and workers and is often formalized by union-management relations.

The Nature of Intergroup Conflict

Intergroup conflict in both vertical and horizontal directions has been studied in a variety of settings. Experimenters and consultants have been able to observe conflict and to test methods for reducing or resolving conflict. This research has provided several insights into the behavioral dynamics that occur within and between groups.

At one time, the U.S. air-traffic controllers union became embroiled in a conflict with the Federal Aviation Administration (FAA). The mismanagement of that intergroup conflict was a disaster for the air-traffic controllers.

IN PRACTICE ◆ 13.1

PATCO

A few years ago, twelve thousand of the United States' air-traffic controllers joined together in a strike against the federal government. They were striking for higher pay and better working conditions. The controllers were supremely confident, dedicated to their cause, and certain they would win.

One month later, the controllers' strike seemed to symbolize a suicide march rather than a courageous mission. The controllers' self-confidence was badly eroded. The reaction of the FAA had been seriously miscalculated. The Professional Air Traffic Controllers Organization (PATCO) was frantically seeking a salvage operation that would save the jobs of the controllers and the dignity of the union.

One year later, the union was dead. Most of its members were fired from their government jobs. The union was found by the courts to have broken the law by striking against the government. It was decertified.

What happened to bring about such a dramatic shift in the prospects of PATCO union members? Why did PATCO leaders miscalculate so badly?

Union members badly overestimated their importance to air travel and their worth to the government. Members genuinely believed the government could not operate the nation's air transport system without the controllers. They also believed their enormous demands were justified. However, while controllers probably do endure more stress than ordinary government workers, they were more highly paid than other workers and also had job security. An average salary of thirty-three thousand dollars didn't seem that low to outsiders.

Several other reasons for PATCO's failure also surfaced. One was extreme internal cohesiveness. When the government issued an ultimatum with the backing of the full power of the presidency and the federal government, PATCO didn't flinch. Instead of compromising, PATCO members pulled together to stick it out. The emotional commitment to union solidarity became more important than the logical rationale for the strike.

Moreover, PATCO members didn't listen. They refused to believe President Ronald Reagan, who insisted that federal strikes were illegal and would be broken regardless of cost. Drew Lewis, secretary of transportation, said that, if a strike were called, the strikers would be dismissed and there would be no amnesty. PATCO didn't gain the support of other unions, such as the Airline Pilots Association or the International Machinist's Union. They were overconfident to the point of believing they could shut down the airline system by themselves. Also, they went on strike in the fall, when air transportation was easy to manage. They should have waited until midwinter when control problems were more severe.

The Professional Air Traffic Controllers Organization made several blunders and miscalculations, with tragic human and financial costs. The union members lost their jobs as air-traffic controllers, and the union itself was dead at the tender age of thirteen.[9]

TYPES OF CHANGES

The **behavioral changes** that took place among PATCO officials and union members during the strike are similar to changes that take place in most conflict situations. The types of changes frequently observed during intergroup conflict are as follows:[10]

1. People strongly identify with a group when members share a common mission or value. Members think of their group as separate and distinct from other groups. They develop pride and show signs of the "we feelings" that characterize an in-group. This in-group identification was very visible among members of PATCO.
2. The presence of another group invites comparison between "we" and "they." Members prefer the in-group to the out-group. The "they" for PATCO members was the Federal Aviation Administration.
3. If a group perceives itself in intense conflict with another group, its members become more closely knit and cohesive. Members pull together to present a solid front to defeat the other group. A group in conflict tends to become more formal and accepting of autocratic leader behavior. This strong internal cohesiveness was clearly visible among members of PATCO.
4. Group members tend to see some other groups as the enemy rather than as a neutral object. PATCO perceived the FAA and the Department of Transportation as adversaries, and members displayed negative sentiments toward them.
5. Group members tend to experience a "superiority complex." They over-estimate their own strengths and achievements and underestimate the strength and achievements of other groups. This certainly took place in PATCO. Overconfidence in their ability and strengths was the biggest mistake PATCO members made.
6. Communication between competing groups will decrease. If such communication does take place, it tends to be characterized by negative statements and

hostility. Members of one group do not listen or give credibility to statements by the other group. PATCO, for example, did not fully assimilate the statements made by President Reagan and Transportation Secretary Lewis.

7. When one group loses in a conflict, members lose cohesion. Group members experience increased tension and conflict among themselves and look for a scapegoat to blame for the group's failure. After the failed strike, PATCO members blamed one another and their leaders for the strike's failure and their loss of jobs.

8. Intergroup conflict and associated changes in perception and hostility are not the result of neurotic tendencies on the part of group members. These processes are natural and occur when group members are normal, healthy, and well-adjusted.

These behavioral outcomes of intergroup conflict research were vividly displayed in PATCO. They also can be observed in other organizations. Members of one high school or college often believe their school is superior to a rival school. Employees in one plant perceive themselves as making a greater contribution to the organization than do employees in other plants. Once these perceptions are understood, they can be managed as a natural part of intergroup dynamics.

MODEL OF INTERGROUP CONFLICT

Exhibit 13.2 illustrates a **model of intergroup conflict.** The boxes on the left of the model are the organizational and intergroup factors that set the stage for intergroup conflict. An intergroup situation typically leads to conflict when a specific incident

Exhibit 13.2   Model of Intergroup Conflict in Organizations.

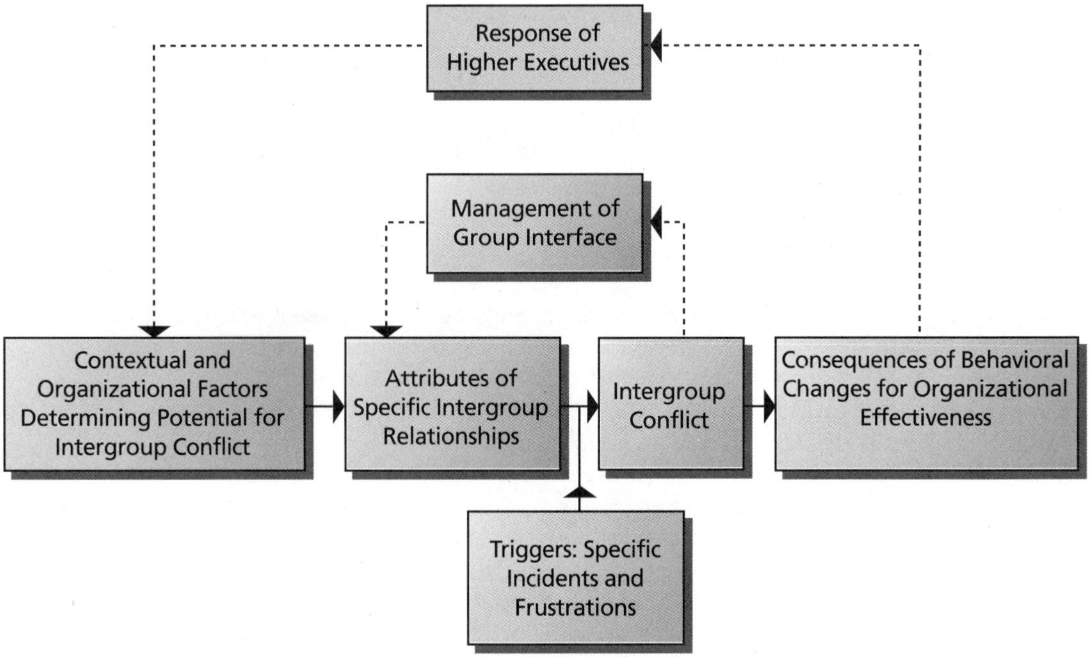

Source: Adapted from Richard E. Walton and John E. Dutton, "The Management of Interdepartmental Conflict," *Administrative Science Quarterly* 14 (1969): 73–84; and Louis R. Pondy, "Organizational Conflict: Concepts and Models," *Administrative Science Quarterly* 12 (1967): 296–320.

or frustration triggers a dispute. The boxes at the top indicate the responses managers can make to control emergent conflict.

A conflict at Apple Computer between the Apple II and Macintosh groups reflects the model in Exhibit 13.2. Organizational factors that led to the conflict were physical separation of the two groups and different goals. The trigger for conflict was an annual meeting in which senior executives devoted most of the program to Macintosh products and ignored Apple II's innovations, which were the backbone of the company at that time. The consequence for Apple was poor morale and decreased performance in the Apple II division. Management responded by paying more attention to Apple II and by changing conditions so the Apple II group would not be physically removed from the rest of the organization.

The remainder of this chapter describes the attributes of organizations in Exhibit 13.2 that lead to conflict, and the responses managers can use to manage or prevent conflict.

Horizontal Conflict

CONTEXTUAL AND ORGANIZATIONAL FACTORS

The potential for horizontal conflict exists in any situation in which separate departments are created, members have an opportunity to compare themselves with other groups, and the goals and values of respective groups appear mutually exclusive. Several of the topics covered in previous chapters explain why organizational groups are in conflict with one another. Five of these topics are reviewed here.

Environment Recall from Chapter 3 that departments are established to interact with major domains in the external environment. As the uncertainty and complexity of the environment increase, greater differences in skills, attitudes, power, and operative goals develop among departments. Each department is tailored to fit its environmental domain and, thus, is differentiated from other organizational groups. Moreover, increased competition, both domestically and internationally, has led to demands for lower prices, improved quality, and better service. These demands translate into more intense goal pressures within an organization and, hence, greater conflict among departments.

Size As organizations increase in size, subdivision into a larger number of departments takes place. Members of departments begin to think of themselves as separate, and they erect walls between themselves and other departments. Employees feel isolated from other people in the organization. The lengthening hierarchy also heightens power and resource differences among departments.

Technology Technology determines task allocation among departments as well as interdependence among departments. Groups that have interdependent tasks interact more often and must share resources. Interdependence creates frequent situations that lead to conflict.

Goals The overall goals of an organization are broken down into operative goals that guide each department. Operative goals pursued by marketing, accounting, legal, and personnel departments often seem mutually exclusive. The accomplishment of operative goals by one department may block goal accomplishment by other departments and, hence, cause conflict. Goals of innovation also often lead to conflict because change requires coordination across departments. Innovation goals cause more conflict than do goals of internal efficiency.

Structure   Organization structure reflects the division of labor as well as the systems to facilitate coordination and control. It defines departmental groupings and, hence, employee loyalty to the defined groups. The choice of a divisional structure, for example, means divisions may be placed in competition for resources from headquarters, and headquarters may devise pay incentives based on competition among divisions.

ATTRIBUTES OF INTERDEPARTMENTAL RELATIONSHIPS

Environment, size, technology, goals, and structure are elements of the organizational context that lead to more or less horizontal conflict between departments. These contextual dimensions determine the specific organizational characteristics that generate conflict, as illustrated in Exhibit 13.3. The organizational context translates into seven attributes of interdepartmental relationships that influence the frequency, extent, and intensity of conflict between departments. These seven **sources of interdepartmental conflict** are operative goal incompatibility, differentiation, task interdependence, resource scarcity, power distribution, uncertainty, and reward system.

Operative Goal Incompatibility   Goal incompatibility is probably the greatest cause of intergroup conflict in organizations.[11] The operative goals of each department reflect the specific objectives members are trying to achieve. The achievement of one department's goal often interferes with another department's goals. University police, for example, have a goal of providing a safe and secure campus. They can achieve their goal by locking all buildings on evenings and weekends and not distributing keys. Without easy access to buildings, however, progress toward the sci-

Exhibit 13.3
Sources of Horizontal Conflict between Departments.

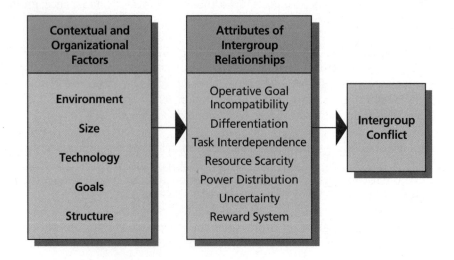

ence department's research goals will proceed slowly. On the other hand, if scientists come and go at all hours and security is ignored, police goals for security will not be met. Goal incompatibility throws the departments into conflict with each other.

The potential for conflict is perhaps greater between marketing and manufacturing than between other departments because the goals of these two departments are frequently at odds. Exhibit 13.4 shows examples of goal conflict between typical marketing and manufacturing departments. Marketing strives to increase the breadth of the product line to meet customer tastes for variety. A broad product line means short production runs, so manufacturing has to bear higher costs.[12] Other areas of goal conflict are quality, cost control, and new products. Goal incompatibility exists among departments in most organizations.

Differentiation   Differentiation was defined in Chapter 2 as "the differences in cognitive and emotional orientations among managers in different functional departments." Functional specialization requires people with specific education, skills, attitudes, and time horizons. For example, people may join a sales department because they have ability and aptitude consistent with sales work. After becoming members of the sales department, they are influenced by departmental norms and values. The underlying values and traits of personnel differ across departments, and these differences lead to horizontal conflicts.[13] Consider an encounter between a sales manager and an R&D scientist about a new product:

> **The sales manager may be outgoing and concerned with maintaining a warm, friendly relationship with the scientist. He may be put off because**

Exhibit 13.4   Marketing-Manufacturing Areas of Potential Goal Conflict.

Goal Conflict	MARKETING versus Operative goal is customer satisfaction.	MANUFACTURING Operative goal is production efficiency.
Conflict Area	*Typical Comment*	*Typical Comment*
1. Breadth of product line	"Our customers demand variety."	"The product line is too broad—all we get are short, uneconomical runs."
2. New product introduction	"New products are our lifeblood."	"Unnecessary design changes are prohibitively expensive."
3. Production scheduling	"We need faster response. Our lead times are too long."	"We need realistic customer commitments that don't change like wind direction."
4. Physical distribution	"Why don't we ever have the right merchandise in inventory?"	"We can't afford to keep huge inventories."
5. Quality	"Why can't we have reasonable quality at low cost?"	"Why must we always offer options that are too expensive and offer little customer utility?"

Source: Based on Benson S. Shapiro, "Can Marketing and Manufacturing Coexist?" *Harvard Business Review* 55 (September–October 1977): 104–14; and Victoria L. Crittenden, Lorraine R. Gardiner, and Antonie Stam, "Reducing Conflict Between Marketing and Manufacturing," *Industrial Marketing Management* 22 (1993): 299–309.

the scientist seems withdrawn and disinclined to talk about anything other than the problems in which he is interested. He may also be annoyed that the scientist seems to have such freedom in choosing what he will work on. Furthermore, the scientist is probably often late for appointments, which, from the salesman's point of view, is no way to run a business. Our scientist, for his part, may feel uncomfortable because the salesman seems to be pressing for immediate answers to technical questions that will take a long time to investigate. All the discomforts are concrete manifestations of the relatively wide differences between these two men in respect to their working and thinking styles. . . .[14]

Task Interdependence   Task interdependence refers to the dependence of one unit on another for materials, resources, or information. As described in Chapter 4 on technology, pooled interdependence means little interaction; sequential interdependence means the output of one department goes to the next department; and reciprocal interdependence means departments mutually exchange materials and information.[15]

Generally, as interdependence increases, the potential for conflict increases.[16] In the case of pooled interdependence, units have little need to interact. Conflict is at a minimum. Sequential and reciprocal interdependence require employees to spend time coordinating and sharing information. Employees must communicate frequently, and differences in goals or attitudes will surface. Conflict is especially likely to occur when agreement is not reached about the coordination of services to each other. Greater interdependence means departments often exert pressure for a fast response because departmental work has to wait on other departments.[17]

The following example of a purchasing department illustrates how the need for purchasing agents and engineers to work together and depend upon each other provided a setting for intergroup conflict.

IN PRACTICE ◆ 13.2
Purchasing Department

The [purchasing department] had two primary functions: (1) to negotiate and place orders at the best possible terms—but only in accordance with specifications set by others—and (2) to expedite orders; that is, to check with suppliers to make sure deliveries are made on time.

Normally orders flow in one direction only, from engineering through scheduling to purchasing; but the agent is dissatisfied with being at the end of the line and seeks to reverse the flow. The purchasing agent would like to suggest alternative materials, changes in specifications, or more economical lot sizes, which is called "value analysis." Value analysis permits him to initiate for others. Such behavior may, however, result in ill feeling on the part of other departments, particularly engineering and production scheduling.

Engineers write up the specifications for the products the agents buy. If the specifications are too tight or, what is worse, if they call for one brand only, agents have little or no freedom to choose among suppliers. Yet engineers find it much easier to write down a well-known brand name than to draw up a lengthy functional specification which lists all the characteristics of the desired item. . . .

The size of the order and the date on which it is to be delivered are typically determined by production scheduling. The agent's chief complaint against scheduling is that delivery is often requested on excessively short notice—that schedulers engage in sloppy planning or "cry wolf" by claiming they need orders earlier than they really do—and thus force the agent to choose from a limited number of suppliers, to pay premium prices, and to ask favors of sales people (thus creating obligations the agent must later repay). Schedulers, on the other hand, claim "short lead times" are not their fault but the fault of the departments further up the line, such as engineering (which delays its blueprints) or sales (which accepts rush orders).[18]

Engineering and production scheduling both depend upon purchasing to acquire products at favorable terms. Purchasing depends upon engineering for specification and production scheduling for delivery dates. These interdependencies cause frequent conflicts.

Resource Scarcity   Another major source of conflict involves competition between groups for what members perceive as limited resources.[19] Organizations have limited money, physical facilities, staff resources, and human resources to share among departments. In their desire to achieve goals, groups want to increase their resources. This throws them into conflict. Managers may develop strategies, such as inflating budget requirements or working behind the scenes, to obtain a desired level of resources. Resources also symbolize power and influence within an organization. The ability to obtain resources enhances prestige. Departments typically believe they have a legitimate claim on additional resources. However, exercising that claim results in conflict. For example, in almost every organization, conflict occurs during the annual budget exercise, often creating the political activities described in Chapter 12.

Power Distribution   As explained in the previous chapter, power differences evolve even when departments are at the same level on the organization chart. Some departments provide a more valuable service or reduce critical uncertainties for the organization. For example, sometimes a conflict builds up between sales and marketing departments because of power differences. Over the past decade, the role of marketing has expanded into the realm of strategic planning, which means more involvement in analyzing the competition with senior management. Sales, meanwhile, focuses on customer needs. Marketing's growing influence has elevated the conflict with sales departments in some companies to a battle for dominance. Power differences often provide a basis for conflict, especially when actual working relationships do not reflect perceived power.[20] In the following case, an engineering department perceived as weak tried to tell a more powerful production department what to do.

IN PRACTICE ◆ 13.3
Engineering Department

In one company, the engineering department took research designs and translated them into parts lists, production drawings, and fabrication and assembly specifications, and in addition processed engineering change orders (ECOs). Much of production's work—both its content and its timing—depended on production engineering's efforts, since product designs were constantly changing.

Engineering was seen by production as telling production what to do and when to do it. On the other hand, engineering was composed of people with skills no greater than—in fact, quite similar to—those possessed by production members. Production felt itself capable of performing not only engineering's tasks but the more important tasks of job design and methods work that were within production's jurisdiction but outside engineering's.

Production managers spent an inordinate amount of time checking for consistency among the various items produced by production engineering. When errors were discovered (as they seldom were), a cry of victory would ring out across the production office. A messenger would be quickly dispatched to carry the offending material back to engineering, amply armed with a message elaborately outlining the stupidity that had produced such an error. The most common topic of production conversation centered about "those goddam ECOs," even though production originated as many ECOs (making changes for its own convenience) as did any other department.[21]

In this case, energies were focused on the impropriety of a less powerful department such as engineering calling the tune for a supposedly more powerful department such as production. Production devoted its energies to rebalancing power between the two departments. Production felt its power could be maintained only by calling more tunes than it danced.

Uncertainty   Another factor for predicting intergroup conflict is the uncertainty and change experienced by organizational departments. When activities are predictable, departments know where they stand. They can rely on rules or previous decisions to resolve disputes that arise. When factors in the environment are rapidly changing or when problems arise that are poorly understood, departments may have to renegotiate their respective tasks.[22] Managers have to sort out how new problems should be handled. The boundaries of a department's territory or jurisdiction become indistinct. Members may reach out to take on more responsibility, only to find other groups feel invaded. In a study of hospital purchasing decisions, managers reported significantly higher levels of conflict when purchases were nonroutine than when purchases were routine.[23] Generally, as uncertainty about departmental relationships increases, conflict can be expected to increase.

Reward System   The reward system governs the degree to which subgroups cooperate or conflict with one another.[24] An experiment with student groups illustrates how incentives influence conflict.[25] In one-half of the groups, called cooperative groups, each student's grade was the grade given for the group's project. All students in those groups, regardless of individual contribution, received the same grade. In the remaining groups, called competitive groups, students were rewarded on the basis of their personal contribution to the group project. Each student was graded individually and could receive a high or low grade regardless of the overall group score.

The outcome of these incentives on conflict was significant. When the incentive system rewarded members for accomplishing the group goal (cooperative groups), coordination among members was better, communication among members was better, productivity was greater, and the quality of the group product was better. When individuals were graded according to their personal contributions to the group (competitive groups), they communicated less with each other and were more frequently in conflict. Members tried to protect themselves and to succeed at the expense of others in the group. Quality of the group project and productivity were lower.

Incentives and rewards have similar impact on conflict between organizational departments. When departmental managers are rewarded for achieving overall organization goals rather than departmental goals, cooperation among departments is greater.[26] Bechtel, for example, provides a bonus system to division managers based upon the achievement of Bechtel's profit goals. Regardless of how well a manager's division does, the manager isn't rewarded unless the corporation performs well. This incentive system motivates division managers to cooperate with each other. If departments are rewarded only for departmental performance, managers are motivated to excel at the expense of the rest of the organization.

The Cooperative Model of Organization

The preceding section looked at several causes and examples of horizontal conflict. The very nature of an organization, with goal incompatibility, task interdependence, scarce resources, and power differences, invites conflict. Conflict is natural and inevitable. Yet an emerging view is that cooperation—not conflict or competition— is the way to achieve high performance. The new trends in management discussed in previous chapters—including clan control, high-involvement corporate cultures, time-based competition, and self-managed teams—all assume employee cooperation is a good thing. This means successful organizations must find healthy ways to confront and resolve conflict. Managers champion a **cooperative model** of organization, meaning they foster cooperation and don't stimulate competition or conflict, which work against the achievement of overall company goals.

Consider the company studied by Rosabeth Moss Kanter, a Harvard professor and consultant. This was a high-flying financial services company that she called Fastbuck. Conflict was initiated to increase performance—and led to disastrous failure.

IN PRACTICE ◆ 13.4
Fastbuck, Incorporated

Top management at Fastbuck took advantage of deregulation to acquire a company that would serve as a hedge against a downturn in the core business. The new and old businesses were set up to compete for resources and the attention of the CEO, and the two business heads were asked to fight for the big prize, taking over the CEO's job. In this organization, cooperation was seen as something soft, for sissies. Survival of the fittest was the style in this company.

Each business was treated as a totally separate organization. Nothing was done to create ties among the people in each group. The two business chiefs developed a strong personal rivalry. Gradually, George, head of the new business, got more attention than Fred, head of the traditional core business. The CEO was enthralled with the risky direction of the new business. George became more outspoken and aggressive; Fred started withdrawing and avoiding the CEO. George got the confidence of his own people and the board of directors. Fred and his business lost stature.

The major problem for Fastbuck was that most revenues and profits were from the traditional business, but those employees perceived themselves as losers and lost energy. Executives became passive, assuming George would soon take over as CEO and things would get even worse. Revenues declined, and a negative cycle began. At this point, George and his division managers were sure he was winning the competition.

Within a few months, Fastbuck hit a major financial crisis because overall business plummeted 20 percent. Something dramatic was needed, so the CEO fired both Fred and George, and the company was reorganized to integrate the two lines of business into one group. A few months later, parts of the new business were sold off because the traditional business was a more important mainstay. Only now the company was weaker and less valuable than before, thanks to the exercise in competition.[27]

The case of Fastbuck illustrates the consequences of conflict described earlier in the chapter. Groups in conflict develop mistrust of one another and pay more attention to beating their rivals than to performing their task. When that happens, the stronger party begins to feel invincible. Competition can sometimes have a healthy effect, but carried to an extreme, it can lead to long-term losses and a detrimental impact on the entire organization. For example, while CS First Boston Group has all the elements of a global financial giant, intense competition among CSFB's three geographic divisions has kept the firm from reaching its potential. A new chairman was hired to try to increase profits by increasing cooperation among the New York, London, and Tokyo divisions.[28]

If an organization achieves an ideal of no conflict, it is probably in trouble. Conflict is a sign of an active, ongoing, forceful organization. However, conflict becomes a problem when there is too much and when it is used for motivational purposes. Exhibit 13.5 summarizes several benefits from cooperation and losses from conflict.

BENEFITS FROM COOPERATION

The new viewpoint about cooperation proposes that internal competition is bad for organizations. The Vince Lombardi philosophy, "Winning isn't everything. It's the only thing," may do more harm than good within companies. One expert argues the ideal amount of competition between departments is zero—none at all.[29] Managers should discourage even informal competition, designing work to encourage cooperation. The reason is that conflict prevents the free exchange of ideas, resources, and skills. Competition and conflict should be with other companies. Employees should identify with the entire organization as one team.

To achieve the cooperative state, for example, managers can design bonuses and incentive systems to enhance cooperation. Incentives should never be designed as prizes that only one department can win, because no department will help any other department. The result will be ill will and declining productivity. Incentives

Exhibit 13.5
Organizational Benefits from Cooperation and Losses from Conflict.

Benefits from Cooperation	Losses from Conflict
1. Productive Task Focus	1. Diversion of Energy
2. Cohesion and Satisfaction	2. Altered Judgment
3. Goal Attainment	3. Loser Effects
4. Innovation and Adaptation	4. Poor Coordination

should be designed so that any department that reaches a certain goal is eligible for the bonus.[30]

The **benefits from cooperation** are as follows:

1. *Productive task focus.*   Departmental employees do not become preoccupied with achieving their own goals. Instead, they are able to focus on the overall goals of the organization. For example, research in employment agencies found that when interviewers worked cooperatively to fill positions, they filled significantly more jobs than did interviewers in an agency that competed fiercely to fill job openings. The sharing of information about candidates and job openings far outweighed the intense effort generated by competition. A study of managers in an engineering firm and a utility company found that a goal of cooperation was associated with more cooperative assistance, exchange of resources and information, and more progress on tasks.[31]

2. *Employee cohesion and satisfaction.*   Under conditions of cooperation, "we-feelings" and in-group identification occur for employees throughout the organization. Members are attracted to the organization as a whole, not just the group, and receive satisfaction from both memberships. Members across departments cooperate with each other and link the achievement of departmental tasks to organizational goals. One study of twenty organizational units found strong social ties between groups in low-conflict organizations and an image of order and meaning about the organization. High-conflict organizations were seen as chaotic by employees, who had only weak ties to other groups.[32] Other research suggests conflict creates stress that often produces negative results. While some employees may seem to work hard under competition, they are less satisfied and are less likely to worry about company goals. A study of supervisors found that supervisors who engendered competitiveness were seen as less effective and as managing less effective departments. Supervisors rated high were able to engender a cooperative orientation. Employees simply enjoyed the cooperative arrangement more. Their jobs were more satisfying, partly because they achieved more.

3. *Organizational goal attainment.*   Under the cooperative model, the organization is able to achieve overall goals because energy is not wasted on interdepartmental rivalries. Competition and conflict are created toward other organizations, not toward other departments within the organization. Moderate competition and conflict against other organizations stimulate participants to work hard.[33] Cohesion results in an enjoyable work atmosphere. The intensity of an athletic team achieving its goal is an example of benefits of competition against other organizations. Cooperation does not mean complacency, which can be as big a problem as internal conflict. An organization can prosper and achieve its overall goals when subgroups are doing their tasks well and cooperating with one another.

4. *Innovation and adaptation.*   Cooperation encourages creativity and innovation, helping organizations develop new technologies, products, and services quickly. As discussed in Chapter 8, when technical, marketing, and production people are sharing information and ideas and working simultaneously on projects, companies are able to speed new products to market for time-based competition. In addition, cooperation among departments is essential for companies to keep pace in today's rapidly changing, competitive environment. When employees are obsessed with their own department's task and with defeating other departments, innovation is stifled, and organizations are not poised to change and grow with

the environment. Today's most successful companies are pushing cooperation to the limit. General Electric, described in the Paradigm Buster, is on the cutting edge, striving to totally eliminate boundaries both within the organization and between GE and its suppliers and customers.

LOSSES FROM CONFLICT

When conflict is too strong, several negative consequences for organizations may arise. These **losses from conflict** are as follows:

1. *Diversion of energy.*   One serious consequence is the diversion of a department's time and effort toward winning a conflict rather than toward achieving organiza-

---

Paradigm Buster

General Electric

Jack Welch, chairman and CEO of General Electric, believes that to win in today's competitive global environment, his company must involve, energize, and reward everyone throughout the company's twelve businesses. One of the principles guiding GE in its efforts to involve everyone is the concept of "boundaryless behavior," which Welch explained to employees and stockholders in GE's 1993 annual report:

"**Boundaryless behavior** is the soul of today's GE. . . . Simply put, people seem compelled to build layers and walls between themselves and others, and that human tendency tends to be magnified in large, old institutions like ours. These walls cramp people, inhibit creativity, waste time, restrict vision, smother dreams, and, above all, slow things down.

"The challenge is to chip away and eventually break down these walls and barriers, both among ourselves and between ourselves and the outside world. The progress we've made so far has released a flood of ideas that is improving every operation in our Company. We've adapted new product introduction techniques from Chrysler and Canon, effective sourcing techniques from GM and Toyota, and approaches to quality from Motorola and Ford. We've moved more effectively into the immense potential markets of China with advice and best practices

from pioneers like IBM, Johnson & Johnson, Xerox and others. . . .

"Internally, boundaryless behavior means piercing the walls of 100-year-old fiefdoms and empires called finance, engineering, manufacturing, marketing, and gathering teams from all those functions in one room, with one shared coffee pot, one shared vision and one consuming passion—to design the world's best jet engine, or ultrasound machine, or refrigerator.

"Boundaryless behavior shows up in the actions of a woman from our appliances business in Hong Kong helping NBC with contacts needed to develop a satellite television service in Asia. On a larger scale, it means labor and management joining hands in the unprofitable Appliance Park complex in Louisville in a joint effort to "Save the Park," with a combination of labor practice changes and GE investment—not two people making a "deal," but 10,721 making a commitment.

"And finally, boundaryless behavior means exploiting one of the unmatchable advantages a multibusiness GE has over almost every other company in the world. Boundaryless behavior combines twelve huge global businesses—each number one or number two in its markets—into a vast laboratory whose principal product is new ideas, coupled with a commitment to spread them throughout the Company."

Source: Jack Welch, "Letter to Shareowners," *General Electric 1993 Annual Report,* p. 2. Used with permission of General Electric.

tional goals.[34] When the most important outcome becomes defeating other departments, no holds barred, resources are wasted. This certainly occurred at Fastbuck. In extreme cases, sabotage, secrecy, and even illegal activities occur. Recall the AIDS laboratory, described at the beginning of this chapter, in which conflict caused research scientists to tamper with and sabotage colleagues' experiments.

2. *Altered judgment.* One finding from intergroup research is that judgment and perceptions become less accurate when conflict becomes more intense. The overconfidence and unrealistic expectations of PATCO members in In Practice 13.1 is an example. Moreover, when a group makes a mistake, it may blame perceived opponents within the organization rather than acknowledge its own shortcomings. People involved in conflict also have a poor understanding of ideas offered by competitors.[35]

3. *Loser Effects.* Another unfortunate aspect of intense interdepartmental conflict is that someone normally loses. The losing department undergoes substantial change. Losers may deny or distort the reality of losing. They may withdraw. They often seek scapegoats, perhaps even members or leaders in their own department. Dissension replaces cohesion. Losers generally tend toward low cooperation and low concern for the needs and interests of other department members.[36]

4. *Poor coordination.* The final problem with conflict is the emphasis given to achieving departmental goals. Departmental goals serve to energize employees, but these goals should not become an all-consuming priority. Departmental goals must be integrated with the goals of the organization. Under intense conflict, coordination does not happen. Collaboration across groups decreases. Groups have less contact, and they are not sympathetic to other points of view. Under intense conflict, achieving departmental goals and defeating the enemy take priority. There is no room for compromise.[37] This lack of cooperation produced the disastrous result at Fastbuck.

Techniques for Managing Conflict among Groups

The ideal situation for most organizations is to have only moderate interunit *competition* and *conflict.* Managers should not let conflict get so great that losses from conflict occur. To the extent possible, they should strive to stimulate cooperation to encourage productive task focus and organizational goal attainment.

Reducing extant conflict is often a challenge. When conflict has been too great, participants may actively dislike each other and may not want to change. The target of conflict management techniques can be either the *behavior* or the *attitude* of group members.[38] By changing behavior, open conflict is reduced or eliminated, but departmental members may still dislike people in other departments. A change in behavior makes the conflict less visible, or keeps the groups separated. A change in attitude is deeper and takes longer. A new attitude is difficult to achieve and requires a positive change in perceptions and feelings about other departments. A change in attitude is the basis for a *true* cooperative organization.

The techniques available for managing conflict are arranged along a scale in Exhibit 13.6. Techniques near the top of the scale, such as formal activity, will change behavior but not attitudes. Techniques near the bottom of the scale, such as

Exhibit 13.6
Strategies for
Managing Con-
flict among
Groups.

Source: Adapted from Eric H. Neilsen, "Understanding and Managing Conflict," in Jay W. Lorsch and Paul R. Lawrence, eds., *Managing Group and Intergroup Relations* (Homewood, Ill.: Irwin and Dorsey, 1972), 329–43.

rotating group members or providing intergroup training, are designed to bring about positive change in cooperative attitudes between groups.

Formal Authority   Formal authority means senior management invokes rules, regulations, and legitimate authority to resolve or suppress a conflict. For example, the advertising and sales departments may disagree about advertising strategy. The sales force may want a strategy based on direct mail, while advertising prefers to use radio and television. This type of conflict can be resolved by passing it to the marketing vice president, who uses legitimate authority to resolve the conflict. The disadvantage of this technique is that it does not change attitudes toward cooperation and may treat only the immediate problem. The formal authority method is effective in the short run when members cannot agree on a solution to a specific conflict.[39]

Limited Communication   Encouraging some communication among conflicting departments prevents the development of misperceptions about the abilities, skills, and traits of other departments. When departments are in severe conflict, controlled interaction can be used to resolve the conflict. Often the interaction can be focused on issues about which the departments have a common goal. A common goal means the departments must talk and cooperate, at least for the achievement of that goal. For example, Datapoint Corporation experiences frequent conflict between the research and development and manufacturing divisions. Since senior managers in these divisions are located in the same city, a forum was devised for them to resolve differences. "Summit meetings" were created where managers could bring their disagreements for discussion and resolution. A dispute about R&D security in a new building was resolved in this fashion. This technique may make a small impact on attitude change.[40]

Integration Devices   As described in Chapter 6, teams, task forces, and project managers who span the boundaries between departments can be used as integration devices. Bringing together representatives from conflicting departments in joint problem-solving teams is an effective way to reduce conflict because the representatives learn to understand each other's point of view.[41] Sometimes a full-time integrator is assigned to achieve cooperation and collaboration by meeting with members of the respective departments and exchanging information. The integrator has to understand each group's problems and must be able to move both groups toward a solution that is mutually acceptable.[42]

As an outgrowth of teams and task forces, many organizations today are restructuring into permanent multidisciplinary, self-managed work teams focused on horizontal process rather than function. One recent book championing the team approach as a way to enhance organization performance is discussed in Book Mark 13.0. Chapter 7 describes these self-managed teams, which eliminate old boundaries between departments by bringing together employees from several functions, such as design, engineering, production, sales, supply, and finance. At Saturn Corporation, teams of about fifteen employees handle everything from production schedules and new car quality to budgeting and hiring new workers.[43]

Teams and task forces reduce conflict and enhance cooperation because they integrate people from different departments. Consider how an old-line insurance company, Aid Association for Lutherans, used the team concept to achieve integration and reduce conflict.

IN PRACTICE ◆ 13.5
Aid Association for Lutherans

For years, employees in the health insurance department at Aid Association for Lutherans (AAL) had little regular contact with their colleagues in other departments. AAL was divided into three functional departments, with employees specializing in health insurance, life insurance, or support services. Although the structure seemed efficient, policyholder inquiries were often passed among several departments and back again. For example, a request to use the cash value of a life policy to pay the premiums for health insurance would bounce through all sections and take at least twenty one days to process—assuming everything went smoothly. But part of the problem at AAL came about because of misunderstandings that would arise among the different departments, causing even further delays.

Top managers decided to risk everything on a team approach. At precisely noon on the appointed day, nearly five hundred clerks, technicians, and managers wheeled their chairs to new locations, becoming part of twenty five-person cross-functional teams, each serving a particular region of the country. Each team has specialists who can handle any of the 167 tasks required for policyholder sales and service. The procedure that used to take twenty one days now takes just five. Misunderstandings that once led to a decline in customer service and provided a breeding ground for conflict among departments are now worked out quickly among team members.[44]

Confrontation and Negotiation   **Confrontation** occurs when parties in conflict directly engage one another and try to work out their differences. **Negotiation** is the

BOOKMARK 13.0

HAVE YOU READ ABOUT THIS?

The Wisdom of Teams: Creating the High-Performance Organization
by Jon R. Katzenbach and Douglas K. Smith

Your group term paper is due in a week and finals begin two days after that. Between now and then, you and two other group members have major papers and presentations due in other classes. The last group member is out in left field, unconcerned with this assignment or anything else. You feel that you've already done your part on the paper, but now neither you nor any of the other members has the time or inclination to do a good job on completing it. Your grade will suffer.

You're living another teamwork horror story. You vow it will not happen again—but it does, in most classes, every term. And the nightmare continues after you reenter the real world. No wonder you've joined the ranks of business people turned off to teams.

Jon R. Katzenbach and Douglas K. Smith take issue with those who are anti-team. Their book, *The Wisdom of Teams,* relies heavily on the distinction between real teams and mere work groups. The latter, which are far more common, include several individuals who interact primarily to share information and help other members handle their responsibilities more effectively. Members of work groups do not share common purposes and goals even when producing joint products, and they are evaluated as individuals. The horror story above was about a group, not a team.

What Makes a Team?

Katzenbach and Smith identify several characteristics that distinguish real teams and lead to success:

- Small size. Successful teams are small, usually with fewer than ten members, to facilitate communication and problem solving.
- Members possess complementary skills. Success depends on team members having three basic skill sets: technical or functional expertise; problem-solving and decision-making skills; and strong interpersonal skills.
- Members share a common purpose and performance goals. As the authors put it, "A team's imme-

diate goal must correlate with its overall purpose. Teams work best when management gives them a broadly defined job to do and lets them do it."
- Members develop a common approach. Team members themselves set the ground rules for workload distribution, schedules, and decision-making procedures.
- Members hold themselves mutually accountable. Members make sincere promises to themselves and the other team members.

Katzenbach and Smith emphasize that focusing on tough performance goals shapes teams and galvanizes members to contribute more than the sum of their individual abilities to the task.

Teams In the Conventional Hierarchy

Despite claims that teamwork and hierarchy are incompatible, the authors believe teams actually complement conventional hierarchy. Cross-functional teams effectively break down barriers and reduce conflict between departments by focusing organizations on key processes. As the authors put it, "Hierarchy and teams go together almost as well as teams and performance. . . . Those who see teams as a replacement for hierarchy are missing the true potential of teams."

Conclusion

Real teams offer the opportunity to raise organizational performance and enhance individual members' skills by putting people with complementary abilities in small units where communication and response are rapid. The authors strongly believe the opportunities of teams outweigh the pitfalls: "The wisdom of teams is . . . in a small group of people so committed to something larger than themselves that they will not be denied."

The Wisdom of Teams by Jon R. Katzenbach and Douglas K. Smith is published by Harvard Business School Press.

bargaining process that often occurs during confrontation and that enables the parties to systematically reach a solution. These techniques bring appointed representatives from the departments together to work out a serious dispute.

Confrontation and negotiation involve some risk. There is no guarantee that discussions will focus on a conflict or that emotions will not get out of hand. However, if members are able to resolve the conflict on the basis of face-to-face discussions, they will find new respect for each other, and future collaboration becomes easier. The beginnings of relatively permanent attitude change are possible through direct negotiation.

Confrontation is successful when managers engage in a "win-win" strategy. Win-win means both departments adopt a positive attitude and strive to resolve the conflict in a way that will benefit each other.[45] If the negotiations deteriorate into a strictly win-lose strategy (each group wants to defeat the other), the confrontation will be ineffective. Top management can urge group members to work toward mutually acceptable outcomes. The differences between win-win and win-lose strategies of negotiation are shown in Exhibit 13.7. With a win-win strategy—which includes defining the problem as mutual, communicating openly, and avoiding threats—understanding can be changed while the dispute is resolved.

Third-Party Consultants   When conflict is intense and enduring, and department members are suspicious and uncooperative, a third-party consultant can be brought in from outside the organization to meet with representatives from both departments. Such consultants should be experts on human behavior, and their advice and actions must be valued by both groups. Third-party consultants can make great progress toward building cooperative attitudes and reducing conflict.[46] Typical activities of third-party consultants are as follows:

- Reestablish broken communication lines between groups.
- Act as interpreter so that messages between groups are correctly understood and are not distorted by preconceived biases.

Win-Win Strategy	Win-Lose Strategy
1. Define the conflict as a mutual problem	1. Define the conflict as a win-lose situation
2. Pursue joint outcomes	2. Pursue own group's outcomes
3. Find creative agreements that satisfy both groups	3. Force the other group into submission
4. Use open, honest, and accurate communication of group's needs, goals, and proposals	4. Use deceitful, inaccurate, and misleading communication of group's needs, goals, and proposals
5. Avoid threats (to reduce the other's defensiveness)	5. Use threats (to force submission)
6. Communicate flexibility of position	6. Communicate high commitment (rigidity) regarding one's position

Exhibit 13.7
Negotiating Strategies.

Source: Adapted from David W. Johnson and Frank P. Johnson, *Joining Together: Group Theory and Group Skills* (Englewood Cliffs, N.J.: Prentice-Hall, 1975), 182–83.

- Challenge and bring into the open the stereotyping done by one group or the other. Exposing stereotypes often leads to their dissolution.
- Bring into awareness the positive acts and intentions of the other group. This forces a cognitive reassessment of one group's stance toward the other group.
- The specific source of conflict must be defined, focused, and resolved.

With negative emotions removed, a cooperative attitude can be established and nurtured to replace the previous conflict.[47]

Member Rotation   Rotation means individuals from one department can be asked to work in another department on a temporary or permanent basis. The advantage is that individuals become submerged in the values, attitudes, problems, and goals of the other department. In addition, individuals can explain the problems and goals of their original departments to their new colleagues. This enables a frank, accurate exchange of views and information.

Rotation works slowly to reduce conflict but is very effective for changing the underlying attitudes and perceptions that promote conflict.[48] The following case illustrates the successful use of member rotation in one company.

IN PRACTICE ◆ 13.6
Canadian-Atlantic

Canadian-Atlantic, a transportation conglomerate headquartered in Vancouver, British Columbia, experienced intense conflict between research managers and operating managers at the home office. Research managers were responsible for developing operational innovations, such as for loading railroad cars, to increase efficiency. Operations managers were responsible for scheduling and running trains.

Operations managers disliked research personnel. They claimed research personnel took far too long to do projects. One manager said, "A 50 percent solution when we need it is much better than a 100 percent solution ten years from now when the crisis is over." Operating managers were also offended by the complicated terminology and jargon used by research personnel. Researchers had developed several useful innovations, such as automated loading platforms and training simulators, but resistance to their innovations was great. Research personnel wanted to cooperate with operations managers but could not go along with certain requests. They refused to release half-completed innovations or to water down their ideas for less well-educated employees in operations. One manager commented that the extent of communication between research and operations "was just about zero, and both groups like it that way."

The vice president of research and development was worried. He believed intergroup hostility was sharply reducing the effectiveness of R&D. Morale in R&D was low, and operations managers had little interest in new developments. The vice president persuaded the president to try rotating managers between operations and research. Initially, one manager from each department was exchanged. Later, two and three were exchanged simultaneously. Each rotation lasted about six months. After two and one-half years, the relationship between the departments was vastly improved. Key individuals now understood both points of view and could work to integrate the differences that existed. One operations manager enjoyed the work in research so much that he asked to stay on, and the operations vice president tried to hire two R&D managers to work permanently in his division.

Shared Mission and Superordinate Goals   Another strategy is for top management to create a shared mission and establish superordinate goals that require cooperation among departments.[49] As discussed in Chapter 10, organizations with strong, adaptive cultures, where employees share a larger vision for their company, are more likely to have a united, cooperative work force. Recent studies have shown that when employees from different departments see that their goals are linked together, they will openly share resources and information.[50] To be effective, superordinate goals must be substantial, and employees must be granted the time to work cooperatively toward those goals. The reward system can also be redesigned to encourage the pursuit of the superordinate goals rather than departmental subgoals.

Perhaps the most powerful superordinate goal is company survival. If an organization is about to fail and jobs will be lost, groups forget their differences and try to save the organization. The goal of survival has improved relationships between groups in meat packing plants and auto supply firms that have been about to go out of business.

Intergroup Training   A strong intervention to reduce conflict is intergroup training. This technique has been developed by such psychologists as Robert Blake, Jane Mouton, and Richard Walton.[51] When other techniques fail to reduce conflict to an appropriate level or do not fit the organization in question, special training of group members may be required. This training requires that department members attend an outside workshop away from day-to-day work problems. The training workshop may last several days, and various activities take place. This technique is expensive, but it has the potential for developing a company-wide cooperative attitude.

Intergroup training is similar to the OD approach described in Chapter 8 on innovation and change. The steps typically associated with an intergroup training session are as follows:

1. The conflicting groups are brought into a training setting with the stated goal of exploring mutual perceptions and relationships.
2. The conflicting groups are then separated, and each group is invited to discuss and make a list of its perceptions of itself and the other group.
3. In the presence of both groups, group representatives publicly share the perceptions of self and other that the groups have generated, while the groups are obligated to remain silent. The objective is simply to report to the other group as accurately as possible the images that each group has developed in private.
4. Before any exchange takes place, the groups return to private sessions to digest and analyze what they have heard; there is great likelihood that the representatives' reports have revealed to each group discrepancies between its self-image and the image the other group holds of it.
5. In public session, again working through representatives, each group shares with the other what discrepancies it has uncovered and the possible reasons for them, focusing on actual, observable behavior.
6. Following this mutual exposure, a more open exploration is permitted between the two groups on the now-shared goal of identifying further reasons for perceptual distortions.
7. A joint exploration is then conducted of how to manage future relations in such a way as to encourage cooperation between groups.[52]

Intergroup training sessions can be quite demanding for everyone involved. It is fairly easy to have conflicting groups list perceptions and identify discrepancies.

But exploring their differences face-to-face and agreeing to change is more difficult. However, if handled correctly, these sessions can help department employees understand each other much better and lead to improved attitudes and better working relationships for years to come.

Vertical Conflict

The discussion so far in this chapter has dealt with horizontal conflict between departments. Vertical conflict occurs among groups at different levels along the vertical hierarchy. Several of the same concepts apply to vertical conflict, but the groups and issues may be different.

Vertical conflict can take various forms. Student groups may find themselves in conflict with faculty or administration about the teaching versus research goals of a university. Individual employees may have conflicts with their bosses. Managers of international divisions often experience conflict with senior executives located at domestic headquarters. Dealers for large computer companies have found themselves in conflict with corporate headquarters in recent years. As computer companies attempt to increase sales by shifting distribution to mail-order sales and volume retailers, their traditional dealers are often left unable to obtain adequate inventory rapidly enough to serve even their long-term customers.[53]

One visible and sometimes troublesome area of conflict within organizations is between management and workers, who are often represented by a union. All too often we see union or management representatives on television explaining why the other side is wrong and why a strike or lockout is necessary. These conflicts often occur in major industries, such as transportation and steel, and in specialized groups, such as football players or television writers. As an example, the United Auto Workers' struggle to save jobs for its members is in serious conflict with General Motors Corporation's strategy to improve domestic productivity and profitability in ways that could eliminate up to 90,000 blue-collar jobs by the late 1990s.[54]

Status and power differences among groups are often greater for vertical conflict than for horizontal conflict. Part of the reason vertical conflict occurs is to equalize power differences; for example, unions try to give workers more power over wages or working conditions. Moreover, the ground rules for conflict between workers and management are formalized by laws and regulations. Formal negotiation procedures are available in which appointed representatives work to resolve differences. The conflict between union and management is thus different from conflict that occurs horizontally across departments.

The following sections explore some of the reasons for worker-management conflicts and techniques for the reduction of those conflicts.

Sources of Worker-Management Conflict

Vertical conflict can exist with or without a union, but conflict is more visible when workers join a union. The union formalizes vertical differences and provides a mechanism for resolving those differences. Workers form into unions for a variety of reasons, which reflect the **sources of vertical conflict:**

1. *Psychological distance.*   Workers often do not feel involved in the organization. They perceive that their needs are not being met. A union is a way of giving voice to those needs. It provides workers with a clear group identity. Once the union is formed, members identify with the union, not the company, and try to achieve gains through the union. This often throws union and management into a win-lose conflict situation.

2. *Power and status.*   Workers are at the bottom of the hierarchy and often feel powerless and alienated. They have little say in decisions about issues that directly affect their lives, such as wages and benefits. Standing together in a union gives them strength that equalizes their power with management's. This power is restricted to areas directly affecting workers, but it is still more power than workers have alone.[55]

3. *Ideology.*   One basic difference between management and workers pertains to values and ideology. This difference represents basic beliefs about the purpose and goals of organizations and unions.[56] Major ideological differences identified in a survey of managers and union members are listed in Exhibit 13.8. Union members strongly believe in seniority, the right to engage in a strike, and union security. Managers believe more strongly in the free enterprise system, the right to work during a strike, management rights, and the use of quotas to measure performance.

   Though recent conflicts between union and management at Caterpillar focused on a host of issues ranging from wages to health care benefits, the real clash was ideological. While the UAW insisted on "pattern bargaining," a process whereby all companies within an industry accept similar union contracts, Caterpillar management refused, firmly reasserting the company's "right to manage." Basic value differences between union and management represent a major conflict that must be overcome before the groups can cooperate successfuly.[57]

4. *Scarce resources.*   Another important issue between unions and management is financial resources. Salary, fringe benefits, and working conditions are dominant bargaining issues. Workers look to the union to obtain financial benefits. Unions may strike if necessary to get the pay and benefits they want. Management, by

Ideological Belief	Strength of Belief	
	Union Members	Management
1. Seniority	High	Low
2. Right to engage in a legal strike or boycott	High	Low
3. Union security	High	Low
4. Free enterprise system	Low	High
5. Right to continue work during a legal strike or boycott	Low	High
6. Management rights	Low	High
7. Use of work quotas to measure performance	Low	High

Exhibit 13.8
Differences in Union and Management Beliefs.

Source: Based on Roger S. Wolters, "Union-Management Ideological Frames of Reference," *Journal of Management* 8 (1982): 21–33.

contrast, feels pressure to reduce costs by holding the line on wages in order to maintain low prices. For example, the United Food and Commercial Workers has squared off with Food Lion, claiming that the chain's steadily growing earnings are due to Food Lion willfully avoiding paying overtime to thousands of hourly workers, in violation of federal labor laws. Food Lion itself is not unionized; the UFCW's primary motive is to slow the chain's rapid expansion, which takes market share—and UFCW members' jobs—away from unionized supermarkets.[58]

Resolution of Worker-Management Conflict

One study that explored the underlying dynamics in union-management relationships was conducted by Blake and Mouton.[59] It involved managers who were placed in groups of from nine to twelve persons. Each group produced a solution to a problem. To simulate the negotiation strategies of unions and management, each group was then asked to elect a representative who would negotiate with a representative from a competing group. The two representatives were asked to select one solution as the winner. An interesting thing happened: representatives stayed loyal to their own groups' solutions. In thirty-three incidents of having group representatives meet, thirty-one representatives remained loyal to their own groups' solutions, regardless of solution quality. The representatives never did agree on a winning solution.

These findings are striking because they emphasize just how difficult it can be for elected representatives to reach a solution when conflict is severe. The first priority for representatives is loyalty to their group. In a recent nonunion example, J. Hugh Liedtke, CEO of Pennzoil, and James W. Kinnear, CEO of Texaco, tried to settle the $10 billion debt Texaco owed Pennzoil. The two representatives were unwilling to reach a compromise; each was afraid to give in to the opposition. Ultimately, after almost two years of negotiation, the two sides settled for $3 billion, and Texaco was driven into bankruptcy. Some commentators believed both companies lost because of the long struggle.[60]

COLLECTIVE BARGAINING

The primary approach to resolving union-management conflict is collective bargaining. **Collective bargaining** is the negotiation of an agreement between management and workers. The bargaining process is usually accomplished through a union, and it follows a prescribed format. Collective bargaining involves at least two parties that have a defined interest. The collective bargaining activity usually begins with the presentation by one party of demands or proposals that are evaluated by the other parties. This is followed by counterproposals and concessions. A rigid agreement is ultimately reached that defines each party's responsibilities for the next two or three years.

COOPERATIVE APPROACHES

Today's economic environment has led to a more cooperative rather than confrontational approach to labor-management relations. These changes have grown from the unions' need to prevent loss of employment and the companies' need to curb labor and production costs. Some of the new approaches to resolving union-management conflict are as follows:

- *Gain sharing.*   Union members receive bonuses and profit sharing rather than guaranteed, flat-rate increases. **Gain sharing** is designed to provide a connection between organization performance and worker compensation. At Volkswagen, for example, workers are paid an annual bonus that reflects a combination of individual performance and company performance.[61]

- *Labor-Management Teams.*   **Labor-management teams** are designed to increase worker participation and provide a "cooperative model" for union-management problems. The main function of teams is to tap workers' knowledge of their jobs to improve productivity. These teams exist at three levels: (1) On the shop floor, teams of perhaps ten workers identify problems and implement solutions, similar to a quality circle approach. At Saturn Corporation, for example, teams of factory workers actively make decisions on tools, supplies and suppliers, factory layout, and other plant matters; (2) Middle managers and local union leaders serve as an advisory team to coordinate programs and implement team suggestions; and (3) At the top, senior corporate executives and top union leaders set long-term policy and plan alternatives to layoffs. This coordinated approach engages union members' participation in the company and increases their identification with the company.[62] For example, in Canada, a cooperative model was developed in the 1980s by a joint Gulf Canada/Union task force. SaskComp Ltd. of Regina used this approach to resolve a labor relations mess. Morale and productivity soon improved, while sick leave declined. Employee grievances, once epidemic, virtually disappeared.[63]

- *Employment security.*   The new trend is away from job security and toward employment security, which means unions allow workers to be reassigned to different positions. Employment security also means there can be no jobs unless the firm is successful. Managers and workers create a "common fate" culture that means they succeed or fail together. This superordinate goal increases employee concern about company productivity and profits. Moreover, employees are given meaningful information on the company's performance.

These new approaches have helped shift management and union leaders away from win-lose negotiating positions toward a win-win attitude to benefit both company and employees.[64] The win-win approach was described in Exhibit 13.7. For example, teams that include both workers and managers are now being tried in hundreds of companies, including AT&T, Goodyear, Ford Motor Company, and Xerox. Union Camp's giant paper plant in Savannah, Georgia, created labor-management teams to find cost-cutting measures that would keep the declining plant from closing. Management agreed to new work rules that give workers more power, and the union agreed to cuts in vacation and lower pay for overtime; working together, management and labor saved thousands of jobs in Savannah. In the steel industry, both LTV and Inland Steel have signed pacts that give labor representatives seats on the board, profit sharing, and strong job security guarantees in return for simpler work rules and job reductions through attrition.[65]

These innovative approaches do not eliminate collective bargaining, but they broaden the bargaining philosophy. As the traditional barriers between union and management are broken down through collaboration and teamwork, companies get increased productivity and workers receive a better quality of work life. The win-win approach is being applied to union-management relationships more than managers would have believed possible just a few years ago.

Summary and Interpretation

This chapter contains several ideas that complement the topics of power and decision making in the two previous chapters. The most important idea is that intergroup conflict is a natural outcome of organizing. Differences in goals, backgrounds, and tasks are necessary for departmental excellence. These differences throw groups into conflict. Some intergroup conflict is healthy and should be directed toward successful outcomes for everyone. Understanding the role of organizational conflict and the importance of achieving appropriate levels of conflict are important lessons from this chapter.

The most recent thinking suggests managers should encourage cooperation within the organization. Conflict and competition should be directed toward other organizations. This approach increases cohesion, satisfaction, and performance for the organization as a whole. Too severe conflict among departments can lead to disregard and dislike for other groups, seeing other departments as inferior, as the enemy; hence, cooperation will decrease. Organizations can manage conflict with techniques such as member rotation or intergroup training. Some organizations are pushing cooperation even further by establishing permanent cross-functional work teams that virtually eliminate boundaries between departments.

Much of the work in organization theory has been concerned with horizontal rather than vertical conflict. Horizontal conflict is the day-to-day preoccupation of most managers. Vertical conflict is reflected in union-management relationships and is also important. Indeed, some of the most exciting developments taking place in the organizational world are techniques for improving union-management relationships. Problem-solving teams, employee gain sharing, and even union membership on the board of directors are steps to achieving collaboration between management and workers.

KEY CONCEPTS

behavioral changes	intergroup conflict
benefits from cooperation	labor-management teams
collective bargaining	losses from conflict
competition	model of intergroup conflict
confrontation	negotiation
cooperative model	sources of interdepartmental conflict
gain sharing	sources of vertical conflict
horizontal conflict	vertical conflict

DISCUSSION QUESTIONS

1. Define *intergroup conflict*. How does this definition compare with that of *competition?* What is vertical as opposed to horizontal conflict?

2. Briefly describe how differences in tasks, personal background, and training lead to conflict between groups. How does task interdependence lead to conflict between groups?

3. What impact does conflict have on people within conflicting groups?

4. Discuss the organizational losses from interdepartmental conflict.

5. Intergroup training is located at a higher level on the scale of conflict-resolution techniques than is member rotation. What does this mean in terms of the impact the two techniques have on behavior versus attitudes? Can you think of situations in which rotation might have greater impact on attitudes than would intergroup training? Discuss.

6. What techniques can be used to overcome conflict between workers and management? Are there similarities to the techniques used to deal with horizontal conflict? Discuss.

7. Do you believe cooperation will stimulate higher performance than competition among departments? Discuss.

 GUIDES TO ACTION

As a manager, keep the following guidelines in mind:

1. Recognize that some interdepartmental conflict is natural but that cooperation among departments is associated with higher performance. Cooperation enhances productive task focus, employee satisfaction, and the attainment of organizational goals more than does competition or conflict.

2. Associate the organizational design characteristics of goal incompatibility, differentiation, task interdependence, resource scarcity, power distribution, and reward systems with greater conflict among groups. Expect to devote more time and energy to resolving conflict in these situations.

3. Do not allow intense conflict to persist. Intense conflict is harmful to an organization because departments direct their resources toward sabotaging or defeating other groups rather than toward working with other departments to achieve company goals. Intervene forcefully with conflict resolution techniques.

4. Manage conflict among departments. Conflict can be reduced with formal authority, limited interaction, integration devices, confrontation, third-party consultants, member rotation, superordinate goals, and intergroup training. Select the techniques that fit the organization and the conflict.

5. Avoid placing groups in direct win-lose situations when managing either horizontal or vertical conflict. Direct the conflict toward enabling both groups to be partial winners. When negotiating, do not place representatives in the dilemma of choosing between loyalty to their group or loyalty to the best interest of the company as a whole. Representatives usually will be loyal to their group, even if their proposals are not the best solutions for the entire company.

Consider these guides when analyzing the following case.

CASE FOR ANALYSIS

Valena Scientific Corporation*

Part I

Valena Scientific Corporation (VSC) is one of the largest manufacturers of health-care products in the world. The health-care market includes hospitals, clinical laboratories, universities, and industry. Clinical laboratories represent fifty-two percent of VSC's sales. The laboratories are located in hospitals and diagnostic centers where blood tests and urine analyses are performed for physicians. Equipment sold to laboratories can range from a five-cent test tube to a $195,000 blood analyzer that performs eighteen blood tests simultaneously.

During the 1970s, many large energy and industrial corporations began to move into the clinical market. Eli Lilly, Dow Chemical, Revlon, and E. I. DuPont shifted more research dollars to medical products. Fifty percent of the nation's health-care bill goes into testing, and the medical profession is demanding more accurate tests as well as tests for a variety of new diseases.

By 1980, the industry experienced a new twist: genetic engineering. New companies, such as Genentech Corporation and Cetus Scientific Laboratories, were created as venture capital companies and were staffed with a handful of university microbiologists. These companies were designed to exploit the commercial potential for gene splicing.

Senior executives at VSC saw the trend developing and late in 1979, decided to create the biotech research department. Skilled microbiologists were scarce, so the department was created with only nine scientists who had experience in the fields of biology and engineering. Twenty technicians, who helped with research at the scientists' direction, were also assigned. The department was divided into three groups: gene splicing, recombination, and fermentation. The biotech research department was the smallest of three research departments at VSC. Its organization chart is shown in Exhibit 13.9.

The most competent personnel had been selected to serve as part of the new department. They would be doing leading-edge research compared with other departments at VSC. The employees from each group were expected to work closely together, although each group was located on a separate floor in the research building. The groups would be located together after a new research wing was constructed sometime in the future.

For the first eighteen months of operation, the work in the biotech department was moderately routine. The department concentrated on applying principles established elsewhere. One example was the production of human insulin by gene splicing. The basic research was performed by a scientist at Harvard. The work required by private companies was to produce insulin in large amounts. Other work included the refinement of blood tests, such as for diabetes

*This case is based on "Genetic Engineering's Manpower Problem," *Dun's Business Month*, January 1982, 92–95; "Reid Scientific" case, distributed by the Intercollegiate Case Clearing House, Soldiers Field, Boston, MA 02163; "Daniels Computer Company," in Robert E. Coffey, Anthony G. Athos, and Peter A. Reynolds, eds., *Behavior in Organizations: A Multidimensional View*, 2d ed. (Englewood Cliffs, N.J.: Prentice-Hall, 1975), 416–20; "Biotech Comes of Age," *Business Week*, 23 January 1984, 84–94; and "Biotech Firms Offer 'Interim' Products," *Dun's Business Month*, May 1984, 103–105.

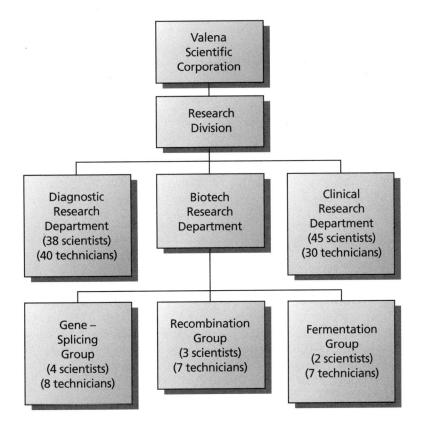

Exhibit 13.9
Organization
Chart of VSC's
Biotech Research
Department.

and for the identification of hereditary diseases (for example, sickle-cell anemia). The initial projects all followed a similar pattern. The work was started in the gene-splicing group, followed by work in recombination, and then in fermentation. Fermentation was used to breed the bacteria created by the other two groups in sufficient numbers to enable mass production.

The senior scientist in each group was appointed group leader, and the three leaders reported to the director of the biotech department, who did not have a scientific background. The structure within each group was very informal and collegial.

The scientists and technicians were enthusiastic about the new department. They felt proud to be selected and quickly identified with the new department. They were happy with the division of labor, but lunch and coffee gatherings included members from all three groups. Group leader meetings were cooperative, quickly resolved any coordination problems, and were conflict-free.

During the summer of 1982, the biotech research department received a special project. Hoffman-LaRoche was developing leukocyte interferon to use as a treatment against cancer. The company was unable to clone the bacteria in its own lab and hired other companies to do the job. VSC contracted with Hoffman-LaRoche to develop a technique for interferon production. The company had only six months to come up with a production technology. Because of the intense time pressure, the research could not be done in the sequence of gene splicing, recombination, and fermentation. Each group remained in its own geographic confines and began immediately to test ideas relevant to its own work. Each group also examined the current research literature and contacted university colleagues in its own area of specialization. The groups were aware that if findings from another group were strong enough to dictate the entire production sequence, the work undertaken by their own group would be lost.

QUESTIONS

1. Would department employees be enthusiastic or unenthusiastic as the interferon project developed? Would they identify more strongly with the department as a whole or with their own subgroup? Explain.
2. Would conflict among group leaders be high or low during this period? Explain.
3. Would social relationships tend to be department-wide or subgroup oriented? Explain.

Part II

In September 1982, the group leaders met for the first time to explore the technical progress and discoveries made by each group. The goal of this meeting was to exchange information and to establish parameters for each group's subsequent research activities. It quickly became apparent that each group had taken a different research direction and had discovered concepts that the group considered paramount. The position of any one group required considerable extra work by the other two groups. The group leaders argued vehemently for their positions, and the meeting was concluded without compromise of original positions.

During the following six weeks, each group worked desperately to complete its research before complementary segments were completed in the other groups. Haste was necessary because the late groups would have to reformulate their research based on what was found by the group that finished first. Future meetings among group leaders were conflict-laden and did not resolve the issues. No research approach was proven to be superior for cloning and manufacturing interferon. All three avenues looked promising but mutually exclusive. A number of personal frictions developed among the groups. Enthusiasm for the project was initially high but gradually dropped off as conflict increased. Social activities were limited to members in each subgroup and were dominated by talk of research and the need to beat the other groups.

On November 15, a Stanford professor with extensive research experience in recombinant DNA technology was hired. His first assignment was to be project leader for the interferon project. His title was chief biologist, and all scientists, engineers, and technicians working on the interferon project were to report to him. The group leaders in each area discussed their work with him. After one week, the chief biologist selected the basic approach that would be taken in future research. The new approach was a technique developed at Stanford and in many ways was similar to the line taken in the fermentation group. Technical objections from the other groups were dismissed. The new approach was to be followed by everyone. Each group was assigned a set of research instructions within the overall research plan. Firm deadlines were established based upon group interdependence. Weekly progress reports were required from each group leader.

For several weeks after the chief biologist decided the direction of the interferon project, the group leaders from gene splicing and recombination disagreed with him. Considerable time was spent trying to find a weakness in the new plan and to prove that their previous research was superior. Few problems in the new plan could be found. The chief biologist defended his position and demanded that deadlines be met.

Schedules were met, and the three groups simultaneously developed the approach in their respective areas. Communication with the chief biologist became more frequent. Communication among groups became common. Problems discovered by one group were communicated to other groups so that effort was not expended needlessly. Group leaders coordinated many problems among themselves.

Cohesion within each group became less pronounced. Lunch and coffee groups including several members of each group began to appear. Group leaders had daily discussions and cooperated on research requirements. Enthusiasm for the department and for the interferon project was expressed by department members.

QUESTIONS

1. What intraorganizational changes in Valena Scientific Corporation led to heightened intergroup conflict? Explain.
2. What factors account for the reduction of conflict after the chief biologist took over?
3. Why couldn't the group leaders resolve the conflict by themselves?

NOTES

1. Jonathan Kwitny, "At CDC's AIDS Lab: Egos, Power, Politics and Lost Experiments," *Wall Street Journal,* 12 December 1986, 1.
2. Clayton T. Alderfer and Ken K. Smith, "Studying Intergroup Relations Imbedded in Organizations," *Administrative Science Quarterly* 27 (1982): 35–65.
3. Muzafer Sherif, "Experiments in Group Conflict," *Scientific American* 195 (1956): 54–58; Edgar H. Schein, *Organizational Psychology,* 3d ed. (Englewood Cliffs, N.J.: Prentice-Hall, 1980).
4. M. Ascalur Rahin, "A Strategy for Managing Conflict in Complex Organizations," *Human Relations* 38 (1985): 81–89; Kenneth Thomas, "Conflict and Conflict Management," in M. D. Dunnette, ed., *Handbook of Industrial and Organizational Psychology* (Chicago: Rand McNally, 1976); Stuart M. Schmidt and Thomas A. Kochan, "Conflict: Toward Conceptual Clarity," *Administrative Science Quarterly* 13 (1972): 359–70.
5. L. David Brown, "Managing Conflict among Groups," in David A. Kolb, Irwin M. Rubin, and James M. McIntyre, eds., *Organizational Psychology: A Book of Readings* (Englewood Cliffs, N.J.: Prentice-Hall, 1979), 377–89.
6. Nathaniel Gilbert, "The Missing Link in Sales and Marketing: Credit Management," *Management Review* (June 1989): 24–30; Robert W. Ruekert and Orville C. Walker, Jr., "Interactions between Marketing and R&D Departments in Implementing Different Business Strategies," *Strategic Management Journal* 8 (1987): 233–48.
7. Brown, "Managing Conflict among Groups."
8. Amy Barrett, "Indigestion at Taco Bell," *Business Week,* 14 December 1994, 66–67; Susan V. Lourenco and John C. Glidewell, "A Dialectical Analysis of Organizational Conflict," *Administrative Science Quarterly* 20 (1975): 489–508.
9. Harry Bernstein, "Union Misjudged Government," *Houston Chronicle,* 4 September 1981, copyright © Los Angeles Times—Washington Post News Service; Paul Galloway, "Negotiating Consultant Says Air Controllers Can't Win Strike," *Houston Chronicle,* 25 August 1981, copyright © Chicago Sun-Times; Susan B. Garland, "Air-Traffic Controllers: Getting Organized Again," *Business Week,* 18 May 1987, 52.
10. These conclusions are summarized from Sherif, "Experiments in Group Conflict"; M. Sherif, O. J. Harvey, B. J. White, W. R. Hood, and C. W. Sherif, *Intergroup Conflict and Cooperation* (Norman, Okla.: University of Oklahoma Books Exchange, 1961); M. Sherif and C. W. Sherif, *Social Psychology* (New York: Harper & Row, 1969); and

Schein, *Organizational Psychology*.

11. Thomas A. Kochan, George P. Huber, and L. L. Cummings, "Determinants of Intraorganizational Conflict in Collective Bargaining in the Public Sector," *Administrative Science Quarterly* 20 (1975): 10–23.

12. Victoria L. Crittenden, Lorraine R. Gardiner, and Antonie Stam, "Reducing Conflict between Marketing and Manufacturing," *Industrial Marketing Management* 22 (1993): 299–309; Benson S. Shapiro, "Can Marketing and Manufacturing Coexist?" *Harvard Business Review* 55 (September-October 1977): 104–14.

13. Eric H. Neilsen, "Understanding and Managing Intergroup Conflict," in Jay W. Lorsch and Paul R. Lawrence, eds., *Managing Group and Intergroup Relations* (Homewood, Ill.: Irwin and Dorsey, 1972), 329–43; Richard E. Walton and John M. Dutton, "The Management of Interdepartmental Conflict: A Model and Review," *Administrative Science Quarterly* 14 (1969): 73–84.

14. Jay W. Lorsch, "Introduction to the Structural Design of Organizations," in Gene W. Dalton, Paul R. Lawrence, and Jay W. Lorsch, eds., *Organization Structure and Design* (Homewood, Ill.: Irwin and Dorsey, 1970), 5.

15. James D. Thompson, *Organizations in Action* (New York: McGraw-Hill, 1967), 54–56.

16. Walton and Dutton, "Management of Interdepartmental Conflict."

17. Joseph McCann and Jay R. Galbraith, "Interdepartmental Relationships," in Paul C. Nystrom and William H. Starbuck, eds., *Handbook of Organizational Design*, vol. 2 (New York: Oxford University Press, 1981), 60–84.

18. George Strauss, "Tactics of Lateral Relationship: The Purchasing Agent," *Administrative Science Quarterly* 7 (1962): 161–86, Quoted by permission.

19. Roderick M. Cramer, "Intergroup Relations and Organizational Dilemmas: The Role of Categorization Processes," in L. L. Cummings and Barry M. Staw, eds., *Research in Organizational Behavior*, vol. 13 (New York: JAI Press, 1991), 191–228; Neilsen, "Understanding and Managing Intergroup Conflict"; Louis R. Pondy, "Organizational Conflict: Concepts and Models," *Administrative Science Quarterly* 12 (1968): 296–320.

20. Richard Devine, "Overcoming Sibling Rivalry between Sales and Marketing," *Management Review*, (June 1989): 36–40; John A. Seiler, "Diagnosing Interdepartmental Conflict," *Harvard Business Review* 41 (September-October 1963): 121–32.

21. Seiler, "Diagnosing Interdepartmental Conflict," 126–27.

22. Walton and Dutton, "Management of Interdepartmental Conflict"; Pondy, "Organizational Conflict"; Kenneth W. Thomas and Louis R. Pondy, "Toward an 'Intent' Model of Conflict Management among Principal Parties," *Human Relations* 30 (1977): 1089–1102.

23. Daniel S. Cochran and Donald D. White, "Intraorganizational Conflict in the Hospital Purchasing Decision Making Process," *Academy of Management Journal* 24 (1981): 324–32.

24. Walton and Dutton, "Management of Interdepartmental Conflict."

25. Morton Deutsch, "The Effects of Cooperation and Competition upon Group Process," in Dorwin Cartwright and Alvin Zander, eds., *Group Dynamics* (New York: Harper & Row, 1968), 461–82.

26. Gordon Cliff, "Managing Organizational Conflict," *Management Review* (May 1987): 51–53.

27. Rosabeth Moss Kanter, *When Giants Learn to Dance* (New York: Simon & Schuster, 1989).

28. Richard A. Melcher with Leah Nathans Spiro, "The New Referee at CS First Boston," *Business Week*, 22 March 1993, 78.

29. Alfie Kohn, "No Contest," *Inc.*, November 1987, 145–48.

30. Alfie Kohn, *No Contest: The Case against Competition* (Boston: Houghton Mifflin, 1986).

31. Dean Tjosvold, "Cooperative and Competitive Interdependence: Collaboration between Departments to Serve Customers," *Group and Organizational Studies* 13 (1988): 274–89.

32. Reed E. Nelson, "The Strength of Strong Ties: Social Networks and Intergroup Conflict in Organizations," *Academy of Management Journal* 32 (1989): 377–401.

33. Joe Kelly, "Make Conflict Work for You," *Harvard Business Review* 48 (July-August 1970): 103–13; Stephen P. Robbins, *Managing Organizational Conflict: A Nontraditional Approach* (Englewood Cliffs, N.J.: Prentice-Hall, 1974).

34. Seiler, "Diagnosing Interdepartment Conflict."

35. Blake and Mouton, "Reactions to Intergroup Competition."

36. Schein, *Organizational Psychology*; Blake and Mouton, "Reactions to Intergroup Competition," 174–75.

37. Pondy, "Organizational Conflict."

38. Neilsen, "Understanding and Managing Intergroup Conflict."

39. Pondy, "Organizational Conflict."

40. Neilsen, "Understanding and Managing Inter-

group Conflict."

41. Robert R. Blake and Jane S. Mouton, "Overcoming Group Warfare," *Harvard Business Review* (November–December 1984): 98–108.

42. Blake and Mouton, "Overcoming Group Warfare"; Paul R. Lawrence and Jay W. Lorsch, "New Management Job: The Integrator," *Harvard Business Review* 45 (November–December 1967): 142–51.

43. David Woodruff, "Saturn: Labor's Love Lost?" *Business Week,* 8 February 1993, 122–24; David Woodruff, James Treece, Sunita Wadekar Bhargava, and Karen Lowery, "Saturn," *Business Week,* 17 August 1992, 87–91.

44. John Hoerr, "Work Teams Can Rev Up Paper Pushers, Too," *Business Week,* 28 November 1988, 64–72.

45. Robert R. Blake, Herbert A. Shepard, and Jane S. Mouton, *Managing Intergroup Conflict in Industry* (Houston: Gulf Publishing, 1964).

46. Leonard Greenhalgh, "Managing Conflict," *Sloan Management Review* 27 (Summer 1986): 45–51.

47. Thomas, "Conflict and Conflict Management."

48. Neilsen, "Understanding and Managing Intergroup Conflict"; Joseph McCann and Jay R. Galbraith, "Interdepartmental Relations."

49. Neilsen, "Understanding and Managing Intergroup Conflict"; McCann and Galbraith, "Interdepartmental Relations"; Sherif et al., *Intergroup Conflict and Cooperation.*

50. Dean Tjosvold, Valerie Dann, and Choy Wong, "Managing Conflict between Departments to Serve Customers," *Human Relations* 45 (1992): 1035–54.

51. Robert R. Blake and Jane S. Mouton, "Overcoming Group Warfare"; Schein, *Organizational Psychology;* Blake, Shepard, and Mouton, *Managing Intergroup Conflict in Industry;* Richard E. Walton, *Interpersonal Peacemaking: Confrontation and Third-Party Consultations* (Reading, Mass.: Addison-Wesley, 1969).

52. Mark S. Plovnick, Ronald E. Fry, and W. Warner Burke, *Organizational Development* (Boston: Little, Brown, 1982), 89–93; Schein, *Organizational*

Psychology, 177–78, reprinted by permission of Prentice-Hall, Inc.

53. Kyle Pope, "Dealers Accuse Compac of Jilting Them," *Wall Street Journal,* 7 April 1993, B1.

54. Neal Templin and Joseph B. White, "GM Drive to Step Up Efficiency is Colliding with UAW Job Fears," *Wall Street Journal,* 23 June 1993, A1.

55. Leon C. Megginson, *Personal and Human Resources Administration* (Homewood, Ill.: Irwin, 1977), 519–20.

56. Roger S. Wolters, "Union-Management Ideological Frames of Reference," *Journal of Management* 8 (1982): 21–33.

57. Kevin Kelly, Aaron Bernstein, and Robert Neff, "Caterpillar's Don Fites: Why He Didn't Blink," *Business Week,* 10 August 1992, 56–57; Kevin Kelly, "Cat May Be Trying to Bulldoze the Immovable," *Business Week,* 2 December 1991, 116.

58. Walecia Konrad, "Much More Than a Day's Work—for Just a Day's Pay?" *Business Week,* 23 September 1991, 40.

59. Blake and Mouton, "Reactions to Intergroup Competition."

60. Stratford P. Sherman, "The Gambler Who Refused $2 Billion," *Fortune,* 11 May 1987, 50–58.

61. Alexander B. Trowbridge, "Avoiding Labor-Management Conflict," *Management Review* (February 1988): 46–49.

62. Barbara Ettorre, "Will Unions Survive?" *Management Review* (August 1993): 9–15; Richard B. Peterson, "Lessons from Labor-Management Cooperation," *California Management Review* (Fall 1988): 40–53.

63. Jim Sutherland, "State of the Union: How One Company Benefits from Continuing Dialogue," *Canadian Business,* June 1990, 153–57.

64. Blake and Mouton, "Reactions to Intergroup Competition."

65. Peter Nulty, "Look What the Unions Want Now," *Fortune,* 8 February 1993, 128–35; Kevin Kelly and Aaron Bernstein, "Labor Deals That Offer a Break from 'Us versus Them'," *Business Week,* 2 August 1993, 30.

PART

6

Strategy and Structure for the Future

CHAPTER 14
Toward the Learning Organization

*T*oward the Learning Organization

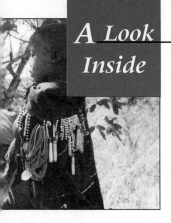
Kalahari Bushmen

For hundreds of years, the Kalahari Bushmen were nomadic hunters and foragers in the harsh, unpredictable Southern African desert. The Bushmen developed the skills to find water during a drought, to live on reptiles and plants in the absence of game, and to fashion bows and arrows from limited sources. They traveled in bands bound together by ties of kinship and friendship. Their mobility and few possessions enabled Bushmen to switch easily to more successful bands, in this way capitalizing on success wherever it was found over a wide geographical area. The flexible band system was enhanced by values of equality, sharing, and gift giving. A hunter's kill would be used to feed neighbors, who would later reciprocate. Gift giving meant that useful artifacts and utensils were widely shared. Hunting camps had grass huts facing the center of a circle where the cooking hearths were hubs of continuous discussion and social exchanges. The Bushmen also bonded through a deep culture in their camps of shared mythology, stories, and dances.

Enter civilization. In recent years, exposure to material wealth has fostered a transformation. Bushmen now accumulate possessions, which hamper mobility, forcing a life-style shift from foraging to farming. A new community structure has evolved, with families living in separate, permanent huts. Entrances are located for privacy, and hearths have been moved inside. Survival skills have deteriorated, with bows and arrows produced only for curio shops. Without sharing and communication, a hierarchy of authority—the chief—is used to resolve disputes. Tension and conflicts have increased, and the tribe's ability to handle drought and disaster today is nonexistent. No longer are there shared stories and mythology that bind the tribespeople into a community.[1]

The emerging herder-farmer society resembles a bureaucracy that excels in a stable, safe environment, leaving the Bushmen vulnerable to sudden environmental changes. The hunter-forager society resembles today's entrepreneurial and learning organization, based on little hierarchy, equality of rewards, shared culture, and a flowing, adaptable structure designed to seize opportunities and handle crises.

Many organizations in industrialized societies have evolved toward bureaucratic forms, as discussed in Chapter 5. And in the face of complex, shifting environments, these organizations no longer work. The hunter-forager society of the Kalahari Bushmen is a metaphor for the learning organization that many companies want to become. Can a bureaucratic herder-farmer society be transformed backward to a skilled, flowing, adaptable hunter-forager society? How can traditional organization structures be transformed into fluid, learning systems?

PURPOSE OF THIS CHAPTER

This chapter explores the trend toward the learning organization. The purpose of this chapter is to integrate materials from previous chapters about organization design and to describe the coming generation of learning organizations. The first section describes how structure, technology, strategy, and other characteristics fit together for organizational effectiveness and identifies the key issues each organization must resolve. Then the learning organization, which resembles the original bands of Kalahari Bushmen , is described. The final sections briefly examine organizational turnaround, the role of organizational leadership in reviving stagnant companies, and the extent to which top management turnover helps organizational performance.

Organizational Design Configurations

In this section, we will integrate concepts from earlier chapters. A key task for top leaders is to decide on goals and strategy, and then to design the organizational form appropriate for the strategy. By fitting the pieces together into the right configuration, an organization can maintain a high level of effectiveness.

STRATEGY FORMULATION AND IMPLEMENTATION

The starting point for defining organizational configuration is **strategy**, which is the current set of plans, decisions, and objectives that have been adopted to achieve the organization's goals. **Strategy formulation** includes the activities that lead to establishment of a firm's overall goals and mission and the development of a specific strategic plan as described in Chapter 2.[2] For example, a firm might formulate a strategy of differentiation, low-cost leadership, or focus. **Strategy implementation** is the use of managerial and organizational tools to direct and allocate resources to accomplish strategic objectives.[3] It is the administration and execution of the strategic plan. The concepts of organization design are especially relevant for implementation. The direction and allocation of resources are accomplished with the tools of organization structure, control systems, culture, technology, and human resources.

ORGANIZATIONAL FORM AND DESIGN

Organizational form and design are the ultimate expression of strategy implementation. Each chapter of this book has dealt with some aspect of design. Top leaders must design the organization so all parts fit together into a coherent whole to achieve the organization's strategy and purpose.

A framework proposed by Henry Mintzberg[4] suggests that every organization has five parts, as illustrated in Exhibit 14.1. Top management is located at the top of the organization. Middle management is at the intermediate levels, and the technical core includes the people who do the basic work of the organization. The technical support staff are the engineers, researchers, and analysts who are responsible for the formal planning and control of the technical core. The administrative support staff provide indirect services and include clerical, maintenance, and mail room employees. The five parts of the organization may vary in size and importance depending upon the overall environment, strategy, and technology.

Mintzberg proposed that these five organizational parts could fit together in five basic configurations, in which environment, goals, power, structure, formalization, technology, and size hang together in identifiable clusters. This framework defines key organizational variables and tells managers the appropriate configuration for specific environments and strategies.

The **five organization configurations** proposed by Mintzberg are entrepreneurial structure, machine bureaucracy, professional bureaucracy, divisional form, and "adhocracy."[5] A brief description of each configuration follows. Specific organizational

Exhibit 14.1
The Five Basic
Parts of an
Organization.

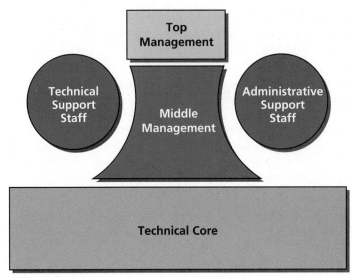

Source: Based on Henry Mintzberg, *The Structuring of Organizations* (Englewood Cliffs, N.J.: Prentice-Hall, 1979), 215–97; and Henry Mintzberg, "Organization Design: Fashion or Fit?" *Harvard Business Review* 59 (January–February 1981): 103–16.

characteristics associated with the appropriate configuration for strategy implementation are summarized in Exhibit 14.2.

1. *Entrepreneurial structure*   The organization with an **entrepreneurial structure** is typically a new, small entrepreneurial company. The organization consists of a top manager and workers in the technical core. Only a few support staff are required. There is little specialization or formalization. Coordination and control come from the top. The founder has the power and creates the culture. Employees have little discretion, although work procedures are typically informal. This organization is suited to a dynamic environment. It can maneuver quickly and compete successfully with larger, less adaptable organizations. Adaptability is required to establish its market. The organization is not powerful and is vulnerable to sudden changes. Unless adaptable, it will fail.

2. *Machine bureaucracy*   **Machine bureaucracy** describes the bureaucratic organization discussed in Chapter 5. This organization is very large, and the technology is routine, often oriented to mass production. Extensive specialization and formalization are present, and key decisions are made at the top. The environment is simple and stable because this organization is not adaptable. The machine bureaucracy is distinguished by large technical and administrative support staffs. Technical support staffs, including engineers, market researchers, financial analysts, and systems analysts are used to scrutinize, routinize, and formalize work in other parts of the organization. The technical support staff is the dominant group in the organization. Machine bureaucracies are often criticized for lack of control by lower employees, lack of innovation, a weak culture, and an alienated work force, but they are suited to large size, a stable environment, and the goal of efficiency.

3. *Professional Bureaucracy*   The distinguishing feature of a **professional bureaucracy** is that the production core is composed of professionals, as in hospitals,

Exhibit 14.2 Dimensions of Five Organizational Types.

Dimension	Entrepreneurial Structure	Machine Bureaucracy	Professional Bureaucracy	Divisional Form	Adhocracy
Strategy and goals:	Growth, survival	Defender; efficiency	Analyzer; effectiveness, quality	Portfolio; profit	Prospector; innovation
Age and size:	Typically young and small	Typically old and large	Varies	Typically old and very large	Typically young
Technology:	Simple	Machines but not automated	Service	Divisible, like machine bureaucracy	Very sophisticated, often automated
Environment:	Simple and dynamic; sometimes hostile	Simple and stable	Complex and stable	Relatively simple and stable; diversified markets	Complex and dynamic
Formalization:	Little	Much	Little	Within divisions	Little
Structure:	Functional	Functional	Functional or product	Product, hybrid	Functional and product (matrix)
Coordination:	Direct supervision	Vertical linkage	Horizontal linkage	Headquarters (HQ) staff	Mutual adjustment
Control:	Clan	Bureaucratic	Clan and bureaucratic	Market and bureaucratic	Clan
Culture:	Developing	Weak	Strong	Subcultures	Strong
Technical support staff:	None	Many	Few	Many at HQ for performance control	Small and within project work
Administrative support staff:	Small	Many	Many to support professionals	Split between HQ and divisions	Many but within project work
Key part of organization:	Top management	Technical staff	Production core	Middle management	Support staff and technical core

Source: Adapted and modified from Henry Mintzberg, The Structuring of Organizations: A Synthesis of the Research (Englewood Cliffs, N.J.: Prentice-Hall, 1979), 466–71.

universities, and consulting firms. While the organization is bureaucratized, people within the production core have autonomy. Long training and experience encourage clan control and a strong culture, thereby reducing the need for bureaucratic control structures. These organizations often provide services rather than tangible products, and they exist in complex environments. Most of the power rests with the professionals in the production core. Technical support groups are small or nonexistent, but a large administrative support staff is needed to handle the organization's routine administrative affairs.

4. Divisional form   Organizations with a **divisional form** are typically large and are subdivided into product or market groups. There are few liaison devices for coordination between divisions, and the divisional emphasis is on market control using profit and loss statements. The divisional form can be quite formalized within divisions because technologies are often routine. The environment for any division will tend to be simple and stable, although the total organization may serve diverse markets. Many large corporations, such as General Motors, Procter and Gamble, Ford, and Westinghouse, are divisional organizations. Each division is somewhat autonomous, with its own subculture. Centralization exists within divisions, and a headquarters staff may retain some functions, such as planning and research.

5. Adhocracy   An **adhocracy** develops to survive in a complex, dynamic environment. The technology is sophisticated, as in the aerospace and electronic industries. Adhocracies are typically young or middle-aged and quite large but need to be adaptable. A team-based structure typically emerges with many horizontal linkages and empowered employees. Both technical support staff and the production core have authority over key production elements. The organization has an elaborate division of labor but is not formalized. Employee professionalism is high, cultural values are strong, and clan control is stressed. With decentralization, people at any level may be involved in decision making. The adhocracy is almost the opposite of the machine bureaucracy in terms of structure, power relationships, and environment. It resembles the horizontal organization described in Chapter 7.

The point of the five configurations is that top management can design an organization to achieve harmony and fit among key elements. For example, a machine bureaucracy is appropriate for a strategy of efficiency in a stable environment; but to impose a machine bureaucracy in a hostile and dynamic environment is a mistake. Managers can implement strategy by designing the correct structural configuration to fit the situation.

THE EFFECTIVE ORGANIZATION

An additional idea proposed by Mintzberg is that for an organization to be effective, it must manage the interplay of seven basic forces.[6] The organization's form can be designed to help manage this interplay as illustrated in Exhibit 14.3.

The first force is direction, which is the sense of vision, goals, and mission for the organization. The entrepreneurial form best typifies a single organizational direction and common purpose.

The next force is efficiency, which is the need to minimize costs and increase benefits. The best known structure for efficiency is the machine bureaucracy because it focuses on rationalization and standardization.

The third force, proficiency, means carrying out tasks with a high level of knowledge and skill. Proficiency is the advantage of the professional bureaucracy, which uses highly trained professionals to achieve excellence.

The fourth force is innovation, the organization's need to develop new products and services to adapt to a changing external environment. The adhocracy form of organization is best for meeting the need for innovation and change.

Exhibit 14.3   A System of Forces and Forms in Organizations.

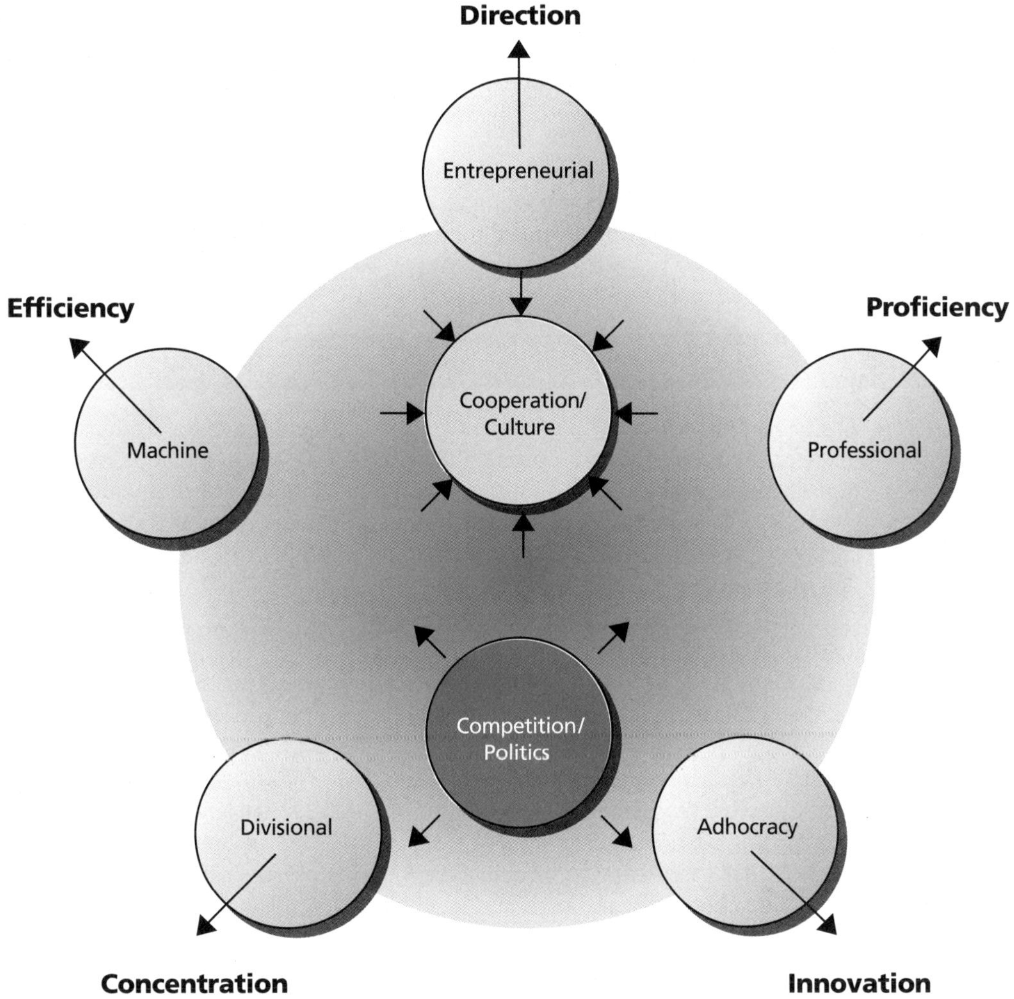

Source: Reprinted from "The Effective Organization: Forces and Forms," by Henry Mintzberg, Copyright © 1991 by the Sloan Management Review Association, Winter, 1991, pp. 54–67 by permission of publisher. All rights reserved.

The fifth force in Exhibit 14.3 is concentration, which means focusing organizational efforts on particular markets. Concentration is the advantage of a divisional organization that focuses its activities on specific products and markets.

Two additional forces within the pentagon of Exhibit 14.3 are cooperation/culture and competition/politics. Cooperation is the result of common culture values and reflects the need for harmony and cooperation among a diverse set of people. Competition can cause politics and a splitting apart of individuals and departments because of the need for individual success and recognition.

An important purpose of organizational form is to enable an organization to achieve the right balance among the seven forces. An effective organization such as 3M stresses innovation, while an organization such as Wal-Mart stresses efficiency and proficiency in its design. A conglomeration such as Hanson Industries stresses concentration; the Daughters of Charity, which runs the fourth largest hospital chain in the United States, is concerned with its mission to provide health care. As we saw in Chapter 13, the pressures for cooperation and competition must be managed, with a cooperative model achieving greater success in many organizations.

Each organization has to find out what works. It cannot maximize all needs simultaneously. By understanding these forces and designing the right structure to achieve strategic outcomes, leaders can create effective organizations. This is a continual leadership process, because a configuration may work for a period of time and then need to be reorganized to achieve a new period of harmony and effectiveness.[7] Ultimately, organizational form will fit the needs of formulated strategy and the environment.

The Learning Organization

The field of management is undergoing a worldwide, fundamental shift. This shift is reflected in the Paradigm Busters throughout this book that describe corporate transformations away from traditional hierarchical management toward full participation by every employee. The shift is also reflected in new organizational forms, such as the modular organization, virtual corporation, and horizontal organization described earlier.

This management shift has been prompted by two accelerating trends. The first is the increasing rate of change brought by global competition. Organizations must adapt faster and be able to do more things well. The second trend is a fundamental change in organizational technologies. Traditional organizations were designed to manage machine-based technologies, with a primary need for stable and efficient use of physical resources, such as in mass production. However, new organizations are knowledge-based, which means they are designed to handle ideas and information, with each employee becoming an expert in one or several conceptual tasks. Rather than striving for efficiency, each employee in knowledge-based companies must continuously learn and be able to identify and solve problems in his or her domain of activity.[8]

In this new world order, the responsibility of management is to create organizational learning capability. In many industries, the ability to learn and change faster than competitors may be the only sustainable competitive advantage. Hence, many companies are redesigning themselves toward something called the learning organization. There is no single model of learning organization. The learning organization is an attitude or philosophy about what an organization is and the role of employees. The notion of learning organization may replace any of the designs described in Exhibit 14.2. The learning organization is a paradigm shift to a new way of thinking about organizations.

In the **learning organization,** everyone is engaged in identifying and solving problems, enabling the organization to continuously experiment, improve, and increase its capability. The essential value of the learning organization is problem solving, in contrast to the traditional organization that was designed for efficiency. In the learning organization, employees engage in problem identification, which means understanding customer needs. Employees also solve problems, which means putting things together in unique ways to meet customer needs. The organization in this way adds value by defining new needs and solving them, which is accomplished more often with ideas and information than with physical products. When physical products are produced, ideas and information still provide the competitive advantage because products are changing to meet new and challenging needs in the environment.[9]

WHY CREATE LEARNING CAPABILITY?

Consider three traditional ways of gaining competitive advantage through financial, marketing, and technological capabilities, as illustrated in Exhibit 14.4.[10] These traditional sources of competitive advantage are taught in most business schools. Financial capability pertains to financial efficiencies as reflected in wise investment decisions and a profitable return to investors. Marketing capability pertains to building the right products, establishing a close relationship with customers, and effectively marketing products and services. Technology capability refers to technical innovation, research and development, new products, and up-to-date production technologies.

But in a world that is shifting from machines to ideas, these traditional capabilities now require organizational learning capability, also illustrated in Exhibit 14.4. The learning component of competitive advantage refers to the ability to advance financial, marketing, and technological capabilities to a higher level by disengaging employees from traditional notions of efficiency and engaging them in active problem solving that helps the organization change. The more learning capability is increased, the more adaptable and successful the organization.

Learning capability is not about learning the principles of accounting or marketing. It means enhancing the organization's and each person's capacity to do things

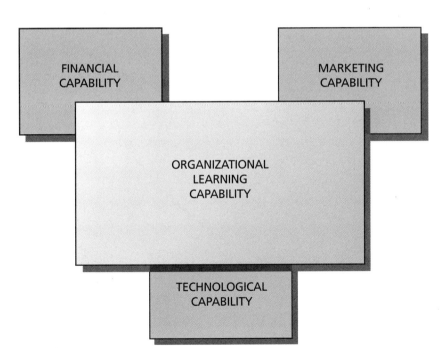

Exhibit 14.4
Organizational Learning Capability Is a Critical Source of Competitive Advantage.

Source: Adapted from Dave Ulrich and Dale Lake, "Organizational Capability: Creating Competitive Advantage," *Academy of Management Executive* 5, no. 1 (1991): 77. Used by permission.

they were not able to do previously. This is knowledge acquired not from textbooks and past experience but from actually engaging in independent action, experimenting, and using trial and error. Experimentation extends from an accounting clerk trying a new software program to the organization's strategy to always modify and update products to meet changing customer needs. Increasing knowledge is not something stored intellectually or in computers; it reflects expanding know-how, similar to the increase in capability gained from learning to ride a bike or paint a portrait.[11]

Although the learning organization cannot be precisely defined, it is an extension of the concepts described in this book and is typically associated with certain characteristics. Exhibit 14.5 indicates how the learning organization goes beyond both the traditional hierarchy and the horizontal organization described in Chapters 6 and 7. In the traditional hierarchy, top management was responsible for directing organizational strategy and took responsibility for thinking and acting. Employees were simply factors of efficient production to be assigned to routine tasks that did not change. The breakthrough of the horizontal organization is that employees are

Exhibit 14.5   Evolution of the Learning Organization.

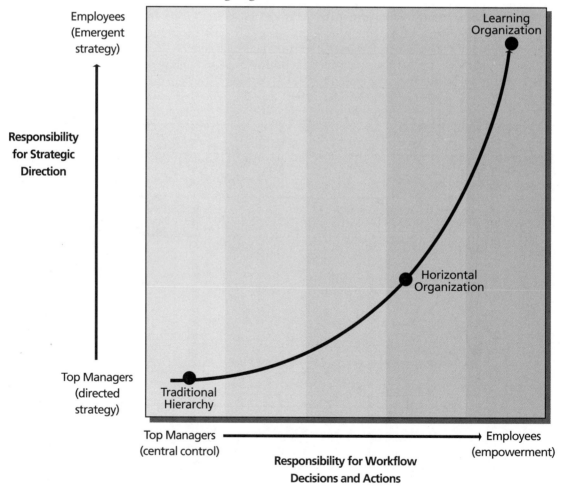

empowered to think and act to design work methods on behalf of the organization. Although top managers still provide a primary strategic direction, employees have great latitude in executing this direction and can sometimes identify and anticipate customer needs.

The further breakthrough of the learning organization is that employees contribute to strategic direction to an extent not before achieved. Employees identify needs so that strategy emerges from the accumulated activities of employee teams serving customers.[12] The strategy emerges within the overall vision of the organization's future that all employees share, so innovations and improvements by respective teams add to the organizational whole. Different parts of the organization are adapting and changing independently while at the same time contributing to the company mission.

In addition to increased employee responsibility over both organizational means and ends, the shift to a learning organization philosophy is associated with mindful leadership, a strong culture, widespread information sharing, and a systematic shift in formal structures and systems. Each of these characteristics of the learning organization is described below.

MINDFUL LEADERSHIP

The learning organization starts in the minds of the organization's leaders. The learning organization requires mindful leadership—people who understand it and can help other people succeed. Leaders in a learning organization have three distinct roles.

1. Design the social architecture   The social architecture pertains to behind-the-scenes behavior and attitudes. The first task of organization design is to develop the governing ideas of purpose, mission, and core values by which employees will be guided. The mindful leader defines the foundation of purpose and core values. Second, new policies, strategies, and structures that support the learning organization are designed and put into place. These structures reinforce new behavior. Third, leaders design effective learning processes. Creating learning processes and ensuring they are improved and understood requires leader initiative. With these design actions, the learning organization idea can take hold.[13]

2. Create a shared vision   The shared vision is a picture of an ideal future for the organization. This may be created by the leader or by employee discussion, but the company vision must be widely understood and imprinted throughout the organization. This vision represents desired long-term outcomes, hence employees are free to identify and solve immediate problems on their own that help achieve the vision. However, without a shared vision that provides harmony and unity of mind, employee actions will not add to the whole. Without a strong vision, employees may fragment and move in different directions.

3. Servant leadership   Learning organizations are built by servant leaders who devote themselves to others and to the organization's vision. The image of a leader as a single actor who builds an organization by herself is not appropriate for the learning organization. Leaders give away power, ideas, and information. The learning organization requires leaders who devote themselves to the organization. Indeed, many people become leaders who serve others and the organization.[14] One example of a servant leader is George Sztykiel, chairman of Spartan Motors.

Spartan builds chassis for fire trucks and motor homes. Sztykiel's attitude is reflected in his statements to new employees: "Welcome. We think this is a good corporation. It is run on the same principles that a family is, because we think that's the most effective way human beings have managed to get along." Sztykiel also said, "I am not the boss. I am the number one servant of this corporation." At Spartan, everyone has equal opportunity, and all share in the gains of continuous learning.[15] The attitude of servant leadership was captured by Max DePree, who spent many years as chairman of Herman Miller Company. His philosophy is described in Book Mark 14.0.

EMPOWER AND RESPECT PEOPLE

The learning organization uses empowerment to an extraordinary degree. The process of empowerment was described in Chapter 12. In the learning organization, cross-functional teams become the basic unit. People work together to identify needs and solve problems. In the learning organization, leaders know that people are born with curiosity and they experience joy in learning. The learning organization develops this intrinsic motivation and curiosity. Employees are respected and trusted. They are given opportunities for growth. They are selected and trained based upon their ability to grow and learn.[16] A firm like McDougal, Littel & Company, a publisher of educational materials, sends every employee to a day-long accounting class so they can interpret the company financial statements. Learning organizations invest heavily in training, providing abundant learning opportunities for everyone.[17]

At Springfield Remanufacturing Corporation, 30 percent of everyone's job is learning. People are expected to think and act as owners of their part of the business, because real owners need not be told what to do. They can figure it out for themselves. Employees are given the knowledge and information needed to make a decision and are trusted to act in the best interest of the company.[18] At Granite Rock Company, virtually all decisions are made by teams at low levels. There are no budgets. A team of drivers and mechanics makes decisions about buying trucks. A team of workers selected the quarry's $850,000 bulldozer. Granite Rock uses more than one hundred teams to share knowledge and make decisions.[19] As illustrated in Exhibit 14.5, the learning organization goes beyond traditional organizations in giving away responsibility for thinking and acting to achieve the company's vision.

EMERGENT STRATEGY

Business strategy emerges bottom up as well as top down. Since many employees are in touch with customers, suppliers, and new technologies, they identify needs and solutions. Customer needs may result in new products that define the company's strategy. Employees at the top and the bottom develop sensitive antennae for technological and market change. They look at what customers ask for, and they look at what the customer may need tomorrow. Hundreds, perhaps thousands of people are in touch with the environment, providing much data about external needs. This information accumulates into the strategy. For example, Nucor Steel developed a strategy of low-cost production that reflects the vision of CEO Ken Iverson, who heard about and took a $270 million chance on new technology for a thin-slab minimill. But employees helped acquire the new technology and found new products and

HAVE YOU READ ABOUT THIS?

Leadership Is an Art*
by Max DePree

"Leadership is much more of an art, a belief, a condition of the heart, than a set of things to do," writes Max DePree, author of Leadership Is an Art and CEO of Herman Miller Company. Herman Miller was recognized by Fortune magazine as one of the ten best managed, most innovative companies in America. In fact, $100 invested in Herman Miller stock in 1975 would have yielded $4,854 in 1986. DePree would say that these accomplishments are the result of empowered employees striving to reach their potential. Six of his major premises about leadership are as follows:

The Leader as Servant

This book is about empowerment and participative management, about values and beliefs—beliefs about people and their inherent need to contribute. DePree feels the result is a leader who becomes a servant and debtor to the people comprising his or her organization. "The first responsibility of a leader is to define reality. The last is to say thank you. In between the two, the leader must become a servant and a debtor."

True Participative Management Begins in the Heart

For DePree, participative management is not a tool, technique, or even a process; it is a way of life. The leader must respect people, understand that beliefs precede practice, agree on the rights of work, understand the difference between contracts and covenants, and understand that personal relationships count more than formal structure. In his words, "Participative management arises out of the heart of a personal philosophy about people."

The Workers' Bill of Rights

DePree believes that, to empower employees, the leader must not only confer the individual's basic rights, he or she must expand those rights to include the following: the right to be needed and involved, the right to a covenantal relationship with one's employer, the right to understand and be accountable, the right to appeal, the right to make a commitment, and the right to affect one's own destiny. ". . . [t]he needs of the team are best met when we meet the needs of individual persons."

Roving Leadership Is the Backbone of Participative Management

DePree describes roving leaders as the unrecognized people in organizations who act quickly and decisively when needed. The top leader must identify, support, and follow roving leaders, enabling them to lead. "More than simple initiative, roving leadership is a key element in the day-to-day expression of a participative process."

Realization of Potential Comes Only with Intimacy

DePree develops the concept of intimacy with work as that essential, powerful ingredient that must precede competence, commitment, and ownership. Intimacy enables one to realize his or her full potential. Intimacy is the machine operator who knows, by virtue of past necessity, exactly what makes his machine tick. DePree says it best: "Intimacy is the experience of ownership. . . . A key component of intimacy is passion. . . . Intimacy is at the heart of competence."

The art of leadership involves "liberating people to do what is required of them in the most effective and humane way possible." The leader as servant removes obstacles that prevent followers from excelling at their jobs. The leader works to create an environment in which employees are able, and believe they are able, to do their best. What does DePree's book teach today's college students, especially business students? "Managers who have no beliefs but only understand methodology and quantification are modern-day eunuchs." Perhaps most important, "Our companies can never be anything we do not want ourselves to be."

---

*A warm thanks to Vanderbilt Executive MBA students Bill Luckey, Bryan Mulroy, Cliff Finney, John Morgan, Steve Mitchell, and Vance LaVelle for their review from which this Book Mark is adapted.

Leadership Is an Art by Max DePree is published by Doubleday.

processes that used it. The result was astonishing, with Nucor producing a ton of sheet steel in forty-five man-minutes versus three man-hours for big steelmakers.[20]

Strategy also emerges from a network of partnerships with suppliers, customers, and even competitors. Organizations develop partnerships—sometimes with legal contracts, sometimes with informal agreements—that share information and create emerging strategies. The learning organization does not act autonomously. Information from partners provides data to the organization about new strategic needs and directions.[21] More companies are evolving into alliances, joint ventures, and electronic linkages, which were discussed in Chapters 7 and 9. Organizations become collaborators rather than competitors, experimenting to find the best way to learn and adapt. Strategy in the learning organization can emerge from anywhere.

STRONG CULTURE

What does the culture of a learning organization look like? Corporate cultures were described in Chapter 10, and the learning organization reflects those values and more. To really become a learning organization, a company must have the following values:

1. The whole is more valuable than the part, and boundaries are minimized.[22] The learning organization stresses the company as a whole system. Only by understanding the overall vision and learning to improve the whole will the learning organization succeed. The culture also reduces boundaries. The move toward a "boundaryless" organization was discussed in the Chapter 13 Paradigm Buster about General Electric. CEO Jack Welch is striving to break down barriers between departments, divisions, and with external organizations. Removing boundaries enables the free flow of people, ideas, and information that allows coordinated action to innovate and adapt to an uncertain and changing environment. Reducing boundaries also means more partnerships with suppliers, customers, and competitors.
2. The culture also values a sense of community and compassion and caring for one another.[23] People like to belong to something, and the learning organization becomes a place for creating a web of relationships that nurtures and develops each person within the community. Love and caring provide the safety for experimentation, frequent mistakes, and failures that enable learning. People learn and experiment as part of a team and as part of a larger community.

FULL INFORMATION SHARING

The learning organization is flooded with information. To identify needs and solve problems, people have to be aware of what's going on. Formal data about budgets, profits, and departmental expenses are available to everyone. Each person is free to exchange information with anyone in the company. In the move toward information- and idea-based organizations, information sharing reaches extraordinary levels. Like the oil in a car's engine, information is not allowed to get low. Managers believe too much information sharing is better than too little. Employees can pick what they need for their tasks.

The president of Quad/Graphics is hooked via e-mail to sixty-five hundred employees. He receives and answers approximately sixty messages a day.[24] At Four-Gen Technologies Software, employee computers have an electronic mailbox. People feel free to contribute advice to other employees, no matter where they work. Good ideas are shared widely and may be implemented anywhere.[25] Many organizations like McDougal, Littel & Company discussed above train employees so they can use the voluminous information available to them. At Granite Rock, employees are flooded with information that includes survey feedback from customers, the charting of one hundred operational variables within the company, and outside speakers talking about changes in the industry. Each employee is informed of events in the company and its environment.[26] At Springfield Remanufacturing, employees meet in group sessions where department heads go over all production and financial figures, encouraging questions. Employees also have access to daily printouts from cost accounting that detail every job in the plant.[27] The days of managers hoarding data to make decisions are long gone in learning organizations.

NEW STRUCTURES AND SYSTEMS

In the learning organization, the formal vertical structure that created distance between managers and workers is disbanded. So too are pay and budget systems that pit individual against individual and department against department. As described in Chapter 7, teams are the fundamental structure in a horizontal organization. People work together along a production process to create an output for a customer. Teams of employees produce the product or service, and they deal with the customer, making changes and improvements as they go along. In learning companies, bosses are practically eliminated, with team members taking responsibility for training, safety, scheduling vacations, purchases, and decisions about work and pay.

Incentive systems are changed also. At Spartan Motors, employees share 10 percent of quarterly profits. Perhaps even more important, the chief executive earns only four times as much as the lowest-paid worker.[28] This narrow pay range signals the egalitarian nature of the company. At Springfield Remanufacturing, employees get 10 percent bonuses when company goals are met. Learning is further enhanced by paying five hundred dollars for each new idea adopted. One employee made a quick seventy-five hundred dollars and appreciated being rewarded for thinking and acting.[29] Solar Press Inc. went through pay system transformations to find an incentive system that encouraged growth and learning of employees. The initial system gave a bonus to each employee without regard to company performance or employee learning. A new system awarded production bonuses by team. This increased productivity but also pitted teams against one another and became an administrative nightmare. The final system gives profit-sharing bonuses to everyone in the company based on company performance. This system emphasizes teamwork and interdepartmental coordination.[30] Some companies are moving to a system called pay for knowledge, which gives employees a raise for each task learned.

Although no organization represents a perfect example of a learning organization, one excellent example is Chaparral Steel, which has been called a learning laboratory.

IN PRACTICE ♦ 14.1
Chaparral Steel

Chaparral Steel is the tenth largest U.S. steel producer, and it has won significant international recognition for quality and productivity. Chaparral produces eleven hundred tons of steel per worker each year compared to the U.S. average of 350 tons. Started nearly twenty years ago, it has become an experimental laboratory for the latest techniques of learning organizations.

What makes Chaparral so effective? Managers articulate a clear vision—to lead the world in the low-cost, safe production of high-quality steel—along with the values of egalitarianism and respect for the individual. Everyone participates. Everyone takes responsibility for solving problems. When a cooling hose burst, a group of operators, a welder, a foreman, and a buyer all responded because they saw the problem. There is no assumption that other people are expected to do a job. Since employees know the vision and values, supervisors do not micromanage. The organization has few supervisors, and only two levels of hierarchy separate the CEO from operators in the rolling mill.

Employees are rewarded for learning new skills and for performance. Ideas are contributed by just about everybody. Everyone is paid a salary rather than an hourly wage—hence, everyone acts like owners and managers. People are also rewarded with bonuses from company profits, which are shared with the entire community, including janitors and secretaries.

Everyone contributes to developing and sharing knowledge. A steel plant is deliberately held to fewer than one thousand employees so that people can share information easily. An employee experimenting with new equipment will tell other people how it works. Employees who visit a competitor explain to others what they learned. There are no staff positions and no boundaries between departments because there are few departments. Everyone is considered a salesperson and is free to interact with potential customers. Security guards do data entry while on night duty. There is no research and development department because employees on the line are responsible for experimenting with new techniques and products. To reinforce continuous learning, most employees attend some school, and many are teachers of other employees in formal classes. Moreover, using new ideas to benefit the company takes precedence over individual ownership of ideas, so knowledge is shared liberally.

Experimentation is rampant. The cultural value is: if you have an idea, try it. First-level managers can authorize thousands of dollars for employee experiments. Everyone is encouraged to push beyond current knowledge. This involves risk, which is another cultural value. Employees learn to tolerate, even welcome, risk on a production line that is very expensive to shut down.

Chaparral also networks outside the organization. Employees travel constantly, scanning for new ideas at trade shows and other companies. Teams of employees that include vice presidents and shop people travel together to investigate a new technology.

Chaparral is so good at what it does that it welcomes competitors to visit. A competitor can be shown everything it does and yet take away nothing. The reason is that the learning organization must be created by leadership, culture, and empowered people. Most other steelmakers have been unable to achieve this, because they don't have the commitment or the vision.[31]

Chaparral Steel illustrates the extension of an organization beyond horizontal organizing toward a true learning organization. The leadership provides organization design, a shared vision, and an attitude of serving employees. The culture emphasizes community values, providing the caring and compassion that supports risk taking. And there are no boundaries separating departments. People are empowered to the point where no one has to take orders if he or she feels the order is wrong. Everyone operates autonomously yet is part of a team and a community doing what is best for the whole. Chaparral is flooded with information from internal experiments and external companies. The formal structure and systems reinforce horizontal teams and companywide performance.

Organizational Revitalization and Leadership

Many organizations are not yet ready to implement the learning organization philosophy. They don't know how. Or they are just struggling to survive. Companies may be in a period of decline because of poor economic conditions, global competition, or bad management. Or senior executives do not understand the skills needed to implement the learning organization philosophy. For companies like these, the dominant issue is revitalization. Revitalization is typically completed in three stages of recovery under the guidance of a charismatic or transformational leader.

TURNAROUND AND RECOVERY

The revitalization and turnaround of an organization suffering from decline typically involve three phases.[32] The first is **crisis** in which managers downsize the work force, cut out several layers of management, and lower production costs. The old mold is broken. Moving through the crisis involves simplification by reducing functions and product lines. Costs are reduced by instituting controls and lowering expenses. Assets may be sold and some units may be relocated or shut down. Also during this period the problems are analyzed by leaders to plan the subsequent turnaround. Leaders also create a new vision about what the organization can become in the future.

The second phase is to **reinvest** organizational capability. Now that the firm's competitive scope has been simplified, expenses are under control, and size has been reduced, the organization stabilizes. Top leaders will mobilize commitment to the new vision, using symbolic management techniques described in Chapter 10. Organization structure and corporate culture will be changed to reflect the new mission and goals. Leaders will invest in new equipment to enhance technological capability and in new marketing and financial programs to improve sales and show a profit. The most important focus of this phase, however, is investing in human factors and organizational capability by implementing a shared mind-set, empowering workers, and creating capacity for change and future growth.

The final phase is **rebuilding,** wherein the organization begins to grow. The focus shifts away from efficiency toward innovation and branching out for growth. New cultural values are reaffirmed. Leaders may reposition products or decrease prices to penetrate new markets or may add new product lines. Organizational expansion becomes the priority, with new people hired and support functions such as research and development and human resource management increased.

Each company undergoes turnaround in its own way, but some aspects of these three stages are typically present. A major turnaround took place for Navistar International Corporation, previously known as International Harvester, during the 1980s.

IN PRACTICE ◆ 14.2
Navistar International Corporation

In the early 1980s, Navistar was forced to the brink of bankruptcy by mismanagement, a strike, soaring interest rates, and increased competition. To stave off bankruptcy, the company was restructured and downsized. Several businesses were divested, plants were closed, and staff was reduced. In one decision, fully half of the company was divested by the sale of its tractor division to Tenneco.

The reduction in work force was handled well. Outplacement centers were established to help all employees, severance pay was provided, and health and life insurance benefits were extended.

After the initial crisis and trauma, Navistar moved into a stable position and began reinvesting in organizational capability. Team-building workshops and staff effectiveness sessions were held. These activities mobilized commitment against the traditional hierarchical, nonparticipative management philosophy that had been deeply ingrained. Even some board members went to off-site retreats to identify new values for the future. A new statement of values was written, as was a new mission statement, which helped institutionalize the new concern for employees. More power was given to the human resource department, and corporate decision making was decentralized.

By 1987, Navistar was growing again. It introduced three new truck products. A new performance evaluation and compensation system was installed that gave leaders flexibility to reward high performance. Continuous improvement teams were formed to make Navistar competitive. Moreover, Navistar focused exclusively on truck and engine manufacturing, devoting all of its energies to grow in those businesses rather than branch out to other fields.

The outcome was an astonishing success. Against all odds, Navistar went from precipitous decline to revitalization and is now a growing, healthy, self-renewing organization.[33]

Navistar had reached a crisis and yet was able to rebound through decisive contraction, the intelligent reconstruction of organizational capability, and rebuilding with a new focus on trucks and engines. It is an exceptional story of what leaders can do to save a major company.

CHARISMATIC AND TRANSFORMATIONAL LEADERSHIP

Leadership is perhaps the most widely studied topic in the organization sciences. What kind of people can lead an organization through major changes? Types of leadership that have substantial impact on organizations are charismatic and transformational.

Charismatic leadership is defined as the force of personality that induces a high degree of loyalty, commitment, and devotion to the leader; identification of people with the leader and the leader's mission; adoption of the leader's values, goals, and behavior; a sense of being inspired by the leader; a sense of self-esteem from relationships with the leader and the leader's mission; and a high degree of trust in the leader and the correctness of the leader's beliefs.[34] In addition, charismatic leadership is sometimes associated with a crisis and championing a radical solution to the crisis. Followers are open to a leader with the force of personality to lead them from a difficult situation.[35] Research on charismatic leaders suggest they also are willing to take great personal risks, are eloquent and emotionally expressive, are self-confident, and have a high energy level.[36]

Transformational leaders are similar to charismatic leaders but are distinguished by the ability to bring about change, innovation, and entrepreneurship. Transformational leaders motivate followers to not just follow them personally but to believe in the vision of corporate transformation, to recognize the need for revitalization, to sign on for the new vision, and to help institutionalize a new organizational process.[37]

Throughout previous chapters, we have discussed the need for large-scale changes in organizations—whether to implement a new corporate culture or self-managed team structure, grow to a new stage in the life cycle, or expand internationally. A massive administrative change involves a fundamental transformation of mission, structure, and the political and cultural systems of an organization to provide a new level of organizational capability.[38] In a situation of crisis or rapid change, a transformational leader should emerge who can impose major changes on the organization. To do so, the transformational leader must successfully achieve the following three activities.[39]

1. Creation of a new vision   The vision of a desired future state will articulate that the organization must break free of previous patterns and that old structures, processes, and activities are no longer useful. The leader must be able to spread the vision throughout the organization. In the early 1980s at General Motors, for example, a new strategic vision was articulated under the leadership of Roger Smith. At Chrysler, Lee Iacocca developed a new vision for transformation. In both cases, the leaders took time to involve managers and employees through numerous task forces, but they alone were ultimately responsible for initiating the new vision.

2. Mobilization of commitment   Widespread acceptance of the new mission and vision is critical. At General Motors, Roger Smith took nine hundred top executives on a five-day retreat to discuss the vision and gain their commitment. Large-scale, discontinuous change requires special commitment, or it will be resisted as inconsistent with traditional organizational goals and activities.

3. Institutionalization of change   The new practices, actions, and values must be permanently adopted. This means major resources must be devoted to training programs, retreats, and employee gatherings to implement the new organizational style. Changes may involve the technical, financial, and marketing systems as well as administrative structures and control systems. A long time period, perhaps several years, may be required for the leader to bring about full implementation. The transformational leader must be persistent to move the organization toward a new way of doing and thinking. The new system may alter power and status and revise interaction patterns. New executives may be hired who display values and behaviors appropriate for the new order of things. The new system is then institutionalized and made permanent.

One example of a leadership with both charismatic and transformational elements that exists right now in the business world is the chairman of Blockbuster Entertainment Corporation.

IN PRACTICE ◆ 14.3
Blockbuster Entertainment Corporation

Wayne Huizenga (HI-zing-a) first built Waste Management into the largest company of its kind and more recently has made Blockbuster the largest national video store chain. When Huizenga bought into Blockbuster, it controlled seventeen stores; just a few years later, it controls more than seventeen hundred. Descriptions of Huizenga by his managers indicate that his leadership is the secret ingredient that made both Waste Management and Blockbuster Entertainment extraordinary successes.

A former president of Blockbuster said, "Wayne creates discontent. He leaves you feeling . . . that you can do more—quicker." A senior vice president describes his boss as follows: "He takes your thoughts one step further, and you have to work hard to catch up with him."

Wayne Huizenga has enormous capacity for hard work, and his enormous energy inspires others. He works twelve- to fourteen-hour days. The chief marketing officer says, "This place is run like a presidential campaign, twenty-four hours a day. We get in early, go home late, travel after hours, have meetings on the plane. Wayne sets the pace and everybody needs to move at that pace."

Huizenga's vision for Blockbuster is that he wants to build something "good" and have a successful product. To that end, X-rated videos are not available at Blockbuster, and his office is furnished with a scratched desk and other furniture acquired at auction. Personal aggrandizement is not his style.

Interestingly, Huizenga shows no charisma in everyday conversation; but those who work with him see differently and agree that his remarkable abilities must fit the right situation. His leadership works best for a business ready for rapid growth or change. Huizenga even recognizes his own limitations. "I enjoy building more than managing." What he has learned is to bring good people in to manage the organization that the force of his personality and energy created. Fortunately, his charismatic personality enables him to recruit whomever he wants for management jobs. All it takes is two hours over dinner and the candidate is hooked.[40]

Does Top Manager Turnover Make a Difference?

So far, this chapter has described how top managers are responsible for leading an organization, creating organizational learning capability, and defining organizational design configurations. This final section of the chapter briefly explores the research on top executive turnover to understand whether a top manager truly has positive impact on organizational performance.

SUCCESSION AND ADAPTATION

One finding from succession research is that, for an organization as a whole, periodic management turnover is a form of organizational adaptation. In organizations characterized by turbulent environments, the turnover of organizational leaders is greater.[41] Such organizations are more difficult to manage, so new energy and vitality are needed on a frequent basis.

Top manager turnover also allows an organization to cope with new contingencies. The selection of a new chief executive may reflect the need for a specific skill or specialization.[42] For example, if the dominant issue confronting an organization is financing mergers, choosing a finance person as chief executive gives priority to financial activities. Historically, CEO backgrounds have changed with business conditions. Early in this century, large firms were controlled by people who came up through manufacturing. In the middle decades, sales and marketing people were more frequently selected as chief executive officers. In the past twenty years, finance personnel have become increasingly dominant.[43] The major issues confronting business organizations were first manufacturing technology, then sales, and now finance.

Turnover every few years can have a positive effect. If a chief executive and top management team serve too long, say over ten years, organizational stagnation may begin. New executives are not coming in to provide fresh energy, new strategies, or expertise for new environmental situations.

One example of how management succession is used for adaptation is Coca-Cola Company. Until a few years ago, Coca-Cola was a tradition-bound, stagnating corporation. The firm was not adapting to its turbulent international environment and was losing ground to PepsiCo in the U.S. market. That all changed with the appointment of new top executives who provided new blood and an international perspective. The new chief executive of Coca-Cola was born in Havana, Cuba. The chief financial officer is Egyptian. The president of Coke USA is an Argentine. The marketing vice president is a Mexican. These changes in top management revitalized Coca-Cola in both the U.S. and foreign markets.[44]

SUCCESSION AND PERFORMANCE

In recent years, companies such as Continental Airlines, Kodak, DEC, Celanese, Tiger International, Baldwin-United, and Northwest Energy had turnover at the top.[45] Replacement of the top executive makes a difference to the performance of companies, especially since turnover may be associated with firm decline and eventual turnaround.

Athletic Team Performance   One type of organization that can help answer the question of whether manager turnover influences performance is an athletic team. The coach is the top manager of the team, and coaches are regularly replaced in both college and professional sports. Several studies have analyzed coaching changes to see whether they lead to an improvement in performance. The general finding is that manager (coach) turnover does not lead to improved performance unless the new coach is exceptionally competent.[46] If the coach has prior experience and has brought about improvements in other teams, then the coach can make a difference. However, most manager replacements do not lead to improved performance.

Another finding from those studies is that performance leads to turnover.[47] Teams with poor records experience greater succession because a poor record often leads to the firing of the old coach. Firing the previous coach serves as a symbol that the team is trying to improve. The term **ritual scapegoating** describes how turnover signals to fans and others that efforts are being made to improve the team's performance record.[48] Corporations also use ritual scapegoating, in the sense that poor performance causes turnover.[49] For example, the board fired the CEO at Allegheny to signal to stockholders and the press that it was attempting to make changes that would correct ethical problems and improve performance.

Corporations and Performance   A corporation is much larger and more diverse than an athletic team. Can the chief executive make a difference to performance in a corporate setting? Several studies of chief executive turnover have been conducted, including a sample of 167 corporations studied over a twenty-year period, 193 manufacturing companies, a large sample of Methodist churches, and retail firms in the United Kingdom.[50] These studies found that leader succession was associated with improved profits and stock prices and, in the case of churches, by improved attendance, membership, and donations. It was also found that performance was improved by good economic conditions and industry circumstances, but the chief executive officer had impact beyond these environmental factors. Overall, when research has been carefully done, there has been a finding that leadership succession explains 20 percent to 45 percent of the variance in an organization's outcomes.[51]

An interesting corollary is that the importance of chief executives means turnover in some cases may lead to poorer performance. In a study of managerial succession in local newspapers, when the founder who created and developed the organization left, performance dropped. In the early stages of the organizational life cycle, an organization depends heavily on the special skills of its founder. A new top manager is unable to achieve the same level of performance.[52]

A realistic interpretation of these findings is the conclusion that corporate performance is the result of many factors. General economic and industry conditions outside the control of the chief executive do affect sales and net earnings. However, outcomes under the control of executive strategy—such as net profit—are influenced by the chief executive. The impact of chief executives on performance is also greater in smaller organizations where chief executives can directly formulate and implement strategy and can use symbolic action to affect the direction and performance of the company.

Summary and Interpretation

This chapter covered several topics concerning organizational forms relevant to the future, the trend toward learning organizations, and organizational revitalization and leadership. Top leaders are responsible for the organization's design configuration. They decide on strategy formulation and then implement strategy by selecting organizational structure and form. Five forms described in the chapter are entrepreneurial, professional bureaucracy, adhocracy, divisional form, and machine bureaucracy. The selection of the configurations among these forms helps managers deal with basic forces, such as efficiency, direction, and innovation.

The paradigm shift occurring in the field of management has resulted in the learning organization. Enhanced learning capability is associated with mindful leadership, empowered people, emergent strategy, strong culture, full information sharing, and new structures and systems.

Some organizations are engaged in revitalization, which includes the three stages of crisis, reinvestment, and rebuilding. The process of turnaround and recovery is often led by a charismatic or transformational leader.

Finally, recent research has explored the impact of top managers on organizations. Top management turnover provides new energy and perspectives for organizational leadership. Succession also provides new skills to cope with changing environmental conditions and may symbolize a new organizational direction.

KEY CONCEPTS

adhocracy	five organizational configurations
charismatic leadership	learning organization
crisis	machine bureaucracy
divisional form	professional bureaucracy
entrepreneurial structure	rebuilding

reinvest   strategy formulation
ritual scapegoating   strategy implementation
strategy   transformational leadership

DISCUSSION QUESTIONS

1. Is charismatic leadership a realistic concept in today's organizations, especially in an era of teamwork? Discuss.

2. Do you agree that creating organizational learning capability is more important for competitive advantage than is creating financial, marketing, or technological capability? Explain.

3. How do the five organizational forms proposed by Mintzberg help an organization deal with the system of seven primary forces?

4. What do you think of the concept of learning organization? Which aspects seem least realistic? Would you like to work in one?

5. What might managers do during the rebuilding stage of turnaround to prevent the problems of the past? Discuss.

6. Why are cultural values of minimal boundaries and compassion and caring important to a learning organization? Discuss.

7. How might top management succession be used for adaptation and ritual scapegoating? Explain.

8. A consultant said, "The individual who occupies the chief executive position can have more impact on profits than on total sales." Explain why you agree or disagree with this statement.

 GUIDES TO ACTION

As an organization's top manager, keep these guides in mind:

1. Take responsibility for designing organization form to fit strategy and environment. Five organizational types to choose from are entrepreneurial, machine bureaucracy, professional bureaucracy, divisional form, and adhocracy.

2. Make sure the organization is effective by managing the interplay among and needs for the seven basic forces of direction, proficiency, innovation, concentration, efficiency, cooperation/culture, and competition/politics.

3. Create organizational learning capability beyond that provided by technology, financial, and marketing capabilities by developing mindful leadership, empowered employees, emergent strategy, strong culture, information sharing, and new structures and systems.

4. When an organization needs revitalization, begin implementing the three stages of crisis, reinvestment, and rebuilding. Depending on your personality characteristics, behave as a charismatic or transformational leader.

5. Encourage periodic top management succession to ensure a flow of fresh energy and ideas into the upper ranks. Adapt to specific problems by bringing needed skills and experience into the chief executive position. Remember that chief executive succession is typically associated with improved organizational performance.

Consider these guides when analyzing the following case.

Harley-Davidson*

Part I

Way back in the 1960s, Harley-Davidson had 50 percent of the motorcycle market with its American cruiser bike. The bike rumbled at stop signs and was a favorite of blue-collar workers and motorcycle gangs.

By the 1970s, the Japanese changed the motorcycle image with ads like, "You meet the nicest people on a Honda." The Japanese created a large market for small cycles and encroached on Harley's big-bike territory. The Japanese manufacturers lowered prices to increase market share. They were unrelenting and would happily put Harley-Davidson out of business. Within ten years, Harley-Davidson's "hogs" had a measly 3.8 percent of the motorcycle market.

During the early 1980s, Harley-Davidson's CEO Vaughn Beals and other executives purchased Harley-Davidson to see if they could turn it around. Their challenge was enormous. Not only did Harley have an almost nonexistent share of the market, but dealers and bikers disliked the company's poor service and shoddy workmanship.

Harley's negative reputation was well deserved. Engines vibrated wildly, the bikes were unstable, and gaskets leaked. Half the hogs coming off the assembly line had to be reworked. One reason quality was abysmal was that labor relations were terrible. Labor and management were hostile toward one another. Employee complaints and absenteeism were rampant. Management felt lucky when a motorcycle came off the line defect-free.

QUESTIONS

1. Draw on concepts in this chapter to suggest approaches CEO Vaughn Beals might take to salvage Harley-Davidson.
2. How would you rate the probability of a successful turnaround at Harley? Why?

Part II

One of the first things President Vaughn Beals did was a surprise. He and other top executives visited Japan's motorcycle factories to see what they could learn. They discovered the real secret of Japanese success was not technology but intelligent organizational approaches and highly motivated employees.

After his return, Beals identified two immediate problems: labor-management tension and lousy quality. Two longer-range problems also had to be managed: unrelenting competition from the Japanese and poor customer relationships.

Vaughn Beals had a vision that Harley-Davidson could produce high-quality motorcycles at a competitive price. Since future improvement was contingent upon employee cooperation, that was where Beals started.

Beals first initiated an open-door policy. His open door gave workers a chance to air their grievances while he learned about the underlying problems. His goal was to develop a more participative, less hierarchical, and less adversarial

---

* Based on Michael Oneal, "Full Cycle," Continental, November 1987, 20–24; Rod Willis, "Harley-Davidson Comes Roaring Back," Management Review (March 1986): 20–27.

working relationship. Other initiatives included the agreement to put a union label on all bikes. Management also voluntarily shared financial information with union leaders. Managers and supervisors were taught to treat workers in a humane and considerate way. In addition, a number of human relations programs were undertaken, including a voluntary peer review system, a tuition refund program, a savings plan, cross-training opportunities, outplacement assistance for anyone who left, a task force to improve job security, and employee assistance programs to help with personal or family problems.

These programs had enormous impact on Harley's culture. The peer review system, for example, created a strong teamwork orientation. Another move was to do away with the traditional vertical hierarchy, thereby giving each employee a sense of ownership in running an efficient operation. Each plant was divided into from four to seven areas, with each area responsible for everything that took place. Company-level staff jobs were cut. If staff functions were needed, they were accomplished by the people in each area. Employees in each area determined the best way to set up their own work, what their job descriptions should be, and what work rates were optimal. This approach applied to sales as well as production employees.

Additional steps were to force a shallower organization chart by eliminating unneeded levels. Quality circles were implemented, and these became a source of bottom-up ideas for improving efficiency. The quality circles also proved to be a tremendous factor in breaking down barriers between workers and supervisors.

To attack the quality problems, executives sought employee help for installing a just-in-time inventory system and statistical process control techniques. The just-in-time system meant that raw materials arrived only as needed for currently assembled motorcycles. This system produced an enormous savings in inventory. Employee coordination with suppliers and dealers was so good that inventory and stockrooms were eliminated. Statistical process control is a systematic way to monitor quality and make immediate corrections. Harley-Davidson also gradually invested in new technology, such as robots and computers to aid motorcycle design and manufacturing. As a result, dealers claim quality has gone up over 100 percent. They have few warranty claims and can get needed parts right away. Harley-Davidson has improved efficiency as well. Inventory costs are way down, the break-even point is lower, and higher-quality bikes are sold at lower costs.

To deal with the Japanese onslaught, Beals got help from the U.S. government. The Reagan administration found that Japanese were dumping (selling below cost) excess bikes in the United States, and it responded with a five-year tariff on heavyweight motorcycles. This gave Harley some temporary breathing room.

Customer relationships have been repaired by personal visits of Beals and his staff at motorcycle rallies and meetings of Harley riders. Sales managers take a van full of hogs for riders to demonstrate; and, unlike the previous CEO who attended rallies in a black limo and a business suit, Beals rides his own 1340 cc Electra Glide. His jeans and leather jacket help build a relationship with customers. Harley-Davidson's dramatically improved quality has also helped the relationship with both dealers and customers. In addition, the company has formed the Harley Owners Group (H.O.G.), which now has more than seventy-five thousand members, to sponsor rides and activities for customers.

Harley is profitable again and has regained 37 percent of the large-bike market. Harley is also becoming more innovative with new product designs. It achieved new designs through "simultaneous engineering," which has engineering and manufacturing work together from the start. This ensures that components are satisfactory for the customer but also simpler and less expensive to produce.

Although Harley experienced a miracle recovery, the future is not so bright. Harley's turnaround led CEO Beals to call for an early elimination of tariffs on large Japanese motorcycles. This was an excellent public relations move and showed that Harley could survive on its own. However, the Japanese stand poised to try again to dominate the large-motorcycle market.

More bad news is the shrinking size of the market. Registrations of large bikes have dropped 25 percent since 1983. One strategy Harley has adopted in response is diversification. Beals moved the company into unrelated fields, such as manufacturing rocket engines for target drones and casings for artillery shells. He hopes this will forestall the gradual shrinkage of market size for large bikes. In another move, Beals tried to gain synergy by buying Holiday Rambler Corporation, a company that makes luxury motor homes. "It makes big toys for big boys," says Beals—which is exactly what Harley does, so Beals expects Harley to do well in that market.

QUESTIONS

1. What concepts from this chapter explain the successful turnaround of Harley-Davidson?
2. What problems do you foresee for Harley-Davidson? What recommendations would you make to CEO Beals for the future?

NOTES

1. David K. Hurst, "Cautionary Tales from the Kalahari: How Hunters Become Herders (and May Have Trouble Changing Back Again)," Academy of Management Executive 3, no. 5 (1991): 74–86.
2. Milton Leontiades, "The Confusing Words of Business Policy," Academy of Management Review 7 (1982): 45–48.
3. Lawrence G. Hrebiniak and William F. Joyce, Implementing Strategy (New York: Macmillan, 1984).
4. Henry Mintzberg, The Structure of Organizations (Englewood Cliffs, N.J.: Prentice-Hall, 1979), 215–97; idem, "Organization Design: Fashion or Fit?" Harvard Business Review 59 (January-February 1981): 103–16.
5. Mintzberg, The Structure of Organizations; idem, "Organization Design."
6. Based on Henry Mintzberg, "The Effective Organization: Forces and Forms," Sloan Management Review (Winter 1991): 54–67.
7. Danny Miller, "Organizational Configurations: Cohesion, Change, and Prediction," Human Relations 43 (1990): 771–89.

8. Peter M. Senge, "Transforming the Practice of Management," Human Resource Development Quarterly 4 (Spring 1993): 5–32.
9. Robert B. Reich, "The Real Economy," Atlantic Monthly, February 1991, 35–52.
10. Dave Ulrich and Dale Lake, "Organizational Capability: Creating Competitive Advantage," Academy of Management Executive 5, no. 1 (1991): 77–92.
11. Senge, "Transforming the Practice of Management."
12. Ken Peattie, "Strategic Planning: Its Role in Organizational Politics," Long Range Planning 26, no. 3 (1993): 10–17.
13. Peter M. Senge, "The Leader's New Work: Building Learning Organizations," Sloan Management Review (Fall 1990): 7–23.
14. Ibid.
15. Edward O. Welles, "The Shape of Things to Come," Inc., February 1992, 66–74.
16. Senge, "Transforming the Practice of Management."
17. Lucien Rhodes with Patricia Amend, "The Turnaround," Inc., August 1986, 42–48.

18. Jack Stack, "The Great Game of Business," Inc., June 1992, 53–66.

19. John Case, "The Change Masters," Inc., March 1992, 58–70.

20. Myron Magnet, "Meet the New Revolutionaries," Fortune, 24 February 1992, 94–101.

21. Marc S. Gerstein and Robert B. Shaw, "Organizational Architectures for the Twenty-First Century," in David A. Nadler, Marc S. Gerstein, Robert B. Shaw, and associates, eds., Organizational Architecture: Designs for Changing Organizations (San Francisco: Jossey-Bass, 1992), 263–74.

22. Mary Anne Devanna and Noel Tichy, "Creating the Competitive Organization of the 21st Century: The Boundaryless Corporation," Human Resource Management 29 (Winter 1990): 455–71; Fred Kofman and Peter M. Senge, "Communities of Commitment: The Heart of Learning Organizations," Organizational Dynamics (Autumn 1993): 4–23.

23. Kofman and Senge, "Communities of Commitment."

24. "Interview with Harry V. Quadracci," Business Ethics (May-June 1993): 19–21.

25. Jenny C. McCune, "More Power to Them," Small Business Reports, November 1992, 51–59.

26. Case, "The Change Masters."

27. Rhodes with Amend, "The Turnaround."

28. Welles, "The Shape of Things to Come."

29. Rhodes with Amend, "The Turnaround."

30. Bruce G. Posner, "If at First You Don't Succeed," Inc., May 1989, 132–34.

31. Dorothy Leonard-Barton, "The Factory as a Learning Laboratory," Sloan Management Review (Fall 1992): 23–38.

32. Brian Dumaine, "The New Turnaround Champs," Fortune, 16 July 1990, 36–44; John M. Stopford and Charles Baden-Fuller, "Corporate Rejuvenation," Journal of Management Studies 27 (1990): 399–415; Richard C. Hoffman, "Strategies for Corporate Turnarounds: What Do We Know about Them?" Journal of General Management 14 (Spring 1989): 46–66.

33. Chet Borucki and Carole K. Barnett, "Restructuring for Self-Renewal: Navistar International Corporation," Academy of Management Executive 4 (February 1990): 36–49.

34. Robert J. House and Jitendra V. Singh, "Organizational Behavioral: Some New Directions for I/O Psychology," Annual Review of Psychology 38 (1987): 669–718.

35. Bernard M. Bass, Bass & Stogdill's Handbook of Leadership: Theory, Research, and Managerial Appli-

cations, 3d ed. (New York: Free Press, 1990).

36. Bass, Bass & Stogdill's Handbook of Leadership; Jay A. Conger and Rabindra N. Kanungo, "Toward a Behavioral Theory of Charismatic Leadership in Organizational Settings," Academy of Management Review 12 (1987): 637–47.

37. House and Singh, "Organizational Behavioral"; Bass, Bass & Stogdill's Handbook of Leadership; Joseph Seltzer and Bernard M. Bass, "Transformational Leadership: Beyond Initiation and Consideration," Journal of Management 16 (1990): 693–703.

38. Noel M. Tichy and Mary Ann Devanna, The Transformational Leader (New York: John Wiley, 1986).

39. Noel M. Tichy and David O. Ulrich, "The Leadership Challenge—A Call for the Transformational Leader," Sloan Management Review 26 (Fall 1984): 59–64.

40. Richard Sandomior, "Wayne Huizenga's Growth Complex," New York Times Magazine: Part II, The Business World, 9 June 1991, 22–25.

41. Gerald R. Salancik, Barry M. Staw, and Louis R. Pondy, "Administrative Turnover as a Response to Unmanaged Organizational Interdependence," Academy of Management Journal 23 (1980): 422–37; Jeffrey Pfeffer and William L. Moore, "Average Tenure of Academic Department Heads: The Effects of Paradigm, Size, and Departmental Philosophy," Administrative Science Quarterly 25 (1980): 387–406.

42. Jeffrey Pfeffer and Gerald R. Salancik, "Organizational Context and the Characteristics and Tenure of Hospital Administrators," Academy of Management Journal 20 (1977): 74–88.

43. Neil Fligstein, "The Intraorganizational Power Struggle: Rise of Finance Personnel to Top Leadership in Large Corporations, 1919–1979," American Sociological Review 52 (1987): 44–58.

44. Ann B. Fischer, "Coke's Brand-Loyalty Lesson," Fortune, 5 August 1985, 44–46; John Huey, "New Top Executives Shake up Old Order at Soft-Drink Giant," Wall Street Journal, 6 November 1981, 1.

45. "Turnover at the Top," Business Week, 19 December 1983, 104–10.

46. Jeffrey Pfeffer and Alison Davis-Blake, "Administrative Succession and Organizational Performance: How Administrator Experience Mediates the Succession Effect," Academy of Management Journal 29 (1986): 72–83; Michael Patrick Allen, Sharon K. Panian, and Roy E. Lotz, "Managerial Succession and Organizational Performance: A Recalcitrant Problem Revisited," Administrative Science Quarterly 24 (1979): 167–80; M. Craig

Brown, "Administrative Succession and Organizational Performance: The Succession Effect," Administrative Science Quarterly 27 (1982): 1–16.

47. David R. James and Michael Soref, "Profit Constraints on Managerial Autonomy: Managerial Theory and the Unmaking of the Corporation President," American Sociological Review 46 (1981): 1–18; Oscar Grusky, "Managerial Succession and Organizational Effectiveness," American Journal of Sociology 69 (1963): 21–31.

48. Brown, "Administrative Succession and Organizational Performance"; William Gamson and Norman Scotch, "Scapegoating in Baseball," American Journal of Sociology 70 (1964): 69–72.

49. J. Richard Harrison, David L. Torres, and Sal Kukalis, "The Changing of the Guard: Turnover and Structural Change in the Top-Management Positions," Administrative Science Quarterly 33 (1988): 211–32.

50. Stanley Lieberson and James F. O'Connor, "Leadership and Organizational Performance: A Study of Large Corporations," American Sociological Review 37 (1972): 119; Nan Weiner and Thomas A. Mahoney, "A Model of Corporate Performance as a Function of Environmental, Organizational, and Leadership Influences," Academy of Management Journal 24 (1981): 453–70; Jonathan E. Smith, Kenneth P. Carson, and Ralph A. Alexander, "Leadership: It Can Make a Difference," Academy of Management Journal 27 (1984): 765–76; Alan Berkeley Thomas, "Does Leadership Make a Difference to Organizational Performance?" Administrative Science Quarterly 33 (1988): 388–400.

51. David V. Day and Robert G. Lord, "Executive Leadership and Organizational Performance: Suggestions for a New Theory and Methodology," Journal of Management 14 (1988): 453–64.

52. Glenn E. Carroll, "Dynamics of Publishers Succession in Newspaper Organizations," Administrative Science Quarterly 29 (1984): 93–113.

INTEGRATIVE CASES

It is a highly motivated, successful engineering team which has utilized a new way of working with international teams, flexible workforce and concurrent engineering to develop a very large, complex client/server software system on-time to our Japanese customer. This is a team that is expert in the need for speed.

From group résumé drafted by the engineering manager

As the Common Utility System (CUS) engineering team was winding down its activities, the engineering manager Maureen Schultz put together a group résumé to be circulated within the organization. Schultz hoped to keep the team together to ensure that it would continue to contribute to the organization in other capacities. She believed that this was a high-performing team that had accomplished major breakthroughs in time to market and quality control on the project. Back in April 1992, no one thought that the project would succeed, but they did it against all odds. The product group manager had told her frequently that CUS was the model for future software product development teams. As Schultz reflected on what had happened to CUS, she wondered what things she would do differently, if she had the opportunity to handle another similar team.

BACKGROUND INFORMATION

The Organization. CUS is a project team in a computer product organization that is portrayed by the industry as a product-driven and technologically oriented company. The organizational structure is complex. It is headed by a newly appointed CEO with about fifty senior vice presidents managing the functional areas of engineering, manufacturing, field service and sales, finance, human resources, international groups, and product marketing. Because this is a technical company, engineering is the most influential at the corporate level. Engineering comprises a number of product groups that design and develop products. Each product group is managed by development managers who run a number of projects. One such product group is the Transaction System that manages this CUS project. For each project, there is a group of engineers working on the design and development of a product. Typically, a project team is managed by a supervisor who assumes managerial responsibilities and a project leader who handles the technical respon-

sibilities. Project teams usually stay together for the development process, which could be from a few months to many years.

How It All Started. The organization is part of an international consortium known as Multi-Vendor Innovative Architecture. In the summer of 1991, the vice president of the product group was in Japan for one of the meetings when he agreed to a request by the Japanese partner of the consortium to do some development work that uses this new architecture. When he came back, he assigned a program manager, Roger Best, to liaise with the Japanese and at the same time come up with a proposal. Best got in touch with the Japanese subsidiary of the organization, which quickly got itself involved in the preliminary work. It saw this as an opportunity to establish itself in Japan. In December 1991, Best received a call from the Japanese subsidiary asking for cost estimates for the kind of development work that they had discussed so far. Without giving a second thought, Best estimated some cost figures, dates, and engineers' requirements and gave it to them. A week later, he was shocked to receive a call from the subsidiary that they were awarded a fixed-price contract for the development project. The task was vaguely to functionally specify and design a utility program to be delivered in February 1993.

Best was furious that he had no prior knowledge of the contract and his estimates were being used to price it. He strongly suggested that the product group should not have anything to do with the project and the Japanese subsidiary rescind the contract. He found it hard to believe that anyone would sign a contract where the scope of the work was not clear but the costs were determined in some arbitrary manner. The Japanese subsidiary went to the vice president, explaining that fixed-price contracts and vague requirements were part of the Japanese mode of doing business. Moreover, it was important for the organization to get the contract as a way to show that it could design complex software systems and wanted to do business with the Japanese. The vice president of the product group opted to stay with the project. A U.S. project team was set up to do the development work, while the Japanese subsidiary assumed the responsibility for fulfilling the contract and carried out all negotiations with the Japanese customer. This occurred despite the continuing objections raised by Best that the product group just did not have a charter for a customer-driven product and was not competent to handle it. In late December 1991, an engineering manager, Martha Lowell, and a project leader, Thomas Roberts, were assigned to work on the project, and the CUS team was officially in existence.

The Contract. While the project was vague, the schedule was clear. For phase one, a functional specification was to be delivered in April 1992. The purpose of the functional specification was to take all the customer's requirements and provide a design structure for the software. The final product was to be delivered in February 1993.

PHASE ONE: DEFINITION OF FUNCTIONAL SPECIFICATION

The first task facing Lowell and Roberts was to make sense of the requirements given by the Japanese customer. The requirements were very general in nature and translated from Japanese. Roberts started the preliminary work for the functional specifications by trying to identify all the components of the product. Lowell spent much of her time clarifying the requirements with the Japanese subsidiary, which tried to provide the required information. Only when it became necessary did the Japanese subsidiary seek clarifications from the Japanese customer. For both Lowell and Roberts, this was the first time they had to deal with a Japanese customer and a product dictated by the customer. The organization's model for developing products was that engineering drives the product, but in this project, essentially, the customer was driving engineering. It was a frustrating time and resulted in much conflict between Lowell and Roberts. Lowell had on numerous occasions muttered, "We just have to make Japan do it the American way." It took about a month before they finally understood the scope of the project and came up with a prototype and estimates of the work. They identified nine components (AP control, code conversion, console, EDF, file transfer, OLSM, On-line Sort, service

API, and schedule management.) and estimated about 100,000 lines of codes would be required. Working on the given schedule, they put in a request for ten engineers. Management evaluated the request and allowed only five engineers. Two reasons were given: financial constraints because of the project's price and the project appeared doable with five engineers.

In February 1992, five engineers came on board. They first attended a class to familiarize everyone with the new architecture. Roberts assigned each engineer responsibility for a few components, and they started working on the functional design immediately (see Exhibit 1 for the group structure). At the same time, Lowell took a three-month leave of absence for personal reasons. When she came back, she was reassigned to another group. Management felt that she did not have the skills for the job. During her absence, the product group manager took over as the acting manager. Unfortunately, at about the same time, Roberts was out sick for a long period, and the team was very much on its own. The five members worked on their assigned tasks, frequently coming together to discuss their work and seeking advice from each other. The team's philosophy was "one for all and all for one."

In April 1992, the Japanese customer began to raise concerns about the commitment of the team to the project, judging from the team's weekly progress reports. Management decided to recruit a supervisor, Alfred Taurus, to handle the managerial responsibility. This was neglected as the team focused on the technical aspects of the project. The team continued to work for long hours, and in late April 1992, they came up with a first draft of the functional design. The members vividly remembered the candid comment from the Japanese customer: "You must obey our requirements. Give us what we want, not what you think we want." It was back to the drawing board and Roberts, together with Best, identified some of the conflicting details and renegotiated a new date of July 1992 for delivering the functional specification.

Exhibit 1   Structure of CUS in February 1992.

Name	Responsibilities
Martha Lowell	Engineering Manager
Thomas Roberts	Project Leader
Bryan Wheeler	File Transfer
Leonard Custer	On-line Server
Mary Euler	Console
Albert Steel	Testing
Anna Key	EDF

In June 1992, Roberts left the team. It did not come as shock to the team. Roberts had dropped hints about it when he came back from his sickness, and he did not hide his feelings toward management and the way they handled the project. He was sure that the project would fail. Except for the renegotiation, he kept a low profile and left much of the work to the team. As a parting gift, he handed a note to management complaining about the lack of management support for the project (lack of hardware, personnel), as well as no engineering manager to provide input to the management. With Roberts's departure, the team was left with no engineering manager and no project leader.

The product group manager quickly brought in two corporate consulting engineers, Bill McKenzie and Lauriet Woods, who were familiar with the new architecture. They provided the technical support for the project. Taurus took over the duties of the engineering manager, and Bryan Wheeler became the acting project leader. McKenzie reviewed what had been done so far and realized that the scope of the project had been underestimated. While the components were identified appropriately, the source codes required were about 250,000 lines instead of 100,000 lines. McKenzie quickly got the engineers together and worked out a new plan based on this information so that the specification could be delivered in July 1992. He approached the product group manager for fifteen additional engineers for the team but was told that it was not going to be possible because of a hiring freeze in the organization. The organization had lost money for the last two years and was downsizing every quarter. At the same time, he pushed for direct communication with the customer. The existing system of communicating via the Japanese subsidiary was cumbersome and time-consuming. Sometimes the messages were misinterpreted, while at other times they simply took too long being transmitted to be of any use. It was finally agreed that all three parties would attend a weekly videoconference where issues could be resolved face-to-face. McKenzie also used the opportunity to point out the underestimation of the project size and that it was just impossible to deliver the final product by February 1993. All the parties agreed to renegotiate the deadline after the functional specification was completed in July 1992. Following the new guidelines, the engineers worked diligently and completed the functional specification in late June 1992.

In the first week of July 1992, McKenzie, Wheeler, Woods, Leonard Custer, and Albert Steel flew to Japan to negotiate and discuss the specifications. On their return, they had to do some updating to the specifications. This lasted till the middle of August 1992, when the Japanese customer accepted the functional specification.

THE BREAK

Completing phase one was a major milestone. No one thought they could make it, but they did. The Japanese customer appreciated the effort by the team and communicated this to management. This gained the team much visibility with management and made a significant difference. The members were given two weeks off, and McKenzie and Woods were reassigned back to their original responsibilities. Eleven engineers and an engineering manager were assigned to the team. They were all from another product group in the organization that was affected by the September 1992 downsizing. Because of the hiring freeze, the product group manager had been negotiating with other groups since July for the additional personnel needed for the project. This group was all that he could get. Schultz, the new engineering manager, worked together with Taurus and Wheeler to put a new working structure in place for the design phase of the project (see Exhibit 2). The team was divided into two subgroups, led by two supervisors. One was the development group and the other was the delivery group. The development group wrote the codes, while the delivery group attended to the building, testing, packaging, and delivery of these codes. Each of the groups had smaller subgroups based on the components of the software program. It was agreed that the original five members would become the leaders for the individual components that they had functionally specified. There was also a clear distinction between administrative and technical work. The engineering manager, supervisors, and all the subgroup leaders were administrators; they did not do any of the detailed designing work.

The structure of the team had become complex and hierarchical. Members discussed their problems with their component leaders, who would then present them to the supervisors in the daily component meetings. If a problem could not be resolved, the supervisors would discuss it with the engineering manager at the weekly management meeting. With this new structure, the members became more specialized.

During the two weeks, all the newcomers were given copies of the requirements and functional specification to familiarize them with what was done and get them actively involved in the work as soon as possible. In the first week of September 1992, all the members came back from their vacations. Schultz got everyone together and organized some activities to

Exhibit 2   Structure of CUS in August 1992.

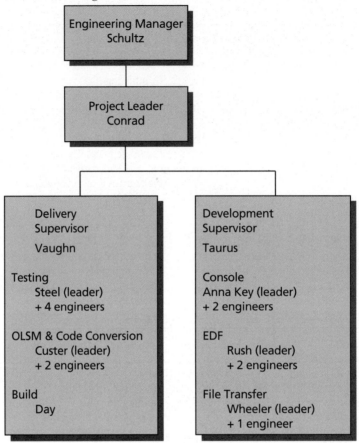

integrate the team. She recognized that the members who came over with her still were unhappy about the downsizing of their previous group. All of them joined this group because the alternative was to be laid off. Some of them were not happy with the task assignments and the choices of component leaders. The initial five members saw themselves as the "founder-members" and generally found it difficult to accept the newcomers.

PHASE TWO: DETAILED DESIGN

Phase two started in September 1992 and was completed in January 1993. The functional specification basically laid out what needed to be done at a high level. Phase two involved planning in detail how these things needed to be done. All the subgroups worked on their tasks separately. In October 1992, Schultz realized that it was difficult to keep track of the progress of the project. She had each subgroup work

out a schedule, which was possible now that the scope of the work was much more defined. In a series of meetings, the team put together a schedule by which the project would be completed in November 1993. Schultz took this schedule to the Japanese customer, and after a lengthy discussion, they decided that the delivery of the product would be done in two stages, the first in April 1993 and the second in August 1993. The project was to be completed by November 26, 1993 (see Exhibit 3).

The component subgroup leaders worked closely with the Japanese customer's engineers. They communicated daily using electronic mail. Issues that could not be resolved were discussed at the weekly videoconferences. The American engineers began to learn more about their Japanese counterparts, which was a cultural breakthrough. For example, the U.S. engineers realized that the Japanese were willing to negotiate the scope of work to be delivered but not the deadline. They also learned that in Japan, the conditions of a con-

Exhibit 3   Renegotiated Project Schedule in October 1992.

Event	Start Date	Completion Date
Stage 1 "Early release" Delivery		3/31/93
Stage 1 Delivery		4/15/93
Stage 1 Customer Integration Phase	4/15/93	6/30/93
Stage 2 "Early release" Delivery		6/30/93
Stage 2 Delivery		8/15/93
Stage 2 Customer Integration Phase	9/01/93	10/31/93
Acceptance Tests	10/01/93	10/31/93
End of Project		11/26/93

tract are not all binding, as in the United States, but can be renegotiated.

During the last week of December 1992, the Japanese engineers came for a detailed design walk-through. For three days, they sat through presentations of the various component designs and how the overall software would function. At the same time, they met with the whole team face-to-face for the first time. The walkthrough went well, and the team started on the implementation phase in January 1993.

PHASE THREE: DESIGN IMPLEMENTATION

The first delivery was in April 1993. The team decided to concentrate on those components that were scheduled for that delivery. Management allowed them to hire seven additional engineers for the work. These engineers were from outside the organization and had the skills and knowledge to start work immediately. All of them were paid hourly and initially had six-month contracts.

Two weeks before the delivery date, an engineer, Dave Day, was assigned to build the program. This involved putting the different parts together and running the program in an actual operating environment. Day found that the program could not run. He started meeting with the subgroups together, and they realized that no one had considered the compatibility of the different components. The team spent the rest of the time making the program run. A day before the program was due to be delivered in April, they still had not gotten the program to run. They tried to negotiate for a later day to deliver, but the Japanese customer told them that was impossible because it had to meet a certain deadline: "Just deliver to us what you have,

and we will see what happens." Somehow, the customer managed to run the program on its system.

By now, the team realized that they could not meet the deadlines given. Schultz and the product group manager went to Japan to present their case and try to negotiate for new dates. Instead of just one more delivery stage, there would be four more (see Exhibit 4): June 1993 for stage 2 delivery; August 1993 for stage 3 delivery; September 1993 for stage 4 delivery; and November 20, 1993 for stage 5 delivery. The final delivery of the fully functional system was still to be November 26, 1993.

During the June 1993 organizational downsizing, all the engineers were assured by management that they would not be affected because the priority was to deliver the product on time. Only one of the supervisors was laid off. The team worked hard and made the stage 2 delivery on June 30, 1993. This was very significant for the team. It was the first time the product was tested and the performance assessed before delivery. There was now optimism in the group, and they began to believe that the team could succeed in the project. Previously, there had been a feeling that the project would fail because they really did not understand the requirements and the deadlines seemed impossible to meet.

In high spirits and morale, the team strived on and made the deliveries for stages 3, 4, and 5. In November 1993, two weeks before the date of the final delivery, the team members got together to discuss what would happen to them. Management had told the team of their intention to keep the team together and were negotiating a few projects for them. That was a few weeks ago, and the team had not heard from them since. Everyone was sold on the idea that the team would be kept together, and no one had made any attempts to seek new jobs. The members con-

Exhibit 4   Actual Project Schedule.

Event	Start Date	Completion Date	Actual Delivery
Stage 1 Delivery		4/16/93	4/16/93
Stage 1 Update		4/30/93	5/25/93
Stage 1 Customer Integration Phase	4/15/93	6/30/93	
Stage 2 Delivery		6/30/93	6/30/93
Stage 2 Update		8/03/93	8/03/93
Stage 2 Customer Integration Phase	7/01/93	8/30/93	
Stage 3 Delivery		8/30/93	9/15/93
Stage 3 Customer Integration Phase	9/01/93	9/30/93	
Stage 4 Delivery		9/30/93	10/15/93
Stage 4 Customer Integration Phase	10/01/93	10/30/93	
Stage 5 Delivery		10/30/93	11/10/93
Stage 5 Customer Integration Phase	11/01/93	11/26/93	
End of Project		11/26/93	

fronted Schultz and the product group manager and pushed them to make a statement about the situation. A day later, Schultz and the product group manager held a meeting and told them that though they had not been successful so far, they would try to keep everyone on the support team until February 1994. Members were left feeling frustrated, and there was a marked change in their commitment to the task. It was only a week before the final delivery and much work was left to be done, but members started working on their résumés and actively looking for jobs. They were more

concerned about their future than the end of the project. Somehow the final delivery was made on November 26. However, the product was conditionally accepted, and the Japanese customer set a new deadline of December 18 for fixing all the reported bugs.

The team was kept together to do support work on the product until February 1994. Though Schultz was trying to sell the team, most of the members started looking for jobs. Support work was minimal, and most members spent their time applying for jobs and attending interviews.

Exhibit 5   Person-Month Chart.

Activity	Functional Design	Detailed Design	Implementation	Total
Administrative[1]	17	20	44	81
Technical[2]	46	64	245	355
Test	10	20	50	80
Total	73	104	339	516

[1]Program management, supervision, nontechnical consulting
[2]Engineers, technical consulting

INTEGRATIVE CASE 2.0
The Audubon Zoo, 1993*

The Audubon Zoo was the focus of national concern in the early 1970s, with well documented stories of animals kept in conditions which were variously termed an "animal ghetto,"[1] "the New Orleans anti-quarium," and even "an animal concentration camp."[2] In 1971, the Bureau of Governmental Research recommended a $5.6 million zoo improvement plan to the Audubon Park Commission and the City Council of New Orleans. The local Times Picayune commented on the new zoo: "It's not going to be quite like the Planet of the Apes situation in which the apes caged and studied human beings but something along those broad general lines."[3] The new zoo confined people to bridges and walkways while the animals roamed amidst grass, shrubs, trees, pools, and fake rocks. The gracefully curving pathways, generously lined with luxuriant plantings, gave the visitor a sense of being alone in a wilderness, although crowds of visitors might be only a few yards away.

THE DECISION

The Audubon Park Commission launched a $5.6 million development program, based on the Bureau of Governmental Research plan for the zoo, in March 1972. A bond issue and a property tax dedicated to the zoo were put before the voters on November 7, 1972. When it passed by an overwhelming majority, serious discussions began about what should be done. The New Orleans City Planning Commission finally approved the master plan for the Audubon Park Zoo in September 1973. But the institution of the master plan was far from smooth.

The Zoo Question Goes Public

Over two dozen special interests were ultimately involved in choosing whether to renovate/expand the existing facilities or move to another site. Expansion became a major community controversy. Some residents opposed the zoo expansion, fearing "loss of

*By Claire J. Anderson, Old Dominion University, and Caroline Fisher, Loyola University, New Orleans. © 1993, 1991, 1989, 1987, Claire J. Anderson and Caroline Fisher. This case was designed for classroom discussion only, not to depict effective or ineffective handling of administrative situations.

green space" would affect the secluded character of the neighborhood. Others opposed the loss of what they saw as an attractive and educational facility.

Most of the opposition came from the zoo's affluent neighbors. Zoo Director John Moore ascribed the criticism to "a select few people who have the money and power to make a lot of noise." He went on to say "[T]he real basis behind the problem is that the neighbors who live around the edge of the park have a selfish concern because they want the park as their private back yard." Legal battles over the expansion plans continued until early 1976. At that time, the 4th Circuit Court of Appeals ruled that the expansion was legal.[3] An out-of-court agreement with the zoo's neighbors (the Upper Audubon Association) followed shortly.

Physical Facilities

The expansion of the Audubon Park Zoo took it from fourteen to fifty-eight acres. The zoo was laid out in geographic sections: the Asian Domain, World of Primates, World's Grasslands, Savannah, North American Prairie, South American Pampas, and Louisiana Swamp, according to the zoo master plan developed by the Bureau of Governmental Research. Additional exhibits included the Wisner Discovery Zoo, Sea Lion exhibit, and Flight Cage. Exhibit 1 is a map of the new zoo.

PURPOSE OF THE ZOO

The main outward purpose of the Audubon Park Zoo was entertainment. Many of the promotional efforts of the zoo were aimed at creating an image of the zoo as an entertaining place to go. Obviously, such a campaign was necessary to attract visitors to the zoo. Behind the scenes, the zoo also preserved and bred many animals species, conducted research, and educated the public. The mission statement of the Audubon Institute is given in Exhibit 2.

NEW DIRECTIONS

A chronology of major events in the life of the Audubon Zoo is given in Exhibit.[3] One of the first significant changes made was the institution of an admission charge in 1972. Admission to the zoo had

Exhibit 1   The Audubon Park Zoo.

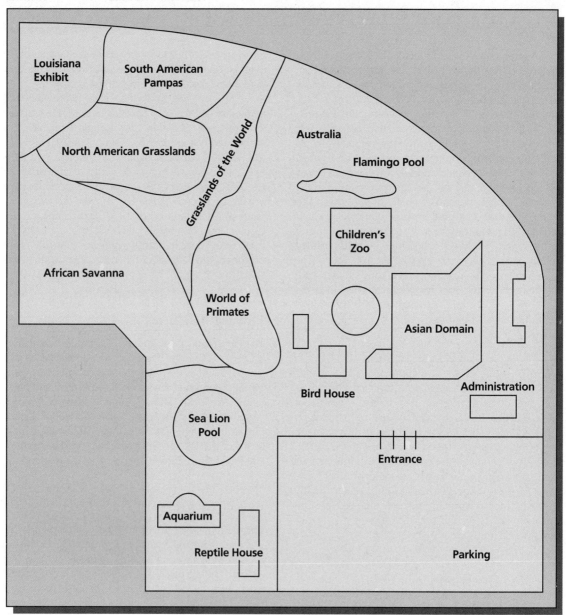

been free to anyone prior to the adoption of the renovation plan. Ostensibly, the initial purpose behind instituting the admission charge was to prevent vandalism,[4] but the need for additional income was also apparent. Despite the institution of and increases in admission charges, attendance increased dramatically (see Exhibit 4).

OPERATIONS

Friends of the Zoo

The Friends of the Zoo was formed in 1974 and incorporated in 1975 with four hundred members. The stated purpose of the group was to increase support

Exhibit 2   Audubon Institute Mission Statement.

The mission of the Audubon Institute is to cultivate awareness and appreciation of life and the earth's resources and to help conserve and enrich our natural world. The Institute's primary objectives toward this are:

Conservation: To participate in the global effort to conserve natural resources by developing and maintaining captive stocks of endangered plants, animals and marine life, and by cooperating with related projects in the wild.

Education: To impart knowledge and understanding of the interaction of nature and man through programs, exhibits and publications and to encourage public participation in global conservation efforts.

Research: To foster the collection and dissemination of scientific information that will enhance the conservation and educational objectives of the facilities of the Audubon Institute.

Economics: To insure long-range financial security by sound fiscal management and continued development, funding through creative means that encourage corporate, foundation and individual support.

Leadership: To serve as a model in the civic and professional communities. To foster a spirit of cooperation, participation and pride.

Source: The Audubon Institute

Exhibit 3   Chronology of Major Events for the Zoo.

1972	Voters approved a referendum to provide tax dollars to renovate and expand the Zoo. The first Zoo-To-Do was held. An admission charge was instituted.
1973	The City Planning Commission approved the initial master plan for the Audubon Park Zoo calling for $3.4 million for upgrading. Later phases called for an additional $2.1 million.
1974	Friends of the Zoo formed with 400 members to increase support and awareness of Zoo.
1975	Renovations began with $25 million public and private funds; 14 acres to be expanded to 58 acres.
1976	The Friends of the Zoo assumed responsibility for concessions.
1977	John Moore went to Albuquerque, Ron Forman took over as Park and Zoo director.
1980	First full-time education staff assumed duties at the Zoo.
1980	Last animal removed from antiquated cage, a turning point in Zoo history.
1981	Contract signed allowing New Orleans Steamboat Company to bring passengers from downtown to the Park.
1981	Delegates from the American Association of Zoological Parks and Aquariums ranked the Audubon Zoo as one of the top three zoos in America of its size.
1981	Zoo accredited.
1982	The Audubon Park Commission reorganized under Act 352 which required the Commission to contract with a non-profit organization for the daily management of the Park.
1985	The Zoo was designated as a Rescue Center for Endangered and Threatened Plants.
1986	Voters approved a $25 million bond issue for the Aquarium.
1988	The Friends of the Zoo became The Audubon Institute.
1990	The Aquarium of the Americas opened in September.

Source: The Audubon Institute

Exhibit 4   Admission Charges.

ADMISSION CHARGES		
Year	Adult	Child
1972	$0.75	$0.25
1978	1.00	0.50
1979	1.50	0.75
1980	2.00	1.00
1981	2.50	1.25
1982	3.00	1.50
1983	3.50	1.75
1984	4.00	2.00
1985	4.50	2.00
1986	5.00	2.50
1987	5.50	2.50
1988	5.50	2.50
1989	6.00	3.00
1990	6.50	3.00
1991	7.00	3.25

ADMISSIONS		
Year	Number of Paid Admissions	Number of Member Admissions
1972	163,000	
1973	310,000	
1974	345,000	
1975	324,000	
1976	381,000	
1977	502,000	
1978	456,000	
1979	561,000	
1980	707,000	
1981	741,000	
1982	740,339	78,950
1983	835,044	118,665
1984	813,025	128,538
1985	856,064	145,020
1986	916,865	187,119
1987	902,744	193,926
1988	899,181	173,313
1989	711,709	239,718
1990	725,469	219,668

Source: The Audubon Institute

and awareness of the Audubon Park Zoo. Initially, the Friends of the Zoo tried to increase interest in and commitment to the zoo, but its activities increased dramatically over the following years to where it was involved in funding, operating, and governing the zoo.

The Friends of the Zoo had a 24-member governing board. Yearly elections were held for six members of the board, who served four-year terms. The board oversaw the policies of the zoo and set guidelines for memberships, concessions, fund-raising, and marketing. Actual policy making and operations were controlled by the Audubon Park Commission, however, which set zoo hours, admission prices, and so forth.

Through its volunteer programs, the Friends of the Zoo staffed many of the zoo's programs. Members of the Friends of the Zoo served as "edZOOcators,"

Exhibit 5   Membership Fees and Membership.

Year	Family Membership Fees	Individual Membership Fees	Number of Membersnips
1979	$ 20	$ 10	1,000
1980	20	10	7,000
1981	20	10	11,000
1982	25	15	18,000
1983	30	15	22,000
1984	35	20	26,000
1985	40	20	27,000
1986	45	25	28,616
1987	45	25	29,318
1988	45	25	33,314
1989	49	29	35,935
1990	49	29	38,154

Source: The Audubon Institute

education volunteers who were specially trained to conduct interpretive educational programs, and "Zoo Area Patrollers," who provided general information at the zoo and helped with crowd control. Other volunteers assisted in the commissary, the Animal Health Care Center and Wild Bird Rehabilitation Center or helped with membership, public relations, graphics, clerical work, research, or horticulture.

In 1988, the name of the Friends of the Zoo was changed to the Audubon Institute to reflect its growing interest in activities beyond the zoo alone. It planned to promote the development of other facilities and manage these facilities once they were a reality.

Fund-Raising. The Audubon Park Zoo and the Friends of the Zoo raised funds through five major types of activities: Friends of the Zoo membership, concessions, "Adopt an Animal," "Zoo-to-Do," and capital fund drives. Zoo managers from around the country came to the Audubon Park Zoo for tips on fund-raising.

Membership. Membership in the Friends of the Zoo was open to anyone. The membership fees increased over the years as summarized in Exhibit 5, yet the number of members increased steadily from the original four hundred members in 1974 to thirty-eight thousand members in 1990, but declined to 28,000 in 1992. Membership allowed free entry to the Audubon Park Zoo and many other zoos around the United States. Participation in Zoobilations (annual members-only evenings at the zoo) and the many volunteer programs described earlier were other benefits of membership.

Expanding membership required a special approach to marketing the zoo. Chip Weigand, director of marketing for the zoo, stated,

. . . [I]n marketing memberships we try to encourage repeat visitations, the feeling that one can visit as often as one wants, the idea that the zoo changes from visit to visit and that there are good reasons to make one large payment or donation for a membership card, rather than paying for each visit. . . . [T]he overwhelming factor is a good zoo that people want to visit often, so that a membership makes good economical sense.

Results of research on visitors to the zoo are contained in Exhibits 6 and 7.

In 1985, the zoo announced a new membership designed for business, the Audubon Zoo Curator Club, with four categories of membership: bronze, $250; silver, $500; gold, $1,000 and platinum, $2,500 and more.

Concessions. The Friends of the Zoo took over the Audubon Park Zoo concessions for refreshments and gifts in 1976 through a public bidding process. The concessions were run by volunteer members of the Friends of the Zoo and all profits went directly to the zoo. Before 1976, concession rentals brought in fifteen hundred dollars in a good year. Profits from operation of the concessions by the Friends of the Zoo brought in $400,000 a year by 1980 and almost $700,000 in profits in 1988. In 1993, FOTZ was considering leasing the concessions to a third party vendor.

Adopt an Animal. Zoo Parents paid a fee to "adopt" an animal, the fee varying with the animal chosen. Zoo Parents' names were listed on a large sign inside the zoo. They also had their own annual celebration, Zoo Parents Day.

Zoo-to-Do. Zoo-to-Do was an annual black-tie fund-raiser held with live music, food and drink, and original, high-class souvenirs, such as posters or

Exhibit 6   Respondent Characteristics of Zoo Visitors According to Visitation Frequency (in %).

Number of Zoo visits over past two years Respondent Characteristic	Four or More	Two or Three	One or None	Never Visited Zoo
Age				
Under 27	26	35	31	9
27 to 35	55	27	15	3
36 to 45	48	32	11	9
46 to 55	18	20	37	25
Over 55	27	29	30	14
Marital Status				
Married	41	28	20	11
Not Married	30	34	24	13
Children at Home				
Yes	46	30	15	9
No	34	28	27	12
Interest in Visiting New Orleans Aquarium				
Very, with Emphasis	47	26	18	9
Very, without Emphasis	45	24	23	12
Somewhat	28	37	14	11
Not Too	19	32	27	22
Member of Friends of the Zoo				
Yes	67	24	5	4
No, but Heard of It	35	30	24	12
Never Heard of It	25	28	35	13
Would You Be Interested in Joining FOTZ (Non-Members Only)				
Very/Somewhat	50	28	14	8
No/Don't Know	33	29	26	12

Source: The Audubon Institute

ceramic necklaces. Admission tickets, limited to three thousand annually, were priced starting at one hundred dollars per person. A raffle was conducted in conjunction with the Zoo-to-Do, with raffle items varying from an opportunity to be zoo curator for a day to the use of a Mercedes Benz for a year. Despite the rather stiff price, the Zoo-to-Do was a popular sellout every year. Local restaurants and other businesses donated most of the necessary supplies, decreasing the cost of the affair. In 1985, the Zoo-to-Do raised almost $500,000 in one night, more money than any other nonmedical fund-raiser in the county.[5]

Advertising

The Audubon Zoo launched impressive marketing campaigns in the 1980s. The zoo received ADDY awards from the New Orleans Advertising Club year after year.[6] In 1986, the film Urban Eden, produced by Alford Advertising and Buckholtz Productions Inc. in New Orleans, finished first among forty entries in the "documentary films, public relations" category of the Eighth Annual Houston International Film Festival. The first-place Gold Award recognized the film for vividly portraying Audubon Zoo as a conservation, rather than a confining, environment.

Exhibit 7   Relative Importance of Seven Reasons as to Why Respondent Does not Visit the Zoo More Often (in %).

Reason (Close Ended)	Very Imp. w/ Emphasis	Very Imp. w/o Emphasis	Somewhat Important	Un-Important
The distance of the Zoo's location from where you live	7	11	21	60
The cost of a Zoo visit	4	8	22	66
Not being all that interested in Zoo animals	2	12	18	67
The parking problem on weekends	7	11	19	62
The idea that you get tired of seeing the same exhibits over and over	5	18	28	49
It's too hot during the summer months	25	23	22	30
Just not having the idea occur to you	8	19	26	48

Source: The Audubon Institute

During the same year, local television affiliates of ABC, CBS and NBC produced independent TV spots using the theme: "One of the World's Greatest Zoos Is in Your Own Back Yard . . . Audubon Zoo!" Along with some innovative views of the Audubon Zoo being in someone's "backyard," local news anchor personalities enjoyed "monkeying around" with the animals, and the zoo enjoyed some welcome free exposure.[7]

In 1993 the marketing budget was over $800,000, including group sales, public relations, advertising, and special events. Not included in this budget was developmental fund-raising or membership. Percentage breakdowns of the marketing budget can be found in Exhibit 8.

The American Association of Zoological Parks and Aquariums reported that most zoos find the majority of their visitors live within a single population center in close proximity to the park.[8] Thus, to sustain attendance over the years, zoos must attract the same visitors repeatedly. A large number of the zoo's promotional programs and special events were aimed at just that.

Progress was slow among non-natives. For example, Simon & Schuster, a reputable publishing firm, in its 218-page [Frommer's] 1983–84 Guide to

New Orleans, managed only a three-word allusion to a "very nice zoo." A 1984 study found that only 36 percent of the visitors were tourists, and even this number was probably influenced to some extent by an overflow from the World's Fair.

Promotional Programs

The Audubon Park Zoo and the Friends of the Zoo conducted a multitude of very successful promotional programs. The effect was to have continual parties and celebrations going on, attracting a variety of people to the zoo (and raising additional revenue). Exhibit 9 lists the major annual promotional programs conducted by the zoo.

In addition to these annual promotions, the zoo scheduled concerts of well-known musicians, such as Irma Thomas, Pete Fountain, The Monkeys, and Manhattan Transfer, and other special events throughout the year. As a result, a variety of events occurred each month.

Many educational activities were conducted all year long. These included (1) a junior zoo keeper program for seventh and eighth graders, (2) a student

Exhibit 8   1991 Marketing Budget.

Marketing	
General and Administrative	$ 30,900
Sales	96,300
Public Relations	109,250
Advertising	304,800
Special Events	157,900
TOTAL	$ 699,150

Public Relations	
Education, Travel and Subscriptions	$ 5,200
Printing and Duplicating	64,000
Professional Services	15,000
Delivery and Postage	3,000
Telephone	1,250
Entertainment	2,000
Supplies	16,600
Miscellaneous	2,200
TOTAL	$ 109,250

Advertising	
Media	$ 244,000
Production	50,000
Account Service	10,800
TOTAL	$ 304,800

Special Events	
General and Administrative	$ 27,900
LA Swamp Fest	35,000
Earthfest	25,000
Ninja Turtle Breakfast	20,000
Jazz Search	15,000
Fiesta Latina	10,000
Crescent City Cats	10,000
Other Events	15,000
TOTAL	$ 157,900

Source: The Audubon Institute

intern program for high school and college students, and (3) a ZOOmobile that took live animals to such locations as special education classes, hospitals, and nursing homes.

Admission Policy

The commission recommended the institution of an admission charge. Arguments generally advanced against such a charge held that it results in an overall decline in attendance and a reduction of nongate revenues. Proponents held that gate charges control vandalism, produce greater revenues, and result in increased public awareness and appreciation of the facility In the early 1970s, no major international zoo failed to charge admission, and 73 percent of the 125 zoos in the United States charged admission.

The commission argued that there is no such thing as a free zoo; someone must pay. If the zoo is tax-supported, then locals carry a disproportionate share

Exhibit 9   Selected Audubon Park Zoo Promotional Programs.

Month	Activity
March	Louisiana Black Heritage Festival. A two day celebration of Louisiana's Black history and its native contributions through food, music, and arts and crafts.
March	Earth Fest. The environment and our planet are the focus of this fun-filled and educational event. Recycling, conservation displays, and puppet shows.
April	Jazz Search. This entertainment series is aimed at finding the best new talent in the area with the winners featured at the New Orleans' Jazz & Heritage Festival.
April	Zoo-To-Do for Kids. At this "pint-sized" version of the Zoo-To-Do, fun and games abound for kids.
May	Zoo-To-Do. Annual black tie fundraiser featuring over 100 of New Orleans' finest restaurants and three music stages.
May	Irma Thomas Mother's Day Concert. The annual celebration of Mother's Day with a buffet.
August	Lego Invitational. Architectural firms turn thousands of Lego pieces into original creations.
Sept.	Fiesta Latina. Experience the best the Hispanic community has to offer through music, cuisine, and arts and crafts.
October	Louisiana Swamp Festival. Cajun food, music, and crafts highlight this four-day salute to Louisiana's bayou country; features hands-on contact with live swamp animals.
October	Boo at the Zoo. This annual Halloween extravaganza features games, special entertainment, trick or treat, a haunted house, and the Zoo's Spook Train.

Source: The Audubon Institute

of the cost. At the time, neighboring Jefferson Parish was growing by leaps and bounds and surely would bring a large, non-paying [constituency] to the new zoo. Further, since most zoos are tourist attractions, tourists should pay since they contribute little to the local tax revenues.

The average yearly attendance for a zoo may be estimated using projected population figures multiplied by a "visitor generating factor." The average visitor generating factor of fourteen zoos similar in size and climate to the Audubon Zoo was 1.34, with a rather wide range from a low of 0.58 in the cities of Phoenix and Miami to a high of 2.80 in Jackson, Mississippi.

Attracting More Tourists and Other Visitors

A riverboat ride on the romantic paddle wheeler Cotton Blossom took visitors from downtown New Orleans to the zoo. Originally, the trip began at a dock in the French Quarter, but it was later moved to a dock immediately adjacent to New Orleans's newest attraction, the Riverwalk, a Rouse development, on the site of the 1984 Louisiana World Exposition. Not only was the riverboat ride great fun, it also lured tourists and conventioneers from the downtown attractions of the French Quarter and the new Riverwalk to the zoo, some six miles upstream. A further allure of the riverboat ride was a return trip to downtown on the New Orleans Streetcar, one of the few remaining trolley cars in the United States. The Zoo Cruise not only drew more visitors but also generated additional revenue through landing fees paid by the New Orleans Steam boat Company and [helped keep] traffic out of uptown New Orleans.[9]

FINANCIAL

The zoo's ability to generate operating funds has been ascribed to the dedication of the Friends of the Zoo, continuing increases in attendance, and creative special events and programs. A history of adequate operating funds allowed the zoo to guarantee capital donors that their gifts would be used to build and maintain top-notch exhibits. A comparison of the 1989 and 1990 Statements of Operating Income and Expense for the Audubon Institute is in Exhibit 10.

Capital Fund Drives

The Audubon Zoo Development Fund was established in 1973. Corporate/Industrial support of the zoo has

Exhibit 10   The Audubon Institute, Inc. The Audubon Park and Zoological Garden Statement of Operating Income and Expenses.

	1989	1990 (ZOO)	1990 (AQU.)
OPERATING INCOME			
Admissions	$2,952,000	$3,587,000	$3,664,000
Food & Gift Operations	$2,706,000	$3,495,500	$711,000
Membership	$1,476,000	$1,932,000	$2,318,000
Recreational Programs	$410,000	$396,000	$0
Visitor Services	$246,000	$218,000	$0
Other	$410,000	$32,000	$650,000
TOTAL INCOME	$8,200,000	$9,660,500	$7,343,000
OPERATING EXPENSES			
Maintenance	$1,394,000	$1,444,000	$1,316,000
Educational/Curatorial	$2,296,000	$2,527,500	$2,783,000
Food & Gift Operations	$1,804,000	$2,375,000	$483,000
Membership	$574,000	$840,000	$631,000
Recreational	$328,000	$358,000	$362,000
Marketing	$410,000	$633,000	$593,000
Visitor Services	$574,000	$373,000	$125,000
Administration	$820,000	$1,110,000	$1,050,000
TOTAL EXPENSES	$8,200,000	$9,660,500	$7,343,000

been very strong—many corporations have underwritten construction of zoo displays and facilities. A partial list of major corporate sponsors is in Exhibit 11. A sponsorship was considered to be for the life of the exhibit. The development department operated on a 12 percent overhead rate, which meant 88 cents of every dollar raised went toward the projects. By 1989, the master plan for development was 75 percent complete. The fund-raising goal for the zoo in 1989 was $1,500,000.

MANAGEMENT

The Zoo Director

Ron Forman, Audubon Zoo director, was called a "zoomaster extraordinaire" and was described by the press as a "cross between Doctor Doolittle and the Wizard of Oz," as a "practical visionary," and as "serious, but with a sense of humor."[10] A native New Orleanian, . . . Forman quit an MBA program to join the city government as an administrative assistant and

found himself doing a business analysis project on the Audubon Park. Once the city was committed to a new zoo, Forman was placed on board as an assistant to the zoo director, John Moore. In early 1977, Moore gave up the battle between the "animal people" and the "people people,"[11] and Forman took over as park and zoo director.

Forman was said to bring an MBA-meets-menagerie style to the zoo, which was responsible for transforming it from a public burden into an almost completely self-sustaining operation. The result not only benefited the citizens of the city but also added a major tourist attraction to the economically troubled city of the 1980s.

Staffing

The zoo used two classes of employees, civil service, through the Audubon Park Commission, and noncivil service. The civil service employees included the curators and zoo keepers. They fell under the jurisdiction of the city civil service system but were paid out of the budget of the Friends of the Zoo. Employees who

Exhibit 11   Major Corporate Sponsors.

Amoco Foundation
American Express
Anheuser-Busch, Inc.
Arthur Anderson and Company
J. Aron Charitable Foundation, Inc.
Bell South Corporation
BP America
Chevron USA, Inc.
Conoco, Inc.
Consolidated Natural Gas Corporation
Entergy Corporation
Exxon Company, USA
Freeport-McMoRan, Inc.
Host International, Inc.
Kentwood Spring Water
Louisiana Coca-Cola Bottling Company, Ltd.
Louisiana Land and Exploration Company
Martin Marietta Manned Space Systems
McDonald's Operators of New Orleans
Mobil Foundation, Inc.
National Endowment for the Arts
National Science Foundation
Ozone Spring Water
Pan American Life Insurance Company
Phillip Morris Companies Inc.
Shell Companies Foundation, Inc.
Tenneco, Inc.
Texaco USA
USF&G Corporation
Wendy's of New Orleans, Inc.

Source: The Audubon Institute

worked in public relations, advertising, concessions, fund-raising, and so on were hired through the Friends of the Zoo and were not part of the civil service system. See Exhibit 12 for further data on staffing patterns.

THE ZOO IN THE LATE '80S

A visitor to the new Audubon Park Zoo could quickly see why New Orleanians were so proud of their zoo. In a city that was termed among the dirtiest in the nation, the zoo was virtually spotless. This was a result of adequate staffing and the clear pride of both those who worked at and those who visited the zoo. One of the first points made by volunteers guiding school groups was that anyone seeing a piece of trash on the ground must pick it up.[12] A 1986 city poll showed

that 93 percent of the citizens surveyed gave the zoo a high approval rating—an extremely high rating for any public facility.

Kudos came from groups outside the local area as well. Delegates from the American Association of Zoological Parks and Aquariums ranked the Audubon Park Zoo as one of the three top zoos of its size in America. In 1982, the American Association of Nurserymen gave the zoo a Special Judges Award for its use of plant materials. In 1985, the Audubon Park Zoo received the Phoenix Award from the Society of American Travel Writers for its achievements in conservation, preservation, and beautification.

By 1987, the zoo was virtually self-sufficient. The small amount of money received from government grants amounted to less than 10 percent of the budget. The master plan for the development of the zoo was 75 percent complete, and the reptile exhibit

Exhibit 12   Employee Structure.

Year	# of Paid Employees	Number of Volunteers
1972	36	
1973	49	
1974	69	
1975	90	
1976	143	
1977	193	
1978	184	
1979	189	
1980	198	
1981	245	
1982	305	
1983	302	56
1984	419	120
1985	454	126
1986	426	250
1987	431	300
1988	462	310
1989	300	270
1990	450	350

Source: The Audubon Institute

was scheduled for completion in the fall. The organization had expanded with a full complement of professionals and managers. (See Exhibit 13 for the organizational structure of the zoo.)

While the zoo made great progress in fifteen years, all was not quiet on the political front. In a court battle, the city won over the state on the issue of who wielded ultimate authority over Audubon Park and Zoo. Indeed, the zoo benefited from three friendly mayors in a row, starting with Moon Landrieu, who championed the new zoo, to Ernest "Dutch" Morial, to Sidney Barthelemy who threw his support to both the zoo and the aquarium proposal championed by Ron Forman.

THE FUTURE

New Directions for the Zoo

Zoo Director Ron Forman demonstrated that zoos have almost unlimited potential. A 1980 New Orleans magazine article cited some of Forman's ideas, ranging from a safari train to a breeding center for rare animals. The latter has an added attraction as a potential money-maker since an Asiatic lion cub, for example, sells for around ten thousand dollars. This wealth of ideas was important because expanded facilities and programs are required to maintain attendance at any public attraction. The most ambitious of Forman's ideas was for an aquarium and riverfront park to be located at the foot of Canal Street.

Although the zoo enjoyed political support in 1992, New Orleans was still suffering from a high unemployment rate and a generally depressed economy resulting from the slump in the oil industry. Some economists predicted the beginning of a gradual turn around in 1988, but any significant improvement in the economy was still forcasted to be years away in 1993. (A few facts about New Orleans are given in Exhibit 14.) In addition, the zoo operated in a city where many attractions competed for the leisure dollar of citizens and visitors. The Audubon Zoological Garden had to vie with the French Quarter, Dixieland jazz, the Superdome, and even the greatest of all attractions in the city—Mardi Gras.

The New Orleans Aquarium

In 1986, Forman and a group of supporters proposed the development of an aquarium and riverfront park to the New Orleans City Council. In November 1986, the electorate voted to fund an aquarium and a riverfront park by a 70 percent margin—one of the largest mar-

Exhibit 13   Audubon Park Commission.

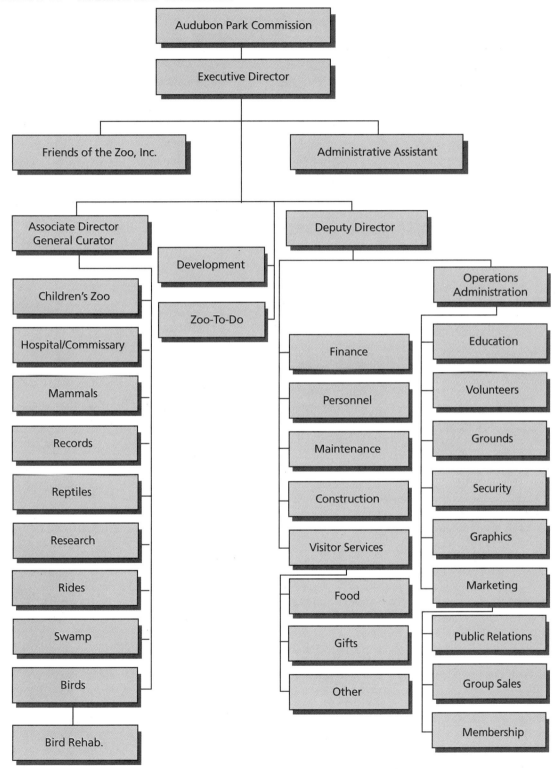

Exhibit 14   A Few Facts About the New Orleans MSA.

Population	1,324,400
Households	489,900
Median Age	30.8 years
Median Household EBI	$29,130
Average Temperature	70 degrees
Average Annual Rainfall	63 inches
Average Elevation	5 feet below sea level
Area	363.5 square miles
	199.4 square miles of land

Major Economic Activities

Tourism (5 million visitors per year)
Oil and Gas Industry
The Port of New Orleans (170 million tons of cargo/year)

Taxes

State Sales Tax	4.0%
Parish (County) Sales Tax	5.0% (Orleans)
	4.0% (Jefferson)
State Income Tax	2.1–2.6% on first $20,000
	3.0–3.5% on next $30,000
	6.0% on $51,000 & over

Parish Property Tax of 126.15 mills (Orleans) is based on 10% of appraised value over $ 75,000 homestead exemption.

Source: Sales and Marketing Management. South Central Bell Yellow Pages, 1991.

gins the city has ever given to any tax proposal. Forman[13] hailed this vote of confidence from the citizens as a mandate to build a world-class aquarium that would produce new jobs, stimulate the local economy, and create an educational resource for the children of the city.

The Aquarium of the Americas opened in September 1990. The $40 million aquarium project was located providing a logical pedestrian link for visitors between [major] attractions of the Riverwalk and the Jax Brewery, a shopping center in the French Quarter. Management of the aquarium was placed under the Audubon Institute, the same organization that ran the Audubon Zoo. A feasibility study prepared by Harrison Price Company[14] projected a probable 863,000 visitors by the year 1990, with 75 percent of the visitors coming from outside the metropolitan area. That attendance figure was reached in only four months and six days from the grand opening. Attendance remained strong through 1992, after a slight drop from the initial grand opening figures.

Meanwhile, the zoo had its own future to plan. The new physical facilities and professional care paid off handsomely in increased attendance and new animal births. But the zoo could not expand at its existing location because of lack of land within the city. Forman and the zoo staff considered several alternatives. One was little "neighborhood" zoos to be located all over the city. A second was a special survival center, a separate breeding area to be located outside the city boundaries where land was available.

Forman presented . . . plans for a project called Riverfront 2000, which included expansion of the aquarium, the Woldenberg Riverfront Park, a species survival center, an arboretum, an insectarium, a natural history museum, and a further expansion of the zoo. With the zoo running smoothly, the staff seemed to need new challenges to tackle, and the zoo needed new facilities or programs to continue to increase attendance.

1. Millie Ball, "The New Zoo of '82," Dixie Magazine, Sunday Times-Picayune, 24 June 1979.

2. Merikaye Presley, "Neighbors Objecting to Audubon Zoo Expansion Project in Midst of Work," Times-Picayune, 30 March 1975, p. A3.

3. "Zoo Expansion Is Ruled Illegal," Times-Picayune, 20 January 1976.

4. "Society Seeks Change at Zoo," Times-Picayune, 29 April 1972, p. D25.

5. "Zoo Thrives Despite Tough Times in New Orleans," Jefferson Business, August 1985, p. A1.

6. Ibid.

7. Sharon Donovan, "New Orleans Affiliates Monkey Around for Zoo," Advertising Age, 17 March 1986.

8. Karen Sausmann, ed., Zoological Park and Aquarium Fundamentals (Wheeling, W. Va.: American Association of Zoological Parks and Aquariums, 1982), p. 111.

9. Diane Luope, "Riverboat Rides to Zoo Are Planned," Times-Picayune, 30 November 1981, p. A17.

10. Steve Brooks, "Don't Say 'No Can Do' to Audubon Zoo Chief," Jefferson Business, 5 May 1986, p. 1.

11. Ross Yuchey, "No Longer Is Heard a Discouraging Word at the Audubon Zoo," New Orleans, August 1980, p. 53.

12. Ibid., p. 49.

13. At the Zoo, Winter 1987.

14. Feasibility Analysis and Conceptual Planning for a Major Aquarium Attraction, prepared for the City of New Orleans, March 1985.

REFERENCES

Beaulieu, Lovell. "It's All Happening at the Zoo", The Times Picayune, Sunday, January 28, 1978.

Ball, Millie. "The New Zoo of '82", Dixie Magazine, Sunday Times Picayune, June 24, 1978.

Brooks, Steve. "Don't Say 'No Can Do' to Audubon Zoo Chief," Jefferson Business, May 5, 1986.

Bureau of Governmental Research, City of New Orleans. Audubon Park Zoo Study, Part I, Zoo Improvement Plan. August 1971. New Orleans: Bureau of Governmental Research.

Bureau of Governmental Research, City of New Orleans. Audubon Park Zoo Study, Part II, An Operational Analysis. August 1971 New Orleans: Bureau of Governmental Research.

Donovan, S. "The Audubon Zoo: A Dream Come True," New Orleans, May 1986, pp. 52–66.

Feasibility Analysis and Conceptual Planning for a Major Aquarium Attraction, prepared for the City of New Orleans, March 1985.

Forman, R., J. Logsdon and J. Wilds. Audubon Park: An Urban Eden, 1985, New Orleans: The Friends of the Zoo.

Poole, Susan. Frommer's 1983–84 Guide to New Orleans, 1983, New York: Simon & Schuster.

Sausmann, K., ed. Zoological Park and Aquarium Fundamentals, 1982, Wheeling, West Virginia: American Association of Zoological Parks and Aquariums.

Yuchey, R. "No Longer Is Heard a Discouraging Word at the Audubon Zoo", New Orleans, August, 1980, pp. 49–60.

Zuckerman, S., ed., Great Zoos of the World, 1980, Colorado: Westview Press.

INTEGRATIVE CASE 3.0
Shoe Corporation of Illinois*

Shoe Corporation of Illinois produces a line of women's shoes that sell in the lower-price market for $11.95 to $13.95 per pair. Profits averaged twenty-five cents to thirty cents per pair ten years ago, but according to the president and the controller, labor and materials costs have risen so much in the intervening period that profits today average only fifteen cents to twenty cents per pair.

Production at both the company's plants totals 12,500 pairs per day. The two factories are located within a radius of sixty miles of Chicago: one at Centerville, which produces 4,500 pairs per day, and the other at Meadowvale, which produces 8,000 pairs per day. Company headquarters is located in a building adjacent to the Centerville plant.

It is difficult to give an accurate picture of the number of items in the company's product line. Shoes change in style perhaps more rapidly than any other style product, including garments. This is so chiefly because it is possible to change production processes quickly and because, historically, each company, in attempting to get ahead of competitors, gradually made style changes ever more frequently. At present, including both major and minor style changes, S.C.I. offers 100 [to] 120 different products to customers each year.

A partial organizational chart, showing the departments involved in this case, appears in Exhibit 1.

COMPETITIVE STRUCTURE OF THE INDUSTRY

Very large general shoe houses, such as International and Brown, carry a line of ladies' shoes and are able to undercut prices charged by Shoe Corporation of Illinois, principally because of the policy in the big companies of producing large numbers of "stable" shoes, such as the plain pump and the loafer. They do not attempt to change styles as rapidly as their smaller competitors. Thus, without constant changes in production processes and sales presentations, they are able to keep costs substantially lower.

Charles F. Allison, the president of Shoe Corporation of Illinois, feels that the only way for a small

independent company to be competitive is to change styles frequently, taking advantage of the flexibility of a small organization to create designs that appeal to customers. Thus, demand can be created, and a price set high enough, to make a profit. Allison, incidentally, appears to have an artistic talent in styling and a record of successful judgments in approving high-volume styles over the years.

Regarding [SCI's] differences from its large competitors, Allison says:

> You see, Brown and International Shoe Company both produce hundreds of thousands of the same pair of shoes. They store them in inventory at their factories. Their customers, the large wholesalers and retailers, simply know their line and send in orders. They do not have to change styles nearly as often as we do. Sometimes I wish we could do that, too. It makes for a much more stable and orderly system. There is also less friction between people inside the company. The [sales people] always know what they're selling, the production people know what is expected of them. The plant personnel are not shook up so often by someone coming in one morning and tampering with their machine lines or their schedules. The styling people are not shook up so often by the plant saying, "We can't do your new style the way you want it."

MAJOR STYLE CHANGES

The decision about whether to put a certain style into production requires information from a number of different people. Here is what typically happens in the company. It may be helpful to follow the organization chart in tracing the procedure.

M. T. Lawson, the style manager, and his designer, John Flynn, originate most of the ideas about shape, size of heel, use of flat sole or heels, and findings (the term used for ornaments attached to, but not part of, the shoes—bows, straps, and so forth). They get their ideas principally from reading style and trade magazines or by copying a top-flight designer. Lawson corresponds with publications and friends in large stores in New York, Rome, and Paris in order to obtain by air mail pictures and samples of up-to-the-minute style innovations.

Source: Written by Charles E. Summer. Copyright 1978. Used with permission.

Exhibit 1   Partial Organization Chart of Shoe Corporation of Illinois.

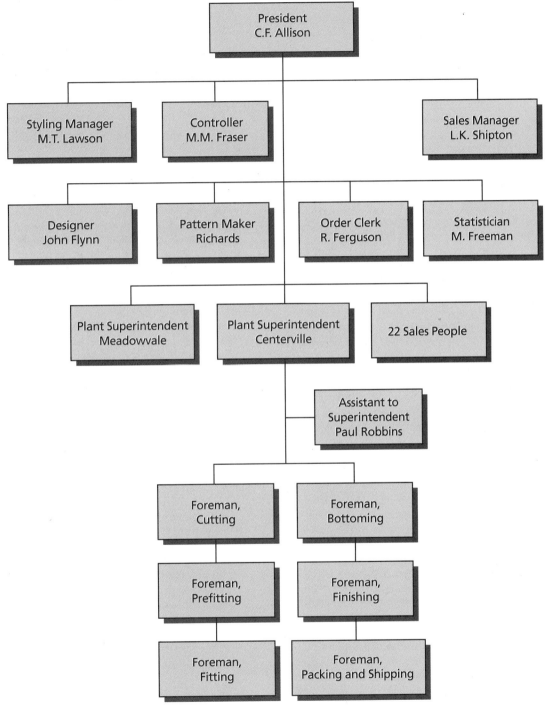

When Lawson decides on a design, he takes a sketch to Allison, who either approves or disapproves it. If Allison approves, he (Allison) then passes the sketch on to Shipton, the sales manager, to find out what lasts (widths) should be chosen. Shipton, in turn, simply forwards the design to Martin Freeman, a statistician in the sales department, who maintains summary information on customer demand for colors and lasts.

To compile this information, Freeman visits [sales people] twice a year to get their opinions on the colors and lasts that are selling best, and he keeps records of shipments by color and by last. For these needs, he simply totals data that is sent to him by the shipping foreman in each of the two plants.

When Freeman has decided on the lasts and colors, he sends Allison a form that lists the colors and lasts in which the shoe should be produced. Allison, if he approves this list, forwards the information to Lawson, who passes it on to Richards, an expert pattern maker. Richards makes a paper pattern and constructs a prototype in leather and paper, sends this to Lawson, who in turn approves or disapproves it. He forwards any approved prototype to Allison. Allison, if he too approves, notifies Lawson, who takes the prototype to Paul Robbins, assistant to the superintendent of the Centerville plant. Only this plant produces small quantities of new or experimental shoe styles. Such production is referred to as a "pilot run" by executives at the plant.

Robbins then literally carries the prototype through the six production departments of the plant—from cutting to finish—discussing it with each foreman, who in turn works with men on the machines in having a sample lot of several thousand pairs made.

When the finished lot is delivered by the finishing foreman to the shipping foreman (because of the importance of styling, Allison has directed that each foreman personally deliver styling goods in process to the foreman of the next department), the latter holds the inventory in storage and sends one pair each to Allison and Lawson. If they approve of the finished product, Allison instructs the shipping foreman to mail samples to each the company's twenty-two [sales people] throughout the country. [Sales people] have instructions to take the samples immediately (within one week) to at least ten customers. Orders for already established shoes are normally sent to Ralph Ferguson, a clerk in Shipton's office, who records them and forwards them to the plant superintendents for production. In the case of first orders on new styles, however, [sales people] have found by experience that Martin Freeman has a greater interest in the success of new "trials," so they rush orders to him, air mail, and he in turn places the first orders for a new style in the interoffice mail to the plant superintendents. He then sends a duplicate of the order, mailed in by the [sales peo-

ple], to Ferguson for entering in his statistical record of all orders received by the company.

Three weeks after the [sales people] receive samples, Allison requires Ralph Ferguson to give him a tabulation of orders. At that time, he decides whether the [sales people] should push the item and the superintendents should produce large quantities, or whether he will tell them that although existing orders will be produced, the item will be discontinued in a short time.

The procedures outlined here have, according to Allison:

. . . worked reasonably well. The average time from when Lawson decides on a design until we notify the Centerville plant to produce the pilot run is two weeks to a month. Of course, if we could speed that up, it would make the company just that much more secure in staying in the game against the big companies, and in taking sales away from our competitors. There seems to be endless bickering among people around here involved in the styling phase of the business. That's to be expected when you have to move fast—there isn't much time to stop and observe all of the social amenities. I have never thought that a formal organization chart would be good in this company—we've worked out a customary system here that functions well.

M. T. Lawson, manager of styling, says that within his department all work seems to get out in minimum time; he also states that both Flynn and Richards are good employees and skilled in their work. He mentioned that Flynn had been in to see him twice in the last year:

. . . to inquire about his (Flynn's) future in the company. He is thirty-three years old and has three children. I know that he is eager to make money, and I assured him that over the years we can raise him right along from the $35,000 we are now paying. Actually, he has learned a lot about shoe styles since we hired him from the design department of a fabric company six years ago.

John Flynn revealed that:

I was actually becoming dissatisfied with this job. All shoe companies copy styles—it's generally accepted practice within the industry. But I've picked up a real feel for designs, and several times I've suggested that the company make all its own original styles. We could make [SCI] a style leader and also increase our volume. When I ask Lawson about this, he says it takes too much time for the designer to create originals—that we have all we can handle to do research in trade magazines and maintain contracts feeding us the results of experts. Besides, he says our styles are standing the test of the marketplace.

"PROJECTS X AND Y"

Flynn also said that he and Martin Freeman had frequently talked about the styling problem. They felt that:

> Allison is really a great president, and the company surely would be lost without him. However, we've seen times when he lost a lot of money on bad judgments in styles. Not many times—perhaps six or seven times in the last 18 months. Also, he is, of course, extremely busy as president of the corporation. He must look after everything from financing from the banks to bargaining with the union. The result is that he is sometimes unavailable to do his styling approvals for several days, or even two weeks. In a business like this, that kind of delay can cost money. It also makes him slightly edgy. It tends, at times when he has many other things to do, to make him look quickly at the styles we submit, or the prototypes Richards makes, or even the finished shoes that are sent for approval by the shipping foreman. Sometimes I worry that he makes two kinds of errors. He simply rubber stamps what we've done, in which sending them to him is simply a waste of time. At other times he makes snap judgments of his own, overruling those of us who have spent so much time and expertise on the shoe. We do think he has good judgment, but he himself has said at times that he wishes he had more time to concentrate on styling and approval of prototypes and final products.

Flynn further explained (and this was corroborated by Freeman) that the two had worked out two plans, which they referred to as "project X" and "project Y." In the first, Flynn created an original design that was not copied from existing styles. Freeman then gave special attention to color and last research for the shoe and recommended a color line that didn't exactly fit past records on consumer purchases—but one he and Flynn thought would provide "great consumer appeal." This design and color recommendation were accepted by Lawson and Allison; the shoe went into production and was one of the three top sellers during the calendar year. The latter two men did not know that the shoe was styled in a different way from the usual procedure.

The result of a second, similar project (Y) was put into production the next year, but this times sales were discontinued after three weeks.

PROBLEM BETWEEN LAWSON AND ROBBINS

Frequently, perhaps ten to twelve times a year, disagreement arises between Mel Lawson, manager of styling, and Paul Robbins, assistant to the superintendent of the Centerville plant. Robbins says that:

> The styling people don't understand what it means to produce a shoe in the quantities that we do, and to make the changes in production that we have to. They dream up a style quickly, out of thin air. They do not realize that we have a lot of machines that have to be adjusted, and that some things they dream up take much longer on certain machines than others, thus creating a bottleneck in the production line. If they put a bow or strap in one position rather than others, it may mean we have to keep people idle on later machines while there is a pile-up on the sewing machines on which this complicated little operation is performed. This costs the plant money. Furthermore, there are times when they get the prototype here late, and the foremen and I either have to work overtime or the trial run won't get through in time to have new production runs on new styles, to take the plant capacity liberated by our stopping production on old styles. Lawson doesn't know much about production and sales and the whole company. I think all he does is to bring shoes down here to the plant sort of like a messenger boy. Why should he be so hard to get along with? He isn't getting paid any more than I am, and my position in the plant is just as important as his.

Lawson, in turn says that he has a difficult time getting along with Robbins:

> There are many times when Robbins is just unreasonable. I take prototypes to him five or six times a month, and other minor style changes to him six or eight times. I tell him

every time that we have problems in getting these ready, but he knows only about the plant, and telling him doesn't seem to do any good. When we first joined the company, we got along all right, but he has gotten harder and harder to get along with.

CERTAIN OTHER PROBLEMS THAT HAVE ARISEN

Ralph Ferguson, the clerk in the sales department who receives orders from [sales people] and forwards totals for production schedules to the two plant superintendents, has complained that the [sales people] and Freeman are bypassing him in their practice of sending experimental shoe orders to Freeman. He insists that his job description (one of only two written descriptions in the company) gives him responsibility for receiving all orders throughout the company and for maintaining historical statistics on shipments.

Both the [sales people] and Freeman, on the other hand, say that before they started the new practice (that is, when Ferguson still received the experi-

mental shoe orders), there were at least eight or ten instances a year when these were delayed from one to three days on Ferguson's desk. They report that Ferguson just wasn't interested in new styles, so the [sales people] "just started sending them to Freeman." Ferguson acknowledged that there were times of short delay, but there were good reasons for them:

They ([sales people] and Freeman) are so interested in new designs, colors, and lasts, that they can't understand the importance of a systematic handling of the whole order procedure, including both old and new shoe styles. There must be accuracy. Sure, I give some priority to experimental orders, but sometimes when rush orders for existing company products are piling up, and when there's a lot of planning I have to do to allocate production between Centerville and Meadowvale, I decide which comes first—processing of these, or processing the experimental shoe orders. Shipton is my boss, not the [sales people] or Freeman. I'm going to insist that these orders come to me.

"One cup of coffee just won't do it this morning," thought Tom Bell as he studied the memorandum he had been given the previous Friday afternoon. It was 7:30 Monday morning, May [18], 1986, and Bell had scheduled a meeting for 9:00 AM to brief the new task force on the job that lay ahead.

Last Friday afternoon, May 15, T. C. (Tom) Bell had received a memorandum from Mr. James Caldwell, Assistant Controller of Nueces Leasing Company (NLC), one of the largest leasing agencies and developers of commercial office space in the U.S., outlining a decision that had been made by NLC's Management Committee to consolidate various departments within the Land Management and Corporate Control Divisions of the company. One such consolidation would be that of the Property Owner Department, which was currently part of the Land Management Division, and the Investor Relations Department, now part of the Corporate Control group. Bell was informed that he would be the new manager for the consolidated department and was to chair a task force charged with developing a plan of action for the consolidation. A presentation to senior management was to be made by the task force in six weeks, outlining the details of the plan.

INDUSTRY BACKGROUND

The commercial real estate industry was experiencing its worst slump in more than thirty years. Market prices for office space had dropped more than 30% since their peak of $15 per square foot in 1981. This price decline, and subsequent deterioration of profits, was causing a major shake-out and consolidation of unprofitable companies in the industry. The larger, more financially stable companies, such as Nueces Leasing Company, were reacting to these economic forces by significantly reducing overhead costs including the reduction of work forces. NLC's strategy called for a total reorganization of the company's current structure, as shown in Exhibit 1, so as to be ready to take advantage of the upturn in the industry which was projected to take place during the latter part of 1987. The reorganization included a company-wide Voluntary Retirement Program (VRP) which offered

*Copyright 1987 by the Colgate Darden Graduate Business School Sponsors, University of Virginia, Charlottesville.

additional seniority and cash bonuses to those of NLC's 10,000 employees who voluntarily left the company by October 30, 1986. NLC had projected that 1,500 employees would participate in the program by this date. The VRP was specifically constructed to be particularly attractive to those NLC employees who were age 50 or older. These individuals were among the highest salaried personnel in the company.

Bell, who was the Land Management Controller for NLC, had joined the company in 1969 after obtaining his MBA from a well-known midwestern business school. His prior assignments with the company had all been in the Corporate Control Division of Nueces Corporation, the parent company, a large multinational conglomerate. He had spent a number of years overseas with Nueces International in Europe, and with Nueces Corporation in New York before being transferred to the NLC office in Chicago, Illinois only a few months ago.

PROPERTY OWNER DEPARTMENT

The Property Owner Department (POD) provided the lease and land records support to NLC. It had been established by centralizing these functions from all of the Division offices in 1969. POD had always been a department within NLC's Land Management Division. The Land Management Division had for years been the most profitable division within the company. Since the explosion of commercial real estate development in the 1930s, domestic leasing and development activity had increased at a feverish pace until the price collapse of 1981. POD had also grown during this period in order to provide support to the rest of the Land Management Division.

The primary function of POD was to manage the lease and land records of NLC. When a leasing company wanted to develop and lease a commercial site, it first had to secure an agreement from the owner of the property. When the property was successfully developed, the property owner (lessor) and the leasing development company shared in the revenue from the agreement signed by the tenant of the property. From a financial standpoint, the tenant agreement revenues owned by the company constituted the major share of its assets. It was POD's responsibility to steward these records and maintain the leases signed with the property owners by satisfying various conditions within the lease instrument. If meticulous records were not kept,

Exhibit 1   Charge of the Nueces Task Force (A) NLC Structure Prior to Reorganization of 1986

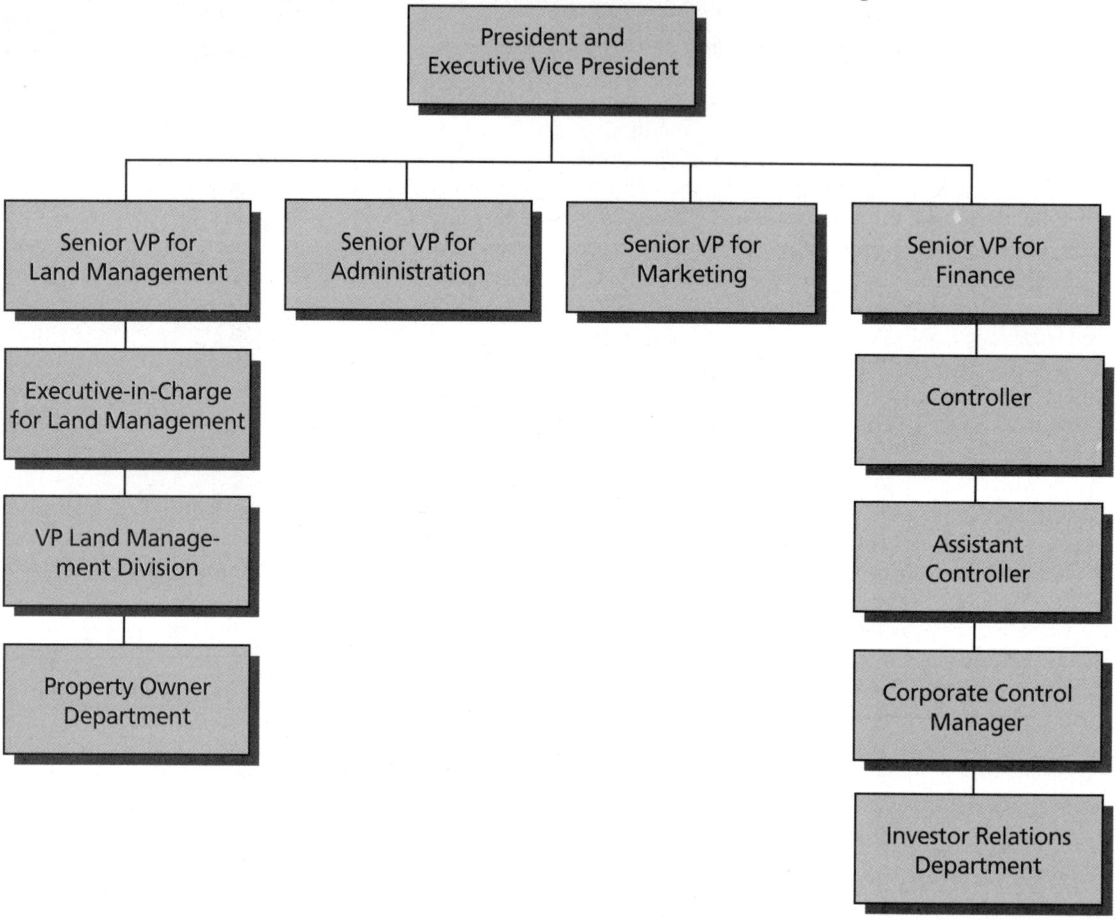

a lease agreement could be forfeited resulting in the loss of thousands, even millions of dollars of the company's assets. POD personnel were obsessed with their duty to maintain the lease records at all costs. This dedication had resulted in only one or two leases, out of a total of 125,000 active leases, being lost since the department was centralized in 1969.

Verification Process. To guarantee that an obligation under an existing lease did not go unattended, POD had an intricate verification process. A lease agreement was mailed to POD from the field office in the area where the lease was taken. The lease would go to either the Undeveloped Property Section, if the lease was not developed at the time, or the Developed Property Section, if the lease was developed when purchased (usually from another company). After a review of the lease was conducted by one of the staff lawyers, the lease would then go to the Contract Compliance group for documentation. The Computer

Systems Unit would then enter the lease information into the computer lease file and send the instrument to the drafting department for mapping. After drafting, the lease would be filed in the record room for future reference. This entire process, from field to file, took approximately 11 months to complete. NLC had recently purchased a number of leases from other companies going out of business. This, along with NLC's own leasing activity, had created, by May of 1986, a backlog of some 11,000 leases waiting to be verified. The number of leases verified, and those left unverified, during the preceding three years, is shown in Table A.

Table A

	1983	1984	1985
New Leases Verified	14,257	18,820	22,290
Unverified Leases	7,723	8,919	9,780

To follow the work flow through POD, management kept track of an assortment of statistics such as total leases received, corrections that needed to be made, letters sent to property owners, number of checks written, number of tracts of land mapped, etc. These figures were not used to evaluate any of the POD managers, but were simply monitored to detect problem areas as soon as possible. Many of the categories of numbers were so broad that it was difficult to determine exactly what activity was being measured.

POD Sections: Undeveloped Property (UP). The acquisition and ownership sections of POD consisted primarily of lawyers and paralegals. Their primary task was to perform a secondary review (the first review being done by the lease-taking personnel in the field) of the documentation regarding the actual lease instruments. The result of this review was to make legal interpretations of the lease agreement. This activity took approximately 55% of the unit's time. The remaining effort was spent analyzing material regarding change of interest ownership.

Isaac Jordan, supervisor for the Southern and Gulf Coast Division areas[s] typified the feeling among the POD personnel: "Our group has the first responsibility for the leases after they are submitted to POD by the division offices. The decisions we make will determine the company's lease maintenance obligations and rights for all of its leases throughout the country. We had better be right."

Developed Property (DP). DP's responsibility was to review all development contracts and trades negotiated and executed by the field personnel, monitor monthly revenue of Nueces properties and other properties in which Nueces had an interest, and . . . handle all matters dealing with commercial property that had been abandoned due to lack of revenue or for other developmental reasons. The DP group was much smaller than the Undeveloped Property group, however, with the current economic forces at play, more and more companies were jointly developing properties or selling developed property, creating a much heavier workload for the DP personnel.

Contract Compliance (CC). CC performed the actual check-writing task for the POD section. Certain provisions of a lease agreement provided for periodic payments to the Lessors to keep the contract in force. Upon authorization by one of the analysts in the Undeveloped or Developed sections, CC would issue the payment to the interested owner. This group also prepared tax information concerning those payments. Very little legal analysis was performed in CC.

Most payments due under conditions of a nondeveloped lease were to be made one year from the original signing date of that lease. If payment was not made on or before the one-year anniversary date, the lease was null and void. The current backlog of leases to be verified was causing CC to have to issue checks very near the one-year expiration date. When this happened, the computerized system that CC employed was circumvented and the checks were written manually, causing a high level of tension and anxiety. The personnel in CC felt that their performance was being hindered by the analysts taking so long to verify leases.

Information Group. Because of the increased number of leases being administered by POD, the decision was made in 1980 to fully automate the department's lease and land records. Since that time, a computerized record system had been developed to take the place of the manual system currently being used. The Computer Systems Unit of the Information Group had the responsibility of being the custodian of this computerized system. The system was currently being utilized for the generation of monthly and ad hoc reports requested by the field offices and senior management. POD personnel, on the other hand, still relied more on the manual system of lease administration for fear that the computerized system would break down or would provide them with inaccurate information, resulting in a lease forfeiture or incorrect payment.

Other functions performed by the Information Group included the mapping of all leases and land record property descriptions, and the filing of hardcopy data for future references.

Computer Systems. Early in 1986, the senior management of the Land Management Division had decided to expand the scope of the computer automation project currently under way in POD to include the activities of the division land offices, creating a company-wide network. The new system, called Systems, Information, General Mapping and Agreements, or SIGMA, was to be written in DB2 computer language, and was estimated to cost $3.5 million. The project was scheduled for completion by late 1990. Bell was concerned that the expansion of the computerization of POD would cause further delay of the group in becoming reliant upon the automated system, rather than utilizing the manual system which was currently the practice. He knew that senior management was intent on cutting operating costs, and switching from a manual record system to an automated system was sure to increase efficiency and reduce expense.

Physical Location. Most of the POD units currently occupied the entire 23rd floor of NLC's headquarters building. The Computer Systems Unit was located on the sixth floor due to a lack of space on 23. Most of the 23rd floor had to have special reinforcements built into it to be able to support the immense weight of the POD electronic file holders. Moving the file holders was a very costly and time-consuming ordeal.

The building was constructed in the early 1960s and at the time was the tallest building in the downtown area. All of the floors had an identical floor plan. All of the offices were created with partitions that ran from floor to ceiling. One could tell a person's seniority by how many panels he or she had in their office (2 panels [by] 3 panels was a middle manager, 3 panels [by] 3 panels a senior manager, and so on). Though considered drab, headquarters was a [desirable] place to be because it was the "hub" of the company's activities.

NLC leased office space in a number of buildings in the city. The reorganization had resulted in a majority of departments having to move into another office or building. This caused a tremendous scheduling problem in trying to coordinate all of the necessary moves.

Personnel. Daniel Cooper, the current manager of POD, had worked his way up through the department since joining the company as a records clerk around 1965. In fact, almost all of the exempt (salaried) personnel working in POD had joined the company in that department. Very few people ever transferred out of POD until they left the company. Cooper had elected to accept the Voluntary Retirement Program and would be leaving at the end of October.

There were currently 104 people working in the POD group as shown in Exhibit 2. [Thirty-five] had law degrees, 5 were paralegals (one of the paralegals also had a computer science degree), 6 had only bachelor's degrees, and 58 were non-degreed. Cooper expected that 11 people from POD (1 law, 4 bachelors, and 6 non-degreed) would be leaving the company under the Voluntary Retirement Program.

Another issue of concern to Bell was that of the contract personnel currently employed by POD. Two vocational education students held positions in POD's file room. There was the possibility that because of the Voluntary Retirement Program senior management may decide to discontinue the hiring of contract personnel.

All employees of NLC were evaluated using a company-wide ranking system. An individual was ranked on a scale of 1–1 to 1–4, based on the following performance measures:

1–1—employee always exceeded job expectations
1–2—employee usually exceeded job expectations
1–3—employee satisfied job expectations
1–4—employee did not satisfy job expectations

All individuals within a department were ranked according to this criteria and were then put on a "standard curve." Employees were then compared to each other and reclassified to "force" 10% 1–1s, 30% 1–2s, 50% 1–3s, and 10% 1–4s. The 1–3s were encouraged to be 1–1s or 1–2s during the next evaluation period. The 1–4s were told to "shape up or ship out." Communication of evaluations between managers and subordinates was left to the discretion of the individual managers. POD managers chose to inform the employees of their final numerical ranking at the end of the process.

Because of the unique nature of POD work, and because most people who worked in POD stayed in POD for the duration of their career, the group was very close-knit. POD parties and picnics were held regularly. Many POD employees lived in the same neighborhood and interacted socially. The Voluntary Retirement Program, the first program to ever effect this group, resulted in many people losing a boss or co-worker that they had known for a long time.

INVESTOR RELATIONS DEPARTMENT

Investor Relations (IR) had been what is now the Corporate Control Division since 1968. The Corporate Control Division of NLC was primarily comprised of financial and accounting managers. Their responsibility was to monitor and evaluate the company's performance based on certain quantitative measures such as business performance indicators (BPIs), forecasts, and budgets.

The major activity of IR was to maintain records of payments resulting from developed lease property as well as any related tax and accounting work needed to perform this task. Once a lease was developed, IR would receive from Land Management a list of to whom to pay unit participations (shares of the lease revenue) and how much to pay them. As revenue information was accumulated on a monthly basis, IR would assemble the data and distribute checks to the various interest owners. IR was also responsible for keeping the revenue records current. Ownership of interests in leased property would change frequently due to a sale of the interest or inheritance. IR would need to be notified of these changes to be able to send a revenue payment to the correct party.

All of the Corporate Control Division's Departments had detailed control systems in place to moni-

Exhibit 2   Charge of the Nueces Task Force (A) POD Structure Prior to Reorganization of 1986

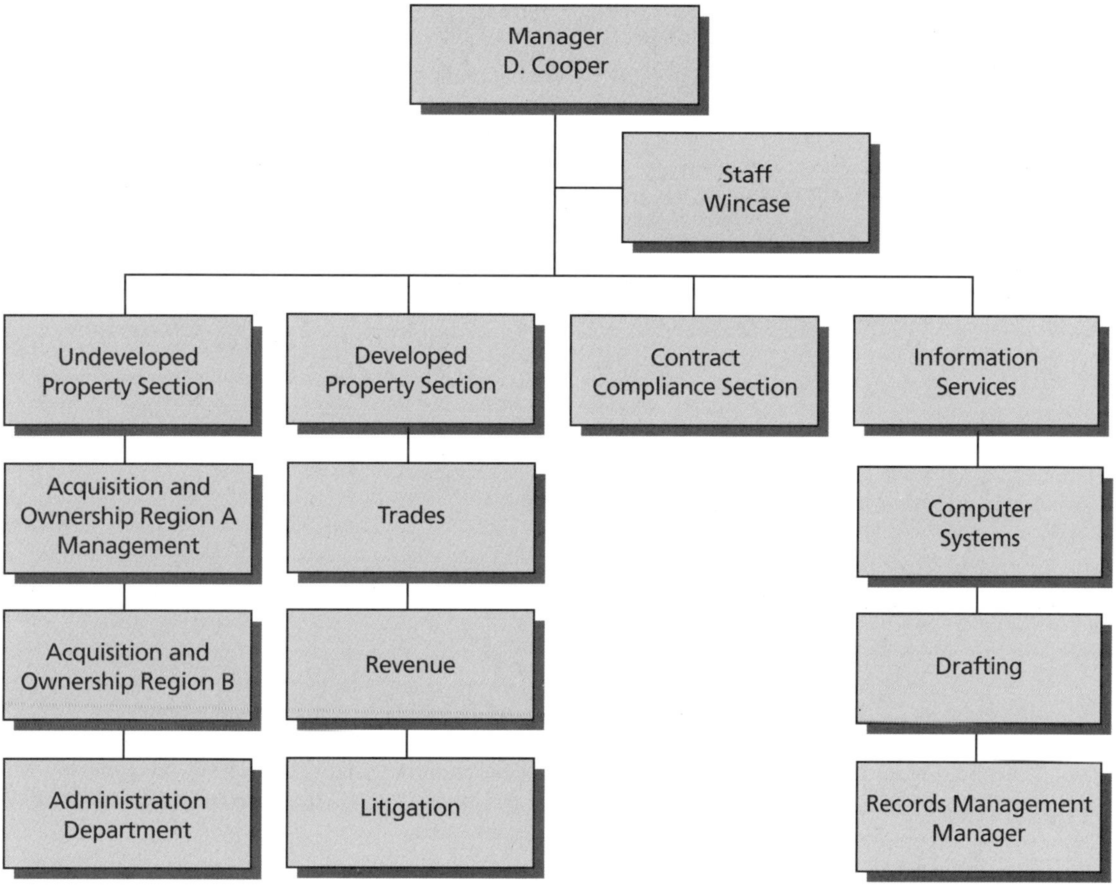

PERSONNEL

Exempt	57
Non-exempt	45
Sub-total	102
Contract	2
Total	104

tor work flow volume and quality. IR's system consisted of a computerized program that tracked legal documents and correspondence through the Unit on a daily basis. When an individual within the group received a document, he or she would access the computer on his/her desk and input a code number for the material to be worked on. This allowed anyone looking for that particular instrument to access the computer and determine the exact whereabouts of the information. It also allowed managers to identify bot-

tlenecks in the data flow process. The code numbers provided historic data on what types of instruments the Unit received and which ones took the most time to handle.

IR Sections. IR was structured primarily on a geographic basis as shown in Exhibit 3, with a communications and administrative group that supported the entire section.

Geographic Units. The primary task of these groups was to set up revenue payment records based

Exhibit 3   Charge of the Nueces Task Force (A) IR Structure Prior to Reorganization of 1986

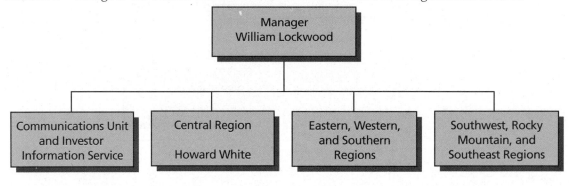

PERSONNEL

Exempt	36
Non-exempt	19
Sub-total	55
Contract	15
Total	70

on lease and property ownership documents received from the field offices and from POD. The group then accumulated monthly revenue information for all of NLC's developed properties, processed that information, and then authorized payment to the interest owners for their proportionate share of the income. All of the payments made by IR were based on developed properties.

The analysts were also responsible for making the necessary changes concerning interest owners, much in the same way as those changes for property were made in POD. In fact, a majority of those persons who signed property leases (POD payees) were also the individuals entitled to receive payments after the lease had become developed (IR payees).

Communication Unit and Investor Information Service. One of IR's business goals for the year was to provide superior service to the company's lease and property interest owners. IR received hundreds of inquiries, by phone and by mail, on a daily basis from these people. It was the job of this group to field questions regarding procedures for changing interest ownership and requests for information from company files. To enhance their image, the Communications Unit had recently produced a pamphlet, to send to all of the company's interest owners, attempting to answer the most frequently asked questions and out-

lining the procedure for changing interest ownership and requesting information from the company. This group was composed almost entirely of non-degreed personnel.

Computer Systems. IR's computer system development program, named INVESTOR, was scheduled to be completed by late 1987 and like the POD system, cost millions of dollars to develop and implement. The system was written in the IMS computer language.

Almost every individual within IR had a personal computer on their desk. There had been a number of early deliverables from the INVESTOR program that had been in use for over a year. To utilize this resource, a large majority of IR personnel had taken company-sponsored computer classes to learn techniques such as computer networking and the use of spreadsheet and word processing packages. Even though IR still maintained a physical file room, all of the information in the files was available on the computer system. Analysts in IR preferred to use the automated data base, unless for legal reasons (to authenticate signatures, etc.) inspection of the original legal document was necessary.

Physical Location. IR currently had its office on the 19th floor of the Grand Plaza Building, across the street from NLC. They had been there only 90 days having moved from another office building across town. The Grand Plaza Building was a new building having been completed during the past year. The architecture was very contemporary and each floor had a unique floor plan. IR's offices were finished in deep pile carpeting and expensive-looking appointments such as solid wood furniture, wall paper, an assortment of plants, and venetian blinds. The group was glad to be finally settled in and was impressed with its new surroundings.

Personnel. The manager of IR, William Lockwood, had recently left the department to undertake a special project. His position was filled by Benjamin Runkle, a seasoned manager who had held many positions within the Corporate Control Division of NLC. The remaining individuals working in IR came from diverse backgrounds. Only a handful of the 70 employees had law degrees; the rest of the group was split 50–50 between those with college degrees and those without. Bell expected that approximately 8 persons would be leaving, from IR, under the VRP (1 law, 6 bachelors, and 1 non-degreed).

There were 15 contract employees working in IR. While the issue of whether or not to continue contract personnel was an important one to POD, it was even more so to IR considering "contracts" made up over 40% of its total workforce. If senior management decided to terminate the contract personnel program at NLC, Bell would have to make the necessary arrangements to ensure that the resources were available for IR to get its job done.

IR personnel were also evaluated on the numerical scale system; however, IR managers had chosen to give employees only descriptive feedback as to their performance, rather than a numerical rating. Runkle had informed Bell that the descriptions used by managers to classify subordinates had not been consistent, leaving some employees not knowing which category they were in (1–1, 1–2, etc.).

The individuals in IR had come from different areas of the organization. Their backgrounds ranged from highly-specialized lawyers to clerical support personnel. The group functioned very well together; however, there was not the camaraderie that was evident in other groups. There was also very little socializing done outside of the workplace.

THE TASK FORCE

Tom Bell looked over the names and positions of those persons who had been assigned as members of the task force. He thought about what biases, expectations, and concerns each one would bring to the group.

Franklin Scobey. Scobey had been transferred to NLC headquarters from the Kansas City Land Office. That office had been closed as a cost-cutting measure during the reorganization. In addition to his position on the task force, Scobey was to assume the management of POD upon Cooper's retirement at the end of July. Upon obtaining his law degree in 1974, Scobey had worked as a leasing agent for NLC, taking leases for development purposes. He had then spent a few years in POD before being transferred to Kansas City to manage that office. While in that position, Scobey had been a member of the study team that recommended the expansion of the POD computer system project to include the division land group.

Scobey was known for his smooth, comforting, yet motivating style of management. Bell had heard that Scobey fostered loyalty from his employees by taking the time to listen to them and from being willing to try something new at their suggestion.

Howard White. White had spent his entire tenure at NLC in the IR department. He had been with NLC for over 30 years and was planning to retire at the end of July. He was, however, to be hired back for an additional six months as a consultant to help Bell with the consolidation. Because of his experience, White was known and trusted by everyone in the IR organization. His current responsibilities within the group included training all new hires, overseeing the computer systems development, as well as representing IR on the task force.

During the period between Lockwood's departure and the arrival of Runkle, Bell knew that White had kept the IR group up and running. He sensed, however, that the six-month extension of White's tenure had been agreed to reluctantly by White.

Lawrence Cross. Cross was a director of a small consulting firm based in Memphis. He was the only non-Nueces employee on the task force. Cross had received his bachelor's degree from a college in upstate New York and had worked at a "Big Eight" accounting firm for a number of years. He and some colleagues left the firm and started their own consulting group specializing in work flow operations and efficiency studies. Cross had worked for Nueces as a consultant for the last year and a half, most recently completing a work flow improvement study for IR, where he got to know a number of the IR managers quite well. White and Runkle had been very involved in Cross' study of IR.

Cross' knowledge of the leasing and development business was limited. The previous work he had done for the company had been in other areas of the organization. The results of his previous studies were focused on the operational aspects of the business rather than the personnel aspects.

Robert Freeman. Freeman had joined NLC as a summer intern between his first and second years at graduate business school. He was assigned to Bell as his assistant for the duration of the summer. Freeman's position on the task force resulted from his experience as a leasing agent before returning to business school. He had provided leasing and revenue payment services to leasing and development companies for three years after graduating with a bachelor of business administration degree in 1982. Bell thought Freeman would be able to provide him with an objective, third-party point of view concerning the consolidation.

Christopher Wincase. The seasoned veteran of the group, Wincase, had been with NLC, in POD, since 1954 when he joined the company at age 18. He was the only one in POD age 50 or older who had not taken retirement under the VRP. Wincase started in POD as a records clerk and currently held the title of senior staff member. This position was given to him after he suffered a heart attack in 1985. He still maintained a very active role in the operations of POD; his responsibilities included training of all new personnel,

overseeing the POD computer systems development, drafting department policy and procedures, and special projects. Bell's chief concern with Wincase would be his adversity to change. Wincase had been known to be objectionable to many new projects in POD, making the statement that ". . . we have always been successful doing it the old way . . .".

SUMMARY

As Bell looked at his watch and saw that it was getting close to 9:00, he began to think over what he thought Caldwell and the other senior managers would want to receive from the task force study. He identified four general areas to concentrate on regarding the new consolidated department: an organizational chart, control systems for work flow and personnel evaluation purposes, how to manage the computer systems development programs currently under way, and the physical location of the new group. He knew it would be necessary to integrate the task force's plan of action with senior management's goals of cost-cutting and streamlining. He asked his secretary to put on another pot of coffee.

INTEGRATIVE CASE 4.2
Charge of the Nueces Task Force (B)*

Last Friday afternoon, May 15, T. C. (Tom) Bell had received a memorandum from Mr. James Caldwell, Assistant Controller of Nueces Leasing Company (NLC), one of the largest leasing agencies and developers of commercial real estate in the U.S. The memo outlined a decision that had been made by NLC's Management Committee to consolidate various departments within the Land Management and Corporate Control Divisions of the Company. One such consolidation would be that of the Property Owner Department, which was currently part of the Land Management Division, and the Investor Relations Department, now part of the Corporate Control group. Bell was informed that he would be the new manager of the consolidated department and that he was to chair a task force charged with developing a plan of action for the consolidation. A presentation to senior management was to be made by the task force in six weeks outlining the details of the plan.[1]

CONTRACT ADMINISTRATION DEPARTMENT

The new organization was named the Contract Administration Department (CAD). The consolidation was scheduled to take place in two phases; a short-term phase to be completed by August 1, 1986, and a long-term phase, which effected only the organizational structure and the physical location of CAD, to be completed over a 1–3 year period.

Organizational Chart. The short-term organizational chart shown in Exhibit 1 was constructed taking into consideration the retirements and transfers resulting from the Voluntary Retirement Program. The new organization was comprised of 90 exempt, 58 non-exempt, and 26 contract personnel, who senior management had decided to retain.

As previously noted, Tom Bell would be the manager for the CAD. Franklin Scobey was to assume the leadership of POD upon the retirement of Daniel

*Copyright 1987 by the Colgate Darden Graduate Business School Sponsors, University of Virginia, Charlottesville.

1. All relevant facts pertaining to this business situation can be found in the case entitled "Charge of the Nueces Task Force (A)," prepared by Frederick Stow, Jr., under the supervision of Associate Professor James G. Clawson.

Cooper on July 31, 1986. IR would be directed by Benjamin Runkle. Eventually, Scobey's position and Runkle's position would no longer be needed. This would happen sometime prior to the long-term phase of the consolidation.

Most of the individuals who chose to leave the company under the Voluntary Retirement Program were in the 50–65 year age range which was expected. Younger managers were hesitant to leave a position for fear that other comparable jobs outside the company were not available due to the industry depression. The loss of the older managers caused a tremendous experience vacuum in all of the departments. For this reason many of the retiring managers were asked to return to the company as consultants to help manage the reorganization and to train new personnel transferred from other departments. The consultants were not counted as "employees" when monitoring departmental costs.

Few organizational changes were made from the original structures other than bringing the two groups together under one manager (Bell). The task force had concluded that any immediate change in the groups' set-up would be detrimental in light of the distinct differences between the two original departments. A more important goal, in the short-run, was to make sure that the day-to-day business of each group was being completed. Of critical concern was the number of leases (11,000) waiting to be verified by the POD analysts. These leases represented approximately six months of backlog to be worked off at present staffing levels.

A noticeable change was the creation of an Operations Support Group, the responsibility of which was to provide information (files and drafting) and systems (computer programming and application development) support to the consolidated organization. This new group was to be managed by the individual who previously headed POD's Information Group. This function, in IR, had previously been assigned to another manager as an auxiliary responsibility.

Other short-term, structural changes were made within each of the consolidated groups. On the POD side of the CAD the acquisition and ownership functions of each regional area in the Undeveloped Property Section were separated and reorganized along functional lines rather than geographic. The administrative group that had supported the Undeveloped Property

Exhibit 1   Charge of the Nueces Task Force (B) Short-term Organizational Chart after Reorganization of 1986

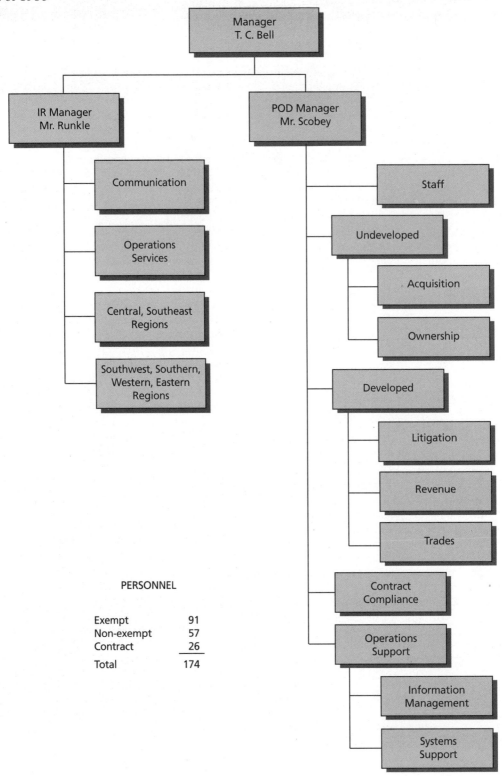

PERSONNEL

Exempt	91
Non-exempt	57
Contract	26
Total	174

Section was now distributed between the new acquisitions unit and the ownership unit. On the IR side, a new Operations Services Unit was formed to give CAD specific hardware and software support services, such as personal computer installation, software selection, training and trouble-shooting problems. This group was necessary because of IR's advances in computer systems automation and implementation.

The long-term view of the organization, shown in Exhibit 2, would be realized after the functional similarities of the two groups had been identified, documented, and integrated. The task force determined that before this type of analysis could be performed the group would need to be physically located together for an extended period of time. This structure designated positions for a total of 161 persons. The reduction

Exhibit 2   Charge of the Nueces Task Force (B) Long-Term Organizational Chart After Reorganization of 1986

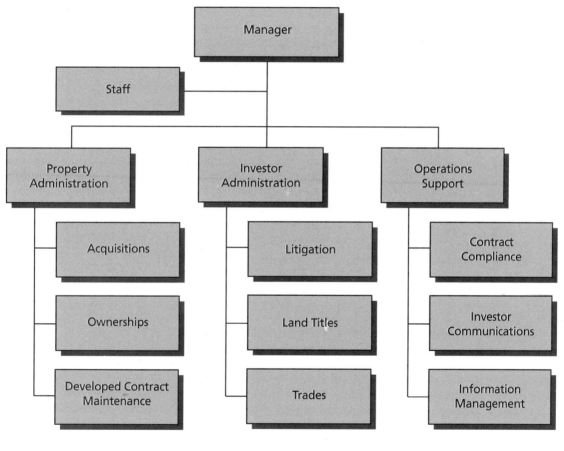

PERSONNEL

Current	174
Additional Work	17
SIGMA Savings	(17)
IR Reductions	(13)
Projected Total	161

from the short-term scenario of 174 persons would be realized as the computer automation projects began to increase efficiency and productivity, and by the elimination of duplication of effort resulting from the consolidation. An increase in the level of company leasing activity, which was expected to occur with the industry upturn later in 1987, had been accounted for in estimating these personnel figures.

The only new group formed under the long-term scenario was the Developed Contract Maintenance Unit. This Unit's responsibility was to maintain all of the company's obligations and agreements pertaining to developed properties owned by NLC or properties in which NLC had an interest.

Personnel Evaluation System. The task force recommended that the complete company evaluation system be applied uniformly across the CAD. Each manager would provide the subordinate with both a verbal description and a numerical ranking of his or her performance at the end of each evaluation period. This solution would provide to the employee more information than he or she had previously been given which would be viewed as a positive addition to the process rather than a change.

Work Evaluation System. Now that POD was a part of the Corporate Control Division, control systems would be designed and implemented to monitor workflow volume and quality. These systems would be designed to be compatible with those already operating in IR. A program would be initiated to track a lease through the various stages of the verification process to determine where bottlenecks were occurring or where a particular instrument was located. This system would be dependent on the office automation efforts currently under way in POD. Other Business Performance Indicators (BPIs) would be used to measure and record such statistics as ownership changes made, number of checks written, number of leases mapped, and the number of errors made/corrected during the course of these activities. The BPIs would be reviewed when evaluating managers and their employee's performance.

Computer Systems. Because automating the physical records and procedures of the groups was critical in increasing efficiency, productivity, and decreasing costs, the task force recommended that both the SIGMA and INVESTOR programs be continued on their respective time schedules. It was, however, inevitable that the POD and IR data bases would at some time need to be merged or, at the very least, be able to be accessed by the same user, on the same terminal. For this reason a study team was to be formed with members of both the SIGMA and INVESTOR teams. The study team was responsible for proposing

recommendations on how to redesign the "architecture" of the two systems so that the two could be connected using software that translates one system's language into that of the other's. A secondary task for this group would be to investigate and analyze who in the new consolidated organization needed to have access to which file within the new merged computer system. This analysis was to be used as a guide in setting up new policies and procedures regarding data security and coordination. The scope of this study team's activities was not expected to add a great deal of time to the length of the automation programs because many of these requirements were already being dealt with by the respective SIGMA and INVESTOR teams. The purpose of the separate team was to integrate the progress made by both groups.

There was also some new technology released onto the market which enabled physical files to be fed into an optical scanning machine which digested the data in the files and then stored the information in a computer. An individual would access the file using a computer terminal thus avoiding the need to leave his or her office and manually extract information from the file room. This information was introduced to the task force during the course of its analysis. It was recommended that a pilot project be scheduled in the IR file room to determine the feasibility of using such technology with their records. If the pilot was successful, larger portions of the IR and POD files would be scanned for viewing on the computer system.

Physical Location. The reorganization of the entire NLC structure had caused almost every individual within the Nueces Building and the Grand Plaza Building to be moved. NLC had hired a consulting firm to do nothing but coordinate the movement of people, furniture, and equipment from one office or building to another. Due to this factor, the task force was limited in its authority to dictate when and where the CAD would be located.

During the short-term phase of the consolidation the two groups would remain physically separated in their current locations with the exception of a handful of administrative personnel who were brought over from IR to the POD offices. These individuals were moved because of their small numbers and because of their functional similarities with their respective POD counterparts.

The Computer Systems Unit was moved up from the sixth floor of the Nueces Building to the 23rd. The group occupied some office space that had been vacated by retiring employees.

Once space became available it appeared that the floor directly below POD in the Nueces Building would be vacant thereby permitting IR to move over from the Grand Plaza Building. The space was expected to be ready in approximately one year. This alternative was the most attractive due to the high cost and risk of moving the large electronic file machines in POD. The contractor for the Grand Plaza Building had informed the task force that there was no guarantee, even with reinforcement, that the floors of the Grand Plaza Building would support the immense weight of the machines. Additionally, because the space in the Nueces Building would not be available for at least a year, IR personnel would not have to move again in a short period of time. Once the move was made, this would precipitate the long-term organizational structure described above.

INTEGRATIVE CASE 5.0
National Bank of San Francisco

The National Bank of San Francisco operates seven branches that receive deposits and make loans to both businesses and individual depositors. Deposits have grown from $14 million to $423 million within the past twenty years, and the directors have opened more branches as population and business activity in the Bay area have increased.

The Bank has generally been characterized by aggressive marketing including give-away promotions for new deposits and extremely competitive interest rates on loans. President E. F. Wellington has prided himself on his ability to appoint entrepreneurial branch managers and loan officers who have pushed new business development.

In response to a question at a board meeting two years ago concerning a noticeable rate of increase in operating and overhead expenses. Wellington announced that he would undertake a study of ways the bank might lower, or at least hold the line on, these costs.

Shortly thereafter, he called in James Nicholson, one of his two assistants, described the general problem of reducing costs, and told him that the bank had reached the size where it needed a man to devote his full time to operating methods and facilities. He said that he had talked this matter over with Mr. Simmons, manager of personnel, and that both of them had agreed "that you would be a fine man for this position." He also explained that Mr. Simmons would be simultaneously promoted to vice president and put in charge of all equipment purchases, the maintenance of all bank buildings, and personnel relations. "Simmons and I feel that you might have a permanent advisory committee made up of one man from each branch, and that such a group can be really effective in deciding on ways to utilize our banking buildings and equipment, and our people, more effectively. Unless you have some objection, each of the branch managers will appoint a man to meet with you regularly."

Within three months of the original reference to the subject at the directors' meeting, Simmons had been promoted to vice president, Nicholson received the title of manager of personnel and equipment planning, and all branch managers had appointed, at Wellington's request, a man to what became known as the "systems committee." At the present time, two years later, the committee appears to have taken its work seriously, as evidenced by

1. a record of regular meetings held over a period of eighteen months;
2. the transcripts of those meetings and exhibits, which show that all seven men entered the discussions;
3. seventeen recommendations in writing, supported by a total of 1,800 pages of research data and reasoning;
4. the fact that meetings often lasted four to five hours, extending after working hours; and
5. the statements of all seven members of the committee to the effect that they enjoyed the work, felt that they were accomplishing something for the bank, and had personally enjoyed being on the committee with the other members.

All men have also expressed their high regard for Jim Nicholson and feel that he has done a good job.

The seventeen recommendations cover such matters as salary scales, a policy on days off for personal business, a policy on central purchasing of janitorial supplies, and a recommendation that certain models of typewriter and dictating machine be adopted uniformly in all branches.

OFFICE SPACE AND FURNISHINGS

About a year ago, both Simmons and Nicholson had made inspection trips to the branches and had come to the conclusion that there was much wasted space in branch offices and that this situation had been brought about principally because office personnel and clerical personnel had been, over a period of years, buying equipment—such as desks, telephone stands, and extra tables—that pleased them personally but that, in many instances, was also "too large and expensive" for what the bank needed to keep up its public appearance. In addition, loan officers in some branches had succeeded in having the managers construct walls for unnecessary private offices. Nicholson had obtained the services of the bank's architect and also of systems engineers from two large equipment manufacturers; together they made a "general estimate, to be confirmed by further fact-finding" that the bank could save $80,000 a year over a thirty-year period if (1) furniture were to be standardized with functional equipment that was modest in design but met the essential requirements of dignity for the branches and if

(2) henceforth, only branch managers could have private offices.

Before the meeting of the systems committee last week, Simmons expressed concern to Nicholson that his committee had not taken up these two problems.

> Your committee could have done some real research on these questions. I hope that you will put them on the agenda right away and agree, let's say in six months, on standard layouts and equipment. You and I both know, for instance, that the loan officers at San Mateo and Menlo Park have entirely too much space, should not be in those large offices, and perhaps should have three standard pieces of equipment—a desk, chair, and small bookcase. There should be no telephone stands like those that were purchased there last year for $90 each.

RELATIONS WITH BRANCH MANAGERS

Branch managers have been kept informed of the committee's general work over the eighteen-month period. Most managers selected a loan officer (assistant manager) to represent them, and these officers made a real effort to let their managers know what was going on. Dick May, representative of the Burlingame branch, reports that he has been spending at least an hour a week with his boss telling him what the committee is doing and asking for his ideas. James Strickland of the Market Street branch says that he has been able to confer briefly with his boss about once a week on the subjects the committee is working on. Other members report that they, too, have been able to keep their managers informed and that the latter exhibit a good deal of interest in the committee's work. In all cases except Burlingame, however, men say that their managers quite naturally do not have the time to go into the details of committee recommendations and that they, the managers, have not been particularly aggressive or enthusiastic about putting any of those recommendations into effect.

The committee has talked about the best way to get its recommendations adopted. Dick May claims that his manager is ready to put many of them into effect immediately and that it is up to each man to convince his own manager. All others say they believe that the president should issue the recommendations as instructions over his signature. The reason given by Strickland is typical:

We're convinced that the recommendations are best for the bank, but the managers just won't buy them. The only way to get the managers to carry them out is to have Mr. Wellington lay them out as official and let it be known that they are going to be put into effect. Of course, they would have to be acknowledged as being drawn up by the Department of Personnel and Equipment, with some advice from our committee.

James Nicholson reported in his own weekly meeting with the president that it looked as if it is going to be "rather touchy" to get managers to accept the recommendations. Mr. Wellington thereupon stated that his own knowledge of the committee recommendations was rather sketchy, even though he had discussed them in part with Nicholson each week for a year. He therefore decided to call a meeting of all branch managers and committee members at the same time so that he and everyone concerned could be acquainted in detail with them. This meeting took place one week ago.

INFORMAL COMMENTS OF BRANCH MANAGERS

Most of the branch managers dropped in to the officers' dining room for lunch before the meeting. After the usual banter, the conversation naturally drifted onto the proposals of the systems committee.

> Sure hope my secretary likes those new typewriters. I can't spell, and if Sally left I'd be sunk.
> So what, Joe, you always talk better than you write.
> Say, I sure hated to come in here this afternoon. Ever since Smedley Scott became president of Menlo Laboratories I've been trying to convince him to do all his banking with us. Had to break a date with him, and in my office, too. If we start spending all our time buying mops, our development program goes out the window.
> How are you making out with your two (officer) trainees, Carl? I have one smart boy coming right along, but he won't be happy under the proposed salary schedule.
> The best young man we have came from the credit department a year ago. He sure gets around. Tennis matches, hospital drives, U.N. meetings; always on the go. I thought

of him when I read that proposal for days off. How do you decide when a guy like that is working? Granted his work gets behind sometimes. That's better than drawing pay for just sitting at his desk. I get a kick out of bringing a man like that along. And he is building a lot of good will for the bank in my area.

Well, I kind of like that days-off rule. It would save a lot of complaints and conversation about grandfather's weak heart.

It might be just fine for you, Tyson, but not so good for Pete. Why not let each manager decide for himself? After all, each of us is paid to run his branch in the best interests of the bank, and we wouldn't be in our present positions if we weren't doing it. What do you think, Oscar?

Guess I have longer service than any of the rest of you. It will be thirty-nine years in September. But I'd say there isn't a manager who doesn't run his branch just as though it was his own business.

And the record is not bad either. Deposits are going up and the bank is making money.

It's making money that counts. (This from a manager of one of the slower-growing branches.)

I heard from somebody about a year ago that the committee was going to study office space and equipment and that someone figured they could save $1 million over a period of years. But apparently they didn't get around to that.

Don't worry. We're building a real base for the future. By the way, did you see the latest report on Zenith Radio?

Just before the meeting with the systems committee, Simmons called Jim Nicholson into his office to have a brief discussion of the recommendations. The two men read over the list of seventeen final recommendations; then Nicholson explained briefly the reasons why each recommendation was made and how it would help the bank to reduce costs.

THE MEETING OF THE COMMITTEE AND BRANCH MANAGERS

The meeting started at 2:00 PM and was scheduled to last until 5:00 PM, but actually ran over until six o'clock. The committee, branch managers, Wellington, and Simmons were present. Wellington opened the meeting by stating that its purpose was to study the

committee recommendations and, it was hoped, to arrive at a decision on whether they should be accepted and put into effect.

In fact, however, after a reading of the seventeen recommendations, the entire meeting was taken up by a discussion of the first two recommendations.

1. It is recommended that the following pay scales be adopted for clerical and nonofficer personnel in all branches. (This was followed by a list of positions and grades—the bank had had some uniformity before, but the recommendations specified absolute uniformity and also changed some of the classifications, thus meaning, for instance, that head tellers would in the future receive more than head bookkeepers, whereas both had received the same in the past.)
2. Employees should be allowed two days per year off with pay for miscellaneous personal business, such days to be granted at the discretion of managers. Because of the possibility of abuse of this privilege, days in excess of two must be taken without pay. This limitation does not apply to sickness or death in the immediate family.

In the discussion, the branch managers found a great many points on which (a) they disagreed among themselves, and (b) they agreed among themselves but disagreed with the committee. For instance, they all agreed that uniformity was in the interest of the bank but disagreed on many of the salary scales and classifications. On this point, they cited many instances in which one competent employee would feel hurt if the scales were arranged in the way the committee recommended.

The committee members had talked confidentially among themselves before the meeting and agreed that Jim Nicholson must be the one to present the findings and, by and large, the one to defend them. This plan was carried out, and after the meeting, the president remarked to Jim that

the combined thinking of the managers, with all of their experience, made quite an impression on Simmons and me. We have confidence in you, and you know that, but I can't help but wonder if your committee really worked out the "best" recommendation for all on this salary matter. If you had, why couldn't you convince the managers instead of raising all of the criticism?

Yesterday, Wellington and Simmons met to consider the recommendations privately. Simmons again expressed the same idea that Wellington passed on to Nicholson, wondered out loud whether the committee should be sent back to do more research on the recommendation. Both men expressed concern that two years had elapsed since the committee was established without any recommendations having been accepted and put into effect.

Source: Written by Charles E. Summer. Copyright 1978. Used with permission.

INTEGRATIVE CASE 6.0
Pierre Dux*

Pierre Dux sat quietly in his office considering the news. A third appointment to regional management had been announced and, once again, the promotion he had expected had been given to someone else. The explanations seemed insufficient this time. Clearly, this signaled the end of his career at INCO. Only one year ago, the company president had arrived at Dux's facility with national press coverage to publicize the success of the innovation he had designed and implemented in the management of manufacturing operations. The intervening year had brought improved operating results and further positive publicity for the corporation but a string of personal disappointments for Pierre Dux.

Four years earlier, the INCO manufacturing plant had been one of the least productive of the 13 facilities operating in Europe. Absenteeism and high employee turnover were symptoms of the low morale among the work group. These factors were reflected in mediocre production levels and the worst quality record in INCO. Pierre Dux had been in his current position one year and had derived his only satisfaction from the fact that these poor results might have been worse had he not instituted minor reforms in organizational communication. These allowed workers and supervisors to vent their concerns and frustrations. Although nothing substantial had changed during that first year, operating results had stabilized, ending a period of rapid decline. But this "honeymoon" was ending. The expectation of significant change was growing, particularly among workers who had been vocal in expressing their dissatisfaction and suggesting concrete proposals for change.

The change process, which had begun three years before, had centered on a redesign of production operations from a single, machine-paced assembly line to a number of semi-autonomous assembly teams. Although the change had been referred to as the INCO "Volvo project" or "INCO's effort at Japanese-style management," it had really been neither of these. Rather, it had been the brainchild of a group of managers, led by Dux, who believed that both productivity and working conditions in the plant could be improved through a single effort. Of course, members of the group had visited other so-called "innovative production facilities," but the new work groups and job classifications had been designed with the particular products and technology at INCO in mind.

After lengthy discussions among the management group, largely dedicated to reaching agreement on the general direction that the new project would take, the actual design began to emerge. Equally lengthy discussions (often referred to as negotiations) with members of the workforce, supervisors, and representatives of the local unions were part of the design process. The first restructuring into smaller work groups was tried in an experimental project that received tentative approval from top management in INCO headquarters and a "wait and see" response from the union. The strongest initial resistance had come from the plant engineers. They were sold neither on the new structure nor on the process of involving the workforce in the design of operating equipment and production methods. Previously, the engineering group had itself fulfilled these functions, and it felt the problems now present were the result of a lack of skill among employees or managerial unwillingness to make the system work.

The experiment was staffed by volunteers supported by a few of the better trained workers in the plant. The latter were necessary to ensure a start-up of the new equipment, which had been modified from the existing technology on the assembly line.

The initial experiment met with limited success. Although the group was able to meet the productivity levels of the existing line within a few weeks, critics of the new plan attributed the minor success to the unrepresentative nature of the experimental group or the newness of the equipment on which they were working. However, even this limited success attracted the attention of numerous people at INCO headquarters and in other plants. All were interested in visiting the new "experiment." Visits soon became a major distraction, and Dux declared a temporary halt to permit the project to proceed, although this produced some muttering at headquarters about his "secretive" and "uncooperative" behavior.

Because of the experiment's success, Dux and his staff prepared to convert the entire production operation to the new system. The enthusiasm of workers in the plant grew as training for the changeover

*This case was prepared by Michael Brimm, Associate Professor at INSEAD. It is intended to be used as a basis for class discussion rather than to illustrate either effective or ineffective handling of an administrative situation. Copyright © 1983 INSEAD Fontainebleau, France. Revised 1987.

proceeded. In fact, a group of production workers asked to help with the installation of the new equipment as a means of learning more about its operation.

Dux and his staff were surprised at the difficulties encountered at this phase. Headquarters seemed to drag their feet in approving the necessary funding for the changeover. Even after the funding was approved, there was a stream of challenges to minor parts of the plan. "Can't you lay the workers off during the changeover?" "Why use workers on overtime to do the changeover when you could hire temporary workers more cheaply?" These criticisms reflected a lack of understanding of the basic operating principles of the new system, and Dux rejected them.

The conversion of the entire assembly line to work groups was finally achieved, with the local management group making few concessions from their stated plans. The initial change and the first days of operation were filled with crisis. The design process had not anticipated many of the problems that arose with full scale operations. However, Dux was pleased to see managers, staff, and workers clustered together at the trouble areas, fine-tuning the design when problems arose. Just as the start-up finally appeared to be moving forward, a change in product specifications from a headquarters group dictated additional changes in the design of the assembly process. The new change was handled quickly and with enthusiasm by the workforce. While the period was exhausting and seemingly endless to those who felt responsible for the change,

the new design took only six months to reach normal operating levels (one year had been forecast as the time needed to reach that level—without the added requirement for a change in product specification).

Within a year, Dux was secure that he had a major success on his hands. Productivity and product quality measures for the plant had greatly improved. In this relatively short period his plant had moved from the worst, according to these indicators, to the third most productive in the INCO system. Absenteeism had dropped only slightly, but turnover had been reduced substantially. Morale was not measured formally but was considered by all members of the management team to be greatly improved. Now, after three years of full operations, the plant was considered the most productive in the entire INCO system.

Dux was a bit surprised when no other facility in INCO initiated a similar effort or called upon him for help. Increases of the early years had leveled off, with the peak being achieved in the early part of year three. Now the facility seemed to have found a new equilibrium. The calm of smoother operations had been a welcome relief to many who had worked so hard to launch the new design. For Dux it provided the time to reflect on his accomplishment and think about his future career.

It was in this context that he considered the news that he had once again been bypassed for promotion to the next level in the INCO hierarchy.

INTEGRATIVE CASE 7.0
Turnaround at Petrus Consumer Goods Division (International)*

Thursday May 5th. 17.30 Cardiff Airport

Three or four passengers waited quietly for the little plane that would return to London in a few minutes. It was the only departure from the airport that evening.

I looked once again over my notes—it had been quite a week.

[Ten] days ago the company's management had decided they had to act. Last Friday my boss had flown West on this little machine and explained to the Managing Director that he had to leave and that his replacement would arrive on Tuesday (Monday was a national holiday).

Jim (aged 46) had worked with the company for 30 years starting at 16 as an office boy and rapidly rising through the salesforce to be Sales Director in the early '80s. After a few years in another UK division he had returned to the business as Managing Director in 1988. Everybody liked him. He had even been kind enough to meet me at the airport, waiting two hours for the delayed flight and driving me to the office in his large white BMW and organizing a meeting with his former management team for me on Tuesday. Then he had left.

The offices were at one end of a run-down industrial complex; the directors' carpark was full of shining expensive motorcars; the large employee carpark was also full with the spaces nearest the offices reserved with initials and full of medium size cars [and] the bicycle sheds right at the other end. Litter everywhere. We walk past the security man without being checked and go to a large corner office full of furniture on the top floor. A sample of each of the 300 products sold by the company seems to have taken over the available space. Anne, Jim's secretary, is crying as she tells me that lunch is served in the Directors' Dining room.

A large table laid for 10, two waitresses in black and white uniforms, and the Directors. I was surprised to see John—he had been fired for incompetence four months ago but, as he explained, the agreement had been that he would keep his office and management position for 6 months. He added that I would see him

every day because he was on the Directors' Floor. The various managers appeared: I introduced myself and confirmed that we would have a management meeting that afternoon. I was surprised to learn that it would have to be after 15.00 because the Directors' Dining room also served as the only conference room. It was 12.30.

Most of the managers chose an aperatif, a glass or two of wine, and [carried on] a desultory conversation about out-of-stocks, customer difficulties, and some problems in the factory.

The management meeting was short. I explained that the Board had asked me to take over the Division on a temporary basis [and] that Jim had been asked to leave, and [I] worked out a schedule for the next two days which allowed me to meet each of the directors in his office.

It took some time to find them. The company employed about 1,200 people of whom 300 were in sales and administration. Managers were located in different buildings on the large site.

On Wednesday morning the Financial Director showed me round his department. It was in a converted bicycle shed. There were two buckets in the middle of the floor [because] "the roof leaks." Some 30 people seemed to be occupied with manual operations relating to invoicing, reconciliation, wages. Some terminals. Passing later in the day I was concerned to see a large pile of unopened mail. The Financial Director was aged 54—25 years in the company, formerly quartermaster in the Navy. Yes, the division had big problems, difficult to quantify, but the last profit forecasts were probably too high by about 3 [to] 4 [million] pounds. Why? Well sales were down and manufacturing costs up. There was also a problem of reconciling book and actual stocks—it would be necessary to make an adjustment of several million pounds. Yes, it should have been made at the end of the previous year but HQ had said leave it. Why was the Division 50% behind budget? The budget had never been possible but HQ had insisted so . . . .

The Personnel Director was about the same age. He explained how the company was implementing the European Manufacturing Strategy which had been dictated by HQ. Some 500 redundancies and the closure of some 10 manufacturing lines. Yes, everything was going according to schedule but it was costing more because final settlements were greatly increased

*Copyright © 1991, by COS. This case was developed for teaching purposes at the Centre for Organisational Studies (COS) Barcelona, under the supervision of José M. de Anzizu.

because of high overtime. About 2 [million pounds]. Morale was pretty low but the company had made a very generous offer and many people—especially skilled technicians—were leaving willingly, earlier than planned. He wondered if HQ appreciated the Division's achievements: during 12 months 500 employees had been made redundant without any significant industrial action and then HQ sacks the MD.

Sales had been very poor in the first five months, running about 85% of previous years and 70% of budget. For the Sales Director, who at 55 had been called back from his job as Managing Director in Taiwan to the division by Jim for whom he had previous[ly] worked, the issue was very simple. The division had one of the best salesforces in the UK but there were far too many out-of-stocks and the company hadn't advertised its main brands for two years now—to make HQ profit targets—so it wasn't surprising. We walked round the department which totalled some 100 people with 35 in administration. Yes, there were a lot of customer complaints and about 30% of all invoices had to be subsequently corrected (credit notes). The out-of stocks were appalling and partly caused by the new warehouse which, as a result of the European Manufacturing Strategy, had been established on a green field site early in the year and still wasn't working properly. The newly established Euro pean focus factories were delivering poor quality products very late. The Key Accounts Manager and the Field Sales Force manager both in their mid 50s confirmed their boss' view but emphasized that with an active promotion programme with the trade, involving special promotion packs, they could generate higher sales and it would only cost 2 [to] 3 [million pounds].

The Marketing Director was younger, Australian, and had been transferred two years previously to the UK after a successful marketing career there. Yes, the division was in a bad way. It was impossible to work with all these old English managers who spent most of the time having lunch and talking. You need guts to run a major business and instead of a stifling bureaucracy and endless discussion what the division needed was leadership and decision making. It took five signatures from four departments to sign off on a Product Managers' expense account. The company was "full of walls" between functions and there was no sense of team among the senior managers. For example the sales department spent all their time imagining new promotions which meant paying the trade for special displays for merchandise that the company couldn't deliver. Then there was the problem of this European production—the products were more expensive than before so the gross margin was lower

and the marketing department could no longer ensure that the products were suitable for the UK market. HQ's European management even wanted the division to use European advertising on British TV!

And so it went on. The IS Director described how the Stock Control system was 25 years old and run on the last remaining IBMX in the country—yes, that had made changing warehouses more difficult. The book stock financial account was on a special package bought 10 years ago that had never worked properly so when "they" started changing the warehouses . . . . But surely this was no surprise? After all HQ Group Internal Audit had had three people in the business for over two months at the end of last year. None of the Directors [was] interested in computers. He noted, smiling, that the Network manager had seen that I had turned on the smart high powered PC on the Managing Directors' desk and logged on—it was the first time this year that the machine had ever been used by anyone other than his own IS people. He added that many of the most skilled employees (like IS staff) had rushed to accept the redundancy offer so that the company no longer had the skilled people nor their knowledge of the company's operations.

The R&D director with 50 people in the lab came from Nestlé some years ago but there hadn't been one successful new product from the lab in the past ten years. The company had a lot of problems but he saw the key issue as being product quality. The new focus factories were not making satisfactory products, the quality control function had been transferred to the shopfloor and it just wasn't working. Was I aware that the company was no longer complying with the national legislation relating to plant hygiene? If the government inspectors or the press . . . . The procurement people were impossible to control—did I know that they had just reduced the quality spec for the most important snack biscuit line so that if they were ever stacked more than two pallets high they were bound to crash and result in broken biscuit ratios exceeding 50%. . .? Sainsbury's, the division's biggest customer, had four level stacking.

And finally the Manufacturing Director, a much respected company veteran who had been with the company 25 years in Planning, Operations and recently been promoted to his current job. He walked around the depressing dirty site for about two hours. He clearly had a good contact with many of the supervisors and there were some interesting conversations. Many of the lines were due to be closed, maintenance and craft skills were being done by contract labour (because the craftsmen had taken up the redundancy offers very quickly) and they didn't know the machines. Remaining employees were often those who couldn't get a job and they were very demotivated. We stopped by a line of a product that was actually out-of-stock; the line was down, embarrassed it became clear that it was sabotage (someone had undone the mixing screws) which would ensure that everybody on the line would have weekend overtime working. Quality? How could you expect quality in such surroundings and circumstances? Reluctantly I was shown a factory employee amenities area—it was absolutely disgusting. Why? Because there are 35 sets of lavatories on the site, the employees don't care any more anyway, and you can't spend all your time just keeping lavatories clean.

The division was the Group's 7th biggest operating company; it delivered (or should deliver) 8% of the worldwide profit; its brands were among the most famous in the UK. A member of the Board had previously run the division, the CEO had been responsible for the UK for 10 years prior to being promoted to CEO eighteen months ago. Overall responsibility for the division had been transferred to my boss who was responsible for having initiated the European Manufacturing Strategy. Tomorrow morning in the HQ the CEO, the Group Personnel Director, and he would expect me to tell them. Tell them what?

Tell them how the managers' carpark was empty at 9.00 AM and at 17.00; tell them of one of the company's chauffeurs who explained to me that he spent most of his time cleaning Directors' cars; tell them of the young product manager who said that the HQ just had never wanted to know about any of the problems—merely wanted to get the profit out. Or tell them that the current profit forecast might be 50% of budget but that it was totally unrealistic and they would be lucky to see any profit from the division in 1990 (and that in a very difficult year for the Group to a CEO determined to make his profit target?). On the CEO's office door was written in large letters "Que Proposez-Vous?" so I knew what he would ask.

The five passengers walked across the tarmac and settled in the seats in the 18 seater plane. Looking out of the window I wondered how I would deal with another conversation this evening. My Italian wife had moved reluctantly to live in central London two years ago, and our four children had, with some difficulty, settled into the only good Italian School in England which was about ten minutes' walk from our house; in good weather the travel time from home to the troubled division's offices was about 5 hours.

INTEGRATIVE CASE 8.0
Chemical™ Bank: Branch Closing*

In mid-1983, Mr. Matthew McPartland, division manager for Chemical Bank's Upper Manhattan/Bronx retail operations, was considering the pros and cons of closing two branches on Jerome Avenue in the West Bronx. Both were unprofitable branches in troubled neighborhoods, and, although closing them would leave Chemical unrepresented in a forty-block market, their projected financial losses for 1983 were approaching $100,000. The losses were especially significant in light of Chemical Bank's recent efforts to cut expenses across-the-board. Mr. McPartland's other option was to consolidate the two branches into one branch on Burnside Drive. The new branch more than likely would still be unprofitable, but at least some expenses would be cut. This option would also be compatible with Chemical's past strategy in the area.

UPPER MANHATTAN/BRONX DIVISION

Mr. McPartland was responsible for twenty-six branches, most of which operated in economically deprived, residential neighborhoods. He firmly supported Chemical's philosophy of active community involvement and participation in community development. Consequently, he and his branch managers had become personally involved with local nonprofit organizations such as United Way and Goodwill Industries, by volunteering their time and expertise—managerial and financial. These efforts had contributed to the bank's reputation for "caring" about the communities it served.

Moreover, the bank had developed good relationships with local politicians and officials monitoring compliance with the Community Reinvestment Act.[1] The CRA had created a legal mechanism for encouraging financial institutions to meet the credit needs of their neighborhoods. Under the CRA, certain federal supervisory agencies were given the power to limit or delay the expansion of banks that had failed to do enough for the communities in which they operated. Mr. McPartland commented:

> We have never had a CRA problem. We can
> show that we have closed fewer branches

than any other large bank and kept open many that are unprofitable because they are serving community needs.

Mr. McPartland had also found that serving community needs brought in new business, which contributed to his "core" of stable retail accounts. He believed that Chemical's success in doing business with more than half of New York's nonprofit organizations was in part a result of its contributions of time and money to nonprofit organizations all over the city. Mr. McPartland acknowledged the use of his contributions efforts as a valuable business tool and saw his large percentage of core deposits as a safety net for bad times. He added, "Even though we have a smaller number of branches in the Bronx than other large banks, we have a bigger market share."

THE OPTIONS

Against this background, Mr. McPartland had to deal with the two unprofitable branches. Commercial business and housing in the area were deteriorating; so the near future offered little chance for economic revival. Consolidation into one branch on Burnside seemed feasible, but with moving and renovation expenses, the new branch would still show a loss for some time. There was also the possibility of lost deposits. The proposed location for the new branch was close to the existing branch at Jerome and Burnside Avenues but was an additional mile from the branch at Jerome and 170th Street. When presented with the possibility of one consolidated branch on Burnside, members of the 170th Street community petitioned Chemical not to close their branch and complained to local politicians. Mr. McPartland had responded by asking the community to help make the branch profitable by bringing in more business, but so far the situation had not improved. He doubted that he could retain all the deposits at the 170th Street branch if he consolidated; on the other hand, one branch would serve the community better than no branches at all.

With Chemical's increasing emphasis on profitability, Mr. McPartland knew he would have to make a decision soon. He could reduce expenses by consolidating, but the only completely profitable alternative was to leave the area entirely. He disliked this last alternative because he and his branch managers had worked closely with this community. Moreover, it

---

1. The Community Reinvestment Act of 1977, 12 U.S. Code Section 2901 et seq. (1976).

seemed contrary to everything Chemical Bank stood
for in the area of community support. Mr. McPartland
wondered if "deserting" the area would undermine
Chemical's good reputation in the community. What
should he do?

*Source: This case was prepared by Susan E. Woodward,
Research Assistant, under the supervision of Lynda Sharp Paine,
Visiting Assistant Professor, and Henry W. Tulloch, Executive
Director, Olsson Center for Applied Ethics. Copyright © 1984
by the Darden Graduate Business School Foundation, Charlottesville, VA. IBM:E–031 UVA E–031, Rev. 9/90. Used by permission.

INTEGRATIVE CASE 9.0
Norman Manufacturing Company*

The Norman Manufacturing Company produces a variety of industrial machinery and equipment, including electrical switches and relay boxes; the small items of coal-mining equipment; and chains, hoists, conveyers and other materials-handling products. In addition to these lines, the company has expanded, through acquisition in the past ten years, into two lines less closely connected with its original product line: the manufacture of sporting goods and of furnishings (hardware, plumbing, furniture) for leisure yachts. At the present . . ., the company employs 1,650 people, and its annual sales have averaged $40 million for the past three years.

Regarding the objectives of the Company, L. D. Norman, Jr., the president, states:

> Since my father's death thirteen years ago, we have endeavored to stress even more strongly the objective of growth over the years. The public now owns 63 percent of our stock, but they, as well as our family and our management, have certain principal accomplishments in mind: to have this company grow in assets, market coverage, profitability, and prestige over the years; and to have it gain a national reputation for quality and service to our customers. This is the reason why we have taken on two new divisions that are not connected with our past experience. We feel that the company has a future in many product lines. Technology and consumer tastes mean you can't stand still with your same traditional products and ways of doing things.

THE LANGE DIVISION

Seven years ago, the Norman Company purchased the Lange Sporting Goods Company and established it as the Lange Division of NMC. The research bulletin of a New York investment firm, at that time, carried the following statement:

> The Lange Company, with a good stable line of products, has suffered in recent years from a lack of vitality in keeping its products, production methods, and advertising up to the

zip displayed by its competitors. We believe that Norman's record of capable and aggressive management should enable this company to show good growth over the intermediate term future.

The management of Lange had been in the hands of four members of the Lange family, all of whom retired at the time of the merger. L. D. Norman, Jr., immediately replaced them with Fred K. Gibbs as general manager of the Lange Division.

Fred Gibbs, forty-two, had been executive vice president of a competing sporting goods manufacturing company. After graduation from Stanford University, he held positions as production-scheduling trainee, salesman, sales manager, and marketing vice president for that company. Reference checks at the time of his employment with Norman Manufacturing Company indicated that he was well liked by his fellow executives.

L. Donald Norman, Jr., has been president of the Norman Manufacturing Company for thirteen years. At age fifty, he has worked for the company twenty-six years, first in the plants, then as a salesman, and for ten years as a staff man to his father, designing and supervising procedures to coordinate production, sales, shipping, and inventories. As president he has spent most of his time planning new customer strategy and sales incentive programs, and projecting financial statements to plan increases in plant investment. Together with T. M. Farish, executive vice president, and C. A. Langford, treasurer, he sits on the executive committee. This committee meets three times a week to discuss all important matters in sales, production, and finance.

Mr. Norman, the minutes also show, gave the committee a summary of the study he had been making of decentralization. He pointed out that such companies as General Motors and Du Pont were able to grow by creating independent divisions, selecting capable [people] to run them, and retaining only very broad measures of performance. In this way, he said, the Norman Company could delegate virtually the entire management task to Fred Gibbs and his team. ["]We do not have to know much about the details of the division, so long as we establish broad controls.["]

In the five months after the acquisition, the three top Norman officials drew up the following control points. They were careful to make clear, Norman says, that Gibb's own performance would be measured

Source: Written by Charles E. Summer, Copyright 1978. Used with permission.

only in terms of these controls. "Everything else—all of the details of running the division—would be left to Fred."

Rate of return on investment: Lange was earning an average of 14 percent (before taxes) on book value, and it was agreed to raise the target to 19 percent within five years.

Sales as a percentage of industry sales: Norman judged that the Lange Company had been performing as indicated below, and new targets were set for Lange's three principal products:

Product	Present Sales	Five Year Target
Tennis equipment	11%	15%
Golf bags	8	12
Gym clothing	10	25

Of the total dollar sales volume of Lange, averaged over the five-year period prior to acquisition, tennis equipment accounted for 40 percent, gym clothing for 45 percent, and golf bags for 15 percent.

In setting these figures, all three executives agreed that there was no accurate way to be scientific about what percentages could be reached. All recognized that the Lange Company had been, in the words of Norman, "conservative, lacking in morale, and complacent. It therefore seemed reasonable that with a hard-hitting management and some new ideas, the targets are neither over- nor understated—they are realistic."

Gibbs at first expressed the idea that the gym clothing sales target was too high, but Langford and Norman showed him the results of their study of profits in this line compared with others. The profitability of selling gym clothing, particularly to institutions, was much higher than the other items. Gibbs, too, agreed that his target was a wise one.

OPERATING RESULTS: FIRST SIX YEARS OF OPERATION

At the time this case is written, Lange Division has been in operation for six fiscal years. Rates of return on investment and percentages of industry sales appear in Exhibit 1 and 2, respectively.

During the first four years, the executive committee of the Norman Company had a verbal agreement, of which they frequently reminded themselves, that none of Norman's management should initiate inquiries about specific operations in Lange. Langford reports, for instance, that when he noticed on the

Exhibit 1   Ratio of Profit (Before Tax) to Investment in the Lange Division.

Year	Method 1*	Method 2**
First	14%	12%
Second	14	11
Third	15	13
Fourth	15	13
Fifth	17	16
Sixth	17	16
Present***	17	16

*Used by Lange Division controller, charging advertising and research to capital investment, the lower half of the ratio.
**Used by Norman Company management, charging advertising and research to current expense, thus decreasing the top of the ratio.
***First quarter adjusted.

expense statements furnished for the first year, that telephone and telegraph expenses of Lange were, in his opinion, far out of line with the rest of the company, he felt that he should not use these statements as detailed controls.

The committee also agreed that Norman should make fairly frequent (perhaps bimonthly) visits to Lange headquarters in Providence for the purpose of inquiring about overall sales improvement. He should also encourage Gibbs to come to New York whenever "he feels the need to discuss any matter, broad, detailed, or otherwise."

As a matter of practice, Norman, Gibbs, and Langford did meet about three times a month, at which times (a) they discussed overall sales results for ten to twenty minutes and (b) they discussed and

Exhibit 2   Sales as a Percentage of Total Industry Sales.

Year	Tennis Equiment	Golf Bags	Gym Clothing
First	11%	9%	10%
Second	12	10	15
Third	12	9	21
Fourth	13	11	22
Fifth	12	10	23
Sixth	12	10	22
Present (1st quarter)	12	10	21

approved lump-sum amounts of money requested by Gibbs to be budgeted for both capital expenditures and current expenses.

At the end of the fourth year, Langford, who had been raising questions with Norman all along about the wisdom of Gibbs's expenditures, suggested that investment return and sales targets were far less than satisfactory. "We have been holding off telling him how to manage various phases of his budget too long. There is little doubt that he has gone too fast and too far in increasing expenditures for advertising, [sales peoples'] bonuses, and [sales peoples'] expense accounts. Furthermore, his expenditures for employee-recreation facilities and increases in factory salaries have been unwise when we are trying to increase return on investment. The former increased the investment side of the ratio, and the latter decreased the income side."

Langford, incidentally, received expense summaries regularly—as he says, "not as control reports, but for the purpose of consolidating the figures with the rest of the company divisions for the profit and loss statement." These summaries contained thirty-five account captions (for excerpts of five captions, see Exhibit 3).

After reviewing Langford's cost statements, the executive committee agreed that "Gibbs needs some helpful guidance." Since Langford knew more about the details of expense and capital budgets, they also agreed that he should visit Gibbs once a month to go over the thirty-five expense accounts and see how each progresses during the year.

Gibbs recalls that, early in his fifth year at Lange, when Langford first came to Providence and told him what the executive committee had decided,

I was surprised. I guess it scared me a little right off the bat, since I had no idea they were thinking like that. The targets weren't being met, but I thought that surely they must know that things were going quite well, considering all of the things which must be done to put this division on a solid footing for the future. After my initial anxiousness and surprise, I got downright mad for a few days.

Gibbs also states that

Early in the fifth year, I began to cut back on some of the spending, inaugurated in the beginning. I got the [sales people] together on four occasions and gave them a talk about the necessity of cutting their expense-account expenditures and the fact that we would have to stop making some of the purely promotional calls and concentrate on

Exhibit 3   Selected Expense Captions and Amounts from Lange Division Expense Tabulation.

Expense Caption	Fourth Year	Year Prior to Merger
Advertising	$280,000	$ 47,000
Salesmen Bonuses	210,000	23,000
Salesmen Expenses	145,000	68,000
Factory Salaries	665,000	550,000*
Employee Service	80,000	2,010

*Average salary per employee in the year prior to merger was $6,540. If this is adjusted for cost-of-living increase from that time to the fourth year, it comes out to an equivalent of $7,185. Average actual salary paid by Lange in the fourth year was $7,540.

those customers that looked more like immediate prospects. I also cut the number of direct-mail promotional brochures from twelve mailings a year to six, and decided to let one man go whom we had hired as a merchandising man. He had helped, in the four years he had been with us, in designing the products for eye appeal, in creating point-of-sale displays, and in improving the eye appeal of our packages. I did not cut down on the number of [sales people] employed, however.

THE QUESTION OF ADVERTISING AND RESEARCH COSTS

As early as February of the second year, Gibbs objected—in his words, "mildly"—to Norman "because of the way Langford entered on certain financial statements the money spent for advertising, the market research department, and the product research department." When the first year statement of return was prepared by Lange's own controller, Gibbs and he felt that the total of $340,000 represented an investment rather than a current operating expense. They reasoned that the increase in new products and the increase in goodwill or consumer acceptance would not begin to pay off for two or three years. Since return on investment is the ratio of income to investment, charging these three items to investment showed a higher performance (14 percent in the first year) than the same statement prepared by Langford (12 percent in the same year). It seemed to Gibbs that subtracting the $340,000 from profits "was a real injustice—Tom

Farish and Norman family stockholders have pretty much stayed out of my end of the business, but I don't want them to get the wrong impression. They will, from that kind of misleading figure."

Gibbs and Langford both feel that, in spite of this disagreement, the relationship of the Norman management group to Gibbs is "a pretty good one." Gibbs states that, as of now,

I pretty much go along with their guidance, though it one time looked like interference.

The only thing I'm still darn mad about is this way of figuring return. Norman overruled me when Langford and I had it out in front of him one time, but it's still such a hot subject that Langford and I won't bring it up anymore. Why, just look at the figures for the whole period that the division has been in existence! (See Exhibit 1.)

VIDEO

CASES

VIDEO CASE 1.0
IBAX Health Care Systems

In 1990, a new leader in information management systems software for the health care industry was announced with great fanfare. With the combined strengths of its two partners—IBM, a technological giant in computer hardware and operating systems, and Baxter Corporation, the world's largest supplier of hospital products—IBAX seemed uniquely positioned to become the worldwide leader in health care applications development, services, and support.

But in its first year, IBAX lost $11 million, and the next year wasn't much better. Customers were unhappy because products were of poor quality, didn't meet their expectations, or didn't perform as promised by the sales force. The morale of the sales people, battered on all sides as market share continued to slip, sank lower and lower. Morale was generally low throughout the company, with employees in several geographically dispersed divisions routinely doing their jobs, feeling little need or desire to cooperate with workers in other divisions and little concern about the overall performance of the company. Fortunately for IBAX and its employees, the principals in the partnership realized that a turnaround was needed.

Enter Jeff Goodman, who took the helm as CEO early in 1991. With a University of Virginia MBA and a General Electric background, Goodman had developed a reputation for turning poorly performing companies into efficient, effective organizations. Within a couple of years, things at IBAX began to turn around. Much of the success can be attributed to changes in organizational design and corporate culture. Goodman's first step was a painful one—consolidating facilities and reducing the work force. But rather than simply slashing nearly two hundred jobs, Goodman actively involved employees in deciding who would stay with the company and how their jobs would be structured. This marked the beginning of a fundamental shift for the company. IBAX had been a functionally organized, highly bureaucratic organization, with rigid policies and procedures and an authoritative, directive management style. Employees were not involved in decision making and had little influence over what happened in the company—in fact, most of them didn't even know what was happening because communication was so poor within the company.

CHANGING THE CULTURE

Goodman realized that developing a strong, adaptive culture at IBAX was critical to all the other changes that needed to be made. The culture at IBAX was fragmented, with no unifying corporate values. Employee commitment was very weak, and employees were described as "generally miserable." There were few performance standards and little effort to hold employees accountable for their efforts. Communication within the company was so inadequate that most employees didn't realize how poorly IBAX was performing. Goodman set out first to educate employees about the severity of the problems. He made financial statements available to all employees and taught workers how to interpret them.

Once employees were convinced that the very survival of the company depended on changes being made, the next surprise was that Goodman asked them how and where to make them. His emphasis on constant, open communication began to develop a greater level of trust within the company; employees began to believe that Goodman truly was committed to involving them in the decision making. Further, he promised to reward employees for their commitment, creativity, and hard work, and he followed through on his promise. Morale improved as employees began to feel a sense of ownership and empowered to make a difference in the company.

CHANGING THE STRUCTURE

Empowered employees can be a strong, positive force in an organization, but Goodman also knew he needed to focus these employees on performance. He believed that a product structure would bring employees closer to the products and the customers that drove IBAX's performance. So, he reorganized the company from a functional structure into six operating units based on three core product lines and three other categories of products. The units were called "businesses" and treated as such—teams of people were identified to run each business; Goodman and other top managers worked with each team to establish performance objectives in terms of such things as quality, revenues, expenses, and customer satisfaction; and then the teams were given the authority to do whatever necessary to make sure their business met the objectives. In addition, Goodman made it clear that these self-managed teams were strictly accountable for the performance of their business. The locus of decision making at IBAX shifted from being highly centralized to being very decentralized.

Once the teams understood their responsibilities, they began to reengineer their units, looking for redundancies in tasks or inefficient processes. Tasks were regrouped and jobs redesigned. When necessary, employees were given additional education and training to perform new tasks or were provided with access to the information and resources they needed to perform effectively.

Human resources management was also decentralized. Rather than providing the traditional services of recruitment, selection, compensation, training, and employee relations centrally, an advisor worked with each business, involving the team members in all elements of the human resources management process. For example, teams assumed responsibility for hiring their own people based on the needs of their particular business.

INSTILLING THE TEAM PHILOSOPHY

Goodman knew he couldn't just put people together into groups and expect them to make major improvements in the company's performance. He needed to turn these groups of people into true teams committed to the company and to each other. He began by taking the senior management group through an intensive off-site team-building program that involved everything from classroom lectures to scaling walls and swinging on ropes, with the intent of building trust and commitment. Eventually, every employee in the company had participated in this team-building program.

By continuing to stress the importance of the team philosophy back in the work environment, Goodman and his senior managers made sure it became a part of the new organizational culture. Formal reward systems and special awards programs were based on team leadership and behavior as well as on performance standards.

By empowering the employees who are closest to the products and customers, and by focusing and rewarding those employees based on team behavior and tough performance standards, IBAX has made significant gains in quality, productivity, financial performance, and customer satisfaction. Today, as stated in IBAX promotional literature, the company truly is "boldly positioned to meet the health care information needs of the 21st century. IBAX is a solid, impressive performer you can choose with confidence." IBAX employees—and customers—can now agree.

"So, what's the problem here? Customers on the West Coast are saying their shipments are being delayed. We've got to find the problem and correct it."

"Well, it's still a relatively small market, and. . . ."

"It doesn't matter how small the market is; those folks want the same quick response our customers everywhere else get."

"Yes, of course. I've done some checking since we first talked, and actually, it's a problem with the computer. Our control systems here cause delays in how the computer handles requests from that region."

"Our computer doesn't work for our control systems; it works for the customer, just like we do. Let's get to work and see what adjustments we can make to fix this."

Soon after a conversation like this occurred at Lanier Worldwide, shipment response time to the West Coast improved, and Lanier once again showed why its customer base continues to grow. With headquarters in Atlanta, Georgia, Lanier has grown from a southern regional sales office to the world's largest independent distributor of office products.

Lanier is a $1 billion wholly owned subsidiary of Harris Corporation that globally markets, sells, and services copying, facsimile, and dictation systems, complete information management systems, and a variety of other office automation products through sixteen hundred centers in eighty countries. Nearly half of the company's business is outside the United States, and Lanier has recently expanded distribution in fast-growing markets in Latin America and Pacific Rim countries.

CUSTOMER VISION

A string of recent letters to newspaper advice columnists has bemoaned the poor quality of newspaper delivery service, with papers landing on snow-covered roofs or under prickly hedges and circulation offices failing to respond to complaints. But Lanier Worldwide's President and CEO Wesley Cantrell learned a valuable lesson from his days as a paperboy in Hiram, Georgia, nearly half a century ago—the customer is always right.

It is this philosophy that drives Lanier and unifies the company's seventy-five hundred employees, whatever their day-to-day responsibilities. The company's clear, straightforward mission is: "To be recognized worldwide as the preferred provider of office solutions, dedicated to total customer satisfaction." Each employee understands his or her responsibilities in achieving the corporate mission. Lanier's unifying work ethic is called "Customer Vision," and it's institutionalized throughout the company. Simply put, "Customer Vision" means looking at Lanier's business through the customers' eyes and actively responding to their needs as a team. But Lanier goes beyond the traditional definition of customers as those who buy its products to include dealers, distributors, shareholders, and even its own employees. Workers in such divisions as finance or human resources, for example, are thought of as serving the needs of Lanier's "internal" customers.

More than any other single factor, it is Customer Vision that has differentiated Lanier from its competitors. As the company approaches its sixtieth anniversary in 1994, the results are persuasive, with the company consistently earning prestigious awards from customers and industry analysts. Lanier was honored for the best overall product line by the Datapro 1993 User Survey; it was the first recipient of DuPont's "Partners in Excellence Award"; and it is only the second U.S. company to win the coveted Buyers Lab "Most Outstanding Copier of the Year" award.

PRODUCTS AND SERVICE

Since Lanier does not manufacture any equipment but buys all the products it sells from such companies as Canon, Toshiba, Kodak, and Matsushita, it can pick the best of the best and have no holes in its product line. But company leaders know that the real key to the company's success is not products per se but service; Lanier doesn't look at the sale as the end of a deal but as the beginning of a relationship. If a new product does not perform to the customer's satisfaction, for whatever reason, Lanier provides a replacement with the same or comparable features at no charge—the customer always makes the decision. The company also guarantees 98 to 100 percent up time; reimbursement for downtime; free loaners; toll-free, after-hours technical assistance year-round; and the availability of parts and supplies for no less than ten years.

Most major copier vendors offer some type of product guarantee. What further sets Lanier Worldwide apart is that it works hard to make sure customers never have to use it. The company maintains a strong commitment to quality assurance and has been known to require manufacturers to make specific changes to meet quality standards before adding machines to its product line. As the president of Buyers Laboratory, Inc. said in a letter defending the company's selection of a distributor rather than a manufacturer for the Most Outstanding Copier Award, ". . . in some cases [Lanier's models] actually perform better than the manufacturer's counterpart because the manufacturer's version is without the enhancements required by Lanier."

"NEVER STOP LEARNING"

According to CEO Cantrell, attaining Lanier's three corporate goals—customer vision, employee satisfaction, and worldwide growth—"depends on our ability to never stop learning." This requires, he says, "communicating within the organization and between divisions, understanding the breadth of Lanier's products and services, knowing how to meet customers' total office automation needs, and working as action-oriented teams to tackle specific issues and opportunities." Extensive training programs enable Lanier's dealers and direct sales personnel to be fast and flexible in responding to changing market conditions.

The company's "Team Management Process" broadens decision making within the organization, empowering teams of employees from all levels to spread knowledge across divisional lines and continuously improve the quality, timeliness, and value of its products and services. Recognition and reward programs are designed to support team-oriented goals and behavior. The ongoing purpose of the Team Management Process is to involve every single employee, as an individual and as part of a team, in the decision making that drives Lanier to reach for its goal of total customer satisfaction.

VIDEO CASE 3.0
Price Costco

Sol Price invented the discount warehouse concept in 1976, when he opened the first Price Club in San Diego. Selling merchandise in bulk at low costs in no-frills warehouses, Price Clubs quickly became a sensation in Southern California. They were the epitome of discount shopping: merchandise offered in bare-bones displays, with no advertising, marketing, and heavy overhead costs to push up prices. Very soon, a multitude of these discount warehouse chains, such as Costco, Pace, and Sam's, were popping up across the country. The 1980s saw major expansion of all these chains, plus a number of smaller ones, with almost everybody making money. But with more stores and more competition, it has been nearly impossible to keep the format profitable. As the chains expanded, they saturated the market and thus began robbing sales from themselves and one another. In the 1990s, growth has been replaced by retrenchment. The industry is now seeing buyouts, mergers, and consolidations where it once saw aggressive expansion.

In the mid-1990s, the battle has come down to two giants: Wal-Mart Store's Sam's Club, which bought out K Mart's Pace Membership Warehouse, and the new Price Costco, which resulted from a merger of the Price Company and Costco Wholesale Corporation in the fall of 1993. In this brutally competitive industry, neither Price nor Costco had the resources alone to fuel growth into a new era. The merger has helped prevent further decline or even failure of the companies and given them the resources and presence to compete with Sam's. With it, Price Costco has the power to cut prices even further by realizing greater purchasing, operating, and distribution efficiencies, as well as the ability to offer a great variety of products and services to consumers. But one of the biggest outcomes is to create a more viable player on the international retailing scene. American retailers have been late getting into international operations, but Price Costco realizes it is in this area that much of its growth must come. Some analysts felt that Price made a big mistake back in the 1970s by not aggressively expanding rapidly enough into other states, thus allowing competitors to take charge of the playing field. Price and Costco, in particular, soon found themselves operating in the same cities, competing fiercely for the same customers. By the time of the merger, it had become clear that no one was going to win; the market simply couldn't support the number of clubs. The Price Costco merger also represents an attempt to prevent the same situation from happening internationally.

As of December 1993, Price Costco operated 218 discount membership warehouses in 21 states, seven Canadian provinces, and the United Kingdom, as well as five warehouses in Mexico through a 50 percent-owned joint venture. Plans call for opening twelve new warehouses in the United States (while closing some unprofitable ones); seven in Canada; two in Mexico (50 percent owned) and one in the United Kingdom (60 percent owned). In addition, the company has signed a licensing agreement with Shinsegae Department Stores to establish warehouse clubs in South Korea, and it's working hard to finalize other international ventures.

While there doesn't seem to be enough business to go around in the United States, opportunities abound internationally for those who can move quickest. Price Costco's warehouse in Thurrock, near London, has been a success, but within months, a British wholesaler opened its first Cargo Club in direct competition and aims to eventually open between thirty to fifty more clubs in Britain. The same process of rapid expansion seen in the United States in the 1980s could now happen on the international scene.

Therefore, both at home and abroad, discount warehouse clubs must struggle to differentiate themselves if they hope to survive. Cargo Club, for example, is aiming itself more toward the general public rather than businesses, offering smaller package sizes and accepting credit cards, to gain an edge. In developing its strategy, Price Costco must look for new ways to stand out in the crowd. One small experiment proposed by a store in Scottsdale, Arizona, set up a real estate service to help members market their homes for a flat fee, much lower than the commission they'd pay by going through a traditional broker. If successful, the concept could be integrated into other stores as a unique service of the club.

In the heated battle with Sam's, Price Costco must develop a strategy that uses its combined strengths and resources to pursue new club-related business opportunities and develop distinct member benefits and services that will give it a competitive edge at home even as it attempts to be a leader in expanding the discount warehouse concept internationally.

VIDEO CASE 4.0
Minnesota Twins

Managing a baseball team may sound like a dream job. But successful businesspeople who have tried to shift their skills to the world of professional baseball find that it truly is a whole new ball game. For one thing, the balance of power they're accustomed to in their usual business world is turned upside down in the world of baseball.

This is an industry where employers have virtually surrendered the right to set salaries of workers with three or more years of experience. Salaries have jumped from an average of twenty-eight thousand dollars in 1970 to over $1 million in 1992, and one in three players now earns $1 million or more a year. Through the process of salary arbitration, a player with three years of service can demand that his salary be set through a process of binding arbitration to which the owners must submit. In arbitration, the ball club makes a dollar offer, the player makes a specific dollar demand, and the arbitrator has to choose one figure or the other—nothing in between. Pay raises average well over 100 percent even when the club's offer is selected, since the clubs offer high amounts to avoid their bid being rejected out-of-hand.

Greater revenues of clubs in large cities, such as New York, Los Angeles, and Chicago, means they can afford to pay big money for players, while smaller clubs see the talent they've helped to develop being drained away. Owners proposed a solution to the problem several years ago in the form of a salary cap, meaning big-market teams like the Yankees could spend no more on players than small-market clubs like the Minnesota Twins. The solution was quickly squashed by the players' union but is still an idea the owners are promoting.

In the meantime, the Minnesota Twins are in the forefront of small-market teams pressing for a revenue-sharing agreement among the owners that would help to level the playing field between large teams and small ones. The Twins have seen a number of players leave because it can't afford their salaries. Nevertheless, this small-market club has been called the "smartest franchise in baseball" and has been able to keep such players as Kent Hrbek and Kirby Puckett for less money than they could get with other ball clubs. The April 1993 issue of Minneapolis/St. Paul Magazine even reported that "free agent stars are initiating negotiations and accepting lower salaries to come to Minneapolis."

The club's cultural values partly account for its continued success in a volatile industry. The Twins have gained a reputation for treating players fairly and honestly. Vice President and General Manager Andy MacPhail knows his club doesn't have the resources to compete financially with larger teams, but he also knows you have to do everything you possibly can within your budget to create a winning atmosphere. A large part of that is dealing openly and aggressively with personnel moves. "We're not afraid to let them go," MacPhail says, referring to the loss of a number of players who have gone to other clubs. "The game turns; it is cyclical, and you have to create spots for others."

This statement reflects another strong value in the Twins' culture: a healthy respect for change. Between the 1987 and the 1991 World Series wins, the Twins had a turnover rate of 72 percent. The Twins recognize that in this age of baseball, sustaining success has become virtually impossible for a small-market team, and they're willing to let the cycle run its course. Twins' management believes you have to be willing to bite the bullet for a year or two and bring in young players rather than importing high-cost veterans to try to sustain a winning streak. Two seasons after their last World Series championship, for example, the Twins lost 91 games. But for the Twins, the goal is not to sustain but to recycle success.

The Twins' emphasis on treating employees fairly and its tolerance for risk and change transfers to the front office as well. As Laura Day, Promotions Manager for the Twins put it, "I have the flexibility to be creative. . . ." A lot of the Twins' employees talk about creativity and flexibility. Because the organization doesn't have major financial resources and employs only about 55 full-time workers, the second-lowest in major-league baseball, workers have to constantly develop creative ways to reach and serve their customers and potential customers. President Jerry Bell believes the only way to encourage creativity is to get all employees involved—to listen to their ideas and recommendations and then act on them. Each of the Twins' 55 employees has a lot of responsibility, but each also has a great deal of flexibility in how he or she does the job. Andy MacPhail summed up the philosophy after he was voted 1991 Sporting News Major League Executive of the Year: "To be a major league executive today is to understand the great volatility in the game in all respects. It is important to have the kind of ownership that is sold on doing things fundamentally right. I think you hire the best people you can and then stay away; give them the freedom to do their jobs as they see fit."

As baseball continues to face major challenges, giving the players, workers, and management the free- dom and power to "do their jobs as they see fit" has helped the Minnesota Twins weather financial difficul- ties and stay in the game.

Glossary

activity grouping structure that places together employees who perform similar functions or work processes or who have similar knowledge and skills.

adaptability culture a culture characterized by strategic focus on the external environment through flexibility and change to meet customer needs.

adhocracy a sophisticated organization that typically uses teams and is designed to survive in a complex, dynamic environment.

administrative principles a closed systems management perspective that focuses on the total organization and grows from the insights of practitioners.

advanced information technology microprocessors and other computer-related information-transmitting devices and systems that have enabled organizations to revolutionize their operations and increase productivity.

advanced manufacturing technology computer systems that link together manufacturing components, such as robots, machines, product design, and engineering analysis.

ambidextrous a characteristic of an organization that can behave both in an organic and a mechanistic way.

ambiguity a situation in which issues cannot be objectively analyzed and understood and additional data cannot be gathered that will resolve the issues.

analyzability a dimension of technology in which work activities can be reduced to mechanical steps and participants can follow an objective, computational procedure to solve problems.

analyzer a business strategy that seeks to maintain a stable business while innovating on the periphery.

authority a force for achieving desired outcomes that is prescribed by the formal hierarchy and reporting relationships.

bargaining a process in which managers with different goals engage in a give-and-take discussion to find a workable basis for achieving their joint interests.

behavior control control that is based on personal observation of employee behavior to see whether an employee follows correct procedures.

behavioral changes alterations in behavior that occur during intergroup conflict.

benchmarking a process whereby companies find out how others do something better than they do and then try to imitate or improve on it.

boundary-spanning roles activities that link and coordinate an organization with key elements in the external environment.

bounded rationality perspective how decisions are made when time is limited, a large number of internal and external factors affect a decision, and the problem is ill-defined.

buffering roles activities that absorb uncertainty from the environment.

bureaucracy an organizational framework marked by rules and procedures, specialization and division of labor, hierarchy of authority, technically qualified personnel, separate position and incumbent, and written communications and records.

bureaucratic control the use of rules, policies, hierarchy of authority, written documentation, standardization, and other bureaucratic mechanisms to standardize behavior and assess performance.

Carnegie model organizational decision making involving many managers and a final choice based on a coalition among those managers.

centrality a trait of a department whose role is in the primary activity of an organization.

centralization refers to the level of hierarchy with authority to make decisions.

change process the way in which changes occur in an organization.

chaos theory a new science that recognizes that randomness and disorder occur within larger patterns of order.

charismatic authority based in devotion to the exemplary character or the heroism of an individual and the order defined by him or her.

charismatic leadership the force of personality that induces a high degree of loyalty, commitment, and devotion to the leader.

clan control the use of social characteristics, such as corporate culture, shared values, commitment, traditions, and beliefs, to control behavior.

closed system a system that is autonomous, enclosed, and not dependent on its environment.

coalition an alliance among several managers who agree through **bargaining** about organizational goals and problem priorities.

collective bargaining the negotiation of an agreement between management and workers.

collectivity stage the life cycle phase in which an organization has strong leadership and begins to develop clear goals and direction.

competing values approach a perspective on organizational effectiveness that combines diverse indicators of performance that represent competing management values.

competition rivalry between groups in the pursuit of a common prize

complexity refers to the number of levels in a hierarchy and the number of departments or jobs.

confrontation when parties in conflict directly engage one another and try to work out their differences.

consistency culture a culture that has an internal focus and a consistency orientation for a stable environment.

consortia groups of firms that venture into new products and technologies together.

contextual dimensions traits that characterize the whole organization, including its size, technology, environment, and goals.

contingency a theory meaning one thing depends on other things; the organization's situation dictates the correct management approach.

contingency control model a model that describes contingencies associated with market, bureaucratic, and clan control.

contingency decision-making framework a perspective that brings together the two organizational dimensions of goal consensus and technical knowledge.

continuous process production a completely mechanized manufacturing process in which there is no starting or stopping.

cooptation occurs when leaders from important sectors in the environment are made part of an organization.

coping with uncertainty a source of power for a department that reduces uncertainty for other departments by obtaining prior information, prevention, and absorption.

craft technology technology characterized by a fairly stable stream of activities but in which the conversion process is not analyzable or well understood.

creative departments organizational departments that initiate change, such as research and development, engineering, design, and systems analysis.

crisis the first of three phases in the revitalization and turnaround of an organization suffering from decline in which managers downsize the work force and lower production costs.

culture strength the degree of agreement among members of an organization about the importance of specific values.

culture the set of values, guiding beliefs, understandings, and ways of thinking that is shared by members of an organization and is taught to new members as correct.

data the input of a communication channel.

decision learning a process of recognizing and admitting mistakes that allows managers and organizations to acquire the experience and knowledge to perform more effectively in the future.

decision premises constraining frames of reference and guidelines placed by top managers on decisions made at lower levels.

decision support system a system that enables managers at all levels of the organization to retrieve, manipulate, and display information from integrated data bases for making specific decisions.

defender a business strategy that seeks stability or even retrenchment rather than innovation or growth.

departmental grouping structure in which employees share a common supervisor and resources, are jointly responsible for performance, and tend to identify and collaborate with each other.

dependent variables organizational characteristics such as structure, control mechanisms, and communications that are influenced by **independent variables**.

differentiation the cognitive and emotional differences among managers in various functional departments of an organization and formal structure differences among these departments.

differentiation strategy a strategy in which organizations attempt to distinguish their products or services from others in the industry.

direct interlock occurs when a member of the board of directors of one company sits on the board of another.

divisional form large organizations that are subdivided into product or market groups.

domain an organization's chosen environmental field of action.

domains of political activity areas in which politics plays a role. The four domains in organizations are: structural change, interdepartmental coordination, management succession, and resource allocation.

domestic stage first stage of international development in which a company is domestically oriented while managers are aware of the global environment.

downsizing laying off employees to whom commitments have been made.

dual-core approach an organizational change perspective that identifies the unique processes associated with administrative change compared to those associated with technical change.

dynamic network a structure in which a free market style replaces the traditional vertical hierarchy.

effectiveness the degree to which an organization realizes its goals.

efficiency the amount of resources used to produce a

unit of output.

elaboration stage   the organizational life cycle phase in which the red tape crisis is resolved through the development of a new sense of teamwork and collaboration.

electronic data interchange   the linking of organizations through computers for the transmission of data without human interference.

empowerment   power sharing; the delegation of power or authority to subordinates.

engineering technology   technology in which there is substantial variety in the tasks performed, but the activities are usually handled on the basis of established formulas, procedures, and techniques.

entrepreneurial stage   the life cycle phase in which an organization is born and its emphasis is on creating a product and surviving in the marketplace.

entrepreneurial structure   typically, a new, small entrepreneurial company consisting of a top manager and workers in the technical core.

escalating commitment   persisting in a course of action when it is failing; occurs because managers block or distort negative information and because consistency and persistence are valued in contemporary society.

ethical dilemma   when each alternative choice or behavior seems undesirable because of a potentially negative ethical consequence.

ethics   the code of moral principles and values that governs the behavior of a person or group with respect to what is right or wrong.

ethics committee   a group of executives appointed to oversee company ethics.

ethics ombudsperson   a single manager who serves as the corporate conscience.

executive information systems   interactive systems that help top managers monitor and control organizational operations by processing and presenting data in usable form.

external adaptation   how an organization meets goals and deals with outsiders.

five organizational configurations   these are entrepreneurial structure, machine bureaucracy, professional bureaucracy, divisional form, and adhocracy.

focus   an organization's dominant perspective value, which may be internal or external.

focus strategy   a strategy in which an organization concentrates on a specific regional market or buyer group.

formalization stage   the phase in an organization's life cycle involving the installation and use of rules, procedures, and control systems.

formalization   the degree to which an organization has rules, procedures, and written documentation.

functional matrix   a structure in which functional bosses have primary authority and product or project managers simply coordinate product activities.

functional structure   the grouping of activities by common function.

gain sharing   an approach to resolving union-management conflict in which union members receive bonuses and prof-

it sharing rather than guaranteed, flat-rate increases.

garbage can model   describes the pattern or flow of multiple decisions within an organization.

general environment   includes those sectors that may not directly affect the daily operations of a firm but will indirectly influence it.

generalist   an organization with a wide niche or domain.

global company   a company that no longer thinks of itself as having a home country.

global geographic structure   a form in which an organization divides its operations into world regions, each of which reports to the CEO.

global heterarchy structure   a form of horizontal organization that has multiple centers, subsidiary managers who initiate strategy for the company as a whole, and coordination and control achieved through corporate culture and shared values.

global matrix structure   a form of horizontal linkage in an international organization in which both product and functional structures (horizontal and vertical) are implemented simultaneously.

global product structure   a form in which product divisions take responsibility for global operations in their specific product areas.

global stage   the stage of international development in which the company transcends any one country.

globalization strategy   the standardization of product design and advertising strategy throughout the world.

goal approach   an approach to organizational effectiveness that is concerned with output and whether the organization achieves its output goals.

goal consensus   the agreement among managers about which organizational goals and outcomes to pursue.

groupware   programs that enable employees on a computer network to interact with one another through their PCs.

heroes   organizational members who serve as models or ideals for serving cultural norms and values.

high tech   technology-based information systems.

high touch   face-to-face discussion.

high-velocity environments   industries in which competitive and technological change is so extreme that market data is either unavailable or obsolete, strategic windows open and shut quickly, and the cost of a decision error is company failure.

horizontal conflict   behavior that occurs between groups or departments at the same level in the hierarchy.

horizontal corporation   a structure in which vertical hierarchy and departmental boundaries are virtually eliminated.

horizontal linkage   the amount of communication and coordination that occurs horizontally across organizational departments.

horizontal linkage model   a model of the three components of organizational design needed to achieve new product innovation: departmental specialization, boundary spanning, and horizontal linkages.

human relations model   an organizational model that

incorporates the values of an internal focus and a flexible structure.

hybrid structure   a structure that combines characteristics of both product and function or geography.

idea champions   organizational members who provide the time and energy to make things happen; sometimes called "advocates," "intrapreneurs," and "change agents."

imitation   the adoption of a decision tried elsewhere in the hope that it will work in the present situation.

incremental change   a series of continual progressions that maintain an organization's general equilibrium and often affect only one organizational part.

incremental decision process model   describes the structured sequence of activities undertaken from the discovery of a problem to its solution.

independent variables   organizational characteristics such as environment and technology that affect other organizational traits.

indirect interlock   occurs when a director of one company and a director of another are both directors of a third company.

informating   a term coined by Shoshana Zuboff to mean providing new streams of data from technology to employees, empowering them to interpret and translate information into action.

information   that which alters or reinforces understanding.

information amount   the volume of data about organizational activities that is gathered and interpreted by organization participants.

information richness   the information carrying capacity of data.

input control   control that uses employee selection and training to regulate the knowledge, skills, abilities, values, and motives of employees.

inspiration   an innovative, creative solution that is not reached by logical means.

institutional perspective   an emerging view that holds that under high uncertainty, organizations imitate others in the same institutional environment.

integration   the quality of collaboration between departments of an organization.

integrator   a position or department created solely to coordinate several departments.

intensive technology   a variety of products or services provided in combination to a client.

interdependence   the extent to which departments depend on each other for resources or materials to accomplish their tasks.

intergroup conflict   behavior that occurs between organizational groups when participants identify with one group and perceive that other groups may block their group's goal achievement or expectations.

interlocking directorate   a formal linkage that occurs when a member of the board of directors of one company sits on the board of another company.

internal integration   a state in which organization members develop a collective identity and know how to

work together effectively.

internal process approach   an approach that looks at internal activities and assesses effectiveness by indicators of internal health and efficiency.

internal process model   an organizational model that reflects the values of internal focus and structural control.

international division   a division that is equal in status to other major departments within a company and has its own hierarchy to handle business in various countries.

international stage   the second stage of international development, in which the company takes exports seriously and begins to think multidomestically.

interorganizational coordination   strategic partnerships between organizations, formed to be more competitive and to share scarce resources.

intuitive decision making   the use of experience and judgment rather than sequential logic or explicit reasoning to solve a problem.

involvement culture   a culture that focuses primarily on the involvement and participation of the organization's members and on rapidly changing expectations from the external environment.

job enrichment   the designing of jobs to increase responsibility, recognition, and opportunities for growth and achievement.

job simplification   the reduction of the number and difficulty of tasks performed by a single person.

joint optimization   the goal of the sociotechnical systems approach, which states that an organization will function best only if its social and technical systems are designed to fit the needs of one another.

joint venture   a separate entity for sharing development and production costs and penetrating new markets that is created with two or more active firms as sponsors.

labor-management teams   a cooperative approach designed to increase worker participation and provide a cooperative model for union-management problems.

language   slogans, sayings, metaphors, or other expressions that convey a special meaning to employees.

large-batch production   a manufacturing process characterized by long production runs of standardized parts.

learning organization   an organization in which everyone is engaged in identifying and solving problems, enabling the organization to continuously experiment, improve, and increase its capability.

legends   stories of events based in history that may have been embellished with fictional details.

level of analysis   in systems theory, the subsystem on which the primary focus is placed; four levels of analysis normally characterize organizations.

liaison role   a person located in one department who is responsible for communicating and achieving coordination with another department.

life cycle   a perspective on organizational growth and change that suggests organizations are born, grow older, and eventually die.

long-linked technology   the combination within one

organization of successive stages of production, with each stage using as its inputs the production of the preceding stage.

losses from conflict   negative consequences of conflict for organizations, including diversion of energy, altered judgment, loser effects, and poor coordination.

low-cost leadership   a strategy that tries to increase market share by emphasizing low cost compared to competitors.

machine bureaucracy   a very large organization in which the technology is routine and often oriented to mass production.

management champion   a manager who acts as a supporter and sponsor of a technical champion to shield and promote an idea within the organization.

management control systems   the formalized routines, reports, and procedures that use information to maintain or alter patterns in organizational activity.

management information system   a system that generally contains comprehensive data about all transactions within an organization.

management science approach   organizational decision making that is the analog to the rational approach by individual managers.

managerial ethics   principles that guide the decisions and behaviors of managers with regard to whether they are morally right or wrong.

market control   occurs when price competition is used to evaluate the output and productivity of an organization.

matrix bosses   department heads and program directors who have complete control over their subordinates.

matrix structure   a strong form of horizontal linkage in which both product and functional structures (horizontal and vertical) are implemented simultaneously.

mechanistic   an organization system marked by rules, procedures, a clear hierarchy of authority, and centralized decision making.

mechanistic management   a tightly controlled management approach.

mediating technology   the provision of products or services that mediate or link clients from the external environment and allow each department to work independently.

mission   the organization's reasons for its existence.

mission culture   a culture that places major importance on a shared vision of organization purpose.

mixed model   a description of an organization that displays both rational and political model characteristics.

model   a simple representation that describes a few important dimensions of an organization.

model of intergroup conflict   a graphic representation of the organizational and intergroup factors that set the stage for intergroup conflict, the triggers that set off a dispute, and the responses managers can make to control emergent conflict.

multidomestic company   a company that deals with competitive issues in each country independent of other countries.

multidomestic strategy   competition in each country is handled independently of competition in other countries.

multifocused grouping   a structure in which an organization embraces structural grouping alternatives simultaneously.

multinational stage   the stage of international development in which a company has marketing and production facilities in many countries and more than one-third of its sales outside its home country.

myths   stories that are consistent with the values and beliefs of the organization but are not supported by facts.

negotiation   the bargaining process that often occurs during confrontation and enables the parties to systematically reach a solution.

network centrality   top managers can increase their power by locating themselves centrally in an organization and surrounding themselves with loyal subordinates.

networking   linking computers within or between organizations.

niche   a domain of unique environmental resources and needs.

nonprogrammed decisions   novel and poorly defined, these are used when no procedure exists for solving the problem.

nonroutine technology   technology in which there is high task variety and the conversion process is not analyzable or well understood.

nonsubstitutability   a trait of a department whose function cannot be performed by other readily available resources.

official goals   the formally stated definition of business scope and outcomes the organization is trying to achieve; another term for **mission**.

open system   a system that must interact with the environment to survive.

open systems model   an organizational model that reflects a combination of external focus and flexible structure.

operational control   a short-term control cycle that includes the four stages of setting targets, measuring performance, comparing performance against standards, and feedback.

operative goals   descriptions of the ends sought through the actual operating procedures of the organization; these explain what the organization is trying to accomplish.

organic   an organization system marked by free-flowing, adaptive processes, an unclear hierarchy of authority, and decentralized decision making.

organic management   a loose, flexible management approach that recognizes the unstable nature of the external environment.

organization theory   a macro approach to organizations that analyzes the whole organization as a unit.

organizational behavior   a micro approach to organizations that focuses on the individuals within organizations as the relevant units of analysis.

organizational change   the adoption of a new idea or behavior by an organization.

organizational decision making   the organizational process of identifying and solving problems.

organizational decline   a condition in which a substantial, absolute decrease in an organization's resource base occurs over a period of time.

organizational development   a behavioral science field devoted to improving performance through trust, open confrontation of problems, employee empowerment and participation, the design of meaningful work, cooperation between groups, and the full use of human potential.

organizational environment   all elements that exist outside the boundary of the organization and have the potential to affect all or part of the organization.

organizational form   an organization's specific technology, structure, products, goals, and personnel.

organizational goal   a desired state of affairs that the organization attempts to reach.

organizational innovation   the adoption of an idea or behavior that is new to an organization's industry, market, or general environment.

organizational politics   activities to acquire, develop, and use power and other resources to obtain one's preferred outcome when there is uncertainty or disagreement about choices.

organizations   social entities that are goal-directed, deliberately structured activity systems with a permeable boundary.

organized anarchy   extremely organic organization characterized by highly uncertain conditions.

output control   control that is based on written records that measure employee outputs and productivity.

output grouping   structure in which people are organized according to what the organization produces.

paradigm   a shared mind-set that represents a fundamental way of thinking, perceiving, and understanding the world.

Parkinson's law   a view that holds that work expands to fill the time available for its completion.

people and culture changes   changes in the values, attitudes, expectations, beliefs, abilities, and behavior of employees.

personnel ratios   the proportions of administrative, clerical, and professional support staff.

political model   a definition of an organization as being made up of groups that have separate interests, goals, and values in which power and influence are needed to reach decisions.

pooled interdependence   the lowest form of interdependence among departments in which work does not flow between units.

population ecology model   a perspective in which the focus is on organizational diversity and adaptation within a community or population of organizations.

power sources   there are five sources of horizontal power in organizations: dependency, financial resources,

centrality, nonsubstitutability, and the ability to cope with uncertainty.

power   the ability of one person or department in an organization to influence others to bring about desired outcomes.

problem identification   the decision-making stage in which information about environmental and organizational conditions is monitored to determine if performance is satisfactory and to diagnose the cause of shortcomings.

problem solution   the decision-making stage in which alternative courses of action are considered and one alternative is selected and implemented.

problemistic search   occurs when managers look around in the immediate environment for a solution to resolve a problem quickly.

product and service changes   changes in an organization's product or service outputs.

product structure   the organization of divisions according to individual products, services, product groups, major projects or programs, divisions, businesses, or profit centers.

professional bureaucracy   an organization in which the production core is composed of professionals.

programmed decisions   repetitive and well-defined procedures that exist for resolving problems.

project matrix   a structure in which the project or product manager has primary responsibility, and functional managers simply assign technical personnel to projects and provide advisory expertise.

prospector   a business strategy characterized by innovation, risk taking, seeking out new opportunities, and growth.

quality circles   groups of six to twelve volunteer workers who meet to analyze and solve problems.

radical change   a breaking of the frame of reference for an organization, often creating a new equilibrium because the entire organization is transformed.

radical-Marxism   a perspective on organizations that holds that managers make decisions to maintain themselves in the capitalist class, keeping power and resources for themselves.

rational approach   a process of decision making that stresses the need for systematic analysis of a problem followed by choice and implementation in a logical sequence.

rational goal model   an organizational model that reflects values of structural control and external focus.

rational model   a description of an organization characterized by a rational approach to decision making, extensive and reliable information systems, central power, a norm of optimization, uniform values across groups, little conflict, and an efficiency orientation.

rational-contingency perspective   an approach to organizations that assumes that managers try to do what is logically best for the organization.

rational-legal authority   based on employees' beliefs in the legality of rules and the right of those in authority to issue commands.

reactor   a business strategy in which environmental threats and opportunities are responded to in an ad hoc fashion.

reasons organizations grow   growth occurs because it is an organizational goal; it is necessary to attract and keep quality managers; or it is necessary to maintain economic health.

rebuilding   the final phase in turnaround and recovery in which the organization begins to grow, moving away from efficiency toward innovation.

reciprocal interdependence   the highest level of interdependence in which the output of one operation is the input of a second, and the output of the second operation is the input of the first (for example, a hospital).

reengineering   the radical redesign of business processes to achieve dramatic improvements in cost, quality, service, and speed.

reinvest   the turnaround and recovery phase in which the organization stabilizes, and its structure and culture are changed to reflect its new mission and goals.

resource dependence   means that organizations depend on the environment but strive to acquire control over resources to minimize their dependence.

retention   the preservation and institutionalization of selected organizational forms.

rites and ceremonies   the elaborate, planned activities that make up a special event and often are conducted for the benefit of an audience.

ritual scapegoating   the functioning of manager turnover as a sign that the organization is trying to improve.

routine technology   technology characterized by little task variety and the use of objective, computational procedures.

rule of law   that which arises from a set of codified principles and regulations that describe how people are required to act, are generally accepted in society, and are enforceable in the courts.

satisficing   the acceptance by organizations of a satisfactory rather than a maximum level of performance.

scientific management   a classical approach that claims decisions about organization and job design should be based on precise, scientific procedures.

sectors   subdivisions of the external environment that contain similar elements.

selection   the process by which organizational variations are determined to fit the external environment; variations that fail to fit the needs of the environment are "selected out" and fail.

self-managed team   a group of workers with different skills who rotate jobs and assume managerial responsibilities as they produce an entire product or service.

sequential interdependence   a serial form of interdependence in which the output of one operation becomes the input to another operation.

service technology   technology characterized by simultaneous production and consumption, customized output, customer participation, intangible output, and being labor intensive.

simple-complex dimension   the number and dissimilarity of external elements relevant to an organization's operations.

small-batch production   a manufacturing process, often custom work, that is not highly mechanized and relies heavily on the human operator.

social responsibility   management's obligation to make choices and take action so that the organization contributes to the welfare and interest of society as well as itself.

sociotechnical systems approach   an approach that combines the needs of people with the needs of technical efficiency.

sources of interdepartmental conflict   seven factors that generate conflict, including operative goal incompatibility, differentiation, task interdependence, resource scarcity, power distribution, uncertainty, and reward system.

sources of vertical conflict   factors within an organization, usually involving workers and management, that cause conflict, including psychological distance, power and status, ideology, and scarce resources.

specialist   an organization that has a narrow range of goods or services or serves a narrow market.

stable-unstable dimension   the state of an organization's environmental elements.

stakeholder   any group within or outside an organization that has a stake in the organization's performance.

stakeholder approach   also called the constituency approach, this perspective assesses the satisfaction of stakeholders as an indicator of the organization's performance.

stories   narratives based on true events that are frequently shared among organizational employees and told to new employees to inform them about an organization.

strategic contingencies   events and activities inside and outside an organization that are essential for attaining organizational goals.

strategic control   the overall evaluation of the strategic plan, organizational activities, and results that provides information for future action.

strategy   a plan for interacting with the competitive environment to achieve organizational goals.

strategy and structure changes   changes in the administrative domain of an organization, including structure, policies, reward systems, labor relations, coordination devices, management information control systems, and accounting and budgeting.

strategy formation   the activities that lead to the establishment of an organization's overall goals and mission and the development of a specific strategic plan.

strategy implementation   the use of managerial and organizational tools to direct and allocate resources to accomplish strategic objectives.

strategy   the current set of plans, decisions, and objectives that have been adopted to achieve the organization's goals.

structural dimensions   descriptions of the internal characteristics of an organization indicating whether stability or flexibility is the dominant organizational value.

structure   the formal reporting relationships, groupings, and systems of an organization.

struggle for existence   a principle of the population ecology model that holds that organizations are engaged in a competitive struggle for resources and fighting to survive.

subsystems   divisions of an organization that perform specific functions for the organization's survival; organizational subsystems perform the essential functions of boundary spanning, production, maintenance, adaptation, and management.

supervisory control   control that focuses on the performance of individual employees.

switching structures   an organization creates an organic structure when such a structure is needed for the initiation of new ideas.

symbol   something that represents another thing.

symbolic leader   one who defines and uses signals and symbols to influence corporate cultures and ethical value systems.

symptoms of structural deficiency   signs of the organizational structure being out of alignment, including delayed or poor-quality decision making, failure to respond innovatively to environmental changes, and too much conflict.

system   a set of interacting elements that acquires inputs from the environment, transforms them, and discharges outputs to the external environment.

system resource approach   an organizational perspective that assesses effectiveness by observing the beginning of the process and evaluating whether the organization effectively obtains resources necessary for high performance.

tactics for increasing the power base   these include: enter areas of high uncertainty, create dependencies, provide resources, and satisfy strategic contingencies.

tactics for using power   these include: build coalitions, expand networks, control decision premises, enhance legitimacy and expertise, and make preferences explicit while keeping power implicit.

task environment   sectors with which the organization interacts directly and that have a direct effect on the organization's ability to achieve its goals.

task force   a temporary committee composed of representatives from each department affected by a problem.

team building   activities that promote the idea that people who work together can work together as a team.

teams   permanent task forces often used in conjunction with a full-time integrator.

technical complexity   the extent of mechanization in the manufacturing process.

technical knowledge   understanding and agreement about how to reach organizational goals.

technical or product champion   a person who generates or adopts and develops an idea for a technological innovation and is devoted to it, even to the extent of risking position or prestige.

technology changes   changes in an organization's production process, including its knowledge and skills base,

that enable distinctive competence.

technology   the tools, techniques, and actions used to transform organizational inputs into outputs.

theory   a description that explains how organizational characteristics or variables are causally related.

top leader   the head of both functional and product command structures in a matrix.

total quality management   an organizational approach in which workers, not managers, are handed the responsibility for achieving standards of quality.

traditional authority   based in the belief in traditions and the legitimacy of the status of people exercising authority through those traditions.

transformational leadership   the ability of leaders to motivate followers to not just follow them personally but to believe in the vision of organizational transformation, to recognize the need for revitalization, to commit to the new vision, and to help institutionalize a new organizational process.

transaction processing systems   automation of the organization's routine, day-to-day business transactions.

transaction-cost economics   a perspective that assumes that individuals act in their self-interest and that exchanges of goods and services theoretically could occur in the free marketplace.

two-boss employees   employees who must maintain effective relationships with both department heads and program directors in a matrix structure.

uncertainty   occurs when decision makers do not have sufficient information about environmental factors and have a difficult time predicting external changes.

user or customer grouping   a structure in which resources are organized to serve a customer or client.

variation   appearance of new organizational forms in response to the needs of the external environment; analogous to mutations in biology.

variety   in terms of tasks, the frequency of unexpected and novel events that occur in the conversion process.

venture teams   a technique to foster creativity within organizations in which a small team is set up as its own company to pursue innovations.

vertical conflict   behavior between groups that arises over issues of control, power, goals, and wages and benefits.

vertical information system   the periodic reports, written information, and computer-based communications distributed to managers.

vertical linkages   communication and coordination activities connecting the top and bottom of an organization.

whistle-blowing   employee disclosure of illegal, immoral, or illegitimate practices on the part of the organization.

work flow automation   a form of advanced information technology in which documents are automatically sent to the correct location for processing.

work flow redesign   reengineering work processes to fit new information technology.

Name Index

A

Abdalla, David, 228n18
Ackerman, Linda S., 212n, 228n24
Adams, Dennis A., 329n16
Adices, Ichak, 189n39
Adler, Nancy J., 242n, 258n25
Adler, Paul S., 128n, 156 nn 16, 22, 158 nn 62, 63
Aiken, Michael, 157n33, 188n22, 293n10, 296n65, 328n4
Akers, John, 4, 6
Akinnusi, David M., 295n46
Alderfer, Clayton T., 477n2
Aldrich, Howard E., 36 nn 18, 19, 113n13, 115 nn 74, 75
Alexander, Keith, 294n33, 399n2, 401n51
Alexander, Ralph A., 510n50
Alexander, Suzanne, 112n2
Allaire, Paul, 210
Allen, Michael Patrick, 509n46
Allen, Robert W., 442 nn 56, 57, 443n62
Allison, Charles F., 534–538
Altier, William J., 227n10
Amend, Patricia, 508n17, 509 nn 27, 29
Ander, George, 293n2
Anderson, Claire J., 519n
Anderson, Martin, 191
Anderson, Paul A., 399n10, 400–401n47
Andrews, Edmund L., 114 nn 40, 54
Anzizu, José de, 558n
Applegate, Lynda M., 158 nn 57, 59
Archer, Ernest R., 399 nn 6, 8
Archer, Lawrence, 358n50

Archibald, Nolan, 262
Argote, Linda, 156n3, 158 nn 39, 45
Argyris, Chris, 59, 75n40
Armstrong, Larry, 187n1
Arnold, Bill, 336
Arnst, Catherine, 36n4, 112n4
Arogyaswamy, Bernard, 356n19
Asch, David, 329n28
Ash, Roy, 348
Astley, W. Graham, 188n29, 441 nn 6, 12, 21
Atkin, Robert S., 115n62
Aubin, Jean, 400 nn 27, 28
Austin, Nancy K., 356n16

B

Babcock, Judith A., 114n52
Babe Ruth, 239
Bacharach, Samuel B., 293n11, 296n65, 328n4
Baden-Fuller, Charles, 509n32
Bailey, Jeff, 113n28
Baker, Edward, 400n27
Ball, Ken, 51
Ball, Millie, 532n1, 533n
Banforth, K., 159n68
Barker, James R., 330n46
Barnett, Carole K., 509n33
Barney, Jay B., 114n38
Barrett, Amy, 477n8
Barrett, Paul M., 188–189n35
Barthelemy, Sidney, 530
Bartimo, Jim, 328n10
Bartlett, Christopher A., 228n29, 252n, 258 nn 40, 41
Bartz, Carol, 280–281

Bass, Bernard M., 509 nn 35–37
Bazerman, Max H., 115n62
Beals, Vaughn, 506–508
Beard, Donald W., 113n15
Beatty, Carol A., 296n63
Beatty, Richard W., 75n30
Beaulieu, Lovell, 533
Becherer, Hans W., 24
Becker, Selwyn W., 187n19, 188n31, 296n66
Beckhard, Richard, 59, 75 nn 40, 42
Bedeian, Arthur G., 36n19, 116n81
Bee Gees, The, 374
Beer, Michael, 295n55, 296n56
Behling, Orlando, 399n13
Bell, Cecil H., Jr., 296n60
Bell, Gerald D., 157n36
Bell, Jerry, 573
Bell, T. C. (Tom), 539, 541, 542, 545–548
Benjamin, Robert I., 329 nn 22, 23
Benner, Susan, 356n16
Bennett, Amanda, 37n33
Bennis, Warren G., 59, 75n40
Bensen, Joe, 111
Benson, Al, 394–398
Bergman, Ingrid, 383
Bernstein, Aaron, 442n55, 479 nn 57, 65
Bernstein, Harry, 477n9
Best, Roger, 513–514
Beyer, Janice M., 335n, 356 nn 5, 12
Bhargava, Sunita Wadekar, 479n43
Birnbaum, Jeffrey H., 115n68
Bisett, M. J., 328n8
Blackburn, Richard S., 441–442n30

Corporate Name Index

$\mathcal{S}$ubject Index

Photo Credits

1 Courtesy of International Business Machines Corporation; 3, 4 Courtesy of International Busines Machines Corporation; 39 Reprinted with permission of Compaq Computer Corporation. All rights reserved; 41, 42 Reprinted with permission of Compaq Computer Corporation. All rights reserved; 77, 78 David R. Frazier Photolibrary; 117 David R. Frazier Photolibrary, 119, 120 Courtesy of General Motors Corporation; 160, 161 Courtesy of Xerox Corporation; 190, 191 Courtesy of Chrysler Corporation; 229, 230 Courtesy of General Electric; 259, 261, 262 Courtesy of Black & Decker Corporation; 297 Courtesy of International Business Machines Corporation; 298 Courtesy of Chrysler Corporation; 331, 332 Courtesy of Ben & Jerry's Homemade, Inc.; 359 Courtesy of Chrysler Corporation; 361, 362 Reprinted with permission of PepsiCo, Inc., 1994; 444, 445 ©James Prince, Photo Researchers, Inc.; 481 Courtesy of Chrysler Corporation; 483, 484 M. Shostak/Anthro-Photo